NORTH CAROLINA COURT OF APPEALS REPORTS

VOLUME 47

3 JUNE 1980

5 AUGUST 1980

RALEIGH
1981

CITE THIS VOLUME
47 N.C. App.

TABLE OF CONTENTS

THE COURT OF APPEALS
OF
NORTH CAROLINA

Chief Judge

NAOMI E. MORRIS

Judges

R.A. HEDRICK

EARL W. VAUGHN

ROBERT M. MARTIN

EDWARD B. CLARK

GERALD ARNOLD

JOHN WEBB

RICHARD C. ERWIN*

HARRY C. MARTIN

HUGH A. WELLS

CECIL J. HILL

WILLIS P. WHICHARD

Retired Judges

HUGH B. CAMPBELL
FRANK M. PARKER

Clerk

FRANCIS E. DAIL

---

*Resigned 30 October 1980

v

TRIAL JUDGES OF THE GENERAL COURT OF JUSTICE

SUPERIOR COURT DIVISION

First Division

DISTRICT	JUDGES	ADDRESS
1	J. HERBERT SMALL	Elizabeth City
2	ELBERT S. PEEL, JR.	Williamston
3	ROBERT D. ROUSE, JR.	Farmville
	DAVID E. REID	Greenville
4	HENRY L. STEVENS III	Kenansville
	JAMES R. STRICKLAND	Jacksonville
5	BRADFORD TILLERY	Wilmington
	N.B. BAREFOOT	Wilmington
6	RICHARD B. ALLSBROOK	Roanoke Rapids
7	GEORGE M. FOUNTAIN	Tarboro
	FRANKLIN R. BROWN	Tarboro
8	R. MICHAEL BRUCE	Mount Olive
	JAMES D. LLEWELLYN	Kinston

Second Division

9	ROBERT H. HOBGOOD	Louisburg
10	JAMES H. POU BAILEY	Raleigh
	A. PILSTON GODWIN, JR.	Raleigh
	EDWIN S. PRESTON, JR.	Raleigh
	ROBERT L. FARMER	Raleigh
11	HARRY E. CANADAY[1]	Smithfield
12	E. MAURICE BRASWELL	Fayetteville
	D.B. HERRING, JR.	Fayetteville
	COY E. BREWER, JR.	Fayetteville
13	GILES R. CLARK	Elizabethtown
14	THOMAS H. LEE	Durham
	ANTHONY M. BRANNON	Bahama
	JOHN C. MARTIN	Durham
15A	D. MARSH McLELLAND	Burlington
15B	F. GORDON BATTLE	Chapel Hill
16	HENRY A. McKINNON, JR.[2]	Lumberton

Third Division

17	JAMES M. LONG	Yanceyville
18	CHARLES T. KIVETT	Greensboro
	W. DOUGLAS ALBRIGHT	Greensboro
	EDWARD K. WASHINGTON	Greensboro
19A	THOMAS W. SEAY, JR.	Spencer
	JAMES C. DAVIS	Concord
19B	HAL HAMMER WALKER	Asheboro

DISTRICT	JUDGES	ADDRESS
20	F. FETZER MILLS	Wadesboro
	WILLIAM H. HELMS	Wingate
21	WILLIAM Z. WOOD	Winston-Salem
	HARVEY A. LUPTON[3]	Winston-Salem
22	ROBERT A. COLLIER, JR.	Statesville
	PETER W. HAIRSTON	Advance
23	JULIUS A. ROUSSEAU	North Wilkesboro

Fourth Division

DISTRICT	JUDGES	ADDRESS
24	RONALD W. HOWELL	Marshall
25	FORREST A. FERRELL	Hickory
	CLAUDE S. SITTON	Morganton
26	WILLIAM T. GRIST	Charlotte
	FRANK W. SNEPP, JR.	Charlotte
	KENNETH A. GRIFFIN	Charlotte
	CLIFTON E. JOHNSON	Charlotte
	ROBERT M. BURROUGHS	Charlotte
27A	ROBERT W. KIRBY	Cherryville
	ROBERT E. GAINES	Gastonia
27B	JOHN R. FRIDAY	Lincolnton
28	ROBERT D. LEWIS	Asheville
	C. WALTER ALLEN	Asheville
29	HOLLIS M. OWENS, JR.	Rutherfordton
30	LACY H. THORNBURG	Webster

SPECIAL JUDGES

DONALD L. SMITH	Raleigh
H.L. RIDDLE, JR.[4]	Morganton
SAMUEL E. BRITT[5]	Lumberton
JUDSON D. DeRAMUS, JR.	Winston-Salem
JOHN R. JOLLY, JR.	Rocky Mount
ARTHUR L. LANE	Fayetteville
CHARLES C. LAMM, JR.	Boone
PRESTON CORNELIUS	Troutman
WILLIAM H. FREEMAN[6]	Winston-Salem

EMERGENCY JUDGES

ALBERT W. COWPER	Wilson
HAMILTON H. HOBGOOD	Louisburg

---

[1]Retired 31 December 1980.
[2]Retired 31 October 1980 and constituted Emergency Judge on that date.
[3]Retired 31 December 1980.
[4]Retired 31 October 1980.
[5]Appointed Resident Judge, Sixteenth District, 21 November 1980.
[6]Appointed 1 December 1980.

vii

DISTRICT COURT DIVISION

DISTRICT	JUDGES	ADDRESS
1	JOHN T. CHAFFIN (Chief)	Elizabeth City
	GRAFTON G. BEAMAN	Elizabeth City
	J. RICHARD PARKER	Manteo
2	HALLETT S. WARD (Chief)	Washington
	CHARLES H. MANNING[1]	Williamston
3	CHARLES H. WHEDBEE (Chief)[2]	Greenville
	HERBERT O. PHILLIPS III[3]	Morehead City
	ROBERT D. WHEELER	Grifton
	E. BURT AYCOCK, JR.	Greenville
	JAMES E. RAGAN III	Oriental
	JAMES E. MARTIN	Bethel
4	KENNETH W. TURNER (Chief)	Rose Hill
	WALTER P. HENDERSON	Trenton
	STEPHEN W. WILLIAMSON	Kenansville
	E. ALEX ERWIN III	Jacksonville
	JAMES NELLO MARTIN	Clinton
5	GILBERT H. BURNETT (Chief)	Wilmington
	JOHN M. WALKER	Wilmington
	CHARLES E. RICE	Wilmington
	CARTER TATE LAMBETH	Wilmington
6	NICHOLAS LONG (Chief)	Roanoke Rapids
	ROBERT E. WILLIFORD	Lewiston
	HAROLD P. MCCOY, JR.	Scotland Neck
7	GEORGE BRITT (Chief)	Tarboro
	ALLEN W. HARRELL	Wilson
	JAMES EZZELL, JR.	Rocky Mount
	ALBERT S. THOMAS, JR.	Wilson
8	JOHN PATRICK EXUM (Chief)	Kinston
	ARNOLD O. JONES	Goldsboro
	KENNETH R. ELLIS	Fremont
	PAUL MICHAEL WRIGHT	Goldsboro
	RODNEY R. GOODMAN, JR.[4]	Kinston
9	CLAUDE W. ALLEN, JR. (Chief)	Oxford
	BEN U. ALLEN	Henderson
	CHARLES W. WILKINSON	Oxford
	J. LARRY SENTER	Louisburg
10	GEORGE F. BASON (Chief)	Raleigh
	HENRY V. BARNETTE, JR.	Raleigh
	STAFFORD G. BULLOCK	Raleigh

viii

District	Judges	Address
	George R. Greene	Raleigh
	John Hill Parker	Raleigh
	Russell G. Sherrill III	Raleigh
11	Elton C. Pridgen (Chief)	Smithfield
	W. Pope Lyon	Smithfield
	William A. Christian	Sanford
	Kelly Edward Greene	Dunn
12	Derb S. Carter (Chief)	Fayetteville
	Joseph E. Dupree	Raeford
	Charles Lee Guy	Fayetteville
	Sol G. Cherry	Fayetteville
	Lacy S. Hair	Fayetteville
13	William E. Wood (Chief)[5]	Whiteville
	J. Wilton Hunt, Sr.	Whiteville
	Roy D. Trest	Shallotte
	William C. Gore, Jr.[6]	Whiteville
14	J. Milton Read, Jr. (Chief)	Durham
	William G. Pearson	Durham
	David Q. LaBarre	Durham
	Karen B. Galloway	Durham
15A	Jasper B. Allen, Jr. (Chief)	Burlington
	William S. Harris	Graham
	S. Kent Washburn	Burlington
15B	Stanley Peele (Chief)	Chapel Hill
	Donald Lee Paschal	Siler City
16	John S. Gardner (Chief)	Lumberton
	Charles G. McLean	Lumberton
	B. Craig Ellis	Laurinburg
	Herbert Lee Richardson	Lumberton
17	Leonard H. van Noppen (Chief)	Danbury
	Foy Clark	Mount Airy
	Peter M. McHugh	Reidsville
	Jerry Cash Martin	Mount Airy
18	Robert L. Cecil (Chief)	High Point
	Elreta M. Alexander Ralston	Greensboro
	John F. Yeattes	Greensboro
	Joseph R. John	Greensboro
	Robert E. Bencini[7]	High Point
	William L. Daisy[8]	Greensboro
	Edmund Lowe[9]	High Point
	Thomas G. Foster, Jr.[10]	Greensboro

DISTRICT	JUDGES	ADDRESS
19A	ROBERT L. WARREN (Chief)	Concord
	FRANK M. MONTGOMERY	Salisbury
	ADAM C. GRANT, JR.	Concord
	L. FRANK FAGGART	Kannapolis
19B	L.T. HAMMOND, JR. (Chief)	Asheboro
	WILLIAM H. HEAFNER[11]	Asheboro
20	DONALD R. HUFFMAN (CHIEF)	Wadesboro
	WALTER M. LAMPLEY	Rockingham
	KENNETH W. HONEYCUTT	Monroe
	RONALD W. BURRIS	Albemarle
21	ABNER ALEXANDER (Chief)	Winston-Salem
	GARY B. TASH	Winston-Salem
	WILLIAM H. FREEMAN[12]	Winston-Salem
	JAMES A. HARRILL, JR.	Winston-Salem
	R. KASON KEIGER	Winston-Salem
	DAVID R. TANIS[13]	Winston-Salem
22	LESTER P. MARTIN, JR. (Chief)	Mocksville
	HUBERT E. OLIVE, JR.	Lexington
	ROBERT W. JOHNSON	Statesville
	SAMUEL ALLEN CATHEY	Statesville
23	RALPH DAVIS (Chief)	North Wilkesboro
	SAMUEL L. OSBORNE	Wilkesboro
	JOHN T. KILBY	Jefferson
24	ROBERT HOWARD LACEY (CHIEF)[14]	Newland
	ALEXANDER LYERLY[15]	Banner Elk
25	LIVINGSTON VERNON (Chief)	Morganton
	BILL J. MARTIN	Hickory
	SAMUEL McD. TATE	Morganton
	L. OLIVER NOBLE, JR.	Hickory
	EDWARD J. CROTTY	Hickory
26	CHASE BOONE SAUNDERS (Chief)	Charlotte
	L. STANLEY BROWN	Charlotte
	LARRY THOMAS BLACK	Charlotte
	JAMES E. LANNING	Charlotte
	WILLIAM G. JONES	Charlotte
	WALTER H. BENNETT, JR.	Charlotte
	DAPHENE L. CANTRELL	Charlotte
	T. MICHAEL TODD	Charlotte
	WILLIAM H. SCARBOROUGH	Charlotte
27A	LEWIS BULWINKLE (Chief)	Gastonia
	J. RALPH PHILLIPS	Gastonia
	DONALD E. RAMSEUR	Gastonia

DISTRICT	JUDGES	ADDRESS
	Berlin H. Carpenter, Jr.	Gastonia
27B	Arnold Max Harris (Chief)	Ellenboro
	George Hamrick	Shelby
	Thomas Bowen	Lincolnton
28	James O. Israel, Jr. (Chief)	Candler
	William Marion Styles	Black Mountain
	Earl Justice Fowler, Jr.	Arden
	Peter L. Roda	Asheville
29	Robert T. Gash (Chief)	Brevard
	Zoro J. Guice, Jr.	Hendersonville
	Thomas N. Hix	Mill Spring
	Loto J. Greenlee	Marion
30	Robert J. Leatherwood III (Chief)	Bryson City
	J. Charles McDarris	Waynesville
	John J. Snow, Jr.	Murphy

EMERGENCY JUDGE

P.B. Beachum, Jr.   Charlotte

[1]Retired 31 December 1980.
[2]Retired November 30, 1980.
[3]Appointed Chief Judge 1 December 1980.
[4]Elected 4 November 1980 and took office 1 December 1980 to succeed Joseph E. Setzer, Jr. whose term expired 30 November 1980.
[5]Appointed Chief Judge 1 December 1980.
[6]Elected 4 November 1980 and took office 1 December 1980 to succeed Frank T. Grady whose term expired 30 November 1980.
[7]Elected 4 November 1980 and took office 1 December 1980 to succeed Frank Allen Campbell whose term expired 30 November 1980.
[8]Elected 4 November 1980 and took office 1 December 1980 to succeed John B. Hatfield whose term expired 30 November 1980.
[9]Elected 4 November 1980 and took office 1 December 1980 to succeed Joseph Andrew Williams whose term expired 30 November 1980.
[10]Elected 4 November 1980 and took office 1 December 1980 to succeed James Samuel Pfaff whose term expired 30 November 1980.
[11]Resigned 30 November 1980.
[12]Appointed Special Judge, Superior Court, 1 December 1980.
[13]Appointed 1 December 1980.
[14]Appointed Chief Judge 1 December 1980.
[15]Elected 4 November 1980 and took office 1 December 1980 to succeed J. Ray Braswell whose term expired 30 November 1980.

ATTORNEY GENERAL OF NORTH CAROLINA

Attorney General

RUFUS L. EDMISTEN

Administrative Deputy Attorney General
CHARLES H. SMITH

Deputy Attorney General For Legal Affairs
JAMES M. WALLACE, JR.

Special Assistant to the Attorney General
JOHN A. ELMORE II

Senior Deputy Attorneys General
JAMES F. BULLOCK
ANDREW A. VANORE, JR.
EUGENE A. SMITH, JR.

Deputy Attorneys General
JEAN A. BENOY
MILLARD R. RICH, JR.
WILLIAM W. MELVIN

Special Deputy Attorneys General

MYRON C. BANKS
T. BUIE COSTEN
JACOB L. SAFRON
JAMES B. RICHMOND
HERBERT LAMSON, JR.
WILLIAM F. O'CONNELL
JOHN R.B. MATTHIS
EDWIN M. SPEAS, JR.
WILLIAM A. RANEY, JR.

LESTER V. CHALMERS, JR.
ANN REED DUNN
CHARLES J. MURRAY
ISAAC T. AVERY III
H. AL COLE, JR.
THOMAS F. MOFFITT
RICHARD N. LEAGUE
CLAUDE W. HARRIS

Assistant Attorneys General

WILLIAM B. RAY
WILLIAM F. BRILEY
THOMAS B. WOOD
CHARLES M. HENSEY
ROBERT G. WEBB
ROY A. GILES, JR.
JAMES E. MAGNER, JR.
GUY A. HAMLIN
ALFRED N. SALLEY
GEORGE W. BOYLAN
RALF F. HASKELL
I.B. HUDSON, JR.
ROBERT R. REILLY, JR.
RICHARD L. GRIFFIN
ARCHIE W. ANDERS
DAVID S. CRUMP
DANIEL C. OAKLEY
ELIZABETH C. BUNTING
ELISHA H. BUNTING JR.

ALAN S. HIRSCH
SANDRA M. KING
JOHN C. DANIEL, JR.
ACIE L. WARD
JOAN H. BYERS
J. MICHAEL CARPENTER
BEN G. IRONS II
DONALD W. GRIMES
NONNIE F. MIDGETTE
JO ANN SANFORD
DOUGLAS A. JOHNSTON
JAMES PEELER SMITH
RUDOLPH A. ASHTON III
FRANK P. GRAHAM
GEORGE W. LENNON
MARILYN Y. RICH
DAVID BLACKWELL
NORMA S. HARRELL
THOMAS H. DAVIS, JR.

JANE R. THOMPSON
DENNIS F. MYERS
KAYE R. WEBB
REBECCA R. BEVACQUA
DANIEL F. McLAWHORN
JEAN W. BOYLES
TIARA B. SMILEY
MARVIN SCHILLER
DONALD W. STEPHENS
HENRY T. ROSSER
HENRY H. BURGWYN
J. GREGORY WALLACE
LUCIEN CAPONE III
FRANCIS W. CRAWLEY
MICHAEL D. GORDON
JAMES C. GULICK
HARRY H. HARKINS, JR.
J. CHRISTOPHER PRATHER
GRAYSON G. KELLEY

DISTRICT ATTORNEYS

DISTRICT	DISTRICT ATTORNEY	ADDRESS
1	THOMAS S. WATTS	Elizabeth City
2	WILLIAM C. GRIFFIN, JR.	Williamston
3	ELI BLOOM	Greenville
4	WILLIAM H. ANDREWS	Jacksonville
5	WILLIAM ALLEN COBB	Wilmington
6	W.H.S. BURGWYN, JR.	Woodland
7	HOWARD S. BONEY, JR.	Tarboro
8	DONALD JACOBS	Goldsboro
9	DAVID WATERS	Oxford
10	RANDOLPH RILEY	Raleigh
11	JOHN W. TWISDALE	Smithfield
12	EDWARD W. GRANNIS, JR.	Fayetteville
13	LEE J. GREER	Whiteville
14	DAN K. EDWARDS, JR.	Durham
15A	HERBERT F. PIERCE	Graham
15B	WADE BARBER, JR.	Pittsboro
16	JOE FREEMAN BRITT	Lumberton
17	FRANKLIN FREEMAN, JR.	Reidsville
18	MICHAEL A. SCHLOSSER	Greensboro
19A	JAMES E. ROBERTS	Kannapolis
19B	RUSSELL G. WALKER, JR.	Asheboro
20	CARROLL R. LOWDER	Monroe
21	DONALD K. TISDALE	Clemmons
22	H.W. ZIMMERMAN, JR.	Lexington
23	MICHAEL A. ASHBURN	Wilkesboro
24	CLYDE M. ROBERTS	Marshall
25	DONALD E. GREENE	Hickory
26	PETER S. GILCHRIST	Charlotte
27A	JOSEPH G. BROWN	Gastonia
27B	W. HAMPTON CHILDS, JR.	Lincolnton
28	RONALD C. BROWN	Asheville
29	M. LEONARD LOWE	Caroleen
30	MARCELLUS BUCHANAN III	Sylva

CASES REPORTED

xiv

CASES REPORTED

xvii

CASES REPORTED WITHOUT PUBLISHED OPINION

CASES REPORTED WITHOUT PUBLISHED OPINION

GENERAL STATUTES CITED AND CONSTRUED

RULES OF CIVIL PROCEDURE
CITED AND CONSTRUED

CONSTITUTION OF NORTH CAROLINA
CITED AND CONSTRUED

CONSTITUTION OF UNITED STATES
CITED AND CONSTRUED

DISPOSITION OF PETITIONS FOR DISCRETIONARY REVIEW UNDER G.S. 7A-31

Case	Reported	Disposition in Supreme Court
Allen Co. v. Quip-Matic, Inc.	47 N.C. App. 40	Denied, 301 N.C. 85 Appeal Dismissed
Baer v. Davis	47 N.C. App. 581	Denied, 301 N.C. 85
Brown v. Motor Inns	47 N.C. App. 115	Denied, 301 N.C. 86
Burcl v. Hospital	47 N.C. App. 127	Denied, 301 N.C. 86 Allowed, 301 N.C. 234
City of Winston-Salem, v. Concrete Co.	47 N.C. App. 405	Denied, 301 N.C. 234
Contractors, Inc. v. Forbes	47 N.C. App. 371	Allowed, 301 N.C. 86
Cox v. Real Estate Licensing Board	47 N.C. App. 135	Denied, 301 N.C. 87
Crumpler v. Turnage	47 N.C. App. 374	Denied, 301 N.C. 87 Appeal Dismissed
Davis v. Siloo Inc.	47 N.C. App. 237	Denied, 301 N.C. 234
Dept. of Transportation v. Lancaster	47 N.C. App. 374	Denied, 301 N.C. 87
Emanuel v. Fellows	47 N.C. App. 340	Denied, 301 N.C. 87
Foust v. City of Greensboro	47 N.C. App. 159	Denied, 301 N.C. 88
Fuller v. Fuller	47 N.C. App. 766	Allowed, 301 N.C. 235
Harris v. Paving Co.	47 N.C. App. 348	Denied, 301 N.C. 88
Holt v. Holt	47 N.C. App. 618	Allowed, 301 N.C. 235
Horner v. Horner	47 N.C. App. 344	Denied, 301 N.C. 89
Hudson v. Downs	47 N.C. App. 207	Denied, 301 N.C. 89
Industries, Inc. v. Tharpe	47 N.C. App. 754	Denied, 301 N.C. 90
In re Calhoun	47 N.C. App. 472	Denied, 301 N.C. 90
In re Foreclosure of Burgess	47 N.C. App. 599	Appeal Dismissed, 301 N.C. 90
In re Kapoor	47 N.C. App. 500	Allowed, 301 N.C. 90
In re Kirkman	47 N.C. App. 479	Allowed, 301 N.C. 91
In re Ridge	47 N.C. App. 183	Allowed, 301 N.C. 91
Joyner v. Insurance	46 N.C. App. 807	Denied, 301 N.C. 91
Lathan v. Bd. of Commissioners	47 N.C. App. 357	Denied, 301 N.C. 92
Lee v. Regan	47 N.C. App. 544	Denied, 301 N.C. 92

Case	Reported	Disposition in Supreme Court
Maxwell v. Woods	47 N.C. App. 495	Denied, 301 N.C. 236
Nova University v. University of North Carolina	47 N.C. App. 638	Allowed, 301 N.C. 94
Odom v. Odom	47 N.C. App. 486	Denied, 301 N.C. 94
Parker v. Sheldon	47 N.C. App. 493	Denied, 301 N.C. 236
Spinks v. Taylor and Richardson v. Taylor Co.	47 N.C. App. 68	Allowed, 301 N.C. 236
Stam v. State	47 N.C. App. 209	Appeal Dismissed, 301 N.C. 95
State v. Bizzell	47 N.C. App. 374	Denied, 301 N.C. 236
State v. Clinding	47 N.C. App. 374	Denied, 301 N.C. 96
State v. Cooley	47 N.C. App. 376	Denied, 301 N.C. 96 Appeal Dismissed
State v. Craven	47 N.C. App. 585	Denied, 301 N.C. 97
State v. Creech	47 N.C. App. 207	Denied, 301 N.C. 97
State v. Culpepper	47 N.C. App. 633	Allowed, 301 N.C. 97
State v. Currie	47 N.C. App. 446	Denied, 301 N.C. 237
State v. Denny	47 N.C. App. 207	Denied, 301 N.C. 98
State v. Dixon	47 N.C. App. 207	Denied, 301 N.C. 98 Appeal Dismissed
State v. Dixon	47 N.C. App. 207	Denied, 301 N.C. 98
State v. Edens	47 N.C. App. 374	Denied, 301 N.C. 98
State v. Efird	37 N.C. App. 66	Denied, 301 N.C. 98
State v. Felmet	47 N.C. App. 201	Allowed, 301 N.C. 99 Appeal Dismissed
State v. Flowers	47 N.C. App. 457	Denied, 301 N.C. 99
State v. Freeman	47 N.C. App. 171	Denied, 301 N.C. 99
State v. George	47 N.C. App. 375	Denied, 301 N.C. 100
State v. Greenwood	47 N.C. App. 731	Allowed, 301 N.C. 237 Appeal Dismissal Denied
State v. Hodgen	47 N.C. App. 329	Denied, 301 N.C. 100
State v. Johnson	47 N.C. App. 297	Denied, 301 N.C. 101
State v. Logue	47 N.C. App. 585	Denied, 301 N.C. 101
State v. McCaskill	47 N.C. App. 289	Denied, 301 N.C. 101
State v. McGee	47 N.C. App. 280	Denied, 301 N.C. 101

Case	Reported	Disposition in Supreme Court
State v. McNeil	47 N.C. App. 30	Denied, 301 N.C. 102 Appeal Dismissed
State v. Mackins	47 N.C. App. 168	Denied, 301 N.C. 102
State v. Martin	47 N.C. App. 223	Denied, 301 N.C. 238 Appeal Dismissed
State v. Maxwell	47 N.C. App. 658	Denied, 301 N.C. 102 Appeal Dismissed
State v. Milby and State v. Boyd	47 N.C. App. 669	Allowed, 301 N.C. 103
State v. Modlin	47 N.C. App. 585	Denied, 301 N.C. 103
State v. Mullen	47 N.C. App. 667	Denied, 301 N.C. 103
State v. Rice	47 N.C. App. 208	Denied, 301 N.C. 238
State v. Rich	47 N.C. App. 767	Denied, 301 N.C. 103
State v. Rucker	47 N.C. App. 585	Denied, 301 N.C. 104 Appeal Dismissed
State v. Street	45 N.C. App. 1	Denied, 301 N.C. 104
State v. Walton	47 N.C. App. 208	Denied, 301 N.C. 104
State v. Williams	47 N.C. App. 205	Denied, 301 N.C. 104
State v. Williams	47 N.C. App. 586	Denied, 301 N.C. 105
State v. Wilson	47 N.C. App. 586	Denied, 301 N.C. 105
Synco, Inc. v. Headen	47 N.C. App. 109	Denied, 301 N.C. 238
Vickery v. Construction Co.	47 N.C. App. 98	Denied, 301 N.C. 106
Walker v. Insurance Co.	47 N.C. App. 375	Denied, 301 N.C. 106 Appeal Dismissed
Watson v. Dept. of Correction	47 N.C. App. 718	Denied, 301 N.C. 239
Wesley v. Greyhound Lines, Inc.	47 N.C. App. 680	Denied, 301 N.C. 239
Wilhite v. Veneer Co.	47 N.C. App. 434	Allowed, 301 N.C. 106
Wojsko v. State	47 N.C. App. 605	Denied, 301 N.C. 239 Appeal Dismissed
Wright v. Wright	47 N.C. App. 367	Allowed, 301 N.C. 240

DISPOSITION OF APPEALS OF RIGHT TO THE SUPREME COURT UNDER G.S. 7A-30

Case	Reported	Disposition on Appeal
Brandon v. Insurance Co.	46 N.C. App. 472	301 N.C. ---
Brenner v. School House, Ltd.	47 N.C. App. 19	Pending
Colson v. Shaw	46 N.C. App. 402	Pending
Etheridge v. Peters, Comr. of Motor Vehicles	45 N.C. App. 358	301 N.C. 76
Hice v. Hi-Mil, Inc.	47 N.C. App. 427	Pending
Kinnard v. Mecklenburg Fair	46 N.C. App. 725	301 N.C. ---
Lovell v. Insurance Co.	46 N.C. App. 150	Pending
Morris v. Morris	46 N.C. App. 701	301 N.C. ---
Morrison v. Burlington Industries	47 N.C. App. 50	Pending
State v. Coats	46 N.C. App. 615	301 N.C. 216
State v. Cummings	46 N.C. App. 680	301 N.C. ---
State v. Lane	46 N.C. App. 501	301 N.C. ---
State v. Lynch	46 N.C. App. 608	301 N.C. ---
Taylor v. Taylor	45 N.C. App. 449	301 N.C. ---
Thornburg v. Lancaster	47 N.C. App. 131	Pending
Town of Scotland Neck v. Surety Co.	46 N.C. App. 124	301 N.C. ---
Utilities Comm. v. Oil Co.	47 N.C. App. 1	Pending
Vassey v. Burch	45 N.C. App. 222	301 N.C. 68

CASES

ARGUED AND DETERMINED IN THE

COURT OF APPEALS

OF

NORTH CAROLINA

AT

RALEIGH

STATE OF NORTH CAROLINA, EX REL. UTILITIES COMMISSION, KENAN
TRANSPORT COMPANY AND NORTH CAROLINA MOTOR CARRIERS
ASSOCIATION, INC., AGENT FOR MOTOR COMMON CARRIERS, APPELLEES V.
BIRD OIL COMPANY, BURKE OIL COMPANY, LAMPLIGHTER OIL
COMPANY, WEIL OIL COMPANY, NORWOOD OIL COMPANY, APPEL-
LANTS

No. 7910UC615

(Filed 3 June 1980)

1. **Carriers § 5.1– common carrier rates – petroleum products – dedicated service
provision – discriminatory and preferential rates**

    The dedicated service provision in the tariff schedule for motor vehicle
common carriers of petroleum products, which provides for a lower rate for
petroleum products when the common carrier assigns a single unit of equipment to the exclusive and continuous use of one shipper for a minimum of 100
hours per week for 20 consecutive weeks, is discriminatory and preferential
in violation of G.S. 62-140 and other statutes relating to motor carriers.

2. **Carriers § 5.1– common carrier rates – petroleum products – dedicated service
provision – new business to common carrier system – sufficient evidence**

    There was not competent, material and substantial evidence in the
record to support a finding that the dedicated service rate provision for
common carriers of petroleum products attracts new business to the common carrier system; furthermore, attracting business to a common carrier is
not a sufficient justification for such a discriminatory rate.

Judge VAUGHN dissenting.

APPEAL from the North Carolina Utilities Commission.
Order entered 11 April 1979. Heard in the Court of Appeals 29
January 1980.

This action involves a challenge to the dedicated service provision in the tariff schedule set by the North Carolina Utilities Commission (NCUC) for motor vehicle common carriers of petroleum products.

Pursuant to Chapter 62 of the North Carolina General Statutes, the North Carolina Utilities Commission has the authority to approve rates, fares and charges for common carriers by motor vehicles (G.S. 62-146), and motor vehicle contract carriers (G.S. 62-147), who engage in intrastate commerce. A "common carrier by motor vehicle" is defined as "any person which holds itself out to the general public to engage in the transportation by motor vehicle in intrastate commerce of persons or property or any class or classes thereof for compensation." G.S. 62-3(7). In contrast, a "contract carrier by motor vehicle" means any person which, in contract with another person or persons, as approved by the Utilities Commission, engages in transportation activities other than common carriages. G.S. 62-3. By way of distinction, a "private carrier" means "any person not included in the definitions of common carrier or contract carrier, which transports in intrastate commerce in its own vehicle or vehicles property of which such person is the owner, lessee, or bailee, when such transportation is for the purpose of sale, lease, rent, or bailment, or when such transportation is purely an incidental adjunct to some other established private business owned and operated by such person other than the transportation of property for compensation." G.S. 62-3(22). The Utilities Commission has no authority to regulate transportation activities of private carriers. G.S. 62-260(a)(16).

In the case before us, the North Carolina Motor Carriers Association (NCMCA) serves as agent for the motor vehicle common carriers which, pursuant to Local Motor Freight Tariff No. 5-0, N.C.U.C. No. 110, transport petroleum and petroleum products in bulk, in tank trucks from, to and between points in North Carolina. Appellee Kenan Transport Company is a motor vehicle common carrier represented by the NCMCA. The appellants, Bird Oil Company, Burke Oil Company, Lamplighter Oil Company, Weil Oil Company and Norwood Oil Company, are all "oil jobbers" who purchase petroleum products from the refinery and distribute the products to retail outlets or individual consumers.

The subject matter of this appeal centers around the following tariff schedule for intrastate common carriers of petroleum products in bulk in tank trucks, Supplement No. 8 to Local Motor Freight Tariff No. 5-0, Item No. 8005A:

"ITEM 8005-A (Cancels Item 8005 of Tariff)

DEDICATED SERVICE

(a) The rates, charges, rules, regulations and provisions of this Section apply to the operation of a single unit of carrier's equipment assigned to the exclusive and continuous use of one shipper and when a combination of loading and unloading facilities are available to the carrier for the operation of that equipment for a minimum of one hundred hours per week ... for 20 consecutive weeks.

(b) A calendar week will begin at 12:01 a.m. Monday and run through 12:00 p.m. Saturday.

(c) The shipper will be deemed to be the party paying the freight charges.

(d) Time of arrival and/or departure of points of loading and/or unloading will be furnished shipper or carrier's forms upon request.

(e) Under the application of dedicated service, carrier will put into effect and operation a plan of unattended loading and/or unloading, only after prior written agreement between carrier, shipper and/or consignee."

The approval of the tariff schedule was based in part on the following findings of fact by the Utilities Commission in 1963:

" '3. The tariff filing offers a somewhat improved service to shippers who are in a position to utilize transportation service consistently and provides a reduced rate for consis-

tently [*sic*] and provides a reduced rate for consistent utilization of carriers' equipment and services, which rates
and services are subject to contract between carrier and
shipper.

4. The proposed rates, considered in connection with the
consistent utilization of carriers' equipment, will be compensatory and are found to be just and reasonable.'"

Docket No. T-825, Sub. 68 (27 September 1963).

In essence, the dedicated service section, Section 8 of Tariff
No. 5-0, provides for a fifteen percent lower rate on gasoline,
kerosene, jet fuel, naphtha, diesel fuel oil No. 1, and fuel oils
Nos. 1, 2 and 3, and a five percent lower rate on fuel oils Nos. 4, 5
and 6 and bunker C, provided that the common carrier assign a
single unit of the carrier's equipment to the exclusive and continuous use of one shipper for a minimum of one hundred hours
per week, for twenty consecutive weeks.

On 5 January 1978 NCMCA proposed a revision in the "Dedicated Service" provision Item 8005-A of Petroleum Tariff No.
5-0 in order to add the following "commingling" provision:

"(f) Hours generated by the dedicated unit of equipment in Interstate Commerce will be applicable in determining the minimum of one hundred hours per week (PF
624-A)."

On 23 January 1978, the NCUC issued an order of suspension, investigation and notice of hearing, suspending Item 8005-
A, dedicated service, Paragraph (f), for a period of 270 days and
set the matter for hearing on 10 May 1978.

On 17 April 1978, the appellants filed a verified protest to
Item 8005-A, moved, pursuant to G.S. 62-136, to expand the
scope of the hearing to include an investigation and hearing of
the existing dedicated service rates found in Section 8 of the
Motor Freight Tariff No. 5-0, and further requested the NCUC
to order the motor vehicle common carrier participants in the
subject tariff to produce certain data.

On 2 May 1978, Kenan Transport Company (hereinafter Kenan Transport) on behalf of itself and other motor vehicle common carriers participating in the dedicated service tariff, filed a response in opposition to the protest.

On 4 May 1978, the NCUC issued an order allowing the protestants to intervene in opposition to the proposed revision in the dedicated service rules, expanded the scope of the hearing pursuant to G.S. 62-136 to include an investigation of the existing dedicated service rates contained in Section 8 of Motor Freight Tariff No. 5-0, ordered the motor vehicle common carriers participating in the tariff to file additional information, and continued the hearing to 2 August 1978.

Pursuant to the order of 4 May 1978, a hearing was held before a Hearing Examiner, Antoinette R. Wike, on 2 August 1978, at which time Kenan Transport presented evidence in support of the existing dedicated service rate and the proposed revision to include the commingling provision. The five oil jobbers, appellants herein, presented evidence in opposition to the existing dedicated service rules, including the proposed commingling provision.

On 5 January 1979, the Hearing Examiner issued a Recommended Order approving the revisions in Item 8005-A, canceling the prior order of suspension and investigation and dismissing the proceeding. The recommended order included the following findings of fact and conclusions of law:

"3. There are approximately eighty carriers in North Carolina having intrastate authority to transport petroleum products. At the time of hearing, three of these carriers had equipment dedicated to shippers. The commingling provision was proposed by Kenan Transport Company.

4. The applicable rates for dedicated service on light petroleum products are 15% lower than the applicable mileage rates. If the dedicated equipment is not utilized 100 hours in a given week, the shipper is billed $5.00 per

one-half hour or fraction thereof for the number of hours below 100.

5. The purpose of the proposed revision in Item 8005-A is to allow the carrier and the shipper to commingle interstate and intrastate traffic on one unit of equipment, with the hours generated by the interstate portion counting toward the 100 hours minimum required for the dedicated intrastate rate.

6. Dedicated service attracts business. By spreading fixed costs over more business, the carriers have achieved and will continue to achieve lower unit costs. Additional costs such as record keeping, associated with a dedicated unit, are minimal.

7. The availability of dedicated service at lower rates has encouraged many shippers to discontinue private carriage thus resulting in an expansion of common carrier operations involving petroleum products. One hundred hours per week approximates the utilization which the oil company would achieve with its own equipment. The 20-week provision of the tariff is designed to encompass the five-month period (November-March) during which more light petroleum products, i.e. heating fuels, move.

8. Generally, shippers able to take advantage of existing dedicated service rates are major oil companies, such as Exxon, Texaco, Union, Phillips, Gulf, Mobile, Amerada Hess, A.T.C. Petroleum, Kenan, and Direct.

9. For the most part, smaller entities, such as the oil jobbers, are unable to take advantage of dedicated service rates since their facilities are open only 40-50 hours per week and they are either unwilling or unable to enter into unattended loading and unloading arrangements with a common carrier.

10. The price paid by the oil jobbers for gasoline is a delivered price less a freight allowance.

11. When the dedicated rate was first approved in 1963, the oil jobbers were receiving the full common carrier rate as a freight allowance from their suppliers. Many, therefore, chose to purchase equipment and engage in the private transport of their products from terminals to their bulk holding facilities. At that time, such operations were a lucrative part of the oil jobbers' business.

12. A few years ago, 1972 in some cases, the petroleum suppliers began to use the lower, dedicated rate as the basis for a freight allowance. This, coupled with rising equipment costs, has created an increasingly disadvantageous situation for oil jobbers who are unable to qualify for the dedicated rate.

13. By increasing the use of such lower rates by the larger shippers, the proposed rules revision will tend to exacerbate the competitive disadvantage of the smaller shippers for whom dedicated service rates remain unavailable.

*   *   *   *

1. The burden of proof is on the NCMCA to show that the proposed revision in dedicated service rules is just and reasonable. The burden of proof is on the Protestants to show that the existing dedicated service rates rules and regulations are unjust and unreasonable. G.S. 62-75.

2. The commingling provision contained in the proposed tariff will enable more petroleum shippers to qualify for dedicated service rates. Increased usage of such service will benefit the carriers by creating more traffic and lowering unit costs. The NCMCA has offered evidence showing that the subject rules revision is in the public interest. The oil jobbers have offered no evidence to the contrary. The Hearing Examiner concludes that the tariff should become effective.

3. The Commission previously has determined that existing dedicated service rates, rules and regulations are

just and reasonable. The oil jobbers have shown that not only are they effectively precluded from doing dedicated service by terms of the rules, the price they pay for certain petroleum products often is based on dedicated rates, thus eliminating any incentive to engage in private carriage and in fact raising their costs. Because their competitors more readily qualify for such rates, the oil jobbers contend that they suffer discrimination in the market place. While the oil jobbers' problem is understandable, it cannot be solved by the Commission's declaring unlawful a tariff which is lawful. The NCMCA has shown in this and earlier proceedings that dedicated service is sufficiently distin- guishable from other common carrier service to warrant a difference in rates. Moreover, the oil jobbers' testimony shows clearly that their real complaint is not against the NCMCA but against the oil companies from whom they purchase petroleum products. They must look directly to their own contractual arrangements for relief."

On 22 January 1979, the appellants filed their exceptions to the Recommended Order. On 21 February 1979, the NCUC set exceptions for oral argument for 2 March 1979. Following the hearing on the exceptions, the NCUC issued the Final Order on 11 April 1979, which overruled and denied appellants' excep- tions and affirmed the Recommended Order.

Pursuant to G.S. 62-90, the appellants, on 10 May 1979, filed their exceptions and notice of appeal of the 11 April 1979 order of the North Carolina Utilities Commission.

Other necessary facts will be stated in the opinion.

Allen, Steed & Allen by Thomas W. Steed, Jr. for plaintiff appellees.

Hatch, Little, Bunn, Jones, Few & Berry by David H. Per- mar for defendant appellants.

CLARK, Judge.

This appeal involves three challenges to the dedicated service rate provision in the Local Motor Freight Tariff for bulk shipment of petroleum and petroleum products in tank trucks:

(1) That the dedicated service rate is discriminatory and preferential in violation of G.S. 62-140 because it allows a lower rate for some shippers than for others providing the same service;

(2) The dedicated rate requires the common carrier to violate its statutory and common law duty to provide equal and impartial service to all members of the general public, by, in effect, converting the common carrier into a contract carrier and allowing the carrier to charge a lower rate than that permitted to a contract carrier; and,

(3) That the order fails to include the requisite findings and conclusions required by G.S. 62-79 by failing to determine whether the commingling provision is just and reasonable as required by G.S. 62-130; that the order fails to determine whether dedicated rates are just, reasonable, sufficient and nondiscriminatory as required by G.S. 62-136; and that the order failed to determine whether a substantial difference in service or conditions existed, as required by G.S. 62-140.

I. TARIFF DISCRIMINATION

[1] It is not for this Court to evaluate the merits of whether this State should in fact regulate motor vehicle common carriers. Our only task in a case of this nature is to ascertain whether the orders of the Utilities Commission conform to the mandate of the General Assembly. Unfortunately, there is a dearth of relevant North Carolina case law to guide us in interpreting the statute in the context of dedicated service. Nonetheless, we hold that the entire dedicated rate provision is discriminatory and preferential in violation of G.S. 62-140 and other applicable portions of the General Statutes pertaining to Motor Carriers.

Stripped of all the jargon, the question before us is whether large shippers can lawfully be given lower common carrier rates because they are larger, and thereby, in effect, be ex-

empted from sharing with smaller shippers the costs of utilizing the common carrier system as a whole. Such a result is not
consonant with our statutory system of regulating common
carriers.

Generally speaking, the present regulatory system is designed to insure that common carriers are available to ship
goods for whomever calls upon their services. It is fundamental
that all who ship goods with common carriers are required to be
treated equally with respect to the same category of service:

> "No public utility shall, as to rates or services, make or
> grant any unreasonable preference or advantage to any
> person or subject any person to any unreasonable pre-
> judice or disadvantage ...." G.S. 62-140(a) (1979 Cum.
> Supp.)

> "In addition to the declaration of policy set forth in G.S.
> 62-2 of Article 1 of Chapter 62, it is declared the policy of the
> State of North Carolina to preserve and continue all motor
> carrier transportation services now afforded this State ...
> to encourage and promote harmony among all carriers and
> to prevent discrimination, undue preferences or advan-
> tages, or unfair and destructive competitive practices be-
> tween all carriers ...." G.S. 62-259.

As explained by W. David Fesperman, Traffic Manager of
Kenan Transport, Inc., "The product involved here and transported whether under the regular rates or the dedicated rates
is the same ... and the products are being carried to ... the
same markets."

Our concern that this dedicated rate provision is discriminatory is triggered by the Commission's own Finding of Fact
No. 13, that "[b]y increasing the use of such lower rates by the
larger shippers, the proposed rules revision will tend to *exacerbate the competitive disadvantage of the smaller shippers* for
whom dedicated service rates remain unavailable." (Emphasis
supplied). This finding, we think, indicates that the dedicated
rate provision contravenes the Commission's mandate "to pre-

serve and continue *all* motor carrier transportation services now afforded this state" and to prevent "undue preferences or advantages, or unfair and destructive competitive practices between all carriers." G.S. 62-259, *supra*. (Emphasis supplied).

The appellees do not dispute this effect. In fact, Kenan's representative even goes so far as to suggest that the best result would be for the small oil jobbers to sell all of their equipment and put all of their volume on common carriers. Kenan, in effect, wants to "attract business" to the common carriers though the effect may be to force small oil jobbers out of the petroleum transportation business. Again, this is not consonant with the Commission's statutory mandate.

Furthermore, it is apparent from Fesperman's testimony that Kenan would like to use the dedicated service provision to capture business for Kenan and to prevent the situation where "someone calls for a shipment and [Kenan doesn't] have a unit available, they go to somebody else." We see no reason under the statutory scheme why other motor vehicle common carriers should not have equal access to shippers of petroleum products.

Kenan argues, however, that there is no unreasonable or undue preference because there is a cost justification for the rate reduction. This argument does not withstand close scrutiny. Kenan presented the following chart of expenses at their Greensboro operation:

	Non-Dedicated	Dedicated
Operating Expenses	$328,062.00	$83,818.00
Other Deductions	320.00	86.00
Overhead	47,888.00	12,806,00
Total Expenses	$376,270.00	$96,710.00
Shipments	$ 5,437.00	$ 1,653.00
Cost per Shipment	$ 69.21	$ 58.51

In explaining this charge, Mr. Fesperman stated:

"There is certainly economic justification for the dedicated rates. Many of the costs involved in operating are *fixed costs,* and the increased utilization of the dedicated unit(s) gives a carrier a broader base over which to spread these fixed costs. Examples of *fixed costs* are mechanics' salaries, terminal managers' salaries, dispatchers' salaries, communication and utilities at the terminal, terminal rent, depreciation, and overhead expenses."

Later in his testimony, Mr. Fesperman stated:

"We are anticipating that we are going to be able to increase our business volume with the dedicated rates. This increased volume will enable us to spread our *fixed costs* over more business with less units. That is a justification for the dedicated rates." (Emphasis supplied).

The above statements emphasize that Kenan's primary economic justification for the dedicated rates is based upon lower average fixed costs;[1] such a justification, however, has been explicitly rejected by a federal court in the context of common carrier regulation under section 2 of the Interstate Commerce Act:[2]

---

[1]"Average variable costs (AVC) are those costs which are attributable to the operation of the enterprise as a productive unit — labor, raw materials, power, etc. — divided by the firm's output. Average fixed costs (AFC), on the other hand, are costs which over the short run would be incurred regardless of the operations *vel non* of the firm — examples of this sort of costs are lease payments, property taxes, investment, debt service, etc. — to get an average, fixed costs are divided by output."

Central & Southern Motor Freight Tariff Association v. United States, 273 F. Supp. 823, 829 (1967) at n. 6.

[2]Section 2 of the Interstate Commerce Act, 49 USC § 2 (1976) provides:

"If any common carrier subject to the provisions of this chapter shall, directly or indirectly, by any special rate, rebate, drawback or other device, charge, demand, collect, or receive from any person or persons a greater or less compensation for any service rendered or to be rendered, in the transportation of passengers or property subject to the provisions of this chapter, than it charges, demands, collects or receives from any other person or persons for doing for him or them a like and contemporaneous service in the transportation of a like kind of traffic under substantially similar circumstances and conditions, such common carrier shall be deemed guilty of unjust discrimination, which is prohibited and declared to be unlawful."

"Reduced average fixed costs — which always accompany increased volume when there is unused capacity — have never been considered an element of cost saving in traditional section 2 analysis. In fact, ... using such 'cost savings' to justify rate reductions would permit any rate reduction — where the carriers' demand curve was the slightest bit price elastic, and the carrier was not operating at full capacity — since rate reductions would increase demand, allowing the carrier to spread its fixed cost over a greater volume of shipping. Further, any such treatment of average fixed cost economics would run counter to the legislative spirit which is the very heart of Section 2."

Central & Southern Motor Freight Tariff Association v. United States, 273 F. Supp. 823, 829 (1967).

Similarly, in *Louisville East and St. Louis Consolidated Railroad Company v. Wilson*, 132 Ind. 517, 32 N.E. 311 (1892), the court held that it was unreasonable and discriminatory for a railroad to charge $14.00 per carload of crossties to one shipper and $24.00 per carload of crossties to another shipper, even though the shipper in whose favor the discrimination is made ships many more cars than any of the others. As pointed out by the court:

"It is contended by the appellant that in view of the fact it is secured by its contract with Dickerson a certain income of $7,000 per month, it could well afford to carry ties for him at $14.00 per car as to carry them for the appellees at $24.00 per car. We find it unnecessary to inquire whether the appellant is correct or otherwise in this contention for, as we understand the law, a railroad company engaged in the business of *a common carrier is not permitted by the law to discriminate in favor of a shipper who is able to furnish a large amount of freight over one engaged in the same business who is unable to furnish the same quantity as that shipped by his more opulent rival.*"

32 N.E. at 314-15. (Emphasis added.) We note that the exception to this rule for broken shipments, discussed in *Louisville, supra*, does not apply herein, because as in *Louisville*, we are talking about the same commodities, "shipped in full carloads, and from the same stations." *Id.*

By its very nature, a common carrier which by statute holds itself out to serve everyone on call cannot obtain the same efficiencies of operation that may be obtained on a single route for a single customer who uses the same equipment with great frequency. Nonetheless, it is fundamental that all shippers, both large and small, share the common burden of the common carrier system. It is also true that with more business attracted to the common carrier system, there will be greater utilization of the equipment of all carriers and there will be lower average costs for all carriers. The dedicated rate provision, however, has the effect of allocating all the efficiencies of higher utilization to the large shippers while at the same time allocating an undue burden of maintaining the common carrier system to the smaller shippers. It is true that the large vertically integrated petroleum companies still have the prerogative to utilize their own private transports rather than rely upon common carrier services. Nonetheless, if they elect to use common carriers of petroleum products they must pay the same rates as other shippers of petroleum products where they ship the same products to the same markets.

The appellees also contend, in line with the Hearing Examiner's Conclusion No. 3, that the appellants must look to their own contractual arrangements for relief. The Commission found that the use of the dedicated rate as the basis for a freight allowance in the contracts between appellants and the petroleum refiners created a disadvantageous situation for oil jobbers unable to qualify for dedicated rates. There is no doubt that this is a matter of private contract, and there is no claim herein of unfair trade practices or antitrust violations on the part of the oil companies. Nonetheless, the contractual provisions are not the only source of discrimination against the appellants: the dedicated rate provision itself unreasonably discriminates against smaller oil jobbers. An oil jobber who does not operate his own petroleum transports must rely upon the petroleum common carriers to transport his product from the pipeline terminal to his bulk plant and filling stations. The fact that he must pay a full tariff, while at the same time some of his competitors such as Exxon and Texaco are paying a fifteen percent lower rate for transportation, means that the product that he sells or distributes must be sold at a higher price. This competitive price disadvantage means that the oil jobber supplied or operated service stations will lose business to the major oil company-owned-or-operated filling station which has its fuel transported under the dedicated service rate.

II. *ATTRACTION OF NEW BUSINESS TO COMMON CARRIERS.*

[2] Appellees also argue, in effect, that the dedicated rate provision is justified because it attracts new business to the common carrier system. There is not "competent, material and substantial" evidence in the record to support the assertions in Findings of Fact Nos. 6 and 7 that the dedicated rate tariffs do or will cause the large oil companies to dispose of their private carriage operations and instead use the services of common carriers. G.S. 62-94(b)(5). Nor is there material and substantial evidence indicating whether revenue earned under dedicated service comes from new business or from business merely shifted from "full fare traffic" to the "dedicated service" traffic which receives a fifteen percent lower rate.

The only testimony in this regard comes from Mr. Fesperman, Kenan's Traffic Manager, who stated as follows:

> "Major oil companies are looking to provisions such as this to match their own utilization factors so that they can get out of private carriage. This would result in an expansion of common carrier operations in North Carolina and would be beneficial to the common carrier system.

> *   *   *   *

> By operating these units 100 hours per week, a common carrier can approach more closely the utilization that an oil company gets on its own equipment. As we approach or pass that utilization, the oil companies tend to eliminate their own private carriage, making more transportation available to the common carriers, and increases our safety and stability within the State of North Carolina.

> *   *   *   *

> I am not familiar with any shipper approaching Kenan

asking us to sponsor the commingling provisions of the dedicated rate. We do specifically have in mind serving North Carolina and Southern Virginia out of the Friendship Terminal under the dedicated rate if the commingling provision is adopted. In my original testimony filed with the Commission, I mentioned Texaco and Exxon as companies that were looking to utilizing the commingling provision of the tariff. Texaco and Exxon have asked us about the availability of the dedicated plans. A commingling proposal is an essential part of getting a dedicated plan to operate to its maximum effectiveness.

* * * *

If we decrease the dedicated service hours and more traffic becomes available to be handled under the dedicated plan, some of that traffic is going to be traffic with common carriers that the common carrier does not handle today. It is going to be traffic that is handled in private carriage."

These hypothetical or theoretical statements by Mr. Fesperman do not establish whether the dedicated rate provision has in fact given the common carriers business that otherwise would have been handled by the oil companies' owned transports. It is one thing for the Commission to base a new experimental rate structure upon such testimony, but it is quite another for the Commission to rely on such hypothetical testimony when the actual tariff structure has been in effect for fifteen years. It would have required little effort on the part of the appellees herein to have requested the testimony of officials from the major petroleum companies pertaining to: (1) the cost of the companies' private carriage operations; (2) the question of whether they have dismantled some of their private carrier operations because of the dedicated rates; or (3) whether because of the rates they have not procured transport equipment they would have otherwise procured. In sum, the statutory words "competent, material and substantial" must be given their literal meaning and applied in substance, particularly where the evidence must justify a finding that a rate provision which is discriminatory on its face is nonetheless reasonable. *See, e.g., Central & Southern Motor Freight Tariff Association,*

Inc. v. United States, 345 F. Supp. 1389, 1393-95 (1972) (appeal after remand).

Nor do we think that appellees may rely upon evidence presented before the Commission prior to its order of 27 September 1963, which order was issued fifteen years before the hearing now controverted and for which the supporting testimony was not included in the record in this appeal. See N.C. Rules App. Proc. 18 (c)(v)-(vii). While we would not go so far as to say that all the evidence must be "new" evidence, the record must nonetheless indicate that the Commission had before it sufficient evidence upon which to base its findings. If testimony from an earlier proceeding is relied upon to justify a finding of fact in a later proceeding (and we have doubts as to the merits of this practice), at the very least, the relevant portions of the earlier testimony must also be included in the record on appeal in a case where the sufficiency of facts to support that finding is challenged.

Even if such evidence were in the record, attracting business to a common carrier is not a sufficient justification for a discriminatory rate. In *State ex rel. Kohler, Attorney General v. Cincinnati, W. & B. Railway Company*, 47 Ohio State 130, 23 N.E. 928 (1890), the common carrier charged a substantially lower rate for transporting petroleum in bulk in tank cars as compared to transporting petroleum in barrels. The court stated:

> "The justification interposed is that this was not done pursuant to any confederacy with the favored shipper, or with any purpose to inflict injury on their competitors, *but in order that the railroad companies might secure freight that would otherwise have been lost to them.* This we do not think sufficient .... As common carriers, their duty is to carry indifferently for all who may apply, and in the order in which the application is made, and upon the same terms; and *the assumption of a right to make discriminations in rates for freight*, such as was claimed and exercised by the defendants in this case, freight, *that it would otherwise lose, is a misue of the rights and privileges conferred upon it by law.*" 23 N.E. at 930. (Emphasis supplied).

This is an old case from another jurisdiction but we can find no compelling reason as to why the principles articulated therein should not be the law in this State at this time.

III. *CONTRACT CARRIAGE AND OTHER USES.*

As we have held that the dedicated rate provision is unreasonably discriminatory we do not need to address the question as to whether the dedication of equipment for a twenty-week period is inconsistent with common carriage. Nor are we compelled to answer the remainder of appellants' challenges.

The Order of the Commission, dated 11 April 1979, in Docket No. T-825, Sub. 226, establishing Paragraphs (a)-(f) of Item 8005-A in Local Motor Freight Tariff No. 5-0, is

Vacated.

Judge HEDRICK concurs.

Judge VAUGHN dissents.

Judge VAUGHN dissenting: I respectfully dissent from the well-written opinion of my learned colleagues. I note first that the existing rate structure is presumed to be just and reasonable and that the burden was upon the appellants to show that it was unlawful. Moreover, the findings of the Commission are conclusive if they are supported by competent material and substantial evidence in view of the entire record, and I conclude that they are so supported in this case. Incentive rate structures based on use intensity are widely authorized, and the question of their employment should generally be a matter for the specialized regulatory agency and not the courts. If appellants pay more for the petroleum they buy than others, that result springs from the pricing policies of the oil companies — a matter beyond the jurisdiction of the Utilities Commission. I vote to affirm the order.

RALPH N. BRENNER, JR. v. THE LITTLE RED SCHOOL HOUSE, LIMITED

No. 7918DC1141

(Filed 3 June 1980)

1. **Contracts § 4.1– nonrefundable tuition – failure of child to attend school – no failure of consideration**

   Where plaintiff entered a contract under the terms of which tuition for plaintiff's child to attend defendant's school was payable in advance and not refundable, plaintiff was not entitled to recover tuition paid to defendant on the ground of failure of consideration because plaintiff's former wife would not let the child attend defendant's school after the school year began.

2. **Contracts § 20.1– frustration – impossibility of performance**

   A contract which required plaintiff to pay tuition in advance with no refund in order for defendant to hold a place in defendant's school for plaintiff's child was not subject to rescission because of frustration when plaintiff's former wife would not permit the child to attend defendant's school, since there was no fundamental change in conditions so that if the child had attended the school the object for which the contract was made would not have been attained. Nor was the contract subject to rescission on the ground of impossibility of performance since defendant was able to perform and plaintiff's inability to deliver the child to the school did not constitute impossibility of performance.

3. **Contracts § 6– nonrefundable tuition – contract not unconscionable**

   A contract requiring plaintiff to pay tuition in advance with no refund in order for defendant to prepare and hold a place in its school for plaintiff's child was not unconscionable.

   Judge MARTIN (Harry C.) dissenting.

APPEAL by defendant from *Hatfield, Judge.* Judgment entered 5 October 1979 in District Court, GUILFORD County. Heard in the Court of Appeals 16 May 1980.

This is an action to recover for tuition paid by plaintiff to defendant to enable the plaintiff's child to attend a school operated by the defendant. Plaintiff and defendant entered into a contract which provided in part as follows:

"We understand that the tuition is $1,080 per year, payable in advance of the first day of school, no portion refundable. We also understand that upon your approval we may elect to pay tuition in $100 per month installments with interest according to your published schedule, but that such an election does not in anywise modify the stipulation that tuition is payable in advance."

The plaintiff is divorced, and his former wife has custody of their child. The plaintiff paid the tuition in advance but after the school year had commenced, his former wife refused to allow the child to enroll in the school. The plaintiff alleged that the headmistress of the school promised to return the tuition but then refused to do so.

Plaintiff also alleged that the contract is unenforceable for lack of consideration or for failure of consideration. He alleged further the failure of the defendant to return the consideration was an unfair trade practice under G.S. 75-1.1 and prayed for treble damages.

Both parties moved for summary judgment, and the defendant moved to dismiss under G.S. 1A-1, Rule 12(b) (6). The court granted the plaintiff's motion for summary judgment. Defendant appealed.

Wyatt, Early, Harris, Wheeler and Hauser, by A. Doyle Early, Jr., for plaintiff appellee.

Max D. Ballinger for defendant appellant.

WEBB, Judge.

[1] We hold the court erred in granting the plaintiff's motion for summary judgment and in not granting the defendant's motion to dismiss pursuant to G.S. 1A-1, Rule 12(b) (6). The complaint shows plaintiff entered into a contract under the terms of which tuition was payable in advance and not refundable. The terms of the contract are not ambiguous and the courts are bound to enforce it as written. *See Loving Co. v.*

Contractor, Inc., 44 N.C. App. 597, 261 S.E. 2d 286 (1980) and *Weyerhaeuser v. Carolina Power and Light Co.,* 257 N.C. 717, 127 S.E. 2d 539 (1962).

[2] The appellee contends the contract should be rescinded because of frustration and impossibility of performance. There was not a fundamental change in conditions so that if the child had attended the school, the object for which the contract had been made would not have been attained. This makes the doctrine of frustration inapplicable. *See McCay v. Morris,* 46 N.C. App. 791, 266 S.E. 2d 5 (1980). Nor do we believe impossibility of performance applies. Impossibility of performance is recognized in this jurisdiction as excusing a party from performing on an executory contract if the subject matter of the contract is destroyed without fault by the party who wishes to be excused from performance. That is not the situation in the case sub judice. The defendant was able to perform. It had saved a place in the school for plaintiff's child. When the plaintiff was unable to deliver the child to the school, this did not constitute impossibility of performance. *See Sechrest v. Furniture Co.,* 264 N.C. 216, 141 S.E. 2d 292 (1965). We believe our holding in the case sub judice is consistent with prior cases in this jurisdiction, *Horner School v. Wescott,* 124 N.C. 518, 32 S.E. 885 (1899) and *Bingham v. Richardson,* 60 N.C. 215 (1864) and the majority of jurisdictions in this country. 69 A.L.R. 714 (1930).

[3] The plaintiff also contends he should be relieved from the terms of the contract because it is unconscionable. There was not a disparity of bargaining power between the parties in this case. The plaintiff could have chosen some other school for his child. He entered into a contract which provided there would not be a refund. This was a reasonable requirement in view of the expense to defendant in preparing for the child and holding a place for him. We hold this provision of the contract is not unconscionable.

The plaintiff argues further that the contract should not be enforced because by requiring the forfeiture of the tuition, it provides for a penalty rather than liquidated damages. The difficulty with this argument is that the defendant is not asking for damages. It is asking that the contract be enforced as written. We hold that it is not unreasonable for the defendant to require payment in advance with no refund in order for the defendant to prepare and hold a place in the school for plaintiff's child.

The plaintiff's last argument is that the headmistress of the school promised to refund the tuition and the failure to do so is a breach of contract by the defendant. Assuming the headmistress was acting within her authority, this promise is unenforceable as being without consideration.

The plaintiff has entered into a contract which is not ambiguous. He is bound by its terms. The defendant's motion to dismiss should have been allowed. We reverse and remand for a judgment consistent with this opinion.

Reversed and remanded.

Judge WELLS concurs.

Judge MARTIN (Harry C.) dissents.

Judge MARTIN (Harry C.) dissenting:

I must respectfully dissent from the opinion of Judge Webb.

Here, we are concerned with a contract between plaintiff and defendant for the education of plaintiff's son, Russ, in the fourth grade. Plaintiff and his former wife, the mother of Russ, were divorced in January 1973, and she had custody of Russ during the time in question in this lawsuit. Plaintiff contracted for defendant to teach his son as a pupil in its school for the school year 1978-79. Defendant agreed to accept Russ as a pupil in its school and to teach him during the school year. Plaintiff agreed to pay, and did pay, $100 as a confirmation fee to secure Russ a place in the school. Thereafter, he paid the full yearly tuition of $972. Shortly after the school term began, Russ's mother refused to allow him to attend defendant's school, and he did not attend the school that year. Russ had attended defendant's school for the past several years.

Brenner v. School House, Ltd.

Plaintiff alleged he made demand for the return of the money he had paid defendant and that Patsy Ballinger, an officer of defendant and head of defendant's school, promised to refund the sum of $1,072 to plaintiff. This allegation is contained in paragraph 5 of plaintiff's complaint. Defendant moved in its answer to strike this paragraph, and the motion was denied. Defendant thereafter attempted to file an amended answer without leave of court, and it was stricken by the court. Defendant failed to deny the allegations contained in plaintiff's paragraph 5. By so doing, defendant admitted the allegations of plaintiff's paragraph 5. N.C. Gen. Stat. 1A-1, Rule 8(d). No further proof of the allegations was required. *Clary v. Board of Education,* 286 N.C. 525, 212 S.E. 2d 160 (1975); *Hill v. Hill,* 11 N.C. App. 1, 180 S.E. 2d 424, *cert. denied,* 279 N.C. 348, 182 S.E. 2d 580 (1971).

In admitting paragraph 5 of the complaint, defendant concedes the applicability of the doctrine of rescission to plaintiff's claim.

In Black on Rescission and Cancellation, sec. 213, it is stated: "The true rule appears to be that rescission or cancellation may properly be ordered where that which was undertaken to be performed in the future was so essential a part of the bargain that the failure of it must be considered as destroying or vitiating the entire consideration of the contract, or so indispensable a part of what the parties intended that the contract would not have been made with that condition omitted."

Jenkins v. Myers, 209 N.C. 312, 318, 183 S.E. 529, 533 (1936).

Judicial decisions and text books on the law of contract are in agreement that where there is a material breach of the contract going to the very heart of the instrument, the other party to the contract may elect to rescind and is not bound to seek relief at law by an award for damages. . . . "A breach of such a covenant amounts to a breach of the entire contract; it gives to the injured party the right to sue at law for damages, or courts of equity may grant rescission in such instances if the remedy at law will not be full and adequate."

Wilson v. Wilson, 261 N.C. 40, 43, 134 S.E. 2d 240, 242-43 (1964).

While it is true that defendant has not breached the contract, it has been breached and the object of it frustrated or destroyed by the action of plaintiff's former wife in not allowing Russ to attend defendant's school. Plaintiff, being an innocent victim of this action, is entitled to the equitable relief of rescission.

Therefore, on the pleadings alone, plaintiff is entitled to recover, and I vote to so hold in this case. The trial court did not err in failing to allow defendant's motion to dismiss plaintiff's complaint for failure to state a claim upon which relief can be granted. N.C. Gen. Stat. 1A-1, Rule 12(b)(6).

As has been demonstrated above, plaintiff was entitled to judgment on the pleadings. I also find the trial court properly allowed plaintiff's motion for summary judgment. The doctrine of frustration of the purpose of the contract is applicable to this case. The majority states that there "was not a fundamental change in conditions so that *if the child had attended the school,* the object for which the contract had been made would not have been attained." (Emphasis added.) Obviously this is true, but the fundamental change in conditions was that the child *was not allowed* to attend the school by his mother, *not* the plaintiff. Just as obviously, this did frustrate the objectives the plaintiff and defendant sought to obtain in their contract.

Frustration of the purpose of a contract is not an everyday event in lawsuits. Therefore, it is not inappropriate to set forth some statements as to the law on this subject:

> *Frustration of purpose or object of contract; commercial frustration.*
>
> Changed conditions supervening during the term of a contract sometimes operate as a defense excusing further performance on the ground that there was an implied condition in the contract that such a subsequent development should excuse performance or be a defense, and this kind of

defense has prevailed in some instances even though the subsequent condition that developed was not one rendering performance impossible, some of the cases not referring in any way to impossibility. In such instances, where performance had not become impossible, but achievement of the object or purpose of the contract was frustrated, the defensive doctrine applied has been variously designated as that of "frustration" of the purpose or object of the contract or "commercial frustration." Accordingly, it has been held that an event which substantially frustrates the objects contemplated by the parties when they made the contract excuses nonperformance of the contract. In such a case it is sometimes said that the foundation of the contract is gone.

Although the doctrines of frustration and impossibility are akin, frustration is not a form of impossibility of performance. It more properly relates to the consideration for performance. Under it performance remains possible, but is excused whenever a fortuitous event supervenes to cause a failure of the consideration or a practically total destruction of the expected value of the performance. The doctrine of commercial frustration is based upon the fundamental premise of giving relief in a situation where the parties could not reasonably have protected themselves by the terms of the contract against contingencies which later arose. Whether the doctrine is applicable depends upon the particular circumstances and conditions of each case. It does not apply where the risk of the event that has supervened to cause the alleged frustration was reasonably foreseeable, and could and should have been anticipated by the parties, and provision made therefor in the agreement which it is contended should be supplemented through operation of the doctrine.

Where "frustration" in the legal sense occurs, it does not merely provide one party with a defense in an action by the other; it kills the contract itself and discharges both parties automatically. *Joseph Constantine S.S. Line, Ltd. v. Imperial Smelting Corp.* [1942] AC 154, [1941] 2 All Eng 165 (HL).

Frustration has been defined as the premature determination of an agreement between parties, lawfully entered into and in course of operation at the time of its premature determination, owing to the occurrence of an intervening event or change of circumstances so fundamental as to be regarded by the law both as striking at the root of the agreement and as entirely beyond what was contemplated by the parties when they entered into the contract. *Cricklewood Property & Invest. Trust, Ltd. v. Leighton's Invest. Trust, Ltd.* [1945] AC 221, 228, [1945] 1 All Eng 252 (HL).

17 Am. Jur. 2d Contracts § 401 and nn. 15 & 16 at 848 (1964).

The doctrine of frustration of purpose excuses a promisor in certain situations where the objectives of the contract have been utterly defeated by circumstances arising after the formation of the agreement, and excuse is allowed under this rule even though there is no impediment to actual performance. *Hess v. Dumouchel Paper Co.*, 154 Conn. 343, 225 A.2d 797.

17 Am. Jur. 2d Contracts § 401, p. 847, n. 11 (1979 Supp.).

Frustration of the Object or Effect of the Contract.

Where the assumed possibility of a desired object or effect to be attained by either party to a contract forms the basis on which both parties enter into it, and this object or effect is or surely will be frustrated, a promisor who is without fault in causing the frustration, and who is harmed thereby, is discharged from the duty of performing his promise unless a contrary intention appears.

Comment:

a. It is not enough in order to make the rule stated in the Section applicable, that one party to the contract has in view a specific object or effect without which he would not enter into the contract, and that the other party knows this. The object or effect to be gained must be so completely the basis of the contract that, as both parties know, without it the contract would have little meaning. The rule stated in the Section is applicable, however, though literal performance is still possible, and though that performance would be as beneficial to one of the parties as if the expected object of the contract were not frustrated.

Restatement of Contracts § 288 and comment a at 427 (1932).

A somewhat useful test of the availability of the defense of frustration has been suggested based upon the injunctive practice obtaining in courts of equity — "a good method of testing each defense based on [frustration] is to consider whether, if law and equity were administered, as of old, in wholly separate courts, a chancellor, by reason of what happened, would have enjoined as unjust the enforcement of a judgment secured at law under the letter of the contract."

The doctrine of frustration has been applied by the courts under a variety of circumstances since the decision of the coronation cases, on the ground that the facts involve a failure of consideration despite the possibility of literal performance.

. . . .

"The relatively modern doctrine of commercial frustration in the law of contracts is similar to the doctrine of impossibility of performance in that both require extreme hardship in order to excuse the promisor. Commercial frustration is different in that it assumes the possibility of literal performance but excuses performance because supervening events have essentially destroyed the purpose for which the contract was made."

The doctrine of frustration has been firmly and definitely qualified in the more significant decisions by interjection and reiteration of the requirement that, to be effective in discharging liability under a contract on the ground of frustration of purpose, the frustration must be substantially complete.

18 Williston on Contracts § 1954 (3d ed. 1978).

The doctrine of frustration, which is of relatively recent growth, excuses performance of a contract, in a proper case, where the purpose of the contract, or of the parties thereto, is frustrated by a supervening event, not readily foreseeable, without fault of the parties.

.   .   .   .

The doctrine provides, generally, that where the existence of a specific thing or condition is, either by the terms of the contract or in the contemplation of the parties, necessary for performance of a promise in the contract, the duty to perform the promise is discharged if the thing or condition is no longer in existence at the time for performance; the doctrine holds that under the implied condition of the continuance of the subject matter of the contract, the contract is dissolved when the subject matter is no longer available. Performance remains possible, but is excused whenever an event not due to the fault of either party supervenes to cause a failure of consideration or destruction of the expected value of performance.

.   .   .   .

Frustration is no defense if the frustrating event was reasonably foreseeable, or if it was controllable by the promisor, ...

A party cannot rest a claim of frustration on a condition which he was responsible for creating; so, to establish the defense of frustration, it must appear that the party asserting it has not been instrumental in bringing about the intervening event, either by positive action or by acquiescence.

17A C.J.S. Contracts § 463 (2) (1963).

The North Carolina Supreme Court has recognized the doctrine of frustration as a part of the law of this state. In *Sechrest v. Furniture Co.*, 264 N.C. 216, 217, 141 S.E. 2d 292, 294 (1965), the Court held:

> The doctrine of frustration is clearly stated in *Sale v. Highway Comm.*, *supra* [242 N.C. 612, 89 S.E. 2d 290 (1955)]: "Where parties contract with reference to specific property and the obligations assumed clearly contemplate its continued existence, if the property is accidentally lost or destroyed by fire or otherwise, rendering performance impossible, the parties are relieved from further obligations concerning it. . . . Before a party can avail himself of such a position, he is required to show that the property was destroyed, and without fault on his part."

I find the purposes of the contract between plaintiff and defendant were frustrated by the act of a third party, Russ's mother, who prevented him from attending defendant's school and thus terminated the contract. The purpose of the contract was to educate Russ by teaching him in defendant's school. Because of the acts of Russ's mother, this purpose was completely frustrated. The parties, particularly the plaintiff, could not have reasonably anticipated that Russ's mother would not let him attend the school. He had so attended for several years before 1978-79. Mrs. Patsy Ballinger's affidavit contains hearsay statements made by plaintiff's former wife after school had started. She (Russ's mother) said she was not allowing Russ to attend school so that she could convince the court (in a pending case between her and plaintiff) that she needed a new car to transport Russ to school. These statements were incompetent on the summary judgment hearing, N.C. Gen. Stat. 1A-1, Rule 56(e); *Page v. Sloan*, 281 N.C. 697, 190 S.E. 2d 189 (1972), but in any event, they refer to developments that occurred after plaintiff entered into the contract with defendant. Therefore, they would not demonstrate that plaintiff at the time the contract was made should have foreseen that Russ's mother would not let Russ attend the school. Reasonable foreseeability of a frustrating occurrence must be determined by facts and circumstances existing at the time the contract was made, not by subsequent events. Plaintiff was in no way at fault in the frustration of the contract. He had no control over where the child attended school. Based on the past attendance of Russ at defendant's school and the actions of his mother in allowing him to attend there, however, plaintiff could have reasonably assumed that she would permit him to attend for the school year 1978-79, and he had a reasonable basis for entering into the contract with defendant.

Defendant is not left without a remedy. It can sue Sheila Brenner Kellam, Russ's mother, for interfering with an advantageous contractual opportunity of defendant. *Walker v. Nicholson*, 257 N.C. 744, 127 S.E. 2d 564 (1962); *Overall Corp. v. Linen Supply, Inc.*, 8 N.C. App. 528, 174 S.E.2d 659 (1970). "When a stranger interferes and prevents performance of a contract, either party to the contract may maintain an action against the stranger for the damages sustained by him or it." *Walker v. Nicholson, supra* at 747, 127 S.E. 2d at 566. *See Keeble v. Hickeringill*, 11 East 574, 103 Eng. Rep. 1127 (K.B. 1809).

The $100 "confirmation fee" paid by plaintiff to defendant was to hold a place for plaintiff's son in defendant's school, and this duty was performed by defendant. Therefore, plaintiff is not entitled to recover the $100 from defendant. Otherwise, the plaintiff is entitled to judgment on the pleadings and summary judgment for damages in the sum of $972. *Kessing v. Mortgage Corp.*, 278 N.C. 523, 180 S.E. 2d 823 (1971).

STATE OF NORTH CAROLINA v. CLARENCE DAVID McNEIL

No. 7910SC968

(Filed 3 June 1980)

1. **Criminal Law § 111.1– court's instructions to prospective jurors – no improper reference to indictments**

    The trial judge did not improperly refer to the bills of indictment re-

State v. McNeil

turned against defendant while informing prospective jurors about the case where the judge summarized the indictments and explained to the jury the circumstances under which defendant was being tried. G.S. 15A-1213.

2. **Criminal Law § 111.1– reading indictment during jury charge – no error**

The prohibition against reading the pleadings to the jury is inapplicable to the judge's jury charge, and defendant therefore could not complain of the judge's reading of the indictments returned against him during the charge to the jury.

3. **Constitutional Law § 28; Criminal Law § 66.12– defendant compelled to exhibit self to jury – no denial of due process**

Defendant was not denied due process of law when he was compelled to exhibit himself to the jury for the purpose of allowing a police officer to identify certain physical characteristics on defendant's person, since such procedure did not offend the "sense of justice" implicit in the due process clause of the Fourteenth Amendment of the U.S. Constitution and Article I, § 19 of the N.C. Constitution, but such procedure was simply a logical extension of the rule that witnesses may testify as to a defendant's physical condition or as to identifying marks on his body.

4. **Narcotics § 3.1– "unusual" amount of traffic around defendant's house – evidence properly admitted**

In a prosecution of defendant for possession with intent to sell and sale of a controlled substance, the trial court did not err in allowing testimony as to whether an "unusual" amount of traffic had been observed around defendant's home during the two months immediately preceding the allegedly illegal transaction, since the court did not abuse its discretion in allowing the leading question which drew the response complained of, and since the testimony objected to did not constitute the expression of an improper opinion.

5. **Narcotics § 4.5– possession and sale of controlled substance – no instruction on unlawfulness – burden of proof not shifted to defendant**

There was no merit to defendant's contention that the trial judge erroneously failed to instruct the jury that defendant's alleged possession of a controlled substance with intent to sell and deliver and defendant's alleged sale and delivery of a controlled substance must have been "unlawful" in order to convict him of those offenses, and that such failure created a presumption of unlawfulness from the mere possession or sale and delivery of the controlled substance, thereby shifting the burden of proof to defendant, since G.S. 90-95 makes it unlawful for any person to possess or sell and deliver any controlled substance except in certain circumstances, G.S. 90-113.1(a) placing the burden of proving an exemption or exception on the person claiming its benefit; this statutory scheme does not run afoul of constitutional standards; and the burden of proving that defendant possessed or sold and delivered a controlled substance is not shifted away from the State.

APPEAL by defendant from *Lee, Judge.* Judgment entered 23 May 1979 in Superior Court, WAKE County. Heard in the Court of Appeals 5 March 1980.

Defendant was charged and convicted under G.S. 90-95(a) (1) and G.S. 90-95(a) (3) for the felonious possession with the intent to sell and deliver and the felonious sale and delivery of phenmetrazine (preludin) a Schedule II controlled substance, and was sentenced to a prison term of not less nor more than two years.

At trial, the State presented evidence which tended to prove the following: On 26 January 1979 Raleigh Police Officer James L. Jordan was working as an undercover agent "making buys of drugs, intoxicating liquors and beverages at different locations." Jordan contacted defendant at approximately noon at 924 S. Blount Street in Raleigh, and negotiated the sale of one preludin pill in exchange for an amount of meat worth approximately $38. After the transaction Officer Jordan returned to his office and met a Detective Weathersbee, and the two officers secured the pill in an evidence envelope. The pill was later examined and found to be preludin. At trial, the pill was identified and admitted into evidence.

Defendant was identified by Officer Jordan during the trial as the person from whom he obtained the controlled substance. The identification was based on Jordan's observation of defendant for approximately three to five minutes at a range of one foot in a well-lighted room.

Defendant presented no evidence.

From the judgment entered upon the jury verdict of guilty to the offenses charged, defendant appeals.

Attorney General Edmisten, by Assistant Attorney General Archie W. Anders, for the State.

Loflin, Loflin, Galloway and Acker, by Thomas F. Loflin, III, and James R. Acker, for defendant appellant.

MORRIS, Chief Judge.

By his first assignment of error, defendant contends that the trial judge improperly referred to the bills of indictment returned against him while informing prospective jurors about the case, and that the trial judge erred by reading the bills of indictment to the jury during his jury charge.

[1] With respect to the trial judge's opening remarks, defendant complains of the following portion:

> The defendant, Clarence David McNeil, is charged in one bill of indictment with the felony possession with intent to sell and deliver a controlled substance, to wit: Phenmetrazine, which is included in Schedule Two of the North Carolina Controlled Substance Act, and in another bill of indictment he is charged with the sale and delivery of that controlled substance. These offenses are alleged to have occurred on or about the 26th day of January, 1979, in Wake County. To all of the charges contained in those bills of indictment . . . .

Contrary to defendant's assertion, the trial judge's opening remarks did not violate G.S. 15A-1213 and G.S. 15A-1221. G.S. 15A-1221 prescribes the order of proceedings in a criminal jury trial, and provides, in pertinent part: "The judge must inform the prospective jurors of the case in accordance with G.S. 15A-1213." G.S. 15A-1213 provides:

> Prior to selection of jurors, the judge must identify the parties and their counsel and briefly inform the prospective jurors, as to each defendant, of the charge, the date of the alleged offense, the name of any victim alleged in the pleading, the defendant's plea to the charge, and any affirmative defense of which the defendant has given pretrial notice as required by Article 52, Motions Practice. The judge may not read the pleadings to the jury.

We find in the Official Commentary published pursuant to these sections an explanation as to the purpose of the prohibition against reading criminal pleadings to the jury, "that jurors hearing the stilted language of indictments and other pleadings and witnessing various motions upon arraignment are likely to get a distorted view of the case." Although the trial judge referred to the indictments, he did not read them. Rather, the trial judge summarized those indictments and explained to the jury the circumstances under which defendant was being tried. This procedure is entirely appropriate and certainly complies with the spirit of G.S. 15A-1213.

[2] With respect to the trial judge's reading the indictments returned against defendant during the charge to the jury, we find that this prohibition against reading the pleadings to the jury is inapplicable to the judge's jury charge. At that phase of the trial, "to infer that they [the jury] would be given a distorted view of the case by a mere reiteration of the charge couched in the words of the indictment would be illogical." *State v. Laughinghouse*, 39 N.C. App. 655, 658, 251 S.E. 2d 667, 669, *cert. denied and appeal dismissed*, 297 N.C. 615, 257 S.E. 2d 438 (1979). Defendant's first assignment of error is, therefore, overruled.

[3] Defendant next argues that his right to due process of law was denied him when he was compelled to exhibit himself to the jury for the purpose of allowing Officer Jordan to identify certain physical characteristics on defendant's person. Defendant argues that the State should have used some alternative means with which to display defendant's physical characteristics. Defendant argues further than even in those situations where exhibition of a defendant's person was held proper, some exigency justified such display. *State v. Cook*, 280 N.C. 642, 187 S.E. 2d 104 (1972); *State v. Sanders*, 280 N.C. 67, 185 S.E. 2d 137 (1971); *State v. Thomas*, 20 N.C. App. 255, 201 S.E. 2d 201 (1973), *cert. denied*, 284 N.C. 622, 202 S.E. 2d 277 (1974). We disagree.

Although defendant's assignment of error is based on due process considerations and not on defendant's Fifth Amendment right to be free from self-incrimination, we note that application of the position of the Court in cases decided under the Fifth Amendment would require the conclusion that requiring defendant to stand before the jury did not violate his constitutional protection against self-incrimination. The privilege against self-incrimination protects an accused only from being compelled to testify against himself or provide the State with evidence which is testimonial or communicative in nature. *Schmerber v. California*, 384 U.S. 757, 16 L.Ed. 2d 908, 86 S.Ct. 1826 (1966); *Holt v. United States*, 218 U.S. 245, 54 L.Ed. 1021, 31 S.Ct. 2 (1910); *State v. Perry*, 291 N.C. 284, 230 S.E. 2d 141 (1976). It is, therefore, proper for the State to require a defendant to stand or otherwise exhibit himself before the jury where such an act is not of a testimonial or communicative nature. *See State v. Perry, supra*, and cases there cited.

With respect to defendant's claim that he was deprived of his liberty without due process of law, defendant contends that the totality of the circumstances prevalent at trial made this identification procedure improperly suggestive and prejudicial. The identification of defendant by Officer Jordan, however, had occurred prior to defendant's having to stand before the jury. The record indicates that when asked if he could identify defendant, the witness requested and was allowed to leave the witness stand, walk over to the defense table, and observe defendant. Upon returning to the witness stand, Officer Jordan stated: "When I looked at the defendant sitting at the table I looked at the dent [scar] over his left eye. That tells me that this is the defendant that I bought from on the 26th." It was only after this identification that Officer Jordan was permitted to illustrate his testimony by pointing out the scar over defendant's left eye.

In *State v. Perry, supra*, defendant was required to stand before the jury and place a stocking mask over his head and face in the way a State's witness had testified it was worn by the man who robbed and assaulted her. The Court cited *Schmerber v. California* in holding that such a procedure did not offend the "sense of justice" implicit in the due process clause of the Fourteenth Amendment to the Constitution of the United States and Article 1, § 19 of the Constitution of North Carolina. *See also Rochin v. California*, 342 U.S. 165, 96 L.Ed. 183, 72 S.Ct. 205 (1952). In the present case, we do not believe the exhibition of certain characteristics of one's person offends the "sense of justice" so as to warrant defendant a new trial. We believe that such a procedure is a logical extension of the rule that witnesses may testify as to a defendant's physical condition or as to identifying marks on his body. *See State v. Floyd*, 246 N.C. 434, 98 S.E. 2d 478 (1957). This assignment of error is overruled.

[4] By his fourth assignment of error defendant contends that the trial court erred in allowing testimony as to whether an "unusual" amount of traffic had been observed around defendant's home during the two months immediately preceding the alleged illegal transaction. Defendant contends that the question asked by the prosecutor was leading, that it elicited a conclusory opinion from the witness, and that the admission of such testimony was prejudicial to him.

Although the question was leading in nature, the control of examination of witnesses is a matter of discretion vested in the trial court, reviewable only for an abuse of discretion. *State v. Painter*, 265 N.C. 277, 144 S.E. 2d 6 (1965). We find no abuse of discretion here.

Nor did the testimony concerning the amount of traffic around defendant's house constitute the expression of an improper opinion. An opinion can be best explained as "any narrative statement by a witness which does not describe facts directly perceived by the senses in the fullest detail that could reasonably be expected of an average witness and reasonably be understood by an average juror." 1 Stansbury's N.C. Evidence § 122 (Brandis rev. 1973). An opinion is inadmissible whenever the witness can relate facts so that the trier of fact will have an understanding of them and the jury is as well qualified as the witness to draw inferences and conclusions from those facts. *State v. Patterson*, 288 N.C. 553, 220 S.E. 2d 600 (1975), *death sentence vacated*, 428 U.S. 904, 49 L.Ed. 2d 1211, 96 S.Ct. 3211 (1976). The response by the witness was as follows:

Yes, sir. We had seen cars come and go, and they would come and go in just for a short while and leave.

Such a response is properly admissible as evidence of an observer testifying to the results of his observation. *See State v. Sasser*, 21 N.C. App. 618, 205 S.E. 2d 565, *cert. denied*, 285 N.C.

667, 207 S.E. 2d 764 (1974). In any event, even if the admission of this evidence were error, we find no prejudice which would justify awarding defendant a new trial. This assignment of error is overruled.

[5] By his fifth assignment of error, defendant contends that the trial judge erroneously failed to instruct the jury that defendant's alleged possession of a controlled substance with intent to sell and deliver, and defendant's alleged sale and delivery of a controlled substance must have been "unlawful" in order to convict him of those offenses. The validity of the court's instruction depends on an analysis of certain provisions of the North Carolina Controlled Substances Act, Article 5, Chapter 90 of the North Carolina General Statutes.

The portion of the trial judge's charge to the jury to which defendant excepts is as follows:

I charge that for you to find the defendant guilty of selling or delivering Phenmetrazine, Preludin, a controlled substance, the State must prove beyond a reasonable doubt that on the date in question, that is, January the 26th, 1979, that this defendant, Clarence David McNeil, knowingly sold or delivered one tablet of Phenmetrazine to Officer J.L. Jordan.

. . .

I charge that for you to find the defendant guilty of possessing Phenmetrazine or Preludin, a controlled substance, with the intent to sell or deliver it, the State must prove two things beyond a reasonable doubt. First, that on January the 26th, 1979, that this defendant, Clarence David McNeil, knowingly possessed Phenmetrazine, a controlled substance. The Court instructs you that Phenmetrazine is a controlled substance. ... A person possesses a substance when he has, either by himself or together with others, both the power and intent to control the disposition or use of that substance. And, second, the State must prove beyond a reasonable doubt that at the time defendant possessed that tablet that he intended to sell or deliver that tablet.

The challenged instructions closely parallel North Carolina Pattern Instructions Nos. 260.21 and 260.15. Nowhere in the charge does the term "unlawfully" appear. Defendant insists that such an omission creates a presumption of unlawfulness from the mere possession or sale and delivery of the controlled substance, thereby shifting the burden of proof to defendant.

G.S. 90-95, upon which defendant's conviction is based, provides, in pertinent part, as follows:

(a) Except as authorized by this Article, it is unlawful for any person:

(1) To manufacture, sell or deliver, or possess with intent to manufacture, sell or deliver, a controlled substance;

(3) To possess a controlled substance.

It is clear that one may be exempt from State prosecution for the possession or the sale or delivery of controlled substances if that person is authorized by the North Carolina Controlled Substances Act to so possess or sell or deliver such substances. See, e.g., G.S. 90-95(a); G.S. 90-113.3(f); State v. Cameron, 283 N.C. 191, 195 S.E. 2d 481 (1973). However, the legislative scheme implicit in the North Carolina Controlled Substances Act provides that, in a prosecution under G.S. 90-95, proof of such exemption through authorization must be provided by the defendant. G.S. 90-113.1(a) provides:

It shall not be necessary for the State to negate any exemption or exception set forth in this Article in any complaint, information, indictment, or other pleading or in any trial, hearing, or other proceeding under this Article, and the burden of proof of any such exemption or exception shall be upon the person claiming its benefit.

It is defendant's position that this section is unconstitutional in that it creates a mandatory presumption of criminality and shifts the burden of proof to defendant to prove lawfulness in order to be acquitted of the crimes charged under G.S. 90-95.

We do not believe this statutory scheme runs afoul of constitutional standards. G.S. 90-95 makes criminal the manufacture, possession, sale or delivery of a controlled substance. Phenmetrazine is listed as a Schedule II controlled substance. G.S. 90-90 (c) (2). The manufacture, possession, sale or delivery of phenmetrazine is unlawful unless and until it is authorized under an appropriate section of the Act. G.S. 90-95. It is only under those circumstances that one may avoid prosecution if he otherwise falls under the provisions of the Act.

In two recent decisions, this Court dealt with the exemption provisions of G.S. 90-113.1 *State v. Best*, 31 N.C. App. 250, 229 S.E. 2d 581 (1976), *reversed on other grounds*, 292 N.C. 294, 233 S.E. 2d 544 (1977); *State v. Richardson*, 23 N.C. App. 33, 208 S.E. 2d 274, *cert. denied and appeal dismissed*, 286 N.C. 213, 209 S.E. 2d 317 (1974). In *State v. Best, supra*, this Court dealt with the matter of exemption for physicians in writing prescriptions for controlled substances during the course of their professional practice. In that case we observed that it was the duty of the defendant to "bring himself within an exception to the foregoing prohibition. G.S. 90-113.1." 31 N.C. App. at 264, 229 S.E. 2d at 589. Similarly, in *State v. Richardson, supra*, defendant appealed from a judgment denying him remission of an automobile confiscated by court order pursuant to G.S. 90-112 (f), which provides for the forfeiture of all conveyances used to transport controlled substances. The Court explained the statutory scheme dealing with forfeitures under Chapter 90 by applying G.S. 90-113.1 (a):

> North Carolina law subjects a vehicle which is found to have been used in the illegal transportation of narcotic drugs to immediate forfeiture. Forfeiture may be defeated if the claimant can show the illegal use occurred without his knowledge or consent, with the claimant having the right to have a jury pass upon his claim . . . The burden is statutorily placed upon the claimant to show the absence of consent or knowledge. G.S. 18A-21 (b); G.S. 90-113.1 (a).

Allen Co. v. Quip-Matic, Inc.

---

23 N.C. App. at 36, 208 S.E. 2d at 276. Although the precise question of this appeal was not before the Court in *Best* and *Richardson*, we agreed with these decisions insofar as they approve of the procedure adopted by G.S. 90-113.1 to establish an exemption status in prosecutions under Chapter 90. Contrary to defendant's contentions, this section does not shift the burden of proof away from the State. G.S. 90-95 makes clear the requirements for finding defendant guilty of the manufacture, possession, sale or delivery of a controlled substance. That burden remains with the State.

Since the statutory scheme implicit in the Controlled Substances Act establishes criminal liability once defendant commits the acts set forth in G.S. 90-95, it is apparent that the trial judge properly instructed the jury as to what it must find in order to find defendant guilty. Where the judge's charge fully instructs the jury on all the substantive areas of the case, and defines and applies the law thereto, it is sufficient. G.S. 15A-1231, -1232; *State v. Garrett*, 5 N.C. App. 367, 168 S.E. 2d 479 (1969).

We find that defendant received a fair trial free from prejudicial error.

No error.

Judges VAUGHN and ARNOLD concur.

H. V. ALLEN COMPANY, INC. v. QUIP-MATIC, INC., D/B/A ROCKFORD
SANITARY SYSTEMS

No. 7918SC869

(Filed 3 June 1980)

1. **Constitutional Law § 24.7– foreign corporation – contract not made in N.C. – no personal jurisdiction**

    G.S. 55–145(a) was inapplicable to give the trial court *in personam* jurisdiction over defendant, an Illinois corporation, when the statute provided for jurisdiction of any cause of action arising out of a contract made in N. C.;

Allen Co. v. Quip-Matic, Inc.

plaintiff alleged that a binding contract was entered into, but defendant vigorously denied any contract; and it therefore could not be stated that a contract was made at all.

2. **Constitutional Law § 24.7– foreign corporation – insufficient minimum contacts – no personal jurisdiction**

In an action to recover against defendant, a foreign corporation, for an alleged breach of an oral contract, defendant had insufficient minimum contacts with North Carolina to justify personal jurisdiction over it where defendant had neither offices nor property in N. C.; over a period of sixteen months it filled orders for six N. C. companies for a total value of only $6200; title to this equipment passed in Illinois, the orders having been accepted in that state and f.o.b. delivery made to common carriers in that state; defendant never sent employees to N.C.; defendant did not advertise for business in N. C.; defendant had made, prior to this lawsuit, only seven long distance phone calls to N.C. and had corresponded with three firms in N.C.; and defendant's written contract with a company in Charlotte making that company defendant's manufacturer's representative in N. C. and S. C. did not establish the company as defendant's agent, and defendant had very little contact with the Charlotte company.

Judge HILL concurring in result.

APPEAL by plaintiff from *Collier, Judge.* Cross-assignment of error by defendant. Order and judgment entered 11 June 1979 in Superior Court, GUILFORD County. Heard in the Court of Appeals 20 March 1980.

Plaintiff, a North Carolina corporation, began this action on 27 July 1977, alleging a breach by defendant of an oral contract to sell equipment and, as a separate claim, plaintiff's justifiable reliance on defendant's oral offer and quotation to supply the equipment. Defendant, an Illinois corporation, is a supplier of pumps and oil separators. Plaintiff is a mechanical contractor who, in connection with a United States government construction project to be performed in Memphis, Tennessee, was provided with price information from defendant on certain of its equipment in January 1977. Plaintiff submitted a bid on the project based upon the oral quotation given by defendant. In late February plaintiff was formally awarded the contract, but when it submitted its purchase order to defendant, defendant refused to supply the equipment at the quoted price. Plaintiff was required to purchase from another supplier at a higher price and was damaged in the amount of $21,252.59.

On 30 August 1978 defendant filed a motion to dismiss for lack of jurisdiction over the person of the defendant. Plaintiff then filed written interrogatories seeking to discover the extent of defendant's activities in North Carolina. Defendant filed further dismissal motions and an answer denying any agreement or promise as alleged by plaintiff, admitting that immediately upon receipt of plaintiff's purported purchase order it notified plaintiff of its objections to the contents, and alleging the defense of the statute of frauds under the Uniform Commerical Code, N.C.G.S. 25–2–201. At the same time defendant moved for summary judgment, expressly reserving its motion to dismiss. On 11 June 1979 Judge Collier, on the basis of the pleadings, interrogatories and affidavits of both parties, denied defendant's motion to dismiss for lack of personal jurisdiction but granted defendant's motion to dismiss for failure to state a claim upon which relief can be granted and motion for summary judgment. Plaintiff appeals from this judgment and defendant cross-assigns error to the order denying its jurisdictional motion.

Block, Meyland & Lloyd, by Michael R. Pendergraft, for plaintiff appellant.

Brooks, Pierce, McLendon, Humphrey & Leonard, by Edward C. Winslow III and Paul E. Marth, for defendant appellee.

Miller, Johnston, Taylor & Allison, by John B. Taylor and James W. Allison, for Associated General Contractors of America, Carolinas Branch, amicus curiae.

MARTIN (Harry C.), Judge.

It is unnecessary that we reach the interesting substantive question posed by plaintiff on this appeal: Is the defendant estopped to plead the Uniform Commercial Code statute of frauds, N.C.G.S. 25–2–201, in this construction bid case? We must address the jurisdictional issue raised on defendant's cross-assignment of error first, and in so doing we find that the trial court erred in not granting defendant's motion to dismiss for lack of *in personam* jurisdiction over it, a foreign corporation not doing business in North Carolina.

Allen Co. v. Quip-Matic, Inc.

[1] Plaintiff contends that either N.C.G.S. 55–145(a) or N.C.G.S. 1–75.4(1)d confers personal jurisdiction over defendant, an Illinois corporation. N.C.G.S. 55–145(a) provides as follows:

> Every foreign corporation shall be subject to suit in this State, whether or not such foreign corporation is transacting or has transacted business in this State and whether or not it is engaged exclusively in interstate or foreign commerce, on any cause of action arising as follows:
>
> (1) Out of any contract made in this State or to be performed in this State; or
>
> (2) Out of any business solicited in this State by mail or otherwise if the corporation has repeatedly so solicited business, whether the orders or offers relating thereto were accepted within or without the State; or
>
> (3) Out of the production, manufacture, or distribution of goods by such corporation with the reasonable expectation that those goods are to be used or consumed in this State and are so used or consumed, regardless of how or where the goods were produced, manufactured, marketed, or sold or whether or not through the medium of independent contractors or dealers; or
>
> (4) Out of tortious conduct in this State, whether arising out of repeated activity or single acts, and whether arising out of misfeasance or nonfeasance.

This section confers jurisdiction over a cause of action arising out of four specific and well-delineated activities. "If one of these four activities is present but the cause of action arises elsewhere, or if none of the four activities is present although others may be present, there is no jurisdictional grant." *Bowman v. Curt G. Joa, Inc.*, 361 F. 2d 706, 714 (4th Cir. 1966), on appeal from Western District of North Carolina. The only possible subsection which might apply in the instant case is subsection (1). Yet the record fails to show that a contract was ever made in North Carolina between plaintiff and defendant. Plaintiff certainly alleged that a binding contract was entered into, but defendant vigorously denied any contract. It cannot be conclusively stated that a contract was made at all, and therefore this subsection is inapplicable.

With this ruling we turn to the question whether N.C.G.S. 1–75.4(1)d is applicable.

N.C.G.S. 1–75.4(1)d confers jurisdiction over defendant upon a court in North Carolina having subject matter jurisdiction as follows:

(1) Local Presence or Status.—In any action, whether the claim arises within or without this State, in which a claim is asserted against a party who when service of process is made upon such party:

.   .   .   .

d. Is engaged in substantial activity within this State, whether such activity is wholly interstate, intrastate, or otherwise.

Our Supreme Court, although taking note of the phrase "substantial activity," has held that N.C.G.S. 1–75.4(1)d grants the courts of North Carolina the opportunity to exercise jurisdiction over a foreign corporation to the extent allowed by due process.

By the enactment of G.S. 1–75.4(1)(d), it is apparent that the General Assembly intended to make available to North Carolina courts the full jurisdictional powers permissible under federal due process. *See* 1 McIntosh, North Carolina Practice and Procedure § 937.5 (Supp. 1970). Thus, we hold that G.S. 1–75.4 (1)(d) applies to defendant and, statutorily, grants the courts of North Carolina the opportunity to exercise jurisdiction over defendant to the extent allowed by due process.

Dillion v. Funding Corp., 291 N.C. 674, 676, 231 S.E. 2d 629, 630–31 (1977). Therefore, the first step of the requisite "two-fold determination" has been met; the statutes of North Carolina permit courts of this jurisdiction to entertain this action against defendant. *Id.* But has the second step been met? Would due process of law be violated by permitting the courts of North Carolina to exercise their power over defendant? *Id.*

In *International Shoe Co. v. Washington*, 326 U.S. 310, 316, 90 L. Ed. 95, 102 (1945), the United States Supreme Court stated:

> [D]ue process requires only that in order to subject a defendant to a judgment *in personam*, if he be not present within the territory of the forum, he have certain minimum contacts with it such that the maintenance of the suit does not offend "traditional notions of fair play and substantial justice."

Our Supreme Court, although noting the trend toward expansion of personal jurisdiction over nonresidents, has echoed the decision in *International Shoe:* "Unless a nonresident defendant has had 'minimum contacts' with the forum state, that state may not exercise jurisdiction over him." *Chadbourn, Inc. v. Katz*, 285 N.C. 700, 705, 208 S.E. 2d 676, 679 (1974). Quoting from *Hanson v. Denckla*, 357 U.S. 235, 253, 2 L. Ed. 2d 1283, 1298 (1958), the Court went on to state that "[a]pplication of the 'minimum contacts' rule 'will vary with the quality and nature of the defendant's activity, but it is essential in each case that there be some act by which the defendant purposefully avails itself of the privilege of conducting activities within the forum State, thus invoking the benefits and protections of its laws.' " 285 N.C. at 705, 208 S.E. 2d at 679. In a very recent decision of the Supreme Court of North Carolina, it was reiterated: "Absent such purposeful activity by defendant in the forum State, there can be no contact with the forum State sufficient to justify personal jurisdiction over defendant." *Buying Group, Inc. v. Coleman*, 296 N.C. 510, 515, 251 S.E. 2d 610, 614 (1979).

[2] The determination of the existence of minimum contacts depends upon the particular facts of each case. *Chadbourn, Inc. v. Katz, supra.* The order of the trial court denying defendant's motion to dismiss for lack of personal jurisdiction contained no findings of fact or conclusions of law. Absent request by a party the court had no duty to make such findings, Rule 52(a)(2), N.C.R. Civ. Proc., and the record reveals no such request. Although the presumption is that the court on proper evidence found facts to support its order, *Leasing Corp. v. Equity Associates*, 36 N.C. App. 713, 245 S.E. 2d 229 (1978), the record may clearly reveal that the court erroneously drew legal conclusions from these facts. We hold that based on the interrogatories and answers that are part of the record, defendant had insufficient minimum contacts to justify personal jurisdiction over it.

Defendant has neither offices nor property in North Carolina. Over a period of sixteen months, it filled orders for six North Carolina companies for a total value of only $6,200. Title to this equipment passed in Illinois, the orders having been accepted in that state and f.o.b. delivery made to common carriers in that state. Defendant never sent employees to North Carolina; neither did it advertise for business in North Carolina. Defendant had made, prior to the initiation of this lawsuit, only seven long-distance telephone calls to North Carolina and had corresponded with three firms in North Carolina.

Defendant does have a written contract with Quality Plumbing Products, Inc. of Charlotte, North Carolina, making it defendant's manufacturer's representative in North Carolina and South Carolina. This contract, however, is not the source of the cause of action in this lawsuit. Quality Plumbing does not operate under the name of defendant. It neither takes orders in defendant's name nor collects funds as an agent of defendant. Defendant has sent equipment to Quality for sale on a consignment basis for a ten-percent commission. This arrangement does not establish that Quality is defendant's agent. *Lindsey v. Leonard*. 235 N.C. 100, 68 S.E. 2d 852 (1952). Quality has actually sold only five units for a total value of $990 between March 1976 and July 1977. Quality does need defendant's approval before extending credit to purchasers. Defendant has sent sales materials to its manufacturer's representative.

We think this activity on defendant's part is *de minimis* and insufficient to justify personal jurisdiction over it. The contact with North Carolina is parallel to that of the defendant Delaware corporation in *Putnam v. Publications,* 245 N.C. 432, 96 S.E. 2d 445 (1957), and in that case insufficient minimum contacts were found to confer personal jurisdiction. Defendant sold its publications to eighteen independent wholesale news dealers in North Carolina by delivering to common carriers in other states. Defendant made no attempts to control the policy of the independent dealers, except for general suggestions. Defendant did not advertise in North Carolina; it had no place of business in North Carolina; it neither owned, leased, nor controlled any property in this state. It did employ three persons as sales promotion representatives who travelled within North Carolina. It also gave credit to the dealers for unsold copies. The Court found these activities incidental and casual, and held it would not be reasonable and just under the notions of fair play for the courts of North Carolina to have personal jurisdiction over defendant.

Plaintiff relies on several cases in which sufficient contacts were found to justify personal jurisdiction. These cases are clearly distinguishable.

In *Byham v. House Corp.,* 265 N.C. 50, 143 S.E. 2d 225, 23 A.L.R. 3d 537 (1965), defendant Tennessee corporation solicited, by mail and newspaper ads, franchise owners in North Carolina. Plaintiff, a North Carolina resident, entered into a contract with defendant to purchase a franchise for an eating establishment in Durham. Defendant dictated all menus and equipment and had a right to examine all books and records; it could also inspect at any time. Plaintiff was to adhere to defendant's advertising policy, and defendant sent a representative to North Carolina to assist in locating plaintiff's franchise. The Court held that by its actions, defendant purposefully availed itself of the privilege of conducting activities in North Carolina and invoked the benefits and protection of her laws. This cause of action had been brought by plaintiff, alleging a breach of this contract with defendant.

In *Goldman v. Parkland*, 277 N.C. 223, 176 S.E. 2d 784 (1970), plaintiff brought suit on a written contract with a Texas corporation whereby plaintiff was to act as manufacturer's representative for defendant in North Carolina and other southeastern states. The Court found the contract in question met the requirement of "substantial connection" with North Carolina.

Defendant in *Byrum v. Truck & Equipment Co.*, 32 N.C. App. 135, 231 S.E. 2d 39 (1977), was a Florida corporation that manufactured trailers, titled them in the name of a North Carolina corporation, and invoiced them to the North Carolina corporation. The North Carolina corporation provided plans for the manufacture of the trailers. The Court held that these transactions between the two corporations met the requirement of " 'some act by which the defendant purposefully avails himself of the privilege of conducting activities within the forum state, invoking the benefits and protection of its laws.' " *Id.* at 138-39, 231 S.E. 2d at 41. In an action by a North Carolina resident to recover for defects in a log trailer purchased from the North Carolina corporation, the defendant had filed a third-party complaint against the Florida corporation, and personal jurisdiction was found to exist.

In *Leasing Corp. v. Equity Associates, supra,* a lease of televisions and an assumption agreement which gave rise to the action were contracts made in North Carolina. Defendants were Texas corporations. The Court found sufficient minimal contacts in the ongoing contractual relations and obligations between plaintiff and defendants. Plaintiff shipped televisions from its North Carolina warehouse, and monthly rentals under the lease were mailed to plaintiff's offices in North Carolina. An additional factor noted by the Court was that the lease expressly provided that North Carolina law would govern in case a dispute arose over the lease.

We note that in a recent decision of the Court of Appeals, *Parris v. Disposal, Inc.*, 40 N.C. App. 282, 253 S.E. 2d 29, *disc. rev. denied, appeal dismissed,* 297 N.C. 455, 256 S.E. 2d 808 (1979), the crucial facts which influenced the Court's finding personal

---

Allen Co. v. Quip-Matic, Inc.

---

jurisdiction over defendant foreign corporation were that defendant had phone listings in the directories of five North Carolina cities, indicating a toll-free number in Connecticut and general agents to contact within various North Carolina cities, defendant had made mailings into the state, issues of its magazines had been received in North Carolina, and an insurance policy from defendant had been mailed to a named person in an envelope with defendant's tradename on it.

The Court in *Parris* distinguished *Putnam* and noted "that the reason courts refuse to uphold the exercise of jurisdiction over nonresident publishers is because of fear of undue burdens imposed upon multi-state publishers of defending suits in distant states when weighed against a need to provide plaintiffs with a convenient forum." 40 N.C. App. at 290, 253 S.E. 2d at 34. It then stated that this rationale does not apply "where foreign corporations launch massive campaigns seeking to influence jury verdicts in our State." *Id.* The instant case contains no such special situation, and even though defendant is not a nonresident publisher, we think *Putnam* is controlling.

We hold that defendant had insufficient minimum contacts with North Carolina, on the facts of this case, to justify the assertion of personal jurisdiction over it. The trial court therefore erred in not granting defendant's motion to dismiss for lack of personal jurisdiction. With this holding, we do not reach the question whether summary judgment for defendant was proper.

The result is: plaintiff's action is dismissed for lack of jurisdiction over defendant. The court's dismissal of plaintiff's action is therefore

Affirmed.

Judge PARKER concurs.

Judge HILL concurs in the result.

Judge HILL concurring in the result:

In my opinion, the trial judge was correct in denying the defendant's motion to dismiss for lack of personal jurisdiction under the facts of this case. There were sufficient minimum contacts. I conclude further that the trial judge was correct in granting defendant's motion to dismiss for failure to state a claim upon which relief can be granted and the motion for summary judgment.

ELSIE T. MORRISON, Employee, Plaintiff, v. BURLINGTON INDUS-
TRIES, Employer, and LIBERTY MUTUAL INSURANCE COMPANY,
Carrier, Defendants

No. 7910IC1167

(Filed 3 June 1980)

**Master and Servant § 68– workers' compensation – disability to work – portion
caused by occupational disease – right to compensation for total disability**

    If an employee's incapacity to work is total and that incapacity is occa-
sioned by a compensable injury or disease, the employee's incapacity to work
cannot be apportioned to other pre-existing or latent illnesses or infirmities,
nor may the entitlement to compensation be dismissed for such conditions.
Therefore, where the Industrial Commission found that plaintiff was totally
disabled to work, that 55% of her disability was due to her occupational
disease, and that 45% of her disability was due to physical infirmities not
related to her work, the Commission erred in holding that plaintiff was
entitled only to compensation for partial rather than total disability.

Chief Judge Morris dissenting.

Appeal by plaintiff from Full Industrial Commission order of 18 June 1979. Heard in the Court of Appeals 24 March 1980.

The record discloses that there were three initial hearings in this case. The first, before Commissioner Robert S. Brown, on 25 and 26 July 1977; the second before Deputy Commissioner Richard B. Conely on 18 November 1977; and a third before Deputy Commissioner Christine Y. Denson on 7 June 1978. At the conclusion of the third hearing, Commissioner Brown en-tered an order in which he found and concluded that plaintiff was totally disabled for work due to chronic obstructive lung disease resulting from her exposure to cotton dust while in defendant's employ. He found her average weekly wage to be in the sum of $119.77, and awarded her compensation at the rate of $79.85 per week for the number of weeks provided by law or until such time as plaintiff has a change of condition. Upon review by the Full Commission, its order found and concluded that fifty-five percent of plaintiff's disability to work was due to her occupational disease and that forty-five percent of her disability was due to physical infirmities not related to her employment. Plaintiff's compensation was reduced to $43.92 per week.

Davis, Hassell & Hudson, by Charles R. Hassell, Jr. and Robin E. Hudson, for the plaintiff appellant.

Teague, Campbell, Conely & Dennis, by C. Woodrow Teague and George W. Dennis III, for the defendant appellees.

WELLS, Judge.

The sole issue presented in this appeal is whether the Industrial Commission erred as a matter of law in apportioning and reducing plaintiff's compensation for total disability. In order to address the question of law at issue, it is necessary to review the evidence upon which the Commission acted.

Plaintiff was employed in defendant Burlington Industries Mill in Erwin for twenty-seven years. She worked in the cotton spinning department. She last worked on 24 April 1975. At the July 1977 hearing, Henderson D. Mabe, Jr., M.D., testified for plaintiff that he has treated plaintiff since 1965. In January 1975, plaintiff was hospitalized under his treatment. He diagnosed recent upper respiratory infection superimposed on chronic bronchitis, diabetes controlled by diet, and suspected possible byssinosis with history of exposure to lint. In addition to her lung problem, she suffered from phlebitis of the left leg. She was unable to work at her job as of 24 April 1975. The leg problem would not have totally disabled her but was an added factor *in her disability.*

At the June 1978 hearing, Mario C. Battigelli, M.D., testified for defendants that he was a professor of medicine at the University of North Carolina and was one of the panel of physicians to whom the Industrial Commission refers claimants who make claims for byssinosis. He specialized in pulmonary diseases. He examined plaintiff on 8 April 1975. He filed a report following that examination which included a finding of "4. Chronic obstructive lung disorder, bronchitis in type, in cigarette smoker with aggravation on dust exposure" and a conclusion that "[s]he does not present cyclic disorder which would allow the diagnosis of byssinosis." At the hearing, Dr. Battigelli testified that:

> If the Commission should find that Mrs. Morrison is either totally or partially disabled, my opinion, satisfactory to myself to a reasonable degree of medical certainty, as to what percentage of her disability which can be traced or is due to her exposure to cotton dust is that it could be quite miniscule, if not negligible. With luck, between 0 and 20% in percentage terms.

> I suggested that she be relocated to a similar activity in a more sheltered environment, that is not only less exposure to cotton dust, but also not involving a static standing position or anything that was displeasing Mrs. Morrison.

At the November 1977 hearing, Herbert O. Sieker, M.D., testified for plaintiff that he was a professor of medicine at Duke University, specializing in chest and allergic diseases. He examined plaintiff in January 1977 and determined that plaintiff was suffering from severe respiratory disability, that cotton dust was a causitive factor in her lung disease, that she was disabled, and that her disability was due to her chronic lung disease. He estimated that somewhere between fifty and sixty percent of her disability was related to cotton dust exposure.

Commissioner Brown's order of 18 December 1978 contains the following pertinent findings and conclusions:

> 6. On 24 April 1975, plaintiff was totally disabled for work due to her chronic obstructive lung disease resulting

from her exposure to cotton dust while in defendant's employ and has since remained so disabled.

7. Plaintiff suffers from chronic obstructive lung disease, an occupational disease due to causes and conditions characteristic of and peculiar to her particular trade, occupation or employment in the textile industry. Her disease is not an ordinary disease of life to which the general public is equally exposed outside of such employment.

8. Due to the occupational disease suffered by plaintiff, she has no earning capacity in any employment for which she can qualify in the labor market.

* * *

CONCLUSIONS OF LAW

1. The compensable occupational disease from which plaintiff suffers is due to causes and conditions which are characteristic of and peculiar to her particular trade, occupation or employment and is not an ordinary disease of life to which the general public outside of such employment is equally exposed. G.S. 97–53(13).

2. As a result of her occupational disease plaintiff is disabled and has been so disabled from 24 April 1975. She is entitled to compensation at the rate of $79.85 per week for such disability for the number of weeks by law provided or until such time as plaintiff has a change of condition. G.S. 97–52; G.S. 97–29; G.S. 97–2(9).

The Full Commission order of 18 June 1979 contains the following pertinent entries:

...After reviewing all the competent evidence received in this case, it is the opinion of the Full Commission that while plaintiff does suffer from an occupational disease and is entitled to compensation, it is further the opinion of the Full Commission that plaintiff is not totally disabled by reason of such occupational disease. The Opinion and

Award heretofore filed in this case is therefore amended as follows:

* * *

(3) Finding of Fact No. 6, as the same appears on Page 4 of the Opinion and Award, is hereby stricken out in its entirety and there is substituted in lieu thereof the following:

6. In addition to her chronic obstructive lung disease, plaintiff suffers and has suffered for some time from phlebitis, varicose veins and diabetes. Such conditions constitute an added factor in causing her disability.

(4) Finding of Fact No. 8, as the same appears on Page 4 of the Opinion and Award, is hereby stricken out in its entirety and there is substituted in lieu thereof a new Finding of Fact as follows:

8. Due to the occupational disease suffered by plaintiff and due to her other physical infirmities, including bronchitis, phlebitis, varicose veins and diabetes, plaintiff has no earning capacity in any employment for which she can qualify in the labor market. Fifty-five percent of such disability is due to her occupational disease and 45 percent of such disability is due to her physical infirmities not related to her employment with defendant-employer.

(5) A new Finding of Fact is added immediately following Finding of Fact No. 9, as the same appears on Page 4 of the Opinion and Award, as follows:

10. As a result of the occupational disease giving rise hereto, plaintiff has sustained a 55 percent loss of wage-earning capacity or ability to earn wages. Her average weekly wage-earning capacity has been reduced by 55 percent of $119.77 or $65.87 per week. The

balance of her wage loss is not a result of her occupational disease.

(6) Conclusion of Law No. 2, as the same appears on Page 5 of the Opinion and Award, is hereby stricken out in its entirety and there is substituted in lieu thereafter a new Conclusion of Law as follows:

2. As a result of her occupational disease, plaintiff has sustained an average weekly wage loss of $65.87 and such temporary partial disability commenced 24 April 1975. She is therefore entitled to compensation at the rate of $43.92 per week for such temporary partial disability commencing 24 April 1975 and the payment of such compensation should continue until such time as plaintiff sustains a change of condition; provided, however, that such payments shall not exceed 300 weeks. G.S. 97-52; G.S. 97-30; G.S. 97-2(9).

As a result of the Full Commission's amendments to Commissioner Brown's order, the Commission has found that plaintiff is totally disabled from work, that her disability was in part caused by occupational disease compensable under the law and in part caused by other noncompensable illnesses, and therefore plaintiff is only entitled to compensation for partial, not total, disability. The Commission erred in this conclusion.

Our courts have historically and consistently held that the disability of the injured employee is to be measured by his capacity or incapacity to earn the wages he was receiving at the time of the injury and that loss of earning capacity is the criterion. *See, Ashely v. Rent-A-Car Co.*, 271 N.C. 76, 155 S.E. 2d 755 (1967) and cases cited therein. From the wording of the pertinent provisions of the statute it is clear that the Commission can only apportion when the claimant retains some capacity to work. G.S. 97-29 provides, ". . . where the incapacity for work resulting from injury is total, the employer shall pay or cause to be paid . . . to the injured employee during such total disability a weekly compensation equal to sixty-six and two-thirds percent (66⅔%) of his average weekly wages. . . ." G.S. 97-30 provides, " . . . where the incapacity for work resulting from the injury is partial, the employer shall pay . . . to the injured employee during such disability, a weekly compensation equal to sixty-six and two-thirds percent (66⅔%) of the difference between his average weekly wages before the injury *and the average weekly wages which he is able to earn thereafter . . . .*" [Emphasis added.] In the case *sub judice*, the Comission's findings of fact clearly establish the link between plaintiff's occupational disease and her incapacity to work. Once that link is established, our law does not contemplate that the Commission shall act as a board of medical inquiry, assigning or proportioning a worker's incapacity to work to other discernable infirmities. If the worker's incapacity to work is total and if that incapacity is occasioned by a compensable injury or disease, the worker's incapacity to work cannot be apportioned to other preexisting or latent illnesses or infirmities, nor may the entitlement to compensation be diminished for such conditions. *Little v. Food Service*, 295 N.C. 527, 246 S.E. 2d 743 (1978); *Mabe v. Granite Corp.*, 15 N.C. App. 253, 189 S.E. 2d 804 (1972); *Martin v. Service Co.*, 17 N.C. App 359, 194 S.E. 2d 223 (1973), *disc. rev. denied*, 283 N.C. 257, 195 S.E. 2d 690 (1973); *Pruitt v. Publishing Co.*, 27 N.C. App. 254, 218 S.E. 2d 876 (1975), *rev'd on other grounds*, 289 N.C. 254, 221 S.E. 2d 355 (1976).

The Commission's findings that plaintiff was totally incapacitated for gainful employment and that she suffers from a compensable disease compel the conclusion that she is entitled to compensation for total incapacity as provided by law.

This matter is remanded to the Industrial Commission for entry of an order consistent with this opinion.

Reversed and remanded.

Judge PARKER concurs.

Chief Judge MORRIS dissenting.

Chief Judge MORRIS dissenting:

I do not disagree with the statement of the majority that "[i]f the worker's incapacity to work is total *and if that incapacity to work is occasioned by a compensable injury or disease,* the worker's incapacity to work cannot be apportioned to other pre-existing or latent illnesses or infirmities, nor may the entitlement to compensation be diminished for such condition." (Emphasis supplied.) Nor do I disagree with the holdings of the cases cited as supportive authority. I simply do not think the statement and the case have any applicability to the case before us.

In *Mabe v. Granite Corp.,* 15 N.C. App. 253, 189 S.E. 2d 804 (1972), the only case cited by the majority dealing with occupational disease, and the case closest to the one *sub judice,* this Court did affirm an order to the Industrial Commission awarding total disability benefits upon a finding of total incapacity for work *because* of silicosis. There the employee had worked as a stone cutter for the defendant for some 30 to 35 years. He terminated his employment with defendant in 1968 and thereafter filed a claim against defendant for compensation because of disability caused by silicosis. Medical testimony established that he was 40% disabled for employment "in his previous or any other occupation." His testimony was that he had not held regular employment since he quit working for defendant because, "due to a shortness of breath and a lack of strength, he can no longer perform hard labor." He had only a fifth grade education, could read a little, but could not "write much", and didn't "know nothing but hard labor" and could not get "a job like that." We said:

> Defendant contends that elements of age and poor education are factors which are beyond the control of an employer and cannot be considered in determining an employee's disability. The answer to this is that an employer accepts an employee as he is. If a compensable injury precipitates a latent physical condition, such as heart disease, cancer, back weakness and the like, the entire disability is compensable and no attempt is made to weigh the relative contribution of the accident and the pre-existing condition. 2 Larson, Workmen's Compensation Law, § 59.20, p. 88.109.

By the same token, *if an industrial disease renders an employee actually incapacitated* to earn any wages, the employer may not ask that a portion of the disability be charged to the employee's advanced age and poor learning on the grounds that if it were not for these factors he might still retain some earning capacity. (Emphasis supplied.)

15 N.C. App. at 256, 189 S.E. 2d at 807. In *Mabe*, the Court was not faced with the question now before us. There was no additional disease or physical condition totally unrelated to the employment which contributed in large measure to the incapacity. Here the majority of claimant's disability is due to factors other than her employment. In the mid sixties she went to Duke Hospital, "but not for a breathing problem." She was told she had bronchitis. She worked until 24 April 1975. She smoked about a pack and one-half of cigarettes a day. Along about 1967 she had a "a vein stripping in her leg" done at Duke Hospital. She did not recover as expected and had to return to the hospital, at which time it was discovered that she had diabetes. The doctors would tell her to stop smoking and she would stop and then start back and continued to smoke to the date of hearing. In addition to the phlebitis and severe venous deficiency in her lower extremities, diabetes, and bronchitis, claimant had had other illnesses, some involving surgical procedures. She had undergone a hysterectomy because of the presence of fibroid tumors in the womb. She had had tumors removed from both breasts and in 1953 had had cancer diagnosed. She had also had diagnosed left ventribular enlargement with a systolic ejection murmur.

Dr. Sieker testified that only 50 to 60 percent of her disability was due to cotton dust, and the rest was due to factors totally unrelated to employment. Dr. Battigelli testified that the percentage of her disability due to her employment was from 0 to 20 percent, "quite miniscule, if not negligible". These two medical experts clearly testified that claimant's incapacity *resulting* from occupational disease is not total. It is also clear that all of the evidence clearly showed that claimant did not actually become incapacitated *because* of byssinosis. When the General Assembly amended the Worker's Compensation Act to include specified occupational diseases, it did not, by so doing,

Oliver v. Powell

remove the requirement that compensation is payable only where there is causal connection between injury and employment. *See Duncan v. City of Charlotte*, 234 N.C. 86, 66 S.E. 2d 22 (1951).

In my opinion, the Worker's Compensation Act is not intended to require that employers provide general health insurance for employees whose disability stems from causes other than causes connected with and resulting from employment. This would be the result of the majority non-apportionment rule. *See* dissent by Clark, Judge, in *Pruitt v. Knight Publishing Co.*, 27 N.C. App. 254, 218 S.E. 2d 876 (1975), *reversed on other grounds*, 289 N.C. 254, 221 S.E. 2d 355 (1976). Nor do I think *Mabe* requires the result reached by the majority. It seems clear that G.S. 97-29 and G.S. 97-30 mandate that benefits are to be provided only for incapacity "resulting from the injury." This the full Commission did. Its facts are supported by the evidence and the facts found support the conclusions and the award.

I agree with the full Commission that claimant be compensated only for that portion of her disability which is related to and results from her employment.

TERRY OLIVER, Administrator of the Estate of WILLIAM ALFRED OLIVER, SR. v. ROBERT HENRY POWELL

No. 7918SC1084

(Filed 3 June 1980)

1. **Automobiles § 46– striking of pedestrian – opinion testimony as to speed – exclusion error**

    In an action to recover for the wrongful death of a pedestrian who was struck by defendant's automobile, the trial court erred in excluding testimony by an eyewitness to the accident concerning the speed of defendant's vehicle, but the court did not err in excluding testimony by the witness that he saw what looked like beer cans in the backseat of defendant's car, since this testimony was the only evidence that defendant was intoxicated at the time of the accident, was irrelevant and too remote, and did not raise even a conjecture that defendant was under the influence of alcohol at the time of the collision.

2. **Automobiles § 62.2– pedestrian crossing highway – sufficiency of evidence of driver's negligence**

In an action to recover for the wrongful death of a pedestrian who was struck by defendant's vehicle, evidence was sufficient to be submitted to the jury and did not show that the pedestrian was contributorily negligent as a matter of law where the evidence tended to show that deceased was crossing a four lane highway at a point where he would be visible to defendant for 1500 feet at night; defendant, exceeding the maximum speed of 45 mph by 15 mph, bore down on deceased who was able to reach the median before defendant was upon him; deceased, standing on the median, was looking for traffic in the lanes opposite the lane defendant was traveling in and opposite those lanes he had just crossed; and defendant meanwhile applied his brakes on seeing the pedestrian, swerved upon the median and there struck deceased in the back as he stood on the median of the divided four lane highway.

APPEAL by plaintiff from *Davis, Judge.* Judgment entered 13 June 1979 in Superior Court, GUILFORD County. Heard in the Court of Appeals 13 May 1980.

Plaintiff, the administrator of the estate of William Alfred Oliver, Sr., who died on 14 March 1977 as a result of injuries received from being struck by defendant's automobile, brought this action against defendant for the wrongful death of William Alfred Oliver, Sr. Plaintiff alleged negligence which defendant denied in his answer. Defendant also alleged contributory negligence as an affirmative defense. Last clear chance was not pled as an issue in the case.

The following was stipulated as fact by the parties. At approximately 10:45 p.m. on 14 March 1977, an accident occurred on Wendover Avenue near its intersection with Maple Street in Greensboro, North Carolina. A 1966 Volkswagen owned and operated by defendant struck plaintiff's intestate. Prior to the accident, plaintiff's intestate was crossing Wendover Avenue on foot from north to south. The Volkswagen was traveling west on Wendover Avenue in the far left lane next to the median. The maximum posted speed on Wendover at the point of the accident is forty-five miles per hour. There are no municipal streetlights in the area of the accident. At the point where plaintiff's intestate was crossing Wendover, he was not within a marked crosswalk or unmarked crosswalk at an intersection. Plaintiff's intestate died as a result of injuries suffered in the accident.

Plaintiff's evidence consisted of the testimony of Roland Smith (by deposition), three investigating police officers and plaintiff. Their testimony, in pertinent part, can be summarized as follows.

Through deposition, Roland Smith testified he remembered an accident on Wendover Avenue sometime in 1977 though he did not remember the date. He specifically recalled that it was drizzling rain that night, a condition he particularly does not like to drive in. He was on his way to pick up his wife after she got off work at 11:00 p.m. This put him on Wendover Avenue between 10:30 and 10:40 p.m. He was traveling approximately fifty miles per hour to the right of a light-colored Volkswagen which was in the left lane next to the median. They both ran through a yellow light and proceeded on to the Summit Avenue underpass. The Volkswagen was two car lengths in front of him as both cars went under the Summit Avenue underpass. From the Summit Avenue underpass to the Maple Street intersection, Wendover is straight. The area is dimly lit. He saw the Volkswagen car lights shine on the figure of a person three car lengths ahead who was crossing the street from the direction of the Cone Mill plant at the Maple Street intersection with Wendover. The pedestrian was "just about to the median and had jumped up on the median and was watching traffic coming the other way." "When his light hit the pedestrian, I saw the man step up" on the median. The Volkswagen brake lights came on when the pedestrian came into view. Smith hit his brakes, pulled to the right and went past the Maple Street entrance onto Wendover. "I remember applying my brakes and moving over into the next lane and then seeing a car go up on a median and hit the pedestrian." He later testified he did not see the pedestrian being hit but only heard the thud when he was hit. Five or six seconds passed from the time the pedestrian came into view until Smith heard the thud. He pulled to the side of the road past Maple Street. He crossed the road to the accident site and observed the pedestrian lying in the lane closest to the median opposite to the direction in which the

Volkswagen and his car were traveling. Four or five people were present, so he got back in his car and went to pick up his wife. After picking up his wife, they came back by the accident but did not stop. An ambulance and police car were there. He did not notice whether the pedestrian's clothes were light or dark. Testimony by Smith to the effect that the Volkswagen was "doing about fifty-five or close to sixty" in the forty-five mile per hour zone and that he saw what looked like two beer cans in the backseat was excluded by the trial judge over objection by plaintiff. When shown the description and diagram of the 14 March 1977 accident contained in the police report, Smith testified it did not correspond to what he remembered seeing in that "when I saw the pedestrian, he was up on the median." Smith was discovered as a witness by mere coincidence. The wife of plaintiff's intestate happened to be at the police department trying to find out why no one had been charged in the death of her husband on a day when Smith came in to get a copy of a police report of an accident involving his daughter. He described the accident he had seen on Wendover and gave the wife of plaintiff's intestate his phone number.

Thomas H. Eanes testified that he arrived at the scene on the night in question sometime after 11:00 and began taking photographs. He was at that time an Identification Specialist for the city police department. On arriving, he observed "a 1966 Volkswagen automobile sitting crossways with the front wheels up on the center median." There were skid marks leading up to the wheels of the Volkswagen which was damaged in the front and on the windshield. There was what appeared to be blood on the street which was otherwise dry. He described Wendover Avenue at that point as a four lane highway, two lanes going east and two going west with an additional left turn lane for eastbound traffic. After photographing the scene of the accident, he went to the hospital to photograph the deceased pedestrian. Eanes could not remember exactly what clothing the deceased was wearing. He observed injuries to the back of the deceased's head, his left arm, right shoulder and back. He did not remember any injuries to the front of deceased's body.

Police Officer D.A. Denny testified that he arrived on the scene about 10:53 p.m. and was the second officer on the scene.

It was a dry night. He could find no eyewitnesses to the accident. He began making measurements of the area. He found a white Volkswagen in the inside westbound lane of Wendover with its front end up on a concrete median where Wendover and Maple Street meet in a T intersection. The front hood was dented, the windshield shattered and the right front bumper was clean of road grime. He measured four different skid marks. The first skid mark measured twenty-nine feet, ten inches and was located next to the median just before the intersection of Wendover and Maple. There was then a break of eight to ten feet followed by three more skid marks which began in the middle of the intersection. One skid mark went for fifty-seven feet, five inches and went up to the right rear tire of the Volkswagen. Another skid mark to the far left of this one went for twenty-eight feet, one inch to the concrete median. The tire leaving this skid mark went onto the concrete median where the median began at the west margin of the intersection. Between these two was another skid mark measuring more than twenty feet, which stopped at about the west side of where the median began. The total distance of skid marks to the right rear tire of the Volkswagen was eighty feet, six inches. The Volkswagen tires did not appear slick to the point they were unsafe or unlawful. Denny described that vicinity of Wendover as a very dark roadway at night. According to his testimony, Wendover, as you come under the Summit Avenue bridge headed west toward the Maple Street intersection, develops a third lane for westbound traffic. In the other direction going towards the summit Avenue bridge, there are two lanes for eastbound traffic, a left turn lane for vehicles turning onto Maple and a lane to the south for those vehicles exiting onto Summit.

Police Officer Q.J. Parlier testified that he assisted in the investigation of the accident in question. He found all the tires on the Volkswagen except the left front tire had the required amount of tread. It had not been raining at all the night of the accident. The unobstructed view for traffic going west, as was defendant, to the point of the accident was approximately 1500 feet that night. He testified that plaintiff's intestate was wearing dark work clothes.

Plaintiff testified that he is the twenty-nine-year-old son of the pedestrian hit and killed by defendant's car. His father worked at the Cone Mill plant located right off Wendover on Maple Street. His father walked to and from work from his home which was only four or five blocks away. On learning of the accident, he went to the scene of the accident where Officer Parlier told him what happened. The area had enough light from several sources that he could see a puddle of blood in the street and blood spattered over the median.

At the close of plaintiff's evidence, defendant moved for directed verdict on the grounds (1) that the plaintiff had failed to introduce any evidence of negligence on the part of defendant as a proximate cause of the collision and death of defendant and (2) that plaintiff's own evidence established contributory negligence on the part of plaintiff's intestate as a matter of law. The trial court granted the motion for directed verdict and plaintiff appeals.

Graham, Cooke, Miles and Daisy, by James W. Miles, Jr., for plaintiff appellant.

Smith, Moore, Smith, Schell and Hunter, by Robert A. Wicker, for defendant appellee.

VAUGHN, Judge.

The principal question raised on this appeal is whether the trial court erred in granting defendant's motion for directed verdict. Before we reach this issue, we must address the issue of whether the trial court properly excluded certain evidence offered by plaintiff through the deposition of Roland Smith.

Defendant, at the outset, contends Roland Smith was not testifying about the same accident. Smith remembered an accident in 1977 on Wendover Avenue where it intersects with Maple Street involving a light-colored Volkswagen and a pedestrian. Smith did not remember the exact date and he recalled that it was drizzling rain that night and that the pavement was glistening because of the rain. All the investigating police officers testified it was not raining at all that night and that the pavement was dry. The police report diagram did not correspond with his recollection of the accident. Except for these details, the testimony of the accident Smith observed is substantially the same as the testimony of the investigating officers about the accident scene they observed. The testimony of the officers and Smith was identical in respect to the time of the accident, the make of car, its light color, the exact location of the accident and the positions at which the pedestrian and the car which hit him came to rest after the collision. The evidence presents a sufficient foundation that Smith was testifying about the accident involving defendant and plaintiff's intestate. The jury could, of course, find otherwise and choose to ignore the testimony. He was, however, a competent witness to testify about the accident. *See Honeycutt v. Strube,* 261 N.C. 59, 134 S.E. 2d 110 (1964).

[1] The question thus becomes whether it was proper for the trial court to exclude certain evidence offered by this witness. This evidence is crucial for it presents some evidence of negligence on the part of defendant pled by plaintiff.

The trial court excluded testimony by Smith that defendant was "doing about fifty-five or close to sixty because I was doing fifty and it was in front of me." The posted maximum speed on Wendover at that point was forty-five. Any person of ordinary intelligence, who has an opportunity to observe a vehicle, is competent to testify as to the rate of speed of such vehicle and can express an opinion as to its speed. *Honeycutt v. Strube, supra; Lookabill v. Regan,* 247 N.C. 199, 100 S.E. 2d 521 (1957). Smith had a reasonable opportunity to observe the Volkswagen which traveled beside his car and then pulled ahead of his car. It was error for the trial court not to admit this testimony of the speed of the Volkswagen. Other testimony concerning skid marks and the time between which Smith saw the Volkswagen brake lights come on and he heard the thud or actually saw the car hit the pedestrian does not make the opinion on speed of the car inherently incredible or contradictory to the physical evidence. What Smith, who had problems measuring distance, described as three car lengths, one of the investigating officers described as a distance of 1500 feet. The skid marks do not give a conclusive indication of speed and stopping time because of the collision with the median. *Contrast Jones v. Schaffer*, 252 N.C. 368, 114 S.E. 2d 105 (1960); *Hall v. Kimber*, 6 N.C. App. 669, 171 S.E. 2d 99 (1969).

The trial court also excluded testimony that Smith saw what looked like beer cans in the backseat of defendant's car. Plaintiff contends this was relevant evidence that defendant was intoxicated at the time of the collision. This is the only evidence of such and the trial court properly excluded it as irrelevant and too remote. *Merchants Distributors v. Hutchinson*, 16 N.C. App. 655, 193 S.E. 2d 436 (1972). The proffered evidence did not raise even a conjecture that defendant was under the influence of alcohol at the time of the collision.

[2] The central question of this case is whether the directed verdict was proper because plaintiff did not present sufficient proof of defendant's negligence or because the evidence demonstrates that plaintiff's intestate was contributorily negligent as a matter of law. We hold it was error to grant the directed verdict for defendant for the evidence in a light most favorable to plaintiff presents questions of fact on both the issue of negligence and contributory negligence which entitled plaintiff to have the case presented to a jury.

Duties are imposed on both a motorist and a pedestrian to be reasonably prudent persons in the use of the highways of the State. These duties are codified in part in G.S. 20-174, which provides in part the following.

(a) Every pedestrian crossing a roadway at any point other than within a marked crosswalk or within an unmarked crosswalk at an intersection shall yield the right-of-way to all vehicles upon the roadway. . . .

(e) Notwithstanding the provisions of this section, every driver of a vehicle shall exercise due care to avoid colliding with any pedestrian upon any roadway, and shall give warning by sounding the horn when necessary. . . .

As stated in *Blake v. Mallard*, 262 N.C. 62, 65, 136 S.E. 2d 214, 216 (1964) (citations omitted),

> [t]he failure of a pedestrian crossing a roadway at a point other than a crosswalk to yield the right of way to a motor vehicle is not contributory negligence *per se;* it is only evidence of negligence. However, the court will non-suit a plaintiff-pedestrian on the ground of contributory negligence when all the evidence so clearly establishes his failure to yield the right of way as one of the proximate causes of his injuries that no other reasonable conclusion is possible.

Our courts have considered many cases involving pedestrians being hit by automobiles. The case at hand, when considered in a light most favorable to plaintiff, presents the following situation.

Plaintiff's intestate was crossing Wendover Avenue near its intersection with Maple Street at a point where he would be visible to defendant for 1500 feet at night. Defendant, exceeding the maximum speed of forty-five miles per hour by fifteen miles per hour, bore down on plaintiff's intestate who was able to reach the median before defendant was upon him. Plaintiff's intestate, standing on the median, was looking for traffic in the lanes opposite the lane defendant was traveling in and opposite those lanes he had just crossed. Defendant, meanwhile, applied his brakes on seeing plaintiff's intestate, swerved upon the median and there struck plaintiff in the back as he stood on the median of the divided four lane highway. An inference from this evidence is that plaintiff's intestate had yielded the right-of-way but was struck when defendant lost control of his car.

We hold the evidence in a light most favorable to plaintiff presents clear evidence of negligence on the part of defendant in the control of his car. It does not demonstrate that plaintiff's intestate was contributorily negligent as a matter of law. This holding is consistent with the holdings of the courts of this State in similar factual situations. *Ragland v. Moore*, 299 N.C. 360, 261 S.E. 2d 666 (1980); *Landini v. Steelman*, 243 N.C. 146, 90

S.E. 2d 377 (1955); *Goodson v. Williams*, 237 N.C. 291, 74 S.E. 2d 762 (1953); *Williams v. Henderson*, 230 N.C. 707, 55 S.E. 2d 462 (1949); *Morris v. Minix*, 4 N.C. App. 634, 167 S.E. 2d 494 (1969); *contrast Anderson v. Carter*, 272 N.C. 426, 158 S.E. 2d 607 (1968); *Blake v. Mallard, supra; Gentry v. Hackenburg*, 23 N.C. App. 96, 208 S.E. 2d 279 (1974).

The case of *Gentry v. Hackenburg, supra,* involved a situation where a directed verdict was affirmed where the plaintiff was struck while attempting to cross a roadway. Gentry was crossing at a point where the view was unobstructed for three quarters of a mile. She saw Hackenburg's car coming but crossed the road in front of it. She was not struck until she reached the shoulder of the road and she was struck by Hackenburg's left rear fender. He applied his brakes, drove entirely off the road to avoid hitting plaintiff and the court held Gentry's disregard of the approach of the oncoming car in her attempt to cross the road to be contributory negligence as a matter of law. The case is factually similar only to the extent that both pedestrians were struck somewhere off the main traveled portion of the road. The evidence is uncontradicted that the pedestrian in the *Hackenburg* case did not yield the right-of-way as required by G.S. 20-174(a). The testimony of the plaintiff and the testimony of the driver who hit her made this clear. In the present case, the evidence of such is contradicted and presented a jury question.

Reversed and remanded.

Judges PARKER and HEDRICK concur.

———————

CASSAUNDRA SPINKS v. JOHN R. TAYLOR, JR., TRADING AS TAYLOR REALTY

DOROTHY L. RICHARDSON v. JOHN R. TAYLOR COMPANY, INC.

No. 7918DC1063

(Filed 3 June 1980)

1. **Landlord and Tenant § 18– notice to tenant of padlocked premises – no simulation of court document**

Defendant's use of the words "Legal Notice" on a padlocking notice posted on the doors of tenants who were late paying their rent did not violate G.S. 75-54 which prohibits the use of false representations in efforts to collect debts and the use of paper writings that simulate documents authorized or issued by a court or other legal authority, since the notice in question clearly was not a simulated court notice.

2. **Landlord and Tenant § 18– nonpayment of rent – provision for termination and padlocking of premises – provision not unconscionable**

There was no merit to plaintiff's contention that the termination provision of their lease, which allowed for padlocking of the premises upon failure to pay rent and after notice by the landlord, was unconscionable and therefore unenforceable as violative of public policy, since it was not the padlocking procedures that deprived plaintiffs of a place to live but their failure to pay rent, and a tenant in N.C. cannot retain possession of premises without paying rent, even to protest alleged wrongful acts of the landlord in providing substandard conditions in the premises.

3. **Landlord and Tenant § 19– failure to pay rent – landlord's exercise of self-help proper**

A landlord can lawfully exercise peaceful, nonviolent self-help in N.C. to regain possession of leased premises where the tenant fails to pay rent.

APPEAL by plaintiffs from *Cecil, Judge.* Judgments entered 14 August 1979 in District Court, GUILFORD County. Heard in the Court of Appeals 24 April 1980.

These two actions were consolidated for trial and appeal as they involve common questions of law and fact. Plaintiffs seek damages from defendant for breach of rental agreements by wrongfully padlocking plaintiffs' apartments and depriving them of possession and use of the apartments and their personal property. Although plaintiff Spinks sued John R. Taylor Company; Inc., plaintiff's amended complaint and defendant's amended answer establish that John R. Taylor rents the apartments in dispute and that he is the proper party defendant.

In the Spinks case the parties stipulated defendant leased an apartment to Spinks 1 November 1976 and she occupied it until 1 August 1977. On 16 May 1977 defendant padlocked the apartment, without judicial process, and after Spinks paid the past-due rent, the padlock was removed. On 15 July 1977 defendant again padlocked the apartment without judicial process. At least ten days prior to the padlocking, defendant had given Spinks notice of default and demand for payment.

The stipulation in the Richardson case is essentially the same, except that Richardson's apartment was only padlocked once, after which she paid the past-due rent and the padlock was removed.

The leases involved contain the following provisions:

15. RULES AND REGULATIONS: The various rules and regulations which are attached to this Lease and such alterations, additions, and modifications thereof as may be from time to time made by the Agent, shall be considered a part of this agreement, with the same effect as though written herein, and the Resident covenants that said rules and regulations shall be faithfully observed by the Resident, the employees of the Resident, and all persons invited by the Resident on or in said premises. The right is reserved by the Agent to add to, alter, modify or rescind from time to time, said rules and regulations. The Agent, however, shall have the right to change said rules and regulations and to waive in writing any or all of said rules and regulations and to waive in writing any or all of said rules and regulations in the case of any one or more residents.

. . . .

19. TERMINATION BY AGENT (DEFAULT, OBJEC-TIONABLE CONDUCT, RE-ENTRY): If the Resident defaults in the payment of rent after the same becomes due, or if the Resident violates the covenants of this Lease, or if the Agent at any time shall deem the conduct of the Resident or visitor ... the Resident objectionable or improper, the Agent may give the Resident five (5) days written notice of the Agent's intention to terminate this Lease, and this Lease shall terminate at the expiration of such five-day period, anything to the contrary herein notwithstanding. At such time, the Agent shall have the right to re-enter and take possession of the leased premises, without process or by legal process from the Court having jurisdiction over the premises. In the event of re-entry by the Agent as provided in this and the next paragraph, the Resident shall

be liable in damages to the Agent and Owner for all losses sustained.

    . . . .

    22. NOTICES: ... The Resident agrees to accept as sufficient notice required by law any written notice delivered personally to the Resident or mailed to the premises.

Plaintiffs and defendant filed motions for summary judgment. Spinks's complaint was verified; Richardson's was not. Defendant offered the affidavits of defendant Taylor and R. Walton McNairy.

Taylor's affidavit showed that he managed the apartment complexes where plaintiffs had lived and was familiar with the rules and regulations which the tenants were required to follow. When delinquency in rentals and the increase in evictions became unmanageable, he sought legal advice, and the witness McNairy established the self-help remedies Taylor later adopted. These procedures for self-help were carefully explained to all apartment managers. The rent is due in full on the first day of the month. Tenants who have not paid by the eighth of the month are given notice that unless the rent is paid before the date set, the apartment will be padlocked on the last Tuesday of the month. This gives tenant a notice of the impending padlocking of from sixteen to twenty-three days, depending upon the month. At least ten days' notice of the proposed padlocking is always given. On the day scheduled for the padlocking the manager goes to the apartment and knocks loudly, identifying himself and the purpose of the visit. If tenant then pays the rent, the procedure ends. If tenant indicates he intends to stay in possession of the apartment, the manager ceases the padlocking, tells tenant that court proceedings will be begun, and leaves. If no one answers the manager's knock on the door, manager opens the door to the apartment and again announces the purpose of his presence. Then he carefully checks to see that no animals or persons, particularly small children, are present. If the tenant has vacated the apartment, it is not padlocked; otherwise, it is. Notice of the padlocking is taped on the door. Then, the manager attempts to personally notify tenant of the padlocking. If the tenant requests personal property from the padlocked apartment, the tenant may enter and remove this property without payment of the past-due rent. If the tenant, after entering to retrieve personal property, refuses to leave the apartment, the manager tells tenant that court proceedings will be started and the padlock is removed. Once a tenant objects to padlocking, the self-help procedures end and resort is made to the courts. Usually, most tenants pay once the padlocking procedures begin; only an average of one tenant per month is evicted by padlocking. Basically, this is because rent is not allowed to accumulate for more than one month. When court proceedings are required, several months' rent accumulates and tenants are not financially able to pay.

After considering the materials before it, the trial court denied plaintiffs' motions for summary judgment and allowed the summary judgment motions of defendant. Plaintiffs appeal.

Central Carolina Legal Services, by Robert S. Payne, and Ling & Farran, by Jeffery P. Farran, for plaintiff appellants.

Smith, Moore, Smith, Schell & Hunter, by Bynum M. Hunter, Jeri L. Whitfield and Suzanne Reynolds, for defendant appellee.

MARTIN (Harry C.), Judge.

Plaintiffs contend the self-help eviction procedures of defendant are contrary to the law of North Carolina and, therefore, the court erred in denying their motions for summary judgment and in allowing summary judgment for defendant.

They first argue defendant's agents who carry out the padlocking procedures are "debt collectors" as defined by N.C.G.S. 75-50 (3) and therefore bound by the provisions of Article 2 of Chapter 75. We do not decide whether defendant's agents are "debt collectors" within the meaning of the statute because the record fails to show any violations of Article 2 by them. N.C.G.S. 75-51 (1) prohibits the use or threat of violence of illegal means to cause harm to any person, his reputation, or his property.

Plaintiffs make no allegations of violence by defendant's agents and, as will be hereinafter discussed, the padlocking procedures are not illegal. Nor has there been any representation of seizure of property as proscribed by N.C.G.S. 75-51 (6), or threat of illegal action prohibited by N.C.G.S. 75-51 (8).

[1] N.C.G.S. 75-54 (4) and (5) prohibit the use of false representations in efforts to collect debts and the use of paper writings that simulate documents authorized or issued by a court or other legal authority. Plaintiffs argue defendant's use of the words "Legal Notice" on the notice of padlocking violates this statute. We do not agree. The notice used by defendant is well within the bounds established in *State v. Watts*, 38 N.C. App. 561, 248 S.E. 2d 354 (1978), *disc. rev. denied*, 296 N.C. 414, 251 S.E. 2d 473 (1979). There the notice to vacate was drawn in the form of the usual notice used in court proceedings except for the absence of a case heading and docket number. The Court in *Watts* held it was obvious the notice was issued not by a court official but by the agent of the owner. The padlock notice here at issue reads:

GUILFORD COUNTY   PADLOCKED APARTMENT

NORTH CAROLINA   LEGAL NOTICE

This apartment has been padlocked for nonpayment of rent. ANYONE ENTERING THE APARTMENT IS A TRESPASSER AND WILL BE PROSECUTED.

The previous resident may regain legal possession of the apartment by immediately paying the past due rent.

The previous resident can recover any personal property left in the apartment by immediately contacting the resident manager.

The notice is clearly not a simulated court notice.

Plaintiffs urge us to find N.C.G.S. 75-1.1 applicable to the facts of this case, relying upon *Love v. Pressley*, 34 N.C. App. 503,

239 S.E. 2d 574 (1977), *disc. rev. denied*, 294 N.C. 441, 241 S.E. 2d 843 (1978). In *Love*, the tenants were not in default on their lease and were in rightful possession of the premises. In our case, plaintiffs do not deny that they were in default on their rent. *Love* is distinguishable from this case and we find no merit in plaintiffs' arguments concerning the applicability of N.C.G.S. 75-1.1.

[2] Next, plaintiffs argue that paragraph 19 of the lease, the termination provision, is unconscionable and therefore unenforceable as violative of public policy. The law argued by plaintiffs on unconscionable contracts is accurate but has no application to the facts of plaintiffs' cases. Here, it is not the padlocking procedures that deprive plaintiffs of a place to live, but their failure to pay the rent. Plaintiffs offer no reason for failing to pay their rent. In North Carolina a tenant cannot retain possession of premises without paying rent, even to protest alleged wrongful acts of the landlord in providing substandard conditions in the premises. *Thompson v. Shoemaker*, 7 N.C. App. 687, 173 S.E. 2d 627 (1970). We must reject plaintiffs' argument that paragraph 19 is unconscionable and unenforceable.

[3] Last, plaintiffs contend the public policy and law of North Carolina prevent remedies of self-help as used by defendant. Obviously, a landlord cannot without judicial process seize and sell a tenant's personal property to collect delinquent rent. *Dalgleish v. Grandy*, 1 N.C. 249 (1800). There has been no effort by defendant here to seize plaintiffs' personal property for the purpose of collecting past-due rent, either by sale of the property or by holding it till the rent was paid. A landlord can lawfully exercise peaceful, nonviolent self-help in North Carolina to regain possession of leased premises where the tenant fails to pay rent. *Mosseller v. Deaver*, 106 N.C. 494, 11 S.E. 529 (1890). In *Mosseller*, defendants had used force to eject plaintiff from possession, and plaintiff sued for damages. The trial court instructed the jury that defendants had the right to use force to remove plaintiff, but no more force than was necessary. On appeal, the Supreme Court ordered a new trial, holding the instruction to be error and stating: "[W]e cannot approve of the instruction given, as it is not only opposed to the public policy, which requires the owner to use *peaceful means* or resort to the

courts in order to regain his possession, ..." *Id.* at 495, 11 S.E. at 530 (emphasis added). Thus, while North Carolina rejects the use of force to regain possession, peaceful means by an owner may be utilized. Plaintiffs do not contend defendant used force to regain possession of the premises.

North Carolina has held the changing of locks on a door to keep out an occupant is not a forcible entry within the meaning of the criminal laws. For there to be a forcible entry there must be some force or violence in excess of a simple trespass. *State v. Leary*, 136 N.C. 578, 48 S.E. 570 (1904). The placing of the padlock by defendant is the basic act that deprived plaintiffs of possession. Under *Leary*, this appears to be a peaceful means.

We believe that under the common law of North Carolina when a tenant fails to pay rent and to vacate leased property, the owner may use peaceful means to regain possession of the property. Upon failure to regain possession thereby, he may resort to the courts. *Mosseller, supra.* This is in accord with other common law jurisdictions. *See Krasner v. Gurley*, 252 Ala. 235, 40 So. 2d 328 (1949); *Calef v. Jesswein*, 93 Ind. App. 514, 176 N.E. 632 (1931); *Paddock v. Clay*, 138 Mont. 541, 357 P. 2d 1 (1960); *Liberty Ind. Park Corp. v. Protective Pkg. Corp.*, 71 Misc. 2d 116, 335 N.Y.S. 2d 333 (1972), *aff'd*, 351 N.Y.S. 2d 944 (1974). The rule is succinctly stated in 50 Am. Jur. 2d Landlord and Tenant § 1220 (1970), as follows:

> According to many cases, where a landlord is wrongfully held out of possession by an overstaying tenant, he may, when the opportunity presents itself, gain possession of the leased premises by peaceable means, and necessity for recourse to legal process exists only where peaceable means fail and force would be necessary; thus, where the tenant's right of possession has terminated, the landlord has the right to re-enter the leased premises peaceably, as where the tenant is absent.

In a case similar to the one *sub judice*, the Missouri Supreme Court in *Chappee v. Lubrite Refining Co.*, 337 Mo. 791, 85 S.W. 2d 1034, 101 A.L.R. 471 (1935), held a tenant whose lease had been rightfully terminated is not entitled to recover damages for the act of the lessor in peaceably taking possession of the premises, although against the lessee's will.

In addition, the modern policy of diverting conflicts away from the courts supports lawful self-help remedies. This theory, utilizing arbitration, "citizen courts," referees, traffic offense commissions, debt-counselling services, tax conferences, and other non-court methods of resolving disputes, recognizes that the courts cannot resolve every dispute between persons or between persons and the state. Proper and peaceful self-help remedies by landlords have a place in this scheme. Where a dispute can be properly resolved in a peaceful manner, one is not required to seek the services of the courts. Here, plaintiffs do not deny that they were delinquent in their rent payments and that defendant was entitled to possession of the premises. They only insist defendant could not use peaceful self-help to regain possession of the premises and that he must resort to the courts for this purpose. Under the facts of this case, we reject plaintiff's argument.

The court properly denied plaintiffs' motions for summary judgment and properly granted summary judgment for defendant. *Kessing v. Mortgage Corp.* 278 N.C. 523, 180 S.E. 2d 823 (1971).

Affirmed.

Judges VAUGHN and CLARK concur.

JAMES F. STUTTS v. DUKE POWER COMPANY, A CORPORATION, AND ROBERT ACREE

No. 7926SC1008

(Filed 3 June 1980)

1. **Rules of Civil Procedure § 41.1– voluntary dismissal – new action brought within one year – actions not based on same claim**

   A new action commenced by plaintiff within one year after his voluntary dismissal without prejudice was not based on the same claim as the first

---

Stutts v. Power Co.

---

action, and the second action was therefore barred by the statute of limitations, where the gist of plaintiff's first complaint was that because defendant
power company filled out plaintiff's discharge slip, stating thereon that
plaintiff was discharged for misconduct and a dishonest act, plaintiff was
denied unemployment compensation benefits, while plaintiff's second complaint alleged that defendant power company, through its employees and
agents, slandered plaintiff.

2. **Libel and Slander § 6– statements made by employee – publication not attributable to employer**

   In an action for slander the trial court properly determined that any
   publication of the alleged defamatory statements by the individual defendant which possibly would bring defendant power company, as employer of
   the individual defendant, within the statute of limitations was not attributable to defendant power company, since any idle statements made by individual defendant a month to six weeks after plaintiff's discharge were not
   made within the scope of the individual defendant's employment and, consequently, were not attributable to defendant power company.

3. **Libel and Slander § 5.2– plaintiff called dishonest and unreliable employee –
   statements not actionable per se**

   Alleged false statements made by a defendant calling a plaintiff dishonest or charging that plaintiff was untruthful and an unreliable employee are
   not actionable per se.

4. **Libel and Slander § 14– slanderous words not alleged verbatim in complaint**

   In an action for slander plaintiff's failure to state the defamatory words
   verbatim in the complaint did not render it fatally defective since the words
   attributed to defendant must be alleged only substantially or with sufficient
   particularity to enable the court to determine whether the statement was
   defamatory.

APPEAL by plaintiff from *Graham, Judge.* Judgment entered
19 July 1979 in Superior Court, MECKLENBURG County. Cross-
appeal by defendants. Order entered 17 July 1979. Heard in the
Court of Appeals 17 April 1980.

Plaintiff was employed as a plumber and pipe fitter by
defendant Duke Power Company at its McGuire Nuclear Construction Project. When plaintiff arrived for work on 1 September 1976, he told a fellow worker that he was sick and asked him
to tell plaintiff's foreman or someone in his crew that he would
not be at work that day. Defendant Robert Acree, plaintiff's
foreman, was not informed that day of plaintiff's absence, and
Acree himself was absent the next two workdays. On 8 September Acree questioned plaintiff about his not working one day

---

---

during the previous week. Plaintiff replied that he did pick up his "brass" if he indeed worked, and Acree later informed plaintiff that he had the matter "straightened out." Plaintiff, questioned by other superiors over the next two days, told them he was not at work on 1 September. On 10 September Acree told plaintiff, in the company of other workers, "We are fired, both of us, for a dishonest act and falsifying the records." Plaintiff was then terminated by Duke Power.

Plaintiff filed a complaint against Duke Power on 30 November 1976, alleging a wrongful discharge and false, malicious and libelous statements in charging plaintiff with a dishonest act in connection with his work. After Duke Power filed its answer, plaintiff took a voluntary dismissal without prejudice pursuant to N.C.G.S. 1A-1, Rule 41.

Plaintiff subsequently filed the complaint in this action on 22 September 1977. The first claim for relief was based upon allegations of "false, libelous, slanderous and defamatory statements" made by both Duke Power and Robert Acree. The second and alternative claim for relief was based upon allegations of negligence against both defendants. Defendants' subsequent motion for summary judgment as to the second claim was granted, but Judge Grist denied motions for summary judgment on the defamation claim made by both plaintiff and defendants.

A final pretrial conference was held on 16 July 1979, and on 17 July 1979 defendants' motion to dismiss filed pursuant to Rule 12(b) was denied in open court by Judge Graham. Both defendants entered notice of appeal from that ruling. Plaintiff put on evidence at trial, and at the close of plaintiff's evidence both defendants made motions under Rule 50 for a directed verdict. The court granted these motions, and plaintiff appeals from this judgment.

McConnell, Howard, Pruett & Bragg, by Ellis M. Bragg and Scott MacG. Stevenson, for plaintiff appellant.

William I. Ward, Jr. and W. Edward Poe, Jr. for defendant appellee Duke Power Company.

Henderson, Henderson & Shuford, by Charles J. Henderson and Robert E. Henderson, for defendant appellee Robert Acree.

MARTIN (Harry C.), Judge.

Plaintiff's principal argument on appeal is that the trial court improperly entered directed verdicts in defendants' favor. After careful review of the record, we conclude that plaintiff's argument is unpersuasive and that the trial court was correct in its decision.

[1] Counsel for plaintiff and defendants stipulated that Duke Power Company moved for directed verdict upon the ground that the claim of plaintiff as to matters prior to 23 September 1976 is barred by the one-year statute of limitations. The complaint in this action was filed 22 September 1977; it alleges certain defamatory statements made by Duke Power "on or about September 10th, 1976." On its face the complaint reveals that N.C.G.S. 1-54 (3) has not been complied with. Plaintiff, however, argues that his action is salvaged because it was based on the same claim filed originally on 30 November 1976. He cites Rule 41 (a) (1), providing that if an action brought within the applicable statute of limitations is voluntarily dismissed without prejudice, a new action based on the same claim may be commenced within one year of such dismissal.

Whereas plaintiff contends that the two causes of action alleged in the 30 November 1976 and 22 September 1977 complaints are based upon the same claim, Duke Power insists that plaintiff's new action is not based on the same claim as the original. Defendant admits that the alleged slanderous and libelous acts in both complaints "stemmed" from Duke's discharge of plaintiff on 10 September 1976, but notes that "there the similarity ends." We agree with defendant and hold that plaintiff's second complaint did not allege "a new action based on the same claim," required under Rule 41 (a) (1).

The gist of plaintiff's first complaint was that because Duke Power filled out plaintiff's discharge slip, stating thereon "Discharged for misconduct" and "a dishonest act," plaintiff was denied unemployment compensation benefits. This denial set

into motion a chain of events whereby plaintiff was forced to
request a hearing before the North Carolina Employment
Security Commission, to engage an attorney, and to be present
at the hearing where defendant "reasserted the false and libelous allegations against the Plaintiff to the effect that he had
been discharged for misconduct and was guilty of a dishonest
act." The first action, then, was based upon proceedings before
the Employment Security Commission and what was said by
defendant in those proceedings. The complaint also alleged a
violation of plaintiff's constitutional rights by defendant in its
methods of interrogating him before his discharge.

The second complaint focuses on paragraphs 9, 10 and 12:

  9. That on or about September 10th, 1976, the Defendant, Duke Power Company through its agents and employees terminated the Plaintiff and entered in his employment record that the reason for his termination was for
"dishonest act — intentionally falsifying records" and "terminated, dishonest act saying that he was on the job when
he was absent from work 9-10-76."

  10: That in particular the corporate Defendant's agent,
the Defendant Robert Acree, made a notation on the corporate Defendant's "Field Termination Notice" that the
Plaintiff had been discharged for "dishonest act including
falsifying records."

  12. That the Defendant, Duke Power Company,
through its employees and agents and the Defendant,
Robert Acree, have on numerous occasions since on or about
September 10th, 1976 told the Plaintiff's fellow workers
at the McGuire Nuclear Construction Project and the
Plaintiff's prospective employers that the Plaintiff was discharged from his employment with the corporate Defendant because of a dishonest act, saying that he was on the
job when he was absent from work, and that said slanderous and defamatory statements are without foundation in
truth, and have caused the Plaintiff severe embarrass-
ment, humiliation and pain and suffering, and have severely and permanently impaired the Plaintiff's good reputa-

tion and have seriously and permanently impaired the Plaintiff's ability to obtain other employment.

A comparison of the two complaints reveals, and we so hold, that the new action commenced by plaintiff within one year after his voluntary dismissal without prejudice is not based on the same claim as the first. Therefore, plaintiff's action against Duke Power is barred by the one-year statute of limitations.

[2] The trial court was also correct in its determination that any publication of the alleged defamatory statements by Robert Acree, which possibly would bring Duke Power within the statute of limitations, was not attributable to Duke Power.

Plaintiff introduced testimony by employees of Duke Power that Acree had made slanderous statements about plaintiff on occasions in October or November, 1976. Plaintiff argues that the issue whether Acree was within his scope of employment when he made these statements, thereby making them attributable to Duke Power, is a question of fact for the jury. Defendant counters that Duke Power cannot be held liable, under North Carolina case law, for "idle statements" made by Acree a month to six weeks after plaintiff's discharge and unauthorized by Duke Power.

We think the case of *Strickland v. Kress*, 183 N.C. 534, 112 S.E. 30 (1922), answers this question squarely in defendant's favor. In *Strickland*, the manager of one of the stores of a corporation, after the dismissal of an employee, stated to the employee's husband, within the hearing of other employees, that she had taken company money and lied about it. The trial court as a matter of law set aside a jury verdict against the corporation as to slander. The Supreme Court found no error, on the basis that the facts showed the employee's discharge was a closed incident so far as the manager's official duties were concerned. What was said related to an event that had passed and could not be considered as within the course and scope of the manager's employment. In the case *sub judice*, any remarks made by Acree in the months after plaintiff's discharge were, as a matter of law, not made within Acree's scope of employment and, consequently, not attributable to Duke Power.

The parties also stipulated that defendant Robert Acree, in addition to asserting the same grounds as those asserted by Duke Power, moved for a directed verdict on the grounds that plaintiff made no showing of damages. Plaintiff argues that Acree's slanderous statements were actionable per se, entitling plaintiff to recover without proof of damages. We cannot agree with this argument.

[3] North Carolina cases have held consistently that alleged false statements made by defendants, calling plaintiff "dishonest" or charging that plaintiff was untruthful and an unreliable employee, are not actionable per se. *See Satterfield v. McLellan Stores*, 215 N.C. 582, 2 S.E. 2d 709 (1939); *Ringgold v. Land*, 212 N.C. 369, 193 S.E. 267 (1937). Such false statements may be actionable *per quod;* if so, some special damages must be pleaded and proved. *Ringgold, supra.* In the law of defamation, special damage means pecuniary loss, as distinguished from humiliation. *Williams v. Freight Lines and Willard v. Freight Lines*, 10 N.C. App. 384, 179 S.E. 2d 319 (1971). As we shall discuss later, plaintiff adequately pleaded special damages. He failed, however, to produce any testimony that he suffered pecuniary loss as a result of defendant Acree's statements made to employees of Duke Power after his discharge. Because the record is devoid of evidence of special damages resulting from Acree's statements, it was proper for the court to direct a verdict in Acree's favor.

The trial court admitted into evidence certain exhibits and answers to questions as to Duke Power Company but sustained objections to the admission of this testimony as to Acree. Plaintiff argues that this was error, because the offered testimony and exhibits would have tended to show actual malice on Acree's part. We note that plaintiff inconsistently argues elsewhere that Acree's statements are slanderous per se, thereby presuming malice and dispensing with its proof. Because we have held that plaintiff failed to prove special damages, he would not be aided by the admission of this excluded evidence arguably tending to prove malice. Even assuming that the court erred in excluding this evidence, the error would be harmless.

We turn now to the question raised on defendants' cross-appeal. Should the trial court have granted defendants' motion to dismiss pursuant to Rule 12 (b)? We think the court's refusal to grant this motion was proper.

Defendants contend that plaintiff's complaint was subject to dismissal for three reasons: it contains no allegations of time and place; it fails to state the words of slander or libel allegedly made; and it fails to allege special damages although it appears to allege slander *per quod*.

We think that plaintiff's use of the date "September 10th, 1976" and reference to "numerous occasions since on or about September 10th, 1976" satisfy the time requirement. Similarly, plaintiff's allegation that defendants "told the Plaintiff's fellow workers at the McGuire Nuclear Construction Project," satisfies the place requirement. Rule 9(f) was sufficiently complied with.

Likewise, in paragraphs 15 and 16, plaintiff alleges that he sustained a direct loss of earnings of no less than $13,000 per year and a loss of earnings of not less than $200,000 during his normal work expectancy as a result of defendants' defamatory statements. Surely plaintiff has adequately pleaded special damages.

[4] Our final query is whether plaintiff's failure to state the defamatory words in the complaint renders it fatally defective. Actually, the specific words alleged are stated in paragraphs 9 and 10. In paragraph 12, however, set out in full earlier in this opinion, plaintiff paraphrases defendant Acree's statement.

Defendants cite two North Carolina cases, decided before the new Rules of Civil Procedure took effect in this state, standing for the proposition that the actionable words spoken or written must be alleged. *See Scott v. Veneer Co.*, 240 N.C. 73, 81 S.E. 2d 146 (1954), and *Burns v. Williams*, 88 N.C. 159 (1883). Defendants concede that no court decisions in North Carolina pertaining to the necessity to plead the slanderous words verbatim have been reached since the new rules went into effect, but they point to federal court opinions calling for allegations of the false words *in haec verba*. We read these cases to require that the words attributed to defendant be alleged "substantial-ly" *in haec verba*, or with sufficient particularity to enable the court to determine whether the statement was defamatory. In *Drummond v. Spero*, 350 F. Supp. 844 (D. Ct. Vt. 1972), the court found neither specific language nor an attempt to paraphrase the claimed slanderous words with any degree of particularity, indica-ting that a paraphrase could be sufficient. And in *Scott, supra,* the North Carolina Supreme Court pointed out that plaintiff failed to set forth either the exact language or the "substance" of the libelous language. A review of paragraph 12 of the complaint in this action leads us to the conclusion that plaintiff adequately alleged the slanderous statement.

We hold that under the notice theory of pleading, plaintiff's statement of a defamation claim was adequate. The trial court properly refused to grant defendants' motion to dismiss.

Affirmed as to appellant and cross-appellants.

Judges VAUGHN and CLARK concur.

PAUL I. PARSLOW v. MILDRED M. PARSLOW

No. 7915DC832

(Filed 3 June 1980)

1. **Quasi Contracts § 5– unjust enrichment – contributions to improvements on wife's properties – equitable lien**

    Plaintiff's forecast of evidence on motion for summary judgment was sufficient to support a claim for an equitable lien on properties owned by his former wife based on unjust enrichment for contributions to improvements on the properties made by plaintiff while the parties were married to each other.

2. **Partition § 3.1– property in Florida – no jurisdiction to partition**

    The courts of this State do not have jurisdiction to order a partition or partition sale of real property located in Florida.

3. **Estates § 8; Tenants in Common § 1– tenant in common – procedure for division of personalty**

The appropriate procedure for a tenant in common seeking a division of personal property is to file a petition in the superior court for that purpose pursuant to Art. 4 of G.S. Ch. 46.

APPEAL by plaintiff from *Harris (W.S.), Judge.* Order entered 5 June 1979 in District Court, ALAMANCE County. Heard in the Court of Appeals 7 March 1980.

On 13 September 1977 plaintiff filed an action seeking absolute divorce from defendant, as well as liquidation and division of certain assets. Pursuant to Rule 42(b), the trial court entered an order on 16 May 1979 separating the trial of issues pertaining to absolute divorce from those pertaining to interests in certain property. On 5 June 1979 the trial court entered a judgment of absolute divorce. On the same day, the trial court had a hearing on defendant's Rule 12(b)(6) motion, heard arguments, considered affidavits and accepted the written briefs of both parties. The court then ordered the dismissal of all of plaintiff's claims pertaining to the division of properties. This latter order is the subject of this appeal.

The pleadings, interrogatories and affidavits of the parties tend to indicate that, prior to the marriage of Paul and Mildred Parslow, Mildred Parslow owned a house on 512 Alamance Road and a one-sixth undivided interest in land which, after partition, is now situated at 2601 Hoskins Road, both properties being located in Alamance County, North Carolina. Paul also owned a small tract of land in Orange County, Florida.

The plaintiff asserted that the parties were married on 14 February 1959. In 1964 they purchased a home on Lake Fairview, 4546 Edgewater Drive, in Orlando, Florida for $22,500. There was an $18,000 mortgage and a down-payment of $4,500 was made. The down-payment funds came from a loan from First Federal of Burlington and Paul Parslow's cashed-in endowment policy with the United States Marine Corps. Paul Parslow paid the mortgage on the house from 1964 to 1972 with his earnings from the Marine Corps, Woods of Florida, Allison's Plating and the Bendix Corporation. In 1971 Paul Parslow sold his small tract of land in Florida, and used part of the proceeds to retire the promissory note to First Federal.

Paul Parslow's sworn statements indicated that he contributed to improvements on Mildred Parslow's real estate in the following manner:

First, in 1972 the Parslows spent approximately $5,000.00 in renovating Mildred Parslow's rental property at 512 Alamance Street. Paul Parslow expended considerable labor and supervision time in this effort. The money for the renovation came in large part from insurance proceeds from damages and personal property loss associated with the burglary of their mobile home which was owned jointly by the parties. Plaintiff had paid approximately $5,000.00 of the $8,000.00 cost of the mobile home with his earnings at the Bendix Corporation and with part of the proceeds from the sale of his Florida property.

Second, in 1975 the parties built a new house on Mildred Parslow's property at 2601 Hoskins Drive. The house was built for a contract price of $34,210.00 of which $20,000 was paid by First Federal pursuant to a promissory note signed by both of the parties. The balance of the funds came from, among other sources, $5,800.00 from the sale of the mobile home and $5,300.00 from funds placed in a savings account left over from the sale of the house owned by the parties in Orlando, Florida. Mildred Parslow made the subsequent mortgage payments on the house but Paul Parslow paid all of the other household expenses.

In addition to the above described real property, the parties own a 1973 Holiday Rambler and a 1973 Buick Electra, purchased for $8,000.00 and $5,100.00 respectively with the proceeds from the sale of the Florida house. The parties also own 749 shares of Bank of Beaufort stock worth approximately $8,000.00 The initial 25 shares were given to Paul Parslow by his mother in 1969. The remainder came from reinvested dividends, stock splits and new purchases by the Parslows. The parties are also joint owners of one-half of a building lot in Cape Coral, Florida.

Shoffner & Moseley by W. Phillip Moseley and Daniel H. Monroe for plaintiff appellant.

Parslow v. Parslow

Holt, Spencer & Longest by W. Clary Holt for defendant appellee.

CLARK, Judge.

Three categories of property are involved in this case: personal property owned in common by the parties, improvements on real property for which the title is held by Mildred Parslow, and real property in Florida jointly owned by the parties.

We begin with the more difficult question pertaining to the improvements on real property at 512 Alamance Street and 2601 Hoskins Drive in which Mildred Parslow held record title and on which improvements were added with a substantial contribution by Paul Parslow. With respect to the house and lot on 512 Alamance Street the appellant seeks $7,000.00 for the improvements and appreciation which result from the investment and personal labor of the appellant. With respect to the house constructed at 2601 Hoskins Drive, appellant asserts that the land and the residential dwelling place constructed thereon were at all times considered the joint properties of the parties, that the defendant holds the properties in constructive trust, or in the alternative, in a resulting trust, in favor of the parties, share and share alike, and that the properties should be sold, the outstanding Note and Deed of Trust be satisfied from the proceeds, and the balance be divided between the parties.

The general rule in North Carolina has been stated as follows:

"If the husband pays the purchase price, and a deed of conveyance is made to himself and his wife, the law presumes the creation of a tenancy by the entirety, presuming that the husband intended to make a gift to the benefit of the wife to the extent of her interest in the tenancy by the entirety. On the other hand, if the wife furnishes the purchase price, the law makes no presumption that a tenancy by the entirety was created, but instead presumes that the wife intended to place title in the husband and herself on a resulting trust for the wife."

Webster, Real Estate Law in North Carolina § 102 (1971); *Tarkington v. Tarkington*, 45 N.C. App. 476, 263 S.E. 2d 294 (1980). This rule was tacitly criticized in *Tarkington, supra*, and there is a substantial question as to whether this rule denies equal protection of the laws to male spouses in view of recent Supreme Court decisions, *see, e.g., Wengler v. Druggists Mutual Insurance Company*,   U.S.   (No. 79-381, 48 U.S.L.W. 4459 (1980), and *Orr v. Orr*, 440 U.S. 268, 99 S. Ct. 1102, 59 L. Ed. 2d 306 (1979). We cannot, however, reach this question at this time because constitutional objections may not be raised for the first time on appeal and there is nothing in the record to indicate that this question was ever adjudicated by the trial court. *See, Brice v. Moore*, 30 N.C. App. 365, 226 S.E. 2d 882 (1976), involving this very same question. *See also*, 1 Strong's N.C. Index 3d, *Appeal and Error* §§ 2-3 (1976).

Nonetheless, even assuming that the above-stated rule applies to create a presumption that Paul Parslow's contributions to the improvements on Mildred's property were a gift to her, this presumption is rebuttable. *Tarkington, supra*. The question is therefore whether under Rule 56 the pleadings, answers to interrogatories, and admissions on file, together with the affidavits tend to rebut the presumption of gift and raise a genuine issue of material fact. If so, the order dismissing this claim was improvidently entered. It is noted that the order refers to defendant's Rule 12 (b) (6) motion to dismiss for failure to state a claim, but Rule 12 (b) provides that on such motion if matters outside the pleadings are presented to and considered by the court, the motion will be treated as one for summary judgment and disposed of as provided in Rule 56. Therefore, the order appealed from is treated by us as a motion for summary judgment.

[1] We find that the supporting materials presented to and considered by the court raise a genuine issue of material fact in that the matters favorable to plaintiff's claim tend to show unjust enrichment and would support the creation of an equitable lien on the real property of the defendant to enforce plaintiff's right to compensation for the value of the improvements made by him. No contract, oral or written, enforceable or not, is

necessary to support a recovery based upon unjust enrichment. "Such a recovery is founded on the equitable theory of estoppel and not on principles of quasi or implied contract." *Clontz v. Clontz*, 44 N.C. App. 573, 578, 261 S.E. 2d 695, 698 (1980).

If the plaintiff-appellant herein possessed a good faith belief that he owned or would own a one-half interest in the value of the improvements made by him on his wife's property, or that an interest in the property was promised by her to him, "and such improvements inure to defendant's benefit, [this factor] is sufficient to support recovery under the unjust enrichment doctrine." *Id.* If so, the plaintiff-husband would be entitled to an equitable lien on the realty as an aid in enforcing his rights, but such lien is not an estate in the land and may not be the basis of a beneficial interest. *Fulp v. Fulp*, 264 N.C. 20, 140 S.E. 2d 708 (1965); 5 Scott, *The Law of Trusts* (3d ed.) § 454.7 at 3387. Plaintiff's supporting materials tend to show an equitable lien for unjust enrichment rather than a constructive or a resulting trust and this trial court erred in dismissing this claim by summary judgment.

[2] Second, the courts of this State do not have jurisdiction to order a partition or partition sale of the real property in Florida. The trial court did not err in dismissing this aspect of plaintiff's claim.

Third, the District Court erred in dismissing the plaintiff's claims pertaining to the personal property. "In this State a tenancy by the entirety may exist only in land and not in personalty of any kind. If a husband and a wife are co-owners of personal property, nothing else appearing, they hold as tenants in common." 2 Lee, *North Carolina Family Law* § 114 (1963) at 67. "One cotenant is as much entitled to the possession of the common property as the other, and the law will not take from the one so as to give the other property owned in common. The proper remedy is by a special proceeding to divide or to sell for division." *Coulbourn v. Armstrong*, 243 N.C. 663, 667, 91 S.E. 2d 912, 915 (1956).

[3] The appropriate procedure, provided in Article 4 of Chapter 46 of the General Statutes, is for the tenant in common seeking

a division of personal property to file a petition in the *superior* court for that purpose. This action was brought in the district court, and while the parties could have moved pursuant to G.S. § 7A-258 to transfer the case to the proper division while the case was pending in the improper division, the parties waived this right after the case had been called for trial, and the defect is not jurisdictional. *Stanback v. Stanback*, 287 N.C. 448, 215 S.E. 2d 30 (1975).

The plaintiff has joined in the District Court one cause of action for an equitable lien for the value of improvements made on realty with another cause of action for the partition of personal property. The two causes of action depend upon different facts and principles of law, and they should be severed. Since the judgment is reversed and the action remanded, if the plaintiff elects to proceed with his claim for partition of personal property, it is ordered that this cause be severed by plaintiff taking a voluntary dismissal without prejudice under G.S. 1A-1, Rule 41(a)(1) and by filing his petition for division in the Superior Court as provided by Article 4 of Chapter 46 of the General Statutes.

So much of the judgment dismissing the claim for partition of jointly-owned realty in the State of Florida is affirmed; so much of the judgment dismissing the claims for equitable lien for unjust enrichment and partition of personal property is reversed and the case remanded for further proceedings in compliance with this decision.

Affirmed in part; Reversed in part.

Judges MARTIN (Robert M.) and ERWIN concur.

CAROLYN S. CORNELISON v. LEO DOYLE CORNELISON

No. 7926DC1203

(Filed 3 June 1980)

1. **Divorce and Alimony § 18.12– alimony pendente lite – constructive abandonment – indignities**

   The trial court's conclusions in an alimony *pendente lite* action that defendant constructively abandoned plaintiff and subjected her to such indignities as to render her condition intolerable and her life burdensome were supported by the court's findings, which in turn were supported by competent evidence, that plaintiff removed herself from the marital home because of defendant's yelling and cursing and refusal to permit plaintiff to sleep, that for a period of at least two years defendant failed to come home in the evenings until very late or until the early morning hours and was away on the weekends, that defendant would constantly interrupt plaintiff's sleep when he came home late at night or early in the morning, and that defendant evidenced a total absence of consideration and affection concerning plaintiff's mental problems and hospitalizations caused by those problems, it being unnecessary for the court to make additional negative findings that plaintiff was without fault or that she did not provoke the defendant's behavior.

2. **Divorce and Alimony §§ 18.13, 18.16– amount of alimony pendente lite and counsel fees – sufficiency of evidence and findings**

   The evidence and findings were sufficient to support the court's order requiring defendant husband to pay plaintiff wife $335 per month as alimony *pendente lite* and $1250 for counsel fees.

APPEAL by defendant from *Lanning, Judge.* Order entered 10 September 1979 in District Court, MECKLENBURG County. Heard in the Court of Appeals on 13 May 1980.

This is a domestic action initiated 27 April 1979 by the plaintiff, Carolyn Cornelison, in which she seeks to recover temporary and permanent alimony and counsel fees from the defendant. Plaintiff alleged in a verified complaint that she and the defendant were married on 28 May 1955, that they separated in April 1978, and that their separation resulted from acts and conduct of the defendant which constituted a "constructive abandonment" of plaintiff, thus entitling her to alimony and alimony *pendente lite.*

Defendant filed a verified answer on 17 August 1979 wherein he alleged that the plaintiff had left the marital home in April 1978 "without any justifiable cause or excuse and without fault or provocation on the part of defendant," and thus was not entitled to an award of alimony or alimony *pendente lite.*

The matter was heard on plaintiff's motion for alimony *pendente lite* and counsel fees on 20 August 1979. To the extent that evidence presented at the hearing is necessary for the decision in this case, it will be set out in the opinion to follow.

On 10 September 1979 the trial court entered an order directing that defendant pay plaintiff $335 per month as alimony *pendente lite* and $1250 counsel fees. Defendant appealed.

Stack and Stephens, by Richard D. Stephens, for the plaintiff appellee.

James B. Ledford and W. M. Nicholson for the defendant appellant.

HEDRICK, Judge.

Defendant assigns error to the award to plaintiff of alimony *pendente lite* and argues that plaintiff failed to establish her entitlement to such an award for the reason that she offered no evidence of her conduct at the time of the parties' separation, nor did she show that she "had not done anything to provoke any of the conduct of Defendant about which she complains."

The statutory provision governing awards of alimony *pendente lite*, G.S. § 50-16.3, provides in pertinent part as follows:

(a) A dependent spouse who is a party to an action for absolute divorce, divorce from bed and board, annulment, or alimony without divorce, shall be entitled to an order for alimony pendente lite when:

(1) It shall appear from all the evidence ... that such spouse in entitled to the relief demanded ... and

(2) It shall appear that the dependent spouse has not sufficient means whereon to subsist during the prosecution or defense of the suit and to defray the necessary expenses thereof.

(b) The determination of the amount and the payment of alimony pendente lite shall be in the same manner as alimony, . . .

We have interpreted the statute to require the trial judge to conclude as a matter of law that the spouse seeking alimony *pendente lite* is the dependent spouse within the meaning of G.S. § 50-16.1(3); that such spouse is a party in an action for absolute divorce, divorce from bed and board, annulment, or alimony without divorce; that such spouse is entitled to the relief demanded; and that such spouse is shown to lack sufficient means whereon to subsist during the course of the litigation. *Gardner v. Gardner*, 40 N.C. App. 334, 252 S.E. 2d 867, *cert. denied*, 297 N.C. 299, 254 S.E. 2d 917 (1979); *Steele v. Steele*, 36 N.C. App. 601, 244 S.E. 2d 466 (1978). These conclusions must, of course, be supported by specific findings of fact. If the findings are supported by competent evidence, they are conclusive on appeal even though the evidence would support contrary findings. *Gardner v. Gardner, supra.* While the sufficiency of the findings to support the award is reviewable on appeal, *Rickert v. Rickert*, 282 N.C. 373, 193 S.E. 2d 79 (1972), the weight to be accorded the evidence is solely for the trier of the facts. *Rauchfuss v. Rauchfuss*, 33 N.C. App. 108, 234 S.E. 2d 423 (1977).

[1] The defendant in the case at bar does not argue that the trial judge failed to draw the necessary conclusions of law, and the Order appealed from demonstrates that the judge did enter the appropriate conclusions. Rather, the defendant contends that the findings of fact necessary to support the following conclusions of law are not supported by competent evidence of record, and thus these conclusions similarly are unsupported by proper findings of fact:

3. That from all of the evidence presented . . . the plaintiff is entitled to the relief demanded in this suit . . . .

4. That the defendant has offered the plaintiff indignities such as to render her condition intolerable and life burdensome.

5. That the defendant constructively abandoned the plaintiff on or about April, 1978.

6. That the defendant has wilfully [sic] failed to provide the plaintiff with necessary subsistence according to [his] means and conditions so as to render her condition intolerable and life burdensome.

If these conclusions are supported by specific findings of fact which, in turn, are supported by competent evidence, then the plaintiff is *prima facie* entitled to an award of temporary alimony. In other words, the trial judge is not required to make additional negative findings and conclusions that the plaintiff was without fault or that she did not provoke the defendant's behavior.

In this case, the following findings of fact clearly support the contested conclusions:

4. That the plaintiff separated herself from the defendant in about April, 1978, because of the defendant's yelling and cursing and refusal to permit the plaintiff to sleep, which forced her to remove herself from the marital home in order to preserve her mental and physical well being. That said acts on the part of the defendant were wilful [sic] and without provocation.

5. That for a period of time of at least two years prior to their separation in April, 1978, the defendant failed and refused to come home in the evenings until very late or until the early morning hours and was away from home on the weekends.

6. That when the defendant would come home late at night or early in the morning, he would constantly interrupt the plaintiff's sleep.

. . .

8. That the defendant evidenced a total absence of consideration and affection with regard to the plaintiff's mental problems and her hospitalizations.

The court made further findings regarding the failure of the defendant to provide adequately for the plaintiff's support.

These findings in turn are supported by competent and uncontradicted evidence. Regarding the circumstances which apparently initiated the separation, plaintiff testified that she had suffered mental and emotional problems which had required several hospitalizations and that in April 1978 she had been home from a stay at Broughton Hospital for about three days when defendant came in one night "raising cain, drinking." She testified that she "got scared," called the police and left the next day. She lived with a relative for a while, then took an apartment to herself. The parties have remained separated since that time. Plaintiff also testified that, in the two years prior to the separation, the defendant "wasn't around very much"; that he made her life "unbearable" when he was at home staying out nights until between 11:30 p.m. and 2:00 a.m. and by turning the T.V. "wide open" when he did come home; and that, as a result of such conduct, she was unable to sleep. She said that following her release from Broughton Hospital on a prior occasion, the defendant's attitude and conduct was the same, that he "just wasn't around and wouldn't give me any money and wouldn't take me anywhere . . . ." When abdominal problems necessitated surgery for plaintiff in January 1978, the defendant "did nothing to help me get ready to go in the hospiyal [sic] . . . . [Instead], [h]e left town, ..."

This evidence, which the defendant did not dispute in his testimony or through his witnesses, is clearly sufficient to support the findings of fact set out above. Moreover, the findings provide a basis for the court's conclusion that the defendant had "constructively abandoned" the plaintiff and, considering all the circumstances of the case as we must do, *Presson v. Presson*, 12 N.C. App. 109, 182 S.E. 2d 614 (1971), we think the court was correct in concluding that the plaintiff had been subjected to such indignities over a period of time "as to render her condition intolerable and life burdensome." Furthermore, even though defendant contends on appeal that the court should have made findings regarding the plaintiff's conduct at the time of the parties' separation, including findings as to whether plaintiff did or did not provoke the defendant's conduct, we note that the defendant offered no evidence of provocation on the part of plaintiff, nor did he complain of her conduct. Such evidence is in the nature of a defense to her claim for relief and thus is properly allocated to the defendant's burden of proof. We hold that the requisite conclusions of law to support an award of alimony *pendente lite* are fully supported by specific findings of fact which are amply supported by competent evidence.

[2] Likewise, and contrary to the defendant's contentions, we find the findings of fact sufficient and the evidence plenary to support the amount of temporary alimony awarded. While the amount to be awarded rests within the sound discretion of the trial judge, *Self v. Self*, 37 N.C. App. 199, 245 S.E. 2d 541, *cert. denied*, 295 N.C. 648, 248 S.E. 2d 253 (1978), it is true, as defendant argues, that the judge must take into consideration a number of factors, including the accustomed standard of living of the parties and the estate of earnings of each party. G.S. §§ 50-16.3(b), 50-16.5(a). "The amount to be awarded is a question of fairness to the parties, and, so long as the court has properly taken into consideration the factors enumerated by statute, the award will not be distrubed absent an abuse of discretion." *Gardner v. Gardner*, *supra* at 340, 252 S.E. 2d at 871.

The Order in this case contains specific findings regarding the income and living expenses of each spouse. Moreover, it contains findings regarding the ability of the defendant to pay the ordered amount in that he is the "principal figure in and general manager of" his corporation, that he still lives in the marital home on which he has made all the mortgage payments and which has a fair market value in excess of $40,000, and that he has access to funds from the sale of other property, even though those funds are currently being held by his mother. Similarly, the Order contains findings as to the relative inability of the plaintiff to fully support herself. It is clear that all the necessary factors relating to the award of alimony *pendente lite* were considered, and that the findings of fact as to each factor are amply supported by competent evidence. We find no abuse of discretion in the court's ordering the defendant to pay $335 per month, which represents the difference between the plaintiff's monthly income and her estimated monthly expenses.

With respect to the award of counsel fees in the amount of $1250, we hold that this award also is supported by sufficient findings of fact showing that the fee is allowable and that the amount awarded is reasonable. *Self v. Self, supra; Upchurch v. Upchurch*, 34 N.C. App. 658, 239 S.E. 2d 701 (1977), *cert. denied*, 294 N.C. 363, 242 S.E.2d 634 (1978). *See* G.S. § 50-16.4. The fee is allowable because the plaintiff has established her entitlement to an award of alimony *pendente lite. Upchurch v. Upchurch, supra.* As to the reasonableness of the award, the court found as follows:

> That the plaintiff's counsel, ... has rendered valuable legal services to the plaintiff in this action, ... that he is known to the Court to be familiar with matters of this kind, that his average hourly rate is approximately Sixty ($60.00) Dollars per hour and that is in line with charges of similar lawyers with similar experience ..., that he has conferred on numerous occasions with his client, has represented her interest in this Court proceeding ..., prepared for same and attempted to undertake discovery to discover the defendant's assets, has spent at lease 29 hours working on this case, and the Court finds that the reasonable value of his services is at least $1250.00.

These findings are supported by the evidence and plainly support the award. Defendant's contentions are without merit.

The Order entered 10 September 1979 is in all respects affirmed.

Affirmed.

Judges PARKER and VAUGHN concur.

Vickery v. Construction Co.

MICHAEL D. VICKERY and wife, DIANE A. VICKERY, Plaintiffs v. OLIN
HILL CONSTRUCTION COMPANY, INC., a corporation; MOORE INSUR-
ANCE & REALTY COMPANY, INC., a corporation; and REBECCA HIN-
SON, Defendants v. CLIFFORD McCLAIN HELMS and wife, MARIANNE
H. HELMS; MOORE INSURANCE & REALTY COMPANY, INC., Third-
Party Defendants

No. 7920SC789

(FILED 3 JUNE 1980)

1. **Principal and Agent § 4– sale of land by realtor – realtor as agent of landowner
or realty company – jury question**

   In an action to recover for fraud, negligence, breach of contract, and
   unfair and deceptive trade practices in the sale of a lot and house, the trial
   court erred in directing verdict in favor of defendants where there was a jury
   question as to whether the realty company employee who sold the property
   to plaintiffs was acting as an employee or agent of the realty company, or as
   agent of the owner of the property, or as an independent contractor.

2. **Fraud § 12– sale of lot and house – misrepresentation as to inclusion of driveway – sufficiency of evidence of fraud**

   Evidence was sufficient for the jury in an action to recover for fraud in
   the sale of a house and lot where such evidence tended to show that the agent
   who sold the property to plaintiffs was very familiar with it, and the driveway had achieved significant notoriety; in selling the property to plaintiffs,
   the agent did not simply state her opinion that the property included the
   driveway, but she used a plat showing the driveway to be included, told
   plaintiffs she had measured the property line and that her measurement
   showed the driveway to be included, and drew plaintiffs' attention to a stake
   on the ground at a spot which would have included the driveway within the
   property; and plaintiffs presented two witnesses who testified they had
   informed the agent, prior to purchase of the land by plaintiffs, that the
   driveway was not on the property.

3. **Fraud § 5– reliance on misrepresentation – reasonableness – jury question**

   In an action to recover for fraud in the sale of a house and a lot to
   plaintiffs where plaintiffs claimed that defendant misrepresented to them
   that the property in question included a driveway which plaintiffs viewed
   during their inspection of the land prior to purchasing it, the trial court
   erred in directing verdict for defendants, since whether plaintiffs' reliance
   on defendant's representations was reasonable was a question to be resolved
   by the jury.

4. **Principal and Agent § 5.2– sale of house and lot by agent – breach of contract by
landowner**

   Evidence was sufficient to take the case to the jury on plaintiffs' cause of action for breach of contract against defendant landowner where plaintiffs' evidence tended to show that defendant realtor had represented to plaintiffs that the land in question included a driveway, and the realtor was acting as the owner's agent, since, if a contract is made with a known agent acting within the scope of his authority for a disclosed principal, the contract is that of the principal alone.

APPEAL by plaintiffs from *Seay, Judge.* Judgment and orders entered 20 April 1979 in Superior Court, UNION County. Heard in the Court of Appeals 4 March 1980.

This action arises out of plaintiffs' purchase of a house and lot owned by defendant Olin Hill Construction Company, Inc. (Hill). Plaintiffs allege in their complaint that Hill employed defendant Moore Insurance and Realty Company, Inc. (Moore) to sell the property and that they dealt with defendant Moore through an employee and agent, Rebecca Hinson. Plaintiffs aver that Hinson had misrepresented to them that a certain parcel of land which they were considering purchasing included a driveway which plaintiffs had viewed during their inspection of the property. Plaintiffs asserted four theories of recovery — fraud, negligence, breach of contract, and unfair and deceptive trade practices under G.S. 75-1.1, *et seq.*

Defendant Hill answered and impleaded the parties from whom it purchased the property, Clifford Helms and wife, Marianne Helms, as well as defendant Moore, alleging that the Helms had employed Moore to act as their agent in the sale of the subject property and that Moore had represented to Hill that the driveway was located on the property. Moore, answering plaintiffs' complaint, denied the essential allegations and additionally defended on grounds that Hinson, as agent of the defendants Helms, had originally sold the property to Hill and subsequently sold the property to plaintiffs as Hill's agent. Moore averred that it was not involved in either transaction, that it did not enter into a contract with any party with respect to the sale of the property, and that it did not make any representations to any party with respect to the property. Moore alleged that Hinson was an independent contractor and was not its agent or employee. Defendant Moore cross-claimed against Hinson and Hill.

Upon defendants' motions, the trial court entered directed verdicts in favor of all defendants and against the plaintiff at the close of the plaintiffs' evidence. Plaintiffs appeal.

Casstevens & Hanner, P.A., by Robert P. Hanner II, for the plaintiff appellants.

Thomas, Harrington & Biedler, by Larry E. Harrington, for defendant Olin Hill Construction Company, Inc.

Griffin, Caldwell & Helder, P.A., by C. Frank Griffin, H. Ligon Bundy, and James E. Griffin, for defendants Moore Insurance and Realty Company and Rebecca Hinson.

Robert L. Holland for third-party defendants Clifford McClain Helms and wife, Marianne H. Helms.

WELLS, Judge.

On a defendant's motion for directed verdict at the close of a plaintiff's evidence, the evidence must be taken as true and considered in the light most favorable to the plaintiff, and the motion may be granted only if, as a matter of law, the evidence is insufficient to justify a verdict for the plaintiff. *Dickinson v. Pake*, 284 N.C. 576, 201 S.E. 2d 897 (1974). A plaintiff is entitled to the benefit of every reasonable inference which may legitimately be drawn from his evidence. *Bowen v. Gardner*, 275 N.C. 363, 168 S.E. 2d 47 (1969); *Jenkins v. Starrett Corp.* 13 N.C. App. 437, 186 S.E. 2d 198 (1972).

[1] We first examine the evidence in support of plaintiffs' theory that defendant Hinson was acting as the agent of Hill and Moore in these transactions. On this issue, plaintiffs' evidence tended to show that they first learned of the subject property through an advertisement placed by Moore in the local newspaper. The newspaper ad set out the names of two persons — Roy Moore, Jr. and Rebecca Hinson. Plaintiff Michael Vickery telephoned Moore's office and Hinson answered the phone. Later, Moore joined an offer to purchase, executed by plaintiffs and defendant Hill, as escrow agent to

acknowledge receipt of the deposit. Hinson, testifying as a witness for plaintiffs, stated that her work with Moore began in 1971, that there was a verbal agreement between Hill, Moore and herself, that she was compensated through real estate commissions, and that she sold the subject property from the Helms to Hill and then from Hill to plaintiffs, splitting the commissions with Moore. From this evidence, a jury question is presented as to whether Hinson was acting as an employee or agent of defendant Moore, or as the agent of Hill, or as an independent contractor. *See, Vaughn v. Dept of Human Resources,* 37 N.C. App. 86, 245 S.E. 2d 892 (1978), *aff'd,* 296 N.C. 683, 252 S.E. 2d 792 (1979).

[2] We next examine whether plaintiffs' evidence was sufficient to take the case to the jury on the theory of fraud as against defendants Hinson, Hill, and Moore. Plaintiffs presented evidence that Hinson was very familiar with the property and that the disputed driveway had achieved significant notoriety. In selling the property to plaintiffs, Hinson did not simply state her opinion that the property included the driveway, but she used a plat showing the driveway to be included, she told plaintiffs she had measured the property line and that her measurement showed the driveway to be included, and she drew plaintiffs' attention to a stake on the ground at a spot which would have included the driveway within the property. Plaintiffs presented two witnesses who testified they had informed Hinson, prior to the purchase of the land by plaintiffs, that the driveway was not on the property. This evidence is sufficient to make out a case of actionable fraud in that defendant Hinson made a definite and specific representation that the driveway was on the property, the representation was false and was made either with knowledge of its falsity or in culpable ignorance of its truth, the representation was made with the intent to deceive, and it was reasonably relied upon by plaintiffs to their deception and damage. *See, Odom v. Little Rock & I-85 Corp.,* 299 N.C. 86, 261 S.E. 2d 99 (1980); *Johnson v. Owens,* 263 N.C. 754, 140 S.E. 2d 311 (1965); *see also, Kleinfelter v. Developers, Inc.,* 44 N.C. App. 561, 261, S.E. 2d 498 (1980); *Woodward v. Pressley,* 39 N.C. App. 61, 249 S.E. 2d 471 (1978); *Parker v. Bennett,* 32 N.C. App. 46, 231 S.E. 2d 10 (1977), *disc. rev. denied,* 292 N.C. 266, 233 S.E. 2d 393 (1977). If the jury should find that

plaintiffs were injured by the fraudulent representations of Hinson, then both Moore and Hill, as principals, must be held answerable for the fraudulent act of their agent.

> The general rule is that a principal is responsible to third parties for injuries resulting from the fraud of his agent committed during the existence of the agency and within the scope of the agent's actual or apparent authority from the principal, even though the principal did not know or authorize the commission of the fraudulent acts. *Thrower v. Dairy Products*, 249 N.C. 109, 105 S.E. 2d 428; *King v. Motley*, 233 N.C. 42, 62 S.E. 2d 540; *Dickerson v. Refining Co.*, 201 N.C. 90, 159 S.E. 446; 3 C.J.S., Agency, § 257; 3 Am. Jur. 2d, Agency, §§ 261 and 264.

Norburn v. Mackie, 262 N.C. 16, 23, 136 S.E. 2d 279, 284-285 (1964). *See also, Parsons v. Bailey*, 30 N.C. App. 497, 227 S.E. 2d 166 (1976), *disc. rev. denied*, 291 N.C. 176, 229 S.E. 2d 689 (1976); 37 Am.Jur. 2d, Fraud and Deceit §§ 311 and 312, pp. 411-414 (1968).

[3] Defendants Hinson and Moore argue that even if there were false representations made as to the inclusion of the driveway, they should not be held accountable because plaintiffs had a responsibility to make their own investigation to determine the truth of the matter, citing *Calloway v. Wyatt*, 246 N.C. 129, 97 S.E. 2d 881 (1957). We do not think *Calloway* is applicable here. A thorough discussion of the principles of law involved in this question may be found in *Kleinfelter v. Developers, Inc., supra. Kleinfelter* and the authorities discussed and cited therein may be distilled into this holding applicable to the facts of this case: Whether plaintiffs' reliance on Hinson's representation was reasonable or not is a question to be resolved by the jury.

The determination of the question of plaintiffs' cause of action for unfair trade practices under G.S. 75-1.1 is dependent upon the jury's response to the issue of fraud. If, on remand, the jury answers this issue in plaintiffs' favor, plaintiffs will be entitled to Chapter 75 damages. *Hardy v. Toler*, 288 N.C. 303, 218 S.E. 2d 342 (1975); *Kleinfelter v. Developers, Inc., supra.*

Vickery v. Construction Co.

[4] We also find the evidence sufficient to take the case to the jury on plaintiffs' cause of action for breach of contract against defendant Hill. Plaintiffs' evidence tends to show that Hill had listed the property with defendant Moore, and that Hinson, as their agent, had represented to plaintiffs that the driveway was included in the property conveyed. *See, Emerson v. Carras,* 33 N.C. App. 91, 234 S.E. 2d 642 (1977). Plaintiffs have not made out a case of breach of contract against defendants Hinson and Moore, as all of the evidence tends to show that they were acting as Hill's agents. If a contract is made with a known agent acting within the scope of his authority for a disclosed principal, the contract is that of the principal alone. *Jenkins v. Henderson,* 214 N.C. 244, 199 S.E. 37 (1938); *Way v. Ramsey,* 192 N.C. 549, 135 S.E. 454 (1926).

We do not believe that plaintiffs have presented sufficient evidence for the case to have been submitted to the jury on the theory of negligence. Actionable negligence presupposes the existence of a legal relationship between the parties by which the injured party is owed a duty which either arises out of a contract or by operation of law. *Pinnix v. Toomey,* 242 N.C. 358, 87 S.E. 2d 893 (1955). In the case *sub judice* there was no relationship between defendants and plaintiffs which would support a duty cognizable under our law of negligence.

As to Vickery, et ux v. Olin Hill Construction Company, Inc.; Moore Realty and Insurance Company, Inc.; and Rebecca Hinson; new trial.

As to defendants Helms; no error.

Judges HEDRICK and WEBB concur.

BASSETT FURNITURE INDUSTRIES OF NORTH CAROLINA, INC. v.
JAMES HUGH GRIGGS

No. 7915SC899

(Filed 3 June 1980)

1. Frauds, Statute of § 3– pleading – summary judgment – issue first raised by affidavit

   While the statute of frauds is an affirmative defense which ordinarily must be pleaded, the N.C. Supreme Court has held that, for the purpose of ruling on a motion for summary judgment, an affirmative defense may be raised for the first time by affidavit.

2. Frauds, Statute of § 5.1– oral guaranty – main purpose rule – sufficient interest in transaction

   In an action to recover upon defendant's alleged oral guarantee to pay the debt of a corporation which sold furniture and appliances in which defendant was alleged to possess a substantial interest, there was a genuine issue of material fact as to whether defendant had such a personal, immediate, and pecuniary interest in the transaction so as to bring his promise within the operation of the main purpose rule and thus except it from the statute of frauds where plaintiff offered evidence that defendant was the furniture and appliance corporation's managing director, owned half the stock, and received from it a monthly salary of $3000; the furniture and appliance corporation engaged in repeated and substantial transactions with a corporation in which defendant was the sole stockholder; and defendant's comment allegedly made to plaintiff's employees that defendant wanted to be a millionaire before the age of forty was evidence that defendant himself believed that he had a substantial personal interest in the extension of additional credit to the furniture and appliance corporation.

APPEAL by plaintiff from *Herring, Judge.* Judgment entered 24 July 1979 in Superior Court, ALAMANCE County. Heard in the Court of Appeals 24 March 1980.

Plaintiff corporation brought suit based upon the defendant's alleged oral guarantee to pay the debt of a corporation in which defendant was alleged to possess a substantial interest. In its complaint, plaintiff alleged that defendant was an officer and director of Big Jim's, Inc., a domestic corporation in the business of selling furniture and appliances. Plaintiff further alleged that all of the stock in Big Jim's was owned by Homeway-Carolina, Inc., a corporation in which defendant was also an officer and director, and that all of the shares of Homeway-Carolina were in turn owned by Tire Sales Company, Inc., a corporation in which defendant owned all of the stock and was an officer and director. In a verified affidavit, an employee of plaintiff stated that defendant, in trying to obtain additional credit from plaintiff for Big Jim's stated:

> You'll never get stuck for a penny. I want to be a millionaire by the time that I am 40 years old and I am two-thirds of the way there. If something ever happens, I'll pay you every penny myself.

Relying on this promise, plaintiff's employee stated that plaintiff extended over $30,000 in credit to defendant which defendant never repaid.

Defendant, answering plaintiff's complaint, admitted that Big Jim's owed plaintiff some amount, that all of the shares of Big Jim's were owned by Homeway-Carolina, that defendant owned all of the stock of Tire Sales Company, and that he was an officer and director of Homeway-Carolina and Tire Sales Company. Defendant, however, denied that Tire Sales Company owned all of the shares of Homeway-Carolina, or that he had orally guaranteed the payment of Big Jim's debt. Defendant did not plead the statute of frauds as an affirmative defense to plaintiff's claim. In an affidavit, defendant admitted that he received a monthly salary from Big Jim's of $3,000, that Tire Sales Company owned half of the shares of Homeway-Carolina and thus that he indirectly owned a one-half interest in Big Jim's, and that there were substantial and recurring intercorporate transactions between Big Jim's and Tire Sales Company. Plaintiff has presented no forecast of evidence which would be available to it at trial to show that defendant owned any more than a one-half interest in Big Jim's. From the trial court's granting of defendant's motion for summary judgment, plaintiff appeals.

Clifton & Singer, by Richard G. Singer, for plaintiff appellant.

Latham, Wood & Balog, by Steve A. Balog, for defendant appellee.

WELLS, Judge.

Plaintiff first argues that the trial court erred in granting defendant's motion for summary judgment because defendant failed to plead the statute of frauds as an affirmative defense. Pursuant to G.S. 22-1,

> [n]o action shall be brought ... to charge any defendant upon a special promise to answer the debt, default or miscarriage of another person, unless the agreement upon which such action shall be brought, or some memorandum or note thereof, shall be in writing, and signed by the party charged therewith or some other person thereunto by him lawfully authorized.

[1] While the statute of frauds is an affirmative defense which ordinarily must be pleaded, G.S. 1A-1, Rule 8(c), our Supreme Court held that for the purpose of ruling on a motion for summary judgment, an affirmative defense may be raised for the first time by affidavit. *Bank v. Gillespie*, 291 N.C. 303, 230 S.E. 2d 375 (1976); *accord, Cooke v. Cooke*, 34 N.C. App. 124, 237 S.E. 2d 323 (1977), *disc. rev. denied*, 293 N.C. 740, 241 S.E. 2d 513 (1977). As the court explained in *Gillespie*, however, the preferred practice is to require a formal amendment to the pleadings.

[2] Plaintiff next argues that the papers before the trial court demonstrated the existence of a genuine issue of material fact as to whether defendant had such a personal, immediate, and pecuniary interest in the transaction as to bring his promise within the operation of the "main purpose rule" and thus except it from the requirements of the statute of frauds. North Carolina has long recognized the exception to the statute of frauds generally referred to as either the "main purpose rule" or the "leading object rule." *Burlington Industries v. Foil*, 284 N.C. 740, 202 S.E. 2d 591 (1974). The general application of the rule was set out in *Burlington Industries* as follows:

> Generally, if it is concluded that the promisor has the requisite personal, immediate, and pecuniary interest in the transaction in which a third party is the primary obligor, then the promise is said to be original rather than collater-

al and therefore need not be in writing to be binding. Professor Lee, in North Carolina Law of Suretyship 12 (3d Ed. 1970), notes that the main purpose rule is applicable when a court has determined that the promisor's "answering for the debt or default of another is merely incidental to his broader purposes. He is participating in the principal contract and making its obligation his own. The expected advantage to the promisor must be such as to justify the conclusion that his main purpose in making the promise is to advance his own interests."

Id., 284 N.C. at 748-749, 202 S.E. 2d at 597. In *Burlington Industries,* the defendant stockholder and director owned a 16⅔ percent interest in the corporation whose debt he allegedly guaranteed, but his investment in the corporation totalled only $750, while credit extended by the plaintiff to the corporation amounted to $125,000. Justice Moore, writing for the Court, held that such an interest was too indirect and remote to invoke application of the main purpose rule.

In *Burlington Industries,* the Court discussed at length the development and application of the main purpose rule in North Carolina. Justice Moore, quoting from Annot., 35 A.L.R. 2d 906, 910-911, 914 (1954), pointed out an important distinction in the rule recognized by our Supreme Court

"As applied to promises by stockholders, officers, or directors, to pay a debt of the corporation, it may be said that the promise is original where the promisor's primary object was to secure some direct and personal benefit from the performance by the promisee of his contract with the corporation, or from the latter's refraining from exercising against the corporation some right existing in him by virtue of the contract. *The benefit to the promisor is to be distinguished from the indirect benefit which would accrue to him merely by virtue of his position as a stockholder, officer, or director.* If the benefit accruing is direct and personal, then the promise is original within the rule above discussed, and the validity thereof is not affected by the statute of frauds." (Emphasis added.) [Citation omitted.]

"Where an oral promise by a stockholder, officer, or director of a corporation is collateral in form and effect, and the consideration was not intended to secure or promote some personal object or advantage of the promisor — as distinguished from the benefit accruing to a person from the mere fact of his being a stockholder, officer or director —, the promise is collateral and within the statute of frauds." [Citation omitted.]

Id., 284 N.C. at 749-750, 202 S.E. 2d at 598.

The foregoing comments provide the basis upon which the ultimate disposition of the issue by the Court in *Burlington Industries* may be reconciled with other cases in which the transaction has been held to be sufficiently direct and personal to come within the operation of the main purpose rule. In *Studio, Inc. v. School of Heavy Equipment*, 25 N.C. App. 544, 214 S.E. 2d 192 (1975) one of the individual defendants orally guaranteed the debt of a corporation in which he served as chairman of the board of directors, drew a monthly salary of $2,000, and owned all of one class of stock and 49 percent of another class of stock. We held that the trial court had improvidently granted this defendant's motion for a directed verdict, since a jury could have found that the defendant's interest in the corporation was sufficient to allow application of the main purpose rule. In *Studio, Inc.*, we recognized the thrust of *Burlington Industries*:

> *Burlington Industries v. Foil, supra,* a 1974 decision, culminates a line of cases which have developed the "main purpose rule" and prescribed its limitations. The *Foil* case holds that the benefit accruing to a party merely by virtue of his position as a stockholder, officer, or director is not alone such personal, immediate and pecuniary benefit as to invoke the main purpose rule. . . .

Id., 25 N.C. App. at 547, 214 S.E. 2d at 194; *accord, Warren v. White*, 251 N.C. 729, 112 S.E. 2d 522 (1960); *Supply Co. v. Motel Development*, 32 N.C. App. 199, 231 S.E. 2d 201 (1977); *see*, Note, *Statute of Frauds — The Main Purpose Doctrine in North Carolina*, 13 N.C.L. REV. 263 (1935).

In the case *sub judice* there was evidence that defendant was Big Jim's managing director, owned half of the stock, and received from it a monthly salary of $3,000. There was also evidence that Big Jim's engaged in repeated and substantial transactions with a corporation in which defendant was the sole stockholder. The comment which defendant allegedly made to plaintiff's employees, that defendant wanted to be a millionaire before the age of forty, is evidence that defendant himself believed that he had a substantial personal interest in the extension of additional credit to Big Jim's. Considered as a whole, the evidence in this case tends to show such direct, personal, and immediate interest on the part of defendant as to distinguish it from *Burlington Industries* and present a question for the jury concerning the application of the main purpose rule. Accordingly, we hold that summary judgment was improvidently granted.

Reversed.

Chief Judge MORRIS and Judge PARKER concur.

SYNCO, INC., A CORPORATION; AND SYNCO, INC., A CORPORATION, AS THE GENERAL PARTNER OF AND ON BEHALF OF ASSOCIATED APARTMENT INVESTORS/SHADOWOOD, A LIMITED PARTNERSHIP, PLAINTIFFS v. FRANK L. HEADEN, JAMES M. SHANNONHOUSE, JR., JOSEPH W. TERRELL III AND TERRELL CONSTRUCTION COMPANY, A NORTH CAROLINA CORPORATION, DEFENDANTS AND JAMES M. SHANNONHOUSE, JR., THIRD-PARTY PLAINTIFF v. HAROLD L. COOLER, THIRD PARTY DEFENDANT

SYNCO, INC., A CORPORATION; AND SYNCO, INC., A CORPORATION, AS THE GENERAL PARTNER OF AND ON BEHALF OF ASSOCIATED APARTMENT INVESTORS/HOLLYWOOD, A LIMITED PARTNERSHIP, PLAINTIFFS v. FRANK L. HEADEN, JAMES M. SHANNONHOUSE, JR., JOSEPH W. TERRELL, III AND TERRELL CONSTRUCTION COMPANY, A NORTH CAROLINA CORPORATION, DEFENDANTS

No. 7926SC802

(Filed 3 June 1980)

1. **Reference § 3.2; Rules of Civil Procedure § 53– compulsory reference – long or complicated account**

In an action to recover for breach of written warranties in connection with the construction and sale to plaintiffs of two apartment complexes, the trial court, after hearing evidence presented by plaintiffs for three and one-half days, did not err in ordering a compulsory reference on the ground that resolution of the case depended upon findings as to a large number of separate transactions by plaintiffs for repairs to the apartments and some of the appliances therein. G.S. 1A-1, Rule 53(a)(2)(a).

2. **Reference § 7; Rules of Civil Procedure § 53– compulsory reference – report of referee – necessity for transcript of evidence**

The referee in a compulsory reference is required under G.S. 1A-1, Rule 53(f)(3) to file a transcript of the evidence with his report, and the referee's notes summarizing the testimony of the witnesses in the hearing before him are not a proper substitute for the transcript of the evidence.

3. **Reference § 7; Rules of Civil Procedure § 53 – compulsory reference – referee's duty to have reporter submit transcript**

It was the duty of the referee in a compulsory reference, with the assistance of the trial court if needed, to have the reporter who recorded the hearing testimony to submit a copy or copies of the transcript of evidence at the hearing, and any controversy as to the cost of the transcript was not a private matter between the parties to the action but was a question for determination by the referee and the trial court. Therefore, the trial court erred in dismissing plaintiffs' actions for failure to offer at trial a transcript of the evidence heard by the referee.

4. **Reference §7; Rules of Civil Procedure § 53– compulsory reference – waiver of transcript**

The requirement that a transcript of the evidence in a compulsory reference be filed with the referee's report may be waived by the parties.

5. **Reference § 7; Rules of Civil Procedure § 53 – compulsory reference – necessity for transcript of evidence – agreement to use referee's notes**

The parties were entitled to have all appropriate issues determined by the jury upon the report of the referee with the transcript of the evidence unless the parties agreed, as indicated by the referee's report, that the report would be accompanied by the referee's notes without a transcript of the evidence.

APPEAL by plaintiffs from *Snepp, Judge.* Order entered 12 November 1976 from Kirby, Judge. Judgment entered 13 June 1979, in Superior Court, MECKLENBURG County. Heard in the Court of Appeals 5 March 1980.

Plaintiffs filed complaints seeking to recover damages for breach of certain written warranties in connection with the construction and sale to them of two apartment complexes known as "Shadowood" and "Hollywood" in Charlotte.

Defendants admitted the sale of the two apartment complexes to plaintiffs and the execution of the warranty agreements but denied liability.

The two actions were consolidated and trial began before Judge Snepp without a jury, and plaintiffs had presented evidence for three and one-half days when Judge Snepp declared a mistrial and entered on 12 November 1976 an order of compulsory reference. Both parties objected and excepted to the order.

The Referee heard evidence in June and July 1977 for a total of nine days. Louise G. Johnson and Associates recorded the proceedings, but a transcript of the evidence was not prepared. Other facts relating to the absence of such transcript are included in the opinion. The Referee filed his report on 13 October 1977. Both parties objected and filed exceptions to the Report and demanded jury trial.

At trial the plaintiff offered the oral testimony since there was no transcript of the evidence before the Referee. Defendants moved under Rule 50 to dismiss for failure to present any evidence. The motion was allowed, and plaintiffs appeal from the judgment dismissing both actions.

Cole & Chesson by Calvin W. Chesson; Hicks & Harris by Eugene C. Hicks III for plaintiff appellants.

Caudle, Underwood & Kinsey by Lloyd C. Caudle; Williams, Kratt & Parker by Neil C. Williams; Kennedy, Covington, Lobdell & Hickman by Wayne P. Huckel for defendant appellees.

CLARK, Judge.

[1] This appeal raises two questions: did the trial court err (1) in ordering the compulsory reference, and (2) in dismissing plaintiffs' actions for failure to offer at trial a transcript of the evidence heard by the Referee?

The written warranties, which are the subject of the actions before us, relate to the plans and specifications for the apartment complexes including certain appliances and equipment in each unit.

The reason for the mistrial and reference are stated in the two opening paragraphs of the order of reference as follows:

"After three and a half days of trial before the Court without a jury, and the Plaintiffs not having yet concluded the presentation of their evidence, the Court is of the opinion that upon the evidence which has been presented, this case cannot be resolved with substantial justice to either party upon any permissible legal theory. The Court, therefore, in its discretion, declares a mistrial.

It being apparent to the Court that the resolution of these suits will depend upon findings as to a large number of individual transactions on the part of the Plaintiffs for repairs to the premises in question and to some of the appliances therein, the cases can only be resolved through reference."

In 1967 the statutes relating to reference were repealed (1967 N.C. Sess. Laws, c. 954), but the statutory provisions were substantially retained and incorporated in G.S. 1A-1, Rule 53, entitled "Referees." The long-standing statutory provision that the trial court may order a compulsory reference where the trial of an issue requires the examination of a "long account" was retained in substance in Rule 53(a)(2)(a), which now provides "long or complicated account."

There is no statutory or judicial definition of a "long account." *Dayton Rubber Mfg. Co. v. Horn,* 203 N.C. 732, 167 S.E. 42 (1932). It is clear, however, that the exact words of the statute do not characterize a case for compulsory reference, and that a "long account" does not restrict the reference to an action on an account. See 11 Strong's N.C. Index 3d *Reference* § 3.2 (1978); *Shute v. Fisher,* 270 N.C. 247, 154 S.E. 2d 75 (1967) (an action against the endorsers and guarantors of a note); *Rudisill v. Hoyle,* 254 N.C. 33, 118 S.E. 2d 145 (1961) (an action for accounting against the personal representative of an estate of a decedent); *Pack v. Katzin,* 215 N.C. 233, 1 S.E. 2d 566 (1939) (an action to recover upon a construction contract).

The case *sub judice* has some features similar to *Shute v. Fisher, supra,* where Judge Brock (now Justice Brock) heard plaintiff's evidence for two days, and then ordered a reference. In upholding the reference the Supreme Court commented that the action required the examination of a long account, numerous calculations of interest, and numerous exhibits, and commented that such examination "would be the *equivalent* of 'the examination of a long account.' " (Emphasis added.)

We find that the trial judge did not abuse his discretion in ordering the reference and appointing a Referee. The plaintiffs and defendants collectively were ordered to advance $500 each toward costs.

The Referee engaged Louise G. Johnson and Associates to record the evidence at the hearing, and the firm had a reporter present during the nine days of oral testimony which was recorded on tape by steno mark.

Defendants requested a transcript of the evidence and Johnson and Associates quoted a price which defendants considered unreasonable. Defendants brought action against Johnson and Associates seeking to buy the tapes or have them deposited with the court. The action was dismissed for failure to state a claim in the trial court and was affirmed on appeal by this Court in an unpublished opinion.

The record on appeal does not reveal that either the Referee or the trial court in the case *sub judice* has made any request for a transcript of the evidence or for the tapes.

[2] G.S. 1A-1, Rule 53(f)(3) provides: "The testimony of all witnesses must be reduced to writing by the referee, or by someone acting under his direction and shall be filed in the cause and constitute a part of the record." We hold that the Referee under this Rule is required to file a transcript of the evidence with his

report. This rule follows from *American Trust Co. v. Jenkins*, 196 N.C. 428, 430, 146 S.E. 68, 69 (1929), where Brogden, J., for the Court, stated: "While the referee has power to rule upon the competency of evidence offered by a party or to exclude such testimony from his consideration in making up his report, nevertheless this power must be exercised in subjection to the ultimate right of the parties to have the trial judge to 'review the report, and set aside, modify or confirm it in whole or in part,' . . . The Trial judge cannot intelligently review the report, modify or confirm it, unless the evidence offered by the parties is before him. . . ."

The referee submitted with his report as an exhibit his notes which purportedly consisted of a summary of the testimony of the various witnesses in the hearing before him; such notes, however, are not a proper substitute for the transcript of the evidence and do not meet the requirements of G.S. 1A-1, Rule 53.

[3] It was the duty of the Referee, with assistance from the trial court if needed, to have Louise G. Johnson and Associates submit a copy or copies of the transcript of evidence. Any controversy as to the cost of the transcript was not a private matter between the reporter and the parties to this action but was a question for determination by the Referee and the trial court. We find that the trial court erred in thereafter adopting the Referee's report, in placing the matter on the ready calendar for trial, and in beginning trial and directing verdicts for defendants.

[4] The transcript requirement of Rule 53 may, however, be waived by agreement of the parties. It is noted that the Referee began his report with the statement that he "was notified by counsel that he should make his report based on his notes taken at the hearing. . . ." In contrast, the defendants in their exceptions and objections to the report stated that they did not so notify the Referee but instead "merely advised that the court reporter has refused to supply the transcript of the evidence at a proper price or deliver the tapes to the Clerk of Superior Court so that they could be transcribed. . . ."

[5] In the record before us we do not find a waiver of rights by either the plaintiffs or the defendants which would deprive them of their right to have all appropriate issues determined by the jury upon the report of the Referee with the transcript of the evidence as provided by Rule 53, unless the parties agreed, as indicated by the Referee, that the report would be accompanied by the Referee's notes without a transcript of the evidence.

The judgment dismissing the actions is reversed and the causes are remanded for determination of whether the parties agreed to the submission of the Referee's report "based on his notes" without a transcript of the evidence. If such an agreement were made, the parties will proceed subject to the agreement, but if the court determines there was no such agreement, then the Referee and the court shall order the preparation and filing of a transcript of the evidence presented by the parties at the hearing before the Referee with appropriate advances to be made by the parties for all anticipated costs. The transcript shall be filed with the court as a part of the Referee's report, which shall constitute a filing of the report under G.S. 1A-1, Rule 53 (g)(1). The clerk shall mail notice of the filing to all parties, who may then proceed with exceptions and review as provided by law.

Reversed and Remanded.

Judges MARTIN (Robert M.) and ERWIN concur.

MARY LOUISE BROWN, ADMINISTRATRIX FOR THE ESTATE OF WILLIAM OSCAR BROWN v. MOTOR INNS OF CAROLINA, INC.

No. 792SC714

(Filed 3 June 1980)

Master and Servant § 87.1– employee drowning in pool – no work related injury – no exclusive jurisdiction in Industrial Commission

In an action to recover for the wrongful death of plaintiff's intestate who drowned in defendant employer's swimming pool after he had completed his day's work and while he was attending a birthday party for another employee, the death of plaintiff's intestate occurred outside the employment contract, and plaintiff's claim therefore fell outside the exclusive jurisdictional provisions of the Workers' Compensation Act.

APPEAL by plaintiff from *Fountain, Judge.* Judgment entered 21 May 1979 in Superior Court, MARTIN County. Heard in the Court of Appeals 25 February 1980.

On 8 June 1978 plaintiff filed this negligence action to recover damages for the wrongful death of her intestate, William Oscar Brown, who died on 16 June 1976 as a result of suffocation by drowning in defendant's swimming pool. The incident occurred after plaintiff's intestate, an employee of defendant, had completed his day's work and while he was attending an impromptu birthday celebration given for another employee at the pool area. Defendant answered, denying negligence on its part, and asserted that plaintiff's intestate was contributorily negligent.

In addition, defendant moved to dismiss the action for want of subject matter jurisdiction in that plaintiff's rights, if any, were governed by the Workers' Compensation Act. Defendant's motion was based on a denial of plaintiff's previous claim for compensation benefits against defendant and defendant's insurance carrier. In an opinion dated 25 March 1977, the Deputy Commissioner ruled that the death of plaintiff's intestate "did not arise out of and in the course of the employment because the social event attended by him after work was not a regular incident of the employment, was not required as a condition of employment, did not constitute remuneration in lieu of wages and did not involve substantial direct benefit to the employer." No appeal was taken from this order.

By agreement between the parties, the trial court treated defendant's motion to dismiss as a motion for summary judgment under G.S. 1A-1, Rule 12(b) and G.S. 1A-1, Rule 56 of the North Carolina Rules of Civil Procedure. The court considered, in addition to the pleadings, the opinion of the Deputy Commissioner denying plaintiff's claim for benefits. That order included the stipulation of the parties that they were "bound by and subject to the provisions of the North Carolina Work[ers']

Compensation Act." On 21 May 1979, the trial court entered summary judgment in favor of defendant and dismissed plaintiff's claim with prejudice. Plaintiff appeals.

Hulse and Hulse, by Herbert B. Hulse, and Duke and Brown, by John E. Duke, for plaintiff appellant.

Battle, Winslow, Scott and Wiley, by Samuel S. Woodley, for defendant appellee.

MORRIS, Chief Judge.

Plaintiff assigns error to the trial court's granting summary judgment in favor of defendant. Although the judgment is not clear as to the basis for the court's ruling, both plaintiff and defendant address in their briefs the issue of whether the disposition of plaintiff's previous claim for death benefits under the Workers' Compensation Act [the Act] precludes plaintiff's present tort action to recover for the wrongful death of her intestate.

The question of coverage under the Worker's Compensation Act is commonly raised by a defendant who seeks to defend a negligence action by alleging exclusive jurisdiction in the Industrial Commission because of plaintiff's employment by defendant at the time the injuries were incurred, thus limiting plaintiff to recovery of compensation benefits. *E.g., Horney v. Meredith Swimming Pool Co.*, 267 N.C. 521, 148 S.E. 2d 554 (1966); *Barber v. Minges*, 223 N.C. 213, 25 S.E. 2d 837 (1943); *McCune v. Rhodes-Rhyne Manufacturing Co.*, 217 N.C. 351, 8 S.E. 2d 219 (1940); *Francis v. Carolina Wood Turning Co.*, 208 N.C. 517, 181 S.E. 628 (1935). Exclusive jurisdiction is based on G.S. 97-10.1, which provides as follows:

> If the employee and the employer are subject to and have complied with the provisions of this Article, then the rights and remedies herein granted to the employee, his dependents, next of kin, or personal representative shall exclude all other rights and remedies of the employee, his dependents, next of kin, or representative as against the em-

ployer at common law or otherwise on account of such injury or death.

This section implements the purpose of the Act, which is to provide certain limited benefits to an injured employee regardless of negligence on the part of the employer, and simultaneously to deprive the employee of certain rights he had at the common law. *Bryant v. Dougherty*, 267 N.C. 545, 148 S.E. 2d 548 (1966); *Hicks v. Guilford County*, 267 N.C. 364, 148 S.E. 2d 240 (1966).

Our Supreme Court has created an exception to the operation of G.S. 97-10.1 in cases where the injury arises from activities disconnected with the employment. In *Barber v. Minges*, *supra*, plaintiff's intestate died as a result of an accident occurring while he was on a fishing trip as a guest of his employer, who customarily provided an annual outing for his employees and their families "in the promotion of good will". In a subsequent negligence suit against defendant and his company, the trial court granted defendants' motion to dismiss based on the ground that the North Carolina Industrial Commission had exclusive jurisdiction over the case under the Workers' Compensation Act. On appeal, defendants contended that the Act "excludes all remedies other than through the Industrial Commission, whether plaintiff be invitee or licensee; whether he be on the job, or off the job; whether the accident arises out of employment, or independently of employment." 223 N.C. at 215, 25 S.E. 2d at 838. The Court rejected this argument, stating:

Carried to its logical extreme, this would confer immunity from liability upon an employer who inflicts a negligent injury on an employee while the latter is not engaged in any activity of his employment and is far from the scene of his duties, while he is on the way to the grocer or to church, or wherever he has the right to be in the pursuit of his own affairs. The contention is too sweeping to merit serious attention except for the fact that counsel for defense cite certain decisions of this Court which have been recognized as having that significance. *Pilley v. Cotton Mills*, 201 N.C., 426, 160 S.E., 479; *Francis v. Wood Turning Co.*, 208 N.C., 517, 181 S.E., 628.

Brown v. Motor Inns
---

223 N.C. at 215, 25 S.E. 2d at 838. The Court characterized the Act as concerning itself with the relation of master and servant and their mutual rights and liabilities, which in the Court's opinion, did not extend beyond the context of "employment":

> The incidence of the law is on the status created by the contract of employment. It deals with the incidents and risks of that employment, in which concededly is included the negligence of the employer in that relation. It has no application outside the field of industrial accident; and does not intend, by its general terms, to take away common law or other rights which pertain to the parties only as members of the general public, disconnected with the employment ... Expressions in [the Act] regarding the surrender of the right to maintain common law or statutory actions against the employer are not absolute — not words of universal import, making no contact with time, place or circumstance. They must be construed within the framework of the Act, and as qualified by its subject and purposes.

223 N.C. at 216, 25 S.E. 2d at 839. Distinguishing prior cases which held the Act controlling on the issue of jurisdiction, the Court ruled that the Act was inapplicable to the facts of that case, in that the outing sponsored by defendant occurred on Sunday, plaintiff's intestate was not paid for attendance, but was merely invited, plaintiff's intestate was not under the control and direction of defendant during the outing, and plaintiff's intestate owed no duty to defendant or to other invited guests.

In *Bryant v. Dougherty, supra,* the *Barber* decision was applied to determine the jurisdiction of the Industrial Commission in a malpractice action against a physician who was not employed by defendant but was merely selected by defendant to treat an employee for injuries received while in defendant's employ. In holding that the Act did not confer upon the Industrial Commission jurisdiction over an action by an injured employee against a physician for injuries due to the physician's negligence in treating the employee, the Court reiterated its position regarding the dispositive nature of the employer-employee realtionship:

The Workmen's Compensation Act relates to the rights and liabilities of employee and employer by reason of injuries and disabilities arising out of and in the course of the employment relation. Where that relation does not exist the Act has no application. *Hicks v. Guilford County*, 267 N.C. 364, 148 S.E. 2d 240. Where the employer and the employee are subject to and have accepted and complied with the provisions of the Act, the rights and remedies therein granted to the employee exclude all other rights and remedies in his favor against the employer. G.S. 97-10.1. The Act does not, however, take away any common law right of the employee, even as against the employer, provided the right be one which is disconnected with the employment and pertains to the employee, not as an employee but as a member of the public. [Citations omitted.]

267 N.C. at 548, 148 S.E. 2d at 551. The findings adopted by the trial court in the case before us reveal that the death of plaintiff's intestate occurred outside the employment context. Therefore, under the rationale in *Barber* and *Bryant*, it is our opinion that plaintiff's claim falls outside the exclusive jurisdictional provisions of the Workers' Compensation Act.

Defendant argues in addition that, even if the Industrial Commission lacked jurisdiction and plaintiff's action is not precluded on this ground, plaintiff's action is barred because defendant owed no duty to plaintiff's intestate from which a breach of duty could be established and that plaintiff's intestate contributed to his own death. From our review of the pleadings presented on motion for summary judgment, we find that substantial questions of material fact exist concerning the knowledge of both plaintiff's intestate and defendant of the condition of the pool area at the time plaintiff's intestate entered the pool. These issues should be developed at trial.

We, therefore, reverse the decision of the trial court and remand this action to the Superior Court for further proceedings not inconsistent with this opinion.

Reversed and remanded.

Judges VAUGHN and ARNOLD concur.

State v. Harris

STATE OF NORTH CAROLINA v. JAMES EARL HARRIS

No. 7917SC1152

(Filed 3 June 1980)

1. **Homicide § 21.7– second degree murder – sufficiency of evidence**

    The State's evidence was sufficient for the jury on the issue of defendant's guilt of second degree murder by stabbing deceased with a knife.

2. **Homicide § 28.1– self-defense – requested instructions given in substance**

    The trial court in substance gave defendant's requested instructions on self-defense.

3. **Homicide § 24.1 – instructions – presumptions of malice and unlawfulness**

    In instructing the jury on the presumptions of malice and unlawfulness arising upon proof of a killing by the intentional use of a deadly weapon, the trial court did not fail to place the burden of proof of malice on the State in instructing that "if nothing else appears the defendant would be guilty of second degree murder."

4. **Homicide § 19– nature and customs of area — incompetency**

    Evidence in a homicide case as to the nature and customs of the area in which the crime occurred did not relate to defendant's state of mind in relation to his plea of self-defense and was properly excluded by the court.

APPEAL by defendant from *Albright, Judge.* Judgment entered 8 March 1979 in Superior Court, ROCKINGHAM County. Heard in the Court of Appeals 22 April 1980.

Defendant was charged with the offense of murder in the first degree of one Clifford Neal and was tried for and convicted of the offense of murder in the second degree.

The State's evidence tended to show from the testimony of four witnesses: that on the night of 7 December 1978, they were at The Spot, a beer establishment in Reidsville; that they saw deceased and Gerald Hairston standing in a booth talking; and that defendant then reached over Hairston and stabbed deceased with a knife. Defendant then left The Spot, and deceased asked someone to take him to the hospital. In a statement given by these witnesses to police officers, they indicated that deceased and Hairston were arguing when defendant stabbed him. The deceased died later the same evening from loss of blood caused by the knife wound under his collarbone on the right side. Deceased had been drinking.

Defendant testified: that prior to 7 December 1978, he had known deceased several weeks; that deceased was at least four inches taller than he and was older; that when defendant lived next to deceased in a trailer park, deceased came over to his trailer and threatened to kill him several weeks prior to 7 December 1978; and that he had heard that deceased had kidnapped a girl and had a reputation for violence. On 7 December 1978, defendant saw deceased in an alley. Deceased pulled a gun on him, and defendant then walked away. Later, defendant went to The Spot and left when he saw deceased walk in. Defendant returned an hour or so later. When he entered The Spot, he saw deceased and Hairston arguing. Defendant walked past the two men and heard deceased say, "'[Y]ou too, [M.F.].'" Deceased turned toward defendant and started toward his (deceased's) pocket. Defendant stabbed him with a seven-inch knife, because he thought deceased was reaching for a gun. Defendant stated that he stabbed deceased in the shoulder, not intending to kill him. Defendant admitted that he had been convicted of assault, larceny, and driving without a license.

A police officer testified that he knew the deceased and that from what he had read and heard about deceased, he had a reputation for being a dangerous and violent fighting man.

Defendant's other evidence tended to show that the deceased jumped up from the booth and reached in his pocket when defendant walked in.

From an active prison sentence of not less than 60 years nor more than 80 years, defendant appealed.

Attorney General Edmisten, by Assistant Attorney General Tiare B. Smiley, for the State.

Bethea, Robinson, Moore & Sands, by Alexander P. Sands III, for defendant appellant.

ERWIN, Judge.

Defendant presents five questions for our determination on his appeal.

[1] The evidence, when considered in the light most favorable to the State, giving the State the benefit of every reasonable inference to be drawn therefrom, was sufficient to submit the case to the jury and to support a verdict thereon. *State v. Hunter*, 290 N.C. 556, 227 S.E. 2d 535 (1976). The trial court properly denied defendant's motion for judgment of nonsuit at the close of all the evidence. This assignment of error is without merit.

[2] Defendant contends that the trial court committed error in its charge by failing to instruct the jury in accordance with his request. The record shows that after the court had instructed the jury, it asked: "Now anything further for the defendant? MR. SANDS: No, sir, Your Honor." The jury was excused to consider the case. The record shows the following:

"REQUEST FOR JURY INSTRUCTIONS

The defendant hereby requests the Court to instruct the jury with regards to self-defense as follows: As contained in the case of *State v. Terrell*, 212 NC 145 (1937) beginning with the last paragraph on page 149 and the remaining part of that paragraph on page 150 as underlined in the attached exhibit.

[The defendant also requests the court to charge the following:

'It may justify the use of a deadly weapon in self defense when assaulted by a person of larger size or of greater strength, although such person may be unarmed.' *S. v. Miller*, 221 NC 356, 358, (1942)]

Court did not give this requested instruction. EXECPTION NO. 17"

Requests for special instructions must be in writing and must be submitted before the beginning of the charge by the court. G.S. 15A-1231(a); *State v. Jackson*, 30 N.C. App. 187, 266 S.E. 2d 543 (1976). The purpose of an instruction is to clarify the issues for the jury and to apply the law to the facts of the case. *State v. Cousin*, 292 N.C. 461, 233 S.E. 2d 554 (1977); *State v.*

Britt, 285 N.C. 256, 204 S.E. 2d 817 (1974). The law requires the trial judge to clarify and explain the law arising on the evidence. *State v. Harrill*, 289 N.C. 186, 221 S.E. 2d 325 (1976), *modified*, 428 U.S. 904, 49 L. Ed. 2d 1211, 96 S.Ct. 3212 (1976). We hold that the court charged in substance on the matters as requested by defendant; and as a result thereof, we find no error.

[3] Defendant contends that the court erred in failing to properly place the burden of proof on the State with regard to the element of murder in the second degree. We glean from defendant's brief that he complains of the following portion of the court's instructions.

> "Now members of the jury, if the State proves beyond a reasonable doubt or it is admitted that the defendant intentionally killed Clifford Neal with a deadly weapon or intentionally inflicted a wound upon Clifford Neal with a deadly weapon that proximately caused his death you may, but need not infer, first that the killing was unlawful and second that it was done with malice. And if nothing else appears the defendant would be guilty of second degree murder."

We note that the court charged in part as follows following the above complained of charge:

> "Now members of the jury, the defendant contends that the stabbing of Clifford Neal was done in lawful self-defense. I charge you that if the defendant acted lawfully in self-defense his actions are excused and he is not guilty.

> * * *

> Now members of the jury, the burden is on the State to prove beyond a reasonable doubt that the defendant did not act in self-defense. However, if the State proves beyond a reasonable doubt that the defendant though otherwise acting in self-defense used excessive force or was the aggressor, though he had no murderous intent when he entered the fight, the defendant would be guilty of voluntary manslaughter.

So then members of the jury, I charge you if you find from the evidence and beyond a reasonable doubt that on or about December 7, 1978, James Earl Harris intentionally and with malice and without justification or excuse stabbed Clifford Neal with a knife, thereby proximately causing Clifford Neal's death, it would be your duty to return a verdict of guilty of second degree murder."

When the entire charge is considered, we do not conclude that the phrase, "and *if* nothing else appears the defendant would be guilty of second degree murder" (emphasis added), creates an impermissible presumption of malice against defendant. The logical inferences from the fact of an intentional infliction of a wound which proximately resulted in death remains and may be weighed against the evidence of self-defense. The jury was required by the charge to consider all of the evidence presented by the State and defendant. We hold that the entire charge, when considered as a whole, is without error. *See State v. Slade*, 291 N.C. 275, 229 S.E. 2d 921 (1976).

[4] Defendant assigns as error the court's failing to permit the defendant to introduce evidence as to the nature of the area and customs therein where the alleged crime occurred. We do not find error.

The record reveals several exceptions based on objections sustained by the trial court to questions propounded by defense counsel. This ordinarily means that the answers the witnesses would have given should be made a part of the record. This applies not only to direct examination but also to cross-examination. *State v. Little*, 286 N.C. 185, 209 S.E. 2d 749 (1974), *reh. denied*, 286 N.C. 548 (1975); *State v. Robinson*, 280 N.C. 718, 187 S.E. 2d 20 (1972); 1 Stansbury's N.C. Evidence (Brandis Rev. 1973), § 26. Here, the answers were not made a part of the record; therefore, these exceptions are not before us.

The record shows the following with reference to Exception No. 10:

"THE JURY LEFT THE COURTROOM.

COURT: Let the record show the following takes place in the absence of the jury.
EXCEPTION NO. 10"

Four pages of questions and answers follow. The jury returned to open court. The questions propounded in the absence of the jury were not repeated after the jury returned. The court did state, "I will sustain an objection to that also. I don't know of any theory of law that lets in the reputation of some area." Defendant did not attempt to explain any personal knowledge or fears he had concerning the nature of the area. This offered and excluded testimony is irrelevant. Defendant did not carry a knife because the area was dangerous. Defendant testified: "As to why I stabbed him, well I didn't have a reason, I stabbed because I thought he was going to shoot me, he had drawed a gun on me before so I thought that he was going back after me." To us, the evidence offered did not in any way relate to defendant's state of mind in relation to his plea of self-defense. *Cf. State v. Miller*, 282 N.C. 633, 194 S.E. 2d 353 (1973).

We have considered all other assignments of error as contended by defendant and find no error in any of them.

In the trial of defendant, we find no prejudicial error.

No error.

Judges HEDRICK and ARNOLD concur.

Burcl v. Hospital

TRACY BURCL, Administratrix of the Estate of PATRICIA B. HYLTON v. NORTH CAROLINA BAPTIST HOSPITAL, INC.: DR. KATHRYN W. COLLIER; DR. JOHN S. COMPERE; DR. DAVID M. DEWAN; DR. DONALD A. DEWHURST; DR. C. NASH HERNDON, Associate Dean; DR. LAURENCE F. HILLER; DR. JAMES J. HUTSON; DR. THOMAS H. IRVING, Chairman of the Department of Anesthesiology; DR. RICHARD JANEWAY, Dean of Bowman Gray School of Medicine; DR. WAYNE JARMAN; DR. JOSEPH E. JOHNSON, III, Chairman of the Department of Medicine; DR. JULIAN F. KEITH, Chairman of the Department of Family and Community Medicine; FAYE L. MAGNESON; DR. MANSON MEADS, Director of Medical Center Board; DR. JESSE H. MEREDITH; DR. JOHN C. MUELLER; DR. JOHN MUSTOL; DR. RICHARD T. MYERS, Chairman of the Department of Surgery; DR. PATRICIA POTTER; DR. THOMAS J. POULTON; DR. RICHARD PROCTOR, Chairman of the Department of Psychiatry; DR. L. EARL WATTS; JOHN LYNCH, Administrator of North Carolina Baptist Hospital, Inc.; and WAKE FOREST UNIVERSITY, INC., d/b/a BOWMAN GRAY SCHOOL OF MEDICINE OF WAKE FOREST UNIVERSITY

No. 7921SC1107

(Filed 3 June 1980)

Death § 4.3; Executors and Administrators § 3– action for wrongful death – nonresident administrator – qualification as ancillary administrator – no amendment of pleadings

The trial court did not err in granting defendant's motion to dismiss and in denying the motion of plaintiff, the duly qualified Virginia administratrix of her daughter's estate, to amend her pleadings in this wrongful death action to allege her subsequent appointment as ancillary administratrix in N. C. and to have her amendment relate back to the original institution of this action so that her claim would not be barred by the statute of limitations.

APPEAL by plaintiff from *Hairston, Judge.* Order entered 11 October 1979 in Superior Court, FORSYTH County. Heard in the Court of Appeals 14 May 1980.

Plaintiff's complaint alleged that her daughter, Ms. Hylton, had undergone a gastric bypass operation at Baptist Hospital in Winston-Salem; that within 36 hours of the operation, she had gone into shock and had undergone emergency surgery, which revealed a perforation in her small intestine; and that she had died of acute peritonitis and septicemia soon afterward. Plaintiff alleged that her daughter had not been fully informed of the risks of the operation and that she had not been psychologically able to decide whether to have the operation. A psychologist who examined Ms. Hylton as part of the pre-operative procedure had recommended that measures other than surgery be taken. More conservative measures were available. Further, Ms. Hylton was not given proper care during and after the procedure.

Plaintiff was granted a stay of this action until jurisdictional issues raised in a virtually identical federal action could be determined.

Defendants moved to dismiss this action on the ground that no administratrix had been appointed in North Carolina.

Plaintiff moved to amend her complaint and to have the amendment relate back. In her affidavit, she stated that she had begun the action in Federal Court, then discovered that she lacked diversity. She did not know that a North Carolina administratrix had to be appointed. She had already been appointed in Virginia and has now been appointed in North Carolina.

Plaintiff's motions were denied, and defendants' motion to dismiss was granted. Plaintiff appealed.

Tornow & Lewis, by Michael J. Lewis for plaintiff appellant.

Hudson, Petree, Stockton, Stockton & Robinson, by R. M. Stockton, Jr. and Robert J. Lawing, for North Carolina Baptist Hospital, Inc., Dr. Kathryn W. Collier, Dr. David M. Dewan, Dr. Laurence F. Hiller, Dr. James J. Hutson, Dr. Wayne Jarman, Faye L. Magneson, Dr. John Mustol, Dr. Thomas J. Poulton, and John Lynch, defendant appellees.

Hutchins, Tyndall, Bell, Davis & Pitt, by William Kearns Davis, for Dr. Donald A. Dewhurst, Dr. C. Nash Herndon, Dr. Thomas H. Irving, Dr. Richard Janeway, Dr. Joseph E. Johnson III, Dr. Julian F. Keith, Dr. Manson Meads, Dr. John C. Mueller, Dr. Patricia Potter, Dr. Richard Proctor, Dr. L. Earl Watts, and Wake Forest University, Inc., d/b/a Bowman Gray School of Medicine of Wake Forest University, defendant appellees.

Frank B. Aycock III, for Dr. John S. Compere, defendant appellee.

Smith, Anderson, Blount, Dorsett, Mitchell & Jernigan, by James D. Blount, Jr. and Nigle B. Barrow, Jr., for Dr. Jesse H. Meredith and Dr. Richard T. Myers, defendant appellees.

ERWIN, Judge.

Plaintiff states the only question for our decision:

"Did the trial court err in granting defendant's motion to dismiss and in denying the motion of the plaintiff, the duly qualified Virginia administratrix of her daughter's estate, to amend her pleadings in this wrongful death action to allege her subsequent appointment as ancillary administratrix in North Carolina, and have this amendment relate back to the original institution of this action, so that her claim will not be barred by the statute of limitations?"

We answer, "No," and affirm the order entered by the trial court.

G.S. 28A-18-2(a) provides in pertinent part:

"(a) When the death of a person is caused by a wrongful act, neglect or default of another, such as would, if the injured person had lived, have entitled him to an action for damages therefor, the person or corporation that would have been so liable, and his or their personal representatives or collectors, shall be liable to an action for damages, to be brought by the personal representative or collector of the decedent; and this notwithstanding the death, and although the wrongful act, neglect or default, causing the death, amounts in law to a felony."

The record clearly shows the following without dispute: (1) that Patricia B. Hylton died in this State on 29 July 1977; (2) that on 7 February 1978, Tracy Burcl qualified as administratrix of the estate of Patricia B. Hylton in the Circuit Court, Henry County, Virginia; (3) that the instant action was filed on 25 July 1979 in Superior Court, Forsyth County by plaintiff in her capacity as a Virginia administratrix; (4) that on 20 September 1979, Tracy Burcl qualified an ancillary administratrix of the estate of Patricia B. Hylton before the Clerk of Superior Court, Forsyth County; (5) that the qualification as ancillary administratrix in Forsyth County occurred more than two years after the death of Ms. Hylton; and (6) that on 21 September 1979, plaintiff moved to amend her complaint to allege that she had been appointed ancillary administratrix in North Carolina and further moved that the amendment be allowed to relate back to the filing of her complaint so that she could avoid the running of the statute of limitations.

Plaintiff argues honestly and forcefully that the order entered in the case *sub judice* should be reversed by this Court for the following reasons: (1) Plaintiff had in fact qualified as administratrix in Virginia prior to filing this action. (2) Plaintiff acted in good faith and was not aware that she had to qualify in the State of· North Carolina prior to filing her action in the capacity of administratrix. (3) Defendants are not prejudiced by her request to amend her complaint and to let such amendment relate back.

Plaintiff contends that her case is distinguishable from our decisions in *Reid v. Smith*, 5 N.C. App. 646, 169 S.E. 2d 14 (1969); *Merchants Distributors v. Hutchinson and Lewis v. Hutchinson*, 16 N.C. App. 655, 193 S.E. 2d 436 (1972); and *Sims v. Construction Co.*, 25 N.C. App. 472, 213 S.E. 2d 398 (1975). We conclude there are some differences in the cases cited, but these differences do not rise to the status of a distinction. The questions raised in the case *sub judice* were answered in *Sims v. Construction Co.*, 25 N.C. App. 472, 473, 213 S.E. 2d 398, 399 (1975):

> "The right of action for wrongful death is purely statutory. *Graves v. Welborn*, 260 N.C. 688, 133 S.E. 2d 761 (1963). In North Carolina, an administrator appointed by the court of another state may not maintain an action for wrongful death occurring in North Carolina. *Monfils v. Hazlewood*, 218 N.C. 215, 10 S.E. 2d 673 (1940), *cert. denied*

312 U.S. 684. The commencement of a wrongful death action by a foreign administrator in North Carolina will not operate to bar the running of the applicable two-year statute of limitations set forth in G.S. 1-53, such action being a nullity and subject to dismissal. *Merchants Distributors v. Hutchinson* and *Lewis v. Hutchinson*, 16 N.C. App. 655, 193 S.E. 2d 436 (1972).

Since no attempt was made to qualify a resident administrator until after expiration of the statute of limitations set forth in G.S. 1-53(4), substitution of the resident administrator would not relate back and validate the present unathorized action. *Johnson v. Trust Co.*, 22 N.C. App. 8, 205 S.E. 2d 353 (1974). It follows that the trial court did not err in refusing to substitute the resident administrator as party plaintiff and did not err in granting defendant's motion for summary judgment and for dismissal."

Judgment affirmed.

Chief Judge Morris and Judge Clark concur.

SHARRON Y. THORNBURG v. ROBERT ALEXANDER LANCASTER and MARTHA MITCHELL LANCASTER

No. 7918SC893

(Filed 3 June 1980)

1. **Torts § 7.7– settlement as partial or complete – issue of fact – reimbursement order improper**

   In an action to recover for injuries sustained by plaintiff in an automobile accident where defendants claimed a complete settlement with their insurer, the trial court's order requiring plaintiff to return the money paid to her by defendants' insurer was invalid where there was an issue of fact as to whether the payment to plaintiff was converted to an advance or partial payment. G.S. 1-540.3.

2. **Rules of Civil Procedure § 41– failure to comply with erroneous order of trial court – order of dismissal vacated**

   The trial court's Rule 41(b) dismissal of plaintiff's action for failure to comply with the trial court's invalid order of reimbursement is vacated and the case is remanded for a determination as to whether plaintiff's failure to comply with the erroneous reimbursement order calls for dismissal with prejudice.

Judge CLARK dissenting.

APPEAL by plaintiff from *Collier, Judge.* Order entered 7 June 1979 in Superior Court, GUILFORD County. Heard in the Court of Appeals 21 March 1980.

Plaintiff seeks to recover for personal injuries she sustained in a collision between her automobile and a car driven by the male defendant and owned by the female defendant. Defendants by their answer alleged that plaintiff is barred from bringing this action, because she has entered into a settlement agreement with defendants' insurance carrier and has been paid $3,394.50 in full settlement of her claim.

Defendants moved for dismissal or for summary judgment. At the hearing on the motions, Shirley Bennett, a claim representative for defendant's insurer, testified that she handled plaintiff's claim and that plaintiff furnished her with medical reports and bills — a $321 bill from Dr. Faga and $73.50 in other medical bills. Plaintiff and Bennett agreed to settle for $3,000 over the medical bills, and on 23 June 1977, Bennett mailed a draft and releases to plaintiff. On 26 July 1977, plaintiff called Bennett and said she had had further medical bills and had been in the hospital for surgery from the accident. Bennett told her that if she was not satisfied with the settlement, "to send everything back." Plaintiff returned the releases with her additional medical bills on 15 August 1977 and, by telephone, informed Bennett that she had deposited the draft in her bank account.

Plaintiff testified that she called Bennett "around the first week in July" to tell her that there would be additional medical expenses and that Bennett told her to go ahead and cash the draft and send the releases back with the additional bills, which she did. Plaintiff's husband testified that he also spoke to Bennett and that she told him to keep the draft and send the releases back unsigned.

On 4 April 1979, the court denied defendants' motions and ordered plaintiff to "reimburse the defendant" the $3,073.50 paid to her and the $320 paid to her doctor by defendants' insurer. On 3 May 1979, defendants moved to have plaintiff's action dismissed with prejudice for her failure to comply with the reimbursement order. Plaintiff filed an affidavit attesting that she does not have and has been unable to borrow sufficient funds to comply with the order. On 7 June 1979, the court entered an order dismissing plaintiff's action unless within ten days she complied with the reimbursement order. Plaintiff did not comply, her action was dismissed, and she appeals. Defendants make cross-assignments of error.

Gerald S. Schafer, for plaintiff appellant.

Tuggle, Duggins, Meschan, Thornton & Elrod, by Richard L. Vanore, for defendant appellees.

ERWIN, Judge.

[1] In connection with its denial of defendant's motions for dismissal under G.S. 1A-1, Rule 12, of the Rules of Civil Procedure and for summary judgment, the trial court ordered plaintiff to return the money paid to her by defendants' insurer. Plaintiff contends that G.S. 1-540.3 makes this order improper.

G.S. 1-540.3(a) provides that in bodily injury claims, advance or partial payments may be made and that the receipt of such advance or partial payment shall not act as a bar to an action on the claim unless there is executed an agreement to show that the payment was accepted in full settlement. G.S. 1-540.3(b) provides that no claim for reimbursement of such an advance or partial payment shall be allowed except in the case of fraud. Since fraud was never alleged in this case, the reimbursement order is improper if the payment to plaintiff from defendants' insurer was an advance or partial payment.

All the evidence presented at the hearing on defendants' motions was to the effect that at the time payment was made to plaintiff, the parties had agreed that the payment would be a full settlement of plaintiff's claim. The evidence is conflicting, however, as to what occurred when plaintiff contacted the insurer about her newly discovered injury and additional medical bills. The insurer's claim adjuster testified that she told plaintiff to return the draft and releases. Plaintiff and her husband both testified, on the other hand, that each of them was told by the adjuster to keep the draft and send back the unsigned releases. Thus, an issue of fact arises as to whether the payment was converted to an advance or partial payment. Because the court does not find facts on either a motion for summary judgment or a motion for a Rule 12 dismissal, the trial court here properly could not have made the factual determination which was necessary prior to the entry of a reimbursement order. Accordingly, the reimbursement order entered is invalid.

[2] The question then remains whether a Rule 41(b) dismissal for failure to comply with a court order can be upheld where the original order has been found to be invalid. We have found no North Carolina case on point nor have we found a federal case which has addressed this question in applying Federal Rule 41(b). While it is certainly true that one cannot take it upon himself to ignore an erroneous order or judgment, *State v. Goff*, 264 N.C. 563, 142 S.E. 2d (1965), in light of the fact that a dismissal with prejudice under Rule 41(b) is an extreme sanction, we find it appropriate in this case to vacate the trial court's ruling on defendants' Rule 41(b) motion and remand for a new ruling. Whether the plaintiff's failure to comply with the erroneous reimbursement order calls for a dismissal with prejudice can then be determined in the trial court's discretion.

Defendants' cross-assignments of error — that the trial court erred in denying its motions to dismiss and for summary judgment — are without merit. As set out above, a genuine issue of material fact does exist. The trier of fact must determine whether the payment to plaintiff constituted a full settlement of her claim or was an advance or partial payment. There are also the issues of fact relating to negligence which are raised by plaintiff's complaint. Denial of the motion to dismiss was proper, as the complaint does state a claim upon which relief can be granted.

The order of the trial court was erroneous and is

Reversed.

Judge Martin (Robert M.) concurs.

Judge Clark dissents.

Judge Clark dissenting:

In the hearing plaintiff admitted that after a settlement agreement on 23 June 1977 the claims agent for defendants' insurer mailed to plaintiff a transmittal letter with a "Full and Final Release of All Claims" and a draft in the amount agreed. The draft was endorsed by plaintiff, deposited in her checking account, and cleared on 30 June 1977. Plaintiff failed to sign the release and return it to the agent and thereby breached the settlement agreement.

The draft was not an advance or a partial payment, and in my opinion G.S. 1-540.3 does not apply. Under these circumstances the trial court had the authority to order that the plaintiff make a reimbursement even though the court recognized that a material issue of fact was raised as to whether subsequently plaintiff was told by the agent that she could retain the money. I vote to affirm the dismissal.

SHIRLEY T. COX Petitioner v. NORTH CAROLINA REAL ESTATE LICENSING BOARD Respondent

No. 7910SC1165

(Filed 3 June 1980)

Brokers and Factors § 8– real estate broker's license – misconduct in sale – realty owned by corporation – shareholder not exempted from broker licensing statutes

A shareholder is not an owner of realty of the corporation in which the shares are held so as to bring the shareholder within the "owner" exemption provisions of the real estate brokers and salesmen licensing statutes. Therefore, the Real Estate Licensing Board had jurisdiction to revoke petitioner's real estate broker's license for encouraging and assisting a purchaser to furnish false information to a lending institution in connection with the sale of realty owned by a corporation in which petitioner owned 7.8% of the outstanding stock. G.S. 93A-2(a) and (c).

APPEAL by petitioner from *Canaday, Judge.* Judgment entered 19 November 1979 in the Superior Court, WAKE County. Heard in the Court of Appeals 20 May 1980.

This is an appeal by the petitioner, Shirley T. Cox, from a judgment of the superior court affirming the decision and order of the North Carolina Real Estate Licensing Board which revoked her real estate broker's license.

In its order revoking petitioner's license, which was entered after a hearing at which the Board heard sworn testimony and at which petitioner was present and represented by counsel, the Board made findings of fact which are in substance as follows:

In July 1978 the petitioner, a licensed real estate broker, showed a house and lot in Lee County owned by Van Harris Realty, Inc., to a Mr. and Mrs. Gerald V. Arnette, who submitted an offer through petitioner to purchase the property for $47,100.00. This offer was accepted on behalf of the seller, Van Harris Realty, Inc., by its president, Milton Van Harris. At the time the offer was made, Mr. and Mrs. Arnette made an earnest money deposit of $500.00, which deposit was placed in the escrow account of Van Harris Realty, Inc. Mr. and Mrs. Arnette told petitioner Cox that they only had $500.00 in cash with which to purchase the property. She told them that she could arrange matters so that they would be able to obtain 100% financing. She instructed Mr. Arnette to apply for a mortgage loan at Sanford Savings and Loan Association and to tell the loan officer that the purchase price of the house was $49,600.00, that they had made a deposit with Van Harris Realty, Inc. of $2,500.00, and ask for a loan of $47,100.00. Petitioner Cox gave Mr. Arnette a card which recited that the sales price was $49,600.00, that the loan amount needed was $47,100.00, and that $2,500.00 was "on deposit with Van Harris Realty." Mr. Arnette showed this card to the loan officer and used the information contained thereon in applying for the loan. Mr.

Cox v. Real Estate Licensing Board

Arnette knew that he was giving false information to the lender and that it was wrong for him to do so, but he did so at the petitioner Cox's direction and on her assurance that the transaction could be arranged so that the Arnettes would not have to furnish any more money. Sanford Savings and Loan Association, intending to make a loan of 95% of the supposed purchase price of $49,600.00, approved a loan for $47,100.00. Petitioner Cox encouraged and assisted Mr. Arnette to provide false information to Sanford Savings and Loan Association so that the Arnettes would be able to obtain a loan with little or no down payment.

At the time of the foregoing transactions, petitioner Cox was vice-president and secretary of Van Harris Realty, Inc. and owned 7.8% of the outstanding stock in that corporation. Milton Van Harris was the president and owned 92.1% of the stock. Other persons owned the remaining .1% of the stock.

On the basis of the foregoing findings of fact, the Board concluded that Shirley T. Cox was guilty of violating G.S. 93A-6(a)(8) and (10) in that she encouraged and assisted Gerald V. Arnette to furnish false information to a lending institution. On these findings and conclusions, the Board ordered her real estate broker's license revoked.

In apt time petitioner Cox filed her petition pursuant to G.S. 150A-43 *et. seq.* for judicial review of the Board's order. After a hearing in the superior court, the court entered judgment ruling that the Board's findings of fact were supported by substantial, material, and competent evidence in view of the entire record, that its conclusions of law were supported by the findings of fact, and that the Board had jurisdiction to take disciplinary action against petitioner in this matter. Accordingly, the court affirmed the Board's order. From this judgment, petitioner appeals.

Love & Wicker by Jimmy L. Love for petitioner appellant.

Attorney General Edmisten by Associate Attorney Harry H. Harkins, Jr. for the North Carolina Real Estate Licensing Board, appellee.

PARKER, Judge.

On this appeal appellant does not challenge any of the Board's findings of fact, nor does she contend that her conduct as disclosed by those findings of fact would not furnish adequate grounds under G.S. Ch. 93A for revoking her real estate broker's license had such conduct been engaged in by her while negotiating the sale of real property belonging to another. Her sole contention is that the Board lacked jurisdiction to revoke her real estate broker's license in this case because it arose as the result of a sale of property in which she had an ownership interest. We do not agree.

In support of her contention, appellant points to the language in G.S. 93A-2(a) which defines a real estate broker as "any person ... who for a compensation or valuable consideration ... sells or offers to sell, ... or negotiates the purchase or sale or exchange of real estate ... for others." She emphasizes the words "for others" and contends that her activities which led the Board's action against her in the present case were not "for others" but for herself and the corporation in which she is a stockholder. She further points to the language in G.S. 93A-2(c) which states that the provisions of G.S. Ch. 93A "shall not apply to and shall not include any person, partnership, association or corporation, who, as owner or lessor, shall perform any of the acts aforesaid with reference to property owned or leased by them, where such acts are performed in the regular course of or as an incident to the management of such property and the investment therein ...," and she contends that this language directly applies to exclude her activities in the present case from coverage by G.S. Ch. 93A.

We find these "owner exemption" clauses in the statute upon which appellant relies inapplicable in the present case. Appellant acted as a real estate broker, not as an owner, in negotiating the sale of the house and lot to Mr. and Mrs. Arnette. She was not the owner of the house and lot in question. It was owned by a corporation in which she owned less than 8% of the stock. It is elementary that "[a] corporation is an entity distinct from the shareholders which own it." *Board of Transportation v. Martin*, 296 N.C. 20, 28, 249 S.E. 2d 390, 396 (1978).

Although the Board found that appellant is vice-president and secretary of the corporation, it did not find that she acted on behalf of the corporation in her capacity as one of its officers in showing the house and lot to Mr. and Mrs. Arnette. On the contrary, it found that she acted as "sales agent," that Mr. and Mrs. Arnette submitted an offer "through" her to purchase the property, and that the offer was accepted by the president of the selling corporation. As already noted, appellant has not challenged any of the Board's findings of fact on this appeal. Such findings of fact are presently conclusive.

Our holding that a shareholder is not an owner of land of the corporation in which the shares are held so as to bring the shareholder within the "owner" exemption provisions of our real estate brokers and salesmen licensing statutes is supported by the decision of the Supreme Court of Virginia in *Grenco Real Estate Inv. v. Nathaniel Greene*, 218 Va. 228, 237 S.E. 2d 107 (1977). Interpreting the "owner" exception in the Virginia real estate brokers licensing statute, Va. Code § 54-734, which in pertinent part is in all material respects identical to the above quoted portion of G.S. 93A-2(c), the Supreme Court of Virginia said:

> Thus, the question presented . . . is whether, within the meaning of Va. Code §54-734, a shareholder is an owner of land of the corporation in which the shares are held.

> The mere statement of this question suggests a negative answer. Nothing in the statutory language employed in §54-734 displays any intent to ascribe to the word "owner" a meaning different from what it enjoys in ordinary legal contemplation. Even if, because of the licensing statute's penal nature, we construe the word "owner" liberally in favor of an exemption, we cannot conclude that a shareholder is an owner of land of the corporation in which the shares are held. Such a construction not only would subvert the shareholder's traditional status vis-a-vis the corporation but also would thwart the salutary purpose of the licensing requirement, *viz.*, "to protect the public from the fraud, misrepresentation and imposition of dishonest and incompetent persons."

218 Va. at 231, 237 S.E. 2d at 109.

We note in passing that the "owner exemption" clauses of G.S. Ch. 93A upon which appellant here attempts to rely have now been effectively eliminated from our statute insofar as licensed real estate brokers and salesmen are concerned. By Sec. 6 of Ch. 616 of the 1979 Session Laws, our General Assembly, effective 21 May 1979, has expressly provided that, notwithstanding anything to the contrary in G.S. Ch. 93A, the Board shall have the power to suspend or revoke the license of a real estate broker or real estate salesman who violates any of the provisions of G.S. Ch. 93A when selling or leasing his own property.

The judgment of the superior court affirming the decision and order of the North Carolina Real Estate Licensing Board revoking appellant's real estate broker's license is

Affirmed.

Judges HEDRICK and VAUGHN concur.

KENNETH G. PORTERFIELD v. RPC CORPORATION AND STANDARD FIRE INSURANCE COMPANY

No. 7910IC931

(Filed 3 June 1980)

Master and Servant § 65.1– workers' compensation – hernia – no loss of important part of body

In order for plaintiff to be entitled to workers' compensation pursuant to G.S. 97-31(24), he must show from medical evidence that he has loss of or permanent injury to an *important* external or internal organ or part of his body for which no compensation is payable under any other subdivision of G.S. 97-31; evidence was sufficient to support the Industrial Commission's finding that repair of plaintiff's third hernia, which resulted in loss of or injury to abdominal muscle and tissue, was not a loss of or permanent injury to an important organ or part of his body in view of his prior operations.

APPEAL by plaintiff from the North Carolina Industrial Commission. Opinion and award filed 7 August 1979. Heard in the Court of Appeals 27 March 1980.

This is an appeal from a decision of the Industrial Commission rejecting an opinion and award entered by Deputy Commissioner Haigh in favor of plaintiff.

The evidence presented before the deputy commissioner tended to show that plaintiff, a welder at RPC Corporation on 21 October 1977, was fabricating a corner housing (used for loading containers onto ships) which weighed about 100 pounds. Plaintiff normally had a small crane or a helper to assist in lifting objects that heavy, but both the crane and the helper were unavailable. He felt a sharp pain in his groin as he lifted the housing and immediately set it down. He continued to work that day, but avoided lifting heavy objects. Dr. Alan Lesage discovered and repaired the hernia but told plaintiff not to lift more than 30 to 35 pounds. The doctor was not sure of his instructions to plaintiff after the 1976 repair but thought he would have told plaintiff not to lift more than 30 or 35 pounds, because he usually told patients with hernias not to lift anything heavy. He usually hesitated to put a time limit on the lifting restriction, because some patients eventually returned to work. In this case, he thought the restriction would be permanent.

Deputy Commissioner Haigh filed an opinion and award in which he found that plaintiff had suffered a permanent injury to an important part of his body, the abdominal muscle and tissue, concluded that compensation was proper under G.S. 97-31(24), and awarded plaintiff $3,000 plus sums for a temporary period of total disability and for attorney fees. The full Commission accepted only the award for temporary, total disability and for attorney fees. The award for compensation under G.S. 97-31(24) was rejected as unsupported by the evidence. Plaintiff appealed from the full Commission.

Burke & King, by Ronnie P. King, for plaintiff appellant.

John H. Pike, for defendant appellees.

ERWIN, Judge.

Plaintiff presents one issue for our determination: "Did the Full Commission of the North Carolina Industrial Commission err in its ruling that, FINDING OF FACT NUMBER 17, in the Opinion and Award filed by Deputy Commissioner William L. Haig [sic], as filed on October 27, 1978, was not supported by evidence?" We find no error and affirm the Commission.

G.S. 97-31(24) provides *inter alia:*

"§ 97-31. *Schedule of injuries; rate and period of compensation.* — In cases included by the following schedule the compensation in each case shall be paid for disability during the healing period and in addition the disability shall be deemed to continue for the period specified, and shall be in lieu of all other compensation, including disfigurement, to wit:

* * *

(24) In case of the loss of or permanent injury to any important external or internal organ or part of the body for which no compensation is payable under any other subdivision of this section, the Industrial Commission may award proper and equitable compensation not to exceed ten thousand dollars ($10,000)."

The Commission is the fact-finding body under the Workers' Compensation Act. *Brewer v. Trucking Co.*, 256 N.C. 175, 123 S.E. 2d 608 (1962). The rule is, as fixed by statute and case law of this State, that findings of fact made by the Commission are conclusive on appeal when supported by competent evidence. G.S. 97-86; *McMahan v. Supermarket*, 24 N.C. App. 113, 210 S.E. 2d 214 (1974). The Commission's legal conclusions are subject to court review. *Jackson v. Highway Commission*, 272 N.C. 697, 158 S.E. 2d 865 (1968).

In order for plaintiff to be entitled to compensation pursuant to G.S. 97-31(24), he must show from medical evidence that he has loss of or permanent injury to an *important* external or internal organ or part of his body for which no compensation is payable under any other subdivision of G.S. 97-31. The record reveals that plaintiff was suffering from his third right inguinal hernia, that such was repaired with a Teflon mesh, and that plaintiff was directed not to lift more than 30 to 35 pounds. Following his 1976 hernia repair, plaintiff was also advised not to lift more than 30 or 35 pounds. The third recurrent inguinal hernia did not reduce plaintiff's ability to lift any objects that were not restricted by his prior 1976 limitation. From this record, the Commission did not find that the repair of plaintiff's hernia in 1978 was a loss of or permanent injury to an important organ or part of plaintiff's body in view of his prior operations. The evidence in the record supports the negative finding.

Webster's Third New International Dictionary (1976) defines "important" as "valuable in content or relationship." The evidence in the record before us does not show how much muscle or tissue was removed from plaintiff's body, and if not removed, the degree of injury to the muscle or tissue. The record is completely devoid of any evidence as to the value of the muscle or tissue in question to the body of plaintiff. Unless the importance of the muscle and tissue is shown, an award for compensation will not lie under G.S. 97-31(24); otherwise, all injuries could fall within G.S. 97-31(24). This, in our opinion, was not the intent of the Legislature when it enacted G.S. 97-31(24).

This statement written by Justice Higgins in *Cates v. Construction Co.*, 267 N.C. 560, 563, 148 S.E. 2d 604, 607 (1966), is as true today as the day the case was decided:

"It must be remembered the Workmen's [now Workers'] Compensation Act requires the Industrial Commission and the courts to construe the compensation act liberally in favor of the injured workman. 'The Act "should be liberally construed to the end that the benefits thereof shall not be denied upon technical, narrow, and strict interpretation.'" *Guest v. Iron & Metal Co.*, 241 N.C. 448, 85 S.E. 2d 596; *Henry v. Leather Co.*, 231 N.C. 477, 57 S.E. 2d 760. The philosophy which supports the Workmen's Compensation Act is that the wear and tear of the workman, as well as the machinery, shall be charged to the industry. *Vause v. Equipment Co.*, 233 N.C. 88, 63 S.E. 2d 173."

The philosophy which supports the Workers' Compensation Act is not authority in and of itself to permit the Commission to make an award to plaintiff unless the medical evidence shows to some degree of certainty that his injury falls within the meaning of G.S. 97-31(24).

Upon review of the opinion and award of the full Commission, this Court does not weigh the evidence, but may only determine whether there is evidence in the record to support the findings made by the Commission. If there is any evidence of substance which directly or by reasonable inference tends to support the findings, this Court is bound by such evidence, even though there is evidence that would have supported a finding to the contrary. *Willis v. Drapery Plant*, 29 N.C. App. 386, 224 S.E. 2d 287 (1976).

Plaintiff's reliance on *Cates v. Construction Co.*, 267 N.C. 560, 148 S.E. 2d 604 (1966), is misplaced. In *Cates*, plaintiff was allowed recovery for loss of his kidney. There is not any dispute among medical authorities that a kidney is an important part of one's body. In the case *sub judice*, the importance of the "abdominal muscle and tissue" to the other parts of the body is unknown.

The order of the full Commission is

Affirmed.

Judges HEDRICK and ARNOLD concur.

ESSIE MAE WHITAKER v. CHARLES A. BLACKBURN, JR., AND MRS. CHARLES A. BLACKBURN, JR.

No. 7910DC1099

(Filed 3 June 1980)

1. **Rules of Civil Procedure § 56.6– summary judgment –negligence cases**

Summary judgment may be appropriate in negligence cases when it appears there can be no recovery for plaintiff even if the facts as claimed by plaintiff are accepted as true.

2. **Master and Servant § 23.1– duties of employer to employee – safe place to work – warning of dangers**

While an employer is not an insurer of his employee's safety, he does have a duty to exercise ordinary care to provide his employee with a reasonably safe place to work and to warn the employee of any dangers which are known to the employer and not to the employee.

3. **Master and Servant § 26.1– injury to domestic servant – absence of negligence by employers**

Summary judgment was properly entered for defendants in an action to recover for injuries suffered by plaintiff when a stairstep in defendants' dwelling collapsed and caused plaintiff to fall while she was doing domestic work for defendants where the evidence on motion for summary judgment showed that the stairstep came out of its grooves in the framework of the stairs; the stairsteps were wrapped by carpet which concealed the grooves and nails securing them; although defendants made no formal inspection of the stairway, they did use it and observe it daily; and defendants had never observed any defects or indications of possible defects in the stairs, the evidence being insufficient to show that a reasonable inspection would have disclosed the hidden defect which caused plaintiff's fall.

APPEAL by plaintiff from *Barnette, Judge.* Judgment filed 25 September 1979 in District Court, WAKE County. Heard in the Court of Appeals 14 May 1980.

Plaintiff brings this action to recover damages for injuries suffered when she fell while employed by defendants. She was standing on a stairstep near the top of the third floor of the stairway, when it collapsed and she fell to the basement, resulting in injuries to her foot and other bodily injuries.

Defendants allege that they leased the dwelling in question and had no knowledge of any defect in the stairs.

Defendants moved for summary judgment, and at the hearing the court had before it the pleadings, affidavit and deposition of plaintiff, and affidavit of defendant Charles A. Blackburn, Jr.

The evidence of plaintiff showed that she had been doing domestic work for defendants for about a year before the accident on 10 February 1978. Defendants were living in a rented house and she had worked there three or four times on Fridays. She did general cleaning work in the home. As a part of her duties, she cleaned the stairway by sweeping it. On the day she was hurt, she had started sweeping the stairs, backing down. As she stepped on the third or fourth step from the top, the whole step gave way. The treads on the stairs had no backs on them and "you could fall right through them." They were covered with carpet all the way around.

When she landed, the step fell on top of her; it had not broken, but had come off the sides of the supporting framework of the stairs. In going up and down the stairs, she never noticed anything that looked wrong with them or "heard them creak or make any funny dangerous sounds." She suffered injuries to her right foot and other bruises and injuries to her body, requiring treatment by physicians and medical expenses. After she fell, Mr. Blackburn told her he had heard one of the steps near the top "creak or crack" when he stepped on it earlier that same day. She had never heard any of the steps creak or crack before she fell.

Defendants' evidence showed that they were living in a condominium when the accident occurred and had been there about one month. After the accident, Mr. Blackburn found that the stairs are constructed with two parallel "strings" or "bridgeboards" connected on their inner sufaces by open-backed steps or treads. The steps are flat boards, unconnected to each other by risers. The steps are supported by grooves on the inside of the bridgeboards, the grooves being relatively shallow and only long enough to contain the width of each step. The steps are secured in the grooves by nails. When defendants moved in, the steps were wrapped by carpet that concealed the grooves and nails. Even the most careful inspection of the steps would not have disclosed any defective method of construction.

When Mr. Blackburn saw that plaintiff had fallen, he went to her and found a step that had slipped out of its grooves. He weighs about 200 pounds, some 50 pounds more than plaintiff, and had come down the steps about ten minutes before she fell. He had no knowledge prior to her fall that the staircase could be of defective construction. Defendants had never heard any noises, such as "creaks," while using the stairs, nor had they felt a step "give" under them. None of the other persons in the condominium complex had experienced any similar problems with their staircases.

After the hearing, the court entered summary judgment for defendants. Plaintiff appeals.

Kimzey, Smith & McMillan, by Duncan A. McMillan, for plaintiff appellant.

Johnson, Patterson, Dilthey & Clay, by D. James Jones, Jr., for defendant appellees.

MARTIN (Harry C.), Judge.

[1] The only question on appeal is whether the court erred in granting summary judgment for defendants. Generally, summary judgment is not appropriate in negligence cases where the standard of the reasonably prudent man is to be applied to the facts. *Page v. Sloan,* 281 N.C. 697, 190 S.E. 2d 189 (1972); *Robinson v. McMahan,* 11 N.C. App. 275, 181 S.E. 2d 147, *cert. denied,* 279 N.C. 395, 183 S.E. 2d 243 (1971). However, summary judgment may be appropriate in negligence cases when it appears there can be no recovery for plaintiff even if the facts as claimed by plaintiff are accepted as true. *Pridgen v. Hughes,* 9 N.C. App. 635, 177 S.E. 2d 425 (1970). If the materials before the court at the summary judgment hearing would require a directed verdict for defendants at trial, defendants are entitled to summary judgment. *Id.* The holding in *Pridgen* has been followed in *Gibson v. Tucker,* 42 N.C. App. 214, 256 S.E. 2d 288 (1979); *Gladstein v. South Square Assoc.,* 39 N.C. App. 171, 249 S.E. 2d 827 (1978), *disc. rev. denied,* 296 N.C. 736, 254 S.E. 2d 178 (1979); *Robinson v. Moving and Storage, Inc.,* 37 N.C. App. 638, 246 S.E. 2d 839 (1978); *Forte v. Paper Co.,* 35 N.C. App. 340, 241 S.E. 2d 394, *disc. rev. denied,* 295 N.C. 89, 244 S.E. 2d 258 (1978); *Joyce v. City of High Point,* 30 N.C. App. 346, 226 S.E. 2d 856 (1976); *Town of Southern Pines v. Mohr,* 30 N.C. App. 342, 226 S.E. 2d 865 (1976); *Kiser v. Snyder,* 17 N.C. App. 445, 194 S.E. 2d 638, *cert.*

denied, 283 N.C. 257, 195 S.E. 2d 689 (1973), and is now firmly embedded in our body of law.

[2] An employer is not an insurer of his employee's safety, but he does have a duty to exercise ordinary care to provide his employee with a reasonably safe place to work, *Gaither v. Clement,* 183 N.C. 450, 111 S.E. 782 (1922), and to warn the employee of any dangers which are known to the employer and not to the employee. *Clark v. Roberts,* 263 N.C. 336, 139 S.E. 2d 593 (1965). As a concomitant part of their duty to provide plaintiff with a reasonably safe place in which to work, defendants must make a reasonable inspection of the premises to determine the presence of any dangerous conditions. *Burgess v. Power Co.,* 193 N.C. 223, 136 S.E. 711 (1927); *Orr v. Rumbough,* 172 N.C. 754, 90 S.E. 911 (1916). The defendants must make such inspection that a reasonably prudent person would make under the same or similar circumstances. *Young v. Barrier,* 268 N.C. 406, 150 S.E. 2d 734 (1966). Defendants' duty is to exercise ordinary care to keep the premises in a reasonably safe condition and to give warning or notice of hidden perils or unsafe conditions insofar as they can be ascertained by reasonable inspection and supervision. *Spell v. Smith-Douglas Co.,* 250 N.C. 269, 108 S.E. 2d 434 (1959).

[3] Applying these rulings to the facts of this case, we hold the summary judgment for defendants was properly granted. Although there is a factual dispute whether Mr. Blackburn heard *a* stairstep creak earlier in the day, it is not a material question of fact. There is no evidence that he heard a creak from the stairstep that gave way under plaintiff. Plaintiff stated in her affidavit that Mr. Blackburn told her he had heard "one of the steps at the top of the stairs creak" earlier that same day. Assuming the stair did so creak, it does not help plaintiff's case. If a reasonable inspection of the stairway is required by the creak, it would not have disclosed the hidden defect that plaintiff contends caused her fall. The stairs were completely wrapped in carpet, preventing defendants from seeing the manner of construction of the stairsteps and their condition. Although defendants made no formal inspection of the stairway, they did use it and observe it daily. Defendants had never observed any defects or indications of any possible defects in the stairs.

Frissell v. Frissell

The mere existence of a condition which causes an injury is not negligence per se, and the occurrence of the injury does not raise a presumption of negligence. *Spell v. Contractors*, 261 N.C. 589, 135 S.E. 2d 544 (1964). Plaintiff has the burden to prove a breach of duty by defendants, and in this case must show that defendants knew of the defect in the stairway that caused her injury, or that they could have discovered it by the exercise of ordinary care. *Orr v. Rumbough, supra*. Plaintiff has failed so to do. The evidence before the trial court is insufficient to show that a reasonable inspection would have disclosed the hidden defect which caused plaintiff's fall. *Spell v. Smith-Douglas Co., supra*. The evidence and materials before the trial court would have required a directed verdict for defendants at trial. The entry of summary judgment for defendants was proper. *Kessing v. Mortgage Corp.*, 278 N.C. 523, 180 S.E. 2d 823 (1971); *Pridgen v. Hughes, supra*.

Affirmed.

Judges WEBB and WELLS concur.

HARRY M. FRISSELL v. ELEANOR SUSAN LINDLEY FRISSELL

No. 8010DC37

(Filed 3 June 1980)

Jury § 1.3; Rules of Civil Procedure § 38– permanent alimony – jury trial – waiver by failure to appear

   In addition to the waiver of right to jury trial established by G.S. 1A-1, Rules 38(d) and 39(a), a party may waive his right to a jury trial by failing to appear at trial. Therefore, plaintiff waived his right to a jury trial in a hearing on permanent alimony by his failure to appear at the hearing either personally or by counsel. The decision of *Heidler v. Heidler*, 42 N.C. App. 481, is overruled insofar as it is inconsistent with this opinion.

APPEAL by plaintiff from *Parker, John H., Judge*. Order entered 27 August 1979 in District Court, WAKE County. Heard in the Court of Appeals 16 May 1980.

On 13 March 1973 plaintiff began this action for absolute divorce on the grounds of one year's separation. Plaintiff alleged he was a resident of Wake County, North Carolina, and that defendant was a resident of Pennsylvania. Plaintiff did not request a jury trial in his complaint or reply.

Defendant answered, alleged a counterclaim for alimony without divorce, and requested a jury trial. On 16 June 1975, after hearing with both plaintiff and defendant represented by counsel, an order was entered finding facts, making conclusions of law, and ordering plaintiff to pay alimony pendente lite for the benefit of defendant. Thereafter, on 7 November 1975, defendant filed a motion for a contempt show cause order against plaintiff. A copy of this motion was served upon plaintiff's then attorney, Philip O. Redwine, of Raleigh, North Carolina. This motion was allowed the same date and plaintiff was ordered to appear on 9 December 1975 and show cause why he should not be punished for contempt for failing to comply with the alimony pendente lite order.

Meanwhile, the cause had been placed upon the district court trial calendar for Tuesday, 9 December 1975, for hearing on the question of permanent alimony. Defendant's counsel wrote plaintiff's counsel on 27 October 1975, advising him that the case was so calendared. On 30 October 1975, plaintiff's counsel, Mr. Redwine, wrote plaintiff notifying him that his case was set for 9 December 1975 on the question of permanent alimony. On 7 November 1975 both plaintiff and his counsel were again notified that the case was still scheduled for 9 December 1975. On 19 November 1975, plaintiff wrote Honorable Stafford G. Bullock, District Court Judge, acknowledging the receipt of a court order for his appearance at the 9 December 1975 contempt hearing. He also stated his work in Japan was more important to him than "being in Court in Raleigh, N.C. 9 Dec. 1975."

On 2 December 1975, Mr. Redwine filed a motion to be allowed to withdraw as counsel for plaintiff. This motion was allowed prior to the permanent alimony hearing. On 31 December 1975, an order (dated 29 December 1975) was filed, awarding defendant permanent alimony. This order recited that the alimony hearing was heard at the 9 December 1975 term of Wake

County District Court. The hearing was conducted by the court without a jury. Although defendant's attorney was present and participated in the hearing, neither plaintiff nor counsel for him appeared. On 31 December 1975 the court adjudicated plaintiff was in contempt for failing to comply with the 16 June 1975 alimony pendente lite order.

On 25 June 1979, plaintiff filed a motion seeking to vacate the permanent alimony order filed 31 December 1975, contending the court erred in holding the proceeding without a jury. By order of 27 August 1979, the district court denied plaintiff's motion to vacate the alimony order, and plaintiff appeals to this Court.

Ward and Smith, by J. Randall Hiner, for plaintiff appellant.

Broughton, Wilkins & Crampton, by Charles P. Wilkins and H. Julian Philpott, Jr., for defendant appellee.

MARTIN (Harry C.), Judge.

The question raised on this appeal is whether plaintiff waived his right to a jury trial on the issue of permanent alimony. The district court, in its order denying plaintiff's motion to vacate the permanent alimony order, concluded as a matter of law that plaintiff had waived his right to a jury trial by his failure to appear, either personally or by counsel, when the issue of permanent alimony was decided by the district court.

Plaintiff insists there was no waiver of jury trial and relies upon *Heidler v. Heidler*, 42 N.C. App. 481, 256 S.E. 2d 833 (1979). In *Heidler*, the Court, of which this writer was a member of the panel, was faced with facts similar to those of the case at bar. Plaintiff husband brought an action for absolute divorce and his wife counterclaimed for alimony. Plaintiff was a resident of North Carolina; defendant lived in Illinois. Plaintiff did not request a jury trial in either his complaint or reply; however, defendant did ask for a jury trial in her answer. Plaintiff's counsel requested to withdraw as attorney for plaintiff and was allowed to do so. Thereafter the case came on for hearing with defendant and her counsel present but plaintiff not appearing either in person or by counsel. Defendant waived her right to jury trial; the court heard the case without a jury and entered judgment awarding defendant permanent alimony. Plaintiff Heidler appealed, contending he was deprived of jury trial as he had not given his consent to the withdrawal of defendant's jury trial demand as required by N.C.G.S. 1A-1, Rule 38(d). The Court held that N.C.G.S. 1A-1, Rules 38(d) and 39(a), "do not provide that failure to appear at the trial constitutes consent to a withdrawal of a valid jury trial demand . . . ." *Id.* at 486, 256 S.E. 2d at 835.

This Court in *Heidler* was correct in its holding with respect to Rules 38(d) and 39(a). However, the Court did not consider grounds for the waiver of right to jury trial outside the Rules of Civil Procedure.

The Rules of Civil Procedure are not the exclusive authority on the question of waiver of right to jury trial. The Rules became effective 1 January 1970 and apply to all actions pending on that date. 1969 N.C. Sess. Laws ch. 803, § 1. *Sykes v. Belk*, 278 N.C. 106, 179 S.E. 2d 439 (1971), was tried at the 27 August 1970 session of Superior Court of Mecklenburg County. In *Sykes*, the plaintiffs contended the trial court erred in denying their timely motion for jury trial. In discussing waiver of jury trial, the Court stated:

> North Carolina Constitution, Art. I, § 19, guarantees to every person the "sacred and inviolable" right to demand a jury trial of issues of fact arising in all controversies at law respecting property.
>
> A party may waive his right to jury trial by (1) failing to appear at the trial, (2) by written consent filed with the clerk, (3) by oral consent entered in the minutes of the court, (4) by failing to demand a jury trial pursuant to G.S. 1A-1, Rule 38(b). Art. IV, § 12, North Carolina Constitution; *Driller Co. v. Worth*, 117 N.C. 515, 23 S.E. 427.

Id. at 123, 179 S.E. 2d at 449. By its reference to Rule 38(b), the Court obviously was aware of the provisions of the Rules concerning jury trial waiver, and by its holding did not limit itself to the provisions of the Rules. In *Ervin Co. v. Hunt*, 26 N.C. App. 755, 217 S.E. 2d 93, *cert. denied*, 288 N.C. 511, 219 S.E. 2d 346 (1975), the Court of Appeals ruled that a party could waive trial by jury by failing to appear at trial, relying upon *Sykes.*

We hold that in addition to the waiver of right to jury trial as established by N.C.G.S. 1A-1, Rules 38(d) and 39(a), as set forth in *Heidler*, a party may waive his right to jury trial by failing to appear at trial. *Sykes v. Belk, supra.* Insofar as *Heidler* is inconsistent with this opinion, it is expressly overruled. Chief Judge Morris, Judges Parker and Martin (Harry C.), who constituted the Court in *Heidler*, join and concur in this holding.

Plaintiff Frissell, after proper notice, failed to appear at the 9 December 1975 hearing for permanent alimony. He thereby waived his right to trial by jury. With this holding we do not discuss the contention of laches on the part of plaintiff.

The trial court did not err in denying plaintiff's motion to vacate the order for permanent alimony.

Affirmed.

Judges WEBB and WELLS concur.

GENERAL ELECTRIC COMPANY, A NEW YORK CORPORATION v. LOCAL 182 INTERNATIONAL UNION OF ELECTRICAL, RADIO AND MACHINE WORKERS, INTERNATIONAL UNION OF ELECTRICAL, RADIO AND MACHINE WORKERS, CHARLES BUFF AND EARL WHITE

No. 7925SC1064

(Filed 3 June 1980)

1. **Master and Servant § 17.1– enjoining union's mass picketing and other strike activities – jurisdiction of State courts**

   The courts of this State had jurisdiction of an action to enjoin defendant union from mass picketing at plaintiff's plant and to prohibit the union from interfering with ingress and egress at the plant, assaulting or intimidating workers, blocking public or private roads, damaging motor vehicles entering or leaving plaintiff's plant and resisting law enforcement officers in the lawful discharge of their duties.

2. **Master and Servant § 17– permanent injunction against union two years after strike ended**

 The trial court erred in entering a permanent injunction prohibiting defendant union from mass picketing at plaintiff's plant, limiting the number of pickets to six, and prohibiting the union from interfering with ingress and egress at the plant, assaulting or intimidating workers, blocking roads and interfering with police officers in the lawful discharge of their duties where the permanent injunction was entered almost two years after the settlement of the strike which gave rise to the action for an injunction and the controversy resulting in the court's prior temporary restraining order had ceased to exist.

APPEAL by defendants from *Griffin, Judge.* Judgment entered 29 June 1979 in Superior Court, CATAWBA County. Heard in the Court of Appeals 24 April 1980.

This appeal arises from the granting of a permanent injunction sought by plaintiff which enjoins defendants from engaging in certain activities. Plaintiff operates a plant in Hickory, North Carolina, where some of its employees are members of the defendant union. The plant is located approximately 1425 feet down an access road off Fairgrove Church Road. Approximately one quarter mile to the north on Fairgrove Church Road is the Catawba Memorial Hospital. To the south, the road goes to major U.S. highways (U.S. 64 and U.S. 70) and crosses an interstate (I 40), to which it has access.

On 24 October 1977, at approximately 10:00 p.m., a strike was called by the defendant union against plaintiff because of a grievance over welding job classifications. Plaintiff was given notice of the strike pursuant to the collective bargaining agreement between the parties. A picket line was set up outside the plant at the intersection of Fairgrove Church Road and the plant's access road. Up to seventy-nine pickets marched in an elliptical formation, creating a double line at the entrance of the access road into Fairgrove Church Road. An equal number of people were crossing back and forth to the picket line from the other side of Fairgrove Church Road. A state road crew was also working in the intersection.

At rush hour on the morning of the strike, the area was clogged by considerable traffic congestion. Access to plaintiff's plant was effectively impeded and employees of the nearby hospital were late for work that morning. This was also the same route emergency vehicles would use. The picketers, as well as impeding the flow of traffic, engaged in other illegal and violent acts. They were reported to have damaged vehicles entering the plant, thrown rocks and threatened nonunion employees.

On 25 October, plaintiff filed a complaint in Superior Court against the union, its president and its vice president. A temporary restraining order was obtained at 2:55 p.m. that day from Judge William T. Grist which prevented defendants from mass picketing and limited the number of pickets to six or fewer. They were not to picket in the road. The temporary restraining order prohibited the union from interfering with ingress and egress at the plant, assaulting or intimidating workers, blocking public or private roads, damaging motor vehicles entering or leaving plaintiff's plant and resisting law enforcement officers in the lawful discharge of their duties. A hearing was held before Superior Court Judge George M. Fountain on 3 November 1977, at which time the temporary restraining order was continued in effect as a preliminary injunction. The strike ended on 28 October.

The union, its president and its vice president filed motions for summary judgment which were denied on 10 August 1978 by Superior Court Judge Sam J. Ervin III, except as to defendant Charles Buff who was no longer an officer of the union. Superior Court Judge Kenneth A. Griffin tried the case on its merits and, after hearing evidence from both sides, found for plaintiff. The preliminary injunction was continued as a permanent injunction by order of the trial court on 29 June 1979. The defendants and others acting in concert with them were permanently restrained and enjoined in the following manner:

1. From preventing or attempting to prevent by mass picketing, violence, intimidation or coercion any person or

persons from freely and peacefully entering or leaving the GE plant.

2. In the event defendants wish to picket the GE plant they shall use not more than six walking pickets at any one time; pickets may walk only on the shoulders of that portion of the GE access road from its intersection with Fairgrove Church Road to the fence at the plant entrance and on the outside of the guard rails of the access road. Replacement pickets shall not be replaced at intervals of less than two hours except in an emergency situation. One person but no more may be stationed at or near the plant gate for the purpose of observing and maintaining a front picket line or giving information or other assistance to pickets.

3. Persons working, seeking to work, doing business with or seeking to do business with GE at this plant shall not be assaulted or intimidated in any way.

4. Vehicles seeking to enter or leave the GE plant by means of the access road into Fairgrove Church Road shall not be blocked or impeded in any manner and shall not be damaged in any way.

5. There shall be no resistance or other interference with state or county law enforcement officers in the lawful discharge of their duties in maintaining peace and order in the event of another strike.

6. Defendants shall not aid, procure or cause to be done any act which they are hereby restrained or enjoined from doing themselves.

Defendants appealed the granting of this permanent injunction.

Weinstein, Sturges, Odom, Bigger, Jonas and Campbell, by William W. Sturges and Hugh B. Campbell, Jr., for plaintiff appellee.

Judith E. Kincaid, for defendant appellants.

General Electric Co. v. Union

VAUGHN, Judge.

[1] At the outset, this Court is faced with the question of whether our State courts have jurisdiction over the subject matter of this action or whether jurisdiction is preempted by the National Labor Relations Act of 1935, 29 USC § 151 *et seq.*, and vested in the National Labor Relations Board. The federal labor relations statutes do not deprive a state of the power to enjoin mass picketing or picketing involving violence, notwithstanding that interstate commerce is affected by the picketing. *Youngdahl v. Rainfair*, 355 U.S. 131, 2 L. Ed. 2d 151, 78 S. Ct. 206 (1957); *United A.A. & A.I.W. v. Wisconsin Employment Relations Board*, 351 U.S. 266, 100 L. Ed. 1162, 76 S. Ct. 794 (1956); *Allen-Bradley Local v. Wisconsin Employment Relations Board*, 315 U.S. 740, 86 L. Ed. 1154, 62 S. Ct. 820 (1942). The State is not preempted by the National Labor Relations Act from exercising its historic powers of maintaining peace and order within its jurisdiction and protecting its citizens in the free, rightful and safe use of the public roads and highways. The courts of a state cannot regulate orderly and peaceful picketing. But, where picketing results in heavy traffic congestion, damage to property and threats of physical violence as occurred in this case, the State courts have the power to enforce the laws of this State which protect the public welfare and to enjoin acts of violence and civil disobedience.

> [O]rderly and peaceful picketing to obtain a lawful result is but the exercise of constitutional rights and cannot be prohibited; but when picketing, for a lawful purpose, is such as to disturb the public peace, it can and has repeatedly been enjoined or otherwise punished. But the power of a court of equity to enjoin is not exhausted merely because violence is not present .... "Wrongful acts which may also be criminal, but which threaten injury to private property rights may invoke the aid of equity to prevent irreparable loss."

Aircraft Co. v. Union, 247 N.C. 620, 626, 101 S.E. 2d 800, 805 (1958) (citations omitted). The trial court and consequently this Court has jurisdiction in this case of threatened and actual violence where the picketing could not be characterized as peaceful. The clause in the temporary restraining order and preliminary injunction which limited the number of pickets, restricted their placement and provided the method for their replacement was a valid order for the protection of the public safety of the working employees and those citizens traveling upon the public highways. The other enjoined acts were criminal acts and were appropriate matters of state jurisdiction and not the National Labor Relations Board.

[2] We now turn to whether it was appropriate for the trial court to enter a permanent injunction in this case. We hold this was not an appropriate circumstance for the issuance of a permanent injunction.

In reversing the entry of a permanent injunction, our Supreme Court has said, "[t]he injunction is an extraordinary remedy and will not be granted except in cases where adequate relief cannot be had without it." *Smith v. Rockingham*, 268 N.C. 697, 699-700, 151 S.E. 2d 568, 570 (1966). Where permanent injunction is the sole relief sought and the evidence at the final hearing fails to make out a cause of action, the action should be dismissed. *Greene Co. v. Kelley*, 261 N.C. 166, 134 S.E. 2d 166 (1964).

In this case, a cause of action for a permanent injunction was not established. The order was entered almost two years after the strike had been settled and the controversy resulting in the temporary restraining order had ceased to exist. The strike and picketing having ended, the subject matter of the lawsuit no longer existed. A trial court sitting in equity has no powers to issue an injunction when only abstract rights are involved. Plaintiff demonstrated no then existing acts by defendants justifying the permanent injunction. The record indicates there was a similar strike at plaintiff's Hickory plant in late 1969 and early 1970 for which a preliminary injunction was obtained. We also note that the strike in question began on 24 October at about 10:00 p.m. and by 2:55 p.m. the very next day, plaintiffs had a temporary restraining order. Strikes against plaintiff by defendant appear from the record to be frequent but not every strike is accompanied by picketing. The plant experiences a one percent turnover in its labor force every month and the union office holders frequently change. Both the individual defendants are no longer union officers. With these constant changes, we do not discern the need for such prohibitive restrictions to be permanently placed upon defendants. Plaintiff's injunctive remedy arises only as each cause of action arises, *i.e.*, each time violent picketing or irreparable injury to persons and property appears likely or actually occurs. The circumstances will be different each time. The trial court should not have entered a permanent injunction. The action should have been dismissed.

Reversed and remanded.

Judges CLARK and MARTIN (Harry C.) concur.

STEVEN M. FOUST v. CITY OF GREENSBORO

No. 7918SC1094

(Filed 3 June 1980)

Administrative Law § 8; Appeal and Error § 21– discharged fire department employee – departmental hearing not judicial or quasi-judicial – no review

The trial court did not err in ruling that it did not have jurisdiction over the subject matter of this action by a discharged fire department employee on the ground that executive actions in personnel matters are not appealable on a writ of certiorari to the courts, and there was no merit to petitioner's contention that a departmental hearing conducted by the fire department was a judicial or quasi-judicial function which would permit review by certiorari.

APPEAL by petitioner from *Albright, Judge.* Order entered 7 September 1979 in Superior Court, GUILFORD County. Heard in the Court of Appeals 13 May 1980.

This is an appeal from an order dismissing a petition for a writ of certiorari pursuant to Rule 12(b). The petitioner, Steven M. Foust, was terminated from employment by R. Powell, Chief of the Greensboro Fire Department, on or about 26 April 1979. The termination was the result of petitioner's violation of the Greensboro Fire Department Rules, Regulations, Practices, and Procedures arising out of an incident occurring on 5 March

1979. On that day Chief Reese Kent received a telephone call from an employee of Catherine's Stout Shop complaining that a yellow fire department vehicle was parked behind the building; that a man and woman were engaged in sexual intercourse in an adjacent car; and that upon completion of the act, the man drove away in the fire department vehicle. A check of the license number revealed the vehicle belonged to petitioner. Petitioner denied participation in the incident, and Chief Powell requested the Internal Affairs Division of the Police Department to investigate the matter. As a result of the investigation, petitioner was charged with the violation referred to above, and in addition, another charge of insubordination.

The Departmental Hearing Board of the Fire Department conducted an inquiry into the violations on 26 April 1979, and found that the petitioner had committed the violations as charged, including the insubordination charge.

Chief Powell, after considering the findings of the Hearing Board and other circumstances surrounding the case, discharged the petitioner. The petitioner appealed to the public safety director who upheld the chief's decision. Petitioner then appealed the decision to the city manager who found him guilty of the offenses charged except for the insubordination charge. The city manager upheld the decision of the fire chief in terminating the petitioner's employment with the city.

The petition for a writ of certiorari to the superior court was dismissed on motion of respondent pursuant to Rule 12(b) of the North Carolina Rules of Civil Procedure for lack of jurisdiction on the grounds that executive actions in personnel matters are not appealable on a writ of certiorari to the courts. Petitioner appealed.

Ben D. Haines for petitioner appellant.

Linda K. Avery, Assistant City Attorney, for respondent appellee.

HILL, Judge.

Petitioner contends the trial judge erred in ruling that he did not have jurisdiction over the subject matter of this action and in dismissing the proceeding. We do not agree.

Petitioner than cites from *In Re Burris*, 261, N.C. 450, 453, 130, 59 S.E. 2d 589 (1950), which states that:

> G.S. 1-269 expressly stipulates that 'writs of *certiorari* . . . are authorized as heretofore in use.' It is well settled in this jurisdiction that *certiorari* is the appropriate process to review the proceedings of inferior courts and of bodies and officers exercising judicial or *quasi*-judicial functions in cases when no appeal is provided by law. (Citations omitted.)

Petitioner then refers to the record of the departmental hearing held 26 April 1979, at which time the petitioner and his attorney were present. The record states:

> [T]his hearing is being held in accordance with the Rules, Regulations, Practices and Procedures of the Greensboro Fire Department as set out in Article 24, Sections 13 and 14.
>
> This Hearing is an administrative hearing to serve an investigative as well as *adjudicatory* function, and as such, is not bound by strict rules of evidence applicable to a criminal or civil trial. (Emphasis added.)

Relying on the record of the hearing, together with the order of procedure before the board at the hearing, together with the orderly review of the findings of the board thereafter, petitioner contends that the departmental hearing constituted a judicial or quasi-judicial board.

Petitioner then cites from *In Re Burris*, 261, N.C. 450, 453, 135 S.E. 2d 27 (1964), as follows:

> [I]t is said in McQuillin, Municipal Corporations, section 12.267, page 397, et seq.:

'In most jurisdictions *certiorari* to review removal proceedings is sanctioned. *The general rule is that if the act of removal is executive it is not reviewable on certiorari, but if it is on a hearing and formal findings, it is so reviewable.* Stated in another way, the writ may be invoked only to review acts which are clearly judicial or *quasi*-judicial.' (Emphasis added.)

A careful reading of the record nowhere reveals any evidence that the Rules, Regulations, Practices and Procedures of the Greensboro Fire Department are ordinances of the city, or that they are in any way binding. In fact, it would appear that they are not binding in any manner, for the city manager declined to accept a finding that the petitioner was insubordinate. Nowhere do we find that the hearing board acted in any capacity other than as an investigative board. The board made no recommendation as to disciplinary action. Neither did it take any such action.

The fire chief dismissed the petitioner. The public safety director and city manager upheld the action of dismissal by the fire chief — although the manager did not concur in the finding of insurbordination by the board. It would appear that if the city manager could eliminate the hearing board's finding of insubordination, he could eliminate all the findings. This power tends to confirm our conclusion that the authority of the hearing board is limited to that of an investigative body alone. The hearing board cannot simply assume adjudicatory functions as it appears to have done.

The general rule in North Carolina is that, nothing else appearing, a contract of employment is terminable at the will of either party. *Still v. Lance,* 279 N.C. 254, 259, 182 S.E. 2d 403 (1971). Nevertheless, the Supreme Court of the United States in Board of *Regents v. Roth,* 408 U.S. 564, 33 L.Ed. 2d 548, 92 S. Ct. 2701 (1972), and *Bishop v. Wood,* 426 U.S. 341, 48 L.Ed. 2d 684, 96 S.Ct. 2074 (1976), has determined that when a liberty interest or a property right exists, the right to some kind of hearing prior to discharge is paramount.

Certainly, there is no liberty interest involved here. Further, in this case nothing rebuts the fact that the contract of employment was terminable at the will of either party. If the contract is terminable at will, there is no vested right to future employment, and no property right exists. Certainly, courts would recognize the right to recover for services rendered to the date of discharge, but that is not the question here.

"In the absence of any claim that the public employer was motivated by a desire to curtail or to penalize the exercise of an employee's constitutionally protected rights, we must presume that official action was regular and, if erroneous, can best be corrected in other ways." *Bishop v. Wood, supra,* at p. 350.

The decision of the trial judge is

Affirmed.

Judges MARTIN (Robert M.) and ARNOLD concur.

———

IN THE MATTER OF: SUE S. CLARK
POST OFFICE BOX 502, BOONE, NORTH CAROLINA 28607
SS No. 237-50-4231, APPELLEE
AND
DEPARTMENT OF SOCIAL SERVICES
COURTHOUSE ANNEX, BOONE, NORTH CAROLINA 28607
AND
EMPLOYMENT SECURITY COMMISSION OF NORTH CAROLINA
POST OFFICE BOX 25903, RALEIGH, NORTH CAROLINA 27611, APPELLANTS

No. 7924SC932

(Filed 3 June 1980)

Master and Servant § 108– unemployment compensation – resignation from work – good cause attributable to employer

Claimant voluntarily left work as a county social worker for good cause attributable to her employer and was thus entitled to unemployment compensation where she resigned her position because she was instructed by her supervisor to initiate custody proceedings for certain children after she had secured voluntary, revocable Board Home Agreements from the mothers to place their children in the temporary custody of others upon her assurances to the mothers that the children would be returned to the mothers upon request, and because she felt that the actions she was required to take violated the ethical standards of her profession.

APPEAL by the Department of Social Services and the Employment Security Commission from *Johnson (Clifton E.)*, *Judge*. Judgment entered 3 July 1979 in Superior Court, WATAUGA County. Heard in the Court of Appeals 27 March 1980.

Claimant, a former social worker with the Watauga County Department of Social Services, filed a claim with the Employment Security Commission (Commission) to collect unemployment compensation. The Commission denied claimant's claim for compensation stating that claimant was disqualified from receiving unemployment insurance benefits, because she had left her last job voluntarily and without good cause attributable to her employer.

The Commission's denial of compensation was based on the following findings of fact:

"3. On June 5, 1978, the claimant submitted a letter of resignation to the director of the Department of Social Services, stating that she was resigning her position because, in her opinion, she was being required to act in a manner not consistent with the ethical standards of her profession.

. . . .

5. On May 1, 1978, the claimant's work came under a new supervisor. In the cases of two clients, cases in which the claimant was the assigned social worker, the claimant and the new supervisor disagreed over how the cases should be handled. In both cases, the claimant had induced the parties involved to sign 'boarding home agreements,' to place their children in the temporary care of other people. These agreements are voluntary and provide for children to be placed in foster homes during periods when the parent is incapacitated or otherwise unable to care for them. These agreements are severable at will by the parents.

6. In both of these cases, after having secured these agreements, the claimant's supervisor and the Department director reached the conclusion that the parents involved should not be allowed to regain custody of their children. In at least one of the cases, the claimant was asked to initiate immediate custody proceedings to remove the children in question from their parents' care. These decisions were discussed at meetings during which the claimant, her supervisor, and the director of the Department were present and given an opportunity to voice their opinions.

7. The claimant disagreed with these decisions, although she did not indicate her disagreements to her supervisor during the above mentioned discussions. The claimant quit her job on the basis of these two cases and the basis of her understanding of the above-cited ethical standard."

Claimant appealed the Commission's decision to the Superior Court for judicial review. Judge Johnson entered a judgment wherein he found that: (1) there was no evidence to support the Commission's finding that claimant had not indicated her disagreements with her employer's actions; and (2) the precipitating causes of claimant's resignation were (a) her being ordered to prepare and sign a petition for a temporary custody order on certain children after she, as an agent of the employer and at the employer's direction, had secured a voluntary, revocable Boarding Home Agreement from the mother based upon her assurances to the mother that the children could and would be returned to the mother upon request, and (b) her feelings that the actions she was required to take violated her ethical standards and those of her profession.

Additional findings made by Judge Johnson are not dispositive of this appeal.

Based on the foregoing findings, Judge Johnson reversed and remanded the Commission's decision. The Commission and the Watauga County Department of Social Services appealed.

V. Henry Gransee, Jr., for petitioner appellant, Employment Security Commission of North Carolina.

Stacy C. Eggers III, for petitioner appellant, Watauga County Department of Social Services.

Isenhower & Long, by Samuel H. Long III, for respondent appellee.

ERWIN, Judge.

The question which will dispose of this appeal is whether the claimant voluntarily left work because of good cause attributable to her employer. We hold that she did.

G.S. 96-14(1) disqualifies an individual who has voluntarily left his work, *i.e.*, quit his job, without *good cause attributable to the employer.*

"Good cause" is a reason which would be deemed by reasonable men and women valid and not indicative of an unwillingness to work. *In re Watson*, 273 N.C. 629, 161 S.E. 2d 1 (1968). If a claimant leaves his work voluntarily, but for good cause attributable to the employer, then a claimant is not disqualifed from receiving unemployment benefits under the Employment Security Commission Law. Thus, to determine claimant's entitlement, we must examine her reason for leaving her work.

The Commission found that claimant had induced two clients to sign Boarding Home Agreements to place their children in the temporary care of other people. In the first case, the record indicates that the mother had fled from home with her five minor children because of her husband's drinking. At the time of flight, the mother was ill to the point that she was unable to take care of her children. Claimant had visited the mother in her hospital room and had secured the boarding agreement only upon the assurance that the mother would be able to re-obtain the children and that the agreement was merely a contract to arrange for care for the children while she was incapacitated and unable to care for them.

In the second case, claimant had procured the agreement of a mother, who was subject to psychological breakdowns, for temporary foster care of the mother's child while the mother was in the hospital. Again, this procurement was obtained after assurances that the child could be re-obtained when the mother got out of the hospital.

In both cases, claimant was instructed to initiate custody proceedings by her supervisor, even though she informed the supervisor of the Boarding Home Agreements and her assurances that custody proceedings would not be initiated as a means of obtaining them. Entry of the agreements was in accordance with previous departmental policy. Claimant also informed her supervisor that the children were in good health.

Based upon the foregoing incidents, claimant felt that she could no longer ethically continue her employment with her employer and tendered her resignation.

Our objective view of the foregoing circumstances leads us to believe, and we so hold, that claimant's reason for leaving her work was one which would be deemed by reasonable men and women to be valid and not indicative of an unwillingness to work. Claimant's resignation was clearly attributable to her employer, and the Commission's own findings of fact support this conclusion.

Appellants' argument that there is evidence to support the Commission's finding that claimant failed to try to resolve the conflict, even if true, would not aid them in this appeal. In *In re Werner*, 44 N.C. App. 723, 263 S.E. 2d 4 (1980), we rejected this same argument in the context of failure to exhaust the employer's grievance machinery.

The judgment entered below is

Affirmed.

Judges HEDRICK and ARNOLD concur.

STATE OF NORTH CAROLINA v. LORENZO MACKINS

No. 8026SC61

(Filed 3 June 1980)

1. Constitutional Law § 53– delay in trial caused by defendant – no denial of speedy trial

Defendant was not denied his right to a speedy trial where he was charged on 28 June 1978 and tried in September 1979, since the case was continued only once on the motion of the State, and defendant moved to continue the case twice, waiving his right to dismiss for failure to grant a speedy trial when he made his second motion to continue.

2. Criminal Law § 66.1– identification testimony – opportunity for observation

Identification testimony of an assault victim was admissible where the victim was shot while he was in an automobile parked in the street; he testified that a street light and a light in the house from which the shots came were on; and though the record did not show how close the victim was to the person in the house, he was within the range of a .16 gauge shotgun.

3. Searches and Seizures § 10– search of house without warrant – exigent circumstances

The fact that officers were standing under a light on a porch of a house from which a short time previously two shots had been fired, killing one person and seriously wounding another, was such an exigent circumstance that the officers were justified in entering the home and searching it to make sure no one else, including the officers, would be shot; and since the officers saw a shotgun in the house in plain view, evidence in regard to the gun was admissible.

APPEAL by defendant from *Howell, Judge.* Judgment entered 15 September 1979 in Superior Court, MECKLENBURG County. Heard in the Court of Appeals 21 May 1980.

Defendant was tried on bills of indictment for murder and assault with a deadly weapon with intent to kill inflicting serious injury. The evidence showed that on 27 June 1978, Tommy Lisenby was riding in an automobile with Ruth Wilson. Ms. Wilson was in the process of stopping the automobile so that Mr. Lisenby could get out when Mr. Lisenby heard what sounded as if it were the firing of a shotgun. He looked toward the house in front of which the automobile was coming to a stop. He testified the street light and the light in the house were on, and he was able to identify the defendant as the man who was standing at the window. As Mr. Lisenby looked at the man in the window, he saw the flash of a gun, and he was shot. Mr. Lisenby also noticed that Ms. Wilson was slumped in her seat and was bleeding. He was able to leave the scene by pushing Ms. Wilson's foot on the accelerator. After the automobile had moved approximately one block, he stopped it and went into the house of a friend for help. The friend called the police who arrived a few minutes later. Ms. Wilson died.

Mr. Lisenby pointed out to the officers the house from which the shots had come and they surrounded the house. The officers called on the occupants of the house to come outside, and after they had been on the scene approximately one hour, the defendant came out of the house. As he was standing on the front porch, he was handcuffed by the officers. One of the officers stated that they "were sitting ducks" standing on the porch under the light, and the officers went inside the house and searched it. They found a .16-gauge shotgun propped against the wall. The defendant made a motion to suppress any evidence as to what the officers found after they entered the house. The court held a *voir dire* hearing out of the presence of the jury. The court found facts based on the evidence and concluded that the officers "had reasonable grounds to believe at the time [they] entered the house on Rosada Drive, that there might be danger to officers or other persons as a result of information ..." they had received. The court allowed the testimony into evidence that the officers found a .16-gauge shotgun in the house.

The defendant was convicted of second degree murder and assault with a deadly weapon with intent to kill inflicting serious injury. From a sentence imposed, the defendant appealed.

Attorney General Edmisten, by Associate Attorney J. Chris Prather, for the State.

Robert M. Talford and Charles V. Bell for defendant appellant.

WEBB, Judge.

[1] The defendant's first assignment of error is to the court's failure to dismiss because the defendant was denied a speedy trial. Factors to be considered in determining whether a criminal action should be dismissed for failure to grant the defendant a speedy trial are: (1) the length of the delay; (2) the reason for the delay; (3) prejudice to the defendant; and (4) waiver by the defendant. *See State v. Brown*, 282 N.C. 117, 191 S.E. 2d 659 (1972). In the case sub judice, defendant was charged on 28 June 1978. In October 1978, defendant became disenchanted with his attorneys, and they moved to withdraw. In December 1978, defendant made a motion to have his bond reduced which was allowed. In January 1979, defendant moved for a continuance, which motion was granted. In March 1979, defendant had retained new counsel and made a motion to continue the case, waiving his right to dismiss for failure to grant a speedy trial. The case was set for trial in August 1979 and was continued on motion of the State because one of its witnesses was on vacation. The case was tried in September 1979. In the case sub judice, it appears that the case was continued only once on the motion of the State. We hold it was not error to deny the defendant's motion to dismiss for failure to grant a speedy trial.

[2] The defendant's second assignment of error is to the court's allowing the identification testimony of Tommy Lisenby. Defendant relies on *State v. Miller*, 270 N.C. 726, 154 S.E. 2d 902 (1967). In *Miller*, our Supreme Court held that identification testimony should have been excluded as having no probative force when all the evidence showed the witness attempted to identify a person he had observed from a distance of 286 feet at night. In this case, Mr. Lisenby testified a street light and a light in the house were on. The record does not disclose how close Mr. Lisenby was to the person in the house, but he was within range of a .16-gauge shotgun. We believe *State v. Miller, supra*, is distinguishable from the case sub judice. We hold the identification testimony of Mr. Lisenby was properly admitted into evidence.

[3] Defendant also assigns as error the admission of the testimony that the officers found the shotgun in the house. The defendant contends the shotgun was the fruit of an illegal

search and should have been excluded under *Payton v. New York*, U.S., 100 S.Ct. 1371, 63 L.Ed. 2d 639 (1980). *Payton* held that an entry into a home to make a routine arrest for a felony without a warrant violates the Fourth Amendment to the United States Consitution, made applicable to the states by the Fourteenth Amendment. In that case the Supreme Court struck down a New York statute, very similar to G.S. 15A-401(b) and (e), allowing entry into homes without a warrant to make felony arrests. *Payton* pointed out that there were no exigent circumstances in that case justifying an entry without a warrant. In the case sub judice, the officers did not enter to make an arrest. We hold there were exigent circumstances justifying entry. The officers were standing under a light on a porch of a house from which a short time previously two shots had been fired, killing one person and seriously wounding another. We hold this was such an exigent circumstance that the officers were justified in entering the home and searching it to make sure no one else, including the officers, would be shot. As they saw the shotgun in plain view, evidence in regard to the shotgun was admissible.

The defendant also assigns as error the admission into evidence of certain pictures. We hold these were properly admitted to illustrate the testimony of the witnesses.

The defendant's last assignment of error is to the denial of his motion to dismiss both charges. We find no error in the denial of this motion.

No error.

Judges Martin (Harry C.) and Wells concur.

STATE OF NORTH CAROLINA v. JOYCE FREEMAN

No. 8013SC25

(Filed 3 June 1980)

1. Criminal Law § 143.5– probation revocation – no jury trial – quantum of proof – rules of evidence

In a probation revocation hearing, a jury trial is not required, proof of a probation violation need not be beyond a reasonable doubt, and the rules of evidence need not be strictly enforced.

2. **Criminal Law § 143.10– probation revocation – monthly payments – gainful employment**

The evidence supported the court's revocation of defendant's probation for violation of conditions of her probation that she make monthly payments on costs, fines and restitution and that she remain gainfully employed.

APPEAL by defendant from Godwin, Judge. Judgment entered 3 October 1979 in Superior Court, BLADEN County. Heard in the Court of Appeals 15 May 1980.

Defendant was charged with obtaining assistance to which she was not entitled from the Bladen County Department of Social Services. She pled guilty to misdemeanor fraud before District Court Judge J. Wilton Hunt, Sr., who sentenced her to twelve months in prison, suspended for three years on condition that she not violate certain specified conditions of probation. Those conditions of probation were:

(a) cooperate with and truthfully report to the Probation–Parole Officer as directed, and permit the Probation–Parole Officer to visit at his–her home or elsewhere;

(b) remain within the County of Bladen and not change his/her residence without permission of the Probation/Parole Officer;

(c) violate no penal law of any state or of the Federal Government;

(d) remain gainfully employed, or in full-time school status, and support his/her dependents, if any;

(e) pay a fine of $50.00;

(f) pay costs of court of $27.00;

Additional conditions:

State v. Freeman

(g) Become gainfully employed and stop taking assistance from the Department of Social Services.

(h) Make restitution in the amount of $75.00 to reimburse the State for counsel's fees.

(i) Make restitution to the Clerk of Court in the amount of $587.00 to reimburse the Department of Social Services for loss caused by this offense.

(j) Pay fine, costs, restitution and counsel's fees into the office of the Clerk of Superior Court, Elizabethtown, N.C. at the rate of no less than $30.00 per month. A payment of no less than $30.00 is due on or before September 5, 1978 and no less than $30.00 is due on or before the 5th day of each succeeding month thereafter until the total amount due is paid in full.

On 20 April 1979, Probation Officer Thomas F. Adams filed a violation report requesting that defendant's probation be revoked because she had violated condition (j) of her probation by falling into arrears and failing to make her monthly payments to cover the fine, court costs, restitution and counsel fees. On 15 August 1979, Officer Adams filed another violation report requesting that defendant's probation be revoked because she violated conditions (d) and (g) of her probation by not remaining gainfully employed and by taking assistance, some for which she was ineligible, from the Bladen County Department of Social Services.

A hearing on the violation reports was held in District Court on 30 August 1979 where defendant was found to have willfully and without just cause violated the provisions of her probationary judgment. The prior suspended sentence was ordered activated. Defendant appealed to Superior Court and a hearing *de novo* was held before Judge Godwin on 3 October 1979.

The only witnesses at the hearing were the probation officer testifying for the State and defendant testifying in her own behalf. The evidence concerning the violations of conditions (d), (g) and (j) was to the following effect. By condition (j), defendant, beginning on or before 5 September 1978, was to pay into the clerk of court $30.00 on or before the fifth of each month until all costs, fines, counsel fees and restitution were paid in full. Defendant made payments until March or April, 1979. During this period, she also purchased a Pontiac Grand Prix for which she made a $500.00 down payment with $170.00 monthly payments which she made in March and April, 1979. She returned the car to the dealer sometime after April of 1979. As of 3 October 1979, defendant was $100.00 in arrears on her payments pursuant to condition (j) of her probation. Defendant testified that she had put in a few job applications and that she had completed her high school education by obtaining an equivalence degree from the local technical college. She further testified that she was prepared to pay the arrearage as of the date of this hearing. Condition (g) of defendant's probation required that she "[b]ecome gainfully employed and stop taking assistance from the Department of Social Services" and condition (d) required her to "remain gainfully employed, or in full-time school status, and support his–her dependents, if any." From the time defendant was put on probation, she held three consecutive jobs until May of 1979 when she voluntarily quit the job she then held. She remained unemployed from May of 1979 until the time of the revocation of probation hearing in early October of 1979. During this period, she received unemployment compensation at a rate of $49.00 per week. She was also receiving assistance for her two minor children from the Department of Social Services. The Department of Social Services reported to the probation officer that as of August of 1979, defendant had received some assistance to which she was not entitled above and beyond the amount which was for the children. Defendant testified she needed to support her two minor children on her unemployment compensation and the money she received from the Department of Social Services.

The trial court found defendant had violated willfully and without just excuse the three conditions of probation. The probationary sentence was revoked and the suspended sentence was activated. From this judgment, defendant appeals.

Attorney General Edmisten, by Associate Attorney Elaine M. Jessee, for the State.

Moore and Melvin, by David Garrett Wall, for defendant appellant.

VAUGHN, Judge.

We find no error in the revocation of defendant's probation. Defendant presents six assignments of error on the part of the trial court in the revocation of her probation but we need not reach all these assigned errors in upholding the probation revocation by the trial court.

[1] Probation is an act of grace by the State to one convicted of a crime. It is a matter of discretion with the trial court. The matter is not governed by the rules of a criminal trial. Consequently, a jury is not required as defendant contends nor must the proof of violation be beyond a reasonable doubt. *State v. Duncan,* 270 N.C. 241, 154 S.E. 2d 53 (1967). The evidence need be such that reasonably satisfies the trial judge in the exercise of his sound discretion that the defendant has violated a valid condition on which the sentence was suspended. Because of this and also because it is a matter which a judge hears and not a jury, the rules of evidence need not be strictly enforced. *State v. Baines,* 40 N.C. App. 545, 253 S.E. 2d 300 (1979).

> All that is required in a hearing of this character is that the evidence be such as to reasonably satisfy the judge in the exercise of his sound discretion that the defendant has violated a valid condition upon which the sentence was suspended. Judicial discretion implies conscientious judgment, not arbitrary or willful action.
>
> It takes account of the law and the particular circumstances of the case and "is directed by the reason and conscience of the judge to a just result."

State v. Duncan, 270 N.C. at 245, 154 S.E. 2d at 57.

[2] The trial court found defendant to have violated three conditions of her probation. The trial court found that defendant failed to make the monthly payments on the costs, fines and restitution, quit her job and continued to take welfare assistance. All these acts would be in violation of her probation conditions. Any one would have been sufficient grounds to revoke defendant's probation. *State v. Braswell*, 283 N.C. 332, 196 S.E. 2d 185 (1973).

There is plenary evidence that defendant did not make the monthly payments as required as a condition of her probation. Only after six months had elapsed and when faced with possible imposition of the prison sentence did defendant offer to make up arrearage. Defendant did not present any evidence of justifiable excuse for her failure to meet this condition of her probation. Also, there is plenary evidence to support the violation of the condition that defendant become and remain gainfully employed. Defendant did not present evidence of a justifiable excuse for quitting her job. Either one of these above would justify a revocation of probation. There can be no doubt that they were both valid conditions of probation. Consequently, we need not consider in this case whether the condition prohibiting defendant from seeking assistance from the Department of Social Services was a valid condition of probation. *State v. Byrd*, 23 N.C. App. 63, 208 S.E. ed 216 (1974).

Affirmed.

Judges PARKER and ERWIN concur.

ROBERT D. WILLIAMS v. SOUTHERN BELL TELEPHONE AND TELEGRAPH COMPANY

No. 7929SC955

(Filed 3 June 1980)

Easements § 8.3– utility easement – permit executed by life tenant – permit invalid upon tenant's death

Defendant utility was not bound by the terms of a general permit to enter property for the purpose of locating and maintaining its lines since plaintiff's predecessor who executed the permit was only a life tenant, and the permit conveyed to defendant an easement for and during her lifetime and no longer.

APPEAL by defendant from *Ferrell, Judge.* Judgment entered 6 February 1979 in Superior Court, HENDERSON County. Heard in the Court of Appeals 14 April 1980.

This civil action was brought for a judgment declaring the rights and duties of the parties under the provisions of a general permit as to which party should bear the cost of relocating the defendant utility's lines and poles located on land owned by plaintiff. The matter was heard before the trial court upon stipulated facts. The trial court made findings of fact and concluded that defendant was responsible for the cost of relocating the lines, in the sum of $4,316.00.

D. Samuel Neill and William H. Miller for plaintiff appellee.

Roberts, Cogburn & Williams, by James W. Williams, for defendant appellant.

WELLS, Judge.

The operative facts stipulated between the parties were as follows: On 5 February 1929, defendant obtained and duly recorded a general permit to enter property owned in fee by plaintiff's predecessors in interest for the purpose of locating and maintaining its lines. The sole grantor of the permit was Ola H. White, who possessed only a life estate in the land. Ola White died 1 October 1935. The permit contained the following provision, "No Fruit Trees To Be Cut, The Said Company agree [*sic*] and has The right To relocate Said line to conform with future building or Street Improvements." On 4 June 1976, plaintiff became the owner in fee of the disputed lands. At the time this action was brought on 29 April 1977, defendant had maintained its lines and poles on the disputed property for more than forty years.

We note that the facts stipulated fail to disclose the original location of the lines upon the subject lands, their current location, or the cost of relocation. In its judgment, the trial court made the following pertinent findings of fact:

1. That the Defendant, Southern Bell Telephone and Telegraph Company entered onto the lands in question under a grant set forth in the General Permit recorded in Book 186, at Page 564, Henderson County Registry.

2. That the grantor in the permit was vested with only a life estate in the lands in question.

* * *

5. That the defendant, Southern Bell Telephone and Telegraph Company, is in fact bound by the permit and that they [*sic*] gain entry to the land and use of the land by permission through the permit and have never disclaimed or changed their character or style of possession or use of said land since obtaining entry to the property through said permit.

The judgment concludes with the following entry:

WHEREFORE, based upon the above findings of fact and stipulations, the Court finds as a matter of law that the Defendant, Southern Bell Telephone and Telegraph Company, is bound by the permit in question and is responsible for the cost of the relocation of said telephone lines in the amount of $4,316.00.

On appeal, defendant has not argued that the wording of the general permit was insufficient to establish its liability to pay for relocating its lines. Defendant's position is that the permit expired upon the death of Ola White and that its present grant is through a prescriptive easement.

The facts as stipulated by the parties lead us to conclude that defendant Southern Bell is not bound by the terms of the general permit. It is settled law that a grantor cannot convey to his grantee an estate of greater dignity than the one he has. *Lovett v. Stone*, 239 N.C. 206, 79 S.E. 2d 479 (1954). The general permit executed by the life tenant, Ola White, conveyed to defendant an easement for and during her lifetime, and for no longer. As a life tenant, she could not create an estate or interest to endure beyond the term of her own estate. 2 Thompson on Real Property § 317, p. 28 (1961); 2 Powell on Real Property ¶ 203[3], p. 130 (1977); 25 Am. Jur. 2d, Easements and Licenses § 15, p. 429 (1966); *cf.*, *Haywood v. Briggs*, 227 N.C. 108, 41 S.E. 2d 289 (1946) (life tenant may not grant a lease to extend beyond the term of the life tenancy). As defendant's rights under the permit terminated upon the death of Ola White, so did its obligations. As between the parties to this action, there are no rights or obligations of any kind based upon the permit.

We note that our determination that the general permit does not obligate defendant to pay for the moving of its lines does not necessarily settle the issue as to which party is liable for the cost of relocation. Plaintiff has not demanded an adjudication as to whether defendant has a right to a prescriptive easement, nor has defendant counterclaimed for such an adjudication. The scope of the present action for a declaratory judgment concerns solely the rights and obligations of the parties under the general permit. The trial court's conclusion that defendant is bound by the permit is in error, and its judgment is

Reversed.

Chief Judge MORRIS and Judge PARKER concur.

———————

DALE M. ELLIS AND WIFE, MARY ELIZABETH ELLIS v. EMMETT NATHAN KIMBROUGH

No. 796SC1206

(Filed 3 June 1980)

Process § § 1.2, 3.1; Rules of Civil Procedure § 4– defect in copy of summons served
  on defendant – alias summons – continuance of action

Where an action was validly commenced by the filing of a complaint on 27 August 1979, well within the period of the statute of limitations, a valid original summons was issued on 28 August 1979, the attempted service of this summons on 3 September 1979 was defective in that the copy of the summons delivered to defendant incorrectly indicated that the action was pending in Pitt rather than in Bertie County, and plaintiffs then procured the issuance of an alias summons which was served on defendant on 29 September 1979, plaintiffs' action was continued in existence as to defendant by the alias summons until valid service of the summons was obtained upon defendant, and the trial court erred in dismissing plaintiffs' action on the ground that it was barred by the statute of limitations. G.S. 1A-1, Rule 4(d)(2).

APPEAL by plaintiffs and defendant from *Small, Judge.* Judgment entered 8 November 1979 in Superior Court, BERTIE County. Heard in the Court of Appeals 22 May 1980.

Plaintiffs commenced this action on 27 August 1979 by filing complaint in the Superior Court in Bertie County in which they alleged they were injured by defendant's negligence in an automobile collision which occurred on 10 September 1976. Original summons was issued by the assistant clerk of superior court of Bertie County on 28 August 1979 and was delivered to the sheriff for service. On 3 September 1979 a deputy sheriff of Bertie County attempted service by delivering a copy of the complaint and what purported to be a copy of the summons to the defendant in Bertie County. The original summons bore the notation at the top, "State of North Carolina, County of Bertie," but the copy delivered to defendant bore the notation, "State of North Carolina, County of Pitt." In all other respects the copy of the summons delivered to defendant was identical to the original summons which had been issued by the assistant clerk of superior court of Bertie County.

On 24 September 1979 defendant moved pursuant to Rules 12(b)(2), (4), and (5) of the Rules of Civil Procedure to quash the summons and the service of summons for lack of jurisdiction over the person of the defendant. On 28 September 1979 an alias summons was issued by the deputy clerk of superior court of Bertie County, and on 29 September 1979 a copy of the alias summons and a copy of the complaint were served on the defendant by a deputy sheriff in Bertie County.

On 10 October 1979 plaintiffs filed a motion to amend the copy of the original summons which had been served on the defendant on 3 September 1979 by changing the word "Pitt" in the upper left-hand corner to the word "Bertie," so that the copy would conform with the original summons in all respects.

On 15 October 1979 defendant filed a motion under Rule 12(b)(6) to dismiss plaintiffs' action for failure to state a claim upon which relief can be granted in that the complaint discloses on its face that the cause of action arose on 10 September 1976 and is barred by the three-year statute of limitations. Plaintiffs responded by requesting that, in the event the court should grant involuntary dismissal of their action, the dismissal be without prejudice and that plaintiffs be allowed one year in which to bring a new action based on the same claim.

All motions came on for hearing before Judge Small, who, on 8 November 1979, entered judgment dismissing the action without prejudice to plaintiffs' right to bring a new action based on the same claim within 30 days from the date of the judgment. From this judgment both plaintiffs and defendant appealed.

Laurence S. Graham and William Sidney Aldridge for plaintiffs.

Gram & Baker by Ronald G. Baker and Pritchett, Cooke and Burch for defendant.

PARKER, Judge.

It was error for the court to dismiss plaintiffs' action. The action was validly commenced when the complaint was filed on 27 August 1979, well within the period of the statute of limitations. A valid original summons was issued on 28 August 1979, within the five day period after the filing of the complaint prescribed by Rule 4(a). True, the attempted service of this summons on 3 September 1979 was defective in that the copy of the summons delivered to defendant incorrectly indicated that the action was pending in Pitt rather than in Bertie County, *see Harrell v. Welstead*, 206 N.C. 817, 175 S.E. 283 (1934); *Brantley v.*

Sawyer, 5 N.C. App. 557, 169 S.E. 2d 55 (1969), but the mistake on the copy did not in any way invalidate the original summons, which was itself in all respects correct. Rule 4(c) of the Rules of Civil Procedure provides that service of summons must be made within 30 days after the date of issuance of the summons (except in certain tax and assessment foreclosure actions not here applicable), "[b]ut the failure to [make service within the time allowed] shall not invalidate the summons."

When plaintiffs learned that the summons had not been validly served within 30 days after the date of its issuance as required by Rule 4(c), they procured the issuance of an alias summons, as they had a right to do under Rule 4(d)(2). That Rule provides:

> (d) ... When any defendant in a civil action is not served within the time allowed for service, *the action may be continued in existence as to such defendant* by either of the following methods of extension:
>
> *   *   *
>
> (2) The plaintiff may sue out an alias or pluries summons returnable in the same manner as the original process. Such alias or pluries summons may be sued out at any time within 90 days after the date of issue of the last preceding summons in the chain of summonses or within 90 days of the last prior endorsement. (Emphasis added.)

By the express language of Rule 4(d), plaintiffs' action, which had been commenced when the complaint was filed on 27 August 1979, was continued in existence as to the defendant when plaintiffs, within the time permitted by Rule 4(d)(2), sued out a valid alias summons. The record reveals that service of this alias summons was made on the defendant on 29 September 1979, and defendant has not questioned the validity of that service. Plaintiffs' action having been commenced within the period permitted by the statute of limitations and having been continued in existence as to the defendant until valid service of summons was obtained upon him, it was error for the court to dismiss the action.

In re Ridge

Mintz v. Frink, 217 N.C. 101, 6 S.E. 2d 804 (1940) and *Lackey v. Cook*, 40 N.C. App. 522, 253 S.E. 2d 335, *cert. denied* 297 N.C. 610, 257 S.E. 2d 218 (1979), are distinguishable from the present case. The plaintiff in each of those cases failed in apt time to sue out a valid alias summons, with the unfortunate result that the original action was discontinued. Plaintiffs in the present action did not make the same mistake.

Holding as we do that the court erred in dismissing plaintiffs' action, we do not reach the question sought to be presented by defendant's appeal from the portion of the court's judgment which permitted plaintiffs to bring a new action within 30 days of the date of the judgment.

The judgment dismissing plaintiff's action is

Reversed.

Judges HEDRICK and VAUGHN concur.

IN THE MATTER OF THE WILL OF MATTIE T. RIDGE, DECEASED

No. 7918SC1065

(Filed 3 June 1980)

Attorneys at Law § 7.5– caveat proceeding – fees awarded caveators' counsel – insufficient findings

   Where the trial court made no finding or conclusion with respect to whether a caveat proceeding was without substantial merit, the court on appeal could not determine whether the trial court properly exercised its discretion in awarding fees to caveators' counsel. G.S. 6-21.

APPEAL by propounders from *Graham, Judge*. Order entered 27 June 1979 in Superior Court, GUILFORD County. Heard in the Court of Appeals 24 April 1980.

Mattie T. Ridge died 28 November 1978, leaving a will and three codicils which were probated in common form. Three of testatrix's nieces filed caveat to the three codicils, alleging they are invalid because of lack of testamentary capacity of

Mattie Ridge, undue influence exerted upon her, and mistake by Mattie as to the nature of the codicils.

In Item VI of the will Mattie left a one-fifth interest in the residue of her estate to Alson M. Thayer, her brother, who was the father of the caveators. The will was executed 28 May 1969. Thereafter she executed the questioned codicils on 13 May 1974, 22 November 1974, and 16 October 1975. The second codicil removed Alson M. Thayer, who had died a few days prior to 22 November 1974, as a devisee under her will. The third codicil confirmed the will and first two codicils and made other changes not affecting caveators.

At trial, the parties entered into stipulations as to all uncontested issues. The caveators withdrew all their grounds for the caveat except that of undue influence. Propounders produced evidence showing the due execution of all four paperwritings as the last will and codicils thereof of Mattie Ridge. All three caveators testified and produced evidence describing the physical condition of Mattie Ridge, but failed to produce any evidence supporting their claim of undue influence, or any other basis for their caveat.

The court peremptorily instructed the jury in favor of propounders on all issues, and verdict was returned accordingly. Caveators gave notice of appeal which was later withdrawn.

At the conclusion of the hearing, propounders' counsel requested attorneys' fees for their services to the estate and objected to any fee on behalf of caveators' counsel. The court overruled their objection, and after hearing entered an order making findings of fact and allowing attorneys for caveators $7,500 legal fees. From this order, propounders appeal.

Wyatt Early Harris Wheeler & Hauser, by William E. Wheeler, for propounder appellants.

Edwards, Greeson, Weeks & Turner, by Elton Edwards, for caveator appellees.

MARTIN (Harry C.), Judge.

Propounders question the propriety of awarding legal fees to caveators' counsel and the amount of the award, to be paid from the assets of the estate.

Both parties rely upon the following statute:

> *Costs allowed either party or apportioned in discretion of court.* — Costs in the following matters shall be taxed against either party, or apportioned among the parties, in the discretion of the court:
>
> . . . .
>
> (2) Caveats to wills and any action or proceeding which may require the construction of any will or trust agreement, or fix the rights and duties of parties thereunder; provided, however, that in any caveat proceeding under this subdivision, if the court finds that the proceeding is without substantial merit, the court may disallow attorneys' fees for the attorneys for the caveators.
>
> . . . .
>
> The word "costs" as the same appears and is used in this section shall be construed to include reasonable attorneys' fees in such amounts as the court shall in its discretion determine and allow: . . . .

N.C. Gen. Stat. 6-21.

This statute authorizes the trial court in its discretion to allow attorneys' fees to counsel for unsuccessful caveators to a will. *In re Will of Slade*, 214 N.C. 361, 199 S.E. 290 (1938). The court is not required to do so. It is a matter in the discretion of the court, both as to whether to allow fees and the amount of such fees. *Godwin v. Trust Co.*, 259 N.C. 520, 131 S.E. 2d 456 (1963); *Mayo v. Jones*, 78 N.C. 406 (1878).

The statute specifically provides that "if the court finds that the proceeding is without *substantial* merit, the court *may* disallow attorneys' fees for the attorneys for the caveators." (Emphasis added.)

Appellants contend the caveat had no merit at all and that the court abused its discretion in allowing counsel fees for caveators. The evidence strongly supports appellants' argument. Caveators, before trial, abandoned their claims of lack of testamentary capacity and mistake on the part of the testatrix. That left remaining their allegation of undue influence exerted upon testatrix. Caveators do not allege who perpetrated this undue influence upon Mattie Ridge. The record is absolutely void of any evidence to substantiate the claim of undue influence. For this reason, the court allowed propounders' motion for peremptory instructions on all issues.

In its order for counsel fees the trial court made no finding or conclusion with respect to whether the proceeding was without "substantial merit." Under the evidence in this case, without such a finding we cannot determine whether the trial court properly exercised its discretion in awarding the counsel fees.

For this reason, the order allowing attorneys' fees for caveators' counsel and costs must be vacated and the cause remanded to the Superior Court of Guilford County for another hearing to determine the propriety of awarding attorneys' fees to counsel for caveators and, if found proper, the amount of such fees. With this ruling, we do not decide nor intimate any opinion as to whether the amount of the attorneys' fees awarded by the trial court was proper. However, we believe the trial court in determining an appropriate fee can properly consider the failure of caveators to present evidence in support of their allegations.

Vacated and remanded.

Judges VAUGHN and CLARK concur.

HARRY L. COOK, Plaintiff v. EXPORT LEAF TOBACCO COMPANY, Defendant and Third-Party Plaintiff v. JOHN L. COOK d/b/a JOHN L. COOK PLUMBING COMPANY, Third-Party Defendant.

No. 797SC1143

(Filed 3 June 1980)

Appeal and Error § 6.2– partial summary judgment – premature appeal

Partial summary judgment holding that third party defendant must indemnify defendant for any judgment on plaintiff's claim is interlocutory and not appealable under G.S. 1-277 or G.S. 7A-27(d) since the judgment will not work injury to third party defendant if not corrected before appeal from a final judgment. Nor was the partial summary judgment appealable under G.S. 1A-1, Rule 54(b), even if the court's finding that third party defendant "shall be entitled to appeal this judgment to the Court of Appeals" constituted a finding that "there is no just reason for delay," since the judgment was not final as to any of the parties.

APPEAL by third-party defendant from *Peel, Judge.* Judgment entered 10 September 1979 in Superior Court, WILSON County. Heard in the Court of Appeals 16 May 1980.

This is an action in which the plaintiff seeks to recover from Export Leaf Tobacco Company (Export) for a personal injury which, as alleged in the complaint, was proximately caused by the negligence of Export. The plaintiff, at the time of the injury, was employed by John L. Cook (Cook) who was doing some repair work on the property of Export. Export made Cook a party to the action alleging, among other things, an agreement between Export and Cook. The agreement provided that Cook would hold Export harmless for any injury or damage which occurred by reason of any act of Cook or his agents in connection with the performance of the contract. Under the agreement, this would be so regardless of whether the injury or damage was caused in part or contributed to by any act or omission of Export. Before any liability of Export to the plaintiff had been determined, the court granted Export's motion for partial summary judgment holding that Cook was bound to indemnify Export for any judgments, costs and attorney fees arising from the incident in regard to which this action was filed. The court also held that Cook "shall be entitled to appeal this judgment to the Court of Appeals . . . ." Cook has appealed.

Hudson, Petree, Stockton, Stockton and Robinson, by Norwood Robinson and Daniel R. Taylor, Jr., for third-party plaintiff appellee.

Moore, Weaver and Beaman, by George A. Weaver, for third-party defendant appellant.

WEBB, Judge.

The partial summary judgment in favor of Export does not dispose of all the issues in the case and is therefore an interlocutory order. The first question we face is whether this appeal should be dismissed as being fragmentary. The appealability of interlocutory decrees has raised troublesome questions in this jurisdiction. The problem has been faced in the following cases. *Whalehead Properties v. Coastland Corp.*, 299 N.C. 270, 261 S.E. 2d 899 (1980); *Industries, Inc. v. Insurance Co.*, 296 N.C. 486, 251 S.E. 2d 443 (1979); *Nasco Equipment Co. v. Mason*, 291 N.C. 145, 229 S.E. 2d 278 (1976); *Newton v. Insurance Co.*, 291 N.C. 105, 229 S.E. 2d 297 (1976); *Oestreicher v. Stores*, 290 N.C. 118, 225 S.E. 2d 797 (1976); *Highway Commission v. Nuckles*, 271 N.C. 1, 155 S.E. 2d 772 (1967); *Nichols v. Credit Union*, 46 N.C. App. 294, 264 S.E. 2d 793 (1980); *Beck v. Assurance Co.*, 36 N.C. App. 218, 243, S.E. 2d 414 (1978). We believe the rule from these cases is that if a trial court enters an order which affects a substantial right and will work injury if not corrected before appeal from a final judgment, it is appealable under G.S. 1-277 and G.S. 7A-27(d). G.S. 1-277(b) also allows an immediate appeal from an adverse ruling as to the jurisdiction of the court over the person or property of the defendant. The cases also hold that G.S. 1A-1, Rule 54(b) provides for an immediate appeal when there are multiple parties or claims and the trial court enters a final judgment as to less than all the parties or claims and determines "there is no just reason for delay."

In this case, we hold the summary judgment will not work injury to appellant if not corrected before appeal from a final judgment. Indeed we cannot say whether or not Cook will be injured until the plaintiff's claim against Export has been determined. The summary judgment is not appealable under G.S.

1-277 or G.S. 7A-27(d). Nor do we believe the summary judgment is appealable under Rule 54(b). The court did make a finding that Cook "shall be entitled to appeal" which might comply with the Rule's requirement that the court determine "there is no just reason for delay." However, the judgment is not final which is also a requirement for appealability under Rule 54(b). The partial summary judgment held that Cook must indemnify Export for the claim of plaintiff in the case sub judice. At this time, Export has not been held liable to plaintiff. Until the amount for which Cook must pay on the indemnity contract has been determined, the partial summary judgment will not be a final judgment which is a requirement for appealability under G.S. 1A-1, Rule 54(b).

When the liability of Cook to Export on the indemnity agreement has been determined, Cook may appeal. His exception to the entry of the partial summary judgment will be preserved.

Appeal dismissed.

Judges MARTIN (Harry C.) and WELLS concur.

STATE OF NORTH CAROLINA v. HOWARD EUGENE SAFRIT

No. 8017SC8

(Filed 3 June 1980)

1. **Criminal Law § 134.4– resentencing proceeding – determination of no benefit from treatment as committed youthful offender**

   In a resentencing proceeding to determine whether defendant should be sentenced as a committed youthful offender, the trial court's finding that "defendant is now 21 years of age, and would not benefit from treatment and supervision . . . as a Committed Youthful Offender" did not show that defendant's age at the time of the resentencing was the primary reason for failure of the court to resentence defendant as a committed youthful offender, and the court's order was sufficient without giving reasons for the "no benefit" finding.

2. **Criminal Law § 138.11– resentencing – harsher punishment statute not violated**

   A notation in an amended judgment and commitment that the maximum penalty for the offense charged was ten years did not show that the court considered imposing a harsher sentence on defendant when he was resentenced but was for the purpose of showing that the sentence imposed was within the statutory maximum, and the harsher punishment statute, G.S. 15A-1335, was not violated where defendant was given the same indeterminate term of imprisonment at his resentencing as that imposed at his original sentencing.

APPEAL by defendant from *Albright, Judge.* Judgment entered 10 May 1979 in Superior Court, CASWELL County. Heard in the Court of Appeals 13 May 1980.

The defendant Safrit and two other men were convicted of assault with a deadly weapon, inflicting serious bodily injury upon Sampson McNeil, while all were inmates at Blanch prison. McNeil testified that when his cell door was opened at breakfast time Safrit and a man named Cagle entered his cell while a man named Spry stood guard at the door. Cagle called McNeil a "rat" and stabbed him with a home-made knife. Safrit dragged McNeil by his feet from the left side of the dormitory to the right side. After the assault, threats were made by the attackers toward McNeil to keep him from testifying against them. Defendant was sentenced to prison for not less than eight years nor more than ten years, to begin at the expiration of any sentences presently being served. Defendant appealed.

This Court, in an unpublished opinion, found no error in Safrit's conviction. *State v. Cagle,* 38 N.C. App. 391, 248 S.E. 2d 472 (1978). Thereafter, the defendant's Pro Se Petition for Discretionary Review was denied by the North Carolina Supreme Court. 296 N.C. 107, 249 S.E. 2d 805 (1978).

Defendant subsequently collaterally attacked his conviction by petition for writ of habeas corpus. The petition was denied, but after considering the petition as a motion for appropriate relief, the judge ordered that defendant be returned to Caswell County for re-sentencing. The trial judge in sentencing defendant had failed to take into account defendant's eligibility for status as a committed youthful offender. The re-sentencing proceedings were limited to the question of whether the defendant should be sentenced as a committed youthful offender.

At the re-sentencing hearing, the State offered evidence concerning numerous infractions committed by the defendant since he went to prison in 1973. The defendant testified that he was sentenced to 12 to 15 years for armed robbery and breaking and entering when he was 15 years old. The defendant is now approximately 21 years of age and incarcerated in Central Prison.

From the re-sentencing judgment imposing the same terms, the defendant *pro se*, but with court appointed counsel standing by, objected and excepted to the judgment and rulings of the court, and the matter is now before this Court.

Attorney General Edmisten, by Assistant Attorney General James L. Stuart, for the State.

Howard Eugene Safrit, defendant appellant pro se.

HILL, Judge.

Here we have another example of the right of unbridled, unrestrained and unlimited appeal, which demonstrates the further need for the North Carolina General Assembly to consider whether the present method of appellate review should be changed in this State. The defendant works (voluntarily) in the law library within the Department of Correction, has the opportunity to read extensively and to seek advice from "jail house lawyers" who, like the defendant, have read much and understand little. In addition, defendant has the benefit of skilled attorneys, provided by the State at great expense to the taxpayers, coupled with the constitutional guarantees provided to all who seek justice in our courts.

[1] Safrit complains at this time that the trial judge committed error by (1) failing to sentence the appellant as a youthful offender at the re-sentencing hearing, and (2) by considering the imposition of a harsher sentence during the re-sentencing hearing. Upon consideration of the evidence presented at the re-sentencing hearing, the trial judge made the following finding:

This Court finds that the defendant is now 21 years of age, and would not benefit from treatment and supervision pursuant to G.S. 148, Article 3B, as a Committed Youthful Offender, and, therefore, this Court expressly does not sentence this defendant as a Committed Youthful Offender.

The question before the re-sentencing court was whether the defendant would benefit from a committed youthful offender sentence. The defendant contends the court improperly considered the defendant's age at the time of re-sentencing, made it the primary reason for denying defendant the many benefits afforded under an Article 3B sentence, and erred by doing so. We do not agree. There is no particular form or wording required of the trial judge in making a determination that a defendant will derive "no benefit" from sentencing under the statute. *State v. White*, 37 N.C. App. 394, 246 S.E. 2d 71 (1978). From the record, it is apparent the re-sentencing judge considered defendant's violent nature in making his decision. The finding is sufficient.

[2] The appellant next contends the trial judge considered imposing a harsher sentence on the appellant in the amended judgment and commitment, and thereby violated G.S. 15A-1335. This contention is not borne out by the facts. Defendant was sentenced to a term of imprisonment following his re-sentencing hearing identical to that ordered in the original sentencing of the appellant. The trial judge's amended judgment and commitment did include a notation that the maximum penalty for the offense charged was ten years' imprisonment, but this was only for the purpose of showing that the sentence imposed was within the maximum statutory penalty.

Affirmed.

Judges MARTIN (Robert M.) and ARNOLD concur.

Herbin v. Farrish

GEORGE HERBIN v. NETTIE FARRISH

No. 7918SC1177

(Filed 3 June 1980)

Banks and Banking § 4– joint account – no right of survivorship

In an action by plaintiff to recover, as joint legatee, funds withdrawn by defendant, another legatee, from a bank account which named testatrix and defendant as joint depositors, the trial court properly entered summary judgment for plaintiff since Ohio law controlled; Ohio cases hold that for there to be a right of survivorship in a joint account, there must be an intention to give the survivor rights fully as great as those of the deceased in the account during the lifetime of the deceased as well as the intent to give the survivor the balance of the account upon the death of the deceased; and by defendant's own testimony, she had to secure permission of the testatrix to withdraw money from the account during testatrix' lifetime, and there was therefore no intent to confer upon defendant a present, vested interest during the life of deceased.

APPEAL by defendant from *Seay, Judge.* Judgment entered 6 November 1979 in Superior Court, GUILFORD County. Heard in the Court of Appeals 20 May 1980.

The plaintiff and defendant, along with Mozelle Moore, are legatees under the will of Maggie Hairston, who died a resident of the State of Ohio. Plaintiff and the testatrix were siblings. Defendant was Hairston's cousin. The will bequeathed to the named legatees,

All the rest of my property ... which includes my savings account ... at the ... Ohio National Bank ... which I may own or have the right to dispose of at the time of my death.

Prior to the death of Maggie Hairston and subsequent to the death of her husband, the name of the defendant, Nettie Farrish, was added to the depositor card at the bank. Defendant, however, never put any money into the account. Defendant testified that while Maggie Hairston was alive she would have had to have Mrs. Hairston's permission to withdraw any funds and that she never went to the bank until after Mrs. Hairston died. Defendant went to the bank on the advice of her attorney after Mrs. Hairston's death and withdrew the deposit, a portion of which was spent on the funeral expenses of Mrs. Hairston. Defendant further testified that her cousin did not want the plaintiff to have any of the proceeds because he drank excessively. Plaintiff sued the defendant to recover one-third of the amount withdrawn by her from the account. Defendant answered, alleging that she was the owner of the account after Mrs. Hairston's death. Plaintiff's motion for summary judgment was allowed, and defendant appealed.

Smith, Patterson, Follin, Curtis, James & Harkavy, by Norman B. Smith, for plaintiff appellee.

Dow M. Spaulding for defendant appellant.

HILL, Judge.

The trial court correctly granted plaintiff's motion for summary judgment. Since the bank account was in Ohio at the time of the death of the testatrix-depositor, the case is governed by the law of that state. *Ellison v. Hunsinger,* 237 N.C. 619, 75 S.E. 2d 884 (1953); 3 Strong's N.C. Index 3d, Courts, Sec. 21.10. Likewise, the law of the state of the situs determines rights of claimants under a will. *Johnson v. Salsbury,* 232 N.C. 432, 61 S.E. 2d 327 (1950); 3 Strong's N.C. Index 3d, Courts, Sec. 21.12.

A joint and survivorship account is created between the co-signators by contract and through that contract the creation gives to the other co-signator a present joint interest in the account equal to his own interest. *Webb v. Webb,* Gdn., 13 Ohio Misc. 1, 231 N.E. 2d 177 (1967). Such an account raises a presumption that the co-owners of the account share equally in the ownership of the funds on deposit. However, the presumption may be rebutted by competent evidence. *Vetter v. Hampton,* 54 Ohio St. 2d 227, 375 N.E. 2d 804 (1978).

A careful reading of the record leads us to conclude that the decedent did not intend that the defendant share equally in the ownership of the bank deposit at the time the name of the defendant was added. We believe the following facts to be controlling:

Herbin v. Farrish

(a) The money in the account was money deposited by Mrs. Hairston alone. The defendant had only one transaction involving the account — the act of withdrawal of funds after the death of Maggie Hairston.

(b) The defendant acknowledged that during the life of Maggie Hairston she would have to secure permission of Maggie Hairston to withdraw any funds.

Ohio cases hold that for there to be right of survivorship in a joint account, there must be an intention to give the survivor rights fully as great as those of the deceased in the account (1) during the lifetime of the deceased, (2) as well as the intent to give the survivor the balance of the account upon the death of the deceased. *Eger v. Eger*, 39 Ohio App. 2d 14, 314 N.E. 2d 394 (1974); *Benson v. Harmon*, 39 Ohio App. 2d 92, 315 N.E. 2d 821 (1974).

We are aware of the defendant's testimony that "she [Maggie Hairston] did not want her brother [plaintiff] to have it because he is a heavy drinker, and he would throw her money away." Nevertheless, the testatrix did not change her will to eliminate plaintiff or restrict his right to inherit thereunder. We conclude that Maggie Hairston must have been referring to all of the deposit when she made this statement. In any event, the statement is of no consequence. The defendant survivor admits there was no intent to confer upon her a present, vested interest during the life of the deceased. There is no question of fact to be determined. *Vetter, supra.*

The entry of the summary judgment is

Affirmed.

Judges MARTIN (Robert M.) and ARNOLD concur.

ERNEST MARSICO D/B/A MACKIE BUILDING & SUPPLY COMPANY v.
FRED M. ADAMS AND WIFE, IRENE ADAMS

No. 7925SC1123

(Filed 3 June 1980)

1. **Contracts § 27.3– breach of contract – nominal damages – failure to award not prejudicial error**

   The trial court erred in failing to award nominal damages to defendants upon finding that plaintiff had breached the contract between the parties but that defendants had suffered no financial loss by reason of the breach; however, failure of the trial court to award such a trivial sum did not constitute prejudicial error.

2. **Costs § 1.2– breach of contract by plaintiff – taxing of costs against plaintiff**

   The trial court should have taxed the costs to plaintiff where the court found that plaintiff breached the contract between the parties but was entitled to recover in quantum meruit, and defendants were therefore entitled to recover nominal damages for the breach.

APPEAL by defendants from *Graham, Judge*. Judgment entered 19 June 1979 in Superior Court, CALDWELL County. Heard in the Court of Appeals 15 May 1980.

The parties entered into a contract on 24 February 1972 whereby plaintiff agreed to construct a house for defendants in consideration of $24,000. Plaintiff completed construction of the foundation, subflooring, roofing and all rough-in work before defendants ordered him to cease work and vacate the premises. At that point in time, defendants had paid plaintiff $8,500 as consideration for partial performance of the contract.

Plaintiff contractor filed this action against defendants, alleging that he had ". . . performed all of his obligations under [the] contract in a reasonable and professional manner . . . ." Plaintiff requested a sum, which, in addition to the money defendants had already paid, would come close to equaling the contract price. Plaintiff also requested attorney's fees plus the costs of the action.

Defendants answered the complaint, alleging breach of the contract by plaintiff. Defendants requested that the action be dismissed and that they ". . . recover their costs and such other relief as the court deems proper." The trial court found that plaintiff had substantially breached the contract but that plaintiff was entitled to recover in quantum meruit. No setoff was granted to defendants, nor were nominal damages awarded for the breach. Defendants appealed from the judgment.

West, Groome & Correll, by H. Houston Groome Jr. and Edward H. Blair Jr., for plaintiff appellee.

Wilson, Palmer & Cannon, by David P. Palmer Jr., for defendant appellants.

HILL, Judge.

Defendants properly bring forth an argument in their appellate brief and state in part that, "... at least nominal damages should be awarded by way of a setoff ...." Defendants base their argument on their assignment of error #13 and exception #28. When we look to the record, however, no exception #28 is apparent.

Appellate Rule 10(b) states that,

Each exception shall be set out immediately following the record of judicial action to which it is addressed .... Exceptions set out in the record on appeal shall be numbered consecutively ....

The Rules of Appellate Procedure are mandatory. *Craver v. Craver*, 298 N.C. 231, 236, 258 S.E. 2d 357 (1979). Failure to follow the Rules subjects defendants' appeal to dismissal. We have decided, however, to treat the purported appeal as a petition for writ of certiorari and allow it in order that we may decide the case on its merits.

[1] The trial court in its conclusions stated that the plaintiff breached the contract between the parties by failing "... to perform the work specified in the contract in a workmanlike manner." The trial court further concluded that plaintiff's

breach was substantial, but found as fact, "[t]hat [d]efendants suffered no financial loss by reason of [p]laintiff's failure to perform the work required by the contract in a workmanlike manner." No exception was taken to any findings of fact, conclusions of law, or to the judgment.

Defendants argue in their appellate brief that nominal damages, at least, should have been awarded to them. We agree. "A party is entitled to nominal damages if the jury [in this case, the trial judge] find that there has been any injury to his legal rights." *Hutton v. Cook*, 173 N.C. 496, 499, 92 S.E. 355 (1917).

Error by the trial judge in failing to grant nominal damages is not reversible error in this case, however. Nominal damages are "... a small trivial sum ..."; a "... trifling amount ..." that is only awarded in recognition of a technical injury. *See Hairston v. Greyhound Corp.*, 220 N.C. 642, 644, 18 S.E. 2d 166 (1942). Such a trivial sum, that is awarded for technical rather than substantial injury, does not in this circumstance constitute prejudicial and reversible error. *Accord see* RESTATEMENT OF CONTRACTS, § 328, Comment b (1932).

[2] We do find, however, that this case must be modified. The trial court taxed the costs of the action to the defendants. Nominal damages, which defendants were entitled to, "... have been described as 'a peg on which to hang costs.'" *Hutton, supra*, at p. 499. Because the court found that plaintiff was in breach of the contract, and because defendants were entitled to nominal damages, the trial court should have taxed the costs to the plaintiff.

Modified and Affirmed.

Judges MARTIN (Robert M.) and ARNOLD concur.

GEORGE THOMAS POYTHRESS v. BURLINGTON INDUSTRIES, INC.

No. 7916SC242

(Filed 3 June 1980)

Negligence § § 30.3, 31– injury from operation of forklift – foreseeability – insufficiency of evidence – inapplicability of res ipsa loquitur

In an action to recover for personal injuries sustained by plaintiff when defendant's forklift operator started forward, the "motor went into high speed," and a metal sheet on which plaintiff was standing was jerked forward, causing plaintiff to fall, directed verdict for defendant was proper since, in order for the evidence to be submitted to the jury, the jury would have to be able to conclude that a reasonable man would not have accelerated the forklift while it was on the metal sheet, knowing the sheet might be pulled forward, causing plaintiff to fall, and the jury could not so conclude on the evidence presented; nor should the case have been submitted to the jury under the doctrine of res ipsa loquitur, since it could be concluded from the evidence what caused the accident.

Judge WELLS concurs in the result.

APPEAL by plaintiff from *Fountain, Judge*. Judgment entered 15 November 1978 in Superior Court, SCOTLAND County. Heard in the Court of Appeals 26 October 1979.

Plaintiff appeals from a verdict directed against him in an action for personal injury. The evidence in the light most favorable to plaintiff showed that plaintiff is a truck driver who delivered a load consisting of pallets of plywood to the defendant on 21 October 1975. Three pallets were to be unloaded at the plant of the defendant. The plywood was unloaded by an agent of the defendant by use of a forklift. A thin metal sheet which had been used to brace the pallets while the tractor-trailer was carrying its load was lying on the floor of the trailer. The first two pallets were unloaded without difficulty. The plaintiff then went into the trailer to help place the third pallet on the forklift. After the pallet was loaded, the plaintiff stepped aside and was standing on the metal sheet. As the forklift operator was backing the forklift out of the trailer, it rolled on the metal sheet. At this time the pallet, which was on the forklift, brushed against the side of the trailer. In an effort to get the forklift off the wall of the trailer, the forklift driver started forward when "all of a sudden the motor went into high speed." The sheet of metal on which the forklift was rolling was jerked forward and from under the plaintiff who fell, suffering personal injury. At the close of the plaintiff's evidence, the court directed a verdict for the defendant.

Mason, Williamson, Etheridge and Moser, by Kenneth S. Etheridge and Daniel B. Dean, for plaintiff appellant.

Hedrick, Parham, Helms, Kellam and Feerick, by J.A. Gardner III, for defendant appellee.

WEBB, Judge.

The question posed by this appeal is whether the jury could have concluded from the evidence that the agent of defendant who was operating the forklift did something which a reasonable man would not have done or failed to do something which a reasonable man would have done which proximately caused the plaintiff's injury. *See* 9 Strong's N.C. Index 3d, Negligence § 1 (1977) for a definition of negligence. The fact that there was an accident is not evidence of negligence. *Pittman v. Frost*, 261 N.C. 349, 134 S.E. 2d 687 (1964). In order for the evidence in the case sub judice to be submitted to the jury, the jury would have to be able to conclude that a reasonable man would not have accelerated the forklift while it was on the metal sheet, knowing the sheet might be pulled forward, causing the plaintiff to fall. We do not believe that the jury could so conclude. We hold that the directed verdict in defendant's favor was proper.

The plaintiff also urges that the case should have been submitted to the jury under the doctrine of res ipsa loquitur. "When an instrumentality which caused an injury to plaintiff is shown to be under the control and operation of the defendant, and the accident is one which, in the ordinary course of events, does not happen if those who have the management of it use the proper care, the occurrence itself is some evidence that it arose from want of care." *Kekelis v. Machine Works*, 273 N.C. 439, 160 S.E. 2d 320 (1968). The difficulty with the application of res ipsa loquitur in the case sub judice is that we can conclude from the evidence what caused the accident. It was caused when the forklift moved forward and pulled the steel plate from under the

State v. Felmet

plaintiff. We have held that this was not enough evidence to submit to the jury.

Affirmed.

Judge ARNOLD concurs.

Judge WELLS concurs in the result.

STATE OF NORTH CAROLINA v. JOE ANDREW FELMET

No. 8021SC9

(Filed 3 June 1980)

1. **Criminal Law § 18.2— misdemeanor trial in superior court – necessity for conviction in district court**

    The superior court has no jurisdiction to try a defendant upon a specific misdemeanor charge on a warrant unless he is first tried and convicted in the district court and then appeals to the superior court from the sentence pronounced against him on his conviction for such misdemeanor in the district court.

2. **Criminal Law § 18.1— appeal from misdemeanor conviction in superior court – failure of record to show jurisdiction in superior court**

    Appeal from conviction of a misdemeanor in the superior court is dismissed for failure of the record to show jurisdiction in the superior court where the record shows that defendant was tried in the superior court upon a warrant issued by a deputy clerk of superior court but fails to show that defendant was first tried and convicted in the district court and then appealed to the superior court.

APPEAL by defendant from *Rousseau, Judge.* Judgment entered 7 September 1979 in Superior Court, FORSYTH County. Heard in the Court of Appeals 14 May 1980.

The record shows that the defendant was tried in this case, docket number 79CRS23904, in the Superior Court of Forsyth County on a *warrant,* issued by a deputy clerk of superior court, charging defendant with trespass by violating N.C.G.S. 14-134, a misdemeanor. The record does not show that defendant was ever tried in the district court on this charge.

Defendant was convicted by the jury in the superior court, a suspended sentence was entered, and defendant appealed.

Attorney General Edmisten, by Assistant Attorney General Roy A. Giles, Jr., for the State.

Pfefferkorn & Cooley, by Robert M. Elliot, for defendant appellant.

MARTIN (Harry C.), Judge.

[1] The superior court has no jurisdiction to try a defendant upon a specific misdemeanor charge on a warrant, unless he is first tried and convicted in the district court, and then appeals to the superior court from the sentence pronounced against him on his conviction for such misdemeanor. *State v. Hall,* 240 N.C. 109, 81 S.E. 2d 189 (1954); *State v. Byrd,* 4 N.C. App. 672, 167 S.E. 2d 522 (1969). Defendant was convicted of trespass, a misdemeanor proscribed by N.C.G.S. 14-134. The district courts of North Carolina have exclusive original jurisdiction of misdemeanors. N.C. Gen. Stat. 7A-272; *State v. McKoy,* 44 N.C. App. 516, 261 S.E. 2d 226, *cert. denied,* 299 N.C. 546, 265 S.E. 2d 405 (1980). The jurisdiction of the superior court for the trial of a specific misdemeanor is derivative and arises only upon an appeal from a conviction of the misdemeanor in the district court. *State v. Guffey,* 283 N.C. 94, 194 S.E. 2d 827 (1973); *State v. McKoy, supra.*

[2] The record fails to disclose jurisdiction in the superior court. As that court had no jurisdiction, insofar as this record discloses, we have none on appeal. Therefore, the appeal must be dismissed. *State v. Banks,* 241 N.C. 572, 86 S.E. 2d 76 (1955); *State v. Byrd, supra.*

The question of jurisdiction is not raised or discussed by the defendant or the Attorney General in the briefs. The Court of Appeals will take notice ex mero motu of the failure of the record to show jurisdiction in the court entering the judgment appealed. *State v. Guffey, supra; State v. Johnson,* 251 N.C. 339, 111 S.E. 2d 297 (1959); *State v. McKoy, supra; State v. Byrd, supra.*

In this case, the appellant had the duty to see that the record on appeal was properly made up and transmitted to this Court. *State v. Stubbs*, 265 N.C. 420, 144 S.E. 2d 262 (1965); *State v. Byrd, supra.*

For the failure of the record to show jurisdiction, the appeal must be dismissed.

Appeal dismissed.

Judges WEBB and WELLS concur.

BEN LLOYD v. CARNATION COMPANY, GARY WILLIER, AND WARREN MANUEL

No. 7915SC1120

(Filed 3 June 1980)

Appeal and Error § 45.1– assignments of error not discussed in brief – appeal dismissed

Defendants' appeal is dismissed where they failed to set forth in their brief the assignments of error and the exception pertinent to their argument.

APPEAL by defendants from *Battle, Judge.* Order entered 25 October 1979 in Superior Court, ORANGE County. Heard in the Court of Appeals 15 May 1980.

From September 1967 until January 1978 plaintiff distributed Carnation's bull semen in the States of Virginia, North Carolina and South Carolina. These states constituted plaintiff's "territory." By 1977, plaintiff and defendant Carnation began having disputes over the exclusivity of plaintiff's distributorship in Virginia. On 19 January 1978, Carnation terminated " ... all prior distribution arrangements written or oral with [plaintiff]."

Plaintiff sued defendants. Defendants answered, and on 3 July 1979 made a Request for Production of Documents. Plaintiff responded on 11 July 1979, stating that he would comply with defendant's request, with certain exceptions.

On 23 July 1979, defendants made a motion pursuant to G.S. 1A-1, Rule 37, to compel discovery. Judge Battle, on 25 October 1979, ordered plaintiff to produce his list of customers in Virginia, but stated that plaintiff was not required to produce his lists of North Carolina and South Carolina customers. Judge Battle stated that plaintiff was not required to produce notes of conversations that were made since litigation had begun and did not require plaintiff to produce those portions of his tax returns "... which make no reference to Plaintiff's bull semen business ...." Defendants appealed from the interlocutory order.

Powe, Porter, Alphin & Whichard, by Charles R. Holton and Eugene F. Dauchert, for plaintiff appellee.

Smith, Moore, Smith, Schell & Hunter, by Jack W. Floyd and Frank J. Sizemore III, for defendant appellants.

HILL, Judge.

Defendants have failed to comply with App. R 28(b)(3). Neither the assignments of error nor the exception pertinent to defendant's argument is set forth in the appellate brief. "Exceptions in the record not set out in appellant's brief ... will be taken as abandoned." App. R. 28(b)(3). The Rules of Appellate Procedure are mandatory. *Craver v. Craver*, 298 N.C. 231, 258 S.E. 2d 357 (1979); *Pruitt v. Wood*, 199 N.C. 788, 156 S.E. 126 (1930); *State v. Brown*, 42 N.C. App. 724, 257 S.E. 2d 668 (1979), *disc. rev. denied, cert. granted*, 299 N.C. 123 (1980).

For failing to comply with the Rules of Appellate Procedure, defendants' appeal is

Dismissed.

Judges MARTIN (Robert M.) and ARNOLD concur.

State v. Williams

STATE OF NORTH CAROLINA v. LARRY WILLIAMS, AKA HOSEAR

No. 808SC50

(Filed 3 June 1980)

Criminal Law § 23– illegal search and seizure – guilty plea not vitiated – other evidence supporting plea

Even if an electric coffee maker was illegally seized from defendant's apartment pursuant to an invalid warrant, defendant's plea of guilty of felonious larceny of certain business machines and the coffee maker by breaking and entering was not thereby vitiated where the business machines were seized from the basement of the apartment house in which defendant lived pursuant to a search conducted with the landlord's written permission, defendant thus had no standing to contest the search of the basement, and evidence relating to the business machines would support the guilty plea.

APPEAL by defendant from *Brown, Judge.* Judgment entered 21 August 1979 in Superior Court, WAYNE County. Heard in the Court of Appeals on 20 May 1980.

Defendant was charged in a proper bill of indictment with the felonious breaking or entering of a building occupied by G.A.B. Business Services, Inc. and the felonious larceny of two dictaphones, two electric calculators, one IBM electric typewriter, and one electric coffee maker. He filed a motion to suppress evidence seized from his apartment pursuant to the execution of a search warrant on the grounds that the warrant insufficiently described the premises to be searched and the confidential informant was not shown to be reliable. After a hearing the trial judge entered an order denying the motion to suppress, and the defendant thereupon entered a plea of guilty to felonious larceny as charged, in accordance with the terms of a "plea bargain" wherein all other charges against the defendant were dismissed. From a judgment imposing a prison sentence of two years, defendant appealed pursuant to the provisions of G.S. § 15A-979(b).

Attorney General Edmisten, by Assistant Attorney General Kaye R. Webb, for the State.

Hulse & Hulse, by H. Bruce Hulse, Jr., for the defendant appellant.

HEDRICK, Judge.

Defendant assigns error to the order denying his motion to suppress. The record discloses that the only evidence seized pursuant to the execution of the challenged search warrant was the coffee pot found in defendant's apartment. The remaining items described in the bill of indictment — that is, the dictaphones and calculators — were seized pursuant to a search of the basement of the apartment house in which the defendant lived. Moreover, the search of the basement was undertaken with the permission of the landlord of the apartments who signed a permission to search form. Defendant does not and cannot challenge the admissibility of the items thereby recovered since he has no standing to contest the consent of the owner. *State v. Bates,* 37 N.C. App. 276, 245 S.E. 2d 827, *cert. denied,* 295 N.C. 735, 248 S.E. 2d 864 (1978); *State v. Little,* 27 N.C. App. 54, 218 S.E. 2d 184, *cert. denied,* 288 N.C. 512, 219 S.E. 2d 347 (1975). Defendant's plea of guilty to larceny of the items seized in the search of the basement obviously supports the judgment entered thereon. Thus, it is not necessary that we reach the question of the validity of the search warrant since, even assuming *arguendo* that the coffee pot was illegally seized because the warrant was somehow invalid, the suppression of that evidence would have no effect on and could not vitiate the plea of guilty to larceny of the remaining items. For this reason the judgment appealed from is affirmed.

Affirmed.

Judges PARKER and VAUGHN concur.

CASES REPORTED WITHOUT PUBLISHED OPINION

FILED 3 JUNE 1980

CHEEK v. CHEEK No. 7910DC1090	Wake (78CVD5817)	Affirmed
CONSTRUCTION CO. v. MASON No. 7919SC1006	Rowan (78CVS602)	New Trial
GOODE v. GOODE No. 8021DC46	Forsyth (76CVD3690)	Vacated and Remanded
HOSPITAL v. MITCHEM No. 7929SC753	Rutherford (77CVS483)	Affirmed
HUDSON v. DOWNS No. 792SC830	Beaufort (78SP58)	Affirmed
IN RE FUTRELL No. 8022DC15	Wake from Davidson (79SP279)	Reversed
IN RE MOORE No. 7921DC1149	Forsyth (79SP501)	Reversed and Vacated
MAYES v. FARMER No. 7930DC920	Swain (78CR1134)	Affirmed
STATE v. BOOMER No. 802SC59	Hyde (79CRS166) (79CRS169)	Judgment Arrested Judgment Reversed
STATE v. CARROLL No. 801SC72	Beaufort (79CRS5940)	Appeal Dismissed
STATE v. CHINN No. 7919SC1052	Montgomery (79CRS107)	No Error
STATE v. CREECH No. 8011SC81	Johnston (78CRS13714)	No Error
STATE v. DENNY No. 8023SC12	Wilkes (79CR3440)	Affirmed and Remanded
STATE v. DIXON No. 7927SC1200	Gaston (79CRS6032)	No Error
STATE v. DIXON No. 805SC7	New Hanover (79CRS9687) (79CRS9699)	No Error

STATE v. GRIER No. 8022SC35	Iredell (79CRS7585)	No Error
STATE v. LEE No. 806SC106	Hertford (79CRS1199)	No Error
STATE v. MITCHELL No. 798SC1011	Wayne (79CR6737) (79CR6740)	No Error
STATE v. RICE No. 8021SC88	Forsyth (79CR18079)	No Error
STATE v. RICHARDSON No. 8019SC56	Cabarrus (79CRS233)	No Error
STATE v. ROGERS No. 8017SC57	Surry (79CRS9340)	No Error
STATE v. SCHAEFER No. 804SC95	Onslow (79CRS16159)	No Error
STATE v. WALTON No. 808SC63	Lenoir (78CRS482)	No Error
STATE v. WARD No. 803SC47	Pitt (79CRS4349) (79CRS10886)	No Error
STATE v. WARD No. 803SC48	Pitt (79CRS2243) (79CRS2244)	No Error
STATE v. WHITE No. 803SC92	Craven (79CRS3296)	No Error

Stam v. State

PAUL STAM, JR. v. THE STATE OF NORTH CAROLINA; JAMES B. HUNT, JR., INDIVIDUALLY AND IN HIS OFFICIAL CAPACITY AS GOVERNOR OF THE STATE OF NORTH CAROLINA; RUFUS EDMISTEN, IN HIS OFFICIAL CAPACITY AS ATTORNEY GENERAL OF THE STATE OF NORTH CAROLINA; SARA MORROW, INDIVIDUALLY AND IN HER OFFICIAL CAPACITY AS SECRETARY OF THE DEPARTMENT OF HUMAN RESOURCES OF THE STATE OF NORTH CAROLINA; NORTH CAROLINA DEPARTMENT OF HUMAN RESOURCES; ROBERT WARD, INDIVIDUALLY AND IN HIS OFFICIAL CAPACITY AS DIRECTOR OF THE DIVISION OF SOCIAL SERVICES OF THE DEPARTMENT OF HUMAN RESOURCES OF THE STATE OF NORTH CAROLINA; SOCIAL SERVICES COMMISSION; JAMES WIGHT, INDIVIDUALLY AND IN HIS OFFICIAL CAPACITY AS DIRECTOR OF THE WAKE COUNTY DEPARTMENT OF SOCIAL SERVICES; WAKE COUNTY, A BODY POLITIC

No. 7910SC546

(Filed 17 June 1980)

1. **Abortion § 4; Constitutional Law § 17– human fetus not "person" – no constitutional bar to State funding of abortions**

   A human fetus is not a "person" within the meaning of Art. I, §§ 1 and 19 of the N. C. Constitution, and the protections of those sections thus do not apply to the fetus so as to prohibit State funding for elective abortions.

2. **Abortion § 4; Taxation § 7– use of State tax monies for elective abortions**

   The funding of elective abortions constitutes a "necessary use and purpose of government" within the meaning of G.S. 105-1, and the appropriation and expenditure of State tax monies for elective abortions does not violate Art. V, § 5 of the N. C. Constitution.

3. **Abortions § 4; Counties § 6.2– State Abortion Fund – expenditures by counties – administrative rules – statutory authority**

   In administering State funds appropriated by the General Assembly for the State Abortion Fund through the county department of social services, a county acts pursuant to administrative rules governing the Fund which were enacted pursuant to statutory authority since (1) the rules are not inconsistent with G.S. 130-254, which provides for the establishment of programs to improve perinatal care for low income pregnant women; (2) the rules are not inconsistent with G.S. 108-61 which adopted provisions of the federal Social Security Act, including a provision prohibiting federal funding of medically unnecessary abortions; and (3) the provision of funding for elective abortions fulfills the purpose stated in G.S. 143B-137 of providing services "in the fields of general and mental health," and the promulgation of administrative rules under G.S. 143B-153 satisfies the requirements of "necessity" to carry out the purposes of the Department of Human Resources in that it provides standards without which the State Abortion Fund could not lawfully be administered.

4. **Abortion § 4; Counties § 6.1; Taxation § 5.2– elective abortions – county's levy of taxes – statutory authority**

A county's levy of taxes with a rate limitation for the purpose of funding elective abortions for indigents is authorized by G.S. 153A-149(c)(30) because the taxation is for the purpose of providing a program of public assistance not required by G.S. Chs. 108 and 111 but which, like those required by Ch. 108, is directed to the problems of poverty; futhermore, the program for elective abortions constitutes a "social service program intended to further the health, welfare, education, safety, comfort, and convenience of its citizens" within the meaning of G.S. 153A-255 and is thus authorized by "other portions of the General Statutes" as required by G.S. 153A-149(g).

APPEAL by plaintiff from *Braswell, Judge.* Judgment entered 18 April 1979 in Superior Court, WAKE County. Heard in the Court of Appeals 17 September 1979.

This declaratory judgment action was brought against the State and against Wake County seeking judgment declaring unlawful the appropriation of State funds by the 1977 session of the General Assembly and the use of supplemental county funds to pay for elective abortions for indigents. Plaintiff is a citizen and taxpayer of North Carolina, residing and paying ad valorem taxes on real and personal property in Wake County, as well as paying miscellaneous State and County taxes.

The appropriations bill passed by the General Assembly for the fiscal year 1978-79, 1977 Sess. Laws (Second Session), Ch. 1136, included an appropriation of $1,000,000.00 for the funding of medically unnecessary abortions for indigent women. In order to implement the disbursement of funding, the Social Services Commission adopted administrative rules effective 1 February 1978, codified as 10 NCAC 42W.0001 et seq. These rules provide that the Fund was to be administered by the county departments of social services to reimburse eligible applicants at the maximum rate of $150.00 for first trimester abortions and $500.00 for second trimester abortions. The provisions, set out at 10 NCAC 42W.0001(3) et seq. specified that only medically unnecessary abortions performed within the first twenty weeks of pregnancy were reimbursable. Eligibility for the State Abortion Fund was to be determined by the county departments of social services on the basis of Title XX eligibility criteria for family planning services. The counties were directed to provide to all eligible applicants family planning counselling, to arrange for the delivery of abortion services through appropriate medical providers, including licensed physicians, licensed hospitals, and certified abortion clinics. 10 NCAC 42W.0003(e)(2) provided that county funds, if needed and available, could be used to supplement the State Abortion Fund.

In his complaint filed 21 December 1978, plaintiff alleged that monies had been paid in the year 1978 out of the tax revenues of the State and of Wake County for the performance of medically unnecessary abortions; that the administrative rules pursuant to which the State Abortion Fund was established are unauthorized by statute; that if the rules are authorized by statute, the statute constitutes an unconstitutional delegation of legislative power; that the application of state monies is unconstitutional in that it violates Article V, § 5 of the State Constitution in failing to be an application for purposes stated in the Act levying the tax; that it is an unlawful drawing of monies from State and County treasuries in violation of Article V, § 7; and that it deprives aborted fetuses of their right to life and right to due process in violation of Article I, §§ 1 and 19 of the State Constitution.

On 6 February 1979, the State moved for summary judgment, and on 20 March 1979 Wake County made a similar motion. Based on pleadings, motions, affidavits, admissions, documents and oral argument, the trial court concluded that there were no genuine issues of material fact and granted summary judgment for the defendants, based on the following conclusions of law:

1. A live human fetus is not a legal "person" within the meaning of the North Carolina Constitution, Article I, Sections 1 & 19, and has no inalienable right to life nor right to due process, and accordingly the expenditure of public funds for medically unnecessary abortions of live human fetuses is not unconstitutional.

2. The application of tax monies for the purchase of medically unnecessary abortions of live human fetuses is

not in violation of Article V, Secion 5, of the North Carolina
Constitution, and the drawing of public monies from the
state and County treasuries for the purchase of medically
unnecessary abortions of live human fetuses is not in violation of the Article V, Section 7, of the North Carolina Constitution, and accordingly the expenditure of public monies
for medically unnecessary abortions of live human fetuses
is not unconstitutional.

3. The legislative intent of the General Assembly as
expressed in GS 130-254, *et seq.*, is not inconstant (sic) with
the expenditure of public funds for medically unnecessary
abortions of live human fetuses, and accordingly such expenditure is lawful.

4. The administrative rules under which the Defendants operate the North Carolina Abortion Fund, codified
as 10 N.C.A.C. 42W.0001, *et seq.*, are fully authorized by GS
143B-153 and GS 14-45.1, are effective, and are the product
of a lawful delegation of legislative authority consistent
with the North Carolina Constitution, Article I, Section 6,
and Article II, Section I, and accordingly the expenditure
of public funds for medically unnecessary abortions of live
human fetuses is not unconstitutional or in violation of
statute.

5. The expenditure of public funds by Wake County for
the abortions of live human fetuses is not *ultra vires.*

Plaintiff appealed from entry of judgment in favor of defendants.

Plaintiff appellant *pro se.*

*Attorney General Edmisten by Associate Attorney Steven
M. Shaber for the State of North Carolina, appellee.*

Michael R. Ferrell for Wake County, Appellee

PARKER, Judge.

[1] Initially, plaintiff contends that the use of state tax monies for the funding of elective abortions through the State Abortion Fund is unconstitutional because a human fetus is a "person" within the meaning of Article I, Sections 1 & 19 of the North Carolina Constitution and is therefore entitled to the constitutional protections of those sections. We note at the outset that there is no federal constitutional requirement that a state provide funding for elective abortions. *Maher v. Roe*, 432 U.S. 464, 97 S. Ct. 2376, 53 L. Ed. 2d 484 (1977). Thus, the narrow question which plaintiff has initially raised on this appeal is whether the North Carolina Constitution affords constitutional protection to fetal life such that the state may not provide funds for the performance of medically unnecessary abortions.

Article I, § 1 of the Constitution of North Carolina provides:

The equality and rights of persons. We hold it to be self-evident that all persons are created equal; that they are endowed by their Creator with certain inalienable rights; that among these are life, liberty, the enjoyment of the fruits of their own labor, and the pursuit of happiness.

Article I, § 19 provides in part:

Law of the land; equal protection of the laws. No person shall be taken, imprisoned, or disseized of his freehold, liberties, or privileges, or outlawed, or exiled, or in any manner deprived of his life, liberty, or property, but by the law of the land.

Although it is basic that constitutional guaranties should be liberally construed, *see, Allred v. Graves*, 261, N.C. 31, 134 S.E. 2d 186 (1964), it is equally basic that such guaranties are not to be construed as absolute or without limitations. In interpreting the meaning of a word or phrase used in a constitutional provision, our courts have often attempted to ascertain the intention of those by whom the constitution was adopted. *Elliott v. Board of Equalization*, 203 N.C. 749, 166 S.E. 918 (1932); *Collie v. Commissioners*, 145 N.C. 170, 59 S.E. 44 (1907). Also, the courts of this State have looked to interpretations of similar words or

phrases in the U.S. Constitution. Although decisions of the
Supreme Court of the United States construing federal constitutional provisions are not binding on our courts in interpreting cognate provisions in the North Carolina Constitution, they
are, nonetheless, highly persuasive. *Watch Co. v. Brand Distributors*, 285 N.C. 467, 206 S.E. 2d 141, (1974). Having considered
both the probable intent of the framers of our Constitution, as
well as the U.S. Supreme Court's interpretation of the similar
wording in the Federal Constitution, we hold that a fetus is not
a "person" within the meaning of Article I §§ 1 and 19 of the
Constitution of North Carolina.

The intention of those by whom our Constitution was
drafted should be determined by looking "to the history, general
spirit of the times, and the prior and the then existing law . . . ."
Perry v. Stancil, 237 N.C. 442, 444, 75 S.E. 2d 512, 514 (1953). The
"Law of the Land" clause was originally adopted as Section 12
of the Declaration of Rights which, by Section 44 of the Constitution of 1776 of North Carolina, was incorporated as a part
of the State Constitution. Originally, the section protected a
"freeman" only; however, in 1868 that limited protection was
extended to protect a "person." In the same year, 1868, Article
I, § 1 was newly added to reinforce the right of "all men" to life.
The 1946 revisions amended the Constitution to the extent of
substituting the word "person" for "men" in Article I, § 1, as
well as in other sections of our Constitution. *See* Gardner, "The
Continuous Revision of Our State Constitution," 36 N.C.L. Rev
297 (1958). Historical precedent persuades us that it was not the
intent of those who drafted the Constitution to protect the
unborn in the full constitutional sense. Although there is some
dispute on the issue, the general conclusion of legal scholars is
that abortion of an unborn child was not homicide at common
law, and that consensual abortion was no crime at all. *See, e.g.*,
Means, "The Phoenix of Abortional Freedom: Is a Penumbral
or Ninth Amendment Right About to Arise from the
Nineteenth-Century Legislative Ashes of a Fourteenth-
Century Common-Law Liberty?," 17 New York Law Forum 335
(1971); Note, "The Law and the Unborn Child: The Legal and
Logical Inconsistencies," 46 Notre Dame Lawyer 349 (1971).

Stam v. State

The first reported case in which our Supreme Court applied the common law of abortion was *State v. Slagle*, 82 N.C. 653 (1880), in which it was held that it was a misdemeanor to administer a noxious drug to a pregnant woman with intent to produce an abortion. Upon later hearing of the same case, reported in 83 N.C. 630 (1880), the Court adopted the view of the courts of Pennsylvania: "It is not the murder of a living child which constitutes the offence (sic), but the destruction of gestation by wicked means and against nature. The moment the womb is instinct with embryo life and gestation has begun, the crime may be perpetrated." 83 N.C. at 632. It is apparent, then, that even though held to be a crime under the common law as adopted by this state, the crime was not murder, the taking of a person's life, but the destruction of the potentiality of life and, as such, merely a misdemeanor. Even when the crime of abortion was made a statutory offense in this State in 1881, it carried a maximum punishment of ten years imprisonment with a fine. 1881 Sess. Laws, c. 351, s. 1.

Neither is there any indication in the history of the civil law in this state that the fetus was ever regarded in the complete sense as a "person" prior to birth. This is not to say that the state did not accord certain rights and protections to the unborn child in anticipation of its eventual birth and capacity to exercise the full rights of a "person." At common law, a child *en ventre sa mere* could not acquire property by deed. *Dupree v. Dupree*, 45 N.C. 164 (1853). Such a child could, however, take by will *contingent upon his live birth. Barringer v. Cowan*, 55 N.C. 436 (1856); *see also, Mackie v. Mackie*, 230 N.C. 152, 52 S.E. 2d 352 (1949). As early as 1809 the North Carolina Supreme Court recognized that after-born children were entitled to a distributive share of an intestate's estate. *Hill v. Moore*, 5 N.C. 233 (1809). The common law as to deeds was changed by N.C. Rev. Code Ch. 43, § 4 (1854) which provided that an unborn infant in *esse "shall be deemed* a person capable of taking by deed or other writing, any estate whatever *in the same manner as if he were born*." (emphasis added). In discussing the modern successor to that statute, G.S. 41-5, our Supreme Court stated:

It seems clear to us that G.S. 41-5 gives to an unborn infant the same capacity to take property by "deed or other writing," as such infant has under the law governing its right to take by inheritance or devise .... By a legal fiction or indulgence, a legal personality is *imputed* to an unborn child as a rule of property for all purposes beneficial to the infant after his birth, but not for purposes working to his detriment. The interest taken by the child at birth dates back to the time of conception or to the later originating of the title, and cannot be defeated by intermediate proceedings to which he was not a party. (Emphasis Added).

Mackie v. Mackie, supra at 154, 55, 52 S.E. 2d at 354.

The view expressed in Mackie, that an unborn child may be a "person" for some purposes, is qualified in one significant respect: Live birth, the event which the "legal fiction" anticipates, is a condition precedent to the exercise of the property rights of the child *en ventre sa mere.* The rule of *Deal v. Sexton,* 144 N.C. 157, 56 S.E. 691 (1907), that an inheritance or estate of such a child may not be destroyed by judicial proceedings to which it was neither a party nor represented by a guardian ad litem is not inconsistent with the view that a fetus was not historically a "person" within the term's full legal meaning. In that case, the living heirs sought partition of a decedent's land prior to the birth of a child of decedent who was at the time of decedent's death *en ventre sa mere.* The court indulged, just as the court in the later *Mackie* case did, in the legal fiction which treats the unborn child *as if* a person in anticipation of the most common end result of human pregnancy, live birth.

Thus, viewing the common law which was in existence in 1776 when the "Law of the Land" clause became part of our Constitution, and early statutory enactments in existence in 1868 when Article I, § 1 was adopted, as well as considering later judicial interpretations of the rights of the unborn, we find no historical indication that the constitutional protections of those sections were intended to extend to the unborn child. This Court is, of course, aware that our State Constitution is an organic document, and that the interpretation of its language is subject to change to include new things and new conditions of the same class as those specified which were not known or contemplated when it was adopted. *Purser v. Ledbetter,* 227 N.C. 1, 40 S.E. 2d 702 (1946). Clearly, the state of medical knowledge concerning fetal development is now far more advanced than at the time the State Constitution was adopted in the eighteenth century and amended in the nineteenth century. If the fact of biological life were the sole consideration here, plaintiff's argument would not fail, yet the reasons are compelling why the fact should not control. If the word "person" in Article I, § § 1 and 19 were now broadened in meaning to include the fetus, such interpretation would indirectly conflict with our federal Constitution. Bound as the courts of this state would be by the U.S. Supreme Court's holding in *Roe v. Wade,* 410 U.S. 113, 93 S. Ct. 705, 35 L. Ed. 2d 147 (1973), that a woman has a substantive due process right to choose whether to have an abortion in the first trimester of pregnancy without any state interference, a fetus could be a "person" within the meaning of Article I, §§ 1 & 19 whose life could be protected from state funding of abortions, but whose life could not be protected in any manner inconsistent with the mother's right under *Roe.* Also, such an interpretation could have troublesome future implications. The State Abortion Fund at present only provides funding for medically unnecessary abortions. 10 NCAC 42 W.0001(3). Medically necessary abortions, those defined as necessary to save the life of the mother, to prevent severe and long-lasting physical health damage, or to terminate a pregnancy caused by reported rape or incest, are currently funded by the federal government. Should Congress ever elect to terminate such funding, a construction of the State Constitution which includes fetuses as "persons" would operate as an absolute bar to state assistance for abortions necessary to save the life of the mother or to terminate pregnancy caused by rape or incest.

Apart from historical and practical considerations, we are also guided by the decision of the U.S. Supreme Court in *Roe v. Wade, supra.* The phrase "The Law of the Land," used in Article I, § 19, of the Constitution of North Carolina, is synonymous with "Due Process of Law." *Watch Co. v. Brand Distributors, supra.* In *Roe v. Wade* the U.S. Supreme Court held that the word "person," as used in the Fourteenth Amendment due process clause, does not include the unborn. In reaching that holding, the Court discussed in detail the background of the treatment of the unborn in light of ancient philosophy, the common law, and American statutory law through the nineteenth century. The Court's conclusion, based on such detailed considerations, as well as our own consideration of the historical background of the law in our own State, persuades us that the word "person" should not have broader meaning in the State Constitution than it has in the U.S. Constitution. Our ruling in the present case in no way implies that the unborn child is to be accorded no rights at all. The General Assembly may, in recognition of the potentiality of life, continue to grant the rights and privileges to the unborn which it chooses. We hold only that the protections of Article I, §§ 1 & 19 do not extend to the fetus so as to prohibit the funding here at issue.

[2] Plaintiff next contends that the appropriation and expenditure of state tax monies for elective abortions violates Article V, § 5 of the N.C. Constitution. That section provides:

Every act of the General Assembly levying a tax shall state the special object to which it is to be applied, and it shall be applied to no other purpose.

The funds appropriated for the funding of abortions for indigents are derived from taxes levied under Chapter 105 of the General Statutes. While certain of the taxes imposed are subject to use for special limited purposes, *e.g.* G.S. 105-164.2 (sales and use tax for the support of the public school system), G.S. 105-435 (fuel tax for the use of the state highways), most of the taxes levied in Chapter 105 are subject only to G.S. 105-1 which provides in part:

The purpose of this Subchapter shall be to raise and provide revenue for the necessary uses and purposes of the government and State of North Carolina . . . .

Plaintiff contends that because the administrative rules, 10 NCAC 42W.0001 *et seq.* specify that medically necessary abortions are not reimbursable through the State Abortion Fund, *a fortiori*, the appropriation of funds for abortions cannot be for the necessary uses and purposes of the State of North Carolina.

To say, as plaintiff does, that pregnancy itself creates no necessity for an abortion, is not to answer the legal issue involved. There is clearly no doubt that the appropriation of funding for other medical services is a legitimate and proper use of state tax monies to aid the poorer citizens of North Carolina. Because there is adequate funding available through Medicaid for medically necessary abortions, the General Assembly, by establishing a fund for elective abortions, has chosen to bridge the gap in coverage to ensure that low-income women have a meaningful opportunity to exercise their constitutional choice to terminate their pregnancies. While there is no doubt that a state may choose to influence a woman's abortion decision, *Maher v. Roe, supra*, by funding childbirth but not abortion, it is clear that if funding for childbirth could be considered a "necessary use and purpose of government," abortion funding is equally so. Admittedly, the State's interest in funding childbirth may be that of encouraging proper medical care to ensure the health of both mother and child, as well as to encourage childbirth itself, both certainly necessary uses and purposes of the government. Equally so, the State's interest in funding elective abortion may be that of ensuring, if an indigent women chooses abortion, that her health is protected through her ability to obtain competent professional medical care.

[3] Plaintiff's final contention on this appeal is that the expenditure of public funds by Wake County for elective abortions is *ultra vires*. The record discloses that the public funds expended by Wake County in 1978-79 included both state funds disbursed through the county department of social services and supplemental county funds derived from local tax revenues.

We consider first the question of the lawfulness of Wake County's use of state funds for this purpose. As an agent of the State, the County has no inherent power, but may exercise only those powers prescribed by statute and those necessarily implied by law. *Insurance Co. v. Guilford County*, 225 N.C. 293, 34 S.E. 2d 430 (1945). In administering state funds appropriated by the General Assembly for the State Abortion Fund, the County has acted pursuant to the administrative rules governing the Fund, 10 NCAC 42W.0001 *et seq*. Thus, whether the County has power to administer these funds appropriated for elective abor-

tions depends upon whether these rules were enacted pursuant
to statutorily granted authority. The rules in question state in
part that they were enacted pursuant to G.S. 143B-153. That
statute creates the Social Services Commission of the Department of Human Resources and authorizes and empowers the
Commission to adopt rules and regulations "under and not
inconsistent with the laws of the State necessary to carry out
the provisions and purposes of this Article." Subsection (7) of
G.S. 143B-153 provides a broad grant of power to the Commission to adopt "rules and regulations consistent with the provisions of this Chapter," as an addition to the specific grants of
rule-making power in subsections (1) through (6).

The purposes of the Article referred to in G.S. 143B-153,
Article 3 of Ch. 143B, are stated in G.S. 143B-137 to be:

It shall be the duty of the Department to provide the necessary management, development of policy, and establishment and enforcement of standards for the provision of
services in the fields of general and mental health and
rehabilitation with the basic goal being to assist all citizens
— as individuals, families, and communities — to achieve
and maintain an adequate level of health, social and economic well-being, and dignity.

Plaintiff contends on this appeal that the rules in question are
neither consistent with state law nor "necessary" to carry out
the above-stated purposes. In support of his contention that the
regulations are inconsistent with state law, plaintiff relies on
G.S. 130-254 which, in recognition of the high mortality rate
among unborn children of mothers from low socioeconomic
backgrounds, mandates the establishment of programs to improve perinatal care. That the State has decided on the one
hand to provide care to low-income pregnant women who
choose to bear children in the interests of promoting the birth of
healthy children is in no way inconsistent with its decision to
ensure proper medical care for those low-income women who
choose to exercise their constitutionally protected right to terminate their pregnancies. Neither are the Rules inconsistent
with provisions of G.S. 108-61 which adopt the provisions of the
federal Social Security Act. It is true that the Social Security

Stam v. State

Act only provides funds for medically necessary abortions and that § 210 of the 1978 Departments of Labor and Health, Education, and Welfare Appropriations Act, Public Law 95-480, prohibits *federal* funding of medically unnecessary abortions; however, nothing in the statute either expressly or impliedly prohibits the states from providing such funds.

Further, that the rules governing administration of the State Abortion Fund provide only for abortions not strictly *medically* necessary does not imply that such rules are not "necessary" to carry out the purposes of the Department of Human Resources as required by G.S. 143B-152. The provision of funding for elective abortions fulfills the purpose stated in G.S. 143B-137 of providing services "in the fields of general and mental health," and the promulgation of administrative rules under G.S. 143B-153 satisfies the requirement of "necessity" in that it provides standards without which the State Abortion Fund could not lawfully be administered. Thus, because the rules empowering counties to apply state funds for elective abortions were duly adopted pursuant to an express grant of statutory authority, plaintiff's argument that the County was without power to use state funds is without merit.

[4] The second issue concerning the county is the lawfulness of the expenditure of its own funds derived from local taxation. Any power which the county has to expend funds to supplement those provided by the State Abortion Fund is granted under G.S. 153A-149. G.S. 153A-149(c)(30) provides that a county may levy property taxes with a rate limitation "to provide for the public welfare through the maintenance and administration of public assistance programs not required by Chapters 108 and 111 of the General Statutes". In turn, G.S. 153A-149(b)(8) authorizes the levy of taxes by counties without restriction as to rate or amount "[t]o provide for public assistance required by Chapters 108 and 111 of the General Statutes." G.S. 153A-149(g) limits the power to tax otherwise conferred in G.S. 153A-149 as follows:

This section [G.S. 153A-149] does not authorize any county to undertake any program, function, joint undertaking, or service not otherwise authorized by law. It is intended only to authorize the levy of property taxes within the limitations set out herein to finance programs, functions, or services authorized by other portions of the General Statutes or by local acts.

The levy of taxes and the expenditure of county revenues to fund a program of elective abortions for indigent women does not fall within the category of programs required by Chapters 108 and 111 of the General Statutes. Thus, G.S. 153A-149(b)(8) is inapplicable in the present case. Chapter 111 is intended to provide solely for aid to the blind. Although G.S. 108-59 requires the establishment of programs of "medical assistance" funded by federal, State, and county appropriations, G.S. 108-60 limits the use of funds to payment of medical expenses for eligible persons "when it is *essential to the health and welfare of such* person that such care be provided." (emphasis added).

We consider, therefore, whether taxation by the county and expenditure of funds for elective abortions for indigents is authorized by the language G.S. 153A-149(c)(30), and if so, whether the program of funding those abortions is "authorized by other portions of the General Statutes" as required by G.S. 153A-149(g). As to the first issue, we hold that the levy of taxes with a rate limitation for this purpose is authorized by G.S. 153A-149(c)(30), because the taxation is for the purpose of providing a program of public assistance not required by Chapters 108 and 111 of the General Statutes, but which, like those required by Chapter 108, is directed to the problems of poverty. *See Hughey v. Cloninger*, 297 N.C. 86, 253 S.E. 2d 898 (1979). Further, the undertaking of the social service through the use of county funds is authorized by "other portions of the General Statutes" as required by G.S. 153A-149(g). G.S. 153A-255 provides:

Each county shall provide social services programs pursuant to Chapter 108 and Chapter 111 *and may otherwise undertake, sponsor, organize, engage in, and support other social service programs intended to further the health, welfare, education, safety, comfort, and convenience of its citizens.*

The grant of power in this provision is sufficiently broad to permit the county to sponsor and support the program established by the State Abortion Fund through the levy of taxes and the expenditure of county funds.

The judgment appealed from is

Affirmed.

Chief Judge MORRIS and Judge MARTIN (Robert M.) concur.

STATE OF NORTH CAROLINA v. ERNEST LEE MARTIN

No. 797SC922

(Filed 17 June 1980)

1. **Robbery § 4.3– armed robbery – money given to defendant by victim – sufficiency of evidence**

   Evidence was sufficient to be submitted to the jury in a prosecution for armed robbery where it tended to show that defendant told the victim that he did not want to hurt him and did not want his money, but defendant was at the same time pointing a sawed-off shotgun at the victim, and the victim was in fear when he subsequently placed his wallet containing money on the front seat of the car which defendant was driving; although defendant did not take possession of the wallet at that time, evidence that the victim was soon thereafter placed in the trunk of the car and that the wallet was gone when the vehicle was later found in a town about thirty miles away was sufficient to permit the inference that a taking occurred at the time the victim was forced into the trunk and was effectively deprived of his wallet and cash therein, and that the taking followed the assault sufficiently closely in time to satisfy the elements of armed robbery.

2. **Robbery § 3.2– armed robbery – gun like one used by defendant – admission not prejudicial**

   In a prosecution for armed robbery, even if an exhibit of the State was not in fact the same shotgun used by defendant, in view of defendant's own testimony that it was "like" the one he had possessed, any error in its admission was harmless.

3. **Kidnapping § 1.3– age of victim – submission of issue not required**

   There was no merit to defendant's contention that the trial court erred in failing to submit the issue of a kidnapping victim's age to the jury, since the victim's age is not an essential element of the crime of kidnapping itself.

4. **Kidnapping § 1.3; Robbery § 5– armed robbery and kidnapping – instructions as to separate crimes proper**

The trial court in an armed robbery and kidnapping case sufficiently instructed the jury that the armed robbery offense must have been completed prior to the beginning of the kidnapping offense where the court instructed the jury that the State was required to prove, among other things, "that [the] carrying or transporting of [the victim] was a separate complete act, independent of and apart from the armed robbery," and that this was done "after committing robbery with a firearm."

5. **Constitutional Law § 34; Criminal Law § 26– double jeopardy – one act violating different statutes.**

If the facts alleged in one indictment, if given in evidence, would sustain a conviction under a second indictment, or if the same evidence would support a conviction in each case, a defendant may not be tried, convicted and punished for both offenses; if, however, a single act constitutes an offense against two statutes and each statute requires proof of an additional fact which the other does not, the offenses are not the same in law and in fact, and a defendant may be convicted and punished for both.

6. **Criminal Law § 26.5; Larceny § 1.1; Robbery § 1.2– armed robbery – larceny of money and automobile – conviction for both offenses double jeopardy**

In a prosecution of defendant for armed robbery and larceny, judgment of the trial court imposing sentence for misdemeanor larceny of the victim's automobile must be arrested, since the evidence necessary to convict defendant of both offenses was substantially the same; inherent in the jury's verdict finding defendant guilty of armed robbery was a finding that defendant took and carried away property consisting of the victims cash and automobile intending to deprive him of the property permanently; and both offenses for which defendant was indicted and convicted arose out of the same continuous course of conduct.

7. **Constitutional Law § 34; Criminal Law § 26– double jeopardy – application to three situations**

There are essentially three contexts in which the N. C. Supreme Court has held that conviction and punishment of a defendant for more than one offense results in impermissible multiple punishment: (1) where a defendant is convicted and sentenced for both felony murder and the underlying felony; (2) where a defendant is convicted and sentenced for two offenses, one being a lesser included offense of the other; and (3) where a defendant is convicted and sentenced for two offenses each arising out of the same conduct but to which the legislature has affixed two criminal labels and prosecutorial abuse is evident.

8. **Criminal Law § 26; Kidnapping § 1; Robbery § 1.2– armed robbery – kidnapping to facilitate flight after armed robbery – two convictions – no double jeopardy**

Defendant was not twice placed in jeopardy when he was tried and convicted of kidnapping for the purpose of facilitating flight following his

State v. Martin

participation in an armed robbery and of armed robbery, since the intent of the legislature in establishing the punishment for kidnapping was to impose an indivisible penalty for restraint and removal for specified purposes, no hypothetical part of which penalty represents a punishment for the felony which gave rise to the flight of defendant and his removal of the victim, and the crimes of armed robbery and kidnapping involve vastly different social implications, and the legislature is clearly free to denounce each as a separately punishable offense. G.S. 14-39(a).

APPEAL by defendant from *Rouse, Judge.* Judgment entered 28 March 1979 in Superior Court, NASH County. Heard in the Court of Appeals 28 February 1980.

In separate bills of indictment returned as true bills defendant was charged as follows:

In Case No. 79CRS610 defendant was charged with having on or about 22 December 1978 unlawfully and feloniously kidnapped Edgar Wells, III, a male person over 16 years of age by unlawfully removing him from one place to another without his consent "for the purpose of facilitating the flight of Earnest [sic] Lee Martin following his participation in the commission of a felony, to wit: robbery with a dangerous weapon."

In Case No. 79CRS611 defendant was charged with having on or about 22 December 1978 willfully and feloniously stolen, taken and carried away one 1962 four-door Mercury sedan, License No. PRE-508, the personal property of Edgar Wells, III, having a value of $300.00.

In Case No. 79CRS612 defendant was charged with having on or about 22 December 1978 wilfully, forcibly and violently taken, stolen, and carried away U.S. Currency in the amount of $120.00 from the person of Edgar Wells, III, with the use and threatened use of a .12 gauge sawed-off shotgun whereby the life of Edgar Wells III, was endangered, and threatened.

Defendant pled not guilty to all charges. The cases were consolidated for trial.

At trial upon these indictments, James Edgar Wells testified that on 22 December 1978 he was working at Strick's Truck
Stop in Rocky Mount, N.C. At about 1:00 a.m. he was working
near the gas pumps and noticed a black male wearing a tobog-
gan, who he identified at trial as the defendant, standing
around in the parking lot area. Wells spoke to him briefly at that
time. Wells's 1962 Mercury Comet was parked in front of the
truck stop building, and defendant asked Wells if it was his car
and if it ran "good," to which Wells responded "Yes." During the
next two hours Wells noticed that the defendant was still on the
truck stop premises. At one point Wells told him to move from
the pit area of the truck stop. At approximately 3:30 a.m. Wells
told defendant that he "was going to have to call somebody if he
didn't go ahead and get out of the way." Defendant told Wells
that he was going to get his knapsack, and defendant went to
the rear of the truck stop. Defendant called Wells to the rear,
and Wells saw him reach down for something. The next thing
Wells saw was defendant holding a faded, chrome-plated,
sawed-off shotgun. Defendant walked toward Wells, pointing
the gun at Wells's heart. Wells had a wallet with him in which he
had about $150 to $160 in cash belonging to Strick's Truck Stop
which he had collected between 8 p.m. and 3 a.m. Wells testified:

> When I first saw that gun or whatever he had, it scared
> me. As soon as I saw that gun I offered him some money. I
> had the money in a truck driver's wallet that had the chain
> missing. I carry it in my back pocket and had it in my back
> pocket. When I first saw the gun I was about 12 feet from
> Lee Martin. As soon as I saw the gun, I did not instantly
> pull out the wallet and say here is the money or something
> to that effect. But I offered him . . . I pulled the wallet out of
> my back pocket and offered him the money. I recall him
> telling me, "I don't want to hurt you." He told me, "I don't
> want to hurt you." We all talked about the money for a few
> minutes. I told him to go on and take the money. He told me,
> "I don't want to hurt you. I don't want your money." I kept
> telling him to take the money. That is the way the conversa-
> tion went. When I first saw the gun he didn't demand the
> money from me. He didn't even ask for it. I offered it to him.
> He told me he didn't want it and he told me he didn't want to
> hurt me.

Then we went back around to the 1962 Comet in front of the building. I laid the truck driver's wallet on the front seat. I laid that on the front seat. I never gave it to Lee. I laid it on the front seat. I never gave it to Lee. I just laid it on the front seat of the car. I drove. I drove around back.

After Wells drove his automobile to the rear of the truck stop as directed by the defendant, defendant told Wells to cut the engine off and get out of the car. Wells did so and was instructed by defendant to go to the rear of the automobile and open the trunk. The defendant ordered Wells to get into the trunk, which Wells did after emptying its contents. Wells lay in the trunk for fifteen or twenty minutes while the vehicle was stationary. After that time, the automobile began to move. After twenty-five or thirty minutes defendant stopped the car for about ten minutes and then drove on another fifteen minutes before stopping again. Defendant then opened the trunk and, pointing the shotgun at Wells, told him to get out. Defendant asked Wells if he knew where he was and then pointed him towards Rocky Mount. The two men shook hands, and defendant drove off. Wells hitchhiked back to Rocky Mount. He testified that, in his opinion, the fair market value of his car was $200.00 or less.

The Deputy Sheriff of Nash County who investigated the matter testified that Wells's car was found in Weldon in front of the home of defendant's sister on 24 December 1978. Wells's wallet was no longer in the vehicle. On 29 December 1978 defendant was arrested.

Defendant testified that he arrived at Strick's Truck Stop at about 11:00 p.m. on 22 December after walking to Rocky Mount from Wendell. He had a sawed-off shotgun with him which he was taking to his mother's home in Weldon to leave. Defendant told Wells that he was trying to find a ride hitchhiking. Defendant stated that when he went around to the rear of the truck stop when Wells told him to leave, Wells followed him. Defendant tried to hide the gun to keep Wells from calling the police. When Wells saw the gun and became frightened, he offered defendant his money and his car. Defendant assured him that he did not want to hurt him, that he was only trying to get a ride. Wells offered to take defendant wherever he wanted to go and told him to take his money. Defendant denied having placed Wells into the trunk of the car, stating that Wells got into the driver's side of the car and defendant sat next to him. After the automobile was moving, Wells asked defendant to drive, and they traded places. The gun lay on the floor on the driver's side. After defendant drove about fifteen miles north on Highway 301 and Interstate 95, he stopped the vehicle. Defendant told Wells that he was going to Weldon to see his mother and his sister to take his gun there. Defendant told Wells to take his car and go home. Wells insisted that he keep the car, and defendant drove on to Weldon to his sister's house. During the entire ride defendant had assured Wells that he did not intend to hurt him.

The jury found defendant guilty of kidnapping, misdemeanor larceny, and armed robbery. The court entered judgment sentencing defendant to prison for not less than twenty nor more than twenty-five years in Case No. 79CRS610, two years in Case No. 79CRS611, and not less than twenty nor more than twenty-five years in Case No. 79CRS612, all sentences to run concurrently. From these judgments defendant appealed.

Attorney General Rufus Edmisten, by Elizabeth C. Bunting, Assistant Attorney General, for the State.

Early and Chandler by John S. Williford, Jr. for defendant appellant.

PARKER, Judge.

Defendant challenges on appeal the sufficiency of the evidence to support his conviction for armed robbery. Although the record does not reflect that defendant renewed his motion to dismiss at the close of all of the evidence, the provisions of G.S. 15A-1227(d) and G.S. 15A-1446(d)(5) allow him to raise this issue on appeal. *State v. Alston,* 44 N.C. App. 72, 259 S.E. 2d 767 (1979). In determining the sufficiency of the evidence to go to the jury, all of the evidence must be considered in the light most favorable to the State, and the State is entitled to every reasonable inference to be drawn from it. *State v. Lee,* 294 N.C. 299, 240 S.E. 2d 449 (1978). When so viewed, that evidence must be sufficient to permit a rational trier of fact to find guilt beyond a reasonable doubt. *Jackson v. Virginia*, 443 U.S. 307, 99 S. Ct. 2781, 61 L. Ed. 2d 560 (1979).

[1] Viewed in the light most favorable to the State, the evidence in the present case was sufficient to permit a rational trier to find defendant guilty of armed robbery beyond a reasonable doubt.

The gist of the offense of robbery with firearms defined by G.S. 14-87 is the accomplishment of the robbery by the use or threatened use of firearms or other dangerous weapons whereby the life of a person is endangered or threatened. *State v. Harris*, 281 N.C. 542, 189 S.E. 2d 249 (1972); *State v. Ballard*, 280 N.C. 479, 186 S.E. 2d 372 (1972). In the present case the State's witness Wells testified that he offered his wallet containing the money when he saw defendant's shotgun pointed at his chest. Although defendant told Wells "I don't want to hurt you, I don't want your money," the State's evidence tends to show that defendant was pointing the sawed-off shotgun at Wells at the same time, and that Wells was in fear when he subsequently placed the wallet containing the money on the seat of the car. Further, although defendant did not take possession of the wallet at that time, the evidence that Wells was soon thereafter placed in the trunk of the car and that the wallet was gone when the vehicle was later found in Weldon is sufficient to permit the inference that a taking occurred at the time Wells was forced into the trunk and was effectively deprived of his wallet and the cash contained therein, and that the taking followed the assault sufficiently closely in time to satisfy the elements of armed robbery. *See State v. Lilly*, 32 N.C. App. 467, 232 S.E. 2d 495, *cert. denied* 292 N.C. 643, 235 S.E. 2d 64 (1977). Defendant's assignment of error directed to the sufficiency of the evidence is overruled.

[2] Defendant also assigns error to the admission of State's Exhibit No. 1, a twelve gauge sawed-off shotgun, on the grounds that insufficient foundation was laid to establish that it was the same weapon in his possession on 22 December 1978. This assignment of error is without merit. Defendant admitted at trial that he had a twelve-gauge sawed-off shotgun with him

on the date in question and that State's Exhibit No. 1 was "like" the one he had, but was not the same gun. Even if it be assumed that State's Exhibit No. 1 was not in fact the same shotgun used by defendant, in view of defendant's own testimony that it was "like" the one he had possessed, any error in its admission was harmless. *State v. Patterson*, 284 N.C. 190, 200 S.E. 2d 16 (1973).

[3] Defendant's several assignments of error to the court's instructions on the kidnapping charge are likewise without merit. He contends that under G.S. 14-39(a)(2) the restraint or removal of the victim must be without his consent if the victim is 16 years of age or over, and that the court erred in failing to submit the issue of Wells's age to the jury where there was no direct evidence establishing that he was over 16 years of age or over, and that the court erred in failing to submit the issue of Wells's age to the jury where there was no direct evidence establishing that he was over 16 years of age. This argument was recently rejected by our Supreme Court in *State v. Hunter*, 299 N.C. 29, 261 S.E. 2d 189 (1980): "[T]he victim's age is not an essential element of the crime of kidnapping itself, but it is, instead, a factor which relates to the state's burden of proof in regard to consent." 299 N.C. at 40, 261 S.E. 2d at 196.

[4] Defendant also argues that the court erred in its instructions on the kidnapping charge in not clearly instructing the jury that the armed robbery offense must have been completed prior to the beginning of the kidnapping offense. We disagree. The court instructed the jury that the State was required to prove, among other things, "that [the] carrying or transporting of Wells was a separate complete act, independent of and apart from the armed robbery," and that this was done "*after* committing robbery with a firearm" (emphasis added). Based on these instructions, we fail to see how the jury could have been misled.

Having determined that the evidence was sufficient to support the conviction for armed robbery, we consider defendant's contention that he was placed in jeopardy more than once on the grounds that the armed robbery and the larceny were part of a single transaction and that the armed robbery was merged into the kidnapping charge. The principle upon which defendant relies was articulated by our Supreme Court in *State v. Summrell*, 282 N.C. 157, 192 S.E. 2d 569 (1972):

> The constitutional guaranty against double jeopardy protects a defendant from multiple punishments for the same offense, a principle recognized in *State v. Parker*, 262 N.C. 679, 138 S.E. 2d 496 (1964). *See also U.S. v. Benz*, 282 U.S. 304, 309, 75 L. Ed. 354, 357, 51 S. Ct. 113, 114 (1931). The fact that concurrent, identical sentences [are] imposed in each case makes this duplication of conviction and punishment no less a violation of defendant's constitutional right not to be put in jeopardy twice for the same offense.

282 N.C. at 173, 192 S.E. 2d at 579. *Accord, State v. Raynor*, 33 N.C. App. 698, 236 S.E. 2d 307 (1977).

[5] The double jeopardy test generally applied is alternative in character: That is, if the facts alleged in one indictment, if given in evidence, would sustain a conviction under a second indictment, *or* if the same evidence would support a conviction in each case, a defendant may not be tried, convicted and punished for both offenses. *State v. Birckhead*, 256 N.C. 494, 124 S.E. 2d 838 (1962); *State v. Hicks*, 233 N.C. 511, 64 S.E. 2d 871 (1951). If, however, a single act constitutes an offense against two statutes and each statute requires proof of an additional fact which the other does not, the offenses are not the same in law and in fact and a defendant may be convicted and punished for both. *State v. Midgett*, 214 N.C. 107, 198 S.E. 613 (1938).

[6] Applying this test in the present case to defendant's convictions for armed robbery and larceny, we conclude that the judgment in Case No. 79CRS611 imposing sentence for misdemeanor larceny of Wells's automobile must be arrested. Although the facts alleged in each indictment may state separate offenses occurring on the same date, the evidence necessary to convict defendant of both offenses was substantially the same. Inherent in the jury's verdict finding defendant guilty of armed robbery was a finding that defendant took and carried away property consisting of cash from Wells's possession intending to deprive him of its use permanently. Equally so, inherent in the jury's verdict finding defendant guilty of larceny

---

State v. Martin

---

was a finding that defendant took and carried away Wells's automobile intending to deprive him of it permanently. Although the taking of the currency and the taking of the automobile may not have occurred at the exact same point in time, both offenses for which defendant was indicted and convicted arose out of the same continuous course of conduct. The verdicts of guilty of two separate offenses have the same effect as if defendant had been found guilty after trial on a single indictment which charged the larceny of both the automobile and the cash. *See, State v. Potter*, 285 N.C. 238, 204 S.E. 2d 649 (1974).

Defendant's argument that he was also placed twice in jeopardy when he was tried, convicted and sentenced for kidnapping in Case No. 79CRS610 and armed robbery in Case No. 79CRS612 rests upon the theory that the State bound itself in the bill of indictment in Case No. 79CRS610 to prove all of the elements of the armed robbery and, therefore, that the armed robbery offense merged into the kidnapping.

The indictment in Case No. 79CRS610 reads as follows:

THE JURORS FOR THE STATE UPON THEIR OATH PRESENT that on or about the 22nd day of December, 1978, in Nash County Earnest [sic] Lee Martin unlawfully and wilfully did feloniously kidnap Edgar Wells, III., a male person who had attained the age of 16 years; by unlawfully removing him from one place to another without his consent; and for the purpose of facilitating the flight of Earnest [sic] Lee Martin following his participation in the commission of a felony, to-wit: robbery with a dangerous weapon. This kidnapping was committed in violation of the following law: GS 14-39

The offense of kidnapping for which defendant was indicted is defined in G.S. 14-39:

§ 14-39. *Kidnapping.* – (a) Any person who shall unlawfully confine, restrain, or remove from one place to another, any other person 16 years of age or over without the consent of such person, or any other person under the age of 16 years without the consent of a parent or legal custodian of such person, shall be guilty of kidnapping if such confinement, restraint or removal is for the purpose of:

> (1) Holding such other person for ransom or as a hostage or using such other person as a shield; or

> (2) Facilitating the commission of any felony or facilitating flight of any person following the commission of a felony; or

> (3) Doing serious bodily harm to or terrorizing the person so confined, restrained or removed or any other person.

The kidnapping statute was enacted by the General Assembly in 1975 Sess. Laws, c. 843, s. 1. Prior to that time, the common law definition of kidnapping governed, which included the elements both of detention and asportation of the victim. *State v. Ingland*, 278 N.C. 42, 178, S.E. 2d 577 (1971); *State v. Murphy*, 280 N.C. 1, 184 S.E. 2d 845 (1971). In adopting the new statute, the General Assembly intended to reject the Supreme Court's holding in *State v. Ingland, supra,* that there must be both detention and asportation of the victim to constitute the substantive offense. *State v. Fulcher*, 294 N.C. 503, 243 S.E. 2d 338 (1978).

Our Supreme Court has had occasion in recent years to review the double jeopardy implications of separate convictions for a felony and for kidnapping under an indictment alleging the confinement, restraint or removal for the purpose of "[f]acilitating the commission of [that]felony." In *State v. Dammons*, 293 N.C. 263, 237 S.E.2d 834 (1977), the Supreme Court found no error in the convictions and sentences for the offenses of felonious assault and kidnapping where the purpose of the kidnapping was to facilitate the commission of the felonious assault:

> In the kidnapping case the felonious assault was alleged in the indictment as being one of the purposes for which defendant removed the victim from one place to another. The felonious assault itself is, therefore, not an element of the

kidnapping offense. It was not necessary for the State to prove the felonious assault in order to convict the defendant of kidnapping. It need only have proved that the *purpose* of the removal was a felonious assault. The assault vis-a-vis the kidnapping charge is mere evidence probative of the defendant's purpose. The purpose proved would, without the assault itself, sustain conviction under the kidnapping statute but not under the assault statute. The felonious assault is, consequently, a separate and distinct offense.

293 N.C. at 275, 237 S.E. 2d at 842. *Accord, State v. Williams*, 295 N.C. 655, 249 S.E. 2d 709 (1978).

Similar reasoning could be applied to defendant's convictions for armed robbery and kidnapping in the present case were it not for the fact that defendant was not indicted under the clause of G.S. 14-39(a) defining kidnapping as confinement, restraint, or removal "for the purpose of . . . [f]acilitating the commission of any felony," but rather under the clause proscribing confinement, restraint or removal "for the purpose of . . . . facilitating flight of any person following the commission of a felony." Unlike the former clause, the latter clause involved here does contemplate the necessity of proof of a completed felony. We hold, however, that principles of double jeopardy still do not apply in a case such as is here presented.

[7] The question of how and when to apply double jeopardy principles to cases in which the issue of multiple punishment is raised may be resolved through consideration of the evils at which the constitutional protection is aimed. There are essentially three contexts in which our Supreme Court has held that conviction and punishment of a defendant for more than one offense results in impermissible multiple punishment: (1) where a defendant is convicted and sentenced for both felony murder and the underlying felony; *e.g. State v. White*, 291 N.C. 118, 229 S.E. 2d 152 (1976); *State v. Woods*, 286 N.C. 612, 213 S.E. 2d 214 (1975); *modified on other grounds*, 428 U.S. 903, 96 S. Ct. 3207, 49 L. Ed. 2d 1208 (1976); (2) where a defendant is convicted and sentenced for two offenses, one offense being a lesser included offense of the other; *e.g. State v. Hatcher*, 277 N.C. 380,

177 S.E. 2d 892 (1970); and (3) where a defendant is convicted and sentenced for two offenses each arising out of the same conduct but to which the legislature has affixed two criminal labels and prosecutorial abuse is evident. *e.g. State v. Summrell, supra; State v. Midyette*, 270 N.C. 229, 154 S.E. 2d 66 (1967). In the first two of these situations our Supreme Court has implicitly recognized that the penalty imposed by the legislature for offense A is hypothetically the sum of a series of penalties, among which is a discrete penalty imposed for offense B. Thus, imposition of a separate penalty for offense B results in the kind of invidious "multiple punishment" which the Fourteenth Amendment to the Federal Constitution and Article I, § 19 of our State Constitution forbid. By way of illustration, the penalty for felony-murder hypothetically includes some sub-penalty representing punishment for the underlying felony. The felony itself substitutes for the elements of premeditation and deliberation which the state would otherwise be required to prove to support a conviction of first degree murder. Similarly, the penalty for rape includes hypothetically discrete penalties for simple assault and for assault with intent to commit rape such that imposition of separate sentences for each offense would run afoul of double jeopardy limitations. In the third situation, the constitutional guaranty against double jeopardy protects a defendant from multiple punishments for what is essentially the same act to which the legislature has affixed more than one criminal label.

In other situations, however, our Supreme Court has recognized that the legislature may intend to punish steps in a single criminal transaction separately, and that the punishment imposed for Offense A, the greater offense, would not include any element of punishment attributable to Offense B which may incidentally be a part of Offense A. Thus, in *State v. Chavis*, 232 N.C. 83, 59 S.E. 2d 348 (1950), the court held that a defendant could be convicted both of unlawfully possessing a quantity of non-taxpaid liquors and unlawfully transporting those same liquors:

> [W]e are not dealing with common law crimes but with statutory offenses; and not with a single *act* with two criminal labels but with *component transactions* violative of

distinct statutory provisions denouncing them as crimes. Neither in fact nor law are they the same. [citation omitted.]. They are not related as different degrees or major and minor parts of the same crime and the doctrine of merger does not apply. The incidental fact that possession goes with the transportation is not significant in law as defeating the legislative right to ban both or either. When the distinction between the offenses is considered in light of their purpose, vastly different social implications are involved and the impact of the crime of greater magnitude on the attempted suppression of the liquor traffic is sufficient to preserve the legislative distinction and intent in denouncing each as a separate punishable offense.

232 N.C. at 85-86, 59 S.E. 2d at 349-350. *Accord, State v. Cameron*, 283 N.C. 191, 195 S.E. 2d 481 (1973).

[8] Viewed in light of the above considerations, defendant's argument that he has been subjected to multiple punishment in violation of his constitutional rights must fail. It is true that the State bound itself in the indictment in Case No. 79CRS610 to prove that defendant restrained or removed Edgar Wells for the purpose of facilitating flight following his participation in the commission of armed robbery. That the armed robbery may technically have become a factual element which the State was required to prove so as to show defendant's *purpose* in restraining and removing Edgar Wells as alleged, however, does not mandate application of principles of double jeopardy to arrest judgment in the armed robbery case. The gist of the offense proscribed by G.S. 14-39 is the unlawful, nonconsensual confinement, restraint or removal of victim, for the purposes of committing certain acts specified in the statute. *State v. Williams*, 295 N.C. 655, 249 S.E. 2d 709 (1978). The penalty provided in G.S. 14-39(b) for the offense of kidnapping differs from those imposed for felony murder and from those imposed for offenses in which other lesser offenses are necessarily included, in that the intent of the legislature in establishing the punishment for kidnapping was to impose an indivisible penalty for restraint and removal for specified purposes, no hypothetical part of which penalty represents a punishment for the felony which gave rise to the flight of the defendant and his removal of the victim. The

crimes of armed robbery and kidnapping involve "vastly different social implications," and the legislature is clearly free to denounce each as a separately punishable offense. As our Supreme Court has recognized, this legislative scheme does create a potential for prosecutorial abuse which would invoke considerations of double jeopardy, in that the legislative elimination of the asportation element from the definition of kidnapping may result in imposition of impermissible multiple punishment in a particular case, as where the removal or restraint alleged is the same conduct relied upon to support the underlying felony. *State v. Fulcher*, 294 N.C. 503, 243 S.E. 2d 338 (1978). In the present case, however, that potential has not been realized.

The result is, the judgments imposing sentences in Case Numbers 79CRS610 and 612 for kidnapping and armed robbery are

Affirmed.

The judgment imposing sentence in Case No. 79CRS611 is

Arrested.

Judges MARTIN (Harry C.) and HILL concur.

SARAH H. DAVIS, ADMINISTRATRIX OF THE ESTATE OF JENNINGS B. REAVES, JR. v. SILOO INCORPORATED, GENUINE PARTS COMPANY, NATIONAL AUTOMOBILE PARTS ASSOCIATION AND HENDERSONVILLE SERVICE PARTS, INC.

No. 7929SC898

(Filed 17 June 1980)

1. **Negligence § 5; Sales § 22– chemical which can cause serious injury upon skin contact – dangerous instrumentality – liability of manufacturer under negligence theory**

    A chemical which, when it comes in contact with the skin of a human being not subject to rare allergenic responses, can cause serious bodily injury, illness or death to a human being is a dangerous instrumentality or substance, and the manufacturer of the dangerous substance will be subject to liability under a negligence theory for damages which proximately result from the failure to provide adequate warnings as to the product's dangerous propensities which are known or which by exercise of care commensurate with the danger should be known by the manufacturer, or from the failure to provide adequate directions for the foreseeable user as to how the dangerous product should or should not be used with respect to foreseeable uses.

2. **Sales § 8– implied warranty – contractual privity**
   Plaintiff's claim for breach of implied warranty of a carburetor and metal cleaner manufactured by defendant was barred by the lack of contractual privity between the plaintiff and defendant manufacturer.

3. **Sales § 5.1– label on product – insufficiency to establish express warranty**
   The label on a can of Petisol 202, a carburetor and metal cleaner manufactured by defendant, was insufficient to create an express warranty that the product would not be harmful when exposed to the skin on the user's arms.

4. **Negligence § 5.2; Sales § 22.1– death from chemical product – no liability by distributors**
   Plaintiff stated no claim for relief against defendant distributors for negligence in the death of plaintiff's intestate allegedly caused by a product distributed by defendant where plaintiff alleged that the product was manufactured and packaged by another, and plaintiff alleged no facts to show any exception to the general rule that the seller of a product manufactured by another who does not know or have reason to know that the product is or is likely to be dangerously defective has no duty to test or inspect it, especially where the product is sold in its original package as it came from the manufacturer and the seller acts as a mere marketing conduit between producer and consumer.

5. **Sales § 5.1; Uniform Commercial Code § 10– warranty not created through advertising**
   Defendant NAPA did not through its advertising create either an express or implied warranty that Petisol 202 was safe for human use where the Petisol 202 in question was merely sold by a retailer who also sells NAPA approved products, and Petisol 202 was not a NAPA line and did not bear the NAPA trade name or mark.

6. **Uniform Commercial Code § 12– implied warranties – employees or purchasers**
   G.S. 25-2-318 does not contemplate extending implied warranties to employees of purchasers.

On writ of certiorari to review proceedings before *Ferrell, Judge.* Judgment entered 16 June 1979 in Superior Court, HENDERSON County. Heard in the Court of Appeals 21 March 1980.

The plaintiff brings suit for wrongful death as administratrix of the Estate of Jennings B. Reaves, Jr. The plaintiff alleges that the decedent was killed by aplastic anemia resulting from the decedent's exposure to Petisol 202 while working at General Heating and Electric Contracting Company on 10 September 1976 in Hendersonville, North Carolina. On that date the decedent was using Petisol 202 as a solvent or bath in a spray gun to keep the spray gun from becoming clogged with hardened glue when the decedent was accidentally sprayed with Petisol 202 on his face, chest, arms and legs. The decedent immediately removed the clothing and washed the areas of skin which had come in contact with the product. The plaintiff further alleges that decedent followed all of the procedures set forth on the label of the container of Petisol 202, which provides as follows:

"PETISOL 202 CARBURETOR & METAL CLEANER is an emulsion-type single-phase, non-caustic, cold-immersion cleaner for the removal of sludge, gums, grease, varnish, carbon and similar residues from carburetors and all metal parts."

"Fast-acting; simple-to-rinse; 'built-in' reserve; long lasting."

"Danger: Harmful or fatal if swallowed, vapor harmful"

"Caution — Combustible mixture"

"Caution: Contains orthodichlorobenzene and xylol. Avoid prolonged breathing of vapor. Use in well-ventilated area. If swallowed, do not induce vomiting. Keep patient warm and quiet in a well ventilated area. Call a physician immediately. Avoid prolonged contact with skin. While Petisol 202 permits the immersion of hands, some dryness of skin may be noticed after prolonged exposure to the cleaner. If sensitive to dryness, simply wash hands in water after use and rub on an oily substance such as lanolin or even ordinary motor oil. If Petisol 202 should be splashed in eyes, simply bathe them with plain cold water."

"Keep away from children."

The plaintiff alleged that the Petisol 202 was purchased by General from defendant Hendersonville Service Parts, Inc. ("Service Parts"). Service Parts in turn purchased the Petisol 202 from Genuine Parts Company ("Genuine Parts"), a distributor in Charlotte, North Carolina. National Auto Parts Association ("NAPA") is a purchasing agent for Genuine Parts.

The plaintiff set forth two claims for relief. In the first claim the plaintiff asserted the following acts of negligence on the part of the defendants:

"a. Manufactured, packaged, distributed and sold a product, Petisol 202, knowing or having reason to know that the product was inherently hazardous and deadly in that it might be absorbed through the skin of a person using the product in an ordinary manner and cause the user to contract aplastic anemia;

b. Knew or should have known that the hazardous and deadly nature of the product would not be apparent to a user thereof and nonetheless failed to provide adequate warnings as to the hazards posed by the product and as to the precautions necessary in the course of its use to prevent absorption through the skin of the user;

c. Caused the product to be packaged, distributed and sold in a container which bore a label stating that, except for a risk of dryness of the skin from prolonged contact, Petisol 202 was not dangerous to a user whose skin was exposed to the product, knowing or having reason to know that a user, including plaintiff's intestate, would rely upon that statement and use the product without taking adequate precautions to prevent contact with his skin;

d. With knowledge of the hazardous and deadly nature of the product, placed it in commerce, knowing or having reason to know that it created an unreasonable risk of injury and death to the purchasers of the product or employees of such purchasers, and more particularly plaintiff's intestate;

e. Failed to comply with the labeling requirements set forth in 15 USC, § 1261, et seq., which provisions were enacted specifically for the protection of users of hazardous products, including Petisol 202, and more particularly for the protection of plaintiff's intestate, JENNINGS B. REAVES, JR.;

f. Undertook by a campaign of advertising in electronic broadcast media and by printed advertising to induce the general public to rely upon and use products distributed under the NAPA distribution system and by that campaign of advertising induced the public generally and particularly JENNINGS B. REAVES, JR., to rely upon the NAPA retailers to supply products which would be safe and suitable when used for the purposes for which those products were marketed and sold."

In her second claim the plaintiff alleged a breach of the implied warranty of merchantability, a breach of the express warranty which leads one to conclude that the product created no danger of illness or death in contacting the skin of the user other than the danger of dryness of the skin after contact, and a breach of the express warranty resulting from its advertising campaign.

In its answer, defendant Service Parts denied negligence, asserted failure to state a claim, and asserted contributory negligence on the part of the decedent by failing to heed the warnings on the label and by using the Petisol as a spray rather than as an immersion cleaner.

Defendant NAPA filed an answer which denied each allegation and contested the sufficiency of process. Defendant NAPA also moved for summary judgment.

On 6 November 1978 Genuine Parts Company, prior to filing an answer, moved pursuant to N.C. Gen. Stat. 1A-1, Rule 12(b), to dismiss plaintiff's first claim for failure to state a claim for relief by not setting forth that: General Parts had a duty to inspect or test such product; that General Parts had knowledge that the product was hazardous, or that the danger to plaintiff was foreseeable; and, that General Parts was negligent in its reliance upon the business reputation and standing of Siloo. As to plaintiff's second claim, Genuine Parts argued that Genuine Parts was not in privity of contract with the decedent and that since the product was not sold or manufactured for human consumption, any warranty would not extend to the plaintiff's intestate.

Defendant Siloo Incorporated, in its answer, denied negligence in the manufacture of Petisol 202, denied that the product was the proximate cause of the decedent's death, and asserted acts of negligence on the part of decedent's employer against whom the decedent has recovered under the Workmen's Compensation Act.

On 9 February 1979, Robert McKenna, Director of Operations of NAPA, filed an affidavit in which he stated, *inter alia*, that Petisol 202 is not a NAPA "line," that NAPA does not buy, sell, approve for sale, advertise, or classify Petisol 202 for itself or any other buyer, that Petisol 202 does not bear the NAPA trade name or mark and that NAPA does not purchase or sell goods in its own right but merely approves goods for sale by its member companies. McKenna also denied any activity by NAPA in North Carolina except as follows: parts bearing the NAPA trademark are manufactured by Wix Filter Company in the State; NAPA advertises in the State through a North Carolina advertising agency; NAPA licenses the use of its trade name and mark to Genuine Parts; written material concerning NAPA parts is sent to Genuine Parts Company in Atlanta and distributed by Genuine Parts to its distribution centers in the State; and, NAPA employees, on an infrequent and irregular basis, have visited the Genuine Parts distribution center in the State for the purpose of providing assistance concerning goods approved by NAPA.

On 1 August 1979 the trial court entered a judgment on several prior orders dismissing plaintiff's action against defendants NAPA, Service Parts, Genuine Parts on all claims and dismissing plaintiff's second claim for breach of warranty against defendant Siloo.

Morris, Golding, Blue and Phillips by William C. Morris, Jr. for plaintiff appellant.

Roberts, Cogburn and Williams by Landon Roberts and James W. Williams for defendant appellee Siloo Incorporated.

Russell & Greene by William E. Greene for defendant appellee Genuine Parts Company.

DuMont, McLean, Leake, Harrell, Talman and Stevenson by Larry Leake for defendant appellee National Automotive Parts Association.

Van Winkle, Buck, Wall, Starnes and Davis by Philip J. Smith for defendant appellee Hendersonville Service Parts, Inc.

CLARK, Judge.

Since the claims asserted by the plaintiff appellant have different applications to each defendant, we elect to consider the potential liability of each defendant separately. We note that the Products Liability Act, Chapter 99B of the North Carolina General Statutes, effective 1 October 1979, is not applicable to this and other actions pending at the effective date.

I. SILOO INCORPORATED

A. *Absolute Liability and Negligence (Manufacturer)*

The Appellate Courts of North Carolina have not gone so far as to adopt a general rule of strict liability of manufacturers of products introduced into the stream of commerce. *Fowler v. General Electric Co.,* 40 N.C. App. 301, 252 S.E. 2d 862 (1979). Nor did the General Assembly elect to create such a rule of strict liability when it recently enacted the new Products Liability Act, *supra.* While we may question this State's rejection of strict liability in light of the relative protections afforded those consumers and innocent bystanders in other states who suffer from product-caused injuries, *see generally,* Annot. 53 A.L.R. 2d 239 (1973), (strict liability for failure to warn of dangerous propensities), it is not for this Court at this time to adopt a rule of strict liability.

There are a few exceptions where strict liability has been imposed upon activity associated with a "dangerous instrumentality" and this occurs most often where explosives or blasting operations are involved. *Guilford Realty and Insurance Co. v. Blythe Brothers Co.*, 260 N.C. 69, 131 S.E. 2d 900 (1963) ("absolute" liability used synonymously with "strict" liability); 9 Strong's N.C. Index 3d *Negligence* § 5.1 (1977). In other cases, however, liability associated with dangerous instrumentalities is predicated upon "negligence" instead of strict liability. *See, e.g., Anderson v. Butler*, 284 N.C. 723, 202 S.E. 2d 585 (1974) (forklift entrusted by parent to an immature child becomes inherently dangerous and the parents' independent negligence is a basis for liability). Other cases have noted that even though a negligence standard is applied, the duty of care is nonetheless commensurate with the degree of danger involved and that a highly dangerous substance, product or instrumentality requires the "highest" care or the "utmost" caution. *Moody v. Kersey*, 270 N.C. 614, 155 S.E. 2d 215 (1967), (crane lifting heavy chute); *Belk v. Boyce*, 263 N.C. 24, 138 S.E. 2d 789 (1964), (firearms); *Luttrell v. Carolina Mineral Co.*, 220 N.C. 782, 18 S.E. 2d 412 (1942), (dynamite caps); *Stroud v. Southern Oil Transportation Company*, 215 N.C. 726, 3 S.E. 2d 297 (1939), (flange of damaged truck wheel).

In accord with this principle, it has been held or noted that a manufacturer may be liable for negligence if he sells a dangerous article likely to cause injury in its ordinary use and the manufacturer fails to guard against hidden defects and fails to give notice of the concealed danger. *Prince v. Smith*, 254 N.C. 768, 119 S.E. 2d 923 (1961); *Tyson v. Long Manufacturing Co.*, 249 N.C. 557, 107 S.E. 2d 170 (1959). Similarly, it has been held that one who puts an inherently dangerous article in the stream of commerce owes a duty of care to all those persons who ought to have been reasonably foreseen as likely to use them. *Stegall v. Catawba Oil Company*, 260 N.C. 459, 133 S.E. 2d 138 (1963); *Wyatt v. Equipment Company*, 253 N.C. 355, 117 S.E. 2d 21 (1960). In this regard, our Supreme Court, in *Corprew v. Geigy Chemical Corporation*, 271 N.C. 485, 491, 157 S.E. 2d 98 (1967), quoted the following from Prosser, Law of Torts (3d Ed. 1964) at 665:

"He [the manufacturer] may be negligent in failing to inspect or test his materials, or the work itself, to discover possible defects, or dangerous propensities. He may fail to use proper care to give adequate warning to the user, not only as to dangers arising from unsafe design, or other negligence, but also as to dangers inseparable from a properly made product. The warning must be sufficient to protect third persons who may reasonably be expected to come in contact with the product and be harmed by it; and the duty continues even after the sale, when the seller first discovers that the product is dangerous. He is also required to give adequate directions for use, when reasonable care calls for them."

In *Whitley v. Cubberly*, 24 N.C. App. 204, 210 S.E. 2d 289 (1974), as in the instant case, the plaintiff's intestate died from aplastic anemia, although in that case the anomaly resulted from a drug administered to the intestate, whereas in this case the anomaly resulted when the subject chemical came in contact with decedent's skin. In *Whitley* Judge Parker explained that summary judgment for the defendant was improper with respect to plaintiff's claim that the drug manufacturer failed to label the drug container adequately, and that the drug manufacturer failed to make adequate warnings about the dangerous properties of the drug to the medical profession and to consumers of the drug. *Accord, Incollingo v. Ewing*, 444 Pa. 263, 282 A. 2d 206 (1971), (death by aplastic anemia, application of § 388 of the Restatement of Torts 2d). *See also*, Annot. 76 A.L.R. 2d 9 (1961). We can see no reason for not imposing the same duty of care on the manufacturer in the instant case when the same anomaly is apparently a potential consequence of defendant's misfeasance or nonfeasance.

[1] We now hold: (1) that a chemical, which, when it comes in contact with the skin of a human being not subject to rare allergenic responses, can cause serious bodily injury, illness or death to the human being, is a dangerous instrumentality or substance; and (2) that the manufacturer of the dangerous substance will be subject to liability under a negligence theory for damages which proximately result from the failure to pro-

vide adequate warnings as to the product's dangerous propensities which are known or which by exercise of care commensurate with the danger should be known by the manufacturer, or from the failure to provide adequate directions for the foreseeable user as to how the dangerous product should or should not be used with respect to foreseeable uses. Consequently, the plaintiff appellant has alleged facts sufficient to state a claim for Siloo's liability predicated upon negligence.

B. *Warranties.*

[2] The trial court did not err in dismissing the plaintiff's claim against the manufacturer for breach of warranty, either express or implied. Plaintiff's claim for breach of implied warranty is barred by the lack of contractual privity between the plaintiff and the manufacturer. While this rule will be changed by the new Products Liability Act, *supra*, the effective date of that Act postdates the filing of this action. Moreover, while the Supreme Court in the recent case of *Kinlaw v. Long Mfg. Co.,* 298 N.C. 494, 259 S.E. 2d 552 (1979), held that the absence of privity will not bar an action on express warranty, the court in *Kinlaw* did not elect to extend this rule to implied warranties.

[3] With respect to plaintiff's claim that the label creates an express warranty that the product Petisol 202 will not be harmful to the skin, we note that a court, as a matter of law, must construe the terms of a contract, and, in construing the above-quoted language on the label of the Petisol 202 container, we hold that the language is not sufficient to create an express warranty that the Petisol 202 will not be harmful when exposed to the skin on a user's arms.

    The purported warranty in this case is distinguishable from that in *Simpson v. American Oil Company,* 217 N.C. 542, 8 S.E. 2d 813 (1940), upon which the plaintiff relies. In *Simpson* the label on a can of insecticide expressly stated: "Amox is made for the purpose of killing insects, *it is not poisonous to human beings* .... *Amox Liquid Spray is non-poisonous to human beings,* but is not suited for internal use. ..." (Emphasis supplied). The Court in *Simpson* focused on the common meaning of "poison" and held that the assurance that the product

---

---

was non-poisonous to human beings constituted a warranty on the part of the original seller. Admittedly, the language in *Simpson* comes close to that found on the label of the Petisol 202; nonetheless, there is nothing on the label of the Petisol 202 can which rises to the level of the express assurance in *Simpson* that the product was non-poisonous, and we cannot accept plaintiff's argument that an express warranty is created by implication from the language on the label.

II. NAPA AND GENUINE PARTS COMPANY
(Distributors)

The trial court did not err in dismissing plaintiff's claims as to NAPA and Genuine Parts Company.

[4] With respect to plaintiff's negligence claims, it is significant that plaintiff alleged that Petisol 202 was manufactured and packaged by Siloo Incorporated. The general rule has been stated as follows: "[T]he seller of a product manufactured by another, who neither knows, nor has reason to know, that the product is, or is likely to be, dangerously defective, has no duty to test or inspect it. Especially is this true where the product is sold in its original package or container, as it came from the manufacturer, and the seller acts as a mere marketing conduit between producer and consumer. Similarly, the seller of a product is ordinarily not liable for his failure to discover, through tests and inspections, product defects which are latent, even where the product is not sold in its original package." Annot. 6 A.L.R. 3d 12, 17 (1966). *See, also, Cockerham v. Ward,* 44 N.C. App. 615, 262 S.E. 2d 651 (1980). This rule is subject to several exceptions: "where the defect is patent, where the seller undertakes to perform auxiliary functions in connection with the sale, such as preparation, installation, or repair, where the duty [to test and inspect] is a matter of statutory law, where the merchandise is used or second hand, where the seller makes representations concerning the product, and where the seller has actual knowledge or is otherwise put on notice of the dangerous nature of the product." Annot. 6 A.L.R. 3d at 17. The plaintiff has alleged no facts which would compel us to apply an exception rather than the general rule. In this case both NAPA and Genuine Parts are "middlemen" and in this role each "is no

more than a conduit, a mere mechanical device through which the thing is to reach the ultimate consumer." *Corprew, supra*, 271 N.C. at 491.

Nor has the plaintiff stated a claim against both NAPA and Genuine Parts Company based on a warranty, either express or implied. As with Siloo Incorporated, the implied warranty claim is barred because plaintiff is not in privity of contract with the two middlemen. Similarly, there are no markings on the label which indicate any representation, much less an express warranty, made by either NAPA or Genuine Parts.

[5] Plaintiff's claim that NAPA made a warranty by undertaking advertising to induce the public to rely upon NAPA retailers to supply products to be safe and suitable is more difficult to resolve. There are numerous cases in which it was held that advertising by the manufacturer or bottler of a specific soft drink constituted a warranty by the manufacturer that the product was safe for consumption. *See, e.g., Tedder v. Bottling Co.*, 270 N.C. 301, 154 S.E. 2d 337 (1967). In those cases, however, a specific product was advertised and the trademark of the manufacturer or bottler appeared on the package itself. In contrast, the uncontested affidavit of NAPA's representative, indicates that "Petisol 202 is not a NAPA line, that NAPA does not buy, sell, approve for sale, advertise, or classify Petisol 202 for itself or for any other buyer; [and] that Petisol 202 does not bear the NAPA trade name or mark." The mere fact that Petisol 202 was sold by a retailer which, *inter alia*, sells NAPA approved parts, is not sufficient for the product to come within a warranty, express or implied, which might be created as a result of NAPA's advertising. *See, generally*, Annot. 75 A.L.R. 2d 112 § 11 (1961).

III. HENDERSONVILLE SERVICE PARTS, INC. (Seller)

[6] For the same reasons discussed in Part II immediately above, we hold that the lower court did not err in dismissing plaintiff's negligence claim against Hendersonville Service Parts, Inc. Similarly, there is no allegation which indicates that any express warranty has been made by Hendersonville Service Parts, Inc. Moreover, G.S. 25-2-318 specifically limits ac-

tions on warranties, either express or implied, to "any natural person who is in the family or household of his buyer or who is a guest in his home. . . ." This section of the North Carolina version of the Uniform Commercial Code does not contemplate extending implied warranties to employees of purchasers, and even if the new Products Liability Act were effective as to this action, the protections of that Act would not extend to the employee of a purchaser where the employee is covered by worker's compensation insurance. G.S. 99B-2(b).

In conclusion we find that part of the judgment dismissing the actions against NAPA, Service Parts, and Genuine Parts is affirmed; that part of the judgment dismissing the action against Siloo Incorporated for breach of express and implied warranty is affirmed; and that part of the judgment which, by omission, denies the motion to dismiss the action against Siloo Incorporated on the first claim for negligence is affirmed.

Affirmed.

Judges MARTIN (Robert M.) and ERWIN concur.

INA LOUISE KOONTZ CLARKE v. KAY DIAMOND CLARKE

No. 7818DC493

(Filed 17 June 1980)

1. **Divorce and Alimony § 18.18– alimony pendente lite order superseded by final judgment**

    Defendant's contention that the pendente lite order entered 12 January 1976 remained in effect and could be enforced by contempt proceedings in the district court until the validity of the final judgment dated 9 November 1977 should be finally determined on appeal was without merit, since the pendente lite order by its express language was effective only "pending the trial of this action," and it was in all respects superseded by the final judgment entered 9 November 1977 from which defendant appealed.

2. **Divorce and Alimony § 21.5; Appeal and Error § 16.1– violations of alimony and child support orders – orders being appealed – punishment for contempt improper**

    Where defendant appealed from final judgment entered on 9 November

1977 providing for divorce from bed and board, alimony and child support, two orders dated 22 December 1977 punishing defendant for contempt are void and must be vacated; however, after determination of the appeal, defendant may be punished for contempt if pending the appeal he has wilfully failed to comply with the terms of the 9 November 1977 judgment.

3. **Rules of Civil Procedure § 33– interrogatories – failure to serve in apt time – no answer required**

In actions for divorce from bed and board, child support and alimony, and to recover damages for assault and battery, the trial court did not err in ruling that plaintiff need not answer interrogatories which defendant had filed in each case, since defendant filed his interrogatories sixteen months after his answer, the last required pleading, had been filed in the alimony case; although only 119 days had elapsed since defendant's answer had been filed in the assault and battery case, no good cause was shown why defendant waited so long to begin discovery; and it was manifest that, having waited so long, defendant would be unable to complete discovery within the 120 day period prescribed in Rule 8 of the General Rules of Practice for the Superior and District Courts.

4. **Assault and Battery § 3.1; Divorce and Alimony § 17.1– alimony action – assault and battery action – sufficiency of evidence**

In actions to recover damages for assault and battery and to recover alimony, evidence was sufficient to be submitted to the jury where it tended to show that defendant deliberately struck plaintiff on the head with a baseball bat after threatening to kill her, causing her serious injuries; defendant testified and admitted he held the bat in his hand when it came in contact with plaintiff's head, though he denied that he had deliberately struck her with it; and plaintiff's evidence showed a long continued course of conduct on the part of defendant characterized by unprovoked physical and verbal abuse of plaintiff by defendant.

5. **Divorce and Alimony § 17.1– dependent and supporting spouses – determination by court**

The trial court in an alimony action did not err in refusing to submit to the jury issues as to plaintiff's status as a dependent spouse and defendant's status as the supporting spouse, since those issues present mixed questions of law and fact which can best be determined by the trial judge when he sets the amount of permanent alimony.

6. **Divorce and Alimony § 17.1– alimony without divorce prayed for – granting of divorce from bed and board improper**

That portion of the trial court's order granting a divorce from bed and board must be vacated, since plaintiff's complaint alleged a claim for alimony without divorce; plaintiff did not ask for a divorce from bed and board in her complaint; and plaintiff's complaint was not verified in the manner required by G.S. 50-8 for actions for divorce.

Clarke v. Clarke

7. **Assault and Battery § 3.1– civil assault action – jury instructions improper**

Defendant is entitled to a new trial in an action for assault and battery since it was error for the trial court to instruct the jury that "if you believe the evidence, you may find that defendant assaulted the plaintiff," since defendant's evidence showed that no assault occurred, and it was error for the court to instruct the jury concerning plaintiff's right to recover for injuries proximately resulting from defendant's negligence, since plaintiff's claim was not based upon any allegations or evidence as to negligence on the part of defendant.

8. **Appeal and Error § 18– unnecessary material in record on appeal – cost of appeal assessed against defendant**

Costs of the appeal were assessed against defendant because his counsel included much unnecessary matter in the record on appeal. Appellate Rule 9(b) (5).

APPEAL by defendant from *Hatfield, Judge.* Judgments entered 7 and 9 November 1977 in District Court, GUILFORD County. Heard in the Court of Appeals 26 February 1979.

Plaintiff-wife instituted Case No. 75CVD6523 on 21 October 1975 by filing complaint seeking alimony without divorce on allegations that defendant-husband had constructively abandoned her, had offered such indignities to her person as to render her condition intolerable and life burdensome, and that by cruel and barbarous treatment he had endangered her life. She alleged that she was the dependent spouse, her husband the supporting spouse, and she prayed for custody of two minor children, child support, and alimony pendente lite. On 5 November 1975 defendant filed answer admitting his marriage to the plaintiff and birth of the children, but otherwise denying the material allegations of the complaint.

On 12 January 1976 a pendente lite order was entered awarding custody of the children to the plaintiff, granting defendant visitation rights, and ordering defendant to pay plaintiff $150.00 per month as temporary support for the plaintiff and $175.00 per month for the support of each of the two minor children pending the trial of this action. Plaintiff was also awarded possession of the home of the parties in Greensboro as temporary support for herself and the two minor children pending the trial of the action, and defendant was ordered to remain away from the home except for purposes of visiting the children or upon the express invitation of the plaintiff. There was no appeal from this order.

While Case No. 75CVD6523 was pending and prior to trial of that case, plaintiff brought Case No. 76CVD5292 by filing complaint on 10 August 1976 in which she alleged that at approximately 4 a.m. on 3 August 1976, while she and defendant were living separate and apart pursuant to the 12 January 1976 order, she was awakened to find that defendant had forcibly entered her home wearing rubber gloves and holding a baseball bat in one hand and a gun in the other, that he told her he had come to kill her, and that he struck her forcefully on the head with the baseball bat causing severe and painful injuries. Plaintiff prayed for recovery of actual and punitive damages. Defendant filed answer on 12 November 1976 denying the material allegations of the complaint in Case No. 76CVD5292. By stipulation of the parties Case No. 76CVD5292 was consolidated for trial with the previously pending Case No. 75CVD6523, and the two cases were tried together at the 24 October 1977 civil jury session of district court in Guilford County.

In Case No. 76CVD5292 the jury answered issues finding that defendant had committed an assault and battery upon the plaintiff and awarding her $5,000.00 actual and $17,500.00 punitive damages. On 7 November 1977 the court entered judgment on the verdict in that case.

In Case No. 75CVD6523 the jury answered issues finding that defendant had willfully abandoned the plaintiff without just cause or provocation and that without provocation he had offered such indignities to her person as to render her condition intolerable and life burdensome. Following rendition of the verdict in Case No. 75CVD6523 the court, sitting without the jury, heard evidence with respect to plaintiff's status as the dependent spouse and the defendant's status as the supporting spouse and the amount of permanent alimony and counsel fees, if any, which should be awarded. On 9 November 1977 the court signed judgment in Case No. 75CVD6523 making detailed findings of fact, on the basis of which, and on the basis of the jury's verdict on the issues of abandonment and indignities, the court concluded as matters of law that plaintiff was entitled to a divorce from bed and board and that she was the dependent and defendant was the supporting spouse. The court's judgment granted plaintiff a divorce from bed and board, ordered defendant to pay her $150.00 per month as permanent alimony, ordered him to pay $175.00 per month per child for the support of the minor children, and awarded plaintiff and the minor children exclusive possession of the homeplace. The judgment also ordered defendant to pay plaintiff on 11 November 1977 the sum of $2,000.00 as permanent alimony in addition to the monthly payments, which sum the court found reasonable to relocate plaintiff and the children into the home which plaintiff had left after defendant had assaulted her on 3 August 1976, and to restore the home to a state of reasonable repair. The court also ordered defendant to pay $5,000.00 counsel fees for plaintiff's attorneys.

In apt time defendant gave notice of appeal from the judgments entered in both Case No. 75CVD6523 and Case No. 76CVD5292. On plaintiff's motion filed in Case No. 75CVD6523, the court entered an order in that case directing defendant to appear and show cause why he should not be held in contempt of court for failure to make the payments as previously ordered in that case. Pursuant to this show cause order, defendant and his counsel appeared before the trial judge, District Judge John B. Hatfield, on 16 December 1977, at which time defendant, through counsel, objected to the contempt proceedings being heard while the case was pending on appeal. The court overruled the objection, and proceeded with the hearing. During the course of the hearing, plaintiff's counsel called the defendant to the stand to testify. On advice of his counsel, defendant refused to testify. Judge Hatfield thereupon entered an order dated 16 December 1977 directing defendant to appear before District Judge Washington on 19 December 1977 to ascertain if defendant was in contempt of court for refusing to obey the court's order that he take the stand. Later, Judge Hatfield on his own motion modified this order to direct defendant to appear before Judge Pfaff rather than before Judge Washington. Following a hearing held 19 December 1977, Judge Pfaff entered an order dated 22 December 1977 finding defendant guilty of contempt for having refused to testify, for which contempt the court imposed a fine of $100.00.

On the same day, 22 December 1977, Judge Hatfield entered an order in Case 75CVD6523 in which he concluded as a matter of law that until the judgment entered in that case on 9 November 1977 should become final pending the disposition of the appeal from that judgment, defendant was required to continue to comply with the pendente lite order which had been entered on 12 January 1976. The court found that defendant had continued to pay the child support payments but since 9 November 1977 had willfully failed to make the payments of alimony which had become due after entry of the 9 November 1977 judgment. On these findings and conclusions, Judge Hatfield found defendant in contempt and ordered him imprisoned for ten days, with execution to be stayed in event defendant should make immediate payment of all arrearages in the payment of alimony.

In apt time defendant noted appeals from the two orders dated 22 December 1977, one entered by Judge Pfaff and the other entered by Judge Hatfield, finding him in contempt.

William W. Jordan for plaintiff appellee.

Samuel M. Moore and Robert S. Cahoon for defendant appellant.

PARKER, Judge.

Defendant appeals from the final judgment entered 7 November 1977 in Case No. 76CVD5292, from the final judgment entered 9 November 1977 in Case No. 75CVD6523, and from the two orders dated 22 December 1977 punishing him for contempt in Case No. 75CVD6523. We shall deal first with the questions raised by defendant's appeal from the two orders finding him in contempt of court.

[1,2] When defendant appealed from the final judgment entered 9 November 1977 in Case No. 75CVD6523, the district court was divested of jurisdiction to hear and determine contempt proceedings in that case. *Beall v. Beall*, 290 N.C. 669, 228 S.E. 2d 407

(1976); *Joyner v. Joyner*, 256 N.C. 588, 124 S.E. 2d 724 (1962); *Lawson v. Lawson*, 244 N.C. 689, 94 S.E. 2d 826 (1956). Plaintiff's contention that the pendente lite order entered 12 January 1976 remained in effect and could be enforced by contempt proceedings in the district court until the validity of the final judgment dated 9 November 1977 should be finally determined on this appeal is without merit. The pendente lite order by its express language was effective only "pending the trial of this action," and it was in all respects superseded by the final judgment entered 9 November 1977 from which defendant appealed. The district court having been rendered *functus officio* by the appeal, the two orders dated 22 December 1977 punishing defendant for contempt of court are void and must be vacated. This is not to say, however, that defendant may not hereafter be punished for contempt if pending this appeal he has wilfully failed to comply with the terms of the 9 November 1977 judgment. As pointed out by our Supreme Court in its opinion in *Joyner*, "taking an appeal does not authorize a violation of the order. One who wilfully violates an order does so at his peril. If the order is upheld by the appellate court, the violation may be inquired into when the case is remanded to the [trial] court." *id.* at 591, 124 S.E. 2d at 727; *See, Traywick v. Traywick*, 31 N.C. App. 363, 229 S.E. 2d 220 (1976).

[3] Turning to the questions raised by defendant's appeal from the final judgment entered 9 November 1977 in Case No. 75CVD6523 and from the final judgment entered 7 November 1977 in Case No. 76CVD5292, we note that by his first assignment of error the defendant challenges a pretrial ruling made by the trial court on 19 March 1977 that plaintiff need not answer interrogatories which defendant had filed in each case. There was no error in this ruling. Rule 8 of the General Rules of Practice for the Superior and District Courts as adopted by our Supreme Court pursuant to G.S. 7A-34 provides:

8. Discovery

All desired discovery shall be completed within 120 days of the date of the last required pleading. For good cause shown, a judge having jurisdiction may enlarge the period of discovery.

Counsel are required to begin promptly such discovery proceedings as should be utilized in each case, and are authorized to begin even before the pleadings are completed. Counsel are not permitted to wait until the pre-trial conference is imminent to initiate discovery.

Defendant here waited until 11 March 1977 to file his interrogatories. This was more than sixteen months after defendant's answer, the last required pleading, had been filed in the alimony case. Although it was only 119 days after his answer had been filed in the assault and battery case, no good cause was shown why defendant waited so long to begin discovery, and it was manifest that, having waited so long, defendant would be unable to complete discovery within the 120 day period prescribed in the rule. Defendant's first assignment of error is overruled.

[4] We also find no error in the denial of defendant's motions for directed verdict in each case. In the assault and battery case, plaintiff's evidence showed that defendant deliberately struck her on the head with a baseball bat after threatening to kill her, causing her serious injuries. Defendant testified and admitted he held the bat in his hand when it came in contact with his wife's head, though he denied that he had deliberately struck her with it. In the alimony case, plaintiff's evidence showed a long continued course of conduct on the part of the defendant characterized by unprovoked physical and verbal abuse of the plaintiff by the defendant. Defendant's evidence was to the contrary. Viewed in the light most favorable to the plaintiff, the evidence was clearly sufficient to require submission of each case to the jury.

[5] Defendant assigns error to the refusal of the court in the alimony case to submit to the jury issues as to plaintiff's status as a dependent spouse and defendant's status as the supporting spouse. We find no error in this ruling. This Court has already held that the issues of who is a "dependent spouse" and who a "supporting spouse" present mixed questions of law and fact which can best be determined by the trial judge when he sets the amount of permanent alimony. *Earles v. Earles*, 26 N.C.

Clarke v. Clarke

App. 559, 216 S.E. 2d 739 (1975), *cert. denied*, 288 N.C. 239, 217 S.E. 2d 679 (1975) *Bennett v. Bennett*, 24 N.C. App. 680, 211 S.E. 2d 835 (1975).

Defendant excepted and assigned error to certain of the court's findings of fact in the alimony case on the basis of which the court concluded that defendant was the supporting and the plaintiff the dependent spouse and on the basis of which the court entered its award of alimony. A careful review of the record reveals that the court's crucial findings of fact are amply supported by competent evidence, and defendant's assignment of error based on exceptions to the court's factual findings is overruled.

[6] Defendant excepted and assigned error to that portion of the judgment in Case No. 75CVD6523 in which the court awarded plaintiff a divorce from bed and board. This assignment of error has merit. Plaintiff's complaint alleged a claim for alimony without divorce. She did not ask for a divorce from bed and board in her complaint, nor was her complaint verified in the manner required by G.S. 50-8 for actions for divorce. Therefore, that portion of the judgment entered in Case No. 75CVD6523 which purports to grant a divorce from bed and board must be vacated.

Defendant noted more than fifty exceptions to the court's charge to the jury and has made a number of these the basis for assignments of error brought forward on this appeal. We have carefully examined all of these and are of the opinion that, insofar as the court's charge to the jury related to the alimony case, no error prejudicial to the defendant occurred. In the court's charge in the assault and battery case, however, we find prejudicial error. In that connection the court charged:

The plaintiff testified that the defendant entered her home without her permission and he struck her with a baseball bat; that he had in his possession rubber gloves, a baseball bat, and a pearl handled pistol. In addition, there was testimony tending to show that there might have been another weapon.

If you believe the evidence, you may find that the defendant assaulted the plaintiff.

If you believe that the defendant pointed the gun at the plaintiff; that he subjected her to some period of — in the bathroom in which he pointed the gun, and if you find that he administered or threatened her with the gun, you may find that he assaulted her.

If you further find from the facts that the defendant struck the plaintiff with the baseball bat as alleged in the Complaint and is alleged from the evidence, you may find that the defendant did commit assault and battery against the plaintiff.

Therefore, I charge you that if you find by the greater weight of the evidence that the defendant threatened or attempted by force or violence to do some injury and apparently had the ability to commit such injury, and if you further find that such was under circumstances that created a reasonable apprehension of injury in the plaintiff, then it would be your duty to answer the issue "Yes" in favor of the plaintiff.

On the other hand, if after considering all of the evidence, the plaintiff has failed to so prove, you will answer this issue "No" in favor of the defendant.

If you further find by the greater weight of the evidence that the defendant touched the plaintiff without her consent in a rude or angry manner, then it would be your duty to answer this issue of battery in favor of the plaintiff.

On the other hand, if after considering all of the evidence, the plaintiff has failed to so prove, you will answer this issue "No" in favor of the defendant. A person who suffers personal injury proximately caused by the negligence of another is entitled to recover in a lump sum the present worth of all damages, past and present, which naturally and proximately resulted from such negligence of such an act.

Clarke v. Clarke

Such damages can include medical expenses, pain and suffering, compensation for scars or disfigurement. Medical expenses include the actual expenses that you find by the greater weight of the evidence that has been paid or incurred by the plaintiff as a proximate result of the defendant's negligence — defendant's deliberate act.

[7] Although the issues in the assault and battery case were simple and it is possible that the jury was not misled by the court's confusing instructions, defendant was nevertheless entitled to have the case submitted to the jury under clear and correct instructions. It was error for the court to instruct the jury that "[i]f you believe the evidence, you may find that the defendant assaulted the plaintiff," since defendant's evidence showed that no assault occurred. It was also error for the court to instruct the jury concerning plaintiff's right to recovery for injuries proximately resulting from defendant's negligence, since plaintiff's claim was not based upon any allegations or evidence as to negligence on the part of the defendant. For error in the charge, defendant must be awarded a new trial in the assault and battery case.

We have examined all of defendant's remaining assignments of error and find them without merit.

[8] Finally, we take note of the fact that defendant's counsel failed in a number of respects to comply with our Rules of Appellate Procedure. For example, Rule 10(c) directs that each assignment of error "shall, so far as practicable, be confined to a single issue of law." A number of defendant's assignments of error present multiple issues of law. Rule 9(b) specifies what shall be included in the record on appeal, and subsection (5) of that Rule provides as follows:

(5) *Inclusion of Unnecessary Matter: Penalty.* It shall be the duty of counsel for all parties to an appeal to avoid including in the record on appeal matter not necessary for an understanding of the errors assigned. The cost of including such matter may be charged as costs to the party or counsel who caused or permitted its inclusion.

In the record on appeal in the present case defendant's counsel have included much unnecessary matter. For example, the entire charge of the court to the jury appears in full twice, Judge Pfaff's order finding defendant in contempt appears in full twice, and the final judgment dated 9 November 1977 entered in the alimony case appears in full three times. Once would have been enough for each. It is possible that this unnecessary repetition was in part due to counsel's failure to heed the admonition in Rule 10(c) that "[i]t is not necessary to include in an assignment of error those portions of the record to which it is directed, a proper listing of the exceptions upon which it is based being sufficient." Whatever the reason, the failure of defendant's counsel to comply with the Rules of Appellate Procedure in preparing the record on appeal has made our task in reviewing the legal issues sought to be presented much more difficult. Because defendant's counsel included much unnecessary matter in the record on appeal, the costs of this appeal will be assessed against the defendant.

The result is:

In Case No. 75CVD6523, the two orders dated 22 December 1977 finding defendant in contempt while this cause was pending on appeal to this Court are vacated; the final judgment dated 9 November 1977 is modified by striking therefrom and vacating that portion thereof which purports to grant a divorce from bed and board; as so modified said judgment is affirmed.

In Case No. 76CVD5292 defendant is awarded a new trial.

Defendant shall pay the costs of this appeal.

Judges HEDRICK and ERWIN concur.

Silver v. Board of Transportation

WILLIAM C. SILVER v. NORTH CAROLINA BOARD OF TRANSPORTA-
TION

No. 7924SC415

(Filed 17 June 1980)

1. **Limitation of Actions § 4.3– breach of contract – accrual of cause of action –
   action not barred by statute of limitations**

   Plaintiff's action to recover for breach of contract was not barred by the
   three year statute of limitations, though the action was brought more than
   three years after the consent judgment embodying the contract was signed,
   since, at the time the consent judgment was signed, no breach of contract
   had yet occurred, and whether the breach occurred at the time construction
   of a dam and pipe by defendant on plaintiff's property was completed in
   October 1975 or early 1976, or at the time the overall highway construction
   project was completed in July 1977, plaintiff's action filed in February 1978
   was brought within the applicable three year period.

2. **Contracts § 26– construction of dam and pipe system – problems with system –
   repairs – admissibility of evidence**

   In an action to recover for breach of contract to construct a dam and pipe
   system to carry water from the dam to plaintiff's mill, the trial court erred in
   permitting plaintiff's expert witness to testify that the system would never
   deliver enough water to the mill to turn the water wheel because the size of
   pipe used was too small, since such testimony directly contradicted the
   parties' contract which unambiguously specified that pipe 30 inches in diameter should be installed; the court did not err in permitting the witness to
   testify that the dam as constructed by defendant needed to be raised and
   that the cost would be $4000 to $5000, since such testimony was relevant not
   only to the issue of breach of contract but also to the issue of what would be
   required to conform the system to the contract and the cost thereof; the trial
   court erred in permitting the witness to testify concerning the necessity for
   a "filtering system and flow straightening system" at the entrance to the
   pipe at the dam, since such testimony was irrelevant to the issues and
   actually contradicted the express terms of the contract which contemplated
   a filtering system consisting only of a grate that would prevent foreign
   objects over three inches in diameter from entering the pipeline; and the
   trial court erred in permitting the witness to testify that a sweeping radius
   pipe was necessary to replace the open raceway area between the 30 inch
   pipe installed by defendant and the old 30 inch pipe running towards the mill
   under the old highway, since the agreement was ambiguous as to whether
   the parties intended that a pipeline be constructed the entire distance from
   the new dam to the mill, and it was for the jury to determine whether the
   contract so required.

3. **Contracts § 27.2– construction of dam and pipe system – breach of contract –
   sufficiency of evidence**

   In an action to recover for breach of contract, the trial court did not err in denying defendant's motion for directed verdict since ample evidence was presented from which the jury could infer that the dam and pipe system as constructed did not substantially conform to the terms of the agreement contained in the consent judgment in that the exit end of the new pipeline was higher than the level of the dam and a slide gate to the dam which was broken during construction was never properly repaired.

APPEAL by defendant from *Howell, Judge.* Judgment entered 8 December 1978 in Superior Court, MADISON County. Heard in the Court of Appeals 5 December 1979.

This is an action to recover damages for an alleged breach of contract. Plaintiff is the owner and operator of a milling business known as Silver's Mill, located on Old N.C. Highway 213 in Petersburg, N.C. On 18 November 1974 plaintiff and the Board of Transportation signed a consent judgment in a proceeding instituted by the State to condemn a portion of the property on which plaintiff's mill was located in connection with a state highway construction project. Under the terms of that consent judgment the Board of Transportation agreed to pay $1,275.00 as a portion of the just compensation for the taking and, as additional compensation, agreed as follows:

[T]he Board of Transportation covenants and agrees that as part of the consideration for the taking of the above described real property, it will construct in good operating condition, a weir dam across Bull Creek at or near the site where the present dam is now located, together with a 30" pipeline with a slide gate, for the conveyance of said water from said dam to Silver's Mill, and provided with a grate or guard over or near the water entrance into the pipe so as to prevent foreign objects over three inches in diameter entering the pipe. Additionally, as a part of the consideration for the taking of the above described property the Board of Transportation gives, grants, and conveys, to the defendants, their heirs, executors and/or assigns, a right and easement for the exclusive use of the water diverted by the above described weir dam as supplied by said pipeline and the right to go upon said premises on which the dam and pipeline are located for the purposes of inspecting, repairing and operating a slidegate and any other apparatus necessary for the complete use of said facility. It is further agreed that any necessary maintenance requirements to the above described 30″ pipe will be handled by the Board of Transportation, through its authorized agents, at no expense to the defendants and through normal maintenance responsibilities.

On 24 February 1978 plaintiff filed the complaint in the present action alleging that the weir dam, slidegate, and other apparatus as constructed by defendant were not in good working condition and provided insufficient water to serve as a power source for the operation of plaintiff's mill. He also alleged that defendant had failed, after repeated requests by plaintiff, to place the apparatus in good working condition or to perform necessary maintenance. Plaintiff prayed that he recover damages in the amount of $20,000.00 from defendant on account of the breach and that defendant be ordered to construct a dam and other apparatus in accordance with the terms of the consent judgment. Defendant denied that the agreement had been breached and alleged that all requirements in the consent judgment had been met.

The case was heard before a jury at the 4 December 1978 session of superior court in Madison County. The evidence presented tended to show:

Plaintiff has been in the milling business for thirty-three years. Prior to the taking of his property, plaintiff used both water power and diesel power to grind corn. Diesel power was used to grind corn during the times of year when there was insufficient water. Prior to the taking, power to turn the water wheel at the mill was provided by means of a log crib type dam, approximately six or seven feet high, located on Bull Creek near the mill. The water from the creek flowed through a wooden drop gate at the dam into an earthen sluice running two to three hundred feet from the dam to old N.C. Highway 213. At that point, the water from the creek entered a thirty-inch pipe fifty to seventy-five feet long which passed under old Highway 213, and then flowed into an open earthen ditch three to five hundred feet long running parallel to the highway. At a point fifty to seventy-five feet above the mill, the water again entered a thirty-inch metal pipe, discharged into a wooden sluiceway and from there flowed over the water wheel of the mill.

After the signing of the consent judgment in November 1974, defendant tore down the old dam and constructed a new concrete and steel dam .3 feet above the level of the old dam and several feet further from the mill. At the top of the dam, defendant installed a thirty-inch pipe, along with a vertical and horizontal grid system of bars at the top of the pipe to filter out debris. This pipe replaced part of the old raceway which was removed by defendant for the construction of a fill to accommodate a new bridge. The thirty-inch pipe was installed to run for a distance of approximately 300 feet under the newly constructed Highway 213 so as to empty the creek water into the pre-existing raceway and thence to direct the water flow into the pre-existing thirty-inch pipe under old N.C. 213. Plaintiff's expert witness Thomas Ray, a civil engineer, testified that the exit point of the new thirty-inch pipe installed by the State was .43 feet higher than the top of the dam. This exit point was also the end point of the State's right of way, approximately 300 feet from the dam. The State made no changes in the existing water flow system beyond the end of its right of way.

Over defendant's objection plaintiff's expert witness was permitted to testify that the system as constructed would never provide enough water to turn the water wheel and to describe a series of modifications which in his opinion would be necessary to develop a sufficient head on the water to furnish power to the mill. Ray did testify from personal observation that the dam appeared in good operating condition and that the grid system installed at the entrance to the thirty-inch pipe at the top of the dam was capable of stopping any object in excess of three inches in diameter. He noticed, however, that the exit end of the pipe was bent or crushed at the top.

Engineers with the State Division of Highways who planned the dam and pipe system constructed on plaintiff's property testified that the project was designed to replace in kind the system existing prior to the highway construction. The pipe was laid on a zero grade on a stone foundation to prevent sagging. As of the completion date of the overall highway construction project on 1 July 1977, the State's engineers were of the opinion that the dam, the gate, and the new pipe were in good operating condition and that water flowed freely throughout the system.

At the close of all of the evidence the trial court denied defendant's motion for a directed verdict and submitted issues which were answered by the jury as follows:

1. Did the Plaintiff and the Defendant enter into a contract on 18 November, 1974, as alleged by the Plaintiff?

ANSWER: YES.

2. At the time of the execution of the contract on the 18th of November, 1974, was it understood and agreed by the Plaintiff and the Defendant that the agreement to "construct in good operating condition a weir dam across Bull Creek at or near the site where the present dam is now located together with a 30 inch pipeline with a slide gate for the conveyance of said water from said dam to Silver's Mill" intended to include the installation of a 30 inch pipeline the entire distance from the dam to the mill as alleged by the Plaintiff?

ANSWER: NO.

3. At the time of the execution of the contract, was it understood and agreed by the Plaintiff and the Defendant that the agreement to "construct in good operating condition a weir dam across Bull Creek at or near where the site where the present dam is now located together with a 30 inch pipeline with a slide gate for the conveyance of said water from said dam to Silver's Mill", intended to include only the area of the old raceway located upon the right of way purchased or owned by the Defendant?

ANSWER: YES.

4. Did the Defendant breach the contract as alleged by the Plaintiff?

ANSWER: YES.

5. What amount of damages is the Plaintiff entitled to recover of the Defendant for breach of contract?

ANSWER: $13,000.00

From judgment on the verdict that plaintiff recover $13,000.00 of defendant, defendant appealed.

Bruce B. Briggs for plaintiff appellee.

Attorney General Edmisten by Senior Deputy Attorney General R. Bruce White, Jr., and Assistant Attorneys General Guy A. Hamlin and Frank P. Graham for defendant appellant.

PARKER, Judge.

[1] Defendant assigns error to the denial of its motion to dismiss plaintiff's action on the ground that it was brought more than three years after the date of the consent judgment. The three-year period of the statute of limitations governing actions based on express contracts does not begin to run until the alleged breach occurs and the cause of action accrues. *Reidsville v. Burton*, 269 N.C. 206, 152 S.E. 2d 147 (1967); *Craig v. Price*, 210 N.C. 739, 188 S.E. 321 (1936). Once the statute is pleaded, the burden is on the plaintiff to show that the action was brought within the applicable period. *Little v. Rose*, 285 N.C. 724, 208 S.E. 2d 666 (1974). In the present case the cause of action could not have accrued at the time the consent judgment embodying the contract was signed, since no breach of the contract had yet occurred. Plaintiff testified at trial that the State ceased work on the project on his property in October 1975 or early 1976, and witnesses for the State testified that the overall highway construction project of which plaintiff's dam and pipeline were only a part, was not completed until 1 July 1977. Whether the breach occurred at the time the construction of the dam and pipe were completed in October 1975 or early

1976, or at the time the overall highway construction was completed in July 1977, plaintiff's action filed in February 1978 was brought within the applicable three-year period provided by G.S. 1-52(1) and was not barred. Defendant's motion to dismiss was properly denied.

[2] Defendant also assigns error to the admission of testimony by plaintiff's expert witness Ray concerning the inability of the dam and pipe system to supply enough water to turn the water wheel at the mill and concerning the engineering modifications necessary to enable it to do so. In response to a question by plaintiff's counsel as to the reason that the system would never deliver enough water to the mill to turn the water wheel, Ray stated that "the total head that you have to work with is not enough with the present size pipe to deliver the amount of water that is necessary." The rule is well-established that "[w]hen the language of a contract is clear and unambiguous, effect must be given to its terms, and the court, under the guise of construction, cannot reject what the parties inserted or what the parties elected to omit." *Weyerhaeuser v. Light Co.*, 257 N.C. 717, 719, 127 S.E. 2d 539, 541 (1962); *accord, Indemnity Co. v. Hood*, 226 N.C. 706, 40 S.E. 2d 198 (1946). Because the relevant provision of the parties' contract unambiguously specified that pipe thirty inches in diameter should be installed, any evidence that thirty-inch pipe was inadequate directly contradicted that written provision and should not have been admitted.

Ray's testimony which followed concerned proposed changes in the system which would increase the head of the water sufficiently to furnish water power to the mill. Defendant contends that such testimony concerning "improvements" was irrelevant in that it introduced matters beyond the scope of the parties' contract. We agree.

The substance of Ray's testimony was as follows: In order to provide sufficient water flow to operate the mill, the dam would have to be raised ten inches, and the entrance to the pipe at the top of the dam would need "a filtering system and a flow straightening system to arrange the water and get the water directed into the entrance of the pipeline without any resistance from surface debris, leaves and that sort of thing." At the point where the thirty-inch pipe built by the State now empties into the old raceway, a "sweeping radius pipe," one with valve arrangements to sweep out silt gathering inside the pipe due to the higher elevation of the exit point, would be required to replace the open raceway area between the new pipe running from the dam and the pipe running under old Highway 213 towards the mill.

The admissibility of this evidence depends upon interpretation of the parties' contract. The State's obligation under the agreement, in essence, was to construct: (1) "a weir dam across Bull Creek in good operating condition at or near the site of the existing dam", (2) "together with a 30″ pipeline with a slide gate, for the conveyance of said water from said dam to Silver's Mill," and (3) "a grate or guard over or near the water entrance into the pipe so as to prevent foreign objects over three inches in diameter entering the pipe." The object of contract construction is to ascertain the intention of the parties "from the expressions used, the subject matter, the end in view, the purpose sought, and the situation of the parties at the time." *Electric Co. v. Insurance Co.*, 229 N.C. 518, 520, 50 S.E. 2d 295, 297 (1948). The clear intention of the parties in including the provisions for dam and pipe construction is stated in the consent judgment itself, that is, to furnish part of the consideration for the taking of plaintiff's property. The record discloses that a new dam was required because the project for which plaintiff's property was taken necessitated the tearing down of the existing dam to accommodate a drainage system for the new highway. Similarly, the purpose of the pipe construction is stated to be "the conveyance of said water [of Bull Creek] from said dam to Silver's Mill." The agreement is ambiguous as to the length of the pipe to be installed. Viewing the language of the agreement in light of the situation of the parties at the time, we conclude that a fair reading of its terms discloses that the parties intended the construction of a dam and a 30-inch pipeline which would permit the waters of Bull Creek to flow unimpeded to

Silver's Mill with whatever force the full capacity of the pipe and the elements of nature should provide. Nothing in the agreement discloses that the parties intended that the State provide a system which would at all times furnish sufficient water to run plaintiff's mill.

Viewing the testimony offered by plaintiff's expert in light of this analysis, we conclude that it is necessary to distinguish those portions of the testimony which injected into the case matters beyond the scope of the contract from those which were relevant to the question of what would be required to conform the project to the terms of the contract. "The fundamental principle which underlies the decisions regarding the measure of damages for defects or omissions in the performance of a building or construction contract is that a party is entitled to have what he contracts for or its equivalent. What the equivalent is depends upon the circumstances of the case." *Robbins v. Trading Post, Inc.*, 251 N.C. 663, 666, 111 S.E. 2d 884, 887 (1960). Although Ray testified that the dam was "in operating condition," he also stated that the exit end of the thirty-inch pipe leading from the dam was higher than the top of the dam by .43 feet, reducing the total head differential of the water flow. This evidence had a direct bearing on the question of whether defendant substantially complied with its contract to construct a system in a good and workmanlike manner. Thus, it was proper for the court to permit Ray to testify that the dam needed to be raised, and that the cost would be approximately $4,000.00 to $5,000.00, since such testimony was relevant not only to the issue of breach of contract, but also to the issue of what would be required to conform the system to the contract and the cost thereof.

Ray's testimony concerning the necessity for a "filtering system and flow straightening system" at the entrance to the pipe at the dam, in contrast, was not only irrelevant to these issues, but actually contradicted the express terms of the contract, which contemplated a filtering system consisting only of a grate or guard that would prevent foreign objects over three inches in diameter from entering the pipeline. Its admission, therefore, was error.

Ray's testimony that a sweeping radius pipe was necessary to replace the open raceway area between the thirty-inch pipe installed by the State and the old thirty-inch pipe running towards the mill under old highway 213 was inadmissible for similar reasons. The agreement was ambiguous as to whether the parties intended that a pipeline be constructed the entire distance from the new dam to the mill, and it was for the jury to determine whether the contract so required. *Root v. Insurance Co.*, 272 N.C. 580, 158 S.E. 2d 829 (1968). Moreover, even if evidence that a pipe should have been installed within the raceway area to which Ray referred was admissible, nothing in the contract required the State to install anything more than the thirty-inch pipe expressly mentioned, and testimony concerning the sweeping radius pipe should have been excluded.

[3] Defendant has also assigned error to the denial of its motion for a directed verdict at the close of all of the evidence on the grounds that the evidence established as a matter of law that defendant fully complied with the terms of the contract. We find no error. Viewed in the light most favorable to plaintiff, the nonmoving party, ample evidence was presented from which the jury could infer that the system as constructed did not substantially conform to the terms of the agreement contained in the consent judgment in that the exit end of the new pipeline was higher than the level of the dam, and a slide gate to the dam which was broken during construction was never properly repaired. In addition, the ambiguity of the contract as to the length of the pipe to be installed was for the jury to resolve.

That the incompetent evidence which was erroneously admitted impermissibly affected the verdict is confirmed by the trial court's instructions to the jury. In those instructions the court referred to the testimony of the witness Ray concerning the complicated filtration and dispersal system and to his testimony concerning the cost of these items. Although the court later properly instructed the jury that "there is no duty on the Defendant to construct a dam sufficient to turn the mill wheel or to install any filter system," it thereafter instructed them that they could award up to $13,000.00 in damages. That $13,000.00 figure to which the trial court referred and which the jury subsequently adopted was based not only on Ray's competent testimony concerning the cost of raising the dam, but also on his incompetent testimony concerning the cost of the filtering and flow straightening system and the sweeping radius pipe.

For errors in the admission of evidence, the defendant is entitled to a

New Trial.

Chief Judge MORRIS and Judge HILL concur.

PATSY E. MEACHAN v. MONTGOMERY COUNTY BOARD OF EDUCATION

No. 7919SC642

(Filed 17 June 1980)

1. **Schools § 13– career teacher – medical leave of absence – granting of disability retirement benefits – resignation by implication**

    The granting of a career teacher's application for disability retirement benefits under the Teachers' and State Employees' Retirement System operated as an acceptance of her resignation by implication and terminated her status as a "career teacher," since a finding that her disability was "likely to be permanent" was implicit in the granting of her application for disability retirement benefits, G.S. 135-5(c), and this finding rendered her status as a disabled retiree wholly inconsistent with her former status as a "career teacher." Because plaintiff's loss of her status as a "career teacher" occurred by operation of law upon her voluntary election to accept retirement benefits, the protections of G.S. 115-142(d)(1) for a career teacher were inapplicable to plaintiff, since that statute by its express terms applies only to actions by school administrators constituting dismissal, demotion or employment on a part-time basis "without the [career teacher's] consent."

2. **Schools § 13– career teacher – medical leave of absence – statutory preservation of career status – inapplicability where disability retirement benefits granted**

    Even if a school board's grant of plaintiff career teacher's request for a medical leave of absence for the second semester of the 1976-77 school year constituted a modification of plaintiff's contract to teach for the full 1976-77 school year, any such contractual modification and any right accruing to plaintiff because of it under G.S. 115-142(c)(5), which preserves the career status of a career teacher who returns to her teaching position at the end of an authorized leave of absence, were superseded by the subsequent granting of plaintiff's application for disability retirement status.

3. **Estoppel § 6– allegation of estoppel not required in complaint**

Plaintiff was not required to allege estoppel to deny her status as a career teacher in her complaint when the answer raising the defense that plaintiff's acceptance of retirement benefits terminated her career status had not yet even been filed, and under G.S. 1A-1, Rule 7, she was precluded from alleging it in a responsive plea to that answer.

4. **Estoppel.§ 4.7; Schools § 13– career teacher status terminated by operation of law – estoppel of school board to deny career teacher status**

Although plaintiff's status as a "career teacher" terminated by operation of law when she was granted disability retirement status after she had received a medical leave of absence, the evidence on motion for summary judgment presented a genuine issue of material fact as to whether defendant school board is estopped from refusing to recognize plaintiff as a "career teacher" where the superintendent of schools and the finance officer for the schools, both agents of defendant board, admitted in their affidavits that they did not know at the time plaintiff talked with them concerning the possibility of disability retirement that she would in effect be resigning her position as a career teacher, and plaintiff's affidavit stated that the finance officer recommended disability retirement to her, assured her that the retirement aspect was just a formality because the State regulations provided that retirement benefits would stop automatically when she returned to work, and did not indicate that her application for retirement benefits would have any bearing on her return to work.

5. **Estoppel § 5.1; Schools § 13– estoppel of school board**

Application of the principles of estoppel to prohibit defendant county school board from refusing to recognize plaintiff as a career teacher although plaintiff's status as a career teacher was terminated by operation of law when she was granted disability retirement status would not impair the exercise of defendant's governmental powers and was therefore proper.

APPEAL by plaintiff from *Wood, Judge.* Judgment signed 27 April 1979 in Superior Court, MONTGOMERY County. Heard in the Court of Appeals 31 January 1980.

This is an appeal from an order granting summary judgment to defendant Montgomery County Board of Education in an action filed by plaintiff seeking a determination that she is and continues to be a teacher employed by the Montgomery County Board of Education and an injunction preventing defendant from treating her otherwise.

Plaintiff filed a complaint on 21 September 1977 alleging the following: She had been employed as a "career teacher" with the Montgomery County School System during the 1974-75, 1975-76, and 1976-77 school years. Effective 1 January 1977 plaintiff was granted a medical leave of absence through the remainder of 1976-77 school year. After having advised the superintendent of schools in July 1977 of her intent to return to work at the beginning of the 1977-78 school year, she reported for work in August and was advised that she had no teaching position. Plaintiff alleged that she is still a career employee of defendant and that defendant's failure to accord her the rights of a career teacher violated the provisions of G.S. 115-142. She prayed for a declaratory judgment that she "is and continues to be a teacher employed by the Montgomery County Board of Education and to enjoin said Board from treating her otherwise."

Defendant answered, admitting the plaintiff was employed as a teacher by defendant during the 1974-75, 1975-76, and portions of the 1976-77 school year, and that plaintiff had been granted a medical leave of absence. The Board raised the defense that plaintiff had, in addition to taking a medical leave of absence, applied for and obtained disability retirement status and retirement benefits effective 1 January 1977, and that at the time of filing suit plaintiff was still retired and had no automatic right to be reinstated and assigned as a classroom teacher.

The record discloses the following: In her second year of teaching at West Montgomery High School plaintiff began to experience severe headaches which caused a drastic change in her teaching performance, behavior, and personal habits. During that year plaintiff met with both the superintendent of the Montgomery County Schools and the principal of West Montgomery High School who discussed with her the problem of her poor teaching performance.

In the fall of the next academic year, 1976-77, neither plaintiff's medical condition nor her teaching performance improved. In November 1976 the superintendent of schools met with plaintiff and informed her that she would be subject to dismissal unless she agreed to take a medical leave of absence for the remainder of the school year. At the superintendent's suggestion, plaintiff met with James B. Woodruff, finance officer of the Montgomery County Schools, who discussed with her the possibility of applying for disability retirement through the state retirement system. At that time neither Mr. Woodruff nor other school officials knew the exact effect of plaintiff's election to accept retirement benefits. Plaintiff thereafter submitted an application for disability retirement to the Teachers' and State Employees' Retirement System and also submitted a letter to the superintendent of schools requesting a medical leave of absence for the second semester of the 1976-77 academic year. On 6 December 1976 at a regularly scheduled meeting of defendant Board of Education, plaintiff's request for a medical leave of absence was granted.

On 15 February 1977 plaintiff's application for disability retirement was approved with benefits payable retroactive to 1 January 1977. Plaintiff underwent surgery for her neurological ailment during the spring of 1977, and her doctors informed the superintendent of schools in May 1977 that she would be able to return to work in August 1977. In the early summer of 1977 plaintiff reapplied for a position with the Montgomery County Schools. School officials determined that other applicants were more qualified than plaintiff, and she was not given a teaching position for the 1977-78 school year.

On 17 March 1979 defendant moved for summary judgment on the grounds that the pleadings, answers to interrogatories, admissions and depositions established as a matter of law that plaintiff had no right to employment as a career teacher after 1 January 1977. That motion was granted on 27 April 1979. From summary judgment dismissing her action, plaintiff appeals.

Chambers, Stein, Ferguson & Becton by James C. Fuller, Jr. for plaintiff appellant.

Golding, Crews, Meekins, Gordon & Gray by John G. Golding and Harvey L. Cosper, Jr. for defendant appellee.

PARKER, Judge.

The propriety of a summary judgment in an action for a declaratory judgment is governed by the same rules applicable to other actions. *Blades v. City of Raleigh*, 280 N.C. 531, 187 S.E. 2d 35 (1972). Thus, the question presented on this appeal is whether defendant, the moving party, has demonstrated that there is no genuine issue as to any material fact and that the movant is entitled to judgment as a matter of law. *Pitts v. Pizza, Inc.*, 296 N.C. 81, 249 S.E. 2d 375 (1978).

Resolution of this question in the present case depends upon the legal effect of plaintiff's election to accept disability retirement and upon the existence of any facts which might alter that legal effect. There is no dispute that prior to 1 January 1977 plaintiff was a "career teacher" within the meaning of G.S. 115-142, known as the Tenure Act. As such, she possessed all of the rights and privileges accorded on account of such status. Plaintiff contends that the action of the School Board in refusing to reinstate her as a career teacher in August 1977 and in treating her as a new applicant denied her several of those rights. She relies upon the following provisions of G.S. 115-142:

G.S. 115-142(c)(5):

Leaves of Absence. — A career teacher who has been granted a leave of absence by a board shall maintain his career status if he returns to his teaching position at the end of the authorized leave.

G.S. 115-142(d)(1):

A career teacher shall not be subjected to the requirement of annual appointment nor shall he or she be dismissed, demoted, or employed on a part-time basis without his or her consent except [for reasons] provided in subsection (e).

The following undisputed facts in the present case are determinative of the applicability of G.S. 115-142(c)(5) and G.S. 115-142(d)(1): Plaintiff submitted her application to the Teachers' and State Employees' Retirement System on 29 November 1976 seeking disability retirement effective 1 January 1977. On 7 December 1976 she was notified by an administrative officer of the System that her application was being reviewed and would be submitted to the System's Medical Review Board for consideration. On 15 February 1977 plaintiff was further notified that her application for retirement had been approved with payment of retirement allowance effective retroactive to 1 January 1977. During the period plaintiff's application for disability retirement was pending, she had submitted a written request to John S. Jones, Superintendent of the Montgomery County Schools, requesting a medical leave of absence "as of December 31st to the end of this school year (1976-'77)," which request was granted at a regular session of the Montgomery County Board of Education on 6 December 1976.

[1] Upon these facts it is clear that defendant did not breach any statutory duty imposed by G.S. 115-142(c)(5) or G.S. 115-142(d)(1) with respect to plaintiff's status as a "career teacher." Plaintiff voluntarily elected to apply for disability retirement status. Article I of Chapter 135 of the General Statutes governs the administration of the Teachers' and State Employees' Retirement System. G.S. 135-5(c) provides that disability retirement benefits are available to any employee eligible by virtue of years of service upon a certification of the System's medical board "that such [person] is mentally or physically incapacitated for the further performance of duty, that such incapacity was incurred at the time of active employment and has been continuous thereafter, *that such incapacity is likely to be permanent,* and that such member should be retired." (emphasis added). Thus, implicit in the granting of plaintiff's application for disability retirement benefits in the present case was a finding that her disability was "likely to be permanent." This finding renders her status as a disabled retiree wholly inconsistent with her former status as a "career teacher." In the absence of any contrary legislative indication in Chapter 115, we hold that the effect of the Retirement System's determination of plaintiff's eligibility to receive disability retirement benefits was to operate as an acceptance of her resignation by implication and to terminate her status as "career teacher" by operation of law. Because plaintiff's loss of her status as a "career teacher" occurred by operation of law upon her voluntary election to accept retirement benefits, the protections of G.S. 115-

142(d)(1) are inapplicable here, since that section by its express terms applies only to *actions* by school administrators consti- tuting dismissal, demotion, or employment on a part-time basis "without the [career teacher's] consent."

[2] Neither is plaintiff aided by G.S. 115-142(c)(5) which pre- serves the career status of a career teacher who returns to her teaching position at the end of an authorized leave of absence. It is true that plaintiff applied for and was granted a medical leave of absence by defendant for the second semester of the 1976 school year. That leave of absence, however, was granted prior to consideration and approval of her application for dis- ability retirement. Even if it be conceded that plaintiff's re- quest for, and the Board's grant of, that leave of absence consti- tuted a modification of plaintiff's contract to teach for the full 1976-77 school year, we conclude that any such contractual modification and any statutory right accruing to plaintiff under G.S. 115-142(c)(5) because of it, were superseded by the grant of disability retirement status on 15 February 1977.

[3] Having determined that plaintiff's status as a "career teacher" terminated by operation of law, we next consider whether, upon this record, defendant may be estopped from denying plaintiff that status. Defendant contends that plaintiff is not entitled to raise the question of estoppel on appeal be- cause she did not plead it. We disagree. Although G.S. 1A-1, Rule 8(c) requires that a party affirmatively plead estoppel, that rule applies only to responsive pleadings. Plaintiff clearly was not required to allege estoppel in her complaint when the answer raising the defense that her acceptance of retirement benefits terminated her career status had not yet even been filed, and under G.S. 1A-1, Rule 7, she was precluded from alleging it in a responsive plea to that answer.

The elements of equitable estoppel were defined by our Supreme Court in *Hawkins v. Finance Corp.* 238 N.C. 174, 77 S.E. 2d 669 (1953): "[T]he essential elements of an equitable estoppel as related to the party estopped are: (1) Conduct which amounts to a false representation or concealment of material facts, or, at least, which is reasonably calculated to convey the impression that the facts are otherwise than, and inconsistent with, those which the party afterwards attempts to assert; (2) intention or expectation that such conduct shall be acted upon by the other party, or conduct which at least is calculated to induce a reasonably prudent person to believe such conduct was intended or expected to be relied and acted upon; (3) knowledge, actual or constructive, of the real facts. As related to the party claiming the estoppel, they are: (1) lack of knowledge and the means of knowledge of the truth as to the facts in question; (2) reliance upon the conduct of the party sought to be estopped; and (3) action based thereon of such a character as to change his position prejudicially." 238 N.C. at 177-178, 77 S.E. 2d at 672. *Accord, Yancey v. Watkins,* 2 N.C. App. 672, 163 S.E. 2d 625 (1968). If the evidence in a particular case raises a permissible inference that these elements exist, but there are other inferences to be drawn from the evidence to the contrary, estoppel is a question of fact for the jury to determine. *Peek v. Trust Co.,* 242 N.C. 1, 86 S.E. 2d 745 (1955).

[4] Applying these principles to the present case, we conclude that there was a genuine issue of material fact as to whether defendant may be estopped from refusing to recognize plaintiff as a "career teacher." Both the superintendent of schools and the finance officer admitted in their affidavits that they did not know at the time plaintiff talked with them concerning the possibility of disability retirement that she would, in effect, be resigning her position as a career teacher. In a verified affidavit submitted in opposition to defendant's motion for summary judgment, plaintiff stated that she met with the finance officer of the Montgomery County Schools, James Woodruff, to whom the superintendent of schools had referred her in late November 1976 to discuss her options during the time she would be receiving medical help. At that meeting they discussed several options and ultimately, Woodruff recommended disability retirement: "He assured me that the retirement aspect was just a formality because the State regulations provide that the benefits stop automatically when one returns to work. He certainly did not indicate that the application, or its acceptance, would have any bearing whatsoever on my return .... Obviously, I would not have pursued disability retirement if I had any suspicion, or if I had been advised, that such would be the case." The finance officer was an agent of defendant, and he is chargeable

with knowledge of the implications of a teacher's election to apply for disability retirement benefits. Plaintiff's sworn statement is sufficient to raise the legitimate inference that the finance officer's representation was false, that it was reasonably calculated to convey the impression that plaintiff would not lose any status previously attained, and that such representation was calculated to and did induce plaintiff to act to her prejudice in electing disability retirement. Although defendant contends that plaintiff did have the means of knowledge of the truth as to the effect of her election, we do not agree that plaintiff was required to make extensive inquiry for herself after being advised that "the retirement aspect was just a formality." There is also evidence in the record that, at the time plaintiff sought to claim the benefits of career status, she continued to receive disability retirement benefits. This fact alone, however, does not defeat her claim of estoppel; rather, it is merely a factor to be considered in determining whether she is entitled to the benefits of equitable principles.

[5] It is true that the Montgomery County Board of Education is an administrative agency of the State, G.S. 115-35, and as such is not subject to an estoppel to the same extent as a private individual or a private corporation. *See, Henderson v. Gill, Comr. of Revenue,* 229 N.C. 313, 49 S.E. 2d 754 (1948). Our Supreme Court has stated however, that "an estoppel may arise against a [governmental entity] out of a transaction in which it acted in a governmental capacity, if an estoppel is necessary to prevent loss to another, and if such estoppel will not impair the exercise of the governmental powers of the [entity]." *Washington v. McLawhorn,* 237 N.C. 449, 454, 75 S.E. 2d 402, 406 (1953). We do not find that application of principles of estoppel in the present case would impair the exercise of defendant's governmental powers.

Because of the existence of disputed issues of material fact, the judgment appealed from is reversed, and the case is remanded.

Reversed and Remanded.

Judges MARTIN (Robert M.) and MARTIN (Harry C.) concur.

State v. McGee

STATE OF NORTH CAROLINA v. CARL EDWARD McGEE

No. 8025SC83

(Filed 17 June 1980)

1. Homicide § 12– indictment for second degree murder – allegation of malice aforethought not required

There was no merit to defendant's contention that the bill of indictment for murder in the second degree should be quashed because it did not contain the word "aforethought" modifying malice, since malice aforethought is required to prove murder in the first degree but is not an element of murder in the second degree.

2. Indictment and Warrant § 1– indictment unaffected by charge at preliminary hearing

There was no merit to defendant's contention that the State should be estopped from prosecuting him on the charge of second degree murder because the district court judge failed to find probable cause on the murder charge and bound defendant over for trial only on a charge of manslaughter, since the actions of a grand jury are not limited by the charges presented or determined at a probable cause hearing in the district court.

3. Homicide § 21.7– second degree murder – sufficiency of evidence

Evidence was sufficient for the jury in a prosecution for second degree murder where it tended to show that defendant was living with deceased's wife in a motel room; upon seeing deceased's truck hit his jeep, defendant took a loaded .12-gauge shotgun and went out of the motel before deceased had gotten out of his vehicle; deceased had only a tire tool, eighteen inches long, in his possession; these events happened in the daytime; defendant shot deceased while he was behind a vehicle some 22 feet away; and there was no evidence deceased was assaulting or threatening to assault defendant in any way.

4. Homicide § 3– tire tool – no deadly weapon as matter of law

The trial court in a second degree murder case properly refused to instruct the jury that a tire tool found in deceased's possession was a deadly weapon as a matter of law.

5. Homicide §§ 28.3, 28.4– second degree murder – deceased as aggressor – defense of habitation – no instructions required

The trial court in a second degree murder case was not required to instruct the jury as a matter of law that deceased was the aggressor under the facts of this case, nor was there any evidence to require a specific instruction that defendant could defend his habitation, a motel room, in order to prevent a forcible entry.

6. Criminal Law § 102.1– State's jury argument – no prejudice to defendant

Defendant was not prejudiced by jury arguments of counsel for the

State since defendant failed to object to some of the arguments at the time they were made; defendant's objections to several of the arguments were sustained and any prejudice to defendant was therefore removed; and the cumulative effect of the contested parts of counsel's arguments was not sufficiently prejudicial to require a new trial.

APPEAL by defendant from *Kirby, Judge*. Judgment entered 12 September 1979 in Superior Court, BURKE County. Heard in the Court of Appeals 23 May 1980.

Defendant was tried and convicted of murder in the second degree. McGee was served with a warrant on the murder charge and upon probable cause hearing was bound over to the superior court on the felony of manslaughter. Thereafter, on 20 August 1979, the grand jury for Burke County returned a true bill of indictment against defendant on the charge of murder in the second degree. Defendant moved to quash the bill and also moved that the state be estopped to proceed on the murder charge. The motions were denied, and upon trial by jury, defendant was convicted of the murder charge.

The state's evidence showed that on 10 July 1979 defendant and Johnny Van Horn's wife, Pat, were staying in the Morganton Motel. In a statement to the investigating officers, defendant said that when he returned to the motel from work, Mrs. Van Horn told him that her husband had been there a short time before and he had threatened to kill him. They talked about this and had decided to leave when defendant saw Van Horn's pickup truck crash into the rear of defendant's jeep parked in front of the motel room. Defendant opened the door and picked up a 12-gauge automatic Browning shotgun; he saw Van Horn come out of the truck with "something long and round and brown." He thought it was a gun. Defendant said for Van Horn to "hold it" and fired.

The investigating officer arrived about 8:15 p.m. and defendant told him that he did the shooting. The shotgun was found in the back of defendant's jeep and had two unfired shells in it. Near the body of Van Horn, the officers found a tire tool, weighing about one-half pound, eighteen inches long, and wrapped on one end with about six inches of white tape. After the shooting, defendant went to Van Horn, who was hit in the shoulder near the neck, and held his hand on the wound until the ambulance arrived.

Sometime before this event, the right foot of Van Horn had been surgically amputated at the ankle and he wore a special fitted shoe. Van Horn died as the result of the gunshot wounds.

Further investigation disclosed that Van Horn was about twenty-two feet from defendant when the shotgun was fired. The spent shotgun shell from defendant's gun was located about seven feet from the motel room door.

The statement by the defendant, offered by the state, showed he and Pat Van Horn had spent Sunday night at the Rainbow Inn and had rented a room for a week at the Morganton Motel. Defendant worked from 7:00 a.m. to 5:30 p.m. In addition to the shotgun, defendant had a .22-caliber pistol in the motel room and a .22-caliber rifle behind the seat of his jeep. After the truck crashed into defendant's jeep and defendant went outside with the shotgun, he saw what he thought was a gun barrel come up over the hood of the truck and he fired at Johnny Van Horn with the shotgun.

From a judgment of imprisonment, defendant appeals.

Attorney General Edmisten, by Special Deputy Attorney General W.A. Raney, Jr., for the State.

Byrd, Byrd, Ervin, Blanton & Whisnant, by Robert B. Byrd and Joe K. Byrd, for defendant appellant.

MARTIN (Harry C.), Judge.

Defendant argues four assignments of error. After a careful consideration of the record, briefs and oral arguments of counsel, we find no error in defendant's trial.

[1,2] First, defendant contends the bill for murder in the second degree should be quashed because it does not contain the word "aforethought," modifying malice. The offense of murder in the second degree requires malice as an element, but not malice aforethought. "Aforethought" means "with premeditation and deliberation" as required in murder in the first degree. It is not an element of murder in the second degree. *State v. Duboise*, 279 N.C. 73, 181 S.E. 2d 393 (1971). Defendant also insists the state should be estopped from prosecuting defendant on the charge of murder in the second degree because the district court judge failed to find probable cause on the murder charge and only bound the defendant over for trial on manslaughter. Defendant's counsel candidly concede this Court has reached a contrary result in *State v. Lee*, 42 N.C. App. 77, 255 S.E. 2d 602 (1979), but request the Court to reconsider this holding. A finding of probable cause by the district court is not a prerequisite to the returning of a true bill of indictment. The actions of a grand jury are not limited by the charges presented or determined at a probable cause hearing in the district court. We see no reason to abandon this beacon of the law to embark on uncharted seas. Defendant contends the present law may result in abuse of authority by the district solicitor. The ballot box is the remedy for such abuse. We find no merit in this assignment of error.

Defendant insists that the trial court erred in denying his motion to dismiss the charges of murder and voluntary manslaughter at the close of all the evidence. On such motion, the state is entitled to every reasonable inference arising from the evidence, which must be considered in the light most favorable to the state. *State v. Witherspoon*, 293 N.C. 321, 237 S.E. 2d 822 (1977). The introduction by the state of exculpatory statements by a defendant does not preclude the state from showing the facts concerning the crime to be different, and does not require nonsuit if the state contradicts or rebuts defendant's exculpatory statements. *State v. May*, 292 N.C. 644, 235 S.E. 2d 178, *cert. denied*, 434 U.S. 928, 54 L. Ed. 2d 288 (1977).

[3] The state's evidence showed defendant to be living with deceased's wife in a motel room. Upon seeing deceased's truck hit his jeep, defendant took an automatic shotgun, loaded with 12-gauge buckshot, and went out of the motel before the deceased had gotten out of his vehicle. Johnny Van Horn only had a tire tool, eighteen inches long, in his possession. These events happened in the daytime, shortly after defendant got off work at 5:30 p.m., daylight saving time, 10 July 1979. Defendant shot

Van Horn while he was behind a vehicle some twenty-two feet away. There is no evidence Van Horn was assaulting or threatening to assault defendant in any way. Defendant voluntarily left the safety of his motel room and could have easily returned there if he feared an assault from Van Horn.

Malice is presumed in the law from the intentional firing of the shotgun resulting in the killing of Van Horn. *State v. Jackson*, 284 N.C. 383, 200 S.E. 2d 596 (1973). The state's evidence is sufficient to throw a different light on the circumstances of the killing and to impeach defendant's exculpatory statements. It was for the jury to say whether defendant's guilt of murder or manslaughter had been proved beyond a reasonable doubt. The assignment of error is overruled.

[4] Defendant makes several exceptions to the court's charge on self-defense. He argues the court should have instructed the jury that the eighteen-inch tire tool was a deadly weapon as a matter of law. From an examination of the tire tool, which was offered into evidence and forwarded to this Court as an exhibit, it is obvious that it is not a deadly weapon as a matter of law. Whether it was a deadly weapon as used in this case depends upon the weapon itself, how it was being used, the size, strength and physical ability of the party using it, Van Horn, as opposed to that of defendant, and the other facts and circumstances of the case. *State v. Cauley*, 244 N.C. 701, 94 S.E. 2d 915 (1956). The court properly refused to instruct the jury that the tire tool was a deadly weapon as a matter of law.

Defendant argues that where there is evidence of self-defense the presumptions of unlawfulness and malice, which arise from the intentional shooting with a deadly weapon, disappear. This argument has been resolved by our Supreme Court in *State v. Hankerson*, 288 N.C. 632, 220 S.E. 2d 575 (1975), *rev'd on other grounds*, 432 U.S. 233, 53 L. Ed. 2d 306 (1977), where the Court held that *Mullaney v. Wilbur*, 421 U.S. 684, 44 L. Ed. 2d 508 (1975), does not preclude the continued use of our traditional presumptions of unlawfulness and malice arising from the intentional use of a deadly weapon resulting in death.

[5] Defendant contends the court should have instructed the jury as a matter of law that Van Horn was the aggressor under the facts of this case. We do not agree. This was properly a question for the jury and the court so instructed.

The court correctly charged the jury on the law of self-defense under the circumstances of this case. There was no evidence to require a specific instruction that defendant could defend his habitation, the motel room, in order to prevent a forcible entry. *State v. Jones*, 299 N.C. 103, 261 S.E. 2d 1 (1980).

> A person has the right to use deadly force in the defense of his habitation in order to prevent a forcible entry, even if the intruder is not armed with a deadly weapon, where the attempted forcible entry is made under such circumstances that the person reasonably apprehends death or great bodily harm to himself or the occupants of the home at the hands of the assailant or believes that the assailant intends to commit a felony. ... The occupant may use deadly force when it is actually or apparently necessary to do so, and the jury is the judge of the reasonableness of the defendant's apprehension. ...

> . . . .

> Thus, when there is competent evidence in the case to raise the issue of defense of home, the jury must be instructed on this defense and the fact that the jury was instructed on defense of a family member does not cure the error.

Id. at 107, 261 S.E. 2d at 5.

In *Jones*, the deceased had made an assault on the house in an effort to force entry; he beat on the door, broke the lock on the door, tore the screen and broke several panes of glass in the front door, all after warning shots had been fired by defendant Jones. In our case, there is no evidence of such attack by Van Horn; he was some twenty-two feet from the motel when killed. The court's instructions were correct.

[6] Last, defendant objects to the jury arguments by counsel for the state. He points out eight places in the arguments, which are part of the record, in which he contends prejudicial error was committed. They read:

[1] Mr. Byrd keeps telling you that the facts are undisputed. Sure the facts are undisputed, but the intent or the truthfulness of the facts might be disputed. You must look at the person, ladies and gentlemen, that's made the statements. Carl McGee is the defendant. He's the man that's on the seat, on the hot seat today. He is the man that has an interest in this case. You must scrutinize very, very carefully, as the Court will instruct you, any person's statements who has an interest in the case.

[2] Now the other statement, Detective Buchanan comes in a little bit later, 9:40, which is some thirty — forty minutes later, and he takes a statement. He says well, let me take a statement here. What's Carl McGee say? Now listen to this second statement. Says Pat and Johnny Van Horn are separated over a month, she went back to Johnny for three days. Talking about Pat there, his roommate. Since Sunday, she left Sunday, — we stayed at the Rainbow Inn Sunday night. Over at the Rainbow Inn, just the two of them. Rented a room then for a week then at the Morganton Motel.

McGee now is making this statement to the officers. Remember again he's an interested witness. He said I signed my name, she didn't sign hers.

[3] I tell you, ladies and gentlemen, this case is clear to me. Johnny Van Horn went over there looking for his wife, he didn't go over there looking for trouble. There is absolutely no evidence of any weapon on the person of Johnny Van Horn. No evidence whatsoever.

[4] Ladies and gentlemen, the defendant Carl McGee shot and killed Johnny Van Horn, and he is guilty of murder. There is no reasonable doubt in my mind that that's not the case.

State v. McGee

[5] There is no self-defense. There is a homicide. Carl McGee has ended a very valuable life. He has done it in a very hostile aggravated manner.

[6] At the very minimum, ladies and gentlemen, from the evidence, if you believe everything that the defendant said, even inconsistencies, if you believe everything to his favor, the statements to the officers, you would have to find him guilty of voluntary manslaughter because he used excessive force. Even if this [tire tool] were thrown at him he used excessive force. He had not at any time been under a deadly attack, a deadly assault. No evidence.

[7] Several things about this case have really bothered me from the standpoint of the contentions made by the defendant. Why, oh why, oh why, Mr. Byrd, did your defendant arm himself with three weapons on this occasion? Why, oh why, Mr. Byrd, did he have two loaded weapons in the motel room, one of them before he ever even talked to Pat Van Horn, the victim's wife, about any threats? Why did he arm himself with three weapons?, when this man had never had any personal contact with him. Had never made a direct threat to him. I think you ladies and gentlemen can see the lies.

[8] I'll have you to recall one thing, the defendant didn't give Johnny Van Horn that right. The defendant, Carl McGee, on this occasion at the Morganton Motel with his twelve gauge shotgun with double-ought buckshot was the jury, the judge, and the executioner.

Defendant did not object to numbers 1, 3, 5, 6 and 7 at the time the statements were made. He objected to numbers 2, 4 and 8; the objections were sustained by the court and on number 8 the court instructed the jury not to consider the argument. Defendant does not argue numbers 1, 3, 5 and 6 in his brief. All four are proper arguments, supported by the evidence in the case. While the statement in number 7 is inappropriate, it does not directly accuse any person or witness of lying. Counsel was only submitting the possibility to the jury for their determination. *State v. Noell*, 284 N.C. 670, 202 S.E. 2d 750 (1974), *death penalty vacated,* 428 U.S. 902, 49 L. Ed. 2d 1205 (1976). Defendant made no objection at the time, and it is not so improper as to require the court to order a mistrial ex mero motu. *State v. Britt,* 291 N.C. 528, 231 S.E. 2d 644 (1977). If a timely objection had been made, the court could have removed any possible prejudice by instructions to the jury. *State v. Miller,* 288 N.C. 582, 220 S.E. 2d 326 (1975). Defendant fails to address number 2 in his brief. In any event, it is a proper argument supported by the facts of this case.

In number 4, state's counsel states his opinion as to the guilt of defendant. The court promptly sustained defendant's objection. No further instruction was requested. We do not believe that the statement, although clearly improper, is so grossly prejudicial as to require a mistrial. *State v. Britt, supra.*

The court sustained defendant's objection to the last quoted statement of counsel, and instructed the jury that they would not consider the argument. Again, although the argument was improper, any possible prejudice was removed by the action of the court and there is not sufficient prejudice to require a new trial.

Nor do we consider the cumulative effect of the contested parts of counsel's arguments to be sufficiently prejudicial to call for a new trial. Jury arguments must be left largely to the control and discretion of the trial judge. Counsel are generally allowed wide latitude in hotly contested cases. *State v. Westbrook,* 279 N.C. 18, 181 S.E. 2d 572 (1971), *death penalty vacated,* 408 U.S. 939, 33 L. Ed. 2d 761 (1972). We hold defendant was not deprived of a fair and impartial trial by counsel's arguments. See the excellent collection of authorities by Justice Copeland in *Reversible Error in Argument to Jury,* Institute of Government, presented at the Conference of Superior Court Judges, Asheville, North Carolina, 22 October 1976.

In defendant's trial, we find

No error.

Judges WEBB and WELLS concur.

State v. McCaskill

STATE OF NORTH CAROLINA v. TERRY McCASKILL

No. 7910SC1161

(Filed 17 June 1980)

1. **Embezzlement § 5– references to defendant as "employee" – no invasion of province of jury**

   In a prosecution for embezzlement in which defendant contended that he was an independent contractor, testimony referring to defendant as an "employee" of the State's witnesses did not invade the province of the jury since the embezzlement statute, G.S. 14-90, requires the establishment of an agency relationship; the question which determined the nature of the relationship between the defendant and the State's witnesses was the ownership of the money in question at the time it came into the hands of defendant; and the reference to defendant as an employee therefore did not infringe upon the jury's responsibility of determining whether defendant was an independent contractor.

2. **Embezzlement § 6– sufficiency of State's evidence**

   The State's evidence was sufficient for the jury in a prosecution for embezzlement where it tended to show that defendant was to procure contracts with retail businesses for promotional services to be rendered by a firm owned by the State's witnesses; defendant was to receive money for such contracts, deliver the money to one State's witness, and receive a commission on the price, or, as later agreed upon, keep any money over a set price; and defendant did receive such money which he did not deliver to the State's witness.

3. **Criminal Law § 102 – permitting only one jury argument by defendant – no violation of statute**

   The purpose of G.S. 84-14 was not to enlarge the number of addresses to the jury but was to limit the number of counsel and the time allowed a defendant's counsel in addressing the jury. Therefore, the trial court did not violate the statute in permitting a defendant who introduced evidence to present only one jury argument.

APPEAL by defendant from *Godwin, Judge.* Judgment entered 19 July 1979 in Superior Court, WAKE County. Heard in the Court of Appeals 23 April 1980.

Defendant was indicted and tried for the felony of embezzlement (G.S. 14-90). The jury returned a verdict of guilty and from a judgment imposing a prison sentence, defendant appealed.

Attorney General Edmisten by Special Deputy Attorney General Charles J. Murray, for the State.

Carlos W. Murray, Jr., for the defendant.

MARTIN (Robert M.), Judge.

[1] Defendant contends the trial court erred in denying defendant's motion to strike the use of the word employment by the State's witnesses. In his arguments I through V defendant contends the references invaded the province of the jury in that whether the defendant was an employee of the State's witnesses was the ultimate question to be decided by the jury. Defendant contends that he was an independent contractor and complains of references to the defendant being an "employee" of Bill Meadors and Perry Walton.

Mr. Meadors testified that he is co-owner of Action Marketing and has been for two months. Prior to that he was President of Carolina Treasure Pak, Inc., a firm which handles promotional mailings for multiple merchants. In September 1978 he hired McCaskill as a sales representative for the Raleigh market of Carolina Treasure Pak, Inc. The following testimony forms the basis for defendant's first four exceptions:

Q. Did you have an oral or written agreement as to terms of employment?

A. Yes, ma'am.

Q. And what type of an agreement?

MR. MURRAY: Your Honor, I would object and move to strike to the use of the word "employment" in the question.

COURT: Overruled.

EXCEPTION NO. 1

Q. Did you have an oral or written agreement with regard to the employment?

A. Yes, ma'am.

Q. And what type of agreement did you have?

A. It was one of employer-employee relationship.

MR. MURRAY: Objection and move to strike.

COURT: The objection is overruled. Motion denied.

EXCEPTION NO. 2

COURT: Was the agreement a written agreement or a parol agreement, that is, a spoken agreement?

A. We had both, sir. We didn't get the written agreement established because the company was just getting off the ground and we wanted to see how the business flowed before we had —

COURT: Then should I understand that in the outset the agreement that you had with the defendant was not reduced to writing?

A. Yes, sir.

EXCEPTION NO. 3

Q. Mr. Meadors, did you have the power to terminate the defendant's employment at any time?

A. Yes, ma'am.

MR. MURRAY: Objection to the use of the word "employment."

COURT: Overruled.

MR. MURRAY: Move to strike.

COURT: Overruled.

EXCEPTION NO. 4

Under G.S. 14-90,

> If ... *any* ... *agent* of a corporation, or *any agent* ... of any person, shall embezzle or fraudulently or knowingly and wilfully ... convert to his own use ... any money ... belonging to any other person or corporation ... which shall have come into his possession or under his care, he shall be guilty of a felony, and shall be punished as in cases of larceny. (Emphasis added)

Defendant contends that he was an independent contractor and the relationship with Carolina Treasure Pak, Inc. was that of a debtor and creditor. Either status, he contends, would take him out of the embezzlement statute. Where an agency is not established, there cannot be a conviction based on that relation within the meaning of a statute prescribing a punishment for embezzlement. An independent contractor is not a servant or agent within the meaning of an embezzlement statute. 26 Am. Jur. 2d, Embezzlement § 26 (1966). Generally, when dealings between two persons create a relation of debtor and creditor, a failure of one of the parties to pay over money does not constitute the crime of embezzlement. Ordinarily, whether the relation of debtor-creditor exists depends upon the facts of the particular case. 26 Am. Jur. 2d, Embezzlement § 17 (1966); *Gray v. Bennett*, 250 N.C. 707, 110 S.E. 2d 324 (1959).

A review of the elements of the offense of embezzlement shows that it is the terms of the relationship that are important and not how the relationship is designated. "In the light of the provisions of this statute, as interpreted and applied by this Court, in order to convict a defendant of embezzlement, as declared in opinion by CLARK, C.J., in *S. v. Blackley, supra,* 'four distinct propositions of fact must be established: (1) that the defendant was the agent of the prosecutor, and (2) by the terms of his employment had received property of his principal; (3) that he received it in the course of his employment; and (4) knowing it was not his own, converted it to his own.' " *State v. Block*, 245 N.C. 661, 663, 97 S.E. 2d 243, 244 (1957), quoting *State v. Blackley*, 138 N.C. 620, 50 S.E. 2d 310 (1905). Since the term "employee" is not used in G.S. 14-90, and because the Court refers to "four distinct propositions of fact," the term "employment" appearing in the second and third elements in *State v. Block, supra,* is used in its broadest sense and is not referring to a strict employee-employer relationship.

The question which determines the nature of the relationship between the defendant and the State's-witnesses is the ownership of the money at the time it came into the hands of the defendant. *Gray v. Bennett, supra.* Therefore, the reference to the defendant as an employee does not infringe upon the jury's responsibility of determining whether or not the defendant was an independent contractor. The court correctly denied defendant's motions to strike.

[2] Defendant contends the court erred in denying defendant's motions to dismiss. In ruling upon a motion to dismiss the evidence is viewed in the most favorable light for the State and contradictions and inconsistencies are ignored. *State v. McKinney,* 288 N.C. 113, 215 S.E. 2d 578 (1975).

The evidence of the State's witnesses showed that the defendant was to procure contracts with various retail businesses for promotional services to be rendered by the firm owned by the State's witnesses Meadors and Walton. The defendant was to receive the money to be delivered to Meadors and he, the defendant, was to receive a commission on the price, or as later agreed upon he was to keep any money over a set price. These terms indicate that the defendant was a sales agent who was to receive money on individual accounts which was to be delivered to the State's witnesses. Further prosecution evidence showed that the defendant did receive money for Meadors which he did not deliver. This evidence, if believed, is sufficient to establish each element of the offense of embezzlement and therefore the case was properly submitted to the jury.

[3] Defendant's eighth assignment of error presents the question whether the trial court properly denied the defendant two arguments to the jury. The defendant introduced evidence, the State waived the opening argument and argued after the defendant argued. At the conclusion of the District Attorney's clos-

ing argument, the defendant moved for permission to make an additional argument to the jury by virtue of the provisions of N.C.G.S. 15A-1230(b) and G.S. 84-14. The motion was denied. It has long been the practice in this State that when a defendant puts on evidence he loses his right to conclude the arguments to the jury. *State v. Curtis*, 18 N.C. App. 116, 196 S.E. 2d 278 (1973). Rule 10, General Rules of Practice for the Superior and District Courts Supplemental to the Rules of Civil Procedure pursuant to G.S. 7A-34.

Defendant argues that G.S. 84-14 clearly says that a defendant in a felony case less than capital has two addresses to the jury. He contends in this case the State, by waiving the opening argument, had two arguments while he had only one. The State, in its brief, contends that G.S. 84-14 provides for "two addresses to the jury," citing Rules 9 and 10 of the General Rules of Practice for the Superior and District Courts which provide for an opening statement and a closing argument. Thus, the State contends that allowing the defendant to make an opening statement prior to the introduction of evidence and a closing argument after the introduction of evidence meets the requirements of G.S. 84-14.

G.S. 15A-1230(b) provides: "Length, numbers, and order of arguments allotted to the parties are governed by G.S. 84-14." G.S. 84-14 provides as follows:

Court's control of argument. — In all trials in the superior courts there shall be allowed two addresses to the jury for the State or plaintiff and two for the defendant, except in capital felonies, when there shall be no limit as to number. The judges of the superior court are authorized to limit the time of argument of counsel to the jury on the trial of actions, civil and criminal as follows: to not less than one hour on each side in misdemeanors and appeals from justices of the peace; to not less than two hours on each side in all other civil actions and in felonies less than capital; in capital felonies, the time of argument of counsel may not be limited otherwise than by consent, except that the court may limit the number of those who may address the jury to three counsel on each side. Where any greater number of addresses or any extension of time are desired, motion shall be made, and it shall be in the discretion of the judge to allow the same or not, as the interests of justice may require. In jury trials the whole case as well as law as of fact may be argued to the jury. (1903, c. 433; Rev., s. 216; C.S., s. 203; 1927, c. 52.)

We interpret G.S. 84-14 by reviewing the history of this legislation. An early statute rendered it unlawful for either party to employ more than one attorney to speak in a suit, and the courts were "directed not to suffer more than one attorney ..." to plead for either party.[1] Thereafter, a law was enacted allowing plaintiff or defendant to employ several attorneys in his case, but not more than one could speak unless allowed by the court.[2]

In *State v. Collins*, 70 N.C. 241 (1874) the court restricted the prisoner's counsel to one hour and a half in addressing the jury, allowing two of the counsel to divide the time between them. The Supreme Court held that it was a power vested in the presiding judge, and that they could not control its exercise. Following this case a statute was enacted giving counsel in civil and criminal cases the right to address the court or jury for such space of time as in his opinion may be necessary for the proper development and presentation of his case.[3]

[1] Revised Statutes of North Carolina ch. 31, § 62, para. 15 (1836-37).

It shall not be lawful for either plaintiff or defendant to employ, in any matter or suit, more than one attorney to speak in such matter or suit in court, and the courts in this State are hereby directed not to suffer more than one attorney as aforesaid, in any matters whatever, to plead for either plaintiff or defendant to any suit, under penalty of a violation of this section.

[2] Revised Code of North Carolina ch. 31, § 57, para. 15 (1855).

The plaintiff or defendant may employ several attorneys in his case, but more than one shall not speak thereto, unless allowed by the court; and in jury trials they may argue to the jury the whole case, as well of law as of fact.

[3] Code of North Carolina v. 1, ch. 4, § 30 (1883).

Any attorney appearing in any civil or criminal action shall be entitled to address the court or the jury for such a space of time as in his opinion may be necessary for the proper development and presentation of his case; and in jury trials he may argue to the jury the whole case as well of law as of fact.

In *State v. Miller,* 75 N.C. 73 (1876), the defendant was represented by three counsel. One of the counsel addressed the jury and at the conclusion of his remarks another of the counsel arose and stated to the court that in order to make a proper presentation of the defendant's case it was necessary that another of the counsel should address the jury, and asked permission to do so. The court refused to hear the counsel. Defendant excepted and the Supreme Court awarded a new trial. The court reviewed the progression of the statutory law. "First, that everyone charged with crime shall be entitled to counsel; but nothing is said about the number. Secondly, we have an act ... allowing him to have as many as he pleases, with the power in the presiding judge to limit the speaking to one; and thirdly, the late act which allows *any* of his counsel appearing in the case to speak as long as *he* pleases." In this case the court observed that the trial judge "thought ... that he would do indirectly what the act prohibited from being done directly — limit the *time* by limiting the *number.*" The court reasoned that the action of the judge was to save the time of the court. "And *that* the Legislature has said he shall not do, so as to deprive any counsel appearing of the right to speak as long as he pleases."

Thus, from the progression of the aforementioned legislation, it is apparent that the purpose of G.S. 84-14 was not to enlarge the number of addresses but rather a limitation on the number of counsel and time allowed a defendant's counsel in addressing the jury. We note the statute gives the court the discretion to allow a greater number of addresses.

We have carefully reviewed defendant's remaining assignments of error and found them to be without merit. In the trial we find no prejudicial error.

No error.

Judges WEBB and HILL concur.

State v. Johnson

STATE OF NORTH CAROLINA v. HOWARD RAY JOHNSON

No. 7926SC1067

(Filed 17 June 1980)

1. **Constitutional Law § 48– codefendants represented by same counsel – no conflict of interest – no denial of effective assistance of counsel**

   Defendant failed to show that he was denied effective assistance of counsel because his attorney also represented his codefendant who was charged with the same offenses, since defendant did not contend that any conflict of interest actually existed or that he was prejudiced in any way by the joint representation.

2. **Criminal Law § 86.2– defendant's prior criminal conduct – examination for impeachment**

   The trial court did not err in permitting the prosecution to examine defendant concerning his prior criminal record and misconduct for the purpose of impeachment.

3. **Criminal Law § 117.2– charge on scrutiny of defendant's testimony – no charge given as to other interested witnesses**

   The trial court did not err in charging the jury that it should scrutinize defendant's testimony in the light of his interest in the outcome of the case, though the court did not instruct the jury that the testimony of other witnesses should be scrutinized as to their interest in the case.

4. **Homicide § 24.1– presumptions arising from use of deadly weapon – jury instructions proper**

   The trial court's use of the phrase, "and, if nothing else appears and you so find beyond a reasonable doubt," did not cause the jury to believe that the burden was on defendant to come forward with evidence disproving unlawfulness and malice arising from the use of a deadly weapon, since the court clearly instructed the jury that they could but need not infer that unlawfulness and malice arose from defendant's use of a deadly weapon.

APPEAL by defendant from *Friday, Judge.* Judgment and commitment entered 4 May 1979 in Superior Court, MECKLEN-BURG County. Heard in the Court of Appeals 26 March 1980.

Defendant was charged upon an indictment with murder, conspiracy to commit murder, and assault with a deadly weapon with intent to kill inflicting serious injury. A codefendant, Danny Ray Anderson, was also indicted for the same offenses, and the cases were consolidated for trial. Both defendants retained and were represented by the same attor-

ney. At trial the State's evidence tended to show that the two
defendants shared an apartment, and on the evening of 19
February 1979 had a run-in' outside of a night club with the
deceased and Earl Lyn Deaton. Later that evening at another
night club the parties confronted again. Still later that night,
while Deaton and the deceased were driving along a road, they
were approached by a vehicle driven by Anderson in which
Johnson was a passenger. When Deaton and the deceased got
out of their vehicle to see who was approaching them, Johnson
and Anderson left their truck and Johnson pointed a gun at the
deceased. Johnson moved closer to the deceased, and when he
was within an arm's length, fired the gun into the decedent's
head. The defendants quickly returned to their vehicle, drove it
at Deaton, striking him, and then fled to Texas. Defendants'
evidence tended to show that Johnson killed the deceased in
self-defense and that Deaton was run over accidentally. The jury
acquitted Anderson of all charges and found defendant Johnson guilty of second degree murder. From the judgment entered upon the verdict, defendant Johnson appeals.

*Lindsey, Schrimsher, Erwin, Bernhardt & Hewitt, P.A., by
Lawrence W. Hewitt, for defendant appellant.*

*Attorney General Rufus L. Edmisten, by Assistant Attor-
ney General Daniel C. Oakley, for the State.*

WELLS, Judge.

[1] In his first assignment of error defendant argues that he
was denied the effective assistance of counsel because his attorney also represented co-defendant Anderson, who was charged
with the same offenses as appellant. Appellant does not argue
that a conflict of interest actually existed as to the joint representation in this case, or that any harm or prejudice in fact
resulted to him. It is defendant's position that the mere *possibility* of such a conflict from which harm *might* have resulted,
no matter how remote this possibility may have been, is sufficient to have violated defendant's Sixth Amendment right to
counsel. We disagree. There is no constitutional mandate requiring co-defendants who have merely potentially conflicting
interests to be represented by separate counsel. As Judge Field
has stated:

The appellants themselves retained their counsel which resulted in the multiple representation, and they, more than anyone, including the court, were in a position to know what facts might be developed at trial. Apparently they concluded that such representation was advantageous, and it should be noted that at no time, either prior to the trial or during the course thereof, was the issue of such multiple representation raised in any fashion. [Citation omitted.] Since we discern no conflict of interest or resultant prejudice to any of the appellants, we cannot accept their contention that they were denied the effective assistance of counsel.

United States v. Atkinson, 565 F. 2d 1283, 1284-1285 (4th Cir. 1977), *cert. denied,* 436 U.S. 944, 56 L. Ed. 2d 785, 98 S. Ct. 2845 (1978); *accord, State v. McKenzie,* 46 N.C. App. 34, 264 S.E. 2d 391 (1980); *State v. Engle,* 5 N.C. App. 101, 167 S.E. 2d 864 (1969). In the case *sub judice,* the testimony of both defendants is virtually identical, and the appellant does not contend that any conflict of interest actually existed or that he was prejudiced in any way by the joint representation. Under these circumstances, ineffective assistance of counsel has not been shown.

[2] Defendant next argues that after defendant took the stand in his own defense the trial court improperly permitted the prosecution to examine him on his prior criminal record and misconduct. The prosecution asked the defendant a number of questions intended to show that defendant had either been charged or convicted with assault on prior occasions. Although defendant's initial response to these questions was consistently negative, on further questioning, his testimony tended to show his involvement but that his recollection of these events was somewhat different than that of the district attorney. In his responses, however, defendant admitted that on direct examination, he had not fully disclosed his prior record.

For impeachment purposes, a witness, including the defendant in a criminal case, may be cross-examined with respect to prior convictions of crime and may be asked disparaging questions concerning collateral matters relating to his criminal and degrading conduct. [Citations omitted.] With respect to such collateral matters, the answers of the witness are conclusive in the sense that the record of his convictions cannot be introduced to contradict him. [Citations omitted.] By appropriate questions, however, the cross-examiner may continue to inquire about specific convictions already denied as well as other prior unrelated criminal convictions so as to "sift the witness." [Citations omitted.]

State v. Currie, 293 N.C. 523, 529, 238 S.E. 2d 477, 480-481 (1977). It is also obvious from the questions asked and defendant's responses to them, that the prosecution was acting upon information and in good faith in its efforts along these lines. *See, State v. Conner*, 244 N.C. 109, 92 S.E. 2d 668 (1956); *State v. Neal*, 222 N.C. 546, 23 S.E. 2d 911 (1943). This assignment is overruled.

[3] The next assignment of error raised by the defendant is that the court erred in charging the jury that it should scrutinize defendants' testimony in light of their interest in the outcome of the case. The court did not instruct the jury that the testimony of other witnesses should be scrutinized as to their interest in the case. While we acknowledge that the rule is different in other jurisdictions, in North Carolina, "the trial court may instruct [the jury] on the defendant's status as an interested witness without being required to give a like instruction, without request, as to possibly interested State's witnesses." *State v. Watson*, 294 N.C. 159, 168, 240 S.E. 2d 440, 446 (1978); *see also, State v. Eakins*, 292 N.C. 445, 233 S.E. 2d 387 (1977). It should also be noted that in the present case the trial court instructed the jury that, if it believed the defendant's testimony, it should give this testimony the same weight as that of the other witnesses, and that it was for the jury, alone, to weigh the credibility and sufficiency of all the evidence in the case.

[4] Defendant also assigns as error a portion of the trial court's charge relating to the elements of second degree murder. The court stated:

Now, members of the jury, in that connection the Court instructs you that if the State proves beyond a reasonable

State v. Johnson

doubt that the Defendant intentionally killed Knighten with a deadly weapon or intentionally inflicted a wound upon Knighten with a deadly weapon that proximately caused his death, you may, but need not, infer, first, that the killing was unlawful; and second, that it was done with malice; and, if nothing else appears and you so find beyond a reasonable doubt, the defendant would be guilty of second-degree murder . . . .

Defendant, relying on *State v. Patterson*, 297 N.C. 247, 254 S.E. 2d 604 (1979), argues that the phrase, "and, if nothing else appears and you so find beyond a reasonable doubt" caused the jury to believe that the burden was on defendant to come forward with evidence disproving unlawfulness and malice.[1] In *Patterson*, the trial court had charged:

Now if the State satisfies you beyond a reasonable doubt that Gregory Patterson intentionally shot Michael Millsap with a deadly weapon or that he intentionally inflicted a wound upon Millsap with a deadly weapon and thereby proximately caused Millsap's death *and there is no other evidence which raises in your mind a reasonable doubt that the defendant acted without malice or without justification or excuse* you may infer that the defendant acted unlawfully, and with malice. [Court's emphasis.].

---

[1] We believe that in this phrase the trial court was referring to the intentional killing of the decedent — that if the jury found, beyond a reasonable doubt, that the defendant intentionally killed the deceased, it could infer unlawfulness and malice. It should be noted that the disputed phrase adds no clarity to the charge and nowhere appears in the North Carolina Pattern Jury Instructions, which provides:

If the State proves beyond a reasonable doubt, or it is admitted, that the defendant intentionally killed *(name victim)* with a deadly weapon or intentionally inflicted a wound upon *(name victim)* with a deadly weapon that proximately caused his death, you may infer first, that the killing was unlawful, and second that it was done with malice, but you are not compelled to do so. You may consider these inferences along with all other facts and circumstances in determining whether the killing was unlawful and whether it was done with malice. If you infer that the killing was unlawful and was done with malice, the defendant would be guilty of second degree murder.

N.C.P.I. — Crim. § 206.10, p. 5 (1979).

297 N.C. at 251, 254 S.E. 2d at 608. The Court held:

Nowhere in his instructions did Judge Snepp tell the jury that it was not compelled to nor need it necessarily infer malice and unlawfulness, *i.e.*, absence of justification. The instructions say, in essence, that unless the jury has a reasonable doubt as to the existence of malice and unlawfulness it "may infer" their existence upon proof of the necessary underlying facts. In this context, it is likely the jury understood the word "may" to mean "should." The complained of instructions are thus susceptible to an interpretation that the jury should infer malice and unlawfulness in the absence of evidence raising a reasonable doubt as to the existence of these elements.

297 N.C. at 252, 254 S.E. 2d at 608.

It is clear that the court's charge in the instant case is substantively distinguishable from the charge disapproved in *Patterson*. In *Patterson*, the Court found that the charge could be construed so as to require the jury to infer unlawfulness and malice. The trial court in *Patterson* never stated to the jury that these inferences were not compelled, but left the impression that the defendant had the burden of persuading the jury that the inferences should not be made. In the present case, the court explicitly charged the jury that it "may, *but need not,* infer" unlawfulness and malice [our emphasis]. Under these circumstances we view the court's charge as sufficiently clear and correct to avoid any prejudice to defendant.

No error.

Chief Judge MORRIS and Judge PARKER concur.

State v. Graham

STATE OF NORTH CAROLINA v. LINWOOD EARL GRAHAM, JR.

No. 798SC1180

(Filed 17 June 1980)

1. **Criminal Law § 17– crimes committed at post office – jurisdiction of State courts**

   The courts of this State had jurisdiction over the crimes of breaking and entering a post office and larceny of property therefrom where the record does not show that the federal government has accepted exclusive jurisdiction over the post office property in accordance with 40 U.S.C. §255. G.S. 104-7.

2. **Arrest and Bail § 5.2– warrantless arrest at home of friend – probable cause**

   The warrantless arrest of defendant at the home of a friend was valid where the friend told the officer about defendant's involvement in certain break-ins, and the officer was afraid defendant would avoid apprehension if not then arrested because defendant had seen his friend arrested and because defendant told the officer that he lived with his mother when the officer knew he did not, since the officer had probable cause to believe that defendant had committed certain felonies and might not be apprehended unless immediately arrested.

3. **Larceny § 7.3– ownership of stolen property – no fatal variance**

   There was no fatal variance where a larceny indictment alleged that stolen money and a stolen radio were the "personal property of Maury Post Office a division of the United States Postal Service" and the evidence showed that the money and radio were the personal property of the postmaster since the property had been left at the post office and the post office was in lawful possession of it at the time it was stolen.

4. **Larceny § 7.3– ownership of stolen property – no fatal variance**

   There was no fatal variance where a larceny indictment alleged that a stolen tire tool was "the personal property of L. A. Moye, L. A. Moye, Jr., and C. L. Stokes t/a Moye and Stokes Store" and the evidence showed that Charles Stokes owned the warehouse from which the tire tool was taken.

5. **Burglary and Unlawful Breakings § 5.7– breaking and entering – intent to steal – ownership of property – no fatal variance**

   There was no fatal variance where the indictment alleged a breaking and entering with intent to steal of a "building occupied by Julian Jones used as a garage" and the evidence showed that the building was a storage shed and no longer used by Mr. Jones, since it was not incumbent on the State to establish the owner of the property defendant intended to steal but only the intent to steal upon breaking or entering.

State v. Graham

6. **Larceny § 4; Receiving Stolen Goods § 2– larceny and receiving – motion to dismiss indictment – reservation of ruling until end of evidence**

The trial court did not err in reserving its ruling on defendant's motion to dismiss indictments charging him with larceny and receiving of the same stolen property until the close of the evidence.

7. **Criminal Law § § 75.2, 75.10– confession – request for counsel – subsequent written waiver – absence of inducement**

The trial court properly admitted defendant's confession where (1) the record shows that defendant was advised of his *Miranda* rights, stated that he wanted to talk to a lawyer but changed his mind, and then signed a written waiver of counsel, and (2) the court found upon conflicting evidence that the officer did not induce defendant's confession by saying that he would put in a good word for defendant in court if he confessed.

8. **Criminal Law § 114.2– instructions – reference to "confession" – no expression of opinion**

The trial court did not express an opinion on the evidence when defendant objected to the court's instruction that the State had presented evidence tending to show that defendant "confessed" to the crimes charged and the court replied, "Well, that's what it is," since defendant's in-custody statement in fact constituted a confession.

APPEAL by defendant from *Barefoot, Judge.* Judgments entered 31 May 1979 in Superior Court, GREENE County. Heard in the Court of Appeals 24 April 1980.

Defendant was tried on two bills of indictment charging breaking and entering and larceny and one bill of indictment charging breaking and entering. Several break-ins occurred in Maury, North Carolina on the night of 27 February 1979. The next morning, the postmaster of Maury discovered the Maury Post Office had been entered. A glass door was knocked out, two record cabinets were opened and mail was strewn on the floor. A safe had been tampered with but was not opened. A radio and twenty dollars which were the personal property of the postmaster were missing. Two sets of shoe prints were all over the floor on the papers. Two sets of shoe prints led from the post office to Charles Stokes' warehouse which had been entered and from which a tire tool was missing. Julian Jones' garage had also been entered but apparently nothing was taken. Defendant was arrested without a warrant at a friend's house after the friend admitted to an investigating officer that he and defendant committed the break-ins and thefts. Defendant was

State v. Graham

questioned and made a statement in which he admitted participating in the alleged crimes. The statement was introduced in
evidence at the trial.

Defendant testified in his own behalf that he did not commit any of the crimes of which he stood charged. He offered the
alibi that he had been in Greenville the night of the break-ins.
He did not know of the break-ins until the next morning. He
admitted to answering part of the questions on the statement
introduced in evidence against him.

The jury found defendant guilty of felonious entry into and
larceny from the Moye-Stokes Store, guilty of felonious entry
into and larceny from the Maury Post Office and guilty of felonious entry into Jones' Garage. Defendant appeals from a judgment imposing an active prison sentence.

*Attorney General Edmisten, by Assistant Attorney General
Roy A. Giles, Jr., for the State.*

William R. Jenkins, for defendant appellant.

VAUGHN, Judge.

Defendant brings forward eight assignments of error in the
trial below. We find the assigned errors without merit.

[1] Defendant contends the courts of this State were without
jurisdiction over the crimes of breaking and entering of and
larceny from the Maury Post Office. The Congress has passed
laws to protect United States post offices from breaking and
entering and larceny. 18 U.S.C. §§ 2115, 1707. Our State, in
compliance with clause seventeen, section eight of the first
article of the United States Constitution, consents to the acquisition of lands within the State by the United States and
cedes exclusive jurisdiction, except for service of civil and criminal process, over lands so acquired to the federal government. G.S. 104-7. The United States may accept exclusive or
partial jurisdiction over lands acquired within a state and 40
U.S.C. § 255 provides that exclusive or partial jurisdiction may
be accepted by giving written notice to the governor of the state

or in such other manner as prescribed by the law of the state in which the land lies of the type of jurisdiction that is being accepted. "Unless and until the United States has accepted jurisdiction over lands hereafter to be acquired as aforesaid, it shall be conclusively presumed that no such jurisdiction has been accepted." *Id.* Until the federal government accepts exclusive jurisdiction in accordance with 40 U.S.C. § 255, our Courts will retain jurisdiction over crimes against the laws of this State committed on Federal lands in this State. *State v. Burell,* 256 N.C. 288, 123 S.E. 2d 795, *cert. den.,* 370 U.S. 961, 8 L. Ed. 2d 827, 82 S. Ct. 1621 (1962). The record does not reveal that the federal government has accepted exclusive jurisdiction over the Maⅼry Post Office property. Defendant maintains we should at least remand the case for a determination by the trial court of whether it had subject matter jurisdiction over the post office offenses. Defendant notes that this was done in a Pennsylvania case involving burglary of a post office. *Commonwealth v. Mangum,* 231 Pa. Super. 162, 332 A. 2d 467 (1974). We do not feel this is necessary because of the differences between the Pennsylvania statute concerning the ceding of jurisdiction over lands to the federal government and interpretations given that statute by Pennsylvania courts and our own G.S. 104-7 concerning the ceding of jurisdiction over lands to the federal government and the interpretation of that statute in *Burell.* Furthermore, the trial court in this case heard defendant's motion to this effect and denied it. Remand to the trial court is not necessary as it has made a ruling on jurisdiction. Upon the record of this case, defendant has no immunity from subject matter jurisdiction of his crimes in our State's courts. There is no showing of acceptance of exclusive jurisdiction by the federal government over the post office.

[2] The arrest of defendant was without a warrant in the home of a friend. Defendant argues illegality in the arrest because the officer lacked probable cause to arrest defendant. According to the arresting officer, he questioned defendant's friend, Tyson, after giving him *Miranda* warnings about his rights. Tyson then told the officer about the crimes and defendant's involvement therein. The officer testified he was afraid defendant would avoid apprehension if not then arrested because defendant had seen his friend Tyson arrested and because de-

fendant had told the officer that he lived with his mother when the officer knew he did not. Upon these facts, the arresting officer had probable cause to believe that defendant had committed the felonies and might not be apprehended unless immediately arrested. The arrest at the home of a friend was a valid warrantless arrest. G.S. 15A-401(b)(2)a; *State v. Phifer*, 290 N.C. 203, 225 S.E. 2d 786 (1976), *cert. den.*, 429 U.S. 1123, 51 L. Ed. 2d 573, 97 S. Ct. 1160 (1977).

[3-5] Defendant contends there is a fatal variance between the allegations of the indictments and the proof at trial. The bill of indictment concerning the theft from the post office building alleged the stolen money and radio were "the personal property of Maury Post Office a division of the United States Postal Service." The evidence was to the effect that the money and radio were the personal property of the postmaster. The fact that the indictment charges defendant with larceny from the post office where evidence is that the post office is not the owner of such property is not a fatal defect in such a case as this where the property stolen was owned by the postmaster and he had left the property in the post office. The post office was in lawful custody and possession of the property at the time it was taken and the indictment is not invalid. *State v. Hauser*, 183 N.C. 769, 111 S.E. 349 (1922); *State v. Robinette*, 33 N.C. App. 42, 234 S.E. 2d 28 (1977); *State v. Dees*, 14 N.C. App. 110, 187 S.E. 2d 433 (1972). The other felonious larceny indictment alleged the tire tool to be "the personal property of L. A. Moye, L. A. Moye, Jr., and C. L. Stokes t/a Moye and Stokes Store." The evidence showed that Charles Stokes owned the warehouse from which the tire tool was taken. There is no fatal variance where as here the indictment alleges ownership in the owners of a business and the proof is that it is taken from the property of one owner personally. *State v. Smith*, 4 N.C. App. 261, 166 S.E. 2d 473 (1969). Finally, the third indictment alleged the breaking and entering of a "building occupied by Julian Jones used as a garage." The evidence was that the building was a storage shed and was not used by Mr. Jones since his health had declined. We find no fatal variance in this indictment. For felonious breaking and entering with intent to steal, it is not incumbent on the State to establish the owner of the property defendant intended to steal but only the intent to steal upon breaking or entering. *State v.*

Crawford, 3 N.C. App. 337, 164 S.E. 2d 625 (1968), *cert. den.*, 275 N.C. 138 (1969).

[6] The grand jury indictments of defendant concerning the crimes committed at the post office and the Moye and Stokes Store contained multiple counts for felonious breaking and entering, felonious larceny, felonious receiving and felonious possession. Prior to trial, defendant moved to dismiss these indictments on the grounds defendant could not be guilty of both the larceny and the receipt of the stolen goods. The trial court reserved ruling on this motion. The prosecutor then indicated the State would proceed on the breaking, entering and larceny counts of the indictments. At the close of the evidence, the trial court ruled it would not charge the jury on the felonious receiving and possession counts leaving the felonious breaking, entering and larceny counts to go to the jury. Defendant contends it was error for the trial judge to reserve ruling on this motion. There is no merit to this argument. A defendant may be found guilty of larceny or receiving but not both. *State v. Meshaw*, 246 N.C. 205, 98 S.E. 2d 13 (1957). An indictment or a jury charge of both larceny and receiving is not improper, depending upon the evidence presented of the two crimes. Consequently, it was not error for the trial court to reserve ruling on the dismissal motion until the evidence indicated whether there was sufficient proof to go to the jury on the crimes properly charged in the indictment.

[7] Defendant in two assignments of error attacks the admissibility of his statement to the arresting officer (1) because it was given without proper *Miranda* warnings or adherence to defendant's right to have counsel present at questioning if requested, and (2) because it was not freely and voluntarily given. We find no merit in these arguments. The record indicates defendant was advised of his *Miranda* rights and stated he wanted to talk to a lawyer but then changed his mind. Defendant was then advised of his rights and expressly waived his right to counsel in a signed written waiver.

Even if we assume that the defendant did request counsel when first advised of his rights, this does not make his subsequent statements inadmissible since the defendant

State v. Graham

initiated the subsequent conversation with officers himself, was once again fully informed of his rights, and expressly waived the right to have counsel present.

State v. Hill, 294 N.C. 320, 328, 240 S.E. 2d 794, 800 (1978). The
evidence is in conflict on whether the officer induced the confession by saying he would put in a good word for defendant in
court if he confessed. The trial court found there was no such
inducement and his finding is supported by ample evidence in
the record. The officer specifically denied making any such
inducement to defendant. The trial court's finding that defendant's confession was freely and voluntarily made is, therefore,
conclusive on appeal. *State v. Rogers*, 23 N.C. App. 142, 208 S.E.
2d 384, *cert. den.*, 286 N.C. 213, 209 S.E. 2d 318 (1974). Defendant's statement was properly admitted into evidence.

[8] When the trial judge summarized the evidence in his charge
to the jury, he stated, "[t]he State has offered evidence *tending
to show* ... that [defendant] *confessed* to the breaking and entering of these places and taking of a radio." (Emphasis added).
Defendant objected to the use of the word "confessed" in the
charge to which the trial judge replied, "Well, that's what it is."
Defendant contends this constitutes a prejudicial expression of
opinion in violation of G.S. 15A-1232. The statement the officer
said defendant made to him which defendant denied making at
trial does amount to a confession and certainly "tends to show
... that he confessed to the breaking and entering." The trial
judge's response to defendant's objection did not constitute
prejudicial error in light of the context of the charge. *State v.
Hamilton*, 298 N.C. 238, 258 S.E. 2d 350 (1979).

The sentence of not less than seven nor more than ten years
by the trial judge was within the maximum limits of punishment for one count of breaking and entering a building with
intent to commit a larceny, G.S. 14-54, and two counts of larceny
upon breaking and entering a building, G.S. 14-72(b)(2). The
maximum punishment and a fine for each felony is ten years
imprisonment. G.S. 14-2. The trial judge could have sentenced
defendant to thirty years imprisonment by imposing consecutive sentences. Rather, he, in his discretion which he did not
abuse, consolidated all of the charges and sentenced defendant

to prison for a period of time below the maximum sentence allowed by law. The sentence must be upheld. *State v. Cradle,* 281 N.C. 198, 188 S.E. 2d 296, *cert. den.*, 409 U.S. 1047, 34 L. Ed. 2d 499, 93 S. Ct. 537 (1972).

No error.

Judges CLARK and MARTIN (Harry C.) concur.

———————

CLIFTON T. WHYBURN v. H. ROSS NORWOOD AND WIFE, STELLA G. NOR-WOOD; RONALD BENOIT; NANCY R. ROBINSON; JUDY R. HARRIS; JOSEPH C. PHILLIPS AND WIFE, TERESA A. PHILLIPS; ROBERT E. TIBBS, SR., AND WIFE, CAROLE R. TIBBS; TIMIR BANERJEE AND WIFE, RITA MARIE BANERJEE; KENNETH W. WATERS AND WIFE, LILA C. WATERS; REGINE NAUMAN HAYES AND HUSBAND, TED W. HAYES; REX E. BROOKS AND WIFE, CAROLYN L. BROOKS; MARY C. WIENTJES; DANIEL A. O'NEAL AND WIFE, JACKIE W. O'NEAL; DYAL JEAN WEAVER; DAVID W. HOLMES AND WIFE, KATHLEEN M. HOLMES; PIERRE MORELL AND WIFE, BONNIE B. MORELL; THE GUARANTY STATE BANK, A NORTH CAROLINA CORPORATION; THE CENTRAL CAROLINA BANK AND TRUST COMPANY, A NORTH CAROLINA CORPORATION

No. 7915SC1175

(Filed 17 June 1980)

1. **Process § 19; Lis Pendens § 1– entire subdivision included in lis pendens – portion of subdivision involved in litigation – no abuse of process**

   Plaintiff's filing of notice of lis pendens which included defendant's entire subdivision did not constitute abuse of process where plaintiff brought an action to remove a cloud on his title to lands constituting a portion of a subdivision which was being developed by defendants; a careful attorney examining title to the lands described in the notice of lis pendens would examine the civil action to which it referred and would identify the exact area which was the subject of pending litigation; if plaintiff prevailed in his lawsuit, it would be proper to remove all restrictive and protective covenants of record affecting plaintiff's property; and the notice of lis pendens was not abusive in calling the pending suit to the attention of prospective purchasers in the subdivision.

2. **Lis Pendens § 1; Malicious Prosecution § 6 – removal of lis pendens from portion of land – appeal dismissed as premature – no termination of action – no malicious prosecution**

   Plaintiff's filing of notice of lis pendens did not constitute an act of malicious prosecution where the trial judge removed notice of lis pendens

Whyburn v. Norwood

from all areas of defendants' subdivision other than the lands specifically described in plaintiff's complaint; plaintiff gave notice of appeal; the appeal was dismissed as interlocutory and premature; there was thus no termination of a former claim favorable to defendants; and defendants' claim of malicious prosecution was therefore premature.

3. Lis Pendens § 1; Slander of Title § 1– filing of lis pendens – insufficient evidence of damages – no slander of title

There was no merit to defendants' contention that filing of plaintiff's notice of lis pendens constituted an injurious falsehood or slander of title, since G.S. 1-116 requires the filing of a separate independent notice (lis pendens) if the public is to be advised of pending litigation in certain types of suits involving real property; the record failed to reveal the name of any person who refused to do business with defendants because of the filing of the lis pendens and the complaint; and allegations by defendant developers that inquiries from prospective purchasers decreased after filing of lis pendens and that the general public had been deterred from dealing with defendants were inconclusive and insufficient to show that their alleged damages were proximately caused by the filing of the complaint and lis pendens.

APPEAL by the defendants from *Battle, Judge.* Order entered 6 August 1979 in Superior Court, CHATHAM County. Heard in the Court of Appeals 20 May 1980.

This is a civil action by which plaintiff seeks to quiet title to lands in Baldwin Township, Chatham County. The defendants Norwood are real estate developers and the owners of a large subdivision known as "River Forest." Plaintiff is an adjoining property owner.

The Norwoods filed a plat of their subdivision in Chatham County along with restrictive and protective covenants restricting use of the land described in the plat. Subsequently, plaintiff filed suit alleging the plat of the defendants was prepared from an erroneous survey, included lands belonging to plaintiff, and that the restrictive and protective covenants restrict the use of the plaintiff's land. Simultaneously with the filing of the complaint, plaintiff filed a notice of lis pendens pursuant to the provisions of G.S. 1-116.

On 31 May 1977, defendants Norwood moved to have the notice of lis pendens canceled as to all portions of "River Forest" except as it applied to those areas for which ownership was in dispute. (This appears to include only about 10 of the approximately 318 acres in the subdivision.) This motion was allowed on 30 June 1977. Plaintiff appealed to this Court, but the Court found the appeal to be interlocutory and premature. *See Whyburn v. Norwood* and *Strowd v. Norwood*, 37 N.C. App. 610, 246 S.E. 2d 540 (1978).

In their seventh defense and counterclaim, defendants Norwood allege the notice of lis pendens is illegal, unreasonable and false, and that filing of the notice of lis pendens exceeds statutory authority and has given rise to what this Court concludes is a counterclaim based on (1) abuse of process; (2) malicious prosecution; and (3) slander of title.

Plaintiff's motion for summary judgment on the counterclaim was allowed, and defendants appealed.

Epting, Hackney & Long, by Joe Hackney, for plaintiff appellee.

Gunn & Messick, by Paul S. Messick Jr. and Billy C. Hamlet, for defendant appellants.

HILL, Judge.

The question on appeal is whether the trial court erred by granting plaintiff's motion for summary judgment dismissing the defendants Norwoods' counterclaim. The issue raises at least three questions of law which must be addressed by this Court, all of which derive their thrust from the lis pendens, filed in this cause.

G.S. 1-116(a) provides that, "[A]ny person desiring the benefit of constructive notice of pending litigation must file a separate, independent notice thereof, which notice shall be cross-indexed in accordance with G. S. 1-117 in the following cases: (1) Actions affecting title to real property."

Plaintiff's right to file the lis pendens is unquestioned. Defendants contend, however, that by including the entire subdivision, plaintiff's filing constitutes a misuse of a legal process for an ulterior purpose, and that this misuse was recognized by the trial judge when he allowed the defendants' motion to remove the lis pendens from the unaffected area. Plaintiff replies that his appeal was dismissed as being interlocutory only, and that the issue is yet to be decided. Plaintiff further points to the language in the notice of lis pendens which shows that not all of "River Forest Subdivision" is intended to be covered in the lawsuit but rather that "Plaintiff will show that a portion of 'River Forest' lands along the western border thereof as shown on the said survey, are owned in fee simple by plaintiff, and that none of the named defendants have any interest or estate therein nor any right to restrict the use thereof."

[1] The first question presented is whether the filing of the notice of lis pendens on 31 March 1979 constituted an abuse of process.

> An abuse of process is some unlawful use of the process for the accomplishment of some end foreign to the purpose for which it may be issued.

Carpenter v. Hanes, 167 N.C. 551, 554, 83 S.E. 577, 579 (1914).

> It consists in the malicious misuse or misapplication of that process *after issuance* to accomplish some purpose not warranted or commanded by the writ. It is the malicious perversion of a legally sound process whereby a result not lawfully or properly obtainable under it is attempted to be secured. (Citations omitted.)

Melton v. Rickman, 225 N.C. 700, 703, 36 S.E. 2d 276 (1945).

The notice of lis pendens and complaint were filed 31 March 1977. The complaint describes with particularity in paragraph 5 the area of ownership in dispute and the adverse claims imposed by the restrictive and protective covenants upon all lot owners in the entire subdivision. The notice of lis pendens clearly states that the purpose of the action is to remove a cloud on plaintiff's title to lands constituting a portion of River Forest Subdivision *along the western border* thereof. A careful attorney examining title to the lands described in the notice of lis pendens would examine the civil action to which it refers and would identify the exact area which is the subject of the pending litigation.

Restrictive and protective covenants are classed as negative easements and affect title to real estate. We do not have the covenants before us, but apparently they apply to all of the lots in River Forest Subdivision, including the lands claimed by the plaintiff. Enforcement is generally left to the lot owners in the subdivision. If the plaintiff prevails in this suit, it will be fitting at that time to remove all limitations of record affecting plaintiff's property. It is apparent that plaintiff's complaint seeks this result, and that the notice of lis pendens is not abusive in calling the pending suit to the attention of prospective purchasers.

On 30 June 1977 the trial judge defined the lands which are the subject of this controversy with greater particularity and excluded areas of River Forest Subdivision from the provisions of the notice of lis pendens. Such removal clarifies the subject of controversy and makes easier an understanding of the matter, but does nothing more. Therefore, we conclude the appellants have failed to state a claim or to raise any genuine issue of material fact as to the tort of abuse of process.

[2] Next, the appellants contend the filing of the notice of lis pendens constituted an act of malicious prosecution. We do not agree.

To sustain an action for malicious prosecution, the plaintiff [defendants in the instant case] must show malice, want of probable cause, and the favorable termination of the former proceeding.

Melton v. Rickman, supra, at p. 703; *Miller v. Greenwood*, 218 N.C. 146, 10 S.E. 2d 708 (1940); *Carpenter, supra*.

When the trial judge removed the notice of lis pendens from all areas other than the lands specifically described in the plaintiff's complaint, plaintiff gave notice of appeal. That appeal was dismissed as being interlocutory and premature. *Whyburn, supra*. The question is yet to be litigated. Thus, defendants' cause for malicious prosecution is premature. There has been no termination of a former claim favorable to them. *Reichler v. Tillman*, 21 N.C. App. 38, 203 S.E. 2d 68 (1974). Plaintiff has retained his right of appeal.

[3] Finally, we are not impressed with the defendants' contention that filing of the notice of lis pendens constituted an injurious falsehood or slander of title. Slander of title occurs when one publishes matter derogatory to the title to real property with the malicious intent to injure the owner thereof and which in fact does cause injury. *Cardon v. McConnell*, 120 N.C. 461, 27 S.E. 109 (1897).

Defendants allege the notice of lis pendens is "illegal, unreasonable and false," and that it exceeds the authority contained in and is implicitly forbidden by G. S. 1-116. We do not read the statute as having this effect. In fact, G. S. 1-116 *requires* the filing of a separate independent notice (lis pendens) if the public is to be advised of pending litigation in certain types of suits involving real property. The complaint is the underlying source of claim, not the notice of lis pendens.

It is well established in North Carolina that one "... who wantonly, maliciously, [and] without cause, commences a civil action and puts upon record a complaint and *lis pendens* for the purpose of injuring and destroying the credit and business of another, whereby that other suffers damage must be liable for the legal consequences." *Estates v. Bank*, 171 N.C. 579, 88 S.E. 783 (1916). We have examined the record in general and the interrogatories directed to the defendants, together with their answers and fail to find the name of any specific person who has refused to do business with the defendants because of the filing of the lis pendens and the complaint. Defendants in their answer to the interrogatories make charges that inquiries from prospective purchasers have decreased since filing of the lis pendens, and the general public has been deterred from dealing with them. They further conclude that their character has been damaged. These charges are inconclusive. There is no evidence that defendants' alleged damages were proximately caused by the filing of the complaint and lis pendens. Neither do we find any evidence of malice on the part of the plaintiff.

The defendants have failed to state a claim or raise any genuine issue of fact with respect to the tort of slander of title.

For the reasons set out above, we conclude that the action of the trial court in granting plaintiff's motion for summary judgment should be

Affirmed.

Judges MARTIN (Robert M.) and ARNOLD concur.

STATE OF NORTH CAROLINA v. FORNEY BUMGARNER GILBERT

No. 8025SC78

(Filed 17 June 1980)

1. **Criminal Law § 101.2– statements by juror in jury room – no violation of right of confrontation**

    The trial court in a homicide case properly found that no evidence came to the attention of the jurors which would violate defendant's right to confront the witnesses against her where defendant contended that one of the jurors stated in the jury room that he realized during the trial that he knew about defendant and that she was not fit to walk the streets and should receive the maximum sentence, and the juror who allegedly made the statements denied on voir dire that he had stated that defendant was not fit to walk the streets and should receive the maximum punishment and testified that he based his verdict on the testimony, arguments of counsel and court's instructions. Furthermore, defendant was not prejudiced by the statements where the juror who allegedly made them was the only juror who voted for a verdict harsher than voluntary manslaughter, the juror eventually also voted with the other jurors for a verdict of voluntary manslaughter, and jurors who purportedly heard the statements did not wish to change their verdict of voluntary manslaughter.

2. **Homicide § 28.2– self-defense – assaults by decedent and another – sufficiency of instructions on reasonable apprehension**

    In a homicide prosecution in which defendant testified that decedent's husband was holding her by the hair while the decedent attempted to hit her with a rock, the trial court did not err in instructing the jury that in determining the reasonableness of defendant's apprehension of death or great bodily harm it should consider the size, age and strength of decedent, rather than of both decedent and her husband, and the fierceness of "the assault" rather than the fierceness of both of their assaults, where the court did

State v. Gilbert

instruct that the jury should consider "the fierceness of the assault, if any, upon the defendant," and that the killing would be entirely excused by self-defense if the circumstances as they appeared to defendant at the time were sufficient to create a belief that defendant had to shoot decedent in order to save herself, and where the court summarized defendant's testimony that decedent's husband was holding her while decedent attempted to hit her with a rock, since the court's instructions would permit the jury to find that independent assaults by decedent and by her husband operated to justify defendant's belief that she had to kill decedent in order to save herself.

3. **Homicide § 19.1– rebuttal evidence – deceased's reputation for peace and quiet – knowledge of deceased on the job – waiver of objections by failure to move to strike answers**

In a homicide prosecution in which defendant presented evidence of self-defense and of deceased's character for violence, defendant's objections to the State's rebuttal evidence of deceased's reputation for peace and quiet based only on the witnesses' knowledge of deceased "on the job" ordinarily would have been well taken, but defendant abandoned her objections by failing to pursue her objections and move to strike the answers.

APPEAL by defendant from *Kirby, Judge.* Judgment entered 24 August 1979 in Superior Court, CATAWBA County. Heard in the Court of Appeals 22 May 1980.

The defendant was indicted for the murder in the second degree of Joan Seitz. Joan and Roy Seitz were married, but had been living separate and apart approximately sixteen months. One child was born to the couple and was visiting Roy on the day Joan Seitz was killed. There was some evidence that Joan and Roy Seitz were considering a reconciliation even though defendant had been living with Roy Seitz at his trailer near Lake Norman for several months. The defendant and Joan Seitz had had previous encounters — one on the day of the shooting — at which time vile language had been used.

Defendant pleaded self-defense. The jury, however, returned a verdict of voluntary manslaughter. Thereafter, the defendant made a motion for a new trial, contending that while in the jury room one of the jurors had stated that he knew the defendant or knew about her, that he realized this after the trial had started, and that defendant was not fit to walk the streets of Catawba County. The judge made findings of fact setting out the unanimous verdict, polling of the jury, the testimony of the witnesses, and concluded that nothing came to the attention of the jurors which would violate the defendant's constitutional rights to confront witnesses against her. Defendant appealed.

Attorney General Edmisten, by Special Deputy Attorney General John R. B. Matthis and Assistant Attorney General Alan S. Hirsch, for the State.

Matthews & Vaught, by Phillip R. Matthews and Curt J. Vaught, for defendant appellant.

HILL, Judge.

[1] The defendant contends that the jury received evidence in violation of her constitutional right to confront all witnesses against her and to receive a trial before an impartial jury panel and that she was thereby entitled to a new trial. G. S. 15A-1240 permits impeachment of a verdict as follows:

(a) Upon an inquiry into the validity of a verdict, no evidence may be received to show the effect of any statement, conduct, event, or condition upon the mind of a juror or concerning the mental processes by which the verdict was determined.

*   *   *   *   *   *   *   *

(c) After the jury has dispersed, the testimony of a juror may be received to impeach the verdict of the jury on which he served, subject to the limitations in subsection (a) only when it concerns:

(1) Matters not in evidence which came to the attention of one or more jurors under circumstances which would violate the defendant's constitutional right to confront the witness against him;

*   *   *   *   *   *   *   *

G. S. 15A-1240 allows the trial judge to admit testimony for the purpose of impeaching the verdict of a jury and nothing more. The judge still has the responsibility to consider all the evidence before him and to decide whether the defendant received a fair trial.

It appeared from testimony on voir dire that the juror who knew of the defendant had first voted for second degree murder, but later joined in the vote with other jurors to make unanimous a vote for voluntary manslaughter. The trial judge swore the accused juror, who testified that while he was being examined as a prospective juror he was asked if he had heard anything about the case or the parties that would prejudice the case or affect his ability to be fair. His answer was that it would not. He further stated that he had heard a little but denied he had stated that the defendant was not fit to walk the streets of Catawba County and that the defendant ought to receive the maximum sentence; that he based his verdict on what came from the witness stand and arguments of counsel and the law given by the court.

The determination of the existence and effect of jury misconduct is primarily for the trial court whose decision will be given great weight on appeal. *State v. Moye,* 12 N.C. App. 178, 191, 182 S.E. 2d 814 (1971), *citing* 5 Am. Jur. 2d, Appeal and Error, § 889.

In passing on a similar question, Justice Denny in the case of *State v. Hill,* 225 N.C. 74, 77, 33 S.E. 2d 470 (1945), stated:

The competency of jurors is a question to be passed upon by the trial judge, and the ruling herein on the evidence and facts therefrom is not reviewable. *State v. De-Graffenreid,* 224 N.C. 517, 31 S.E. 2d 523, and the cases there cited.

"In North Carolina, in instances where the contention was made by the defendant that the jury has been improperly influenced, it has been held that it must be shown that the jury was actually prejudiced against the defendant, to avail the defendant relief from the verdict, and *the findings of the trial judge upon the evidence and facts are conclusive and not reviewable.*" (Citations omitted.) (Emphasis added.) *State v. Hart*, 226 N.C. 200, 203, 37 S.E. 2d 487 (1946).

In the instant case the trial judge examined the jurors who heard the statements causing concern as well as the juror charged with making the statement, and found as a fact that there was no evidence which came to the attention of the jurors that would violate the defendant's constitutional right to confront the witnesses against her. We agree that the findings are conclusive and not reviewable in this case. Furthermore, we find that defendant suffered no prejudice. The juror who purportedly knew of the defendant was the only juror who voted for a sentence harsher than voluntary manslaughter. He was eventually swayed to the position of the other jurors. One of the jurors stated on voir dire that she and another juror who testified on voir dire "... were satisfied with the end result and didn't want to change [their] verdict from voluntary manslaughter."

[2] The defendant contends that the trial court erred in its instruction to the jury concerning the defendant's claim of self-defense. The disputed portion of the charge is as follows:

In making that determination [the reasonableness of the defendant's belief that she was in danger of great bodily harm], you should consider the circumstances as you find them to [have] existed from the evidence, including the size and the age and the strength of the defendant as compared to Joan Seitz; the fierceness of the assault, if any, upon the defendant; whether or not Joan Seitz had a weapon in her possession; and the reputation of Joan Seitz, if any, for danger and violence.

The defendant's requested charge, which is quite similar to the court's actual charge, is set out as follows:

In making this determination, you should consider the circumstances as you find them to have existed from the evidence including the size, age, and strength of the defendant as compared to Joan Seitz and Roy Seitz, the fierceness of the assaults, if any, upon the defendant, whether or not Joan Seitz had a weapon or rock in her possession, the reputation, if any, of Joan Seitz for danger and violence and the previous acts of violence, if any, of Joan Seitz of which the defendant had knowledge . . . .

None of the witnesses other than the defendant testified that Roy Seitz seized the defendant by her hair prior to the shot. Nevertheless, the defendant's testimony must be included in the judge's charge for consideration by the jury.

The difference between the two charges is simple. The defendant believes that because her testimony indicated that Roy Seitz was holding her by the hair while the decedent, Joan Seitz, was bringing a rock down upon her head, that the jury should have been charged that the reasonableness of her apprehension should be based on the size, age, and strength of both Joan and Roy Seitz and upon the fireceness of both of their assaults.

The instruction given by the trial judge fully communicated the essence of the law of self-defense. The judge instructed the jury that it should consider ". . . the fierceness of the assault, if any, upon the defendant . . . ." The judge also instructed the jury that the killing would be entirely excused on the grounds of self-defense if the ". . . circumstances as they appeared to the defendant at the time were sufficient to create . . ." a belief that defendant had to shoot Joan Seitz in order to save herself. In making that determination, the jury was instructed to consider the circumstances as it found them to have existed from the evidence.

Defendant had testified that Roy Seitz was holding her head against her car window in such a way as to place her in danger of being hit in the head by a rock being wielded by Joan Seitz. The trial judge reminded the jury of this testimony in his summary of the evidence. The jury, if it had chosen to believe defendant's evidence, could have found from the circumstances as they were shown by the evidence to have existed, that both Roy and Joan Seitz's independent assaults operated to justify defendant's belief that she had to kill Joan in order to save herself. The instruction was proper.

[3] The defendant contends the trial judge erred by allowing evidence of the deceased's propensity and reputation for peace and quiet. We do not agree. The defendant had testified that Roy Seitz had told her of several threats his wife had made to him and that she was afraid of Joan. In rebuttal, the State called witnesses as to the character and reputation of the deceased. The defendant objected, contending that such rebuttal evidence must be limited to the general reputation of the deceased for peace and quiet and that the rebuttal witnesses only knew deceased "on the job."

It not having been established that the witness had ever observed the deceased except while on the job, it seems obvious that the witness was not qualified to answer the questions, had they otherwise been proper inquiries. It would seem manifest that even a vicious and violent man would not likely display such propensities to or in the presence of his employer.

State v. Thomas, 5 N.C. App. 448, 451, 168 S.E. 2d 459 (1969).

It is settled that where there is evidence of self-defense the State may rebut the defendant's evidence of the deceased's character for violence by evidence of deceased's good character for peace and quiet. State v. Champion, 222 N.C. 160, 22 S.E. 2d 232 (1942); State v. Johnson, 270 N.C. 215, 154 S.E. 2d 48 (1967). Ordinarily, the objection of the defendant to the evidence offered would have been well taken. However, the defendant did not pursue her objections and move to strike the answers. Her objections were thus abandoned. Hudson v. Hudson, 21 N.C. App. 412, 414, 204 S.E. 2d 697 (1974). Defendant further objects to portions of the charge made by the trial judge. We have examined the charge in these respects and find the objections to be without merit.

In the trial of the case we find

No Error.

Judges MARTIN (Robert M.) and ARNOLD concur.

MARION E. BROWN v. HOWARD R. BROWN

No. 804DC97
No. 804DC98

(Filed 17 June 1980)

1. **Rules of Civil Procedure § 52– findings and conclusions – necessity for request**

   Absent a request, the court is not required to find facts and make conclusions of law.

2. **Constitutional Law § 24.7; Divorce and Alimony § 2; Process § 9– nonresident defendant – abandonment of wife in N.C. – minimum contacts sufficient for personal jurisdiction**

   The trial court obtained personal jurisdiction over the nonresident defendant in an action for alimony based on abandonment and for child custody and support where defendant was served with process by registered mail, since an action for alimony on the ground of abandonment was a claim of "injury to person or property" under the long-arm statute, G.S. 1-75.4(3), and defendant's acts of living with and abandoning plaintiff wife in this State met the "minimum contacts" test.

3. **Rules of Civil Procedure § 5– general appearance – service of order on attorney**

   Defendant made a general appearance in an alimony and child custody and support action by filing an answer and counterclaim, and a contempt show cause order was properly served on defendant by hand delivery to his attorney. G.S. 1A-1, Rule 5(b).

4. **Divorce and Alimony § 27– attorney fees – insufficient findings**

   The trial court erred in ordering defendant to pay $100 to plaintiff's attorney for services in bringing contempt proceedings based on defendant's failure to comply with an alimony *pendente lite* and child support order where the court failed to make findings of fact upon which a determination of the reasonableness of the fees can be based, such as the nature of the services rendered and the skill and time required.

APPEAL by defendant from *Henderson, Judge.* Orders entered 16 August 1979 in District Court, ONSLOW County. Heard in the Court of Appeals 4 June 1980.

This is an action for divorce from bed and board, alimony, and child custody and support, brought by a resident of North Carolina against her nonresident husband. The complaint alleged desertion and abandonment of plaintiff by defendant without justifiable cause. The parties stipulated that defendant was served a copy of the complaint and summons by certified mail, restricted delivery, and that defendant signed the return receipt in Cape May, New Jersey.

In his answer and counterclaim, defendant asserted the defense of lack of jurisdiction over the persons of plaintiff and defendant and lack of jurisdiction over the subject matter. Defendant's counsel filed an entry of appearance, purportedly limiting his appearance to "determining the jurisdictional issues only." Plaintiff replied and moved the court for an order awarding her alimony pendente lite, custody of the two minor children and child support during the pendency of the action, and attorney's fees of $500. After hearing on plaintiff's motion, the court, on 2 April 1979, made findings of fact and conclusions of law and awarded plaintiff custody of the children, child support, household furniture under defendant's control in New Jersey, and attorney's fees of $200. In this order, the court also found that defendant had been properly served and concluded that the court had jurisdiction over the parties and the subject matter of this case. The order also found that the parties have agreed to a disposition of the tax refund and requested it be made a part of the order. Defendant did not object to these findings and did not enter notice of appeal from this order within ten days after its entry. Eighteen days after entry of this order, defendant filed a motion to dismiss for lack of personal and subject matter jurisdiction.

On 24 May 1979, after hearing upon verified motion and affidavit of plaintiff seeking a contempt show cause order, Judge Henderson found that such an order should issue. On 16 August 1979 the judge, after evidence and arguments of counsel had been presented, found defendant in willful contempt of court for his failure to comply with the order of 2 April 1979 and ordered defendant to pay $100 to plaintiff's attorney for services rendered in bringing the contempt proceedings. Defendant appeals from this order. Furthermore, on 16 August the judge denied defendant's motion to dismiss; defendant appeals from this ruling also.

Although separate records and two sets of briefs were filed in this action, we decide the two appeals in one opinion.

E. C. Collins for plaintiff appellee.

Patrick M. Donley for defendant appellant.

MARTIN (Harry C.), Judge.

[1] In one of his briefs, defendant argues that the court erred in denying his motion to dismiss this action for lack of jurisdiction over the person of the defendant and lack of jurisdiction over the subject matter. His first contention is that because the court failed to make findings of fact and conclusions of law as required on any motion when requested by a party to that motion, N.C.G.S. 1A-1, Rule 52(a)(2), was not complied with. The record discloses that no findings of fact or conclusions of law were made by the court in denying defendant's motion to dismiss, but, more significantly, the record fails to show that defendant requested such findings and conclusions. Absent request, the court is not required to find facts and make conclusions of law. If the court does not do so in this situation, it is presumed that the court on proper evidence found facts to support its judgment. *Williams v. Bray,* 273 N.C. 198, 159 S.E. 2d 556 (1968); *Sherwood v. Sherwood,* 29 N.C. App. 112, 223 S.E. 2d 509 (1976).

[2] Defendant's additional contention is that jurisdiction over a nonresident that would be sufficient to authorize a North Carolina court to render a personal judgment against him for alimony, child support and attorney's fees can be acquired only by personal service of process within the territorial jurisdiction of the court. This contention cannot be upheld. This Court has previously determined that when defendant personally re-

ceives by registered mail in another state copies of the summons and complaint, this manner of service of process gives the court of North Carolina personal jurisdiction over the defendant which will support a judgment in personam for payment of alimony. *Sherwood, supra.* The Court reached this conclusion after holding that an action for alimony on the ground of abandonment is a claim of "injury to person or property" under N.C.G.S. 1-75.4(3). Because such an action is grounds for personal jurisdiction under N.C.G.S. 1-75.4, the long-arm manner of personal service provided under Rule 4(j)(9)(b) may be utilized. Furthermore, under the circumstances of the *Sherwood* case, the court found that the "minimum contacts" test had been met and that due process had been satisfied. Because the circumstances of this case are essentially identical to those of *Sherwood*, we hold that the service of process on defendant, a nonresident, by certified mail, gave the court personal jurisdiction over him which will support the order for alimony pendente lite, custody, and child support.

Moreover, we think that by defendant's participation in the 2 April 1979 hearing, his agreement with plaintiff as to a disposition of the tax refund for 1978, and his desire that it be incorporated into the 2 April order, he submitted himself to the jurisdiction of the court.

In his other brief, defendant assigns as errors certain findings of fact and conclusions of law made by Judge Henderson in the order adjudicating defendant to be in willful contempt of court. Defendant continues to argue that the order of 2 April 1979 should never have been entered because the court lacked personal jurisdiction over defendant. Because we have held that the court did have personal jurisdiction over defendant, the finding of fact that an order was entered on 2 April 1979 requiring defendant to pay $400 per month for child support and $200 for attorney's fees is supported by competent evidence, perhaps the most competent evidence ever available — the actual inclusion of the order in the record, with its date and specific provisions. The finding, therefore, is conclusive on appeal. *General Specialties Co. v. Teer Co.*, 41 N.C. App. 273, 254 S.E. 2d 658 (1979).

[3] Similarly, the findings that the order to show cause was duly served on defendant and that plaintiff and defendant were both represented by counsel at the hearing on the order are supported by the record. Defendant attempts to persuade us that because his attorney made a limited entry to determine jurisdictional issues only, "service of any other matters must be made personally upon the Defendant and may not be served to the attorney of record who has limited his appearance." The law in North Carolina fails to support this argument. By filing an answer and counterclaim, defendant made a general appearance in this action. A general appearance has consistently been defined as "one whereby the defendant submits his person to the jurisdiction of the court by invoking the judgment of the court in any manner on any question other than that of the jurisdiction of the court over his person." *In re Blalock*, 233 N.C. 493, 504, 64 S.E. 2d 848, 856, 25 A.L.R. 2d 818, 828 (1951); *Swenson v. Thibaut*, 39 N.C. App. 77, 250 S.E. 2d 279 (1978), *disc. rev. denied, appeal dismissed*, 296 N.C. 740, 254 S.E. 2d 182 (1979). Because defendant's appearance was general, service upon him of copies of the order to show cause by hand delivery to his attorney, which service is reflected in the record, complied with N.C.G.S. 1A-1, Rule 5(b), and was therefore valid.

Defendant excepted to the court's finding that defendant had failed to make payments required by the order and was in arrears of $600 for child support and $200 for attorney's fees. The affidavit of plaintiff competently supports this finding of fact. As mentioned earlier in this opinion, defendant failed to timely appeal from the 2 April 1979 order; therefore, the award of attorney's fees to plaintiff, included in that order, cannot now be contested.

[4] Finally, defendant excepted to the finding that plaintiff's attorney had rendered valuable legal services to plaintiff in bringing the contempt proceedings, with a value of no less than $100. This finding in turn underlies the award of $100 attorney's fees to plaintiff's counsel. Defendant's assignment of error based upon this exception must be sustained. An award of attorney's fees here cannot be upheld where the court failed to make findings of fact upon which a determination of the reason-

ableness of the fees can be based, such as the nature and scope of the legal services rendered, and the skill and time required. *Powell v. Powell*, 25 N.C. App. 695, 214 S.E. 2d 808 (1975). The conclusory finding that plaintiff's attorney had rendered "valuable" legal services fails to qualify as a finding upon which a determination of the reasonableness of the $100 fee can be based.

The assignment of error based on defendant's exception to the conclusion of law that his failure to make payments under the 2 April 1979 order "has been willful and without legal justification or excuse" cannot be sustained. The court's finding of fact that "defendant has been gainfully employed on a full-time basis and has had no change in his income or expenses which would justify a refusal to pay the support and attorney fees as ordered" was not excepted to by defendant. It is therefore presumed to be supported by the evidence and is binding on appeal. *James v. Pretlow*, 242 N.C. 102, 86 S.E. 2d 759 (1955). Moreover, the finding supports the conclusion of law based upon it.

The court's denial of defendant's motion to dismiss for lack of personal jurisdiction is affirmed.

The court's order finding defendant in willful contempt of court is affirmed. The award of attorney's fees to plaintiff's counsel in bringing the contempt proceedings is vacated.

Judges WEBB and WELLS concur.

State v. Hodgen

STATE OF NORTH CAROLINA v. GENE OWEN HODGEN

No. 795SC1013

(Filed 17 June 1980)

1. **Criminal Law § 82.2– examination of criminal defendant by psychiatrist – no physician-patient privilege**

   Where the mental capacity of the accused to proceed to trial is questioned on motion of defense counsel and the trial court commits the defendant to a state mental health facility for examination to determine defendant's capacity to proceed, the physician-patient privilege does not preclude the examining psychiatrist from testifying at trial on the insanity issue.

2. **Criminal Law § 82.2– examination of criminal defendant by psychiatrist – intoxication at time of crimes – no physician-patient privilege – constitutional questions not raised by pleading privilege**

   Where defendant was committed to a state mental health facility to determine his capacity to proceed, testimony by a psychiatrist who examined him that defendant told her he was drinking at the time of the events charged did not violate the Sixth Amendment guarantee of right to counsel or the Fifth Amendment privilege against self-incrimination, since the witness testified that she made no attempt in examining defendant to obtain from him any information relating to the alleged crimes; moreover, defendant made no specific objection to the witness's testimony, and any challenge to the evidence on constitutional grounds was not properly raised by defendant's claim of the physician-patient privilege.

3. **Criminal Law § 5.1– insanity defined – instructions on "knowing" and "right or wrong"**

   In a prosecution for armed robbery where defendant pled insanity, the trial court, in defining insanity as not knowing the nature and quality of one's act or not knowing that it was wrong, was not required to instruct that defendant must have "the will and ability to control his conduct," since such an instruction would in effect recognize the "uncontrollable impulse" defense which is not recognized in N. C.; furthermore, the court was not required to instruct that defendant must know that his act was both legally and morally wrong.

APPEAL by defendant from *Strickland, Judge.* Judgment entered 13 April 1979 in Superior Court, NEW HANOVER County. Heard in the Court of Appeals 19 March 1980.

Defendant pled not guilty to charges of (1) armed robbery at Zip Mart on 26 January 1979, and (2) armed robbery at Lee's Grocery Store on 27 January 1979. The jury found defendant guilty as charged. Defendant appeals from judgments imposing concurrent prison terms of not less than 9 nor more than 12 years.

Defendant by petition raised the question of incapacity to proceed (G.S. 15A, Art. 56). He was committed to Dorothea Dix Hospital in February 1979, for observation and treatment, and a ·discharge summary was made by Dr. Mary Rood, forensic psychiatrist, who reported that defendant had an I.Q. of 59 and was able to read at the grade level 4.2, and concluded that "he is competent to proceed in that he understands his legal charges and is able to assist his lawyer." After hearing, the court found that defendant had the capacity to proceed.

Before trial defendant gave notice that he may at trial rely on the defense of insanity. G.S. 15A-959.

At trial the evidence for the State, including confessions made by defendant, established his guilt of both armed robbery charges.

Defendant offered evidence only on the insanity issue. Dr. Rolf H. Fisscher, a psychiatrist, testified that he observed defendant over a period of ten days in August 1977 and found that he was suffering from a catatonic psychosis, which was caused by his wife's abandonment of him the day after their marriage because of his inability to perform sexually. Defendant was sent to Cherry Hospital for treatment. In his opinion defendant could have been suffering from some form of psychosis when the crimes were committed.

Defense witness Dr. William P. Robinson, a psychiatrist, testified that defendant was in Cherry Hospital for 20 days in August 1977 where there was a diagnosis of psychotic depression. Dr. Robinson saw defendant at Southeastern Mental Health Center on 19 March and 30 March 1979, and his diagnosis was chronic undifferentiated schizophrenia, evidenced by defendant's feelings of being possessed by superior powers and by uncontrolled laughter. He was on medication during trial.

Defendant also offered two lay witnesses who testified that defendant was withdrawn and depressed and acted like he had mental problems.

The State in rebuttal offered the testimony of Dr. Mary M. Rood, who had examined defendant at Dix Hospital in February 1979, and found defendant had the capacity to proceed with trial. Defendant objected to her testimony on grounds of the physician-patient privilege. After hearing her testimony, the court found that her testimony was necessary to the proper administration of justice. Dr. Rood testified that defendant answered questions coherently and seemed cheerful. Defendant told her that he had been drinking at the time of the events charged. It was Dr. Rood's opinion that defendant understood the nature of his actions and was able to know whether those actions were right or wrong.

Attorney General Edmisten by Assistant Attorney General Isham B. Hudson, Jr. for the State.

Franklin L. Block for defendant appellant.

CLARK, Judge.

[1] Did the court err in allowing Dr. Rood to testify for the State in violation of the defendant's physician-patient privilege?

Defendant was committed to Dorothea Dix Hospital under G.S. 15A-1002 on petition of his attorney to aid the trial court in determining the capacity of the defendant to proceed. The report to the court, entitled "Discharge Summary," was made by Dr. Mary M. Rood, a forensic psychiatrist on the staff at the hospital. The report was introduced into evidence by the State, after which it became a "public record" as provided by G.S. 15A-1002(d). It was the opinion of Dr. Rood that defendant "is competent to proceed ..." and the court so found.

It further appears from the Discharge Summary that Dr. Rood went beyond the purpose of defendant's commitment to the hospital in that Dr. Rood expressed an opinion as to defendant's mental capacity at the time of the alleged crimes, as follows: "As to his responsibility at the time of the alleged crimes, I believe that he was able to distinguish right from wrong with respect to the acts with which he is charged. He states that he was drinking at the time, and alcohol may have impaired his judgment and self-control to some extent."

Dr. Rood was called as a witness by the State, after defendant had offered evidence of insanity at the times of the offenses, to rebut the defendant's evidence by her testimony that in her opinion defendant was sane at the times of the offenses, some two and one-half months before trial. After Dr. Rood testified about her qualifications and was found to be an expert, she was asked if she examined defendant on 21 February 1979, defense counsel objected and sought to invoke the physician-patient privilege.

Where the mental capacity of the accused to proceed to trial is questioned on motion of defense counsel (G.S. 15A-1002), and the trial court commits the defendant to a State mental health facility for examination to determine the defendant's capacity to proceed, the physician-patient privilege does not preclude the examining psychiatrist from testifying at trial on the insanity issue. This ruling was made in *State v. Newsome*, 195 N.C. 552, 143 S.E. 187 (1928), and recently cited and approved in *State v. Mayhand*, 298 N.C. 418, 259 S.E. 2d 231 (1979), and *In re Johnson*, 36 N.C. App. 133, 243 S.E. 2d 386 (1978). It is noted that the trial judge, pursuant to G.S. 8-53, found that the testimony of Dr. Rood was necessary to the proper administration of justice.

[2] We find that the physician-patient privilege does not preclude the testimony of Dr. Rood. Nor do we find merit in defendant's argument that Dr. Rood's testimony violated the Sixth Amendment guarantee of right to counsel or the Fifth Amendment privilege against self-incrimination. Dr. Rood testified that she made no attempt in examination of defendant to obtain from him any information relating to the alleged crimes. Defendant made no specific objection to the testimony of Dr. Rood that defendant said he had been drinking at the time of the

events charged. Any challenge on constitutional grounds to this evidence was not properly raised by defendant's claim of the physician-patient privilege and should have been raised by proper objection. The failure to make such objection waived the right to raise the question on appeal.

Did the trial court err in failing to give the instructions to the jury requested by the defendant?

[3] The court in instructing the jury gave the usual M'Naghten definition of insanity, that "he either did not know the nature and quality of his act, or did not know that it was wrong." M'Naghten's Case, 8 Eng. Rep. 718, 10 Cl. & Fin. 200 (H.L. 1843); *State v. Willard*, 292 N.C. 567, 234 S.E. 2d 587 (1977). The defendant requested the court to give the following definition of "knowing":

"The definition of 'knowing' in this context requires more than that the accused merely have an awareness or recognition of the act committed. The defendant must also have the will and the ability to control his conduct."

The broad interpretation of "knowing" to encompass the full range of human personality and perceptions has not been accepted in this State. To instruct that defendant must have "the will to control his conduct" would in effect recognize the "uncontrollable impulse" defense which was rejected in *State v. Terry*, 173 N.C. 761, 92 S.E. 154 (1917).

Defendant also contends that the phrase "right or wrong" should have been defined by the court as follows:

"In order for the defendant to know 'right from wrong' the law requires that the defendant have a greater capacity than to merely determine that the act was 'legally' wrong. The defendant must also have comprehended, at the time of the act, that what he was doing was also 'morally' wrong. If he felt himself possessed and could not distinguish between good and evil, he is not guilty of any offense against the law, regardless of how he comprehended the act."

It is not required that the defendant must know that his acts in question were both *legally* wrong and *morally* wrong. The test does not involve the understanding of abstract wrong, but only the moral "wrong" of the particular and specific act. *State v. Barfield*, 298 N.C. 306, 259 S.E. 2d 510 (1979); *State v. Hairston*, 222 N.C. 455, 23 S.E. 2d 885 (1943); *State v. Terry, supra. See* Gardner, *Insanity As A Defense In The North Carolina Criminal Law*, 30 N.C.L. Rev. 4, 11 (1951); *Cf.*, Comment, *The Insanity Defense in North Carolina*, 14 Wake Forest L. Rev. 1157 (1978).

We conclude that defendant had a fair trial free from prejudicial error.

No error.

Judges MARTIN (Robert M.) and ERWIN concur.

CHARLES L. HORNER v. MARGARET HOPE HORNER

No. 7912DC488

(Filed 17 June 1980)

1. **Evidence § 12; Divorce and Alimony § 14.2– spouse's testimony implying adultery – inadmissibility**

    In a divorce action, testimony by a spouse concerning his or her relationship with another party should be excluded under G.S. 50-10 when it clearly implies an act of adultery even though the words "adultery" or "intercourse" are not used.

2. **Evidence § 12; Divorce and Alimony § 14.2– spouse's testimony implying adultery – inadmissibility**

    The trial court in a divorce case erred in permitting defendant to be cross-examined as to whether she had undressed in front of or with various men where adultery was an issue in the case, the court had sustained an objection when defendant was asked whether she had committed adultery, and the cross-examination therefore clearly implied that defendant had committed adultery.

3. Divorce and Alimony § 24.1– child support

　　The trial court did not abuse its discretion in ordering child support because the court first announced the child support would be $200.00 per month and then changed it to $250.00 per month or because the court waited from the day of the verdict on 9 November 1978 until 2 January 1979 to sign the judgment.

4. Divorce and Alimony § 27– child support action – counsel fees – insufficient findings

　　The court erred in awarding counsel fees to the wife in a child support action where the court made no findings as to the wife's ability to pay or the reasonableness of the fees.

APPEAL by plaintiff and defendant from *Guy, Judge*. Judgment entered 2 January 1979 in District Court, CUMBERLAND County. Heard in the Court of Appeals 15 November 1979.

　　This is an action in which the plaintiff sued for divorce on the ground of a one-year separation. The defendant counterclaimed for divorce from bed and board, custody of their child, permanent alimony, and child support. Plaintiff filed a reply in which he denied the allegations of the counterclaim and pled adultery and abandonment by the defendant as affirmative defenses. The jury answered the issues favorably to the plaintiff on his claim for divorce, and against the defendant on her counterclaim for divorce from bed and board. The record does not show that issues were submitted on the plaintiff's affirmative defenses. The court entered a judgment granting the plaintiff a divorce absolute. The court gave the defendant custody of their child and required the plaintiff to pay $250.00 per month in child support and $300.00 for counsel fees. Both parties appealed.

　　Downing, David, Vallery, Maxwell and Hudson, by Edward J. David, for plaintiff appellee and appellant.

　　Pope, Reid, Lewis and Deese, by Renny W. Deese, for defendant appellant.

WEBB, Judge.

DEFENDANT'S APPEAL

[1] Defendant assigns as error the admission of certain testimony which she contends showed the court allowed her to be examined as to her adultery. When the defendant was being cross-examined, plaintiff's counsel asked her if she had committed adultery. The court sustained as objection to this question. Later in the cross-examination, the defendant was examined as follows:

"Q. Did you permit your uncle to touch you?

A. Yes, I did.

Q. Where did you let him touch you?

MR. DEESE: OBJECTION.

COURT: OVERRULED.

* * *

Q. Where would you let him touch you?

A. He would put his arms around me, touch me. Well, what do you want me to say?

Q. The truth.

A. My husband made me document these things. And he even made me say that he touched me on my breast and other places, because it was good for him.

* * *

Q. Now he, — you undressed before your uncle more than one time, did you not?

MR. DEESE: OBJECTION, your Honor.

COURT: OVERRULED.

Horner v. Horner

A. Not to my knowledge.

* * *

Q. You also undressed with the security guard?

Mr. Deese: OBJECTION, your Honor.

Q. — of the PX, did you not?

Court: OVERRULED.

* * *

Q. Do you know a Mr. Conroy?

A. Yes, I do.

Q. Did you undress before him?

Mr. Deese: OBJECTION, your Honor.

Court: OVERRULED.

A. That is the security guard you were talking about.

Q. How many times did you undress for him?

A. Just one time.

Mr. Deese: OBJECTION, your Honor.

Court: OVERRULED.

Q. Just once?

A. Yes, sir.

Q. Now, how many different men have you undressed before, prior to going back to your husband in October, 1976?

* * *

A. (No response).

Q. How many different men did you undress before?

A. When?

Q. Before going back to Germany in October, 1976?

A. This was before May of 1976 when my husband came to the States, there were several. The ones that you mentioned.

Q. And there were others?

A. I'm not sure. I can't remember, sir. During that period I dated several."

The propriety of testimony by parties to a divorce action which tends to prove adultery has been passed on in the following cases. *Traywick v. Traywick*, 28 N.C. App. 291, 221 S.E. 2d 85 (1976); *Earles v. Earles*, 26 N.C. App. 559, 216 S.E. 2d 739 (1975); *Phillips v. Phillips*, 9 N.C. App. 438, 176 S.E. 2d 379 (1970). We believe the rule from these cases is that in a divorce action, testimony by a spouse concerning his or her relationship with another party should be excluded under G.S. 50-10 when it clearly implies an act of adultery, even though the words "adultery" or "intercourse" are not used. Where there is no clear implication of intercourse, the testimony is admissible. In *Phillips*, it was held that it was error to allow a husband to testify he caught his wife in the woods with a man near a church at 9:00 p.m. In *Earles*, testimony by the wife that her husband told her he loved another woman and would continue to see her was held admissible. That was an action for divorce from bed and board and alimony based on abandonment. Adultery was not at issue. This Court said the plaintiff's testimony tended to show defendant saw another woman and loved her, not that he had intercourse with her. In *Traywick*, this Court affirmed a district court judgment for alimony without divorce based on cruel and barbarous treatment and the offering of such indignities as to render plaintiff's condition intolerable and life burdensome. The plaintiff had testified the defendant visited a widow who lived next door every night and would often stay for several hours with no one else present but her two-year-old son. This Court said the plaintiff was not trying to prove her husband had committed adultery but instead that he had offered indignities to her by spending more time with another woman than he did with his wife and making it clear to his wife that he preferred the company of another woman.

[2] Applying the principle stated above to the case sub judice, we hold that allowing the defendant to be cross-examined as set forth above constituted reversible error. The defendant had been asked whether she had committed adultery. An objection was sustained but the jury heard the question. The defendant was then required to answer a series of questions as to whether she had undressed in front of different men. One of the questions was whether she had undressed with a man. Adultery was an issue in the case sub judice. We hold the questions and answers clearly implied the defendant had committed adultery.

The defendant has brought forward other assignments of error which we do not discuss as they may not recur at the subsequent trial.

We hold the defendant must have a new trial.

PLAINTIFF'S APPEAL

[3] Plaintiff has appealed from the order requiring him to pay child support and defendant's counsel fees. Plaintiff contends the court abused its discretion in ordering child support because Judge Guy first announced the child support would be $200.00 per month and then changed it to $250.00 per month, and because Judge Guy waited from the day of the verdict on 9 November 1978 until 2 January 1979 to sign the judgment. We hold this did not constitute abuse of discretion.

[4] As to the order for counsel fees, the court made no findings of fact as to the wife's ability to pay or the reasonableness of the counsel fees. We have held in *Rogers v. Rogers*, 39 N.C. App. 635,

251 S.E. 2d 663 (1979) that such findings of fact are necessary before awarding counsel fees pursuant to G.S. 50-13.6 in actions for child support. We reverse and remand this part of the order without prejudice to the defendant to make another motion for counsel fees.

Plaintiff's appeal is affirmed as to child support; reversed and remanded as to the order for counsel fees.

New trial for the defendant.

Judges VAUGHN and MARTIN (Harry C.) concur.

MICKEY MICHELLE EMANUEL v. NORRIS L. FELLOWS

No. 7914SC1112

(Filed 17 June 1980)

Process § 10.2– service by publication – diligence in determining defendant's whereabouts – sufficiency of evidence

There was no merit to defendant's contention that service of process by publication was improper because plaintiff failed to exercise due diligence to discover defendant's address, whereabouts, dwelling house or usual place of abode where the evidence tended to show that plaintiff attempted to have the sheriff serve defendant personally with process at defendant's old address which was shown in the then current telephone directory; upon learning that the sheriff was unable to serve defendant personally, plaintiff's counsel then placed a call to the number listed for defendant in the then current phone directory; the number was no longer in service; plaintiff's counsel called directory assistance and was told there was no other listing for defendant; counsel then contacted defendant's insurance carrier, but it knew only of defendant's old address; plaintiff then issued a new summons and commenced service by publication; just prior to commencing service by publication, plaintiff mailed a copy of the new summons, complaint and service by publication to defendant's insurance carrier; and a phone directory listing defendant's new address was not published until after service by publication had been completed.

APPEAL by defendant from *Herring, Judge.* Judgment entered 17 September 1979 in Superior Court, DURHAM County. Heard in the Court of Appeals 15 May 1980.

This case reaches us on appeal from an order denying defendant's motion to dismiss pursuant to G.S. 1A-1, Rule 12(b)(2)(4)(5). The trial court made findings of fact to which no exceptions are taken. Those findings are as follows.

　　1. That on April 15, 1976, there was an incident on Rose of Sharon Road near its intersection with Cole Mill Road in the County of Durham in which incident the plaintiff to this action says that she was forced off the road by negligent operation of an automobile on the part of the Defendant and plaintiff says that she was injured thereby.

　　2. Defendant was at the time of the incident complained of, Pastor of Northgate Presbyterian Church in Durham, North Carolina, and remained so employed until October 1977, when he became employed with Rhodes Furniture in Raleigh, to which employment he commuted daily. Defendant's wife is a teacher at Y.E. Smith School of Durham and has been so employed for the past six (6) years.

　　3. At the time of the accident referred to in plaintiff's Complaint and at all times since, the Defendant, Norris L. Fellows, has been a resident of Durham, North Carolina, having lived with his wife and three daughters at 803 Murray Avenue in the City of Durham from September 1968 until June 1978, at which time (June 1978) the Defendant and his wife and children moved to 506 Morreene Road, Durham, North Carolina.

　　4. That the house at 803 Murray Avenue, Durham, was owned by the Northgate Presbyterian Church and that when Defendant moved from that residence to 506 Morreene Road, Durham, in June 1978, he gave his address on Morreene Road to two (2) of his neighbors, to wit: Mr. J. Ben Barnes, 808 Murray Avenue, who lived directly across the street from Mr. Fellows and David G. Coffey of 812 Murray Avenue, who lived across the street and two houses down from Mr. Fellows. Defendant completed a change of address form with the Roxboro Road Post Office which was the post office nearest his home and mail addressed to Defendant at 803 Murray Avenue continued to be for-

warded to him at least through early April 1979. Defendant, when he moved from 803 Murray Avenue to 506 Morreene Road in Durham in June 1978, notified a number of firms and persons as to his new address including the local phone company, the local electric company the local newspaper, and various magazines.

5. The Defendant's name and number at 803 Murray were listed in all telephone books for Durham for the years 1968 through 1978. For some weeks after Defendant's move from 803 Murray to 506 Morreene Road, the Durham telephone company provided a service whereby if an old number was dialed, an operator would answer, ask the person dialing what number he dialed, and then give that person the new phone number.

6. The house at 803 Murray Avenue was owned by the Presbyterian Church and when vacated by the Defendant it was offered for sale by the Presbyterian Church. The selling agent was Jack Johnson of Johnson Realty and Auction Company of 707 North Carolina National Bank Building, Durham, North Carolina. Mr. Johnson's real estate sign showing his name, address and phone number appeared in the front yard at 803 Murray Avenue from the time Defendant moved out of the house in June 1978 until the house was sold in 1979.

7. Mr. Jack Johnson of Johnson Realty knew the Defendant personally and knew that he had moved to Morreene Road in Durham, North Carolina. Mr. Jack Johnson did not know Mr. Fellows' street number on Morreene Road. Morreene Road is several miles in length and contains a number of apartment developments. Mr. Jack Johnson was selling agent for Northgate Presbyterian Church. Upon moving from Murray Avenue to 506 Morreene Road in June 1978, the Defendant informed Northgate Presbyterian Church of his new address at 506 Morreene Road.

8. On October 5, 1978, plaintiff's attorney signed and filed a Complaint in the matter and Summons was issued to the Defendant at 803 Murray Avenue.

9. On October 5, 1978, the Summons was received by the Sheriff of Durham County. The Sheriff of Durham County made his return on October 4, [sic] 1978, indicating that the Defendant was not served for the following reason: "Subject has moved house is For Sale."

10. The Clerk of Superior Court did not send a copy of the Sheriff's Return of Service to plaintiff's attorney as the Clerk had suspended their service because the Clerk was moving from the old Courthouse to a new Courthouse.

11. Plaintiff's attorney checked the Court file in mid-November 1978, and discovered then that the Sheriff had been unable to serve Defendant.

12. That in mid-November 1978, plaintiff's attorney attempted to telephone the Defendant at the telephone number listed for him in the 1978 Durham Telephone Directory and was informed that the number was no longer in service. Plaintiff's attorney then dialed the directory assistance operator and was informed by the directory assistance operator that there was no other listing for the Defendant.

13. That thereafter no other summons was issued or an extension on the existing Summons issued until an Alias and Pluries Summons was issued on January 17, 1979. This Alias and Pluries Summons was not sent to a Sheriff for service.

14. Within a matter of days following the issuance of the Alias and Pluries Summons on January 17, 1979, plaintiff's attorney delivered to the Durham Morning Herald for publication, a Notice of Service of Process by Publication which Notice was published in said newspaper on January 23, January 30, and February 6, 1979.

15. That in late February 1979, the 1979 Durham Telephone Directory was published and delivered throughout Durham County and was then delivered to the office of plaintiff's attorney.

16. On March 2, 1979, an Assistant Clerk of Superior Court extended the time in which the Defendant could answer or otherwise plead up to and including the 5th day of April, 1979.

17. On March 8, 1979, an Assistant Clerk of Superior Court endorsed the reverse side of the October 5, 1978 Summons as follows: "Upon request of the attorney for the plaintiff, the time for serving this Summons is hereby extended the same number of days, from the date of this endorsement, as was originally allowed by law for service."

18. On April 5, 1979, the Court extended the time in which the Defendant could answer or otherwise plead up to and including the 25th day of April, 1979.

19. On April 25, 1979, Defendant filed Rule 12 motions to dismiss for lack of personal jurisdiction, insufficiency of process and insufficiency of service of process, which motion was supported by affidavit of Defendant, Norris L. Fellows. On the same date plaintiff's attorney delivered to the Sheriff of Durham County the Summons originally issued October 5, 1978, and endorsed on the reverse side thereof on March 8, 1979.

20. On May 2, 1979, the Sheriff of Durham County served the Summons originally issued October 5, 1978, and endorsed March 8, 1979, on the Defendant at 506 Morreene Road by leaving copies with Mrs. Norris L. Fellows, who was described by the Sheriff as being a person of suitable age and discretion who resided in the Defendant's dwelling house or usual place of abode.

21. On June 12, 1979, the Defendant renewed his earlier motions under Rule 12.

22. That plaintiff and her attorney have not attempted to mail a copy of Summons or Complaint to Defendant by any type of United States Mail.

Upon these findings of fact, the trial court concluded that the personal service by delivering copies of the 5 October 1978 summons to his wife on 2 May 1979 was ineffective to give the court personal jurisdiction over the defendant. The trial court also concluded that defendant was properly served by publication pursuant to G.S. 1A-1, Rule 4(j)(9)c. Defendant appeals this determination of Jurisdiction over his person pursuant to G.S. 1-277(b).

Randall, Yaeger, Woodson, Jervis and Stout, by John C. Randall, for plaintiff appellee.

Haywood, Denny and Miller, by John D. Haywood, for defendant appellant.

VAUGHN, Judge.

Neither party questions the ruling of the trial court that personal service on defendant by delivering copies to his wife on 2 May 1979 was ineffective to obtain personal jurisdiction over defendant. The summons served on defendant on 2 May 1979 was issued on 5 October 1978 and, therefore, was not served within thirty days after it was issued and it had never been endorsed until 8 March 1979, more than ninety days after its original issuance. The alias and pluries summons issued 17 January 1979 was not served at this time. Both parties submit this personal service was ineffective under *Cole v. Cole*, 37 N.C. App. 737, 247 S.E. 2d 16 (1978).

The sole issue raised by this appeal is whether jurisdiction over the person of defendant was properly obtained through service by publication pursuant to G.S. 1A-1, Rule 4(j)(9)c. We hold there was proper service by publication on defendant and that, therefore, defendant's motion to dismiss for lack of personal jurisdiction, insufficiency of process and insufficiency of service of process pursuant to G.S. 1A-1, Rule 12(b)(2)(4)(5) was properly denied by the trial court.

Service of process by publication is in derogation of the common law and statutes authorizing it are strictly construed both as grants of authority and in determining whether service has been made in conformity with the statute. *Sink v. Easter*, 284 N.C. 555, 202 S.E. 2d 138, *rehearing den.*, 285 N.C. 597 (1974); *Thomas v. Thomas*, 43 N.C. App. 638, 260 S.E. 2d 163 (1979).

A party subject to service of process under this subsection (9) may be served by publication whenever the party's address, whereabouts, dwelling house or usual place of abode is unknown and cannot with due diligence be ascertained, or there has been a diligent but unsuccessful attempt to serve the party under either paragraph a or under paragraph b or under paragraphs a and b of this subsection (9) . . . .

If the party's post-office address is known or can with reasonable diligence be ascertained, there shall be mailed to the party at or immediately prior to the first publication a copy of the notice of service of process by publication. The mailing may be omitted if the post-office address cannot be ascertained with reasonable diligence. Upon completion of such service there shall be filed with the court an affidavit showing the publication and mailing in accordance with the requirements of G.S. 1-75.10(2) and the circumstances warranting the use of service by publication . . . .

G.S. 1A-a, Rule 4(j)(9)c. Defendant contends that the entire publication procedure was improper because in the exercise of due diligence plaintiff could have discovered defendant's address, whereabouts, dwelling house or usual place of abode and could, therefore, have served him with process in a manner more likely to have given him actual notice than did the service by publication. The question is thus whether plaintiff exercised the due diligence required of the statute before service by publication is proper.

Plaintiff, in October 1978, attempted to have the sheriff serve defendant personally with process at 803 Murray Avenue, the address shown in the then current Durham telephone directory. Upon learning that the sheriff was unable to serve defendant personally, plaintiff's counsel placed a call to the number beside defendant's address in the then current Durham telephone directory. The number was revealed to be no longer in service. The directory assistance operator was called. The operator stated there was no other listing for defendant. Plaintiff's counsel, according to his affidavit, then contacted the insurance carrier for defendant which could furnish no other address for defendant other than 803 Murray Avenue. Plaintiff then issued a new summons and commenced service by publication. Just prior to commencing service of process by publication, a copy of the new summons, complaint and notice of service by publication were mailed to defendant's insurance carrier. A telephone directory listing defendant's current address was not published until after service by publication had been completed. We hold these efforts by plaintiff constituted due diligence in attempting to ascertain defendant's address, whereabouts, dwelling place or usual place of abode.

Defendant points to several things he thinks should have been done if the standard of due diligence were to be met by plaintiff. Plaintiff did not, for example, interview or call defendant's old neighbors at 803 Murray Avenue, the realtor selling the 803 Murray Avenue residence or the deputy sheriff who attempted to serve process at this address. Plaintiff did not contact and check the records of any governmental agencies such as the post office, the Department of Transportation in Raleigh or the county register of deeds or clerk of court. Defendant contends he should have done all these things. Such investigation is commendable and should be encouraged. However, we do not wish to make a restrictive mandatory checklist for what constitutes due diligence for purposes of permitting Rule 4(j)(9)c publication. Rather, a case by case analysis is more appropriate. Under the facts and circumstances of this case, when plaintiff's counsel contacted directory assistance and defendant's insurer for his address to no avail, he acted with due diligence in attempting to determine defendant's address, whereabouts or usual place of abode.

Affirmed.

Judges PARKER and HEDRICK concur.

JESSIE R. HARRIS, Widow of GROVER HARRIS, Deceased Employee v. LEE PAVING COMPANY, INC., Employer and U.S. FIRE INSURANCE COMPANY, Carrier

No. 7910IC1127

(Filed 17 June 1980)

1. **Master and Servant § 69– workers' compensation – death benefits – lump sum – unusual case – payment of mortgage of elderly widow**

    The evidence supported the Industrial Commission's finding that this is an "unusual case" which permits an award directing a lump sum payment of death benefits under G.S. 97-44 to the widow of a deceased employee where it tended to show that plaintiff requested a lump sum payment for the purpose of paying the balance due on her home mortgage; plaintiff is 66 years old and the balance of her mortgage will not be paid off until 1992 at which time she will be 80 years old; plaintiff is working full time because she could not meet her payments on the money she received from Social Security and the workers' compensation death benefits; and it appears that plaintiff will probably not be able to retain a sufficient portion of the workers' compensation payments to continue her mortgage payments at the expiration of those benefits when plaintiff will have to make mortgage payments for the remaining nine years at an age at which plaintiff will unlikely be able to support herself from her labors.

2. **Master and Servant § 69– workers' compensation – lump sum – no commutation to present value**

    A lump sum award under G.S. 97-44 need not be commuted to the present value of the future installments which would otherwise be due but can be the uncommuted total of those installments.

APPEAL by defendants from an Order and Award of the North Carolina Industrial Commission filed 26 September 1979. Heard in the Court of Appeals 15 May 1980.

This is a workmen's compensation proceeding in which the defendants have appealed from the Commission's Opinion and Award affirming the lump sum payment of death benefits to the widow and sole dependent of the deceased employee pursuant to G.S. 97-44. The deceased employee was killed in an accident arising out of and in the course of his employment on 3 April 1978. Thereafter, the defendants and the deceased employee's widow filed a Form 23D, Notice of Death Award, on 16 May 1978 with the Industrial Commission in which the parties agreed that the plaintiff would receive weekly compensation of $79.57

for a total of 400 weeks. Subsequently, plaintiff applied to the Industrial Commission for a lump sum award.

On 17 May 1979 Deputy Commissioner Sellers filed her Opinion and Award in which she concluded that a lump sum payment would be appropriate and that plaintiff is entitled to receive a lump sum equal to the uncommuted value of 345 weeks at $79.57 per week or $27,451.65. Upon appeal by the defendants, the Full Commission affirmed the Opinion and Award and added a finding of fact which recites that "this is an unusual case. The Industrial Commission deems it to prevent undue hardship and to be to the best interest of decedent's dependent wife . . . to order payment in a lump sum the uncommuted value of the future installment as due." Defendants appealed.

No brief for plaintiff appellee.

Young, Moore, Henderson & Alvis, by Robert C. Paschal and Walter E. Brock, Jr., for defendant appellants.

MARTIN (Robert M.), Judge.

This appeal involves the propriety of an award of the Industrial Commission directing a lump sum payment of death benefits under G.S. 97-44 to the widow of the deceased employee.

The general theory of the Workers' Compensation Act is to provide for periodic payments of compensation which replace a portion of lost earnings. Experience has taught that the income protection system of the Workers' Compensation Act is best accomplished through periodic payments. The purpose of this method of payment is to prevent the employee or his dependent from dissipating the means for his support and thereby becoming a burden on society. 3 A. Larson, The Law of Workmen's Compensation § 82-71 (1976). The Act, however, does give the Industrial Commission the authority to allow payment of the award in a lump sum pursuant to G.S. 97-44. G.S. 97-44 provides in pertinent part:

Whenever any weekly payment has been continued for not less than six weeks, the liability therefor may, in unusual cases, where the Industrial Commission deems it to be in the best interest of the employee or his dependents, . . . be redeemed, in whole or in part, by the payment by the employer of a lump sum which shall be fixed by the Commission . . .

Thus this section provides that the general statutory scheme for periodic payment of income benefits can be changed to a lump sum payment only in *unusual cases* and when the Commissioner deems it to be in the *best interest* of the employee or his dependents.

[1] The appellants contend the Commission erred in awarding a lump sum payment as the evidence fails to support the Commission's finding that this is an unusual case. The plaintiff in the case *sub judice* requested a lump sum payment for the purpose of paying the balance due on her home mortgage. Defendants argue that claimant's desire to pay off her debts with a lump sum is not such an exceptional circumstance as to justify a lump sum award. It has been stated that commutation will not be made merely because the person receiving compensation desires to pay debts. 82 Am. Jur. 2d, Workmen's Compensation § 654 (1976). We believe, however, that depending on the circumstance, the payment of debts may or may not be an important factor in determining what is an unusual case. *See* 3 A. Larson, *supra;* 69 A.L.R. 547 (1930).

In the case before us plaintiff is a 66 year old widow. Plaintiff testified that she works, when able, for a furniture factory earning approximately $92.00 per week. Plaintiff receives $118.00 per month from Social Security and $79.57 per week from defendant insurance company. Plaintiff's expenses include the house payment of $188.00 per month, payment of two notes which her husband owed at the time of his death, monthly light, heating, water bills and other living expenses. Plaintiff testified that the reason she requested a lump sum is that she is having trouble with her legs and would like to pay off the mortgage on the house. Plaintiff had to start working full time because she could not meet all the payments on the money she received from Social Security and the insurance company. Plaintiff's mortgage is for 20 years beginning July, 1972 and the present balance is $18,690.39.

The foregoing facts show that the balance on plaintiff's mortgage will not be paid off until 1992 at which time plaintiff will be nearly 80 years old. Plaintiff's benefits from the insurance company if paid on the present weekly basis would continue only for an additional 345 weeks ending when plaintiff is in her early seventies. It is apparent that plaintiff's present expenses encumber not only the payments from worker's compensation but also income from other sources. Under these circumstances, it is doubtful that plaintiff will be able to retain a sufficient portion of compensation payments to continue her mortgage payments at the expiration of the worker's compensation benefits at which time plaintiff will have to make mortgage payments for the remaining 9 years at an age when plaintiff will be unlikely to support herself from her labors. There is sufficient evidence to support the finding of the Commission that this is an unusual case within the meaning of the statute. The record convinces us that the relief afforded by a lump sum payment would not be temporary only, bringing about greater economic difficulty in the future, but rather would secure to plaintiff a place to live out her later years.

[2] Defendants next contend that if plaintiff is entitled to a lump sum payment pursuant to G.S. 97-44, plaintiff is entitled to only the present value of the lump sum awarded by the Industrial Commission.

The Industrial Commission concluded that plaintiff is entitled to a lump sum equal to the uncommuted value of 345 weeks at $79.57 per week. In its "Comment" following its finding of fact, the Industrial Commission remarked as follows:

By paying the plaintiff a lump sum award for the uncommuted value of 345 weeks at $79.57 per week, the defendants will lose the use of the money which it would have had if the amount were paid over the 345 week period. But this is not to say that the plaintiff will receive more than the amount provided by law.

With regard to the amount of the lump sum to be awarded by the Commission pursuant to G.S. 97-44, that statute states that the liability for weekly payments "may . . . be redeemed, in whole or in part, by the payment by the employer of a lump sum which shall be fixed by the Commission, but in no case to exceed the uncommuted value of the future installments which may be due under this Article."

Defendants' position that the lump sum award under G.S. 97-44 should be reduced to its present value is not supported by the plain language of G.S. 97-44 which allows an award up to the *uncommuted* value of the future installments. When the Legislature intends a lump sum award to be commuted to its present value, it uses precisely these terms in other sections of the Act as, for example, in G.S. 97-40: "Subject to the provisions of G.S. 97-38, if the deceased employee leaves neither whole nor partial dependents, then the compensation which would be payable under G.S. 97-38 to whole dependents *shall be commuted to its present value* and paid in a lump sum . . . ." Moreover, in 1963 the Legislature changed the language of G.S. 97-44 from a lump sum which shall be fixed by the Commission, but in no case to exceed the "commutable" value of the future installments to the "uncommuted" value of those installments. In so doing the Legislature expressed its intention that the maximum amount of the lump sum under G.S. 97-44 is not its commuted value or its commutable value but rather its uncommuted value.

The award of the Industrial Commission is

Affirmed.

Judges ARNOLD and WELLS concur.

WILLIAM P. GRIMES v. MARY RAKER GRIMES

No. 7922SC736

(Filed 17 June 1980)

1. **Bills and Notes § 8; Uniform Commercial Code § 32; Husband and Wife § 1.1– spouses co-makers of promissory note – wife primarily liable – no presumption of gift from husband to wife**

   When two or more persons execute a note as makers, they are jointly and severally liable unless the language of the note clearly indicates the contrary, and because of the joint and several nature of a maker's obligation under a note, a co-maker who pays the instrument is entitled to contribution from other co-makers; furthermore, a co-maker's right to contribution is unaffected by the marital relationship of the parties to a note, and where the wife executes a promissory note as co-maker with her husband, she is primarily liable thereunder. Therefore, the trial court erred in determining that there was a presumption of gift from plaintiff husband to defendant wife where both executed a promissory note and plaintiff paid the note, and that plaintiff failed to rebut that presumption.

2. **Bills and Notes § 8; Uniform Commercial Code § 32– promissory note executed by spouses – capacity in which wife signed in issue**

   In an action by plaintiff husband to recover from defendant, his former wife, one-half of the amount he paid on a note executed by both plaintiff and defendant while they were separated though still married, the case is remanded for a determination of the capacity in which defendant signed the note, since, as between the parties jointly and severally liable under a note, the true relationship existing between the parties may be revealed to alter the otherwise absolute obligation of the signers.

APPEAL by plaintiff from *Collier, Judge.* Judgment entered 22 March 1979 in Superior Court, DAVIDSON County. Heard in the Court of Appeals 27 February 1980.

Plaintiff seeks to recover from his former wife $13,800, one-half of the amount he paid to retire a debt owed Lexington State Bank of Lexington, North Carolina, in the amount of $27,600. The note was executed by both plaintiff and defendant while they were separated though still married. At a nonjury trial, defendant moved for and was granted an involuntary dismissal under G.S. 1A-1, Rule 41(b). Plaintiff appeals.

Further facts pertinent to this appeal are related below.

Wilson, Biesecker, Tripp and Wall, by Joe E. Biesecker, for plaintiff appellant.

Grubb, Penry and Penry, by Phyllis S. Penry, for defendant appellee.

MORRIS, Chief Judge.

[1] Upon making findings of fact with respect to the circumstances surrounding the execution of the note in question and plaintiff's and defendant's use of the loan proceeds therefrom, the trial judge made the following conclusions of law:

1. That the plaintiff is presumed to be legally obligated for the support of his wife and family.

2. That if a wife receives and uses her husband's money there is a presumption of gift in the absence of the contract to repay.

3. There is no evidence to rebut the above stated presumption and there exist no express contract between the parties for repayment.

4. There is no evidence that the plaintiff [sic] received any benefit other than that accorded to her by her marital status from the loan in question.

We certainly agree with the court and defendant that, nothing else appearing, the law presumes a gift where there is a transfer of realty or personalty from husband to wife. In *Underwood v. Otwell,* 269 N.C. 571, 153 S.E. 2d 40 (1967), the Court stated the following:

It is established law in this State that when a husband purchases land and causes it to be conveyed to his wife, the law presumes that the land is a gift to the wife, and no resulting trust arises. [Citations omitted.] Similarly, a gift is presumed when the husband pays for personalty and procures title either in the wife's name or in their joint names.

269 N.C. at 574, 153 S.E. 2d at 43. It is also true that at common law, a note evidencing a debt executed jointly by husband and wife rendered the husband liable on the note, but not the wife. *See Taft v. Covington*, 199 N.C. 51, 153 S.E. 597 (1930). *See generally* 41 C.J.S., *Husband and Wife* § 185(b) (1944). However, this rule no longer obtains. G.S. 52-2. Now where the wife executes a promissory note as a co-maker, she is primarily liable thereunder. *Taft v. Covington, supra; Union National Bank v. Jonas*, 212 N.C. 394,193 S.E. 265 (1937); *Davis v. Cockman*, 211 N.C. 630, 191 S.E. 322 (1937). *See Wilson v. Vreeland*, 176 N.C. 504, 97 S.E. 427 (1918). This result follows from the rule that, nothing else appearing, a person signing his or her name at the bottom of the face of a promissory note is a maker thereof, and is primarily liable thereon. *Union National Bank v. Jonas, supra. See O'Grady v. First Union National Bank*, 296 N.C. 212, 250 S.E. 2d 587 (1978).

With respect to the applicability of the Uniform Commercial Code, as adopted in North Carolina, on the negotiable note in question, it is clear that the liability of a person signing a negotiable instrument is determined by the capacity in which one executes the instrument. Under G.S. 25-3-413(1), the maker "engages that he will pay the instrument according to its tenor at the time of his engagement . . . ." A maker's liability is unconditional and absolute. When two or more persons execute a note as makers, they are jointly and severally liable, unless the language of the note clearly indicates the contrary. G.S. 25-3-118(e); *O'Grady v. First Union National Bank, supra*. Because of the joint and several nature of a maker's obligation under a note, when one co-maker pays the instrument he is entitled to contribution from other co-makers. *Raleigh Banking and Trust Co. v. York*, 199 N.C. 624, 155 S.E. 263 (1930); *Wachovia Bank and Trust Co. v. Black*, 198 N.C. 219, 151 S.E. 269 (1930); *Lancaster v. Stanfield*, 191 N.C. 340, 132 S.E. 21 (1926). *See Wilson v. Vreeland, supra*.

We are of the opinion that a co-maker's right to contribution is unaffected by the marital relationship of the parties to a note. This case is different from those situations to which a presumption of gift attaches, because in those cases the wife had been given merely a transfer of value from the husband. Here, however, the wife has personally obligated herself under the note. Defendant, as a co-maker, has an absolute and unconditional obligation under the note. The fact that the proceeds from the loan were used during the marriage is of no moment. At any rate, plaintiff and defendant were divorced at the time plaintiff paid the balance due under the note. No presumption of gift arises, therefore, from plaintiff's retiring the debt. Accordingly, we overrule the trial court's conclusions in this regard.

[2] The capacity in which defendant signed the note is a question which must be answered. As between the parties jointly and severally liable under a note, the law is settled that the true relationship existing between the parties may be revealed to alter the otherwise absolute obligation of the signers. Thus, evidence has been held admissible to show that a surety on the face of a note and an accommodation endorser are actually cosureties by virtue of a separate agreement among themselves. *Lancaster v. Stanfield, supra.* We believe justice would be best served if this case were remanded to the trial court for a determination of the capacity in which defendant signed the note, and so hold.

Since the trial judge will be charged with the duty, on remand, to make new findings of fact and conclusions of law based on the evidence adduced on further hearing, we need not discuss defendant's first two assignments of error dealing with certain of the court's findings.

Reversed and remanded.

Judges VAUGHN and ARNOLD concur.

JOSEPH D. LATHAN v. UNION COUNTY BOARD OF COMMISSIONERS
AND UNION COUNTY AND GLADYS NESBIT AND KEITH A. NESBIT

No. 7920SC1181

(Filed 17 June 1980)

Municipal Corporations § 30.9– spot zoning

The rezoning of an 11.42 acre tract from a residential classification to a light industrial classification constituted spot zoning where the surrounding area was zoned residential, and no reasonable basis for the spot zoning existed because a substantial portion of the tract was too low for residential development or because two roads bordered portions of the tract.

APPEAL by defendants from *Wood, Judge.* Judgment signed 17 August 1979 in Superior Count, UNION County. Heard in the Court of Appeals 21 May 1980.

This action for declaratory judgment was brought by plaintiff to determine the validity of the rezoning of a piece of property by the Union County Board of Commissioners.

The facts of this case are not in dispute. Plaintiff and defendants Nesbit are adjoining landowners in Union County. On 25 August 1978 a petition was filed to have the Nesbit property, an 11.412-acre tract, rezoned from R-20 to L-I under the Union County Zoning Ordinance. Property zoned R-20 under the ordinance may be used for detached single-family dwellings, churches, and various forms of agriculture and horticulture. Additional conditional uses are permitted, such as educational institutions, recreational facilities, and emergency stations. The areas zoned L-I (Light Industrial) permit various manufacturing enterprises and wholesale establishments. Additional conditional uses are permitted as well, such as restaurants, service stations, and lumber and planing mills.

The Nesbit property has been owned by the Keith Nesbit family for over fifteen years. A sawmill operation is currently being conducted on a portion of the property as a preexisting nonconforming use.

The Director of the Union County Planning Department, Luther M. McPherson, Jr., visited the Nesbit property after the rezoning petition was filed and subsequently submitted an un-favorable recommendation on the petition to the Planning Board. In his view the property was not a suitable area for future industrial development: it had no access to major trans-portation facilities or public water and sewer services; there was no predominant tendency towards industrial development already in the immediate area; if rezoned, the property would be incompatible with the surrounding residential community. Furthermore, he concluded the rezoning would be unlawful spot zoning. The Planning Board, however, favorably recom-mended the rezoning to the Board of Commissioners, and after a public hearing on 6 November 1978, the county commissioners rezoned the property from R-20 to L-I.

Plaintiff and defendants filed motions for summary judg-ment in this action; the court granted plaintiff's motion and denied defendants' motion. Defendants appealed.

Joe P. McCollum, Jr. for plaintiff appellee.

Griffin, Caldwell & Helder, by Thomas J. Caldwell and H. Ligon Bundy, for defendant appellants Union County Board of Commissioners and Union County.

Smith, Smith, Perry & Helms, by Henry B. Smith, Jr., for defendants appellants Gladys Nesbit and Keith A. Nesbit.

MARTIN (Harry C.), Judge.

Appellants assign as error the trial court's entering sum-mary judgment on behalf of plaintiff and denying appellants' motion for summary judgment. The court granted judgment in favor of plaintiff "as a matter of law in that the property de-scribed in the petition was spot zoned by the defendant, Union County Board of Commissioners."

There is no controversy as to the facts disclosed by the evidence in this case. The only controversy involves the legal significance of the facts; therefore, this action is a proper case for summary judgment. *See Blades v. City of Raleigh*, 280 N.C. 531, 187 S.E. 2d 35 (1972), in which the validity of a City of

Raleigh zoning ordinance was determined on summary judgment. Based on the materials before it, the trial court in the present case ruled that the Nesbit property had been spot zoned. We affirm this ruling.

In the *Blades* case, the Court defined the concept of spot zoning as follows:

> A zoning ordinance, or amendment, which singles out and reclassifies a relatively small tract owned by a single person and surrounded by a much larger area uniformly zoned, so as to impose upon the small tract greater restrictions than those imposed upon the larger area, or so as to relieve the small tract from restrictions to which the rest of the area is subjected, is called "spot zoning."

280 N.C. at 549, 187 S.E. 2d at 45. Spot zoning is beyond the authority of the municipality or county in the absence of a clear showing that a reasonable basis exists for such distinction. *Id.* The question for our determination, then, is whether the record clearly discloses a reasonable basis for spot zoning the Nesbit property. If such a clear showing does not exist, the court appropriately granted summary judgment for plaintiff.

The only evidence in the record that would arguably tend to show a reasonable basis for the rezoning is found in defendant's exhibits. Keith Nesbit stated in an affidavit "[t]hat Cane Creek flows through the property and a substantial portion of the property is unsuitable for residential structures and developments because of the fact that it is too low." Similarly, in the minutes of the Union County Board of Commissioners' meeting, held 6 November 1978, are found the reasons for a favorable recommendation by the Union County Planning Board:

> "(1) Because of how long it has been there. (2) You can't tell a man that he can't grow and will have to go up U.S. 74 to expand. (3) How long they have had the land."

In addition, the zoning maps reveal that a small district, between one and two acres in size, is located across Rocky River Road from the Nesbit property and is zoned B-3, general business district. Two roads, one gravel and one paved, border portions of the Nesbit property; defendants argue that this factor makes the property "peculiarly suited for industrial use" and "sets it apart from the adjoining property."

We think that this evidence falls short of being a clear showing that a reasonable basis exists for spot zoning the Nesbit property. The county, therefore, acted beyond its authority, and the trial court was correct in granting summary judgment for plaintiff on the basis of the unlawful spot zoning.

Affirmed.

Judges WEBB and WELLS concur.

STATE OF NORTH CAROLINA v. DONALD EUGENE CALLIHAN

No. 7910SC1027

(Filed 17 June 1980)

1. **Burglary and Unlawful Breakings § 5.1– burglary – defendant at crime scene – sufficiency of evidence**
    Evidence was sufficient to be submitted to the jury in a burglary prosecution where it tended to show that defendant was apprehended by police at the crime scene, immediately after the crime, dressed the same as the intruder seen by the occupant.

2. **Burglary and Unlawful Breakings § 6.2– nighttime entry accompanied by flight when discovered – evidence of intent – instruction proper**
    The trial court in a burglary prosecution did not err in instructing the jury that "the fact of entry alone in the nighttime accompanied by flight when discovered is some evidence of guilt and in the absence of any other proof or evidence of other intent, and with no explanatory facts or circumstances, may warrant a reasonable inference of guilty intent."

APPEAL by defendant from *Godwin, Judge.* Judgment entered 15 June 1979 in Superior Court, WAKE County. Heard in the Court of Appeals 21 March 1980.

Defendant was charged and convicted of burglary and appeals from judgment imposing a prison term of not less than ten years nor more than life.

State v. Callihan

STATE'S EVIDENCE

Kathleen Hearn operated a boarding house located next to her residence on New Bern Avenue in Raleigh. She rented a room to defendant on 4 February 1979 and saw him three or four times a week. During the early morning of 6 March 1979 she was awakened by the opening and closing of a door. A light was turned on for a few seconds in an adjoining bedroom. She saw a man wearing a brown leather jacket and a black cloth glove. She called the police. She then went to the back yard. The man jumped from the roof and landed on her. She did not see the man's face but she saw the white skin of his neck. She ran back into the house. The police arrived and apprehended in the back yard a man wearing a brown leather jacket. She yelled, "That's him." The man with the police was the defendant.

Joseph Handell, who also had a room in the boarding house, heard a scream. He got up, went to the door, and saw defendant who was standing in the back yard and wearing a brown leather jacket. The police came up and took custody of the defendant. Mrs. Hearn said, "That's him."

A pair of old worn gloves was found in defendant's pants. Glove prints were found on the window of Mrs. Hearn's home.

DEFENDANT'S EVIDENCE

Defendant testified that he was in a local tavern until about 3:30 a.m. He then went to his residence. As soon as he got to his room he heard a scream. He went out the back door and there the police stopped him. At no time that night did he enter Mrs. Hearn's home. He had been convicted of breaking or entering, auto larceny, and escape. Defendant's testimony as to his presence at the tavern until about 3:30 a.m. was corroborated by two witnesses.

Attorney General Edmisten by Assistant Attorney General Ralf F. Haskell for the State.

Hatch, Little, Bunn, Jones, Few & Berry by E. Richard Jones, McDaniel and Heidgerd by C. Diederich Heidgerd for defendant appellant.

CLARK, Judge.

[1] Did the trial court err in denying defendant's motion to dismiss?

The test to be applied in determining whether the evidence is sufficient to warrant the submission of the case to the jury is whether a reasonable inference of defendant's guilt may be drawn from the circumstances. *State v. Cutler*, 271 N.C. 379, 156 S.E. 2d 679 (1967); *State v. Snead*, 295 N.C. 615, 247 S.E. 2d 893 (1978).

We believe that the circumstantial evidence, when viewed in the light most favorable to the State, is sufficient to permit a reasonable inference that defendant was the person who burglarized the home of Mrs. Hearn. We find most significant the apprehension of defendant at the scene, immediately after the crime, dressed the same as the intruder seen by the occupant. The combination of circumstances creates more than a strong suspicion. The motion to dismiss was properly denied.

[2] The defendant assigns as error the instruction to the jury that "the fact of entry alone in the nighttime accompanied by flight when discovered is some evidence of guilt and in the absence of any other proof or evidence of other intent, and with no explanatory facts or circumstances, may warrant a reasonable inference of guilty intent."

Defendant admits that this language is found in numerous cases, including *State v. Accor*, 277 N.C. 65, 175 S.E. 2d 583 (1970), but argues that the language related to the issue of whether there was sufficient evidence to withstand a motion to dismiss rather than to instructing the jury on the element of intent. We do not agree. The court must charge on all the essentials of the case including the intent to commit larceny. There was no evidence that while in the dwelling defendant committed or attempted to commit the crime of larceny or any other crime, but there is evidence that the defendant fled immediately when he was discovered in the building. In instructing on the essential elements of intent the court not only was warranted in, but had the duty of, explaining to the jury that under such circumstances there may be a reasonable inference of guilty intent. If the court may make such inference in ruling on a motion to dismiss, we see no reason why the jury could not make such inference under proper instructions in determining the essential element of intent.

Nor does this instruction reduce the burden of proof on the State in violation of *State v. Hankerson*, 288 N.C. 632, 220 S.E. 2d 575 (1975), *reversed on other grounds*, 432 U.S. 233, 53 L. Ed. 2d 306, 97 S. Ct. 2339 (1977). In *State v. Williams*, 288 N.C. 680, 220 S.E. 2d 558 (1975), it was recognized that certain basic facts in a criminal case may give rise to a presumption or inference. Such presumption or inference may be and should be submitted and explained to the jury for its consideration where the proof necessary to raise the inference is sufficient for rational jurors to find the presumed fact beyond a reasonable doubt. *See State v. Hammonds*, 290 N.C. 1, 224 S.E. 2d 595 (1976), for instructions on the presumptions of malice and unlawfulness arising upon proof of the intentional inflicting of a wound with a deadly weapon proximately causing death.

The trial court properly instructed the jury and did not err in giving the challenged instruction.

We conclude that the defendant had a fair trial free from prejudicial error.

No error.

Judges MARTIN (Robert M.) and ERWIN concur.

STATE OF NORTH CAROLINA v. THOMAS RANDOLPH WINSTON

No. 8026SC87

(Filed 17 June 1980)

1. **Criminal Law § 91.6– time to interview witnesses – denial of continuance – no abuse of discretion**

   In a prosecution for kidnapping and crime against nature in which defendant contended that a third person forced him at gunpoint to take the victim into the woods and perform sexual acts upon the victim, the trial court did not abuse its discretion in the denial of defendant's motion for a continuance to permit defendant to interview three witnesses who furnished descriptions enabling a police artist to prepare a composite sketch of the person suspected of abducting and murdering the victim's ten year old sister eleven days before defendant's trial so that defendant could determine whether such person may have been the same person who defendant contended forced him to commit the crimes charged, since defendant had available in the composite sketch the identical information he sought to obtain from the witnesses, and nothing in the record or defendant's contentions suggests that his interviewing the witnesses would have yielded any information different from that he already had.

2. **Criminal Law § 35– evidence relating to another crime – no tendency to show crimes committed by third person**

In this prosecution for kidnapping and crime against nature, an autopsy report and a pathologist's testimony regarding the murder of the victim's ten year old sister shortly before defendant's trial were not admissible to bolster the credibility of defendant's testimony that a third party forced him at gunpoint to commit the crimes charged and threatened to harm defendant, the victim and their families if they told of the third party's involvement in the crimes, since such testimony did not tend to prove that a third party committed the crimes for which defendant was charged but related to an entirely different offense committed by a person or persons unknown.

APPEAL by defendant from *Ervin, Judge.* Judgments entered 21 August 1979 in Superior Court, MECKLENBURG County. Heard in the Court of Appeals on 3 June 1980.

Defendant was charged in proper bills of indictment with kidnapping, a violation of G.S. § 14-39, and crime against nature, a violation of G.S. § 14-177. He pleaded not guilty and was found guilty as charged.

The assignments of error brought forward and argued make it unnecessary for us to set out the facts of this case in more detail than is done so in the opinion. Defendant appealed from a judgment imposing a prison sentence of not less than 30 nor more than 40 years in the kidnapping case, and not less than nor more than 10 years in the crime against nature case.

Attorney General Edmisten, by Assistant Attorney General Ralf F. Haskell, for the State.

Assistant Public Defender Theo X. Nixon for the defendant appellant.

HEDRICK, Judge.

Eleven days before these cases were called for trial, the victim's ten-year-old sister was apparently abducted from her home and brutally murdered. The perpetrator of this offense had not been apprehended at the time of defendant's trial. However, the police had obtained from three witnesses a sufficient description to enable an artist to prepare a composite sketch of the person suspected to have abducted and murdered the child. This tragic incident forms the basis for defendant's two assignments of error.

[1] First, defendant argues the court erred in denying his pretrial motion to continue. At the hearing on the motion, defendant argued and now argues that he needed additional time to interview the three witnesses who allegedly saw the person who abducted the victim's ten-year-old sister and whose description provided the basis for the composite sketch. The reason defendant gave for needing to interview these witnesses was based on his defense: that is, defendant had maintained from the time of his arrest that a third party had forced him at gun point to take the victim in these cases into the woods and to perform various sexual acts upon the victim. According to defendant, the third party resembled in some respects the person depicted in the composite sketch.

It is well settled and the defendant concedes that a motion for continuance is ordinarily addressed to the sound discretion of the trial judge whose ruling is not subject to review absent an abuse of discretion. *State v. Thomas*, 294 N.C. 105, 240 S.E. 2d 426 (1978). Manifestly, this record fails to demonstrate an abuse of discretion. Even assuming that the record discloses some connection between the crimes for which the defendant was charged and the alleged abduction and murder of the victim's sister, the defendant has not shown that the alleged witnesses' description of the perpetrator of the latter crime would aid the defendant in his defense. Moreover, the record discloses that the defendant had available in the composite sketch the identical information he sought to obtain from the three witnesses, and he offered nothing in support of his motion to show that a continuance was necessary or would in any way aid the preparation of his defense. In short, nothing in the record or defendant's contentions suggests that his interviewing these witnesses would have yielded any information different from or additional to that he already had. *See State v. Thomas, supra.* Defendant must show both error in the denial of his motion to continue and that he was prejudiced thereby before he will be granted a new trial. *State v. Robinson,* 283 N.C. 71, 194 S.E. 2d 811 (1973). He has failed to do so. We find no abuse of discretion on the part of the trial judge in denying the motion.

[2] Next, defendant contends the court erred in not allowing him to introduce into evidence the autopsy report or, alternatively, medical testimony of the pathologist regarding the death of the victim's sister. He argues that it was necessary for him to show the "violent death" of the child in order to bolster his credibility on the witness stand since he had maintained as a part of his defense that the third party who forced him to commit the crimes for which he was charged had threatened to harm the defendant, the victim, and their families if either told of his [third party's] involvement.

While any evidence which tends to shed any light on the crime charged or the defense is relevant and admissible, the question of relevancy is for the trial judge to determine, and again the defendant must prove not only error in the exclusion of evidence but also that he was prejudiced thereby. In this regard, evidence which points to the guilt of third parties may be admissible. However, it is well-settled law that such evidence is not admissible unless it points directly to the guilt of the third party. "[E]vidence which does no more than create an inference or conjecture as to such guilt is inadmissible." *State v. Smith,* 211 N.C. 93, 96, 189 S.E. 175, 176 (1937). *See also State v. Britt,* 42 N.C. App. 637, 257 S.E. 2d 468 (1979); *State v. Couch,* 35 N.C. App. 202, 241 S.E. 2d 105 (1978).

The evidence which defendant argues the court erroneously excluded in this case does not tend to prove that a third party committed the crimes for which the defendant was charged. Indeed, the medical evidence tending to show only that the victim's sister was "strangled" does not even raise an inference that a third party committed or participated in the kidnapping and rape of the victim in these cases. The excluded evidence related to an entirely different offense committed by a person or persons unknown. In short, the entire tragic incident regarding the abduction and murder of the ten-year-old sister of the victim is wholly irrelevant to the charges in the present cases. The trial judge did not err in his exclusion of the evidence challenged by this assignment of error. Defendant's contentions are without merit.

We hold the defendant had a fair trial free from prejudicial error.

No error.

Judges PARKER and VAUGHN concur.

WAYNE R. WRIGHT v. KATHLEEN D. WRIGHT

No. 8021SC14

(Filed 17 June 1980)

Quasi Contracts and Restitution § 1.2– unjust enrichment alleged – improper jury instructions

In an action to recover for unjust enrichment where plaintiff husband alleged that he made substantial improvements with his own labor and money to defendant wife's house and that defendant had been unjustly enriched thereby, the trial court erred in submitting an issue to the jury as to whether defendant agreed with plaintiff to share in the ownership of the real property and erred in instructing the jury that the issue had to be proved by clear, strong and convincing evidence, since no contract, oral or written, enforceable or not, is necessary to support a recovery based on unjust enrichment, and if plaintiff had been successful in rebutting the presumption of gift, all he would have had to show was that the improvements were made upon the good faith belief that an estate in the property was promised him.

Wright v. Wright

APPEAL by plaintiff from *Hairston, Judge.* Judgment entered 15 August 1979 in Superior Court, FORSYTH County. Heard in the Court of Appeals 22 May 1980.

The parties to this action were married in October 1975. Prior to the marriage, defendant and her daughter had been living in the home which is the subject of this controversy, and defendant had apparently completely paid the purchase price. Prior to the parties' marriage, they discussed selling defendant's house at a proposed sales price of $19,000.00, but finally decided to remodel the house and use it as their marital home.

Plaintiff is a carpenter and completed the substantial improvements himself. He added a bedroom, bath, den with fireplace, carport, front porch and brick veneer onto the entire house. Plaintiff's out-of-pocket costs were approximately $15,444.37; his labor costs were approximately $2,147.00

The parties were divorced after thirteen months of marriage. Plaintiff's name was never placed on the deed to the house which he had substantially improved. He has filed this action asking that an equitable lien be put on the property in the amount of $17,270.15. From a judgment denying such relief, plaintiff appealed.

Robert D. Hinshaw for plaintiff appellant.

Harper, Wood, Hux & Brown, by William Z. Wood Jr., for defendant appellee.

HILL, Judge.

Plaintiff appellant's brief fails to comply with App. R. 28(b)(3). "However, rather than [dismiss] the appeal, we have elected to treat it as a petition for *certiorari*, allow it and consider the appeal on its merits." *Insurance Co. v. Webb,* 10 N.C. App. 672, 673, 179 S.E. 2d 803 (1971).

We have examined all of plaintiff's arguments and find one to be dispositive. Plaintiff argues that the trial court erred by failing to submit to the jury issue no. 1 as tendered and by substituting its own instruction. We agree. In his complaint, plaintiff alleged that his wife had been unjustly enriched and asked for equitable relief. Plaintiff's tendered instruction would have required the jury to make a threshold determination of whether plaintiff intended " . . . to make a gift of the labor and materials in improving the home of his wife, the [d]efendant."

The trial court did not submit the issues tendered by plaintiff. Instead, the court asked the jury to resolve the issue of whether " . . . the defendant agreed with the plaintiff to share in the ownership of the real property." To answer that issue in plaintiff's favor, the jury had to find:

> "First, that the defendant . . . promised to share in the property."

> Second, that the defendant's promise " . . . was conditioned on the defendant's furnishing the money to make the betterments."

> Third, that plaintiff had rebutted the presumption " . . . that when a husband makes improvements . . . on his wife's property, he makes a gift to her."

The judge instructed the jury that the main issue, as well as the three preliminary findings, had to be proven by clear, strong and convincing evidence. The jury found that plaintiff did not meet this burden. Thus, the second issue of whether defendant was unjustly enriched, and the third issue concerning the amount of relief plaintiff was entitled to were not reached.

The trial court's substituted issue incorrectly states the law. Plaintiff is not required to show by clear, strong and convincing evidence that his wife " . . . promised to share in the property." "No contract, oral or written, enforceable or not, is necessary to support a recovery based upon unjust enrichment." *Parslow v. Parslow*, 47 N.C. App. 84, 266 S.E. 2d 746 (1980). "Such a recovery is founded on the equitable theory of estoppel and not on principles of quasi or implied contract."

Clontz v. Clontz, 44 N.C. App. 573, 578, 261 S.E. 2d 695 (1980). If plaintiff had been successful in rebutting the presumption of gift, all he would have had to show was that the improvements were made *upon the good faith belief* that an estate in the property was promised him. *See Clontz, supra*, at 578. That showing need not be made by clear, strong and convincing evidence.

This case must be sent back for a new trial. At the conclusion of the evidence, in order to recover, plaintiff must first rebut the presumption that the improvements placed on the wife's house were intended as a gift. *See Shue v. Shue*, 241 N.C. 65, 67, 84 S.E. 2d 302 (1954). If plaintiff rebuts the presumption, or if the trial court finds the presumption to be a denial of equal protection, then plaintiff must go on to show that defendant was unjustly enriched. To make such a showing, defendant must show that he made the improvements on defendant's property "... upon the good faith belief that [an] ... estate in [the] property was promised him, and that [the] improvements inured to defendant['s] benefit ...." *Clontz, supra*, at p. 578.

We note that "... there is a substantial question as to whether this [presumption] denies equal protection of the laws to male spouses ...." *See Parslow, supra.* "We cannot, however, reach this question ... because constitutional objections may not be raised for the first time on appeal and there is nothing in the record to indicate that this question was ever adjudicated by the trial court." *Id.*

Reversed and remanded for New Trial.

Judges MARTIN (Robert M.) and ARNOLD concur.

OUTER BANKS CONTRACTORS, INC. v. SARAH E. FORBES and REGGIE OWENS

No. 791DC158

(Filed 17 June 1980)

Laborers' and Materialmen's Liens § 7– no right to lien as prime contractor
   Plaintiff cannot establish a lien for labor and materials as a prime contractor when its own notice of claim of lien and judicial findings to which plaintiff consented establish it is a subcontractor. However, plaintiff is entitled to try its claim for a money judgment against defendant owner where plaintiff asked for a money judgment in its complaint and stated in answer to interrogatories that it had made a contract with defendant to furnish labor and materials, and defendant in an affidavit denied that she had made a contract with plaintiff.

APPEAL by plaintiff from *Beaman, Judge.* Judgment entered 11 December 1978 in District Court, DARE County. Heard in the Court of Appeals 17 October 1979.

This is an action for a money judgment and to enforce a lien on the real property of the defendant, Sarah E. Forbes. The plaintiff filed a notice on 28 September 1973 which was denominated "Notice of claim of lien by first tier subcontractor" and which claimed a "lien pursuant to North Carolina law and claims all rights of subrogation to which he is entitled under Part 2 of Article 2 of Chapter 44A of the General Statutes of North Carolina." In its complaint, plaintiff alleged that pursuant to a contract between defendant Forbes and plaintiff, the plaintiff had furnished labor and materials to Forbes for construction on the property and prayed for a money judgment and a lien on the property. In her answer, the defendant Forbes denied she had entered into any contract with the plaintiff. She alleged that she had made a contract with Reggie Owens for construction on her property, that any contract plaintiff had made was with Owens, and she had paid Owens in full before she received any notice from the plaintiff that he was due any money as a subcontractor.

A consent order was then entered making Reggie Owens a defendant. This order recited that plaintiff was a subcontractor who furnished labor and materials for the project; that Owens was the prime contractor; and that as the result of a ruling in a separate action between Forbes and Owens, "it would appear that the prime contractor would be responsible for labor and materials that were supplied by the subcontractor . . . ." Plaintiff then filed an amended complaint in which it again alleged its claim against the defendant Forbes and a claim in the alternative against the defendant Owens. In its alternative claim, plaintiff alleged that it, as a subcontractor, made an agreement with Owens as prime contractor to furnish the labor and materials, that plaintiff furnished the labor and materials, and Owens had not paid for them. In answer to interrogatories, plaintiff stated that on 1 April 1977, it entered into an oral contract with defendant Forbes to furnish labor and materials for her property. Defendant Forbes filed an affidavit in which she stated that she had dealt solely with Owens in regard to the contract to furnish the labor and materials, and she did not make any contract with the plaintiff. She also stated she had paid Owens in full before she received any notice of the plaintiff's claim. Defendant moved to strike the plaintiff's amended answer and for summary judgment. Both motions were granted with the court reciting that the amended complaint was filed without leave of the court. Plaintiff appealed.

Aldridge, Seawell and Khoury, by Daniel D. Khoury, for plaintiff appellant.

Leroy, Wells, Shaw, Hornthal, Riley and Shearin, by Norman W. Shearin, Jr., and Ralph T. Baker, for defendant appellee Forbes.

WEBB, Judge.

[1] It appears from the notice of claim of lien filed in the case sub judice that the plaintiff is attempting to enforce a lien pursuant to N.C. General Statute Chap. 44A, Art. 2, Part 2. The lien notice states that plaintiff is a first tier subcontractor and follows the form prescribed by G.S. 44A-19 for filing a lien as a subcontractor. The complaint alleges a claim for a lien as a prime contractor under G.S. 44A, Art. 2, Part 1. An order was then consented to by plaintiff's attorney which recited that plaintiff was a subcontractor and Owens was the prime contrac-

tor who would be responsible for the labor and materials supplied by the subcontractor. This is a judicial finding binding on the parties. We hold that the plaintiff cannot establish a lien as a prime contractor when its own notice of claim of lien and the judicial findings to which it consented establish it is a subcontractor. The claim for a lien was properly dismissed.

In addition to the lien claim, the plaintiff, in its complaint, asked for a money judgment. In answer to interrogatories, the plaintiff stated it had made a contract with defendant Forbes to furnish labor and materials. In her affidavit, defendant Forbes denied she made a contract with plaintiff. We hold this shows a genuine issue which should have been submitted to the jury.

On the record before us, we hold that plaintiff is entitled to try its claim for a money judgment against the defendant Forbes, but it is not entitled to enforce its lien as a subcontractor.

We note that plaintiff made no assignment of error to the order striking its amended complaint. The exception to this order is deemed abandoned. Rule 10(c), N.C. Rules App. Proc.

Affirmed in part; reversed and remanded in part.

Judges ARNOLD and WELLS concur.

CASES REPORTED WITHOUT PUBLISHED OPINION

FILED 17 JUNE 1980

CRUMPLER v. TURNAGE No. 798DC810	Wayne (78CVD465)	Affirmed
DEPT. OF TRANSPORTATION v. LANCASTER No. 7921SC844	Forsyth (77CVS2731)	No Error
HARMON v. SIMPSON No. 8015DC172	Alamance (78CVD1427)	Appeal Dismissed
MARINE RESEARCH v. WAFF BROTHERS No. 7913DC414	Brunswick (75CVD380)	Vacated and Remanded New Trial
MIKEAL v. HAMBY No. 7923DC976	Wilkes (78CVD947)	No Error
MYERS v. MYERS No. 8011DC21	Johnston (79CVD0947)	Dismissed
REED v. MITCHELL No. 7929SC944	Henderson (77CVS458)	Reversed and Remanded
SHARPE v. SHARPE No. 8026DC123	Mecklenburg (78CVD1064)	Affirmed
SMART v. KEZIAH No. 7926DC1077	Mecklenburg (72CVD13164)	Dismissed
STATE v. BIZZELL No. 8011SC214	Johnston (79CR11192)	No Error
STATE v. BLAKENEY No. 7919SC1103	Rowan (79CRS3863)	No Error
STATE v. CLINDING No. 8010SC51	Wake (79CRS35575)	No Error
STATE v. DRAUGHN No. 8026SC217	Mecklenburg (79CRS43218)	No Error
STATE v. EDENS No. 7915SC1133	Alamance (79CRS197) (79CRS198)	No Error
STATE v. FIEDLER No. 8026SC166	Mecklenburg (78CRS136838) (78CRS136839)	Affirmed

STATE v. GEORGE No. 803SC154	Craven (79CRS7237) (79CRS7238)	Appeal Dismissed
STATE v. KING No. 8013SC126	Brunswick (79CRS2137)	No Error
STATE v. McCLAM No. 8021SC112	Forsyth (79CRS29400) (79CRS29401) (79CRS29551)	No Error
STATE v. MITCHELL No. 8017SC116	Stokes (79CR2008)	No Error
STATE v. MURPHY No. 7912SC1108	Hoke (79CRS339)	No Error
STATE v. MURPHY No. 8018SC115	Guilford (79CRS17314)	No Error
STATE v. PACK No. 8017SC62	Stokes (79CR1112)	Appeal Dismissed
STATE v. POWELL No. 8012SC64	Cumberland (78CRS21406)	No Error
STATE v. THOMPSON No. 8016SC135	Robeson (79CR10744) (79CR10745)	No Error
WALKER v. INSURANCE CO. No. 8022DC99	Iredell (79CVD00748)	Dismissed

State v. Cooley

STATE OF NORTH CAROLINA v. CLAUDE VANCE COOLEY

No. 7910SC1057

(Filed 1 July 1980)

1. **Criminal Law § 130 — jury tampering alleged — events not instigated by defendant**

An order of mistrial based upon the provisions of G.S. 15A-1062 would not have been proper in this case, though there was some evidence of jury tampering, since there was no evidence of any connection between defendant or his attorney and the alleged jury tampering, and the possibility or risk that defendant might be the beneficiary of such activity was not sufficient to allow a conclusion that the acts were done at the behest of defendant or his lawyer.

2. **Criminal Law § 130 — misconduct affecting jury — events not instigated by defendant — mistrial proper**

By the enactment of G.S. 15A-1062 and G.S. 15A-1063 the General Assembly did not intend to limit the authority of trial judges to order a mistrial where events not instigated by the defendant or his lawyer have nevertheless colored the proceedings in such a way as to suggest that an impartial trial in accordance with law cannot be had.

3. **Criminal Law § 101; Constitutional Law § 34 — jury tampering alleged — mistrial proper — retrial not denial of constitutional rights**

Where the trial court has reasonable grounds to believe that one or more jurors have been tampered with, it has the constitutional authority, if not the duty, to stop the trial, dismiss the jury, and direct a retrial; in this case testimony by an SBI agent, though hearsay, constituted sufficient basis for the trial court to find that up to three jurors could have been tampered with, and defendant's constitutional rights were not violated where the court declared a mistrial and ordered retrial of defendant.

4. **Conspiracy § 6; Narcotics § 4 — conspiracy to sell contraband — sufficiency of evidence of conspiracy**

In a prosecution for conspiracy to sell controlled substances, evidence was sufficient to establish a conspiracy where it tended to show a close association between defendant and his female coconspirator, defendant's presence during or assistance in telephone conversations during which drug deals were made, and defendant's active participation in various exchanges of drugs for money at which times defendant drove his coconspirator to and from the exchange site or surreptitiously was present at the time several of the exchanges occurred.

APPEAL by defendant from *Braswell and Bailey, Judges.* Order, judgments, and commitments entered 11 April 1979 and 14 June 1979 in Superior Court, WAKE County. Heard in the Court of Appeals 14 April 1980.

Defendant was charged in indictments with twenty-four counts involving the sale, possession with intent to sell, and conspiracy to sell the controlled substances cocaine and BMDA, in violation of the North Carolina Controlled Substances Act, G.S. 90-86 *et seq.* Defendant's first trial commenced at the 2 April 1979 term of court and the State rested its case on 10 April 1979. At the close of the State's evidence the trial court denied defendant's motion to dismiss, but, over defendant's objection, declared a mistrial the following day because of evidence of jury tampering. Upon retrial, the trial court submitted twelve of the indictments for the jury's consideration. Defendant was found not guilty of two of the charges and guilty of the remaining ten. From the order granting the State's motion for a mistrial ending the first trial and the judgments and commitments entered upon the jury's verdict ending the second trial, defendant appeals.

Blanchard, Tucker, Twiggs & Denson, by Irvin B. Tucker, Jr., for the defendant appellant.

Attorney General Rufus L. Edmisten, by Assistant Attorney General Jo Anne Sanford, for the State.

WELLS, Judge.

I. *THE MISTRIAL*

Defendant first assigns as error the action and procedure of the trial court in granting a mistrial. In pertinent part G.S. 15A-1062 provides as follows:

§ 15A-1062. Mistrial for prejudice to the State. — Upon motion of the State, the judge may declare a mistrial if there occurs during the trial, either inside or outside the courtroom, misconduct resulting in substantial and irreparable prejudice to the State's case and the misconduct was by a juror or the defendant, his lawyer, or someone acting at the behest of the defendant or his lawyer ...

Under G.S. 15A-1063:

§ 15A-1063. Mistrial for impossibility of proceeding. —
Upon motion of a party or upon his own motion, a judge may
declare a mistrial if:
> (1) It is impossible for the trial to proceed in conformi-
> ty with law; or
>
> (2) It appears there is no reasonable probability of the
> jury's agreement upon a verdict.

Defendant argues that G.S. 15A-1062 is inapplicable to this
case because the record is devoid of evidence that any alleged
jury tampering occurred "at the behest of the defendant or his
lawyer." The interpretation of this phrase is a question of first
impression before the appellate courts of our State. The word
"behest" has been defined as a "command", "strong often authoritative request", "demand" or "urgent prompting". WEB-
STER'S THIRD INTERNATIONAL DICTIONARY 199 (1967).

After a hearing on the State's motion for a mistrial, the
trial court found, *inter alia*, that:

> 10. SBI Agent Joe Momier testified in substance that
> at approximately 6:55 p.m. on the evening of 10 April 1979,
> that Special SBI Agent J.T. Hawthorne participated in a
> meeting which took place near the intersection of Anson
> and Poole Roads in Raleigh, and in the vicinity of Keith's
> Grocerteria; this meeting took place as part of a special
> investigation which had been requested by the under-
> signed presiding judge. Mr. Momier testified that at the
> conclusion of his meeting he interviewed Mr. Hawthorne
> relative to the events which had just transpired. Based on
> that interview Mr. Momier stated the events as follows: A
> white over blue motor vehicle, Pontiac, approached Mr.
> Hawthorne's location in the vicinity of the Keith's
> Grocerteria, and a white female, later identified as Dorothy
> Tharrington Holden, approached Mr. Hawthorne and
> asked him, quote, Are you Billy Gay, close quote; Mr.
> Hawthorne replied, quote, I'm Billy, close quote; there was
> a discussion between them; they talked about money; the
> woman offered five hundred dollars for a "no vote" and the
> woman, now identified later by arrest as Dorothy Thar-

rington Holden, did thereupon pay five hundred dollars in cash money to J.T. Hawthorne, believing at that time that he was Juror Billy Gay, which money was to buy a "no vote" from Billy Gay in the trial at hand; conversation continued and Dorothy Holden assured Mr. Hawthorne that he was not the only juror who would be voting no, indicating others who were paid were a black male on the jury, and she alluded to a female having been paid; Dorothy Holden indicated that they were using their own money but that they were to be reimbursed and that, quote, he, close quote, had already reimbursed them for monies they had paid and spent for this in the past.

The court took judicial notice that the defendant on trial is a male person. Conversation also included references to a telephone call to Billy Gay at an earlier time in the trial, but Mr. Hawthorne denied having received such a call. Dorothy Holden also referred to the activity which was then taking place between herself and Mr. Hawthorne as a very serious matter, jury tampering. A white male, later identified as Rufus Wade Holden, Sr., was in the above described Pontiac and was observed by Mr. Hawthorne to hand Dorothy Holden what appeared to be cash before Dorothy Holden delivered the five hundred dollars to Mr. Hawthorne and after they had agreed upon that price. When Rufus Holden was later arrested, shortly thereafter, he was found to have had an additional sum of one thousand two dollars in cash on his person.

11. From his own experience, participation and observation, Mr. Momier testified that six SBI Agents maintained surveillance on this meeting and observed the two Holden subjects to enter their Pontiac and leave the area of the meeting with Mr. Hawthorne, and that the Holdens went to the area of Longview Shopping Center where the Holdens were detained and each were [sic] placed under arrest.

12. Formal criminal charges were placed against Dorothy Tharrington Holden and Rufus Wade Holden, Sr., as shown in criminal warrants in court's Exhibits 2

through 8, inclusive, which exhibits were introduced by the State.

Our examination of the record reveals these findings to be supported by the evidence. The court concluded that the jury tampering was attempted "in favor of" and for the "benefit" of the defendant, who "would have been the direct and only beneficiary" of such a scheme.

[1] The statute, G.S. 15A-1062, is based almost verbatim on Rule 541(b) of the Uniform Rules of Criminal Procedure, [1] which was in turn derived from the Idaho and New York rules. [2]

---

[1]   Rule 541 of the Uniform Rules of Criminal Procedure provides:

* * *

(b) For prejudice to State. Upon motion of the State, the court may declare a mistrial if there occurs during the trial, either inside or outside the courtroom, misconduct by the defendant, his lawyer, or someone acting at the behest of the defendant or his lawyer, resulting in substantial and irreparable prejudice to the State's case . . . .

[2]   Rule 29.1 of the Idaho Rules of Criminal Procedure states:

Motion for mistrial. — At any time during a trial, the court may declare a mistrial and order a new trial of the indictment, information or complaint under the following circumstances:

* * *

(b) Upon motion of the state, when there occurs during the trial, either inside or outside the courtroom, misconduct by the defendant, his attorney or attorneys, or some other person acting on his behalf resulting in substantial prejudice to the state's case. . . .

(c) Upon motion of either party or upon the court's own motion, when it is impossible to proceed with the trial in conformity with law.

Section 280.10 of the New York Law of Criminal Procedure provides:

Motion for mistrial. At any time during the trial, the court must declare a mistrial and order a new trial of the indictment under the following circumstances:

* * *

2. Upon motion of the people, when there occurs during the trial, either inside or outside the courtroom, gross misconduct by the defendant or some person acting on his behalf, or by a juror, resulting in substantial and irreparable prejudice to the people's case . . . .

3. Upon motion of either party or upon the court's own motion, when it is physically impossible to proceed with the trial in conformity with law.

Official Commentary to Rule 541(b), Uniform Rules of Criminal Procedure (1974).[3] We believe that the restrictive wording of G.S. 15A-1062 renders the statute inapplicable to this case.[4]

Clearly, the word "behest", implies, at the minimum, that there necessarily be some sort of action or conduct on the part of the defendant or his attorney inducing or prompting the alleged misconduct. There was no evidence here of any connection between the defendant or his attorney and the alleged jury tampering activities of the Holdens. The possibility — or risk — that the defendant might be the beneficiary of such activity is not sufficient to allow us to conclude that these acts were done at the behest of the defendant or his lawyer, and we therefore conclude that an order of mistrial based upon the provisions of G.S. 15A-1062 would not have been proper in this case.

Defendant also argues that the trial court lacked authority to order a mistrial under G.S. 15A-1063(1) for impossibility of proceeding in conformity with law. The trial court concluded that, "in the opinion of this court it is impossible to proceed with the trial of the defendant, Claude Vance Cooley, in conformity with the law" and that it is necessary that a mistrial be de-

---

[3] It is interesting to note that the Idaho and New York rules upon which the Uniform Rule was based both permit the court to declare a mistrial when the misconduct which resulted in substantial and irreparable prejudice to the State was caused by persons merely acting on the defendant's *behalf.* Presumably, under these statutes no prompting need be shown on the part of the defendant or his attorney which induced other persons to engage in the misconduct.

[4] Professor Billings has suggested that the North Carolina rule was adopted soon after the opinion handed down by the Supreme Court of the United States in *United States v. Jorn,* 400 U.S. 470, 27 L.Ed. 2d 543, 91 S.Ct. 547 (1971), which purported to limit severely a court's authority to retry a defendant after a mistrial to which the defendant had objected or refused to consent. However, from the Court's subsequent opinions it became evident that such severe restrictions would not be applied. The result has been that North Carolina has codified a rule more restrictive than that previously imposed on a constitutional basis by the Supreme Court of the United States or the courts of our State. Billings, *Contempt, Order in the Courtroom, Mistrials,* 14 WAKE FOREST L.REV. 909, 948 (1978). Of course, we are bound to follow the policy decisions of our Legislature where they afford greater rights to the accused than those provided by our Constitution.

clared "to attain the ends of justice and the integrity of any
ultimate jury verdict, regardless of whatever the verdict might
be."

There is little question that G.S. 15A-1063(1) was intended
to continue the North Carolina practice of allowing a mistrial
when it becomes physically necessary to do so. The Official
Commentary to G.S. 15A-1063 provides:

* * *

If the prejudice were so total as to make it "impossible" for
the trial to proceed "in conformity with law," then either
party or the judge on his own motion could trigger the
mistrial under subdivision (1) of this section — provided
this would be constitutional.

In its deliberations the Commission was furnished the
following draftman's comment with this section: ... *(This
subparagraph gives) the judge as broad and flexible a power
as possible in impossibility cases consistent with the constitutional rulings concerning former jeopardy."* [Emphasis
added.]

See also, Billings, *Contempt, Order in the Courtroom, Mistrials,*
14 WAKE FOREST L. REV. 909 (1978). Physical impossibility of
trial has been held to occur in North Carolia in situations such
as where a juror became intoxicated, *State v. Tyson,* 138 N.C.
627, 50 S.E. 456 (1905); insane, *State v. Beal,* 199 N.C. 278, 154
S.E. 604 (1930); or ill, *State v. Ledbetter,* 4 N.C. App. 303, 167 S.E.
2d 68 (1969); or upon the illness or incapacity of the judge, *State
v. Boykin,* 255 N.C. 432, 121 S.E. 2d 863 (1961); or codefendant,
State v. Battle, 267 N.C. 513, 148 S.E. 2d '599 (1966).

Prior to the enactment of G.S. 15A-1063 (effective 1 July
1978), our courts had approved the granting of a mistrial, over a
defendant's objection, for "the necessity of doing justice." *State
v. Shuler,* 293 N.C. 34, 235 S.E. 2d 226 (1977). In *Shuler* our
Supreme Court held that the trial court properly granted the
State's motion for a mistrial where a law enforcement officer
had commented in the presence of the jury that the State's case

State v. Cooley

was weak. The rule has never permitted the granting of a mistrial simply upon a whim or at the trial court's unbridled discretion, but has carefully limited the circumstances when it is permissible. Justice (later Chief Justice) Bobbitt has explained:

> It will be observed that "the necessity of doing justice" is not an expression connoting a vague generality but one that relates to a limited subject, namely, the occurrence of some incident of a nature that would render impossible a fair and impartial trial *under the law.* [Emphasis added.]

State v. Crocker, 239 N.C. 446, 450, 80 S.E. 2d 243, 246 (1954). The Court, quoting from *State v. Wiseman,* 68 N.C. 203, 206 (1873), a jury tampering case, stated that the necessity of doing justice, "arises from the duty of the court to 'guard the administration of justice from fraudulent practices; as in the case of tampering with the jury, or keeping back the witnesses on the part of the prosecution.' " *Id.* Thus, when jury tampering has occurred, a case may no longer proceed "in accordance with law."

[2] The question then becomes whether by the enactment of G.S. 15A-1062 and G.S. 15A-1063 the General Assembly intended to limit the authority of trial judges to order a mistrial where events not instigated by the defendant or his lawyer have nevertheless colored the proceedings in such a way as to suggest that an impartial trial in accordance with law could not be had. Professor Billings has commented that since there was no evidence in *Shuler* that the deputy sheriff who made his comment to a juror had done so at the behest of the defendant or his lawyer, a trial court acting on this set of facts could not now declare a mistrial under G.S. 15A-1062. Billings, *Contempt, Order in the Courtroom, Mistrials,* 14 WAKE FOREST L. REV. 909, 945 (1978). However, we do not understand this argument to preclude a court from granting a mistrial on these facts under G.S. 15A-1063(1), where it could reasonably conclude that a fair and impartial trial in accordance with law could not be had. As we view the language of these sections, the draftman's comments, and the prior case law of this State, we do not believe the General Assembly intended to so limit the authority of trial judges to require that jury trials in criminal cases be free of

improper influence. We believe the General Assembly intended to permit trial judges to grant mistrials in cases such as the one *sub judice* under G.S. 15A-1063(1), if constitutionally allowable.

[3] We next address the question of the constitutionality of retrying the defendant after the trial court's action granting a mistrial in the earlier proceedings. We recognize that the Double Jeopardy Clause of the Fifth Amendment[5] precludes retrial of a defendant in some circumstances where the proceedings are terminated prior to judgment.[6] *Arizona v. Washington*, 434 U.S. 497, 54 L.Ed. 2d 717, 98 S.Ct. 824 (1978). The interest of the accused which is protected in such cases is his right to retain a given tribunal. *Crist v. Bretz*, 437 U.S. 28, 57 L.Ed. 2d 24, 98 S.Ct. 2156 (1978); In the Matter of Hunt and In the Matter of Dowd, 46 N.C. App. 732, 266 S.E. 2d 385 1980.

Other circumstances, however, may control. A defendant's "valued right to have the trial concluded by a particular tribunal is sometimes subordinate to the public interest in affording the prosecutor one full and fair opportunity to present his evidence to an impartial jury." *Arizona v. Washington, supra*, 434 U.S. at 505, 54 L.Ed. 2d at 728, 98 S.Ct. at 830. *Accord, Illinois v. Somerville*, 410 U.S. 458, 35 L.Ed. 2d 425, 93 S.Ct. 1066 (1973). In *Washington*, the trial court had granted a mistrial on grounds of prejudicial remarks made by the defendant's attorney during his opening statement. The Court stated that when the prosecution seeks a mistrial, it has the burden of showing a high degree of necessity, although the trial court's decision to declare a mistrial is entitled to substantial deference. *Accord, Gori v. United States*, 367 U.S. 364, 6 L.Ed. 2d 901, 81 S.Ct. 1523 (1961). The Court in *Washington* commented that, "[n]either

---

[5] The Law of the Land Clause of the North Carolina Constitution, N.C. Const. art. 1, § 19, has also been held to embrace the Double Jeopardy Clause of the Fifth Amendment to the United States Constitution. *State v. Cameron*, 283 N.C. 191, 195 S.E. 2d 481 (1973).

[6] This principle represents a departure from the English and early American practice in which the bar of double jeopardy could only be asserted on the basis of an actual verdict of acquittal or conviction. *See, Crist v. Bretz*, 437 U.S. 28, 57 L.Ed. 2d 24, 98 S.Ct. 2156 (1978) (Powell, J., dissenting).

party has a right to have his case decided by a jury which may be tainted by bias . . . ." 434 U.S. at 516, 54 L.Ed. 2d at 734-735, 98 S.Ct. at 835-836. In quoting from *United States v. Morris*, 26 F. Cas. 1323, 1328 (C.C. Mass. 1851) (No. 15815), the Court held that "neither party 'can have a vested right to a corrupt or prejudiced juror, who is not fit to sit in judgment in the case.' " *Id.*, n. 36, 434 U.S. at 516, 54 L.Ed. 2d at 735, 98 S.Ct. at 836. Similarly, in *Illinois v. Somerville, supra,* 410 U.S. at 470, 35 L.Ed. 2d at 434, 93 S.Ct. at 1073 the Court, quoting from *Wade v. Hunter*, 336 U.S. 684, 689, 93 L.Ed. 974, 978, 69 S.Ct. 834, 837 (1949), stated:

> [T]here have been instances where a trial judge has discovered facts during a trial which indicated that one or more members of the jury might be biased against the Government or the defendant. It is settled that the duty of the judge in this event is to discharge the jury and to direct a retrial.

Accord, State v. Shuler, 293 N.C. 34, 235 S.E. 2d 226 (1977). We believe the law is clear that where the trial court has reasonable grounds to believe that one or more jurors have been tampered with, it has the constitutional authority, if not the duty, to stop the trial, dismiss the jury, and direct a retrial.

Defendant argues that his rights to due process of law, confrontation of witnesses, and the effective assistance of counsel were violated by the manner in which the trial court conducted its investigation to determine whether there had been attempts made on behalf of the defendant to bribe jurors. We do not agree. In open court the parties stipulated that after the State had rested its case during the first trial the following events occurred:

> 1. That at the close of court on April 10th, 1979, the judge requested all counsel to meet him in his chambers at 8:30 a.m. on April 11, 1979.

> 2. That shortly before the meeting in chambers on April 11th, 1979, the judge had a brief conference with Assistant District Attorney Jack Hall and SBI Agents Joe Momier and Terry Turbeville.

3. That at or about 8:30 a.m. the judge called all counsel into chambers. Present were Judge E. Maurice Braswell, Assistant District Attorneys Jack Hall and Narley Cashwell, Defense Counsel Irvin B. Tucker, Jr., and W.G. Ransdell, Jr., SBI Agents Joe Momier and Terry Turbeville.

4. That at the conference in chambers Judge Braswell initially advised defense counsel that there was evidence that one and maybe as many as three jurors may have been contacted about voting not guilty in the cases on trial and that it looked like (*sic*) we are probably in a mistrial situation.

5. Defense counsel requested to be advised of the nature of the evidence and pursuant to the judge's request, Jack Hall and Joe Momier disclosed the events that had occurred the prior evening involving a meeting between SBI Agent J.T. Hawthorne and one Dorothy Holden, and others, which events Joe Momier later testified to in court. The defense counsel were not furnished any evidence concerning alleged jury tampering, other than that later testified to in court by Mr. Joe Momier.

6. That the judge and Mr. Hall stated that there was other evidence concerning alleged jury tampering that was not and would not be disclosed because the investigation was ongoing and such disclosure might jeopardize that investigation.

7. That defense counsel advised all present that they had no knowledge of or information about any attempt to tamper with any juror.

8. At the opening of court the State made a motion for mistrial pursuant to 15A-1062 and called Joe Momier in support of that motion. That defense counsel, while cross examining Mr. Momier, asked him the following questions, quote, "Well, do you have any other evidence of contact with any jurors on this case other than what you've — testified

to?" Before the witness answered the question the judge asked counsel to come to the bench, par 9.

9. Before the witness answered the question the judge asked counsel to come to the bench. At the bench conference the judge advised counsel that he would not require the witness to answer the question because the investigation was ongoing and the disclosure might jeopardize the investigation. Defense counsel responded that they were completely in the dark as to what the evidence of jury tampering might be and that they considered it necessary to make a record of that evidence.

10. The Judge then requested that all counsel meet him in his chambers and when in chambers the judge repeated that he would not require the witness to answer the questions because the investigation was ongoing and repeated again that there was evidence which would not be disclosed to defense counsel because such disclosure could jeopardize the investigation. Defense counsel repeated their feeling of a need to make a reviewable record and discussed with those present — the presiding judge, Mr. John T. Hall and Mr. Narley Cashwell of the District Attorney's Office — any alternative ways of making a record that would not jeopardize the ongoing investigation. No way was found to preserve in the court records that information which the investigators had concerning possible jury tampering or attempted jury tampering without such preservation jeopardizing the ongoing investigation and defense counsel withdrew the question to Mr. Momier.

The parties also stipulated that at the time the trial court ruled on the State's motion for a mistrial, he did not have before him the transcript of interviews with the jurors, in which all of the jurors stated that they had not been contacted or bribed.

We hold that the previously quoted testimony of Agent Momier constitutes a sufficient basis for the trial court to have found that up to three jurors could have been tampered with in this case. Momier stated that Agent Hawthorne had been given $500 for a "no vote" by persons later identified as Dorothy and

Rufus Holden, who believed Hawthorne to be juror Billy Gay. According to Momier, Hawthorne was told by the Holdens that he would not be the only person voting in the negative, indicating that a black male and a female had also been paid. The Holdens were later arrested for jury tampering.[7]

We further hold that as long as a reasonable basis appeared in the record for the court's reliance on Agent Momier's testimony, it is not significant that *in this hearing on the State's motion for a mistrial*, the testimony pertaining to what Agent Hawthorne[8] said was hearsay and may have been inadmissible at trial. This testimony was given in the presence of defense counsel, who was allowed to cross-examine the witness.[9] Here, we are dealing with the testimony of an agent of the State Bureau of Investigation as to what he was told to be the personal observation of another named SBI agent. We cannot say that the trial court's reliance upon this detailed testimony was unreasonable, especially in light of the substantial deference which we must afford a trial court's decision declaring a mistrial on grounds of possible jury bias. *Arizona v. Washington*, 434 U.S. 497, 54 L.Ed. 2d 717, 98 S.Ct. 824 (1978); *State v. Shuler*, 293 N.C. 34, 235 S.E. 2d 226 (1977). Nor do we believe that it was error for the trial court to have ruled on the motion prior to

---

[7] The fact that arrest warrants were issued against the Holdens also lends credence to the reasonableness of the court's belief that jury tampering may have occurred. An arrest warrant may only be issued by a judicial official upon a showing of probable cause. G.S. 15A-304(d); *State v. Harvey*,281 N.C. 1, 187 S.E. 2d 706 (1972).

[8] The record shows only that Agent Hawthorne was not available to attend the hearing.

[9] The defendant argues that its questioning of Agent Momier was inhibited by statements made by the trial court that such questioning might jeopardize the ongoing investigation into the alleged jury tampering, which was proceeding at that time. We do not understand the trial court to have done any more than caution the defendant's counsel about the investigation. At no point did the court decline to allow defendant's attorney to ask any question. The testimony of Agent Momier, given in the presence of defendant's counsel and subject to their cross-examination, was the basis for the court's findings of fact. Clearly then; this information was not adduced during a prohibited ex parte investigation, as alleged by defendant. *See, State v. Crocker*, 239 N.C. 446, 80 S.E. 2d 243 (1954).

having considered the testimony of the jurors. It could hardly be expected that jurors who may have accepted payoffs would have freely disclosed such circumstances. For this reason, their testimony was far from conclusive, and would have been of only limited value to the court. [10]

II. *THE TRIAL*

Defendant was originally charged in indictments with twenty-four counts. Two of these counts related to the conspiracy to sell BMDA and cocaine with Teresa Ray, Brenda Johnson, C.J. Overton and C.R. Kimrey. Sixteen counts concerned the sale or possession with intent to sell or deliver cocaine or BMDA through Brenda Johnson. Six counts related to the sale or possession with intent to sell or deliver cocaine or BMDA through Teresa Ray. The trial court submitted to the jury only the eighteen counts concerning the conspiracy, sale, or possession with intent to sell involving Brenda Johnson. The jury determined that defendant was not guilty of two counts pertaining to the sale and possession with intent to sell BMDA on 30 August 1978. The jury found defendant guilty of all the remaining charges. There was no evidence that any drugs were at any time in the actual possession of defendant. Defendant does not maintain that there was insufficient evidence of Brenda Johnson's possession or sale of the drugs on the dates alleged in the indictments. Rather, it is defendant's position that the State failed to show through evidence aliunde that defendant was involved in a conspiracy with her. The defendant argues that he

[10] The situation here is clearly distinguishable from that present in *United States v. Jorn*, 400 U.S. 470, 27 L.Ed. 2d 543, 91 S.Ct. 547 (1971), cited by the defendant. In *Jorn* the trial judge ordered a mistrial when he decided that some of the government's witnesses who might incriminate themselves should not be permitted to testify until they had been counselled by attorneys. The Supreme Court held that there was no necessity for a mistrial because of the availability of a continuance. Thus, in *Jorn*, the reason the trial court's failure to consider a continuance was held to be determinative was that such a continuance would have cured the problem — the witnesses could have consulted counsel. In the present case, however, the juror's testimony which could have been procured during a continuance would, as stated previously, have been of questionable value. Additionally, once the jurors had been questioned about having received bribes, the probability was increased that they became tainted against the accused.

therefore cannot be held to have constructively possessed or sold any of the drugs so possessed and delivered by Johnson, and that his motion to dismiss at the close of the State's evidence should have been allowed.

A conspirator is liable for all of the unlawful acts of his coconspirators committed in furtherance of the conspiracy regardless of whether he was present at the time such illegal acts were committed. *State v. Grier*, 30 N.C. App. 281, 227 S.E. 2d 126 (1976), *cert. denied*, 291 N.C. 177, 229 S.E. 2d 691 (1976). However, before the acts or declarations of coconspirators may be considered as evidence against the conspirator there must be a showing, through evidence independent of the coconspirators' acts or declarations, that a conspiracy existed, that the acts or declarations were made by a party to it in pursuance of its objectives, and that the acts or statements were made while the conspiracy was active. *State v. Tilley*, 292 N.C. 132, 232 S.E. 2d 433 (1977). Independent proof of the existence of a conspiracy may be provided solely by circumstantial evidence. *State v. Horton*, 275 N.C. 651, 170 S.E. 2d 466 (1969), *cert. denied*, 398 U.S. 959, 26 L.Ed. 2d 545, 90 S.Ct. 2175 (1970), *rehearing denied*, 400 U.S. 857, 27 L.Ed. 2d 97, 91 S.Ct. 25 (1970). In the great majority of conspiracies circumstantial evidence is the only mode of proof available. *State v. Smith*, 237 N.C. 1, 74 S.E. 2d 291 (1953).

> Direct proof of the charge is not essential, for such is rarely obtainable. It may be, and generally is, established by a number of indefinite acts, each of which, standing alone, might have little weight, but, taken collectively, they point unerringly to the existence of a conspiracy. [Citation omitted.]

State v. Whiteside, 204 N.C. 710, 712, 169 S.E. 711, 712 (1933); *accord, State v. Grier, supra*. The State's theory of the case is that the defendant's knowledge of and participation in the conspiracy has been shown through circumstantial evidence.

[4] Upon motion for a nonsuit in a criminal action, the court must consider the evidence in the light most favorable to the State, and resolve all contradictions and discrepancies in its favor, giving it the benefit of every reasonable inference which

can be drawn from the evidence. *State v. Abernathy*, 295 N.C. 147, 244 S.E. 2d 373 (1978). In the present case it is undisputed that defendant and Brenda Johnson lived close to one another and were lovers. The record is replete with conversations and transactions which occurred between Johnson and undercover agents Kimrey and Overton of the State Bureau of Investigation involving the purchase of pills and cocaine. The record contains evidence that a conspiracy to sell cocaine and BMDA existed between Johnson and defendant as early as 10 September 1978. On this date Agent Kimrey had a telephone conversation with Johnson during which the sale of pills and cocaine was discussed. Agent Kimrey asked Johnson when she had tried to contact her, and Johnson asked someone in close proximity to her, "Uh, C.V., when did I — what day was it I called that girl to see if she wanted any more of those pills?" Agent Kimrey said that later during the conversation she heard a male voice in the background and Johnson stated, "He just said, you know, if you want it you could pay [for the drugs] with a check or cash." On two occasions during the conversation Johnson used the initials C.V., those of the defendant. These statements are not hearsay and are thus admissible against defendant because they are offered merely to show the presence of the defendant, not to prove the truth of what the matter stated. *State v. Greene*, 30 N.C. App. 507, 227 S.E. 2d 154 (1976); 1 Stansbury's N.C. Evidence § 141, p. 467 (Brandis rev. 1973). Johnson frequently referred to her boyfriend as "C.V."

Independently of the above statements there was sufficient evidence linking defendant to the conspiracy. On 18 September 1978 Agent Kimrey and Brenda Johnson arranged to meet in the restroom of a Raleigh lounge for the purchase of $2,000 worth of cocaine. Johnson was driven by defendant on a motorcycle to the lounge. Two minutes after Johnson entered the lounge, defendant entered. After the sale occurred, defendant and Johnson left the lounge and rode away on the motorcycle. On 2 October 1978 Agents Kimrey and Overton again agreed with Johnson to a sale of BMDA and cocaine. The exchange was to occur at a shopping center parking lot in Raleigh. A car driven by defendant entered the shopping center and parked. Then a vehicle driven by Johnson entered the parking lot, and the sale was completed. Johnson drove her vehicle out of the parking lot, and defendant drove off. Again on 6 October 1978 another drug purchase was arranged between the SBI agents and Johnson at a shopping center parking lot in Raleigh. This time defendant and Johnson drove to the center together. Both exited defendant's vehicle, defendant walking into a fast-food restaurant and Johnson entering the undercover vehicle. Five minutes later defendant left the parking lot. Johnson drove in the undercover vehicle with the agents to another shopping center at which her car was located, and the sale occurred there.

We hold that in this testimony there is sufficient independent evidence from which a jury could reasonably infer that defendant and Brenda Johnson conspired to sell controlled substances. The instant case is similar to *State v. Abernathy*, 295 N.C. 147, 244 S.E. 2d 373 (1978), in which the only evidence against one of the accused coconspirators was testimony showing circumstances from which it could be inferred that he knew of his codefendants' plans to rob a certain residence and that he assisted in the robbery by driving the other defendants to and from the scene of the crime. *Accord, State v. Covington*, 290 N.C. 313, 226 S.E. 2d 629 (1976). In the present action the State's case against defendant rests, in essence, on the close association between defendant and Brenda Johnson, defendant's presence during or assistance in telephone conversations during which drug deals were made, and his active participation in various exchanges of drugs for money at which times he drove Brenda Johnson to and from the exchange site or surreptitiously was present at the time several of the exchanges occurred.[11]

Since we have found that the independent evidence established a *prima facie* case of conspiracy, all of the evidence of Brenda Johnson's actions and statements in furtherance of the conspiracy which occurred during the conspiracy were properly

---

[11]   This evidence of a close and personal involvement of the defendant in Johnson's drug dealings distinguishes the present action from the cases cited by defendant, *e.g., State v. Carey*, 285 N.C. 497, 206 S.E. 2d 213 (1974); *State v. Benson*, 234 N.C. 263, 66 S.E. 2d 893 (1951); *United States v. Gutierrez*, 559 F. 2d 1278 (5th Cir. 1977). Of course, insofar as the Federal cases cited by defendant are not constitutionally based, they are not authoritative on the North Carolina law of conspiracy.

admitted against the defendant by the trial court. *State v. Miley*, 291 N.C. 431, 230 S.E. 2d 537 (1976); *State v. Covington, supra.* Accordingly, the trial court properly submitted the remaining charges pending against the defendant to the jury. We have examined defendant's other assignments of error and have found them to be without merit.

No error.

Chief Judge MORRIS and Judge PARKER concur.

L. JUNE HANKS AND HOBART BOBBITT, D/B/A STOP & SHOP v.
NATIONWIDE MUTUAL FIRE INSURANCE COMPANY

No. 7917SC989

(Filed 1 July 1980)

1. **Insurance § 136– action on fire policy – evidence of prior fire loss by insured – harmless error**

    In an action to recover under a fire insurance policy, error, if any, in the admission of testimony concerning a prior fire loss to property owned by plaintiff in Virginia was harmless where the testimony was admitted on the issue of whether plaintiff burned or procured the burning of the insured property and such issue was answered in plaintiff's favor.

2. **Trial § 16– jury's examination of excluded exhibit – instruction not to consider – absence of prejudice**

    Plaintiff was not prejudiced by the fact that the jury examined a defense exhibit after the court had excluded the exhibit where the court promptly instructed the jury to disregard the exhibit.

3. **Insurance § 136– action on fire policy – issue as to fraudulent misrepresentation of extent of loss**

    In an action to recover under a policy of fire insurance, the trial court properly submitted to the jury an issue as to whether plaintiff intentionally misrepresented the extent of her fire loss for the purpose of defrauding defendant insurer.

4. **Insurance § 136– action on fire policy – instructions – application of law to evidence**

    In an action to recover under a policy of fire insurance, the trial court did not fail to declare and explain the law arising on the evidence by failing to review her evidence in greater detail to point out the "great disparity" between plaintiff's evidence and that of defendant, and the court sufficiently explained to the jury what facts it would have to find to establish a fraudulent misrepresentation as to the extent of the loss.

APPEAL by plaintiff from *Long, Judge.* Judgment entered 2 August 1979 in Superior Court, SURRY County. Heard in the Court of Appeals 16 April 1980.

On 18 November 1977, plaintiffs (hereinafter Ms. Hanks and Bobbitt), operators of a retail grocery store known as Stop and Shop, filed a complaint against defendant (hereinafter Nationwide). Plaintiffs alleged that on 25 February 1977, they contracted with Douglas Anderson, an agent of Nationwide, for the issuance of a fire insurance policy in the sum of $40,000; that the policy covered the merchandise, furniture, and fixtures in the store; that on 14 May 1977, a fire destroyed the insured items; that Ms. Hanks promptly notified Nationwide and submitted a proof of loss on 17 June 1977; that she claimed a loss of $25,996.55; and that Nationwide has refused to pay the claim.

In its answer, Nationwide admitted that the fire destroyed some of the insured items and that Ms. Hanks submitted a proof of loss. Nationwide alleged as defenses that the fire was intentionally set by or at the behest of plaintiffs with the intent to defraud Nationwide; that plaintiffs violated the provisions of the policy by increasing the hazards of the fire and by misrepresenting and concealing material facts pertaining to the extent of the loss claimed and the manner in which the fire occurred; and that at the time the policy was issued, Nationwide was not advised as to the true identity of the co-owners of the store.

In their reply, plaintiffs alleged that prior to the issuance of the policy, Anderson was advised that Ms. Hanks and Bobbitt were co-partners and that both would be active in the business.

At the close of plaintiffs' evidence, the court allowed them to amend their complaint to allege damages of $35,000. The court directed a verdict against Bobbitt, since he was not a named insured in the policies. The jury answered the second issue against plaintiff, and she appealed.

Gardner, Gardner, Johnson & Etringer, by John C.W. Gardner, for plaintiff appellant.

Hudson, Petree, Stockton, Stockton & Robinson, by W.

Thompson Comerford, Jr. and Grover G. Wilson, for defendant appellee.

ERWIN, Judge.

Plaintiff's Evidence

Ms. Hanks testified that on 21 December 1976, she and her brother, Bobbitt, bought all the stock and fixtures of Stop and Shop from Jimmy Akers for $10,000 in cash, although the bill of sale showed a purchase price of $8,500. No inventory was taken of the stock at the time of the sale. After the purchase, Bobbitt invested $7,000 in merchandise for the store. The building and land for the store were leased by plaintiffs.

After the purchase, Anderson tried to sell plaintiffs $50,000 to $60,000 worth of fire insurance on the store. Ms. Hanks finally purchased a $25,000 policy and upped the coverage to $40,000 at the insistence of Anderson, who was told by Ms. Hanks that Bobbitt was a partner. The policies were issued only in Ms. Hanks' name. From late December 1976 until the day of the fire on 14 May 1977, plaintiffs painted the interior and exterior of the building, repaired the bathrooms, and took as little money out of the business as possible. On the morning of 14 May 1977, Ms. Hanks was notified of the fire by the Sheriff's Department. Later in the morning, she notified Anderson. Mr. Gibbs, a claims adjuster with Nationwide, told her to take an inventory of the merchandise and to leave everything alone until after his investigation. Several days after the fire, the Health Department notified plaintiffs and ordered them to remove the goods. Thereafter, plaintiffs inventoried the goods and then removed them to a landfill. After the inventory, Ms. Hanks prepared the proof of loss form showing $25,000 as her loss and mailed it to Gibbs. Ms. Hanks testified that, in her opinion, the fair market value of the goods, merchandise, fixtures, and equipment in the store on 13 May 1977 was $30,000 to $35,000.

On cross-examination, Ms. Hanks testified that there was only one key to the store; that the shelves were stocked at the time of the fire; that they sold beer, wine, groceries, kerosene, and gasoline; and that at the scene of the fire, the fire marshal told her that he thought the fire had originated around the switch box.

Bobbitt testified that on the night before the fire, he closed the store at 11:00 p.m.; that he cut the gasoline and kerosene pumps off and locked the door; that he was notified of the fire; that the North Carolina Department of Agriculture ordered plaintiffs to destroy all foods, drugs, and cosmetics damaged by the fire; and that he estimated the value of the damaged coolers and other equipment and inventory by checking with other stores.

Fletcher Joyce testified that he lived about 100 yards from the store; that prior to the fire, he frequented the store; that after plaintiffs purchased the store, the stock and appearance of the store were ten times better than before; that he helped plaintiffs take the inventory to the landfill after the fire; and that, in his opinion, the coolers in the store were of no value.

Nationwide's Evidence

Paul Gibbs, claims adjuster of Nationwide, testified that he was notified of the fire on 16 May 1977; that he met Ms. Hanks on the following day and took photographs of the fire scene; that he was amazed at the apparent lack of inventory in the store; and that he returned to the store later and took more photographs. The inventory had been removed. However, the photographs taken indicated where items were shelved by the lack of soot.

Jimmy Atkins, the Surry County Fire Marshal on the date of the fire, testified that he and other firemen arrived at the scene of the fire and detected a heavy odor of kerosene; that he found no evidence of malfunction in the fuse box; and that the store appeared to be fifty percent stocked.

Larry Ford, a forensic chemist, testified that he tested four samples of debris taken from the store and that all four samples showed evidence of kerosene.

Joe Farrell, a salvor, testified that in May 1977, he was

contacted by Nationwide to inspect the store. When he inspected the store on 23 May 1977, the inventory had been removed. From his examination of the premises and the photographs taken by Gibbs, he was able to accurately identify fifteen different items in the store and their approximate value. He concluded that their fair market value was $1,903.92.

Mitchell Armeen, an appraiser of grocery store inventories, testified that on 7 July 1977, Nationwide retained him to inspect the store; that on this date, he made an inventory of the equipment and fixtures; that he concluded that their fair market value prior to the fire was $5,140; and that after the fire, their salvage value was roughly $800.

Paul McGraw, a contractor dealing in rebuilding burnouts, testified that he examined the store's fixtures in June 1977 at Nationwide's request. In his opinion, $450 would be the cost of cleaning and painting the fixtures. McGraw admitted that he did not examine the interior damages of the major fixtures nor the wiring system.

David Farris testified that on the date of the fire, he was living next to the store. On the evening before the fire, he saw two people loading several boxes into two cars parked in front of the store. He did not recognize either the cars or the people.

Jimmy Akers testified that when he sold the store to plaintiffs, he received only $8,500 consideration. The stock at the time was valued at $3,500.

Henry Huff testified that prior to the fire, Ms. Hanks told him that their (Ms. Hanks' and Bobbitt's) purpose for buying the store was to obtain a large insurance policy and then burn the store. He also heard Ms. Hanks talk about financial problems she was having between December 1976 and May 1977. Ms. Hanks further told him that in 1975, she hired two men to burn an insured house owned by her. Huff testified that he had been romantically involved with Ms. Hanks' sister for fourteen years; that he does not get along well with Ms. Hanks; that he is presently serving time for assault with intent to kill Ms. Hanks' brother-in-law; that he has been convicted of attempted murder of Ms. Hanks and her sister; and that he has been arrested twenty-eight times. He further testified that on 13 May 1977, Ms. Hanks told him not to come to the store. He denied setting the store on fire.

Posey Green Bobbitt, Jr. testified that he was working in the store with Bobbitt on the evening prior to the fire; that neither he nor Bobbitt removed any merchandise from the store when they closed at 11:00 p.m.; and that the store was well stocked on said date.

Plaintiff's Rebuttal

Ms. Hanks and a woman who lived next to the store testified that in May 1977, Huff fired a gun into the store while Ms. Hanks and her sister were inside. Ms. Hanks' sister testified that prior to the fire, she had discussed purchasing insurance for the store in front of Huff; and that Huff hated her sister.

Results at Trial

At the conclusion of the trial, the jury found that neither Ms. Hanks nor Bobbitt burned or procured the burning of the store, and that Ms. Hanks intentionally misrepresented the extent of her fire loss for the purpose of defrauding Nationwide. The trial court entered a judgment that plaintiff recover nothing.

Assignments of Error

Plaintiff presents five major questions for our determination:

"I. Did the court err in the admission of testimony regarding a prior fire loss in 1975 involving property of the plaintiff in the State of Virginia because such evidence was irrelevant, incompetent and prejudicial?

II. Did the court err in allowing the jury to examine Exhibit # 34 after the court had sustained objections to the introduction of this exhibit?

Hanks v. Insurance Co.

III. Did the court err in its instructions to the jury in that the court did not state and review the evidence to the extent necessary to explain the application of the law regarding the second issue submitted to the jury as required by Rule 51 of the Rules of Civil Procedure?

IV. Did the court err in submitting the second issue to the jury?

    (A) The second issue submitted to the jury does not arise from the pleadings.

    (B) The evidence did not support submission of the second issue.

V. Did the court err in its instruction to the jury as to the second issue by reason of the court's failure to base its charge on the contractual provisions contained in the policy of insurance and by reason of the court's failure to charge the jury as to the specific elements required for fraud?" (Typed from material in all caps)

We answer each question, "No," for the reasons that follow and find no error.

Admission of Testimony

[1] On direct examination of Nationwide's witness, Henry Huff, the record reveals the following:

"Q. Mr. Huff, did Mrs. Hanks at any time in your presence make any statement with regard to a previous fire that she had three years prior to this fire on some property in Virginia?

MR. GARDNER: Objection.

THE COURT: For what purpose is this offered?

MR. COMERFORD: Your Honor, this testimony is offered for the purpose of impeaching the credibility of Mrs. Hanks by showing prior action or conduct.

THE COURT: All right, members of the jury, you may consider this witness's statement as to what Mrs. Hanks may have previously told him for the limited purpose of assisting you, if it does, in deciding whether Mrs. Hanks is a person worthy of belief in this trial, and may not consider it for any other purpose. Overruled.

Q. Mr. Huff, prior to the fire which occurred in May of 1977, did Mrs. Hanks in your presence make any statement about a fire that she had which occurred on some property she owned in Virginia back in 1975?

A. Yes, sir.

Q. What statement did she make in that regard?

MR. GARDNER: Objection for the record, Your Honor.

THE COURT: overruled.

EXCEPTION NO. 1

A. She just had this house up on Piper's Gap Mountain up there and she had a son living with her and she got him to move out, put the old furniture in it, put the good furniture down at her house and had the insurance policy on it; she got these two guys in Mount Airy to burn it down for five hundred dollars and when they went to burn it down they stole the Kelvinator out of it, and when the insurance adjuster went to adjust it, you know, he was asking about the Kelvinator and she told him that she was having the Kelvinator worked on an —"

Plaintiff argues that the trial court erred in the admission of the above statements since such evidence was irrelevent, incompetent, and prejudicial. We do not agree. The evidence was admitted relating to the first issue. Since this issue was answered in favor of plaintiff, error, if any, in the ruling challenged by this assignment of error is harmless. *Wooten V. Cagle*, 268 N.C. 366, 150 S.E. 2d 738 (1966). 1 Strong's N.C. Index 3d, Appeal and Error, § 48, p. 307. We overrule this assignment of error.

Examination of Exhibit No. 34 by the Jury

[2] The record reveals:

"THE COURT: Members of the jury, you have examined these exhibits. There is one which you were allowed to examine which was not received into evidence, that being defendant's exhibit number thirty-four, an inventory of the list made by the defense witness, Joe Ferrell [sic]. You will recall I sustained objections to a good portion of that inventory and the witness was allowed to testify only as to some fifteen or twenty items in which he testified he could identify the number and the item from spots left on the shelves when compared with pictures, the shelves containing the stock before it was removed. I instruct you that as to that exhibit number thirty-four, you may only consider the testimony of the witness as to those items which, according to my notes, included sunglasses, bagged peanuts, stereo tapes, soft drinks, wine, cigarettes, Little Debbie cakes, straws, paper plates, milk, and one hundred and fifty-five six packs of beer. You may not consider anything else about that exhibit which the witness did not testify about. My notes indicate that he testified that his inventory of those items amounted to nineteen hundred and three dollars and ninety-two cents at fair retail price and that the fair wholesale value would be thirty percent less than the retail value. All right, will there be any other evidence for the defense?

EXCEPTION NO. 3"

Defendant specifically contends:

"Although the Court attempted by its instructions to eliminate the prejudice occasioned thereby, it is obvious from the entire record and from the jury verdict on the second issue that the Court did not succeed in disabusing the jury's minds of the prejudice created by an examination of the exhibit."

We do not agree. Where evidence is admitted, but the court

later withdraws the evidence and categorically instructs the jury not to consider such evidence, it will be presumed that the jury followed the instructions of the court, and the admission of the evidence will not ordinarily be held prejudicial. Here, the court's instructions were prompt and precise and were sufficient to cure any error that may have occurred. *Wands v. Cauble*, 270 N.C. 311, 154 S.E. 2d 425 (1967); *Smith v. Perdue* 258 N.C. 686, 129 S.E. 2d 293 (1963); 1 Stansbury's N.C. Evidence (Brandis Rev. 1973), § 28; 12 Strong's N.C. Index 3d, Trial, § 16. It is true Issue No. 2 was answered against plaintiff; however, we cannot hold that the admission of Exhibit 34 for a very short period of time amounted to prejudicial error in view of the court's instructions.

Submission of Issue

[3] Plaintiff contends that the court erred in submitting the following issue to the jury: "Did the plaintiff, L. June Hanks, intentionally misrepresent the extent of her fire loss for the purpose of defrauding the defendant?" The jury answered in the affirmative. We do not find error.

Defendant alleged in its answer.

"[T]hat the plaintiffs committed certain acts in violation of the provisions of the policy by increasing the hazards of fire on or about the premises and on the further grounds that the plaintiff L. June Hanks has misrepresented and concealed certain material facts in violation of the policy provisions, both pertaining to the extent of the loss claimed under the policy and as to the manner in which the fire occurred ... "

The policy introduced into evidence was a standard fire insurance policy. The statutory provisions as required by G.S. 58-176 (c) were incorporated therein, to wit:

"This entire policy shall be void if, whether before or after a loss, the insured has willfully concealed or misrepresented any material fact or circumstance concerning this insurance or the subject thereof, or the interest of the insured therein, or in case of any fraud or false swearing by the insured relating thereto."

The Court reviewed this policy provision recently and stated the following in *Dale v. Insurance Co.*, 40 N.C. App. 715, 717, 254 S.E. 2d 41, 42, *dis. rev. denied*, 297 N.C. 609, 257 S.E. 2d 217 (1979):

"This provision is inserted in the insurance contract by the statute as a part of the public policy of the state. *Green v. Insurance Co.*, 196 N.C. 335, 145 S.E. 616 (1928). This provision is valid, and the rights and liabilities of the parties under the policy must be ascertained and determined in accordance with its terms. *Gardner v. Insurance Co.*, 230 N.C. 750, 55 S.E. 2d 694 (1949). The parties are presumed to know all the terms, provisions and conditions included in the contract of insurance. *Midkiff v. Insurance Company* 197 N.C. 139, 147 S.E. 812 (1929)."

The evidence presented related to this issue and was sufficient for the court to submit the issue to the jury and support a verdict thereon.

We note that neither plaintiff nor defendant objected to the submission of issues to the jury by the court. The record does not show that plaintiff tendered any issues to be submitted as required by better practice. In *Baker v. Construction Corp.*, 255 N.C. 302, 307, 121 S.E. 2d 731, 735 (1961), our Supreme Court stated:

" 'If the parties consent to the issues submitted, or do not object at the time or ask for different or additional issues, the objection cannot be made later.' McIntosh, *opus* cited, § 510. If defendant had not tendered issues or otherwise objected to trial on the issue submitted, it could not do so on this appeal. *Tarkington v. Criffield, supra*, and *Noland Co., Inc. v. Jones*, 211 N.C. 462, 190 S.E. 720."

See Brant v. Compton, 16 N.C. App. 184, 191 S.E. 2d 383 (1972). We overrule this assignment of error.

Instructions to the Jury

[4] Plaintiff contends that the trial court failed to declare and explain the law arising on the evidence as required by G.S. 1A-1, Rule 51(a), of the Rules of Civil Procedure in two events: (1) The Court should have reviewed her evidence in greater detail to point out the "great disparity" between plaintiff's evidence and that of defendant. (2) The court failed to explain to the jury what facts it would have to find to establish an intentional misrepresentation as to the extent of loss in order to constitute fraud. We do not find error.

Plaintiff did not request any special instructions prior to or during the trial. It is the duty of the party desiring instructions on a subordinate feature of the case or greater elaboration on a particular point to aptly tender request for special instructions. *King v. Powell*, 252 N.C. 506, 114 S.E. 2d 265 (1960).

It is well settled in this State that the court's charge must be considered contextually as a whole, and when so considered, if it presents the law of the case in such a manner as to leave no reasonable cause to believe the jury was misled or misinformed, this Court will not sustain an exception on the grounds that the instruction might have been better. *Gregory v. Lynch*, 271 N.C. 198, 155 S.E. 2d 488 (1967); *Jones v. Development Co.*, 16 N.C. App. 80, 191 S.E. 2d 435, *cert. denied*, 282 N.C. 304, 192 S.E. 2d 194 (1972).

We hold that the trial court sufficiently instructed the jury on the material aspects of the case arising on the evidence and fairly applied the law to the factual situation.

Other Assignments of Error

Having answered the above question in the negative, we need not consider plaintiff's other two assignments of error and the one assigned by defendant.

City of Winston-Salem v. Concrete Co.

Conclusion

In the trial, we find no error.

No error.

Judges HEDRICK and ARNOLD concur.

CITY OF WINSTON-SALEM, PLAINTIFF, AND CHARLIE BROWN, CATHER-
INE BROWN, ALBERT PALMER, GLADYS PALMER, VASHTI McNEAL,
AND THE NEIGHBORHOOD COUNCIL OF PINEY GROVE COMMUNITY,
INTERVENORS, v. HOOTS CONCRETE COMPANY INC., DEFENDANT

No. 7921SC1198

(Filed 1 July 1980)

1. **Municipal Corporations § 30.11– permitted use under zoning ordinance – question of law**

    The determination of whether a specific use of a piece of property conforms to the zoning ordinance is a question of law, and as such, the determination is made by the local zoning board and is reviewable by the courts as a matter of law.

2. **Municpal Corporations § 30.11– property used for concrete mixing facility – prior approval – burden of proof on defendant**

    In an action to enjoin the operation of a ready mix concrete batching plant on the ground that such use was not permitted under the city zoning ordinance, the trial court properly placed the burden on defendant of proving that the city had made a determination six years before the action was brought that the operation was permissible and did not violate the zoning ordinance, since this was an affirmative defense to plaintiff's claim that the operation was in violation of the zoning ordinance, and defendant has the burden of establishing all affirmative defenses.

3. **Municipal Corporations § 30.11– use of property for concrete mixing facility – purpose for which action brought – estoppel of city – erroneous instructions**

    In an action to enjoin the operation of a ready mix concrete batching plant on the ground that such use was not permitted under the city zoning ordinance, the trial court's erroneous instruction that the purpose of the case was to determine whether the city was entitled to enforce a zoning ordinance followed by a statement that the city could not be estopped from enforcing the ordinance by the action of its officers was prejudicial to defendant.

4. **Municipal Corporations § 30.11– use of property for concrete mixing facility – approval by zoning officer at issue – evidence improperly excluded**

In an action to enjoin the operation of a ready mix concrete batching plant where defendant alleged that a zoning officer approved the use of the property for such a facility in 1970 but a contrary determination was made in 1976, the trial court erred in excluding (1) evidence concerning the procedure for making a determination when the use applied for was not specifically listed in the ordinance, since such evidence would have been relevant to show how the zoning officer would have acted when application was made by defendant in 1970; (2) evidence concerning similar uses, since the relative similarity of quarry operations in the same zone was relevant to the consideration of whether the zoning official with the power to do so made a determination in 1970 contrary to the determination made in 1976; and (3) evidence that machinery installed on the site in question cost $94,650 and that defendant's total investment in the site was approximately $200,000, since it was relevant evidence that defendant had a determination in 1970 of zoning compliance because the jury might have considered that defendant would not have made the expenditure without it.

APPEAL by defendant from *Hairston, Judge.* Judgment entered 5 September 1979 in Superior Court, FORSYTH County. Heard in the Court of Appeals 22 May 1980.

Plaintiff instituted this civil action on 12 November 1976 to enjoin permanently defendant from using certain real estate for the operation of a ready mix concrete batching plant on the ground that such use was not permitted under the Winston-Salem Zoning Ordinance through which the property in the area in question was zoned I-2, a designation for limited industrial use. The complaint alleged defendant was notified on 2 August 1976 that such a determination of unlawful use of the property had been made and that it must cease the use. Defendant admitted it had been notified in August 1976 that the use was unlawful and that it was continuing to operate the concrete mixing operation on the site. Defendant denied that a concrete mixing plant was an unlawful use in an I-2 district. Defendant in its answer alleged that plaintiff through its zoning officer approved the use of the property for a concrete mixing facility in August 1970. Defendant further alleged that even if the operation did violate the zoning ordinance, plaintiff was estopped to assert the ordinance due to its delay in asserting the ordinance and defendant's detrimental reliance on the August 1970 determination.

Plaintiff filed for summary judgment which was granted by the trial court on 9 May 1977. On appeal to this Court, the entry of summary judgment was reversed. *City of Winston-Salem v. Hoots Concrete Co.*, 37 N.C. App. 186, 245 S.E. 2d 536, *cert. den.*, 295 N.C. 645, 248 S.E. 2d 249 (1978). The Court there outlined the governing provisions of plaintiff's zoning ordinance which were at issue in the case. Subsection G of Section 29-6, Article I, Chapter 29 of the Winston-Salem City Code provides a "Table of Permitted Uses." The table contains three types of industrial districts, to wit: I-1 (Central Limited Industrial District), I-2 (Limited Industrial District) and I-3 (General Industrial District). A concrete mixing operation was not specifically described in any of the three zones. Among the I-2 zoned uses specified were wholesale storage services, storage yards, quarries or other extractive industries and certain fabrication or assembly operations. This Court stated the following in reversing the summary judgment for plaintiff.

We will not enter into a discussion of the varied definitions of some of the words used in describing the permitted uses. Suffice it to say that we are unable to say as a matter of law that defendant's concrete mixing operation is more similar to the permitted uses urged by defendant, or to the permitted use urged by plaintiff. Therefore a triable issue of fact remains as to whether plaintiff's zoning officer approved defendant's concrete mixing operation as a permitted use under I-2. If not, the city cannot be estopped to enforce its zoning ordinance under an appropriate interpretation of the ordinance. If so, the question of estoppel does not arise because the zoning officer, acting under authority of the ordinance, made a reasonable, justifiable and lawful determination as to the classification of the use. Assuming the latter, if the city wishes to amend its ordinance to provide that a concrete mixing operation is a permitted use only under I-1 and/or I-3, then defendant's operation will be a non-conforming use which cannot, under the present circumstances, be enjoined.

37 N.C. App. at 189-90, 245 S.E. 2d at 538.

On remand the case was tried before a jury with the issue

being, as stated in *Hoots,*   whether plaintiff's zoning officers determined in 1970 that defendant could operate the concrete mixing plant in an I-2 zone. The following evidence was
introduced at trial.

The property in question has been zoned I-2 (limited industrial) under the Winston-Salem Zoning Ordinance since 1968.
The Zoning Ordinance as written in 1970 contained Section
29-6-G which provided, in part, the following.

The following uses shall be permitted in the districts as
indicated herein and shall comply with all regulations of
the applicable district. Where a proposed use is covered by
a specific permitted use provision, that provision shall apply, to the exclusion of any provision using general terminology. On receiving an application for a zoning permit for a
use specifically listed in this subsection, the Zoning Officer
shall determine the listed use to which it is most similar
and shall enforce for the requested use all requirements
applicable to the similar use . . . .

The ordinance then contained a table of permitted uses. The
table was introduced into evidence. It does not specifically mention a transit mix concrete batching business. Some of the I-2
uses specified are the following.

— Agriculture or Farming, Including Processing or Sale of
   Products on Premises.

— Broadcasting Studios, Radio or Television.

— Correction Institutions.

— Eating Establishments.

— Landfills, Sanitary.

— Lumber Yards.

— Manufacturing or Processing:

2. Fabrication or Assembly of Products from Prestruc-
tured Materials or Components.

3. Manufacture of Foodstuffs, Textiles, Electrical Components, or Tobacco Products; Fabrication of Wood,
Leather, Paper, Water, or Plastic Products.

— Quarries or Other Extractive Industries.

— Storage Yards, Except Building Material Salvage.

— Welding or Sheet Metal Working.

— Wholesale Storage or Sales, or Storage Services.

Most of these uses were also permitted in an I-3 zone. Some uses
permitted in an I-3 but not in an I-2 zone were the following.

— Flammable Liquids or Gases, Bulk Storage, Above
ground.

— Freight Terminals, Truck or Rail.

— Manufacturing or Processing:

1. Any Processing, or the Manufacture of any Products,
from any Material (Including but Not Limited to Ani-
mal or Vegetable Matter, Chemicals or Chemical Com-
pounds, Glass, Metals, Minerals, Stones, or Earths).

— Motor Vehicles, Agricultural Implements, or Heavy
Machinery, Sale, Repair, Rental, or Storage.

The zoning ordinance also provided that "[a] building permit
issued in accordance with the Building Code shall serve also as
a zoning permit . . . ." Winston-Salem City Code § 29-19-A2a(2).
The ordinance further provided, "[a] *Certificate of Occupancy*
shall be issued by the Zoning Officer upon completion of any
building or other structure, or upon completion of other preparation for site occupancy, if the requirements of this ordinance
and other applicable laws or codes are complied with." *Id.* §
29-19-A2b.

Amos Speas, a Building and Zoning Officer for plaintiff since 1955, testified for plaintiff. He outlined the routine procedure for obtaining permission from the city to make a specified use of property within plaintiff's zoning jurisdiction. In 1970, Mr. Speas was assisted by six building inspectors who had the authority to interpret and apply the zoning ordinance and issue building permits, which also served as zoning permits under the Winston-Salem City Code. This was the case since the issuance of a building permit was dependent upon a prior determination by the inspector that the proposed use for the proposed site was permissible under the zoning ordinance. The inspectors answered telephone inquiries about sites and made zoning determinations over the phone. No formal or written records were kept of the verbal rulings which were relied upon by the individuals making the inquiry. When a person applied for a permit, the application was typed by the clerk, Mary Howerton, who was also authorized to approve routine permits. After a permit is issued for a site, the building inspector assigned to a particular district would visit the site in various periods of the construction to make sure the building code was being complied with and that the use of the property was permissible in the particular zoning district. Finally, a certificate of occupancy which authorized a specific use of the property would be issued after a final inspection. Speas identified two applications for building permits submitted by defendant's corporate predecessor in July and August 1970 for the property in question to erect an office building and a business building and two permits for those proposed uses which were issued. Neither the application nor the permits mentioned a concrete mixing operation. Speas acknowledged that a concrete mixing operation is not within the listed uses for an I-2 zone nor any other zone. Plaintiff's employees could not locate the certificates of occupancy for the buildings in question. Speas denied speaking with any of the inspectors or the clerk authorized to issue permits about the property in question nor did he indicate to any employee of defendant that a concrete mixing operation would be permitted on the site in question.

The six building inspectors employed by plaintiff in 1970 denied speaking with their clerk or any representative of defendant about the property in question. The inspector assigned to the district in which the property was located made four site inspections in July and August of 1970. He denied observing any equipment or structures. He inspected the footings for the proposed office building. He never observed a hopper and conveyor system which would indicate defendant intended to operate a concrete mixing operation on the site. Howerton, the clerk, testified she could not recall typing defendant's application nor talking with Sid Hoots, the principal officer of defendant, about a proposed concrete mixing operation on the site. She testified if she had spoken with him about such, she would have put it on his permit application.

Defendant's evidence tends to show the following. The hopper or storage bin in which sand and gravel are stored was erected in late June or early July 1970. Sid Hoots testified that at the time he applied for the permits in July 1970, he told the clerk and one of the inspectors that one of the buildings would house the controls for his concrete plant. He stated that the clerk and the inspector checked the property for the proposed zoning and issued two building permits for the property.

Defendant's operation consists of the storage of processed and manufactured materials, including sand, gravel and cement. When an order is received, the materials are carried by a conveyor system to a point where they are combined with water and placed in a truck with a revolving chamber. The chemical process of hydration from which concrete is produced takes at least forty-five minutes and occurs while the truck is enroute to its destination.

The case was submitted to the jury on three issues.

1. Did the zoning officer of the City of Winston-Salem make a determination on August 2, 1976 that the defendant's use of the property in question for the operation of a ready-mix concrete batching plant was a violation of the zoning ordinance and did not comply with the zoning classification of I-2 (Limited Industrial)?

2. Is the defendant presently continuing to use the property in question for the operation of a ready-mix batching plant?

3. Did the zoning officer of the City of Winston-Salem, pursuant to two applications made by the defendant in 1970, determine that the transit mix use of the defendant was most nearly similar to a use or uses designated in the Zoning Table of Permitted Uses under Industrial-2 uses?

The jury answered the first two issues in the affirmative and the third issue in the negative. Defendant appeals.

Womble, Carlyle, Sandridge and Rice, by Roddey M. Ligon, Jr., and Anthony H. Brett; Pfefferkorn and Cooley, by William G. Pfefferkorn and J. Wilson Parker, attorneys for plaintiff appellee.

Hutchins, Tyndall, Bell, Davis and Pitt, by Fred S. Hutchins, Jr.; Booe, Mitchell, Goodson and Shugart, by William S. Mitchell, attorneys for defendant appellant.

VAUGHN, Judge.

[1] Defendant contends the issues as submitted were not broad enough to embrace all the relevant evidence and questions involved. It further contends it was improper to submit the first and second issues because those issues were not controverted in the pleadings, were unnecessary and were confusing to the jury. Defendant submitted three alternative issues that essentially required the jury to decide whether defendant's operation was in violation of the zoning ordinance. This was not a determination for the jury. The determination of whether a specific use of a piece of property conforms to the zoning ordinance is a question of law. *Moyer v. Board of Zoning Appeals,* 233 A. 2d 311 (Me 1967); *Crary Home v. Defrees,* 16 Pa. Commw. Ct. 181, 329 A. 2d 874 (1974). As such, the determination is made by the local zoning board and is reviewable by the courts as a matter of law. The issue defendant contends was for the jury was a matter of law for the courts to determine. Defendant did not seek a ruling from the trial court nor did it raise the issue on appeal. The only factual question for the jury was whether a determination was made pursuant to the zoning ordinance in 1970 that the operation of defendant would be permitted. This was the essence of the third issue presented to the jury for determination.

The first and second issues as submitted to the jury did not need resolution. Defendant conceded that a zoning officer made a determination on 2 August 1976 that its ready-mix concrete batching plant was in violation of the zoning ordinance and that it was continuing to operate the facility. Defendant admitted this in the pleadings. It only denied that the use was unlawful. The legality of the determination was not, as we have noted, a question of fact for the jury. Defendant contends it was prejudiced by the submission of these matters on which there was no controversy raised by the pleadings. The trial judge, however, gave the jury what amounted to a peremptory instruction on the two issues. The only instruction on the two issues was the following.

I will discuss these issues one at a time and explain the law which you consider as you deliberate upon your verdict. The first two are going to be very short and very easy to discuss. The burden is on the Plaintiff on the first two issues. The Court instructs you that if you believe what all the evidence tends to show, you will answer Issue No. 1 "Yes" and Issue No. 2 "Yes." If you do not believe any of the evidence, you will of course answer them "No." But if you believe what all the evidence tends to show, you will answer those two "Yes."

Although it would have been better not to have submitted the two issues to the jury, that error, standing alone, would not require a new trial.

[2]   The third issue submitted to the jury was, "Did the zoning officer of the City of Winston-Salem pursuant to two applications made by the defendant in 1970, determine that the transit mix use of the defendant was most nearly similar to a use or uses designated in the Zoning Table of Permitted Uses under Industrial-2 uses?" In his instruction to the jury, the trial judge placed the burden of proof on defendant to prove this issue by the greater weight of the evidence. In his general instruction on burden of proof, the trial judge stated, "If you are not so persuaded, or if you are unable to determine where the truth lies, it would be your duty to answer the issue against the party with the burden of proof." He instructed in part on the third issue,

"If you do not so find or if you are unable to determine where the truth is, then you will answer it 'No' in favor of the plaintiff." Defendant contends the burden of proof of this issue should have been on plaintiff. We disagree. The trial judge properly placed the burden of proof on the third issue on defendant.

Plaintiff alleged that defendant was using the property for the operation of a ready-mix concrete batching plant in violation of the zoning ordinance. Defendant, in its answer, made a denial that its operations violated the zoning ordinance by its specific answers to the paragraphs of plaintiff's complaint. This was followed by a separate defense to the effect that a city zoning officer had made a determination in August 1970 which approved the use of the property as a concrete mixing plant. Defendant pled this defense "in bar of plaintiff's claim for relief." This was an affirmative defense to plaintiff's claim that the operation was in violation of the zoning ordinance. "The defendant, of course, has the burden of establishing all affirmative defenses, whether they relate to the whole case or only to certain issues in the case. As to such defenses, he is the actor and has the laboring oar." *Williams v. Insurance Co.*, 212 N.C. 516, 517-18, S.E. 728, 729 (1937); *Jones v. Insurance Co.*, 254 N.C. 407, 119 S.E. 2d 215 (1961). The city had the burden of proving the existence of an operation in violation of its zoning ordinance. It was defendant's burden to prove the city had already made a determination that the operation was permissible and did not violate the zoning ordinance.

[3] Defendant contends the trial judge erred in his instruction concerning estoppel. Estoppel had been raised as a defense to the action. This issue was completely removed from the case as a defense in the first appeal. A city cannot be estopped to enforce a zoning ordinance against a violator due to the conduct of a zoning official in encouraging or permitting the violation. *Helms v. Charlotte*, 255 N.C. 647, 122 S.E. 817 (1961); *Raleigh v. Fisher*, 232 N.C. 629, 61 S.E. 2d 897 (1950). The Court in the first appeal of the case recognized that estoppel did not bar a city. The Court also noted that in this case, if a zoning officer approved the use in 1970, "the question of estoppel does not arise because the zoning officer, acting under authority of the ordinance, made a reasonable, justifiable and lawful deter-

mination as to the classification of the use." 37 N.C. App. at 190, 245 S.E. 2d at 538. The trial judge instructed the jury on the issue of estoppel in a zoning case to the following effect.

There was evidence then that the Hoots Construction Company, which was the correct and proper corporate name in 1970 when the applications were filed and permits were issued, changed its name but remained the same corporation, changed its name to Hoots Concrete Company, Incorporated. That following this there were some complaints to the City Board and that an investigation followed, as a result of which the zoning officer for the City in August of 1976 made a determination, which you will recall, in writing to Hoots Concrete Company and determined that the defendant's use of the property in question for the operation of a ready-mix concrete batching plant was a violation of the zoning ordinance and did not comply with the zoning ordinance and did not comply with the zoning classification of I-2 (Limited Industrial). That this determination was served on Mr. Hoots and Mr. Hoots took no action with respect to it, and that thereafter he continued to and did operate a transit mix batching plant at the Indiana Avenue address that we are considering. *That thereafter in 1976 the City instituted this action to determine whether or not they were entitled to enforce the provisions of the zoning ordinance.*

.   .   .

Now there is, in addition to this, considerable evidence which may have some bearing on your decision that would indicate that the City with its eyes wide open, buying concrete from Mr. Hoots, accepting revenue from him under his license tax, and with the full knowledge of a number of these inspectors, permitted him to continue to operate out there. This may have some bearing on your decision as to whether or not the zoning officer in fact made a decision, but let me caution you that you should not use it for any other purpose. *It is not proper that the city officials for a period of time failed or even neglected or even intentionally permitted Hoots Concrete Company to violate the law. To*

*put it as our Court does, "The City may not be estopped."
Now an estoppel is nothing more than you take one position
and then you flip-flop and take another. So the fact that he
was permitted to do this does not in any way prevent them
from coming in here now.* (Emphasis added).

Defendant contends this portion of the charge is erroneous and
prejudicial for three reasons. (1) Defendant contends the issues
had been concluded by the decision of this Court in the first
appeal. (2) It was an instruction upon an abstract principle of
law not presented by the evidence, pleadings or issues. (3) The
close proximity of the estoppel instruction to the erroneous
statement that "in 1976 the City instituted this action to determine whether or not they were entitled to enforce the provision
of the zoning ordinance" was unduly prejudicial to defendant.
Defendant's first two objections are without merit. The trial
judge correctly instructed that estoppel was not a defense. It
was a necessary part of the charge. The jurors applying their
own sense of equity and fairness might have decided plaintiff
should have been estopped where there was evidence to the
effect that plaintiff issued business licenses to defendant,
purchased concrete from defendant and allowed the operation
for a number of years. An instruction on estoppel was necessary
in order that the jury would know that the city could not be
estopped for those reasons. In the context in which they were
given, however, the instructions could have been misleading.
The jury could have been led to believe that even if the zoning
officer had approved the concrete plant usage, the city could
"flip-flop" and if it did so, be allowed "to enforce the provisions
of the zoning ordinance" pursuant to the new position it elected
to take. The jury could have been confused and determined they
had to answer the third issue in the negative because they
could not do otherwise or at least such was the opinion of the
trial judge. Plaintiff's suit was not to determine whether they
were *entitled to enforce* the zoning ordinance but to *enforce* the
zoning ordinance by an injunction. The erroneous statement
about the purpose of the case being a determination of whether
the city was entitled to enforce the ordinance followed by a
statement that the city could not be estopped from enforcing
the ordinance by the action of its officers was prejudicial to
defendant.

[4]   The trial judge refused to admit in evidence answers relating to uses listed in the table of uses as permissible in I-2
districts. Defendant's concrete mixing operation was not specifically described in any of the three types of districts zoned
industrial. It was not for the jury to classify the operation. The
issue before it was whether a classification had been made in
1970. Plaintiff contends the admission of the evidence would
invite the jury to consider an issue of law not before it. We think
the excluded evidence should have been admitted in part at
least as far as it concerns the procedure for making a determination when the use applied for is not specifically listed in
the ordinance. This is relevant evidence of how the zoning
officer would have acted when application was made by defendant in 1970. The evidence of similar uses should also have been
admitted. The relative similarity of quarry operations in the
same zone was relevant to the consideration of whether the
zoning official with the power to so do made a determination in
1970 contrary to the determination made in 1976.

The trial judge also excluded testimony that the machinery
installed on the site in question cost $94,650.00 and that the
total investment of defendant in the site was around
$200,000.00. The testimony should have been admitted. It is
relevant evidence that defendant had a determination in 1970
of zoning compliance because the jury might have considered
that defendant would not have made the expenditure without
it. It is not relevant to show detrimental reliance as an element
of estoppel because estoppel is not a bar to the city's enforcement, and the jury should be so instructed.

Defendant's argument that its motion for judgment notwithstanding the verdict should have been granted is without
merit. The evidence was in conflict and should have gone to the
jury for its decision on whether a zoning compliance determination was made in 1970.

For the error in the charge where the estoppel instruction followed an inaccurate statement about the issues in the suit and
for the errors in evidentiary admissions, defendant is entitled to
a new trial. The jury must decide whether a zoning officer
approved defendant's concrete mixing operation in 1970 as a

permitted I-2 use. It is defendant's burden to prove such a determination was made.

New trial.

Judges PARKER and HEDRICK concur.

STATE OF NORTH CAROLINA Ex Rel., UTILITIES COMMISSION AND CONTRACT TRANSPORTER, INC. v M.L. HATCHER PICKUP & DELIVERY SERVICES, INC.

No. 7910UC750

(Filed 1 July 1980)

1. Carriers § 2.7– contract carrier authority – sufficiency of proof

An applicant for authority to operate as a contract carrier under contract with Reynolds Metal Company to transport metal containers between the Reynolds Plant in Salisbury and warehouses in this State to all intrastate points met its burden under NCUC Rule R2-15(b) of proving (1) that Reynolds has a need for a specific type of service and (3) that such service is not otherwise available by existing means of transportation where there was evidence tending to show that the container industry is very competitive and Reynolds needs a carrier with statewide authority; specialized equipment and a carrier with expertise in handling such equipment are necessary to transport the containers; Reynolds needs a carrier which can dedicate equipment to its exclusive use for extended periods of time; protestant common carrier does not have statewide authority and is thus incapable of furnishing the required service; and the type of dedication of equipment which Reynolds needs is not consistent with the concept of common carriage such that protestant can provide the needed service.

2. Carriers § 2.7– contract carrier permit – effect on common carrier

The fact that the grant of authority to applicant to operate as a contract carrier for a can manufacturer will result in denying protestant common carrier the future opportunity to transport the manufacturer's cans does not compel a determination that the grant of such authority will unreasonably impair the efficient service of protestant as a common carrier within the meaning of G.S. 62-262(i).

APPEAL by protestant from Final Order of the Utilities Commission in Docket No. T-1672, Sub. 2 entered 10 April 1979. Heard in the Court of Appeals 28 February 1980.

This is an appeal from an order of the Utilities Commission approving the application of Contract Transporter, Inc. for contract carrier authority.

On 16 May 1978 Contract Transporter, Inc. (CTI), an authorized motor carrier, filed an application with the Utilities Commission seeking authority to operate as a contract carrier under contract with Reynolds Metal Company to transport metal containers and container ends between the Reynolds Metals Company (Reynolds) can plant near Salisbury, North Carolina, and warehouses in this state to all intrastate points. On 7 June 1978, M.L. Hatcher Pickup and Delivery Services, Inc. (Hatcher) of Greensboro filed a Protest and Motion for Intervention in which it stated that it is an irregular route common carrier of property by motor vehicle operating intrastate under a certificate issued by the Commission, that it is authorized to transport the items referred to in CTI's application and between the points referred to therein, and that the proposed service does not conform to the definition of a contract carrier under G.S. 62-262(i) and Rule R2-15(b) of the Commission. The Commission granted protestant's motion for intervention on 16 June 1978.

At a hearing before a hearing examiner held on 17 August 1978, applicant CTI presented evidence as follows:

During the period February through April 1978 Reynolds began negotiating with various carriers for transportation services for its newly constructed can manufacturing facility in Salisbury, North Carolina, which was scheduled to begin production in December 1978. The facility was designed to produce a wide variety of metal containers, including the 12-ounce beer and beverage container. Because of the light weight and the bulk of the product, the practice in the industry is to ship the metal containers in "standard packs," layers of containers which are secured by picture frame-type holders and packed on pallets 44 inches by 56 inches. The transportation of these pallets requires the use of trailers at least 45 feet in length with inside and door opening minimum heights of 110 inches, swing-out doors, square noses, and straight floors without steps. Roy H. Grabman, Division Manager of Transportation and Warehousing for the Can Division of Reynolds, testified that many customers require delivery in trailers equipped with mechanically self-unloading roller devices which increase unloading efficiency and facilitate the distribution of cans within the customers' plants.

At the time of the negotiations, Reynolds was seeking, for both competitive and business reasons, a carrier which could not only provide the necessary equipment, but which could also furnish 24-hour-a-day operation directly from plant or warehouse locations to consignees and drivers trained in handling metal containers, and which could station equipment close to the plant to cover the contingency of short-notice movements. As the witness for Reynolds testified, "[i]f we cannot provide this type of service, our competitors certainly will."

At the time of the negotiations, neither the applicant nor the protestant had the necessary equipment to service Reynolds, although both companies represented that they could obtain it. Both submitted quotations to Reynolds. By late May 1978 applicant had obtained the special trailers and was operating under temporary emergency authority from the Interstate Commerce Commission to transport Reynolds containers received at a warehouse in Greensboro from interstate shipments to Miller Brewing Company in Eden. When protestant's vice-president contacted Reynolds concerning the status of its quotations, he learned that Reynolds intended to support the applicant for intrastate contract carrier authority.

On 12 May 1977 Reynolds and applicant entered into a proposed contract for intrastate service which provides that applicant transport Reynolds's containers, "to and from points in the State of North Carolina at such times, on such schedules, and to such destinations as may from time to time be designated to REYNOLDS." Reynolds made the decision to contract with CTI based upon applicant's greater experience in handling containers, its drivers' experience in operating the unloading system, and its ability to spot equipment at the Salisbury plant for short notice movements and to transport to customers throughout the state. Although at the time of the hearing Reynolds's only customers in North Carolina were the Shasta bottling plant in Charlotte and Miller Brewing Company in Eden, Reynolds produced a list of thirteen other potential customer locations throughout the state. Witness Grabman testified that a carrier with statewide authority such as applicant was needed because Reynolds was unable to foresee when or where new sales would be made, and because it would be necessary at times to lease warehousing space on short notice in various locations in the state from which the carrier can deliver to customers.

The Vice-President of protestant Hatcher offered testimony as follows: Protestant is an irregular route common carrier holding authority for the transportation of general commodities, "except those requiring special equipment," over irregular routes between all points in thirty-seven counties, as well as between all points within a radius of seventy-five miles of Eden, and between Eden and Charlotte. That general authority would permit protestant to transport Reynolds's products from Salisbury to Eden and from Salisbury to Charlotte by way of Eden. Of the thirteen potential geographic customer locations listed by Reynolds, protestant would be able to serve all but five. Protestant can obtain the necessary equipment, and although its terminals are not open twenty-four hours a day, they have answering services which notify persons on call of the shipper's needs. Protestant would be willing to spot equipment at the Reynolds plant in Salisbury. At the time of the hearing, two of protestant's drivers had received instruction in handling the rollerbed equipment, although none of the drivers had actual experience.

Following the hearing, the hearing examiner filed a Recommended Order Denying Contract Carrier Authority based on the conclusion that protestant could amply meet all of Reynolds's needs and that the grant of authority to applicant would detrimentally affect protestant. On appeal to the full Utilities Commission, the Recommended Order was set aside. The Commission, upon findings, of fact, concluded that applicant had met the burden of showing need for contract carrier service and that applicant's proposed operations conformed to the definition of a contract carrier under G.S. 62-3(8). From the Final Order granting the Application of CTI for contract carrier authority, protestant appealed.

Bailey, Dixon, Wooten, McDonald & Fountain by J. Ruffin Bailey and Ralph McDonald for protestant-appellant.

Allen, Steed and Allen by Thomas W. Steed, Jr. and Noah H. Huffstetler III for applicant-appellee.

PARKER, Judge.

G.S. 62-3(8) defines a "contract carrier by motor vehicle" as "any person which, under an individual contract or agreement with another person and with such additional persons as may be approved by the Utilities Commission, engages in the transportation other than [transportation by common carriers], by motor vehicle of persons or property in intrastate commerce for compensation . . . " Under G.S. 62-262, no carrier may transport property in intrastate commerce unless that person has applied for and obtained a certificate or permit. Subsection (i) of G.S. 62-262 specifies what the Utilities Commission must consider before granting a permit to a contract carrier:

> If the application is for a permit, the Commission shall give due consideration to:
>
> (1) Whether the proposed operations conform with the definition in this chapter of a contract carrier,
>
> (2) Whether the proposed operations will unreasonably impair the efficient public service of carriers operating under certificates, or rail carriers,
>
> (3) Whether the proposed service will unreasonably impair the use of the highways by the general public,
>
> (4) Whether the applicant is fit, willing and able to properly perform the service proposed as a contract carrier,
>
> (5) Whether the proposed operations will be consistent

with the public interest and the policy declared in this Chapter, and

(6) Other matters tending to qualify or disqualify the applicant for a permit.

Pursuant to its rulemaking powers under G.S. 62-31, the Utilities Commission has promulgated NCUC Rule R2-15(b) establishing the burden of proof for an applicant seeking contract carrier authority:

If the application is for a permit to operate as a contract carrier, proof of a public demand and need for the service is not required; however, *proof is required that one or more shippers or passengers have a need for a specific type of service not otherwise available by existing means of transportation,* and have entered into and filed with the Commission with a copy to the Public Staff prior to the hearing or at the time of the hearing, a written contract with the applicant for said service, which contract shall provide for rates not less than those charged by common carriers for similar service." (emphasis added).

Unless the requirements of both G.S. 62-262(i) and Rule R2-15(b) are met, the Commission may not grant the authority sought. NCUC Rule R2-10(b). Protestant contends on appeal in the present case that the applicant failed to meet its burden under both G.S. Chap. 62 and the Commission rules in that it did not show the need for a specific type of service, the unavailability of the needed service from existing carriers, or the absence of detrimental effect on common carriers.

[1] In support of its contention that applicant did not carry its burden of showing the need for a specific type of service, protestant challenges the full Commission's findings of fact that Reynolds needs a carrier with statewide authority on the grounds that the findings of Reynolds's need are unsupported by competent, material, and substantial evidence in view of the entire record as submitted. It is well established that if the findings of the Utilities Commission are so supported, they are conclusive and binding upon the appellate court. *Utilities Com-*

mission v. Coach Company, 269 N.C. 717, 153 S.E. 2d 461 (1967). The record discloses that the container industry is highly competitive and that Reynolds must be in a position to provide services comparable to those provided by its competitors. Although at the time of the hearing Reynolds had only two actual North Carolina customer locations, Charlotte and Eden, and the Division Manager of Reynolds's Can Division, Roy Grabman, testified that Reynolds had no present plans to establish warehouses at any specific point in North Carolina, Grabman also testified as follows:

> The demand for metal cans is extremely volatile and varies with the seasons and the weather. Our Salisbury plant will operate three shifts throughout the year, and will warehouse cans produced during the cooler months when demand is relatively low. At the present time, we operate a warehouse at Greensboro, North Carolina, and we anticipate the storage space for considerable number of cans will be available at our Salisbury plant. We also anticipate that from time to time, we will need to lease warehouse space in other locations in the State. Such warehouse locations are usually established on relatively short notice, and the actual location will be dependent on several factors, such as the availability of warehouse space, its proximity to our customers' locations, its costs, and its suitability for storing cans. Since we cannot foretell when or where new sales will be made or the locations of future warehousing operations, we need a carrier who can pick up and deliver shipments at any point in the State of North Carolina.

This testimony, along with evidence of the competitive nature of the container industry, is amply sufficient to support the Commission's finding of Reynolds's statewide need. To limit the scope of Reynolds's needs to its immediate geographic customer locations would be to ignore the realities of the marketing strategy necessary to Reynolds's business.

Protestant next contends that even if the Commission's findings of statewide need are supported by competent, material and substantial evidence, that need is not the type of "specific need" contemplated by NCUC Rule R2-15(b). This contention ignores the fact that the Commission did not rely solely on Reynolds's geographic requirement, but rather considered it as merely one factor along with Reynolds's other special needs. The Commission's order contained extensive findings of fact concerning the specialized equipment necessary to transport Reynolds's containers, the need for a carrier with expertise in handling such specialized equipment, and the need for dedication of equipment to the exclusive use of Reynolds for extended periods of time. This Court has in the past shown deference to the Commission's determination that a need for a specific type of service justifies the grant of contract carrier authority. In *Utilities Comm. v. Transport Co.*, 10 N.C. App. 626, 179 S.E. 2d 799 (1971), the Court held that the applicant for a contract carrier permit had met its burden of proof under G.S. 62-262(i) and NCUC Rule R2-15(b) where the evidence showed that the shipper, a buyer and seller of gas, required a carrier that could deliver liquified petroleum gas within twelve hours and that the permit applicant intended to devote equipment solely for the benefit of the shipper. Viewing the Final Order of the Commission in this case in its entirety, it is manifest that the applicant met its burden of showing that Reynolds has a need for a specific type of service.

The question remains, however, whether the applicant also met its burden under NCUC Rule R2-15(b) of showing that the specific type of service is not otherwise available by existing means of transportation and under G.S. 62-262(i) of showing that its proposed operations will not unreasonably impair the efficient public service of common carriers. Protestant has assigned error to the Commission's finding of fact that "[t]he Protestant and other existing carriers in North Carolina are unable or unwilling to provide the service and the type of equipment that Reynolds Metals needs." It is undisputed that at the time of the hearing protestant did not own any trailers equipped with mechanically self-unloading rollerbed systems such as Reynolds requires, although it was leasing one such trailer and had ordered five more at a cost of $125,000.00. It is also undisputed that Reynolds needs a shipper which can dedicate equipment to its exclusive use. The Commission found that the contract between applicant and Reynolds provides for the dedication of specific pieces of motor vehicle equipment to the exclu-

sive use of Reynolds, and that this provision was inconsistent
with the concept of common carriage. Although protestant contends that a tariff exists providing for the "dedication" of equipment by common carriers, that does not imply that the type of
dedication which Reynolds requires is consistent with the concept of common carriage such that protestant could provide the
needed service. Even if protestant has authority to spot equipment at Reynolds's plant, it nevertheless has a duty as a common carrier to serve the public generally. *Utilities Commission
v. Transport*, 260 N.C. 762, 133 S.E. 2d 692 (1963); *Utilities
Comm. v. McCotter, Inc.*, 16 N.C. App. 475, 192 S.E. 2d 629 (1972);
affirmed, 283 N.C. 104, 194 S.E. 2d 859 (1973). Thus, should any
conflict arise between its duty to the public and its "dedication"
of equipment to Reynolds, the former would prevail to the economic and competitive disadvantage of Reynolds. Further, in
veiw of our determination that the Commission's findings of
fact that Reynolds has a need for a carrier with statewide
authority are supported by competent, material, and substantial evidence, the geographical restrictions on protestant's common carrier authority render it incapable of furnishing the
required services. The facts of the present case distinguish it from
Utilities Comm. v. Petroleum Transportation, Inc., 2 N.C. App. 566,
163 S.E. 2d 526 (1968), in which this Court found insufficient evidence to support the Commission's finding that the shipper had a
need for a specific service not otherwise available.

[2] As to the Commission's conclusion that the grant of contract carrier authority to applicant will not unreasonably impair the efficient public service of common carriers, protestant's only contention is that the grant of contract carrier
authority to applicant will result in denying it the future opportunity to transport Reynolds's cans. A similar contention was
rejected in *Utilities Comm. v. McCotter, Inc., supra*, in which
this court stated.

It is true that protestant might reasonably expect to receive a portion of [the shipper's] business should contract
carrier authority be denied to applicant. This fact alone,
however, does not compel a determination that the efficient service of protestant as a common carrier will be
unreasonably impaired. 'There is no public policy con-

demning competition as such in the field of public utilities; the public policy only condemns unfair or destructive competition.' *Utilities Comm. v. Coach Co.*, 261 N.C. 384, 389, 134 S.E. 2d 689, 694. Neither protestant, nor any other intrastate carrier, has handled any of the shipping which applicant will handle under the contract authority granted herein. Consequently, a continuation of applicant's operations under proper authority could hardly constitute unfair or destructive competition with respect to protestant or other carriers.

16 N.C. App. at 480-481, 192 S.E. 2d at 632-633.

The Commission, upon findings of fact fully supported by competent, material and substantial evidence in view of the record as a whole, concluded that applicant was entitled to the contract carrier authority sought. The Final Order appealed from is

Affirmed.

Judges MARTIN (Harry C.) and HILL concur.

JOHNSIE A. HICE v. HI-MIL, INC.

No. 8025SC109

(Filed 1 July 1980)

1. **Reformation of Instruments § 1.1; Limitation of Actions § 8.1– reformation of deed – mutual mistake – accrual of action from date of discovery**

   Plaintiff's action to reform a deed six years after it was executed was not barred by the statute of limitations, since actions involving mistake are not deemed to have accrued until discovery; the evidence clearly showed that plaintiff did not discover the mistake until six years later when she attempted to sell her home; and she immediately took steps to reform the deed when she learned of the purported conveyance. Furthermore, plaintiff was not estopped to assert her claim simply because, at the time of execution of the deed, she read a long legal document conveying twenty tracts of land, which described them in repetitive and sophisticated language and which included the tract involved in this lawsuit, nor was the fact that plaintiff stopped paying taxes on the tract in question conclusive evidence that plaintiff knew she had conveyed the land six years earlier.

2. **Reformation of Instruments § 7– reformation of deed – mutual mistake – sufficiency of evidence**

Evidence was sufficient to show a mutual mistake in the deed from plaintiff to defendant's predecessors in title where it tended to show that plaintiff intended to convey and grantees intended to receive title to property known as the "Mountain Tract" which consisted of contiguous tracts approximately three miles from plaintiff's homeplace; neither intended for the homeplace to be included in the deed; the attorney who prepared the deed for plaintiff testified that he included 13 acres of plaintiff's homeplace in the deed by mistake; a surveyor for defendant testified that he was unable to fit the 13 acre tract into the plat of the mountain tract prepared for defendant; and defendant's attorney testified that he was unable to fit the 13 acre tract into the boundary as a part of his title examination for defendant.

3. **Reformation of Instruments § 9– reformation of deed – defendant not an innocent bona fide purchaser**

In plaintiff's action to reform a deed conveying a 1200 acre mountain tract which mistakenly included 13 acres of her homeplace, defendant was not an innocent bona fide purchaser for value since (1) through all the mesne conveyances down to defendant, all parties intended to buy only the mountain tract and it was understood that only the mountain tract was being conveyed; there was no direct evidence of any party's intent ever to sell the 13 acre portion of the homeplace and no intention by a party to buy it; it was nevertheless erroneously included in each deed; and (2) knowledge of the mistake was imputed to defendant through plaintiff's grantee who was a shareholder/director/officer of defendant's corporation.

Judge ARNOLD dissents.

APPEAL by defendant from *Riddle, Judge.* Order entered 28 September 1979 in Superior Court, CALDWELL County. Heard in the Court of Appeals 5 June 1980.

Plaintiff seeks to reform a deed on the basis of a mutual mistake. On 27 October 1971 plaintiff took twenty deeds to her lawyer's office and instructed him to prepare a deed from her to Ray Hice and Everette Welch (spelled "Walsh" in the deed) for a tract of land known as her "Mountain Tract," containing approximately 1200 acres. Plaintiff was not aware that one of the deeds delivered to her lawyer — and necessarily one of the tracts included in the deed to Hice and Welch — included a 13-acre parcel constituting a part of her home tract, which was located two or three miles from the mountain tract. The home tract was 25 acres and consisted of a 12-acre tract upon which plaintiff's house is located, and the 13-acre tract referred to above.

Ray Hice subsequently purchased the half interest originally acquired by Everette Welch. Thereafter, in 1973, Ray Hice
and Jack Miller organized the defendant corporation, each owning 50% of the stock, for the purpose of developing the land
know as the "Mountain Tract" and became directors and officers of the corporation. Ray Hice transferred to the corporation
the lands originally acquired from the plaintiff, including the
13-acre tract. Thereafter, Ray Hice sold his stock in the corporation to Jack Miller.

Plaintiff, in late 1977, discovered the 13-acre tract had been
conveyed by the 1971 deed to Ray Hice and Welch. Plaintiff
brings this action, alleging mutual mistake and seeking to reform her deed. The defendant denied plaintiff's allegations,
alleged the plaintiff failed to state a claim upon which relief
could be granted, and further pleaded the statute of limitations
as a bar. Defendant then moved for summary judgment, which
motion was denied. Thereafter, the trial judge sitting without a
jury, heard evidence and arguments of counsel, made findings
of fact and conclusions of law, and entered judgment for the
plaintiff. The defendant appealed.

*West, Groome & Correll, by Ted G. West and Edward H. Blair
Jr., for plaintiff appellee.*

*Billings, Burns & Wells, by Donald R. Billings and R.
Michael Wells, for defendant appellant.*

HILL, Judge.

[1] We first address the question of whether plaintiff's cause of
action is barred by the statute of limitations (G.S. 1-52(9)) and
conclude that it is not. This statute specifically provides that
actions involving fraud or mistake shall not be deemed to have
accrued until discovery. The evidence clearly shows the plaintiff discovered the mistake in 1977 when she attempted to sell
her home and immediately took steps to reform her deed when
she learned of the purported conveyance.

We do not agree with the contention of the defendant that
plaintiff, a 54-year old seamstress, is estopped to assert her
claim now, simply because in 1971 she had read a long legal

document conveying twenty tracts of land, describing them in repetitive and sophisticated language, one tract of which described the parcel involved in this lawsuit. Neither do we conclude the fact that she stopped paying taxes on the 13-acre tract is conclusive evidence that plaintiff knew she had conveyed the land in 1971. There was no evidence that any of the grantees had knowingly exercised acts of ownership over the land in question. This assignment of error is without merit.

[2] Next, we consider whether there was a mutual mistake in the deed from Johnsie A. Hice to Ray Hice and Everette Welch, which included the 13-acre tract. If a solemn document like a deed is to be revised by our courts, proof of mistake must be strong, cogent and convincing. *Hege v. Sellers*, 241 N.C. 240, 84 S.E. 2d 892 (1954). Walker, J., speaking for the Court in *Clements v. Insurance Co.*, 155 N.C. 57, 61, 70 S.E. 1076 (1911), states that:

> There is always a *strong presumption* in favor of the correctness of the instrument as written and executed, for it must be assumed that the parties knew what they had agreed and have chosen fit and proper words to express that agreement in its entirety. (Emphasis added.)

In the case of *Isley v. Brown*, 253 N.C. 791, 793, 117 S.E. 2d 821 (1961), Chief Justice Winborne, quoting Hoke, J., says:

> There is no rule in our system of jurisprudence that has a greater tendency to maintain the stability of titles and the security of investments than that which upholds the integrity of a solemn written deed ...

Defendant contends there was no mistake in the deed from plaintiff to Hice and Welch; that plaintiff selected her own lawyer to prepare the deed and furnished the old deeds for use in preparation; that the tract in question was separated from her homeplace by a stream and was mountainous — just the type of land she intended to convey to Hice, her cousin by marriage, and Welch; and that plaintiff read the deed. Defendant further alleges that Ray Hice was raised on the mountain land, knew where it was, and knew what he was receiving under the deed.

Plaintiff offered evidence which tended to show that she was a 54-year old widow, engaged in settling her husband's estate at the time of the sale; that she had gone no further in school than the seventh grade and was currently employed as a seamstress; that she had not engaged in any real estate transactions prior to this time, and never had been to a lawyer; that she intended to sell the mountain tract, which consisted of 1200 acres, and not her homeplace; that the homeplace had been fenced, and cattle and horses ran on it; and that at the time of the transaction plaintiff was not aware of the fact that her "homeplace" consisted of two tracts.

Dickson Whisnant, a witness for the plaintiff, testified that he was the attorney who prepared the deed to Hice and Welch from deeds brought to him by plaintiff; that all of the land to be sold was contiguous mountain land; that he later (in 1977) discovered the 13-acre tract was not contiguous; that he remarked to plaintiff that this property was not supposed to be in the deed; that including it was his mistake; that he had talked with Mr. Miller who agreed the tract was not supposed to be in the deed (which was denied by Mr. Miller in his testimony); and that he prepared a deed of reconveyance from Hi-Mil, Inc., to plaintiff which was never executed.

A surveyor for the defendant testified that he was unable to fit the 13-acre tract into the plat of the mountain tract prepared for Hi-Mil, Inc. Defendant's attorney further testified that he was unable to fit the 13-acre tract into the boundary as a part of his title examination for Hi-Mil, Inc.

Ray Hice, a cousin of plaintiff's deceased husband, testified that he had lived in the area all his life; that he negotiated for the purchase of the mountain tract; that this tract is approximately three miles from where plaintiff lives and is not contiguous to her homeplace; that the land he purchased consisted of contiguous tracts, totaling 900 acres; that there had not been a survey of the property at the time he purchased it; that none of the 25 acres (homeplace) was to be included; and that he never exercised any dominion over the 25-acre tract where plaintiff's homeplace is.

We conclude there is ample testimony offered by the plaintiff to rebut the presumption relied on by the defendant that the deed is correct as written and executed.

[3] Next, we consider whether Hi-Mil, Inc., is an innocent bona fide purchaser for value. Defendant contends that it is, relying on the presumptions set out above and arguing that the knowledge of any mistake in the deed could not be imputed to the defendant corporation.

It is elementary that as a general rule reformation will not be granted if it appears that the rights of a bona fide purchaser will be prejudiced. *Lowery v. Wilson*, 214 N.C. 800, 200 S.E. 861 (1939); *Dameron v. Lumber Co.*, 161 N.C. 495, 77 S.E. 694 (1913). Plaintiff contends, however, that she presented sufficient evidence of a mistake in the deed from plaintiff to Hice and Welch in 1971, and that such knowledge of the mistake was imputed to the defendant through its shareholder/director/officer, Ray Hice.

Defendant replies, contending that knowledge by Ray Hice of the mistake cannot be imputed for two reasons:

(1) Ray Hice had no knowledge of any mistake at any time until *after* the title was taken by the defendant. Defendant points out that a survey of the mountain tract was not made until *after* the property was purchased by it; that title examination was done simultaneously with the survey; and plaintiff discovered in 1977 the error when she tried to sell her homeplace.

Defendant fails to recognize that the real mistake is plaintiff's conveyance of lands she never intended to sell — not the drafting error by the lawyer. The drafting was merely a ministerial act. A careful reading of all the evidence indicates that Johnsie Hice intended to sell and Ray Hice and Everette Welch intended to purchase the 1200-acre mountain tract. This they did, but more was mistakenly conveyed, and this was error which equity ought to correct. Through all of the mesne conveyances down to the defendant all parties intended to buy only the mountain tract, and it was understood that only the mountain tract was being conveyed. There is no direct evidence of any party's intent ever to sell the 13-acre portion of the homeplace and no intention by any party to buy. In each deed, however, it was erroneously included. Each grantor to a mesne conveyance mistakenly sold more, and each grantee received more than was intended.

(2) Although Ray Hice was a stockholder/director/officer of Hi-Mil, Inc., the corporation was not chargeable with notice of facts known to a director in a transaction between himself and the corporation in which he was acting for himself and not for the corporation. *Gardiner v. Equitable Office Building Corp.*, 273 F. 441 (2nd Cir. 1921).

We do not find the conveyance by Ray Hice to Hi-Mil, Inc., to be strictly at arm's length. Rather, we conclude that Hice's interest and that of the corporation were clearly aligned. Both parties desired to develop the property for their mutual benefit, whether as stockholder or an individual owner. Ray Hice at that time is presumed to have known what he owned and was selling and what the corporation in which he owned 50% of the stock was buying. The knowledge of Ray Hice became the knowledge of the corporation. *Wilson v. Development Co.*, 276 N.C. 198, 171 S.E. 2d 873 (1970); *Whitten v. AMC/Jeep, Inc.*, 292 N.C. 84, 231 S.E. 2d 891 (1977).

The further argument of the appellant that Ray Hice was acting primarily for himself since he would be able to sell his interest in the property and absolve himself from liability for the balance under a mortgage assumed by the defendant and due plaintiff does not impress us. He would still remain secondarily liable.

The defendant has title to a tract of land which it never intended to buy. The plaintiff never intended to sell the 13-acre tract of land. Equity has a duty to correct such mistake as is involved in this case.

We conclude there were issues of fact for the reasons set out above and that Hi-Mil, Inc.'s motion for summary judgment should have been overruled. The trial judge was correct in proceeding to trial. Motions to dismiss made by the defendant at the end of plaintiff's evidence and at the end of all the evidence should have been overruled.

The Order and Judgment of the trial judge are

Affirmed.

Judge MARTIN (Robert M.) concurs.

Judge ARNOLD dissents.

MARY M. WILHITE, WIDOW OF EARNEST WILHITE, DECEASED, PLAINTIFF v. LIBERTY VENEER COMPANY, DEFENDANT-EMPLOYER AND LUMBERMENS MUTUAL CASUALTY COMPANY, DEFENDANT-INSURANCE CARRIER

No. 7910IC911

(Filed 1 July 1980)

1. **Master and Servant § 74– workers' compensation – disfigurement – post mortem award to dependents**

    The dependents of a deceased employee who suffered a serious bodily disfigurement due to an accident covered by the Workers' Compensation Act but who died due to an unrelated cause are entitled to a *post mortem* award for serious bodily disfigurement based on the best possible medical estimate as to the probable residual disability that would have remained had the employee lived to complete his healing period, notwithstanding the employee had not filed a workers' compensation claim for disfigurement before he died.

2. **Master and Servant § 74– workers' compensation – disfigurement – post mortem award – necessary findings**

    A proceeding to recover an award for serious bodily disfigurement suffered by an employee in a compensable accident before his death from an unrelated cuase is remanded for findings as to (1) the state of the employee's recovery at the time of his death; (2) the best possible medical estimate of the probable residual disability which would have remained had the employee lived; and (3) a determination of the effect such disability would have had upon the employee's capacity to earn a living.

APPEAL by defendants from order of North Carolina Industrial Commission entered 15 May 1979. Heard in the Court of Appeals 25 March 1980.

Action by widow of Decedent, Earnest Wilhite, to recover, *inter alia*, an award for serious bodily disfigurement pursuant to N.C. Gen. Stat. § 97-31 (22). It is undisputed that the decedent received second and third degree burns on approximately thirty percent of his body due to an accident which occurred during the course of his employment on 20 June 1975. The decedent had skin grafted from his left thigh with a 100% "take." The deceased was discharged from the hospital on 2 August 1975.

On 25 August 1975 the deceased saw Dr. L.W. Query concerning chest pains. Upon examination, Dr. Query found that the deceased had suffered a heart attack and he was admitted to a local hospital. The deceased was released on 8 September 1975 with a diagnosis of acute myocardial infarction due to hardening of the arteries. The deceased was again admitted to the local hospital on 21 September 1975 due to weakness and shortness of breath, and he died of heart failure on 23 September 1975. Two medical doctors testified that the decedent's death was not causally related to the burns he had suffered.

The Hearing Examiner for the Industrial Commission held that because the death of the deceased was not caused by the burns, the deceased was not entitled to the death benefits of the Workers' Compensation Act, that the serious disfigurement sustained by the deceased did not cause the deceased to suffer a diminution of his future earning power, and that, therefore, no one was entitled to compensation for the serious bodily disfigurement of the deceased. Upon review by the Full Commission, the Full Commission affirmed the Hearing Examiner's causation determination but held that the deceased suffered serious bodily disfigurement which entitled him to an award of $2,250.00.

Although not clearly stated in the record, it is apparent from the arguments of counsel that the deceased received temporary total disability payments up to the date of his death.

Sammie Chess, Jr. for plaintiff appellee.

Tuggle, Duggins, Meschan, Thornton & Elrod by Joseph E.
Elrod, III and Joseph F. Brotherton for defendant appellants.

CLARK, Judge.

[1] This appeal presents a question of first impression in this
jurisdiction: Whether the dependents of an employee who suffers a serious bodily disfigurement due to an accident covered
by the Workers' Compensation Act, but who dies due to an
unrelated cause, are nonetheless entitled to a *post mortem*
award for serious bodily disfigurement?

Several rules of law are undisputed. The purpose of the
Workers' Compensation Act, N.C. Gen. Stat. Ch. 97, is "to furnish compensation for loss of earning capacity." *Branham v.*
Denny Roll & Panel Co., 223 N.C. 233, 236, 25 S.E. 2d 865, 868
(1943). "[U]nder our Act, wages earned, or the capacity to earn
wages, is the test of earning capacity, or, to state it differently,
the diminution of the power or capacity to earn is the measure
of compensability." 223 N.C. at 237, 25 S.E. 2d at 868. This rule
also applies to compensation for serious bodily disfigurement
under N.C. Gen. Stat. § 97-31(22). "Disfigurement alone is not
made compensable by the Act. Before it is compensable it must
be . . . not only (1) marked disfigurement, but also one which (2)
impairs the future usefulness or occupational opportunities of
the injured employee." (Citations and internal quotations omitted) *Davis v. Sanford Construction Company, Inc.*, 247 N.C. 332,
339, 101 S.E. 2d 40, 45 (1957). *See also*, 2 Larson, Workmen's
Compensation Law 58-32 (1976). "[T]here is a serious disfigurement in law only when there is a serious disfigurement in fact.
A serious disfigurement in fact is a disfigurement that . . .
adversely affects the appearance of the injured employee to
such extent that it may be *reasonably presumed* to lessen his
opportunity for remunerative employment . . . . *[N]o present*
loss of wages need be established; but to be *serious*, the
disfigurement must be of such nature that it may be fairly
presumed that the injured employee has suffered a diminution
of his future earning power." (Citations omitted) *Davis, supra*,
247 N.C. at 336, 101 S.E. 2d at 43. The Commission "should take
into consideration the natural physical handicap resulting
from the disfigurement, the age, training, experience, educa-

tion, occupation and adaptability of the employee to obtain and retain employment." *Stanley v. Hyman-Michaels Co.*, 222 N.C. 257, 266, 22 S.E. 2d 570, 576 (1942).

The problem in this case is not one of determining whether the above rules apply, but rather is one of determining *when* they apply. The appellees assert that the proper focus is upon the *post mortem* diminution in earning capacity, and that after one's death there is no earning capacity to be diminished. Appellees also argue that, in any event, no disfigurement award can be made until the decedent had reached maximum medical improvement or the end of the healing period, and since the end of the healing period had not been reached (decedent received temporary total disability payments up to the date of his death), the extent of decedent's disfigurement could not be computed, was therefore premature and was not recoverable. N.C. Gen. Stat. § 97-31 does lend some credence to this argument by providing for compensation during specified periods of time beyond the "healing period." The introductory language of N.C. Gen. Stat. 97-31, however, does not account for the possibility that death from another cause may cut off the healing period. The better rule, we think, is expressed by Professor Larson:

> "[I]f the injured employee dies before stabilization has taken place, the degree of impairment should not be taken as that in effect at the moment of death. The proper procedure is to make the best possible medical estimate of the probable residual disability that would have remained if the employee had lived to complete his healing period."

2 Larson, Workmen's Compensation Law, § 58-40 at 10-258 to -259 (1976). This result, we think, is more consonant with N.C. Gen. Stat. § 97-37, which provides in relevant part:

> *"Where injured employee dies before total compensation is paid.* — When an employee receives or is entitled to compensation under this Article for an injury covered by G.S. 97-31 and *dies from any other cause* than the injury for which he was entitled to compensation, payment of the unpaid balance of compensation shall be made: First to the surviving whole dependents . . . *in lieu of the compensation*

the employee would have been entitled had he lived." (Emphasis supplied.)

This determination, however, does not quite resolve the question before us because no claim for disfigurement was filed before decedent's death and no adjudication of such claim was made before his death. The appellees argue that N.C. Gen. Stat. § 97-37, *supra*, only applies when the "employee *receives* or is *entitled* to compensation" under the Act and that he cannot be so entitled if no adjudication has been made prior to his death. Most courts have held that recovery by a decedent's estate may be had "[i]f a claim [was] filed by the injured worker, but no award [was] made at the time of his death," or if "death occurred after an award was made but while it was pending on appeal, even if the original award was a denial." *Larson, supra*, § 58.40 at 10-255 to -258. *Accord, Inman v. Meares*, 247 N.C. 661, 101 S.E. 2d 692 (1958); *Butts v. Montague Bros.*, 204 N.C. 389, 168 S.E. 215 (1933). In North Carolina, in the situation where a claimant dies after a claim has been filed, the claimant's estate may recover all accrued but unpaid benefits, and all unaccrued benefits to which the employee "would have been entitled" had he lived are payable to decedent's dependents pursuant to N.C. Gen. Stat. 97-37. *McCulloh v. Catawba College*, 266 N.C. 513, 146 S.E. 2d 467 (1966); *Inman v. Meares, supra*.

Generally speaking, a lump sum award made prior to decedent's death is deemed to be an "accrued" benefit, *Larson, supra*, § 58.40 at 10-247; but logic compels us to conclude that if, pursuant to N.C. Gen. Stat. 97-31(22), no determination of the lump sum award for disfigurement had been made prior to death, then such entitlements are "unaccrued" until such time as they are determined, and, for this reason, the payment of the lump sum award for disfigurement would pass to the worker's dependents purusant to N.C. Gen. Stat. 97-37 rather than to the deceased worker's estate.

Whether these principles also apply where no claim had been filed by the worker prior to his death is a novel question in this jurisdiction. We note that some states have permitted recovery in this situation. *Snyder Construction Co. v. Thompson*, 145 Ind. App. 103, 248 N.E. 2d 560 (1969); *Kozielec v. Mack Mfg.*

Corp., 29 N.J. Super. 272, 102 A. 2d 404 (1953). *Contra, Flynn v. Asten Hill Mfg. Co.*, 34 Pa. Commw. Ct. 218, 383 A. 2d 255 (1978), tacitly rejected in *Frederico Granero Company v. Commonwealth, Workmen's Compensation Appeal Board*, 409 A. 2d 1187 (1980). After consideration of this and related authority, we think that allowing the dependent widow of the deceased worker to recover that to which her husband would have been entitled is consistent with the statutory purpose of N.C. Gen. Stat. 97-37, and we hold that plaintiff's claim will not be denied because her husband had not filed a worker's compensation claim for disfigurment before he died. We emphasize that there is no requirement in the statute that a claim be filed before the death of the covered worker.

We note that the plaintiff cannot recover for disfigurement during the period in which the decedent received temporary total disability payments; otherwise the plaintiff would, in effect, be receiving a double recovery for the same injury and such a result has already been rejected by our Supreme Court in *Stanley, supra*, 222 N.C. at 265, 22 S.E. 2d at 576, in the context of an award for disfigurement where permanent total disability payments had been made.

[2] Finally, we have a serious concern as to whether there is sufficient evidence in the record to support an award for disfigurement in accordance with the standards articulated in the second paragraph of this opinion. Appellees point out that no photographs or diagrams of any kind were introduced into evidence and no evidence was adduced as to the state of decedent's recovery at the time of his death from an unrelated cause. Consequently, this case is reversed and remanded to the Industrial Commission and the Industrial Commission is ordered to make additional Findings of Fact concerning: (1) the state of decedent's recovery at the time of his death; (2) the best possible medical estimate as to the probable residual disability that would have remained had the decedent lived; and, (3) a determination of the effect of such disability on the capacity of the decedent to earn a living. Upon such Findings of Fact, the Industrial Commission shall, if necessary, amend the award to the plaintiff for disfigurement suffered by her deceased husband.

The Order of the Commission is

Reversed and Remanded for proceedings consistent with this opinion.

Judges VAUGHN and MARTIN (Harry C.) concur.

ALEX MUMFORD v. HUTTON & BOURBONNAIS COMPANY

No. 8025SC180

(Filed 1 July 1980)

1. **Master and Servant § 10– employment contract – duration not specified – contract terminable at will**

    In an action to recover on an employment contract which plaintiff alleged was to be for a period of three years, plaintiff's complaint was insufficient to state a claim for relief where the time specified in the parties' agreement did not set out a definite term of employment but merely set out a formula for crediting the override account, and the contract was therefore for an indefinite period, and was terminable at the will of either party.

2. **Rules of Civil Procedure § 41– motion to dismiss – hearing not conducted as summary judgment hearing**

    There was no merit to plaintiff's contention that the trial court treated defendant's motion to dismiss under G.S. 1A-1, Rule 12 (b)(6) as a hearing on a motion for summary judgment without giving plaintiff proper notice or a reasonable opportunity to present pertinent evidence, since the trial judge, by asking plaintiff if he desired to present additional evidence or amend his complaint, was doing nothing more than offering plaintiff an opportunity to correct a defective complaint; and there was no matter in the record outside of the pleading which the trial court was considering at that time.

3. **Rules of Civil Procedure § 56.1– notice of summary judgment hearing waived**

    There was no merit to defendant's contention that he was entitled to 10 days' notice of a hearing on a motion to dismiss pursuant to Rule 12 (b)(6) because it was conducted as a hearing on a motion for summary judgment, since plaintiff attended the hearing, made no motion to continue, freely participated in the hearing, and thereby waived any procedural notice required.

4. **Rules of Civil Procedure § 41– dismissal with prejudice – no abuse of discretion**

    The trial court did not abuse its discretion in dismissing plaintiff's action with prejudice where the court gave plaintiff an opportunity to amend his complaint or to offer evidence, and plaintiff declined.

Mumford v. Hutton & Bourbonnais Co.

APPEAL by plaintiff from *Ferrell, Judge.* Orders entered 21 November 1978 and 8 November 1979 in Superior Court, CATAWBA County. Heard in the Court of Appeals 13 June 1980.

This is a suit on an employment contract, which plaintiff alleges was to be for a period of three years. Plaintiff alleges he was wrongfully discharged before the expiration of the contract and seeks damages in the sum of $75,000. A copy of the contract was attached to the complaint and made a part by reference.

Defendant answered the complaint, alleging as a first defense plaintiff's failure to state a claim upon which relief could be granted. The second defense admitted the plaintiff worked for defendant a short while, stated that plaintiff was discharged at will, and denied the existence of the employment contract alleged by the plaintiff. Other defenses were alleged as well as a counterclaim for advances. Plaintiff replied that he had earned the advances set out in the counterclaim. Defendant moved to dismiss the complaint for failure to state a claim upon which relief can be granted pursuant to the provisions of Rule 12 (b)(6).

After hearing arguments of counsel and after inquiring of counsel for the plaintiff in open court whether he desired to make any amendment to the complaint or whether there was any further evidence in regard to the time duration of the contract, and plaintiff through his counsel having advised the court that he desired to make no amendment and that he had no further evidence in regard to the time duration of the contract, the trial judge dismissed plaintiff's action with prejudice. Plaintiff moved for a new trial, and thereafter the same trial judge denied the motion. Plaintiff appealed.

Rudisill & Brackett, by J. Richardson Rudisill Jr., for plaintiff appellant.

Patrick, Harper & Dixon, by James T. Patrick, for defendant appellee.

HILL, Judge.

[1] Plaintiff contends the trial judge erred in dismissing with prejudice his cause of action, pursuant to Rule 12 (b)(6), for failure to state a claim upon which relief can be granted. Plaintiff urges that under the theory of notice pleading he has given sufficient notice of events or transactions which give rise to the claim to enable the adverse party to understand the nature and basis for it, to file a responsive pleading and — by using the rules provided for obtaining pretrial discovery — to get any additional information he may need to prepare for trial. *Sutton v. Duke*, 277 N.C. 94, 176 S.E. 2d 161 (1970).

Nevertheless, a complaint must be dismissed when, on its face, it reveals that no law supports it, that an essential fact is missing, or a fact is disclosed which necessarily defeats it. *Mozingo v. Bank*, 31 N.C. App. 157, 162, 229 S.E. 2d 57 (1976), *disc. rev. denied* 291 N.C. 711 (1977).

Paragraph III of the plaintiff's complaint is as follows:

That on the 23rd day of November, 1976, for good and valuable consideration, the Plaintiff and the Defendant entered into a written contract providing for the employment of the Plaintiff, a copy of which is attached hereto, marked Exhibit 'A' and incorporated herein by reference as if fully set forth herein; that the Plaintiff accepted the employment as outlined by said contract and went to work for the Defendant, pursuant to the terms and provisions of said contract; that the intent of the contract as hereinbefore described was to be a three-year working contract, with both parties having options to review the same at sixty and ninety days; that the Plaintiff has faithfully fulfilled all of his obligations under said contract and was continued by the Defendant after the sixty-day and ninety-day review.

The pertinent parts of Exhibit "A" referred to above are as follows:

4) Hutton & Bourbonnais will start your salary at $12,000.00 per year. If both you and the company are satisfied, this will be raised at the end of a 60 day period to

$15,000.00 per year. Again, if both you and the company are satisfied, this will be raised to $18,000.00 a year at the end of 90 days.

5) In addition to the above salary, Hutton & Bourbonnais will advance $1000.00 per month debit to your over ride account which you may draw against up to the full $1000.00. The company will credit this account as follows:

> For the first year of your employment, you will receive an over ride of 1% on all new accounts (i.e. 76-77 accounts) which have been brought into the company regardless of who is responsible for the account. In the second and third years of your employment you will receive ½ of 1% of these accounts, (i.e. 76-77 account). At the end of the third year, these become house accounts. In the second year of your employment, the same will apply with the new accounts for the 77-78 accounts at the same ½ of 1%; starting point is $4,000,000.00 sales. The company will furnish you a list of present accounts and you will have for your use a computer readout on a weekly basis.

> The company agrees to review this agreement with you at the end of six months. At the end of one year's time and each six months thereafter the draw account will be reconcilled [sic].

The complaint and the exhibit do not indicate a definite term of employment. The time specified in the agreement is nothing more than a formula for crediting the override account. Such a provision as a matter of law does not establish a definite term of employment. *Freeman v. Hardee's Food Systems*, 3 N.C. App. 435, 165 S.E. 2d 39 (1968). When the duration of employment is not definitely specified, the contract is for an indefinite period, terminable at the will of either party. *Freeman, supra.*

Plaintiff contends, however, that the pleadings and exhibit do not include the entire contract between the parties and that part of the contract was oral. Plaintiff further points out that his complaint sets forth " ... that the intent of the contract, as

hereinbefore described, was to be a three-year working contract, with both parties having options to review the same at
sixty and ninety days." The complaint does not refer to an oral
contract, only a written contract, and the reference to the "intent of the contract" refers only to plaintiff's conclusions as to
the effect of its provisions.

At the hearing on the motion, the trial judge asked counsel
for the defendant whether there was further evidence in regard
to time duration other than the written agreement, or whether
plaintiff desired to amend his complaint. Plaintiff's counsel
advised the court that he desired to make no amendment and
had no further evidence in regard to time duration. Plaintiff
now contends that he did have other evidence to complement
the written agreement but was not prepared to offer it at the
time. However, in his motion for a new trial, plaintiff states: "It
is true that at this hearing Plaintiff had available no other
evidence as to the time duration of the contract, but this is not
to say that upon adequate discovery and live testimony at a
trial of this matter, such other evidence could not be presented
. . . ." Plaintiff was given adequate opportunity by the trial
judge to amend his complaint to broaden the terms of the employment contract to show duration. He declined to do so. Plaintiff denied the existence of such evidence then. The trial judge
had every right to believe him. He may not now go on a fishing
expedition to find substantive facts, if any there be, which, due
to the nature of this action, must have been within his personal
knowledge prior to filing his complaint.

Plaintiff's first assignment of error is overruled.

[2] Next, plaintiff contends the trial judge treated the motion
to dismiss under Rule 12 (b)(6) as a hearing on a motion for
summary judgment as provided in Rule 56 without giving the
plaintiff proper notice or a reasonable opportunity to present
pertinent evidence. Counsel for plaintiff argues that he did not
bring evidence of the time duration of the contract with him to
the hearing because he had no notice that such evidence would
be required at the hearing; that when the court asked for further evidence the court was treating the hearing as one for
summary judgment as allowed by Rule 12 (d), and plaintiff was

entitled to be given an opportunity to present all material as provided in Rule 56.

Plaintiff did not request additional time. By asking the plaintiff if he desired to present additional evidence or amend his complaint, the trial judge was doing nothing more than offering the plaintiff an opportunity to correct a defective complaint. We do not observe any matter in the record outside of the pleadings under consideration at that time. This assignment of error is overruled.

[3,4] Plaintiff further argues that even if the dismissal under Rule 12 (b)(6) were warranted, it should have been entered without prejudice. The effect of a dismissal with prejudice is to preclude subsequent litigation to the same extent as if the action had been tried to a final adjudication on the merits, and to make the usual rules of *res judicata* applicable. *Barnes v. McGee*, 21 N.C. App. 287, 289, 204 S.E. 2d 203 (1974). He further contends he was entitled to 10 days' notice since the matter was tried as in summary judgment. (Rule 56) At most, plaintiff argues his was a defective statement of a good cause of action, and he ought to be allowed to amend.

The case was duly calendared for hearing in November 1978. Plaintiff attended the hearing and made no motion to continue. He freely participated in the hearing. By doing so, plaintiff waived any procedural notice required. *Collins v. Highway Commission*, 237 N.C. 277, 74 S.E. 2d 709 (1953); *Raintree Corp. v. Rowe*, 38 N.C. App. 664, 248 S.E. 2d 904 (1978).

As provided under Rule 41 (b), the court in its discretion had authority to dismiss the action with prejudice. The court offered plaintiff an opportunity to amend or to offer evidence, which was declined. We find no error in this assignment.

The trial judge heard plaintiff's motion for a new trial under Rule 59 and denied the motion. The court's decision is not reviewable on appeal, absent manifest abuse of discretion. *Britt v. Allen*, 291 N.C. 630, 231 S.E. 2d 607 (1977). There is no evidence of any abuse of discretion in the record before this Court, and this assignment is denied.

Plaintiff has not set out Assignment of Error No. 1 in his brief, cited authority, nor argued its cause. This assignment is deemed abandoned under Appellate Rule 28 (b)(3).

The orders of the trial judge are

Affirmed.

Judges ARNOLD and ERWIN concur.

STATE OF NORTH CAROLINA v. WAYLAND D. CURRIE

No. 804SC31

(Filed 1 July 1980)

1. **Indictment and Warrant §§ 17.2, 17.3– variance as to time and place of offense**

There was no fatal variance between an indictment charging defendant with felonious possession of a stolen trailer in Duplin County on 21 January 1979 and evidence showing defendant possessed the trailer in Columbus County on 18 February 1979 since (1) defendant presented alibi defenses relating to 21 January and 18 February and therefore did not rely on the date charged in the indictment; (2) defendant was not misled by the allegation of possession in Duplin County because the allegation of place was not descriptive of the offense of felonious possession of stolen property; and (3) the allegation of the county where the offense occurred was essentially one of venue, and the allegation of venue became conclusive under G.S. 15A-135 when defendant failed to make a timely motion to dismiss for improper venue.

2. **Receiving Stolen Goods § 6– possession of stolen goods – date of possession– erroneous instruction – alibi**

Where there was evidence tending to show that defendant possessed a stolen trailer on 18 February 1979 but no evidence that he possessed the trailer on 21 January, the date alleged in the indictment, the trial court erred in submitting the question of defendant's guilt of felonious possession on the date charged in the indictment rather than the date shown by the evidence, since the instruction permitted the jury to convict defendant of possession on a date about which there was no evidence and deprived defendant of the benefit of his alibi because it allowed the jurors to convict even if they believed defendant's alibi for the date on which the State's evidence shows possession occurred.

State v. Currie

APPEAL by defendant from *Allsbrook, Judge*. Judgment entered 5 July 1979 in Superior Court, DUPLIN County. Heard in the Court of Appeals 15 May 1980.

Defendant was indicted for felonious larceny of a 1977 Model Evans Low-Boy Equipment Trailer owned by Bizzelle David Johnson and valued at $13,000 and for felonious possession of said trailer on 21 January 1979 in Duplin County. The original indictment identified the trailer as a 1978 model owned by Nash Johnson and Sons Farms, Inc. A jury found defendant guilty of felonious possession of stolen property, and he was sentenced to a term of not less than 6 nor more than 8 years to be suspended for 5 years on the following conditions: that defendant be placed on probation for 5 years and that he pay certain fines and restitution.

At trial the State presented evidence which tended to show that on or about 20 January 1979, a trailer belonging to Bizzelle Johnson and valued at approximately $14,000 was stolen from behind his office building in Rose Hill. He recovered the trailer in the latter part of February 1979 from C.M. Lindsay in a town outside Lumberton, North Carolina. The recovery was facilitated by information obtained from Pete Williamson, who was paid a $500 reward by Johnson.

Williamson testified that in the latter part of February 1979, defendant told him that he had an Evans Low-Boy Trailer for sale. When Williamson later asked defendant if he had sold the trailer, defendant told him he had sold it to Lindsay. Williamson admitted that he never saw the trailer in defendant's possession.

William Powell testified that around 1 January 1979, defendant told him that he might have a Low-Boy trailer for sale later in the month. Around 1 February 1979 defendant told Powell he had a 40-foot trailer. About a week later Powell and Lindsay rode with defendant to see the trailer. The next day defendant and Powell met with Lindsay in Lumberton. At that time Lindsay made a check out to J. & P. Salvage Company, Powell's business, for $2,500 in return for the trailer. The check was dated 19 February 1979. Powell then gave defendant $2,500 in cash.

Lindsay testified that on 18 February 1979 he viewed the trailer with defendant at the intersection of Highways No. 87 and 74, a place about 16 miles from Wilmington. Defendant told him that he wanted $5,000. Lindsay agreed to pay $4,500. The next day Lindsay picked the trailer up. He drew a check for $2,500 and planned to pay the balance to Powell when he received title. Lindsay testified that he traded the trailer with Powell and never saw defendant get any money. On redirect, Lindsay stated that he was led to believe that defendant owned the trailer.

Defendant then presented the testimony of the Chairman of the Columbus County Board of Education and another man, who both testified that from 7:00 a.m. on 20 January 1979 until 9:00 p.m. on 21 January 1979 they accompanied defendant on a trip to Elbing Park near Beech Mountain and back.

Defendant himself testified as to said trip. He further testified that when he returned home at 9:00 p.m. on 21 January 1979 he spent the night with his wife; that he remembered talking with Williamson at D.P. Currie's Grocery only about high-sided trailers; that on 20 February 1979 he, Powell and a man named Harry Stone drove to Lumberton; that he was not aware of the check drawn by Lindsay until he was shown a copy by Officer Baysden; that on 18 February 1979 he spent the day with his daughter playing in the snow and that he never received any money for Johnson's trailer. Defendant's wife and daughter corroborated his testimony. Defendant then presented testimony of his good character and reputation.

On rebuttal the State presented two witnesses who testified that during the discussion at Currie's Grocery, they heard defendant say that he knew where there was a Low-Boy trailer.

Attorney General Edmisten, by Associate Attorney Grayson G. Kelley, for the State.

Ralph G. Jorgensen for defendant appellant.

MARTIN (Robert M.), Judge.

[1]　Defendant contends the court erred in failing to require the State to prove that defendant had possession of the stolen trailer in Duplin County on 21 January 1979 as charged in the indictment. Defendant argues that a nonsuit should have been granted on the ground that there was no proof that defendant possessed the stolen trailer in Duplin County on 21 January 1979 and that defendant was not connected with the trailer until 18 February 1979 in Columbus County and 19 February 1979 in Robeson County.

A fatal variance between the indictment and the proof is properly raised by motion for judgment of nonsuit. *State v. Cooper,* 275 N.C. 283, 167 S.E. 2d 266 (1969). As to the variance in the time of the offense, where time is not of the essence of the offense charged and the statute of limitations is not involved, a discrepancy between the date in the indictment and the date shown by the State's evidence is ordinarily not fatal. G.S. 15-155; G.S. 15A-924 (a)(4); *State v. Locklear,* 33 N.C. App. 647, 236 S.E. 2d 376, *cert. denied,* 293 N.C. 363, 237 S.E. 2d 851 (1977); 7 Strong's N.C. Index 3d, Indictment and Warrant § 17.3 (1977).

> [T]he time named in a bill of indictment is not usually an essential ingredient of the crime charged, and the State may prove that it was in fact committed on some other date. (Citations omitted). But this salutary rule, preventing a defendant who does not rely on time as a defense from using a discrepancy between the time named in the bill and the time shown by the evidence for the State, cannot be used to ensnare a defendant and thereby deprive him of an opportunity to adequately present his defense.

State v. Whittemore, 255 N.C. 583, 592, 122 S.E. 2d 396, 403 (1961).

In the present case, defendant presented an alibi defense relating to 21 January 1979, the date charged in the indictment. Defendant also presented an alibi defense relating to 18 February 1979, the date shown by the State's evidence on which defendant was in possession of the trailer. Therefore, as in *Locklear, supra,* it is evident defendant did not rely on the date charged in the indictment. The variation in the State's evidence neither deprived defendant of his right adequately to present his defense nor ensnared defendant in any way. Under these circumstances, the variance between the date in the indictment and that shown by the evidence is not prejudicial.

Similarly, we find no merit in defendant's contention that he was entitled to dismissal because the indictment charged that the possession occurred in Duplin County but the proof indicated possession, if any, occurred in Columbus County. The court takes judicial notice that the intersection of Highways 87 and 74 is in Columbus County. "Where an indictment alleges the particular place where an act took place, and such allegation is not descriptive of the offense, and is not required to be proved as laid in order to show the court's jurisdiction . . . a variance which does not mislead accused or expose him to double jeopardy is not material." *State v. Martin*, 270 N.C. 286, 288, 154 S.E. 2d 96, 98 (1967), quoting 42 C.J.S., Indictments and Informations, § 256. In the present case, the allegation in the indictment as to place was not descriptive of the offense of felonious possession of stolen property. The bill of indictment contained a specific description of the stolen property which was identified with sufficient particularity as to enable defendant to prepare his defense. Defendant as shown above was not misled by the allegation of possession in Duplin County.

Moreover, in order to sustain a conviction it is not necessary for the State to prove that the crime occurred in the county where the indictment was drawn. *State v. Ray*, 209 N.C. 772, 184 S.E. 2d 836 (1936). We are not unmindful of G.S. 15A-924 (a)(3) which requires a criminal pleading to contain a statement or cross reference in each count indicating that the offense charged therein was committed in a designated county. We, however, believe that in a criminal pleading, the statement of the county where the charged offense occurred is essentially one of venue. G.S. 15A-135 provides: "Allegations of venue in any criminal pleading become conclusive in the absence of a timely motion to dismiss for improper venue under G.S. 15A-952." The question of venue was not timely raised by defendant's motion to dismiss made at the close of the State's evidence and the allegations of venue became conclusive under G.S. 15A-135. *State v. Morrow*, 31 N.C. App. 654, 230 S.E. 2d 568 (1976). Thus, if the offense of possession had not been committed in Duplin County, defendant waived his objection by not making a timely motion to dismiss for improper venue.

[2] Defendant further contends that the court erred in failing to instruct the jury that in order to convict the defendant of felonious possession of stolen property under the indictment the possession had to be in Duplin County on 21 January 1979. No such instruction was required as to Duplin County. As above noted the allegation of venue contained in the indictment became conclusive. *State v. Morrow, supra.* The judge's charge on the elements of felonious possession of stolen goods followed that in N.C.P.I. — Crim. 216.47 and correctly set forth the elements of that offense. In his final mandate, however, the judge went on to instruct the jury as follows:

> So, I charge that if you find from the evidence and beyond a reasonable doubt that the 1977 Evans Low-Boy trailer was stolen ... and that on or about January 21, 1979, Wayland D. Currie, the defendant, possessed this Low Boy trailer ... it would be your duty to return a verdict of guilty of felonious possession of stolen goods.

While not required to charge on the date of the offense, in so doing, the court submitted the question of defendant's guilt on the date charged in the bill of indictment rather than the date as shown by the evidence. *State v. Overcash,* 182 N.C. 889, 109 S.E. 2d 626 (1921). The evidence conclusively shows that if the defendant possessed the property it was on 18 February 1979. There is no evidence defendant possessed the trailer on or about 21 January 1979. This instruction permitted the jury to disregard the evidence that the offense occurred on 18 February 1979, which was the only evidence of when any offense occurred, and convict defendant of possession on 21 January 1979, about which there was no evidence. It deprived defendant of the benefit of his alibi because it allowed jurors to convict even if they believed defendant's alibi for the date on which the State's evidence shows possession occurred. *State v. Poindexter,* 21 N.C. App. 720, 205 S.E. 2d 145 (1974).

It is not necessary for us to consider defendant's first assignment of error as it may not occur on a new trial.

New trial.

Judges ARNOLD and WELLS concur.

RICHARD H. DeJAAGER v. GHISLAINE M. DeJAAGER

No. 794DC936

(Filed 1 July 1980)

Husband and Wife § 10– separation agreement – no private examination of wife – improper certifying officer – curative statutes inapplicable

The wife's acknowledgement of a separation agreement was fatally defective under former G.S. 52-6 where there was no private examination of the wife and thus no finding as to whether the agreement was unreasonable or injurious to the wife, and where the acknowledgment was certified by a Judge Advocate in the Marine Corps who did not qualify as a "certifying officer" under G.S. 52-6(c) because his position was not that of an "equivalent or corresponding officer" of the jurisdiction where the examination and acknowledgement were to be made. Furthermore, the omission of the private examination and the lack of authority on the part of the certifying officer precludes the use of curative statutes, G.S. 52-8 and G.S. 47-81.2, to validate the agreement.

APPEAL by defendant from *Erwin, Judge.* Judgment entered 17 May 1979 in District Court, ONSLOW County. Heard in the Court of Appeals 11 March 1980.

Plaintiff and defendent were married on 7 June 1955 and lived together until 6 June 1977, the date of their separation. On 10 November 1978, plaintiff sued for divorce based on one year's separation. Defendant answered on 11 January 1979, averring that their separation was due to plaintiff's constructive abandonment of her, and, in addition, counterclaimed for temporary alimony, permanent alimony and attorneys' fees. Plaintiff pleaded a separation agreement dated 26 May 1977 to preclude defendant's claim for alimony, and moved for summary judgment on that ground.

On 22 February 1979, plaintiff was granted an absolute divorce from defendant. On hearing of defendant's claim for temporary alimony, the trial court, on 9 April 1979, awarded defendant $400 per month as temporary alimony plus attorneys' fees. On 17 May 1979, however, the court granted plaintiff's motion for summary judgment on defendant's claim for permanent alimony, based on a finding that the separation agreement was properly acknowledged and otherwise valid. Defendant appeals. Plaintiff cross assigns error to the award of attorneys' fees to defendant in the temporary alimony action.

Other facts necessary to the disposition of this appeal are related below.

Brock, Foy and Proctor, by Jimmy C. Proctor, for plaintiff appellee.

Dixon and Horne, by Phillip R. Dixon, for defendant appellant.

MORRIS, Chief Judge.

The primary question before us is a determination with respect to the validity of the separation agreement entered into by the parties on 26 May 1977, as brought forth by defendant's tenth assignment of error.

The separation agreement dated 26 May 1977 contained the following provision:

The wife accepts the provisions herein made in lieu of and in full settlement and satisfaction of any and all claims and rights against her husband for her support and maintenance and in full settlement and satisfaction of any and all other claims and rights whatsoever.

Plaintiff relies on this provision as a bar to defendant's claim for permanent alimony. Defendant, however, contests the validity of the separation agreement on the ground that it fails to meet the requirements of G.S. 52-6, which provided, at the time the separation agreement was executed, in pertinent part, as follows:

(a) No contract between husband and wife made during their coverture shall be valid to affect or change any part of the real estate of the wife, or the accruing income thereof for a longer time than three years next ensuing the making of such contract, nor shall any separation agreement between husband and wife be valid for any purpose, unless such contract or separation agreement is in writing, and is acknowledged before a certifying officer who shall make a private examination of the wife according to the requirements formerly prevailing for conveyance of land.

(b) The certifying officer examining the wife shall incorporate in his certificate a statement of his conclusions and findings of fact as to whether or not [sic] said contract is unreasonable or injurious to the wife. The certificate of the officer shall be conclusive of the facts therein stated but may be impeached for fraud as other judgments may be.

(c) Such certifying officer must be a justice, judge, magistrate, clerk, assistant clerk or deputy clerk of the General Court of Justice or the equivalent or corresponding officers of the state, territory or foreign country where the acknowledgment and examination are made and such officer must not be a party to the contract.

As originally drawn and signed, the 26 May 1977 separation agreement contains the signatures of, aside from plaintiff and defendant, R.O. Lange and Ferris R. Bond. The following acknowledgment appears in the record:

On this the 26th day of May, 1977, before me, Ferris R. Bond, the undersigned officer, personally appeared Richard H. DeJaager, known to me to be a Retired, Non-Commissioned Officer with the Armed Forces of the United States and his wife, Ghislaine M. DeJaager, who is also known to me and to be the persons whose names are subscribed to the within instrument and acknowledged that they executed the same for the purposes therein contained. And the undersigned does further certify that he is at the date of this certificate a Commissioned Officer of the rank

stated below and is in the active service of the Armed
Forces of the United States.

s/ FERRIS R. BOND CPT, USMCR, Judge Advocate of
the United States Marine Corps stationed at the Joint
Law Center, Marine Corps Air Station, (Helocopter),
New River, North Carolina.

Defendant argues that this acknowledgment is deficient in that
there was no private examination; that it contains no conclusions and findings of fact as to whether the contract is unreasonable or injurious to the wife, as required by G.S. 52-6(b);
and that Ferris R. Bond was not a proper certifying officer, as
required by G.S. 52-6(c). Defendant argues, in addition, that
these defects cannot be cured by the operation of G.S. 52-8 or
G.S. 47-81.2, in that, aside from the defect as to private examination, the separation agreement is not "in all other respects
valid," *citing Mansour v. Rabil*, 277 N.C. 364, 177 S.E. 2d 849
(1970), and *Boone v. Brown*, 11 N.C. App. 355, 181 S.E. 2d 157
(1971).

With respect to the validity of the separation agreement, we
agree with defendant that the failure to comply with G.S. 52-6 in
this instance leaves the purported acknowledgment fatally defective. It is clear that no private examination was conducted in
this case. It necessarily follows that there was not included in
the acknowledgment a statement of the results of such examination. Finally, we find that Ferris R. Bond did not qualify
as a "certifying officer" under G.S. 52-6(c) in that his position as
a Judge Advocate in the Marine Corps was not that of an
"equivalent or corresponding" officer within the jurisidiction
where the acknowledgment and examination were to be made.
See 10 U.S.C. § 936(a)(1); G.S. 47-2, G.S. 10-4(a)(1); G.S. 52-6(c). *See
also Boone v. Brown*, supra (notary public not authorized under
G.S. 52-6 to make required certificate). In any event, the acknowledgment which was executed by Bond and which closely
parallels in substance the form encouraged by G.S. 47-2, is
clearly insufficient for the purposes of the private examination
requirement of G.S. 52-6.

In addition, while we question the continued usefulness of the holdings in *Mansour* and *Boone*, we nevertheless conclude that the curative statute G.S. 52-8 and its counterpart G.S. 47-81.2 are inapplicable to the separation agreement here. In the recent case of *Johnson v. Burrow*, 42 N.C. App. 273, 256 S.E. 2d 811 (1979), our application of the curative statute G.S. 39-13.1(b) was based on our finding that a private examination was conducted by a proper certifying officer, and that the only omission from the requirements of G.S. 52-6 was the certificate that the deed was not unreasonable or injurious to the wife. We held there that the instrument in question was in all other respects proper. In the present case, we hold, under the authority in *Johnson*, that the omission of the private examination and the lack of authority on the part of the officer acknowledging the separation agreement precludes the use of the curative statutes to validate the instrument.

In his brief, plaintiff attacks the constitutionality of G.S. 52-6, but this argument was not advanced at the trial level. "[A]s a general rule this Court will not pass upon a constitutional question not raised and considered in the court from which the appeal was taken." *Brice v. Moore*, 30 N.C. App. 365, 368, 226 S.E. 2d 882, 884 (1976). We adhere to this principle in this case.

Since the separation agreement was not executed in the manner required by G.S. 52-6, and there is not validation under G.S. 52-8, it is void *ab initio*. *Rupert v. Rupert*, 15 N.C. App. 730, 190 S.E. 2d 693 (1972). It follows that the trial court erred in ruling, in its first conclusion of law, that the separation agreement was valid and binding and that it constituted a bar to defendant's counterclaim for permanent alimony. We, therefore, hold that summary judgment was improperly entered against defendant, and we accordingly remand this action for further proceedings not inconsistent with this opinion.

Plaintiff's cross-assignment of error as to the allowance of attorneys' fees in the order of 9 April 1979 awarding temporary alimony is improperly brought forward under North Carolina Appellate Rule 10, which provides that an appellee, without taking an appeal, may bring up within appellant's appeal "any action or omission of the trial court to which an exception was duly taken . . . and which deprived the appellee of an alternative basis in law for supporting the judgment, order, or other determination from which appeal has been taken." The correct avenue of relief from the order would have been a direct appeal. The question is not before us on this appeal.

Reversed and remanded.

Judges VAUGHN and ARNOLD concur.

STATE OF NORTH CAROLINA v. JAMES CHARLES FLOWERS, JR.

No. 7919SC610

(Filed 1 July 1980)

1. **Criminal Law § 63– statements by defendant to police – inadmissibility to show insanity**

    In a prosecution for discharging a firearm into an occupied vehicle where defendant pled insanity, the trial court did not err in refusing to allow a police officer who investigated the crime to testify that defendant admitted shooting a school bus because "he was one of God's children and it was God's bus" since the statement was not so inherently reliable as to be allowed in evidence to show what the witness relied on to form his opinion that defendant was insane.

2. **Criminal Law § 5– insanity – issue for jury determination**

    Defendant's contention that he was entitled to a directed verdict because he offered plenary evidence of insanity which was uncontradicted was without merit.

3. **Criminal Law § 5– defense of insanity – instructions on commitment procedure**

    There was no merit to defendant's contention that he was prejudiced by improper evidence which showed that if he were found not guilty by reason of insanity, he would not be confined, since the testimony of a psychiatrist was not unequivocal that defendant would be released if found not guilty by reason of insanity, and since the court properly charged as to the commitment procedure if defendant were found not guilty by reason of insanity.

4. **Criminal Law § 63– defendant's statements to psychiatrist – admissibility**

    Statements made by defendant to a psychiatrist concerning his use of drugs were inherently reliable, and the trial court did not err in allowing them into evidence.

5. **Criminal Law § 102.6– defendant under influence of drugs – jury argument supported by evidence**

Testimony by a psychiatrist who examined defendant that defendant's conduct was similar to that of a person using PCP, that the psychiatrist suspected the use of PCP because of certain conduct of defendant, and that, in the psychiatrist's opinion, defendant's illness was made worse by some type of drug was sufficient evidence of the use of drugs by defendant at the time of the crime charged so that the district attorney could argue it to the jury and the court should have mentioned it in the charge.

APPEAL by defendant from *Wood, Judge.* Judgment entered 1 March 1979 in Superior Court, ROWAN County. Heard in the Court of Appeals 27 November 1979.

Defendant was charged with having feloniously discharged a firearm into an occupied vehicle. He pled not guilty by reason of insanity. Evidence at trial tended to show that on the morning of 16 October 1978, defendant waited with two school children at a school bus stop in Rowan County and when the bus stopped, he asked for a "lift." When he was told by one of the passengers that he could not ride because "[i]t's illegal," defendant replied that "[i]t's not illegal. This is God's bus. I'm one of God's children. I'm going to blow that stop sign off as a warning to anybody that comes by here." As the bus left the bus stop, the defendant shot at the rear of the bus with a shotgun hitting the area of the right taillight.

The defense called seven witnesses. Each of them testified that at the time of the shooting, defendant did not understand the nature and quality of his act or the difference between right and wrong in relation thereto.

The defendant was found guilty and sentenced to ten years in prison. He has appealed.

Attorney General Edmisten, by Assistant Attorney General George W. Lennon, for the State.

Burke, Donaldson and Holshouser, by William D. Kenerly, for defendant appellant.

WEBB, Judge.

[1] The defendant's first assignment of error deals with the exclusion of testimony by the arresting officer. The State did not call the officer as a witness. He testified as a witness for the defendant to the effect that the defendant was insane at the time of the shooting. The court allowed the officer to testify as to how the defendant acted, looked, and spoke, but refused to allow him to testify that the defendant admitted shooting the bus because "he was one of God's children and it was God's bus." Defendant argues that this testimony should have been admissible as being a statement on which the witness relied to form his opinion that the defendant was insane. Our Supreme Court in *State v. Wade*, 296 N.C. 454, 251 S.E. 2d 407 (1979) recently dealt with the question of the admissibility in evidence of conversations between a psychiatrist and a patient. The psychiatrist had used the conversations to form an opinion that the defendant did not know the difference between right and wrong at the time of an alleged shooting. The Supreme Court held that the psychiatrist should have been allowed to testify to these conversations. The Supreme Court reasoned that statements made to a physician in the course of an examination are inherently reliable and should have been admitted into evidence. The statement made to the officer in the case sub judice was made while the officer was in the presence of the defendant but was not interrogating him. Based on the reasoning of *Wade*, we hold the statement was not so inherently reliable as to be allowed in evidence to show what the witness relied upon in forming his opinion. *Wade* also held that declarations of the defendant may be admitted to show the state of mind of the defendant if the declarations are made prior to the alleged crime. In the case sub judice the statements were made after the alleged crime. The defendant's first assignment of error is overruled.

The defendant's second assignment of error deals with certain questions asked by the court of Dr. James Groce, a psychiatrist who testified that in his opinion the defendant did not know the difference between right and wrong at the time he shot into the bus. During his testimony, the court asked Dr. Groce whether the defendant had been given drugs during the course of his treatment. Dr. Groce then described the type of drugs which were administered to the defendant and his response to the treatment. At another point in his testimony, the court asked Dr. Groce whether PCP could be taken orally. Dr. Groce responded that "it can be swallowed, injected or smoked." The court then asked if the effect is the same and Dr. Groce responded in the affirmative. Defendant contends that the court by its questions expressed an opinion on the evidence. Dr. Groce, at other parts of his testimony, testified as to the drugs he had administered to the defendant and to his investigation as to the possible use by the defendant of PCP. We hold the questions of the court served to clarify the testimony of Dr. Groce and were not expressions of opinion by the court.

[2] The defendant's third assignment of error deals with the denial of his motion for a directed verdict. The defendant contends that he offered plenary evidence of insanity which was uncontradicted and this required that the case be dismissed. We hold that we are bound by *State v. Leonard*, 296 N.C. 58, 248 S.E. 2d 853 (1978). This assignment of error is overruled.

[3] By his fourth assignment of error, defendant contends he was prejudiced by improper evidence that showed that if he were found not guilty by reason of insanity, he would not be confined. He argues further that this error was compounded by allowing the district attorney to argue it to the jury and the court's referring to it in its charge. During the cross-examination of Dr. Groce, the following colloquy occurred:

"Q. So the only way a person can be involuntarily committed against their will is if they are mentally ill or inebriate or imminently dangerous to themselves or others?

A. That's correct.

Q. Now, you indicated at the time you saw the defendant last that that condition did not exist?

A. That's true.

Q. So he was not civilly committable?

A. No, he was not. He had recovered very nicely."

In his argument to the jury the district attorney made the following statement:

> "Dr. Groce released the defendant after his confinement with the statement brought out on cross examination that he was not imminently dangerous to himself or others."

In its charge to the jury, the court stated that Dr. Groce had said:

> "that the last time he was seen that he was not imminently dangerous to himself or others . . . ."

We hold it was not prejudicial error to allow Dr. Groce to testify as he did. The testimony of Dr. Groce was not unequivocal that the defendant would be released if found not guilty by reason of insanity. The court charged as to the commitment procedure if the defendant were found not guilty by reason of insanity. *See State v. Hammonds*, 290 N.C. 1, 224 S.E. 2d 595 (1976). This should have resolved any doubt that was in the jurors' minds. We also hold that the argument of the district attorney and the court's statement were not in error. Neither the district attorney nor the court said the defendant would be released if he were found not guilty. We believe it is speculation that the jury would have interpreted it that way.

[4] The defendant's fifth assignment of error deals with questions on cross–examination of Dr. Groce in regard to drug use by the defendant. During the cross–examination of Dr. Groce, he stated that the defendant told him he had taken PCP and "every other drug that I asked him about." Dr. Groce also said, "I could not exclude any of those drugs from my psychiatric and physical evaluation." Later in the cross–examintion he said that a member of his staff had called the defendant's sister and she told him her brother had taken a drug which Dr. Groce concluded was PCP. Relying on *State v. Wade, supra,* we hold that the statements made by defendant to Dr. Groce were inherently reliable and properly admitted into evidence. The statement made by defendant's sister to a member of Dr. Groce's staff was not so inherently reliable and should have

been excluded. There was sufficient competent evidence of the defendant's use of PCP, however, that we hold this was was harmless error.

[5] The defendant's last assignment of error is to the court's allowing the district attorney to argue that the defendant was under the influence of drugs at the time of the alleged crime and voluntary drug intoxication is not an excuse for a crime. The defendant also contends it was error for the court to charge the jury that there was some evidence the defendant was under the influence of PCP at the time of the alleged crime. Dr. Groce had testified that the defendant's conduct was similar to that of a person using PCP; that he had suspected the use of PCP because of certain conduct of the defendant; and in his opinion, the defendant's illness was made worse by some type of drug. We hold this was sufficient evidence of the use of drugs by the defendant at the time of the shooting so that the district attorney could argue it to the jury and the court should have mentioned it in the charge. The defendant's last assignment of error is overruled.

No error.

Judges VAUGHN and MARTIN (Harry C.) concur.

———————————

SPRINGDALE ESTATES ASSOCIATION v. WAKE COUNTY, NORTH CAROLINA

No. 8010SC43
(Filed 1 July 1980)

1. **Counties § 5.5– county subdivision ordinance – applicability to subdivision**

A subdivision designated as "Springdale Woods" was subject to a county subdivision ordinance where a subdivision plat of a tract known as "Woodbrook Estates" was recorded prior to passage of the ordinance, a plat of "Springdale Woods," which was a combination of previously platted lots in Woodbrook Estates, was recorded after the effective date of the ordinance, and there was no evidence that lots in Springdale Woods equal or exceed the standards of the county as shown in its subdivision regulations so as to exempt Springdale Woods from the subdivision ordinance under G.S. 153A-335(1).

2. **Counties § 5.5– county subdivision ordinance – name closely approximating name of existing subdivision**

The names "Springdale Gardens" and "Springdale Woods" closely approximate the name "Springdale Estates," an existing subdivision so that the use of such names for subdivisions violates Section 3-4-4 of the Wake County Subdivision Regulations.

APPEAL by plaintiff from *Britt (Samuel E.), Judge.* Order entered 17 August 1979 in Superior Court, WAKE County. Heard in the Court of Appeals 3 June 1980.

Plaintiff is an association of homeowners who reside within Springdale Estates Subdivision, and is duly incorporated as a non-profit corporation. The defendant is a political subdivision of the State of North Carolina with all the incident rights, powers, privileges and obligations.

Springdale Estates Subdivision was platted in 1966, and a map of the subdivision was filed in the office of the Register of Deeds for Wake County. The property was developed as a residential subdivision, and, at the time this action was brought, about 275 single family residences had been constructed.

Edd K. Roberts is a real estate developer and owner of two tracts of land adjacent to Springdale Subdivision. At sometime prior to 19 October 1977, the subdivision administrator of the Wake County Planning Department advised Roberts that the name "Springdale Gardens of America, Inc.," by which Roberts planned to designate his tracts, would not be acceptable to the Wake County Planning Board as a name for a subdivision. On 19 October 1977, however, Roberts submitted a preliminary plat entitled "Springdale Gardens" to the Wake County Planning Board, and it was approved. On 15 March 1978 the construction plat of "Springdale Gardens" was approved by the Wake County Planning Director, and a plat thereof recorded on 19 April 1978. A minor subdivision plat was approved by the planning director on 30 January 1978 and recorded.

A subdivision plat of another tract adjacent to Springdale

Estates and known as "Woodbrook Estates" had been recorded in 1964. On 30 June 1978 a plat designated "Springdale Woods" was recorded. The Springdale Woods Subdivision is a combination of previously platted lots in Woodbrook Estates.

Representatives of the plaintiff objected to the use of the names Springdale Gardens and Springdale Woods and sought relief from the Wake County Planning Board and thereafter from the Board of Commissioners. The relief was denied. The plaintiff then filed this complaint and petition to be treated in the alternative as a petition for judicial review or petition in the nature of a writ for certiorari, and seeking an injunction or restraining order prohibiting use of the names "Springdale Gardens" and "Springdale Woods" as had been permitted in a "judgment" entered by the Board of Commissioners of Wake County. Judge Godwin issued a preliminary injunction restraining the defendant from approving or authorizing the use of the names "Springdale Gardens" and "Springdale Woods." Judge Britt subsequently heard the matter on its merits and adopted and approved the "judgment" of the Wake County Board of Commissioners authorizing and allowing the use of the names "Springdale Gardens" and "Springdale Woods." Plaintiff appealed.

C.K. Brown, Jr., for plaintiff appellant.

Arthur M. McGlauflin, Assistant County Attorney, for defendant appellee.

HILL, Judge.

Section 3-4-4 of the Wake County Subdivision Regulations, which were enacted pursuant to G.S. 153-330 and became effective on 1 June 1976, provides as follows:

3-4-4. Name of Subdivision. The name of a subdivision shall not duplicate nor closely approximate the name of an existing subdivision within the County or any municipality within the County.

[1] We first address the question whether Springdale Woods is exempt from the provisions of section 3-4-4. This subdivision

was platted fourteen years prior to passage of the ordinance and appears to have lain dormant for many years prior to this action. Myrick Construction Company later acquired the property and tailored the lots to suit its needs. Myrick also changed the name from Woodbrook Estates to the present name, "Springdale Woods." A new plat was tendered and recorded on 30 June 1978.

G.S. 153A-335 defines "subdivision," and then provides:

However, the following is not included within this definition and is not subject to any regulations enacted pursuant to this Part:

(1) The combination or recombination of portions of previously platted lots if the total number of lots is not increased and the resultant lots are equal to or exceed the standards of the county as shown in its subdivision regulations.

At trial, the parties stipulated among other things:

13.   That the subdivision denominated 'Springdale Woods' is a combination of previously platted lots of a former subdivision plat entitled 'Woodbrook Estates' . . .

It is to be noted that there is no evidence and no finding of fact in the record that the lots in the Springdale Woods Subdivision equal or exceed the standards of the county, as stated in the county's subdivision regulations.

The Wake County Board of Commissioners in its "Judgment" found as a fact:

8.   Woodbrook Estates subdivision was platted and recorded prior to the enactment of a Wake County subdivision ordinance affecting the property.

The Board of Commissioners then concluded that Springdale Woods Subdivision is not subject to Section 3-4-4 of the Wake County Subdivision Regulations because it is exempted from the requirement by virtue of G.S. 153A-335(1). The commissioners finally concluded that the name "Springdale Woods" did not require approval by the Wake County Planning Board. This was error. There is insufficient evidence in the record to support the Commission's finding of fact, and the superior court's ratification of it. Hence, the conclusions of law are invalid, as is the final order. We hold that "Springdale Woods" must conform to the Subdivision Regulation 3-4-4.

[2] We now address the question of whether the names "Springdale Gardens" *and* "Springdale Woods" duplicate or closely approximate the name "Springdale Estates," an existing subdivision, so that approval of these names was violative of Section 3-4-4 of the Wake County Subdivision Regulations as set out above.

The defendant contends that it has been common practice for subdivisions adjacent to each other to carry similar or duplicative names and that the developer of Springdale Estates had granted permission for the use of the name. Furthermore, in its finding of fact no. 7 the Board said:

The intent of Section 3-4-4 of the Wake County Subdivision Regulations was solely to avoid the misdirection of emergency service vehicles which might occur if subdivisions located some distance from each other had names which were duplicative or closely approximate.

The finding apparently is based on the testimony of one of the commissioners made at a public hearing on the subject in which he stated that the intent was that emergency vehicles would not be sent to the wrong area of the county due to similar names. We do not address the admissibility of this testimony for we find it to be of no consequence in reaching a conclusion.

"If the language of a statute is clear and unambiguous, judicial construction is not necessary. Its plain ... meaning controls." *State ex rel Utilities Comm. v. Edmisten, Atty. General*, 291 N.C. 451, 232 S.E. 2d 184 (1977); *Accord State v. Camp*, 286 N.C. 148, 209 S.E. 2d 754 (1974); *Underwood v. Howland, Comr. of Motor Vehicles*, 274 N.C. 473, 164 S.E. 2d 2 (1968); *Wake County v. Ingle*, 273 N.C. 343, 160 S.E. 2d 62 (1968).

Ordinarily, a municipal body, when sitting for the purpose of review, is vested with quasi-judicial powers, and a decision of the board, while subject to review by the courts upon certiorari, will not be disturbed *in the absence* of arbitary, oppressive, or manifest abuse of authority, or *disregard of the law.* The findings of fact made by the commissioners, if supported by evidence introduced at the hearing before the board, are conclusive. But when the findings of the board are not based on competent evidence, the proceedings must be remanded. *See Refining Co. v. Board of Aldermen,* 284 N.C. 458, 469, 202 S.E. 2d 129 (1974); *Jarrell v. Board of Adjustment,* 258 N.C. 476, 480, 128 S.E. 2d 879 (1963).

We find the "judgment" of the board disregarded the ordinance, which plainly states that the name of a subdivision must not duplicate nor *closely approximate* the name of an existing subdivision within the county. When we examine the names of the subdivisions, Springdale Estates, Springdale Gardens, and Springdale Woods, one-half of the name of each subdivision is exactly the same — Springdale. Such usage is "closely approximate" and violates the ordinance. To hold otherwise would condone the use of "Springdale" with a myriad of words to denote other possible subdivisions; e.g., "Springdale Heights," "Springdale Meadows," "Springdale Lake," "Springdale Downs," and "Springdale Forest" — to name a few — presenting possible confusion *ad infinitum.*

The regulation does not address the geographic location of subdivisions or whether it does not apply to contiguous subdivisions. The ordinance plainly states "duplicate" and "closely approximate" names are forbidden.

This case is reversed and remanded to the superior court, directing that court to instruct the Wake County Planning Board not to approve the plats filed herein using the names "Springdale Gardens" or "Springdale Woods."

Reversed and remanded.

Judges MARTIN (Robert M.) and ARNOLD concur.

IN THE MATTER OF: SHIRLEY W. BOLDEN Appellee and J. C. PENNEY COMPANY, INC. Employer and EMPLOYMENT SECURITY COMMISSION OF NORTH CAROLINA Appellant

No. 8026SC146

(Filed 1 July 1980)

1. **Master and Servant § 111.1– unemployment compensation – failure to apply law to "other facts in evidence" – erroneous reversal of decision**

   The superior court erred in reversing a decision of the Employment Security Commission on the ground that the Commission did not properly apply the law to the facts found by the Commission "and other facts in evidence" since the reviewing court may not consider the evidence for the purpose of finding the facts for itself, and if the findings made by the Commission, even though supported by competent evidence in the record, are insufficient to enable the court to determine the rights of the parties upon the matters in controversy, the proceeding should be remanded to the end that the Commission make proper findings.

2. **Master and Servant § 108– unemployment compensation insurance – racial discrimination by employer – necessity for findings**

   Had claimant left her job because of racial discrimination practiced against her by her employer, she would have had good cause attributable to her employer and so would not have been disqualified for unemployment compensation benefits. Claimant's evidence was sufficient to raise a factual issue which the Employment Security Commission was required to resolve where it tended to show that claimant had been employed in the merchandise records section of a department store for three years; she had worked under five different supervisors; she was the only black in the section; and she felt that she had been discriminated against because of her race in not being promoted to supervisor and not being given more pay.

APPEAL by the Employment Security Commission of North Carolina from *Johnson, Judge.* Judgment entered 3 October 1979 in Superior Court, MECKLENBURG County. Heard in the Court of Appeals 11 June 1980.

On 14 April 1978 the claimant, Shirley W. Bolden, left her job as a merchandise records clerk in the Eastland Mall store of J.C. Penney Company in Charlotte, N.C. On 24 May 1978 she filed a claim for unemployment compensation benefits. On 25 July 1978 a hearing on the claim was held before a hearing officer of the Employment Security Commission in Charlotte, at which time the claimant, represented by counsel, appeared and testified concerning her reasons for leaving her employment.

She testified that she had been employed in the merchandise records department of Penney's Eastland Mall store from 19 April 1975 until 14 April 1978, during which time she had worked under five different supervisors. She was the only black in the department, and she felt that she had been discriminated against because of her race in not being promoted to supervisor and in not being given more pay. She also presented the testimony of two other employees, who testified that they felt that the Penney Eastland Mall Store discriminated against its black employees.

On 19 April 1979 the Employment Security Commission entered its Decision No. 8572, holding that claimant was disqualified from receiving unemployment compensation benefits, this decision being based upon the following:

Supporting Findings of Fact:

1. The claim series now under consideration was begun effective May 21, 1978 and extends through May 27, 1978.

2. The claimant last worked with J.C. Penney Company on April 14, 1978. She had been so employed approximately 3 years.

3. The claimant was passed over for a promotion on several occasions and did not receive a raise which she believed she was entitled. On this basis she resigned her job.

Memorandum of Law.

The Employment Security Law provides that a claimant for benefits must be disqualified indefinitely if it is found that she resigned her job without good cause attributable to the employer. G.S. 96-14(1).

In the case at hand in the opinion of the undersigned that although the claimant may have felt she had good personal reasons for resigning, her job situation was not so intolerable or unbearable as to force her to become unemployed at that time.

It is therefore concluded the claimant did resign her last job without good cause attributable to her employer.

Upon claimant's appeal from the decision of the Commission, the Superior Court on 3 October 1979 entered judgment as follows:

The Court, having examined the record on appeal and reviewed the evidence therein contained, finds that the facts found by the Commission in its Decision No. 8572 were based upon competent evidence contained in the record. The Court further finds that the Employment Security Commission did not properly apply the law to those and other facts in evidence and that Decision No. 8572, based on such application of the law to the facts should be reversed.

IT IS NOW, THEREFORE, ORDERED, ADJUDGED, AND DECREED that the decision of the Employment Security Commission under Docket No. 8572 be and the same is reversed, and the cause is remanded to the Employment Security Commission of North Carolina for entry of an Order in accordance with law set forth herein.

From this judgment the Commission, as authorized by G.S. 96-15(i), appealed to the Court of Appeals.

Paul E. Hemphill, Staff Attorney of Legal Services of Southern Piedmont, Inc., for claimant appellee.

Gail C. Arneke, Staff Attorney, for Employment Security Commission of North Carolina, appellant.

PARKER, Judge.

[1] In the judgment appealed from the court expressly found that the facts found by the Commission were based upon competent evidence contained in the record. The court nevertheless reversed the Commission's decision, basing its ruling upon its

finding that the Commission "did not properly apply the law to those *and other facts in evidence.*" (Emphasis added.) In reversing the Commission on the basis of "other facts in evidence," the Court committed error.

In reviewing decisions of the Employment Security Commission as authorized by G.S. 96-15(i), the superior court functions as an appellate court. *In re Enoch*, 36 N.C. App. 255, 243, S.E. 2d 388 (1978). In performing that function, "the reviewing court may determine upon proper exceptions whether the facts found by the Commission were supported by competent evidence and whether the findings so supported sustain the legal conclusions and the award made, but in no event may the reviewing court consider the evidence for the purpose of finding the facts for itself." *Employment Security Comm. v. Young Men's Shop*, 32 N.C. App. 23, 29, 231 S.E. 2d 157, 160 (1977). If the findings of fact made by the Commission, even though supported by competent evidence in the record, are insufficient to enable the court to determine the rights of the parties upon the matters in controversy, the proceeding should be remanded to the end that the Commission make proper findings.

[2]   In the judgment appealed from the court did not specify what were the "other facts in evidence" to which the Commission had failed properly to apply the law. Presumably the court was referring to the evidence presented by the claimant in support of her contention that her employer had unfairly discriminated against her because of her race. The ultimate question for decision in this case was whether the claimant had "left work voluntarily without good cause attributable to [her] employer" within the meaning of G.S. 96-14(1) so as to be disqualified for unemployment compensation benefits by virtue of that section. Had she left her job because of racial discrimination practiced against her by her employer, she would have had good cause attributable to her employer and so would not have been disqualified for beneifts. The Commission made no factual findings on this matter. The question presented for our determination on this appeal thus becomes whether such findings were necessary to determine the rights of the parties upon the matters in controversy in this case. This depends upon whether the evidence presented by the claimant was sufficient to raise a

genuine issue of fact which the Commission was required to resolve as to whether claimant's employer unfairly discriminated against her on account of her race. We find that it was. Although claimant's objective evidence tending to support her subjective feeling that she had been the victim of racial discrimination was minimal indeed and certainly would not compel that conclusion, in our opinion it was sufficient to raise a factual issue which the Commission should have resolved.

Accordingly, the judgment appealed from is vacated and this matter is remanded to the superior court with directions that the superior court further remand this matter to the Employment Security Commission, to the end that the Commission make findings of fact upon all controverted issues required to determine the rights of the parties.

Vacated and remanded.

Judges CLARK and WEBB concur.

IN THE MATTER OF THE WILL OF JOHN R. CALHOUN, DECEASED

No. 8012SC184

(Filed 1 July 1980)

Wills § 16– orphanage not taking under will – no standing to file caveat

The trial court properly dismissed a caveat by an orphanage on the ground that caveator had no standing pursuant to G.S. 31-32 to file a caveat, since the orphanage was not entitled to take under the will or codicil of testator, and the orphanage did not have some pecuniary or beneficial interest in the estate that was detrimentally affected by the will.

APPEAL by caveator from *Lane, Judge.* Order entered 21 January 1980 in Superior Court, CUMBERLAND County. Heard in the Court of Appeals 13 June 1980.

On 9 October 1979, the Oxford Orphanage filed a caveat to the probate of the codicil of the will of John R. Calhoun, alleging undue influence and incapacity to execute the codicil. Propounders of the will filed an answer and motion to dismiss the caveat and the caveator as a party on the grounds that the caveator was not " 'any person entitled under such Will, or interested in the estate' within the meaning of North Carolina General Statute 31-32."

The uncontroverted facts in this case are that: John R. Calhoun died on 3 February 1979; paper writings purporting to be his Last Will and Testament dated 1 June 1978 and a codicil thereto dated 26 January 1979 were admitted to probate; under his will, John Calhoun devised and bequeathed all of his property in fee simple to his wife, Lena G. Calhoun, if she survived him; but, if not, then his estate was devised and bequeathed in fee simple to his sister, Ruby C. Gray, and James Gray, Jr. and wife, Brenda K. Gray. In the purported codicil, John Calhoun changed Article II of his Last Will and Testament which left his entire estate to his wife if she survived him; and in lieu thereof, he devised and bequeathed all of his property in trust to his nephew, James Alexander Gray, Jr., trustee for his wife, Lena G. Calhoun. At her death, the trust was to terminate, and the remaining property was left to Ruby C. Gray, and James Alexander Gray, Jr. and his wife, Brenda Kay Gray, propounders.

Lena Calhoun died on 23 February 1979, shortly after her husband's death. In a purported Last Will and Testament dated 1 June 1978, Lena Calhoun devised and bequeathed all of her property to her husband, John, if he survived her, and if not, then said property was devised and bequeathed to Ruby C. Gray, James A. Gray, Jr., and Brenda Kay Gray. Under a purported Last Will and Testament of Lena G. Calhoun dated 28 April 1975, she devised and bequeathed all of her property to her husband if he survived her, and if not, then said property was devised and bequeathed to a trustee with some income from said trust to be distributed to various churches and the remainder of said income to be distributed to two orphanages, one of which is Oxford Orphanage, caveator herein.

Caveator has also filed a caveat to Lena Calhoun's 1 June 1978 Last Will and Testament, contending that it is not her Last Will and Testament, but that the 28 April 1975 paper writing is.

The trial court entered an order dismissing the caveat, and the caveator appealed.

A. Maxwell Ruppe, for caveator appellant.

Pope, Reid, Lewis & Deese, by Marland C. Reid, for propounder appellees.

ERWIN, Judge.

The record on appeal presents one issue for our determination: whether the trial court erred in dismissing the caveat of Oxford Orphanage on the ground that it had no standing pursuant to G.S. 31-32. We find no error in the judgment entered and affirm the trial court.

G.S. 31-32 provides in pertinent part:

"§ 31-32. *When and by whom caveat filed.* — At the time of application for probate of any will, and the probate thereof in common form, or at any time within three years thereafter, any person entitled under such will, or interested in the estate, may appear in person or by attorney before the clerk of the superior court and enter a caveat to the probate of such will: Provided, that if any person entitled to file a caveat be within the age of 18 years, or insane, or imprisoned, then such person may file a caveat within three years after the removal of such disability."

The caveator concedes that it is not directly entitled to take under the Last Will and Testament or the codicil to the will of John R. Calhoun, but is one of the potential ultimate beneficiaries under the 1975 Last Will and Testament of Lena Calhoun, wife of John Calhoun. The only way that caveator can be successful and receive any benefits from the estate of Lena Calhoun, the following must occur: (1) A court and jury must find that the 26 January 1979 codicil to the Last Will and Testament of John Calhoun is in fact not a codicil to the said Last Will and Testament. (2) Lena Calhoun actually took the estate of her husband in fee simple by reason of his Last Will and Testament dated 1 June 1978, which would only occur if the codicil was found to be invalid. (3) A court and jury must find that the 1 June 1978 Last Will and Testament was in fact not Lena Calhoun's Last Will and Testament. (4) The Last Will and Testament of Lena Calhoun dated 28 April 1975 was in fact her Last Will and Testament. If all of these issues were found in the caveator's favor, it would take under Mrs. Calhoun's 1975 Last Will and Testament.

Our research reveals that a case similar in facts to the one before us has not been decided by our Supreme Court. Caveator calls our attention to *In re Will of Belvin*, 261 N.C. 275, 276, 134 S.E. 2d 225 (1964), wherein our Supreme Court held:

> "Appellees maintain this language excludes all who would benefit by a prior testamentary disposition unless they were (1) heirs of the deceased, or (2) named as beneficiaries in the writing they seek to nullify. The court accepted appellees' interpretation of the statute. This, we think, unduly restricts the phrase 'interested in the estate.' If caveators can establish their allegations of undue influence and lack of mental capacity, the writing which has been probated in common form is not the will of deceased, but proof of that fact alone does not establish their right to take a part of the estate. To establish their interest in the estate they allege they are beneficiaries under the will of deceased made at a time when he possessed mental capacity. If the facts be as caveators allege, they are interested in the estate of Lee D. Belvin." (Citations omitted.)

This Court held in *In re Ashley*, 23 N.C. App. 176, 208 S.E. 2d 398, *cert. denied*, 286 N.C. 335, 210 S.E. 2d 56 (1974), that under G.S. 31-32 which permits the contest of wills by persons interested or claiming to be interested in decedent's estate, the general rule is that a contestant must have some pecuniary or beneficial interest in the estate that is detrimentally affected by the will. Applying this rule, we must conclude that caveator does not come within the meaning of G.S. 31-32 as a person who has standing to caveat Mr. Calhoun's will. Caveator is not the purchaser and holder of land from the testator as was the case in *In re Thompson*, 178 N.C. 540, 101 S.E. 107 (1919). The caveator is a stranger to Mr. Calhoun's estate without any interest therein as contemplated by G.S. 31-32.

The judgment is affirmed.

Affirmed.

Judges ARNOLD and HILL concur.

STATE OF NORTH CAROLINA v. FRANK EVERETTE GRIMES

No. 801SC73

(Filed 1 July 1980)

Constitutional Law § 40– failure to inform defendant of right to counsel – absence of prejudice

Defendant was not prejudiced by the fact that he may not have been informed of his right to be represented by counsel before he entered a guilty plea where defendant has not argued that he was indigent and therefore entitled to appointed counsel at the time he entered his guilty plea or that he lacked the opportunity to retain counsel between the time of his arrest and trial.

APPEAL by defendant from *Strickland, Judge.* Order entered 23 May 1979 in Superior Court, DARE County. Heard in the Court of Appeals 22 May 1980.

Defendant was charged with driving under the influence of intoxicating liquor. G.S. 20-138. He pled guilty and was sentenced to 90 days, suspended on conditions. Defendant moved for a new trial on the ground that he had not been informed of his right to be represented by counsel and was not represented by counsel when he pled guilty. G.S. 15A-1415 (b)(3) and G.S. 15A-1417 (a)(1). In support of his motion he presented his and his wife's affidavits, which indicated that defendant was not represented by counsel, that he did not waive his right to counsel, and that "to the best of [their] recollection[s]" he was not informed of his right to counsel. The State presented the affidavit of the prosecuting attorney in the case, who testified to the routine that was always followed to inform defendants of their right to counsel. He had no specific recollection of defendant's case. Defendant's motion was denied.

Defendant petitioned Superior Court for a writ of certiorari, which was denied. Defendant then petitioned this court for a writ of certiorari, and this petition was allowed.

Attorney General Edmisten, by Assistant Attorney General Jane Rankin Thompson, for the State.

Kellogg, White & Evans, by Thomas N. Barefoot, for defendant appellant.

ARNOLD, Judge.

We note as a preliminary matter that defense counsel's failure to comply with Rule 9 (b)(4) of the Rules of Appellate Procedure has made the record on appeal unnecessarily difficult to follow. Items in the record on appeal should be arranged in chronological order.

The facts in this case give rise not to the question of whether defendant was denied his right to counsel, but instead whether as defendant phrases it, he was denied "his constitutional right to be advised of his right to counsel." Defendant relies upon our decision in *State v. Lee*, 40 N.C. App. 165, 252 S.E. 2d 225 (1979), to support his position that he is entitled to a new trial. Having reviewed that case, however, we disagree with defendant's assertion that the facts in *Lee* are identical to those in the case at bar.

The defendant in *Lee* was charged with failure to support his illegitimate child. The parties stipulated that defendant was not informed of his right to be represented by counsel, and that he did not make a written or oral waiver of his right to counsel. Moreover, the trial court also found that the defendant was not indigent, and this finding was not challenged on appeal.

Additional stipulated facts in *Lee* reveal, however, that defendant was a member of the armed services and that since the time of his arrest he had been unable to employ counsel to represent him. The trial court refused to grant defendant a continuance to employ counsel, thus depriving defendant of his right to counsel. As we noted then, the stipulated facts of *Lee* negated a knowing and intelligent waiver of counsel.

While our decision in *Lee* is consistent with *Argersinger v. Hamlin*, 407 U.S. 25, 32 L.Ed. 2d 530, 92 S. Ct. 2006 (1972), we do not find *Argersinger* helpful in the matter now before us. Neither *Argersinger* nor any other case which we have been able to find holds that a nonindigent defendant must expressly waive his right to counsel before he can enter a plea on his own behalf. On the contrary, G.S. 15A-1012(a) provides that "[a] defendant may not be called upon to plead until he has had an opportunity to retain counsel or, *if he is eligible for assignment of counsel*, until counsel has been assigned or waived." (Emphasis added.)

Defendant here does not argue that he was indigent and therefore entitled to appointed counsel at the time he entered his guilty plea. Nor does he argue that he lacked the opportunity to retain counsel in the twenty days between the time of his arrest and the hearing of his case. He relies solely upon the fact that "to the best of his recollection" he was not informed of his right to be represented by counsel. Although there was some evidence that defendant was so informed, the trial court made no finding on the point. Assuming, however, that for some reason the prosecuting attorney varied from his usual routine and did not inform defendant of his right to be represented by counsel, defendant has not argued any prejudice to him flowing from the omission. Even errors of constitutional dimensions can be harmless, *see* Justice Huskins' dissent in *State v. Hill*, 277 N.C. 547, 178 S.E. 2d 462 (1971), and in the absence of any showing to the contrary we find that to be the case here.

We find no error and conclude that the order of the trial court should be

Affirmed.

Judges MARTIN (Robert M.) and HILL concur.

In re Kirkman

IN THE MATTER OF THE ESTATE OF JOHN C. KIRKMAN, SR.,
DECEASED

No. 7914SC852

(Filed 1 July 1980)

**Wills § 61; Attorneys § 7.5– proceeding to determine spouse's right to dissent –
attorney's fees improperly taxed as costs against estate**

The trial court erred in determining that a proceeding to determine the
right of dissent from a will by a surviving widow is a proceeding within the
meaning of G.S. 6-21(2), and the court erred in taxing the fees for the widow's
attorneys as costs against the estate of the testator, since a spouse's right to
dissent is provided for by G.S. Chapter 30, and a proceeding under that
Chapter is beyond the purview of G.S. 6-21(2), as such a proceeding is not a
caveat to a will, nor does it require the construction of any will or trust
agreement or fix the rights and duties of parties thereunder.

APPEAL by Executor of the Estate of John C. Kirkman, Sr.,
from *Kivett, Judge.* Order entered 13 June 1979 in Superior
Court, DURHAM County. Heard in the Court of Appeals 19 March
1980.

Testator, John C. Kirkman, Sr., died on 12 December 1974
leaving a will which was duly probated on 31 December 1974. On
19 May 1975, testator's surviving spouse, Minnie H. Kirkman,
filed a dissent to the will, as provided for by Chapter 30 of the
North Carolina General Statutes. After substantial litigation,
the wife established her right to dissent from testator's will, as
reported in *In re Kirkman,* 38 N.C. App. 515, 248 S.E. 2d 438
(1978), *cert. denied and appeal dismissed,* 296 N.C. 584, 254 S.E.
2d 31 (1979). Counsel for the widow in the dissent proceedings
filed petitions requesting that their fees resulting from the
litigation be taxed as costs to the estate of testator. On 17 May
1979, the Clerk of Superior Court for Durham County allowed
the requests, concluding as a matter of law that "a proceeding
to determine the right of dissent from a will by a surviving
widow is a proceeding within the meaning of North Carolina
General Statutes 6-21(2) ... ." On 21 May 1979, the executor
filed notice of appeal from the order, and the matter was heard
in the Superior Court. On 13 June 1979, the trial court affirmed
the Clerk's ruling, concluding "as a matter of law that a proceeding to determine the right of dissent from a will by a surviving spouse is a proceeding within the meaning of North Caro-

lina General Statutes 6-21(2), such matter being a proceeding which fixes the rights and duties of the parties under a will . . . ."

From this ruling and an order awarding attorneys' fees as costs of the action executor appeals.

Nancy Fields Fadum for executor appellant.

John C. Randall and E. C. Harris for appellee.

MORRIS, Chief Judge.

The sole question before us is whether a proceeding to determine the right of dissent from a will by a surviving spouse is a proceeding within the meaning of G.S. 6-21(2). We hold that it is not, for the reasons stated below.

G.S. 6-21 (1979 Cum. Supp.) provides, in pertinent part, as follows:

Costs in the following matters shall be taxed against either party, or apportioned among the parties, in the discretion of the court:

. . .

(2) Caveats to wills and any action or proceeding which may require the construction of any will or trust agreement, or fix the rights and duties of parties thereunder; provided, however, that in any caveat proceeding under this subdivision, if the Court finds that the proceeding is without substantial merit, the court may disallow attorneys' fees for the attorneys for the caveators.

G.S. 6-21 provides that "costs" include "reasonable attorneys' fees in such amounts as the court shall in its discretion determine and allow . . . ." This section vests the trial court with the discretionary authority to tax reasonable attorneys' fees as a part of the costs to be paid by the executor of a testator's estate, *McWhirter v. Downs,* 8 N.C. App. 50, 173 S.E. 2d 587 (1970), or the costs incurred in the management of trust estates. *Tripp v. Tripp*, 17 N.C. App. 64, 193 S.E. 2d 366 (1972). This section, however, has been held inapplicable where the particular action involved an instrument which was not sufficient as a trust instrument and was not executed as a will. *See Baxter v. Jones*, 283 N.C. 327, 196 S.E. 2d 193 (1973).

With respect to the present proceeding, a spouse's right of dissent is statutory, and is provided for by Chapter 30 of the North Carolina General Statutes. *See generally Vinson v. Chappell*, 275 N.C. 234, 166 S.E. 2d 686 (1969). To establish the right to dissent, a spouse must make a timely filing pursuant to G.S. 30-2 and must show his or her entitlement to that right under G.S. 30-1. The right of dissent is a matter of mathematical determination, and necessitates a valuation of the property passing to the surviving spouse under the will and outside the will as of the date of the death of the deceased spouse as provided for by statute. *In re Estate of Connor*, 5 N.C. App. 228, 168 S.E. 2d 245 (1969). Determination and establishment of value made by statutory procedures "shall be final for determining the right of dissent and shall be used exclusively for this purpose." G.S. 30-1(c).

It is apparent from the foregoing authority that the purpose and intent in adopting Chapter 30 was to give the surviving spouse an alternative to the amounts which would have been received under the decedent spouse's will. Although certain rights and duties of the parties are determined under Chapter 30, a proceeding to determine the right to dissent does not require a construction of the provisions of the will itself. Unlike a caveat proceeding where the right to inherit at all is determined, a proceeding to determine the right to dissent merely involves a valuation of the property transferred under the will. The use of a will or trust agreement under Chapter 30 is to establish the parties' statutory rights and duties, not to determine what, if any, property is passed by such instruments. We, therefore, believe and so hold that a proceeding under Chapter 30 is beyond the purview of G.S. 6-21(2). Such a proceeding is neither a caveat to a will, nor does it "require the construction of any will or trust agreement, or fix the rights and duties of parties *thereunder*." (Emphasis added.) G.S. 6-21(2).

State v. Allen

It follows, therefore, that the trial court had no authority under G.S. 6-21(2) to tax as costs the attorneys' fees as requested by the widow's attorneys. In addition, we find no other provision in that section which would allow attorneys' fees to be taxed as costs in this situation. In the absence of express statutory authority, attorneys' fees are not allowable as part of the court costs in civil actions. *City of Charlotte v. McNeely*, 281 N.C. 684, 190 S.E. 2d 179 (1972).

Reversed.

Judges VAUGHN and ARNOLD concur.

STATE OF NORTH CAROLINA v. RONNIE LEE ALLEN

No. 8027SC77

(Filed 1 July 1980)

1. **Robbery § 5.4– evidence of armed robbery – no instruction on lesser offenses required**

    The trial court in an armed robbery case was not required to instruct on lesser included offenses where the victims testified that the taking was by two men, one of whom had a gun which he pointed at them; although they expressed some uncertainty as to whether it was defendant or the other man who was armed, their testimony tended to show that the two men acted in concert; and according to the victims' testimony, defendant would be guilty of armed robbery even if it was the other man who held the gun.

2. **Robbery § 5.4– gun in front of pants – evidence of armed robbery – no instruction on lesser offenses required**

    Defendant's statement to a police officer who investigated the armed robbery in question did not show commission of a lesser included offense where, according to the statement, defendant and his brother decided to rob the operator of a grocery store, defendant armed himself with a loaded pistol to carry out the robbery, and he confronted his robbery victim with a pistol stuck in front of his pants and announced a stick up, since the fact that defendant left the pistol stuck in his belt or pants instead of pointing it directly at the victim did not lessen him implied threat to use it or the danger to the life of his victim, and no reasonable view of the evidence would have permitted a verdict other than guilty of armed robbery or not guilty.

APPEAL by defendant from *Ferrell, Judge*. Judgment entered 18 October 1979 in Superior Court, CLEVELAND County. Heard in the Court of Appeals 20 May 1980.

Defendant was tried for armed robbery.

Eunice Earl, age seventy, and her son, Marvin Earl, testified that they were working at a grocery store on 6 September 1979 when defendant and his brother, Levon Allen, entered. Defendant confronted Eunice Earl at the store counter and had a gun in his hand. He said "This is a stick up." He took money and certain other items from the cash register and store counter while Levon Allen took money and a billfold from Marvin Earl's pockets. On cross-examination, both witnesses expressed some uncertainty as to whether it was defendant or his brother who was at the store counter with the gun. Testimony from various officers tended to show that shortly after the robbery they pursued an automobile which Levon Allen was driving and in which defendant was a passenger. That automobile ran off the road and defendant and his brother were arrested. Certain cash, a gun which was identified by Marvin Earl as the robbery weapon and a billfold containing Marvin Earl's identification were found either in or near this automobile. Detective Hugh Buff testified that he took a statement from defendant, which he read into evidence.

Defendant testified in his own behalf. His testimony tended to show that he had nothing to do with the robbery. He stated that he and his brother stopped at a store but that he stayed in the car. He denied making the statement read by Detective Buff and said that it was not true.

Defendant was found guilty as charged. Judgment imposing a prison sentence was entered.

Attorney General Edmisten, by Special Deputy Attorney General Ann Reed, for the State.

Leslie A. Farfour, Jr., for defendant appellant.

VAUGHN, Judge.

[1] The trial judge submitted two possible verdicts to the jury, guilty of armed robbery and not guilty. By his sole argument on appeal, defendant contends that the judge should have instructed on and submitted as possible verdicts the lesser included offenses of armed robbery.

The lesser included offenses of armed robbery include common law robbery, assault with a deadly weapon, larceny from the person, simple larceny and simple assault. *State v. Davis*, 242 N.C. 476, 87 S.E. 2d 906 (1955). In *State v. Hicks*, 241 N.C. 156, 159-60, 84 S.E. 2d 545, 547 (1954) (emphasis original), the following was stated.

The necessity for instructing the jury as to an included crime of lesser degree than that charged arises when and only when there is evidence from which the jury could find that such included crime of lesser degree was committed. The *presence of such evidence* is the determinative factor. Hence, there is no such necessity if the State's evidence tends to show a completed robbery and there is *no conflicting evidence* relating to elements of the crime charged. Mere contention that the jury might accept the State's evidence in part and might reject it in part will not suffice.

The Earls testified that the taking was by two men, one of whom had a gun which he pointed at them. Although they expressed some uncertainty as to whether it was defendant or the other man who was armed, their testimony tended to show that the two men acted in concert and, according to their testimony, defendant would be guilty of armed robbery even if it was the other man who held the gun. The Earls' testimony did not require instructions on any lesser included offense. *See State v. Wilson*, 31 N.C. App. 323, 229 S.E. 2d 314 (1976).

[2] On appeal, defendant points to the statement attributed to him by Detective Buff, which at trial he denied making, as showing a lesser included offense. The statement, offered in evidence by the State, tended to show that defendant and his brother drove up to the store and commented on a money bag. The brother asked defendant if he had left the pistol in the car and defendant said, "Yeah, let me get it in case." Defendant got

State v. Allen

the pistol and put it "down in front of [his] pants." They entered the store and the brother grabbed the man by the arm, and the man told the woman to come out from behind the store counter. Defendant then grabbed the money bag from under the counter. The statement concludes, "I, Ronnie, did not pull the gun out when Levon and I robbed the place. I don't have no reason for taking the gun to the store when Levon and I robbed it."

When considered along with other evidence for the State with which it does not conflict, defendant's own statement either proves armed robbery or it proves nothing. According to the statement, defendant and his brother decided to rob the operator of the store. Defendant armed himself with a loaded pistol to carry out the robbery. Defendant confronted his robbery victim with a pistol stuck in front of his pants and announced, "This is a stick up." His brother grabbed the male victim and defendant took the money. He had the pistol in case he needed it. This conduct constitutes armed robbery. In pertinent part, G.S. 14-87(a) provides:

> Any person ... who, having in possession or with the use or threatened use of any firearms ... whereby the life of a person is endangered or threatened, unlawfully takes or attempts to take personal property from another ... shall be guilty of a felony ....

Threats may be expressed by nonverbal conduct as well as by words. That defendant left the pistol stuck in his belt or pants instead of pointing it directly at his victim did not lessen his implied threat to use it or the danger to the life of his victim had they not yielded. No reasonable view of the evidence would have permitted a verdict other than guilty as charged or not guilty.

No error.

Judges PARKER and HEDRICK concur.

MARY ANN ODOM v. DONALD R. ODOM

No. 808DC36

(Filed 1 July 1980)

Divorce and Alimony § 16.6– alimony action – defendant as spendthrift – insufficient evidence

The evidence in an action for divorce from bed and board and alimony did not require the court to submit to the jury the issue of whether defendant was a spendthrift within the meaning of G.S. 50-16.2(8) or to instruct the jury that defendant's being a spendthrift could be an indignity to plaintiff where plaintiff testified that defendant gave her $500-$1000 per month for her personal use, defendant owned a number of automobiles for the family's use, and on their many vacation trips together defendant took large sums of cash which he spent on whatever they saw that they wanted; no evidence was presented that defendant spent more than he could afford to spend or that he ever exposed his family to want; the evidence showed that defendant paid all the household expenses and gave plaintiff a free hand in spending for herself, the children and items such as household accessories and landscaping; and defendant testified that prior to 1977, when he incurred large medical bills, there was never a year when he spent more money than he made.

APPEAL by plaintiff from *Ellis (Kenneth R.), Judge.* Judgment entered 13 June 1979 in District Court, WAYNE County. Heard in the Court of Appeals 15 May 1980.

Plaintiff seeks a divorce from bed and board, and temporary and permanent alimony. She alleges that defendant committed indignities which made her condition intolerable and life burdensome. Defendant counterclaimed for divorce from bed and board. At trial the jury found that defendant did not constructively abandon plaintiff or commit indignities to her, and that plaintiff abandoned defendant without just cause and committed indignities to him. Accordingly, plaintiff's claims were denied and defendant's counterclaim for divorce from bed and board was granted. Plaintiff appeals.

Kornegay & Rice, by John P. Edwards, Jr., for plaintiff appellant.

Braswell & Taylor, by Roland C. Braswell, for defendant appellee.

Odom v. Odom

ARNOLD, Judge.

G.S. 50-16.2(8) provides that "A dependent spouse is entitled to an order for alimony when . . . [t]he supporting spouse is
a spendthrift." Plaintiff argues on appeal that the court erred
in failing to submit to the jury the issue of whether defendant
was a spendthrift, and in failing to instruct the jury that defendant's being a spendthrift could have been an indignity to the
plaintiff. We find, however, that the evidence would not support
such an issue or instruction.

Black's Law Dictionary 1572 (Rev. 4th ed. 1968) defines
"spendthrift" as "[o]ne who spends money profusely and *improvidently;* . . . one who lavishes or *wastes* his estate." (Emphasis added.) Webster's Third New International Dictionary 2190
(1968) adds the definition "one who spends his estate . . . so as to
expose himself or his family to want or suffering or to become a
charge upon the public." As evidence that defendant here was a
spendthrift, plaintiff points to testimony that he gave her $500-
1000 per month for her personal use, that he owned a number of
automobiles for the family's use, and that on their many vacation trips together defendant took large sums of cash which he
spent on whatever they saw that they wanted. This evidence
does not show that defendant spent wastefully or improvidently, however, and the evidence at trial taken as a whole gives no
indication that defendant met the definition of a spendthrift.
No evidence was presented that defendant spent more than he
could afford to spend, or that he ever approached exposing his
family to want. To the contrary, the evidence showed that defendant paid all the household expenses and in addition gave
plaintiff a free hand in spending for herself, the children, and
items such as household accessories, landscaping, and Christ-
mas decorations. Furthermore, defendant testified that prior
to 1977, when he incurred large medical bills, there was never a
year when he spent more money than he made. In the absence
of evidence that defendant was in fact a spendthrift, no issue or
instruction on that topic would have been proper.

Plaintiff's additional assignments of error, going to the
admission of certain evidence, are without merit. Even if the

evidence was irrelevant and so improperly admitted, we do not find the errors to be prejudicial. Lengthy and detailed testimony was before the jury, and these small portions of the evidence are extremely unlikely to have influenced their decision.

The judgment of the trial court is

Affirmed.

Judges MARTIN (Robert M.) and HILL concur.

HARRY W. BARNES v. CAMPBELL CHAIN COMPANY, INC., LOOS AND COMPANY, AND WEST DURHAM LUMBER COMPANY

No. 7914SC1005

(Filed 1 July 1980)

Partnership § 7– item purchased by partnership – breach of warranty – injury to partner – suit by individual partner proper

    An individual partner may sue to recover damages for his personal injuries which proximately result from the breach of warranty on goods purchased by the partnership with partnership funds.

APPEAL by plaintiff from *Herring (D. B.), Judge.* Judgment entered 27 August 1979 in Superior Court, DURHAM County. Heard in the Court of Appeals 17 April 1980.

Plaintiff, Harry W. Barnes, alleged in his complaint that on 8 July 1976 he was a partner in a partnership trading as Barnes Roofing Company, which partnership purchased a length of vinyl encased cable and a clamp from defendant West Durham Lumber Company and that on 13 July 1974 the length of the aforesaid cable, while being used in the partnership business of Barnes Roofing Company, broke at the point of contact between said clamp and said cable, and that as a consequence, the cable struck and caused injury to plaintiff's eye. The depositions of plaintiff's brother and partner indicate that plaintiff sought relief against defendant West Durham Lumber Company for breach of implied and express warranties. After considering affidavits and interrogatories, the trial court dismissed plaintiff's claims against defendant West Durham Lumber Company. Plaintiff appeals from this judgment.

Other necessary facts will be stated in the opinion.

Spears, Barnes, Baker & Hoof by Alexander H. Barnes for plaintiff appellant.

Maupin, Taylor & Ellis by Armistead, J. Maupin for defendant appellee.

CLARK, Judge.

The primary question in this case is one of first impression in this jurisdiction: Whether an individual partner can sue to recover damages for his personal injuries which proximately result from the breach of warranty on a good purchased by the partnership with partnership funds? We now answer "yes" to this question.

The defendant argues that a partnership is a separate legal entity and that only the partnership may sue in an action arising out of partnership property purchased with partnership funds. This argument does not accurately state the law. In *Threadgill v. Faust,* 213 N.C. 226, 230, 195 S.E. 798, 800 (1938), quoted in defendant's brief, our Supreme Court stated that the "general rule in this jurisdiction is that one partner may not sue in his name, alone, and for his own benefit, upon a cause of action *accruing* to the partnership . . . ." (Emphasis supplied). The crucial distinction in the case *sub judice* is that the partner's personal injury action is not one accruing to the partnership. 60 Am. Jur. 2d *Partnership* § 327 (1972). This is not a suit for recovery of or payment for partnership property, it is a personal injury arising out of the sale of property, and the individual partner, not the partnership was injured. Moreover, while we have not found a similar case in this State, we note that several other states have refused to allow a partnership to bring suit for damages for negligent or unintentional injury to one of its partners. *Id.;* Annot., 36 A.L.R. 3d 1375 (1971). Nor would it be wise public policy to allow all the partners to recover for a personal injury which is suffered by a single partner. Barring some possible exceptions for intentional torts, if anyone can properly sue to recover for personal injury to the partner, it must be the individual partner who is personally injured and not the partnership.

Defendant argues, however, that there is no privity between the defendant-seller and plaintiff since it was the partnership and not the plaintiff which purchased the cable and clamp. We do not agree. It is fundamental that all partners are agents of each other, that a contract entered into by the agent is a contract entered into by the principal and that all partners are liable on any contract executed by a single partner in the name of the partnership. N.C. Gen. Stat. §§ 59-39, 59-45; 10 Strong's N.C. Index 3d *Partnership* § 4 (1977). If a partner may be sued for nonpayment or other breach of the contract, he certainly is privy to the contract.

Defendant next contends that, because of N.C. Gen. Stat. 25-2-318, an employee of the purchaser is barred from suing the seller of a good for breach of warranty, and that, as a consequence, the partner in this case similarly has no horizontal privity and cannot reach the seller in a warranty suit. Again, this argument fails to recognize the fundamental nature of a partnership: the partner is not an employee of the entity; rather, the partner is a tenant in partnership in the entity itself, and as such, the partner is a purchaser, not an employee of the purchaser. The partner here has direct contractual privity.

The judgment by the court below recited that lack of contractual privity was the basis for dismissing plaintiff's claim against defendant West Durham Lumber Company. That judgment is now reversed. Whether the pleadings and depositions indicate that an express or implied warranty was created is not before us at this time.

Reversed.

Judges VAUGHN and MARTIN (Harry C.) concur.

KATHY SUE BOYD and the FORSYTH COUNTY DEPARTMENT OF
SOCIAL SERVICES v. LARRY WAYNE MARSH

No. 7921DC1129

(Filed 1 July 1980)

1. **Rules of Civil Procedure § 60.2– party served with summons – attention required**

    A party served with a summons must give the matter the attention
    which a person of ordinary prudence gives to his important business, and
    failure to do so is not excusable neglect under G.S. 1A-1, Rule 60 (b)(1).

2. **Rules of Civil Procedure § 60.2– failure to file answer – no excusable neglect**

    Defendant's failure to file an answer in a paternity and child support
    action was not the result of excusable neglect where defendant had a ninth
    grade education and could read and write; defendant had employed attor-
    neys in other matters; and defendant testified he failed to file answer be-
    cause he did not believe he could be subject to orders of paternity and child
    support more than seven years after the child was born.

APPEAL by plaintiffs from *Tash, Judge.* Order entered 18
July 1979 in District Court, FORSYTH County. Heard in the Court
of Appeals 15 May 1980.

Plaintiff Boyd brings this action to have defendant adjudged the father of her minor child and to require him to
provide child support. Pursuant to G.S. 110-135, plaintiff Department of Social Services seeks to have defendant declared
the "responsible parent" who must reimburse the State for
public assistance paid to the child. Defendant did not answer
and plaintiffs moved for default, showing by affidavit that personal service was made upon defendant. Entry of default was
made, and paternity and child support default judgments were
entered against defendant.

Defendant moved under Rule 60 to set aside these judgments. At the hearing on the motion defendant testified that in
the seven years between the child's birth and the institution of
this action plaintiff Boyd had never asked him for child support.
He is not the father of the child, though plaintiff has said that
he is. He did not file an answer to plaintiffs' complaint "because
I didn't understand the whole thing and I didn't see how there

was any Court to uphold something like that so long after a child was born and since the child's birth certificate was blank where it says 'father.' ... I didn't see any proof whatsoever that I could possibly be the father." On cross-examination defendant testified that when the Department of Social Services contacted him about child support he told them to take the case to court and let a judge decide who was the father. He had previously employed attorneys in other matters.

The trial court concluded that defendant had a meritorious defense (the three-year statute of limitations set out by G.S. 49-14 (c)(1)) and that "defendant's failure to file answer was due to excusable neglect resulting from his limited education and surprise that he could be subject to orders of paternity and child support when no demands therefor had been made for approximately seven years." The court ordered the default judgments set aside, and plaintiffs appeal.

Bruce E. Colvin for plaintiff appellants.

White & Crumpler, by Edward L. Powell, for defendant appellee.

ARNOLD, Judge.

[1, 2] It is well-established that a party served with a summons must give the matter the attention which a person of ordinary prudence gives to his important business, and failure to do so is not excusable neglect under G.S. 1A-1, Rule 60(b)(1). *See Ellison v. White*, 3 N.C. App. 235, 164 S.E. 2d 511 (1968); *Meir v. Walton*, 2 N.C. App. 578, 163 S.E. 2d 403 (1968) and cases cited therein. In the instant case the facts do not support the court's conclusion that defendant's failure to answer was excusable. Defendant has a ninth grade education and can read and write. He previously has employed attorneys in other matters. The fact that in the present situation he did not believe plaintiffs could prevail does not excuse his failure to file an answer and pursue his defense. Nor does the fact that in his motion he set out a meritorious defense justify the setting aside of the default judgment, since in the absence of a showing of excusable neglect, the ques-

tion of meritorious defense becomes immaterial. *Meir v. Walton, supra.*

The court's order setting aside the default judgment is

Reversed.

Judges MARTIN (Robert M.) and WELLS concur.

GEORGE PARKER AND MEREDITH PARKER v. EVERETT G. SHELDON AND DAISY S. SHELDON AND CARL S. MILSTED, TRUSTEE

No. 794SC1095

(Filed 1 July 1980)

Mortgages and Deeds of Trust § 37– damages for wrongful foreclosure – setting aside foreclosure – election of remedies

Whether, at the beginning of their action, plaintiffs elected to recover damages for wrongful foreclosure or elected to have the foreclosure proceedings set aside, by their failure to assign error to the trial court's order that the sale be set aside they elected to treat the sale as a nullity, and the trial court correctly found that plaintiffs proved no damages as a result of the institution of the foreclosure proceedings.

APPEAL by plaintiffs from *Bruce, Judge.* Judgment entered 14 June 1979 in Superior Court, ONSLOW County. Heard in the Court of Appeals 13 May 1980.

Plaintiffs allege that in 1972 they purchased a piece of property from defendants Sheldon, and that defendant Milsted was made trustee of the deed of trust. They further allege that in 1974 Milsted wrongfully foreclosed on this property, and that the Sheldons were the purchasers at the foreclosure sale. By their original complaint plaintiffs sought to recover $18,000, which is alleged to be the fair market value of the property, and to have the foreclosure proceedings set aside. In 1978 plaintiffs were allowed to amend their complaint, and by their amended complaint they seek only to recover the fair market value, alleged to be $18,000, of the property.

Upon defendant Milsted's Rule 12(b)(6) motion, the action against him was dismissed. The court, sitting without a jury, determined that the manner in which the foreclosure was instituted had denied the plaintiffs due process of law, and set aside the foreclosure. The court also found that plaintiffs had proved no damages from the wrongful institution of foreclosure proceedings. From the court's decision not to award damages, plaintiffs appeal.

Willis A. Talton for plaintiff appellants.

W. M. Cameron, Jr. for defendant appellees.

ARNOLD, Judge.

The trial court found that the institution of foreclosure proceedings violated plaintiff's due process rights because plaintiffs were not notified that the debt was being accelerated and because no hearing was held to determine whether plaintiffs were actually in default. The court concluded: "(5) The institution of foreclosure proceedings being in violation of the constitutional rights of the plaintiffs, the foreclosure is therefore a nullity and the trustee's deed [to the Sheldons] is void," and "(7) The plaintiffs have failed to show that they are entitled to damages as a result of the institution of the foreclosure proceedings in violation of their constitutional rights." Plaintiffs excepted only to Conclusion 7 and the court's resulting denial of damages to them.

Plaintiffs now rely on *Chandler v. Cleveland Savings & Loan Assn.*, 24 N.C. App. 455, 211 S.E. 2d 484 (1975) for the proposition that in the case of a wrongful foreclosure the injured mortgagor who elects not to ratify the sale may elect whether to sue to set the sale aside or to permit the sale to stand and sue to recover damages. Plaintiffs contend that they have made their election to sue for damages and are entitled to recover damages. The proposition set out as dicta in *Chandler* is not pertinent to the present case, however, in the posture in which the case reaches us on appeal.

Plaintiffs did not take exception to the court's conclusion to set the sale aside, and they do not argue on appeal that this portion of the court's judgment was error. Instead, they appear to take the position that once the court found a wrongful foreclosure they became entitled to recover the damages they sought in their complaint, in spite of the fact that the foreclosure sale has been set aside. This is not the law.

Whichever remedy plaintiffs may have elected to pursue at the institution of this action, by their failure to assign error to the trial court's order that the sale be set aside they have now elected to treat the sale as a nullity. The trial court correctly found that plaintiffs have proved no damages "as a result of the *institution* of the foreclosure proceedings" (emphasis added), and the denial of damages to plaintiffs was proper.

Affirmed.

Judges MARTIN (Robert M.) and HILL concur.

HAROLD MAXWELL, JR. v. SANDRA E. WOODS, ALIAS SANDRA E. MAXWELL

No. 793SC1166

(Filed 1 July 1980)

Divorce and Alimony § 29– divorce decree regular on face of record – no collateral attack

Where a divorce decree obtained by defendant wife from her former husband on the ground of separation for one year was in all respects regular on the face of the record, the divorce decree was not void but merely voidable even though there was proof that defendant and her former husband had not lived separate and apart for one year as of the time of the divorce; therefore, plaintiff husband had no standing collaterally to attack the divorce decree to as to show that his subsequent marriage to defendant was void *ab initio.*

APPEAL by plaintiff from *DeRamus, Judge.* Judgment entered 24 October 1979 in Superior Court, CRAVEN County. Heard in the Court of Appeals 20 May 1980.

This action for declaratory judgment brought by plaintiff against his wife sought to establish that a decree of divorce between his wife and her former husband was void and that, therefore, plaintiff's subsequent marriage to defendant was void *ab initio*. Plaintiff also sought to have himself declared fee simple owner of a piece of property which he conveyed to himself and defendant as tenants by the entirety.

Defendant was married to William J. Woods on 6 October 1962. On 19 May 1969, defendant obtained a decree of absolute divorce from Woods by judgment of the District Court for Carteret County on the ground of one year's separation. The record of the divorce, including the complaint, summons, issues and judgment of divorce is regular on its face. Jurisdiction was based on personal service. Approximately five months and one week after the entry of the judgment for absolute divorce, a male child was born to defendant. According to the parties, William J. Woods was the father of the child born to defendant.

Plaintiff and defendant were married on or about 15 March 1974. Sometime thereafter, plaintiff transferred a piece of property to himself and defendant as tenants by the entirety. Plaintiff had purchased the property on 1 March 1974 and executed a note and deed of trust to secure the purchase.

The trial court concluded that plaintiff had no standing to attack collaterally the prior adjudication of divorce between defendant and Woods. Plaintiff appeals.

Dunn and Dunn, by Raymond E. Dunn, Jr., for plaintiff appellant.

Henderson and Baxter, by David S. Henderson, for defendant appellee.

VAUGHN, Judge.

This case is controlled by the case of *Carpenter v. Carpenter*, 244 N.C. 286, 93 S.E. 2d 617 (1956). The trial court found that the judgment role in the Carteret divorce action was in all respects regular on its face. Plaintiff does not contend otherwise. In

Carpenter, our Supreme Court held that, "[a]s against challenge on the ground of false swearing, by way of pleading and of evidence, *relating to the cause or ground for divorce*, a divorce decree, in all respects regular on the face of the judgment roll, is at most voidable, not void." *Id.* at 295, 93 S.E. 2d at 625-26 (emphasis original). Even though there is proof that defendant and Woods had not lived separate and apart for one year as of the time of their divorce, the divorce judgment is not void but merely voidable. *See also Stokely v. Stokely*, 30 N.C. App. 351, 227 S.E. 2d 131 (1976).

Plaintiff does not have standing to attack collaterally the divorce decree between defendant and Woods because he is a stranger to the decree who is not prejudiced as to some pre-existing right by the decree. As stated in *Carpenter*,

> When, in such case, a second spouse can rely upon the divorce decree, we think the sounder view is to require him to do so rather than permit him to attack it at his election, depending on the fortunes or misfortunes of the marriage. We must be mindful of his status where he chooses to maintain the validity of the divorce decree rather than to attack it. It would seem that if this plaintiff has a just grievance, such arises, not on account of the divorce decree and his marriage, but on account of matters arising during the subsistence of such marriage.

Id. at 298, 93 S.E. 2d at 628; *see also* 1 Lee, N.C. Family Law § 92 (4th ed. 1979).

Since the marriage of plaintiff and defendant is not void on the grounds at issue in this appeal, we need not consider plaintiff's claim that he be declared the sole owner of the real estate transferred by him to himself and defendant as tenants by the entirety.

Affirmed.

Judges PARKER and HEDRICK concur.

McCraney v. Flanagan

THERESA McCRANEY v. MICHAEL FLANAGAN and RED SPRINGS MOTORS, INC.

No. 7916SC1171

(Filed 1 July 1980)

Assault and Battery § 3.1; Seduction § 3– willing plaintiff – insufficient evidence of assault or seduction

Summary judgment was appropriate in an action to recover for sexual assault or seduction where the evidence tended to show that plaintiff willingly went to a field with defendant, willingly drank two alcoholic beverages, remembered nothing until she found herself back in town, but subsequently discovered that she had had intercourse, since there was no evidence that plaintiff feared or even knew that harmful or offensive contact might occur, which was required to show an assault, and since there was no evidence that defendant deceived or enticed plaintiff in any way, which was required to show seduction.

APPEAL by plaintiff from *Farmer, Judge.* Judgment entered 27 August 1979 in Superior Court, ROBESON County. Heard in the Court of Appeals 20 May 1980.

Plaintiff alleges that defendant Flanagan, acting within the scope of his employment by the corporate defendant, assaulted her sexually or seduced her, and she seeks to recover damages. Defendants moved for summary judgment, which was granted, and plaintiff appeals from the grant of defendant Flanagan's motion.

James R. Nance, Jr., for plaintiff appellant.

I. Murchison Biggs for defendant appellee.

ARNOLD, Judge.

Plaintiff argues that summary judgment was not appropriate in this case. We find, however, that no genuine issue of material fact exists, *see* G.S. 1A-1, Rule 56(c), and that summary judgment for defendant was proper.

It is undisputed that on the morning of 2 June 1977 the parties agreed to "go somewhere" together, and that they went in defendant's car to a dirt road in a field. Each of them had two drinks of Crown Royal mixed with Coca-Cola. Plaintiff testified on deposition that she took one swallow out of a third drink, and that after that she remembered nothing until she found herself back in town. A subsequent examination by a doctor showed evidence of sperm in plaintiff's vagina, a blood alcohol content of .08 per cent, and no evidence of drugs in her system. Defendant testified on deposition that after reaching the field the parties talked for a while, began kissing, and eventually had intercourse.

This evidence raises no issue of fact as to whether plaintiff was either assaulted or seduced, as she alleges. Plaintiff testified that she has no recollection that defendant ever kissed her, embraced her or had intercourse with her, and that she "had no reason to ask [him] not to touch me because he never tried." The tort of assault occurs when a person is put in apprehension of a harmful or offensive contact, Prosser, Handbook of the Law of Torts § 10 (4th ed. 1971), and there is no evidence here that plaintiff feared, or even knew, that such a contact might occur. She has no recollection at all of the events. "Since the interest involved is the mental one of apprehension of contact, it should follow that the plaintiff must be aware of the defendant's act at the time . . . ." *Id.* at 38-39.

With regard to the tort of seduction, the law is that "the mere proof of intercourse, and no more, is not sufficient to warrant recovery." *Hutchins v. Day*, 269 N.C. 607, 609, 153 S.E. 2d 132, 133 (1967). Plaintiff needed to show "deception, enticement, or other artifice," *id.*, 153 S.E. 2d 134, and she did not do so. The evidence is that she went willingly with defendant to park in the field, willingly drank two alcoholic drinks, and later discovered she had had intercourse. There is no evidence that defendant enticed or deceived her in any way.

Affirmed.

Judges MARTIN (Robert M.) and HILL concur.

IN THE MATTER OF THE DENIAL BY THE SECRETARY OF REVENUE
OF CLAIM FOR REFUND OF NORTH CAROLINA INHERITANCE
TAXES BY THE ESTATE OF SHANKAR N. KAPOOR, DECEASED

No. 8010SC179

(Filed 1 July 1980)

Taxation § 27.1– inheritance taxes – separation agreement – life insurance trust – proceeds not debt of decedent

Where decedent obligated himself in a separation agreement to maintain in full force and effect "a life insurance trust in the amount of at least $150,000" for the benefit of his former wife and his children, this obligation was fulfilled by decedent's payment of the necessary life insurance premiums, and the life insurance proceeds were not a "debt of the decedent" deductible for inheritance tax purposes under G.S. 105-9(4).

APPEAL by respondent from *Hobgood (Hamilton H.), Judge.* Judgment entered 12 November 1979 in Superior Court, WAKE County. Heard in the Court of Appeals 13 June 1980.

Until 1969 decedent was married to Ruth Kapoor, and two children were born of the marriage. Prior to obtaining a divorce, decedent and Ruth Kapoor executed a separation agreement, by the terms of which decedent obligated himself to "maintain in full force and effect . . . a life insurance trust in the amount of at least $150,000.00" for the benefit of Ruth Kapoor and the children. Decedent established such a trust, and at the time of his death all premiums had been paid and policies in the amount of $151,754.63 were in effect.

The trustee of the life insurance trust collected the policy proceeds. Petitioner, the executor of decedent's estate, included the proceeds on both state and federal inheritance and estate tax returns and paid taxes on them. Subsequently, petitioner sought and received a refund of the federal taxes paid on the proceeds, but petitioner's claim for a refund of the state taxes paid was denied.

Upon petitioner's request for review, the Secretary of Revenue and then the Tax Review Board upheld the denial of the refund. Petitioner then sought review in the Superior Court, and the court reversed the denial and ordered that the refund be paid. Respondent appeals.

Haywood, Denny & Miller, by B. M. Sessoms and James H. Johnson III, for petitioner appellee.

Attorney General Edmisten, by Assistant Attorney General George W. Boylan, for the State.

ARNOLD, Judge.

The issue on this appeal is whether the life insurance proceeds are a "debt of the decedent," making them deductible for inheritance tax purposes under G.S. 105-9(4). Our courts have not previously interpreted the word "debt" as it is used in this section. Petitioner argues that G.S. 105-9(4) must be interpreted to include the types of deductions provided for federal estate tax computation by IRC § 2053(a)(3) and (4), but we are unpersuaded that this is what the legislature intended. The language of G.S. 105-9(4) does not parallel that used in the federal statute, and we find no indications otherwise that the legislature intended our state statute to reach the same results as the federal one. Accordingly, federal law is not helpful in interpreting G.S. 105-9(4).

The generally accepted meaning of "debt" is "something owed" from one person to another. See Webster's Third New International Dictionary 583 (1968). Petitioner argues that the life insurance proceeds here are a debt because decedent owed them to Ruth Kapoor under the terms of their separation agreement. Specifically, however, what decedent owed under the pertinent provision of the separation agreement was "a life insurance trust in the amount of at least $150.000.00" maintained in full force and effect, and this obligation was fulfilled by the payment of the necessary life insurance premiums. At the time of decedent's death no debt existed with respect to this obligation.

We hold that since decedent had totally satisfied his contractual obligation, no debt existed and no deduction under G.S. 105-9(4) is proper. The order of the trial court is

Reversed.

Judges ERWIN and HILL concur.

STATE OF NORTH CAROLINA v. DOROTHY M. ALEXANDER

No. 809SC68

(Filed 1 July 1980)

Criminal Law § 142.4– conditions for parole or work release – fine not restitution or reparation

    The imposition of a fine is not "restitution or reparation" within the meaning of G.S. 148-33.2(c); therefore, judgment imposed upon a conviction of voluntary manslaughter is modified by striking that portion ordering the payment of a fine of $4000.

APPEAL by defendant from *Bruce, Judge.* Judgment entered 31 August 1979 in Superior Court, FRANKLIN County. Heard in the Court of Appeals 22 May 1980.

Attorney General Edmisten, by Associate Attorney William R. Shenton, for the State.

Davis, Sturges and Tomlinson, by Conrad B. Sturges, Jr., for defendant appellant.

VAUGHN, Judge.

Defendant was convicted of voluntary manslaughter. Judgment imposing a prison sentence of ten years minimum, twenty years maximum, was entered. The sentence includes the following:

    As to restitution or reparation as a condition of attaining work release privilege or parole, the Court orders the defendant to pay a fine of $4000.00 and the cost of this action; make restitution to the State of North Carolina for attorney fees awarded her court appointed counsel for services to her in connection with this action and to any other court appointed lawyer who may represent her in the future in this matter; make restitution to the personal representative of the deceased Jonas Williams and in an amount equal to the funeral bill of Jonas Williams.

    It is recommended that should she become eligible for Parole or Work Release that she be required to make restitution, to pay fine and cost, and attorney fee under the supervision of a Work Release Counselor or Parole Officer.

When an active sentence is imposed, the judge should consider whether, as a further rehabilitative measure, restitution or reparation should be ordered or recommended to the Parole Commission and the Secretary of Correction to be imposed as a condition of attaining work-release privileges. G.S. 148-33.2(c). We hold, however, that the imposition of a fine is not "restitution or reparation" within the meaning of the statute. We, therefore, modify the judgment by striking that portion ordering the payment of a fine of $4,000.00.

We have examined defendant's other assignments of error and conclude that they fail to disclose prejudicial error.

No error in the trial. The judgment is modified and affirmed.

Judges PARKER and HEDRICK concur.

HAROLD PAGE STUTTS v. GREEN FORD, INC., FORD MOTOR CO., FORD MOTOR CREDIT CO.

No. 7919SC567

(Filed 15 July 1980)

1. **Uniform Commercial Code § 25– oil leak in truck – breach of warranty – repairs by other than selling dealer – directed verdicts for dealer and manufacturer improper**

    Directed verdicts in favor of the seller and manufacturer of a truck were erroneously granted on plaintiff's breach of warranty claim where defendant manufacturer and defendant seller jointly warranted that the seller would repair or replace without charge for parts and labor "any part [found to be defective in factory material or workmanship] during the first 12 months or 12,000 miles of operation"; at the end of the warranty period, plaintiff's truck continued to leak oil despite numerous attempts by two dealers to discover the cause and correct it; the burden was not upon plaintiff, a layman, to identify any specific defective part or workmanship which caused the oil leak in order to recover on his claim; there was evidence from

Stutts v. Green Ford, Inc.

which the jury could infer that defendant seller either refused to perform further repairs on plaintiff's truck or that it failed to make proper repair of defective parts on the truck within a reasonable time, thereby causing plaintiff to seek repairs from another dealer; and plaintiff's refusal to return the vehicle to the selling dealer for further repairs would not preclude him from recovery.

2. **Uniform Commercial Code § 11– limited warranty – duty of warrantor to correct defect**

Although limited warranties are valid, compliance with their covenants to repair and to replace defective parts requires that the warrantor do more than make good faith attempts to repair defects when requested to do so, and a manufacturer or other warrantor may be liable for breach of warranty when it repeatedly fails within a reasonable time to correct a defect as promised; moreover, a party seeking to recover for breach of a limited warranty is not required to give the warrantor unlimited opportunities to attempt to bring the item into compliance with the warranty.

3. **Uniform Commercial Code § 26– truck – breach of warranty – measure of damages – no recovery for loss of use**

Where a defect in a truck was not or could not be repaired within a reasonable period as required by a warranty limiting the remedy available to the purchaser in the event of a breach to repair or replacement of parts, the limited, exclusive remedy "fails of its essential purpose" within the meaning of G.S. 25-2-719(2), and the purchaser is entitled to recover damages as otherwise provided in the Uniform Commercial Code. The appropriate measure of damages in the case would be the difference in the fair market value of the truck in its condition at the time and place of acceptance, increased by the value of repairs and replacements made in compliance with the warranty, and its fair market value had it been as warranted; furthermore, plaintiff would not be entitled to damages for time lost in his business due to his inability to use the truck while it was being repaired, since the warranty provided that loss of use of the vehicle, loss of time, and inconvenience were not covered, and such contractual limitation was valid. G.S. 25-2-714.

4. **Rules of Civil Procedure § 50.2– directed verdict for party with burden of proof**

A trial judge may not direct a verdict in favor of the party having the burden of proof when his right to recover depends upon the credibility of his witnesses, but there are instances in which credibility may be established as a matter of law, as where the non-movant admits the truth of the facts upon which movant's claim rests, where the controlling evidence is documentary and the non–movant does not deny the authenticity of or correctness of the document, or where there are only latent doubts as to the credibility of oral testimony.

5. **Uniform Commercial Code § 45– default under retail sales contract – number of payments made in dispute – directed verdict improper**

In an action to recover damages allegedly resulting from breach of warranty where one defendant counterclaimed for an amount which represented the unpaid balance allegedly due on the retail installment contract executed by plaintiff, the trial court erred in directing verdict for defendant, though defendant's principal evidence was documentary, since that evidence was directly contradicted by plaintiff's testimony that he paid seven monthly installments during a given period rather than six as shown by defendant.

APPEAL by plaintiff from *Walker, Judge.* Judgment signed 6 October 1978 in Superior Court, RANDOLPH County. Heard in the Court of Appeals 17 January 1980.

Plaintiff filed this civil action against defendants Green Ford, Inc. Ford Motor Company, and Ford Motor Credit Company, seeking to recover damages allegedly resulting from breach of warranty and negligence.

On 2 April 1976 plaintiff purchased a 1976 Model F 600 Ford Truck from Green Ford, Inc., paying the sum of $5,073.02 in cash and financing the unpaid balance of $6,500.00 through Ford Motor Credit Company. Under the terms of a Retail Installment Contract signed by plaintiff, plaintiff agreed to make 48 monthly payments of $178.64 beginning 11 May 1976. In connection with the purchase of the truck, plaintiff was issued the following express limited warranty:

Ford and the Selling Dealer jointly warrant for each 1976 model medium and heavier truck sold by Ford that for the following periods from first use or retail delivery, whichever is earliest, the Selling Dealer will repair or replace any of the following parts that are found to be defective in factory material or workmanship under normal use in the United States or Canada on the following basis:

Any part during the first 12 months or 12,000 miles of operation, whichever is earliest (except tire and diesel engines manufactured by others than Ford, which are separately warranted by their manufacturers), without charge for parts and labor.

Any part of the engine block, head and all internal engine parts, water pump, intake and exhaust man-

ifolds, flywheel and flywheel housing, clutch housing
(excludes manual clutch assembly and clutch release
bearing), transmission case and all internal transmission parts (includes auxiliary transmission), transfer
case and all internal parts, drive shaft and drive shaft
support bearings, universal joints, drive axle housing
and all internal parts (excludes drive wheel bearings)
and drive axle shafts, after 12,000 miles and during the
first 12 months or 50,000 miles of operation, whichever
is earliest; for charge of 50 percent of the Dealer's
regular warranty charge to Ford for parts and labor.
(Defective gaskets and seals are covered for the same
warranty period as that of the part with which they
mate.)

. . . .

All Ford and the Selling Dealer require is that you properly
operate, maintain and care for your vechicle, and that you
return for warranty service to your Selling Dealer's place of
business or to any authorized Ford Dealer if you are traveling, have moved a long distance or need emergency repairs.
Waranty repairs will be made with Ford Authorized Service or Remanufactured Parts.

To the extent allowed by law, THIS WARRANTY IS IN
PLACE OF all other warranties, express or implied, including ANY IMPLIED WARRANTY OF MERCHANTABIL-
ITY OR FITNESS. Under this warranty, repair or replacement of parts is the only remedy.

. . . .

Under this warranty, repair or replacement of parts is the
only remedy, and loss of use of the vehicle, loss of time,
inconvenience, commercial loss or consequential damages
are not covered.

In his complaint filed 16 February 1977 plaintiff pled the
limited warranty and the existence of numerous specified defects in workmanship and materials. He alleged that on several

Stutts v. Green Ford, Inc.

occasions he had returned the vehicle to defendant Green Ford, Inc. for repairs, but that Green Ford had negligently failed to repair or refused to repair the defects in workmanship and materials as required by the warranty and that, as a result of such breach, he had suffered damages in the amount of $15,000.00, including time lost in his business due to his inability to use the truck while it was being repaired. Plaintiff prayed that he recover $15,000.00 damages against Ford Motor Company and Green Ford, Inc., and he prayed for a temporary restraining order restraining defendant Ford Motor Credit Company from taking possession of the truck pending final determination of the issues in this case.

Defendant Green Ford, Inc. admitted the sale of the Ford truck to plaintiff in April 1976 and the validity of the warranty, and denied that the warranty had been breached. Defendant Ford Motor Company denied the warranty and, in the alternative, alleged that if it had issued a warranty, its warranty obligations had been fully met. Ford Motor Credit Company and Green Ford, Inc. both admitted the execution of the written Retail Installment Contract and that the unpaid balance on the sales price of the vehicle at the time of sale amounted to $6,500.00. Additionally, Ford Motor Credit Company, by amendment to its answer, alleged that plaintiff had breached the Retail Installment Contract, which had been assigned to Ford Motor Credit Company by Green Ford, Inc. Based on its election to accelerate the debt owing due to plaintiff's breach, Ford Motor Credit Company prayed recovery of $7,486.08 allegedly due under the contract and repossession of the subject property. By way of reply, plaintiff denied that the unpaid balance was due because of defendant Green Ford Inc.'s and Ford Motor Company's breach of warranty.

The case came on for hearing before Judge Hal H. Walker and a jury at the 2 October 1978 civil session of Superior Court in Randolph County. At the close of plaintiff's evidence, all three defendants moved for a directed verdict on plaintiff's claim. The motion was granted as to defendants Ford Motor Company and Ford Motor Credit Company, but denied as to defendant Green Ford, Inc. At the close of all of the evidence, defendant Green Ford, Inc. renewed its motion for a directed verdict, which was granted. At the same time, defendant Ford Motor Credit Company moved for a directed verdict on its counterclaim for the amount due under the Retail Installment Contract. The trial court granted that motion and entered judgment in favor of Ford Motor Credit Company against plaintiff in the amount of $7,190.84 with interest. From judgment that plaintiff recover nothing of the defendants and that Ford Motor Credit Company recover $7,190.84 of plaintiff, plaintiff appealed.

Ottway Burton for plaintiff appellant.

Coggin, Hoyle & Workman, by James W. Workman, Jr. for defendant appellee Green Ford, Inc.

Luke Wright for defendant appellees Ford Motor Company and Ford Motor Credit Company.

PARKER, Judge.

DIRECTED VERDICT ON PLAINTIFF'S CLAIM OF BREACH OF WARRANTY

[1] Motions for directed verdicts were granted in favor of defendant Ford Motor Company at the close of plaintiff's evidence and in favor of defendant Green Ford, Inc. at the close of all of the evidence. The question presented, then, is whether the evidence, viewed in the light most favorable to plaintiff, the nonmovant, so clearly shows the absence of any breach of warranty that it will support no other conclusion as a matter of law. *See, Rose v. Motor Sales*, 288 N.C. 53, 215 S.E. 2d 573 (1975). The evidence, taken as true and interpreted in the light most favorable to the plaintiff, shows the following:

Plaintiff selected a 1976 F600 Ford truck with a heavy duty engine from Green Ford, Inc. in Greensboro for use in his business of transporting furniture to the northeastern United States for sale. In order to adapt the truck to his business, plaintiff ordered a special 25–foot van to be built and installed on the rear of the truck by a body shop in High Point.

On 2 April 1976 plaintiff took delivery of the truck from Green Ford. That same day he discovered wiring problems in the truck affecting the lights and windshield wipers and returned the vehicle to Green Ford for repairs. After the truck was returned to plaintiff ten to twelve days later, he had the van installed on the rear of the truck. In late April 1976 plaintiff began experiencing problems with loud noise and jerking in the transmission when the truck was in low gear, jerking and noise in the speedometer, and steering difficulty which caused the truck to pull to the left. Plaintiff informed Green Ford of these problems, whereupon Green Ford's mechanics replaced several parts in the power steering and the speedometer.

In May 1976 plaintiff continued to experience problems steering the truck, and he noticed oil leakage at the front and the rear. Water overflowed from the engine when it was stationary, and the gears were difficult to shift. Plaintiff also found that the truck lost power when loaded and travelling uphill. All of these problems were brought to the attention of Green Ford on a number of occasions, and the vechicle was in the shop for repairs for a week and a half during that month.

During June and July 1976 the problems with oil leakage, water overflow, speedometer noise, pull in the steering, and difficulty in shifting gears and loss of engine power persisted. In June the truck was in the shop for a week, and in July for two weeks. Although Green Ford did replace a part which was causing the water overflow, the other problems were not fixed.

In August 1976 plaintiff returned from a trip north and again returned the truck to Green Ford for repair of the oil leak, gear shift, and power loss.

During October, gas began leaking from the carburetor, and the oil leak grew worse. Green Ford again attempted repairs on the vehicle. When plaintiff went to pick it up on 25 October 1976 and discovered that the gas leak in the carburetor had not been corrected, plaintiff told Mr. Green, the owner of the dealership, and the service manager that "[he] couldn't imagine someone doing work like that." To this Mr. Green replied, "Why don't you take the truck somewhere else?" At that time the truck had approximately 8,999 miles on it and was still under warranty.

On the same day that Mr. Green had asked him why he didn't take the truck somewhere else, plaintiff took the truck to Piedmont Ford Truck Corporation and asked the service manager if Piedmont would begin to perform repairs on the truck under the warranty. The service manager and assistant service manager of Piedmont Ford agreed, and on 27 October 1976 Piedmont began repairs on the carburetor to stop the gas leak, on the speedometer to stop the jerking, and also attempted to repair a vacuum leak. In November 1976 plaintiff asked Ford representatives to replace the engine or to accept return of the truck and to refund his investment, but they refused to do so. After another trip in December, plaintiff again returned the truck to Piedmont Ford complaining still of loss of power, oil leakage, speedometer noise, vacuum leak and the same power steering problem that Green Ford had failed to repair properly. At that time, Piedmont mechanics, along with Ford factory representatives, discovered that the engine was building pressure in the crank case, contributing to the oil leak, but they were unable to discover the cause. The vacuum leak and the power steering were repaired.

At the time the warranty coverage on all parts ended in approximately February or March 1977, the truck was still leaking oil and losing power going up inclines. Plaintiff's own mechanic testified that the van body which plaintiff had installed would reduce the engine performance and cause the loss of power due to wind resistance.

We find the foregoing evidence sufficient to withstand the motions of Green Ford, Inc. and Ford Motor Company for directed verdicts, and accordingly find error in the granting of such motions.

The validity of the written warranty given by "Ford and the Selling Dealer" in connection with the sale of the truck to plaintiff is governed by the provisions of Article 2 of the Uniform Commercial Code, codified in Chapter 25 of the General

Statutes. Under the terms of the warranty, the obligation of the manufacturer and the dealer during the first 12 months or 12,000 miles of operation is limited to repair or replacement of any part (except tires and diesel engines not manufactured by Ford) that is "found to be defective in factory material or workmanship under normal use." It expressly states that it is in place of all other warranties, express or implied, including any implied warranty of merchantability or fitness. Insofar as the warranty is limited in coverage and disclaims all implied warranties, it is valid under the provisions of G.S. 25-2-316.

Where an aggrieved party seeks to recover damages for breach of an express warranty, limited or otherwise, he must demonstrate both that he has fulfilled his own obligations under it and that he has taken the steps required by Article 2. G.S. 25-2-607(3)(a) requires that a buyer, within reasonable time after he discovers or should have discovered any breach, notify the seller or be barred from any remedy. Where suit is brought to recover damages allegedly suffered as the result of breach of warranty, "[t]he burden is on the buyer to establish any breach with respect to the good accepted." G.S. 25-2-607(4). Arguing within this statutory framework, defendant Green Ford contends that plaintiff has failed to meet his burden of showing that Green Ford failed to repair and replace parts found to be defective as required by the warranty and, further, that plaintiff's refusal to permit Green Ford to perform any further work on the truck after 26 October 1976 relieved it of any liability under the warranty. Likewise, defendant Ford Motor Company contends that its warranty obligation was satisfied when either Green Ford or Piedmont Ford Truck Sales replaced defective parts called to their attention. We disagree.

[2] Although limited warranties are valid, compliance with their covenants to repair and to replace defective parts requires that the warrantor do more than make good faith attempts to repair defects when requested to do so. A manufacturer or other warrantor may be liable for breach of warranty when it repeatedly fails within a reasonable time to correct a defect as promised. *Allen v. Brown*, 181 Kan. 301, 310 P. 2d 923 (1957); *Cannon v. Pulliam Motor Company*, 230 S.C. 131, 94 S.E. 2d 397 (1956); *Givan v. Mack Truck, Inc.*, 569 S.W. 2d 243 (Mo. Ct.

App. 1978). A party seeking to recover for breach of a limited warranty is not required to give the warrantor unlimited opportunities to attempt to bring the item into compliance with the warranty. *Cannon v. Pulliam Motor Co., supra; see generally,* 77 C.J.S. Sales §340–341, pp. 1235,1236.

[1] Application of these principles to the facts shown by the evidence favorable to the plaintiff in the present case discloses that neither defendant Green Ford, Inc. nor Ford Motor Company was entitled to a directed verdict on plaintiff's breach of warranty claim. Ford Motor Company and the Selling Dealer, Green Ford, Inc., jointly warranted that the Selling Dealer would repair or replace without charge for parts and labor "[a]ny part [found to be defective in factory material or workmanship] during the first 12 months or 12,000 miles of operation, whichever is earliest (except tire and diesel engines manufactured by other than Ford . . .)" At the end of the warranty period, in February or March 1977, plaintiff's truck continued to leak oil despite numerous attempts by both Green Ford and Piedmont Ford to discover the cause and to correct it. It is true that plaintiff was unable to identify any specific defective part or workmanship which caused the oil leak; however, we are reluctant to place the undue burden upon a purchaser such as plaintiff, a layman, of doing so in order to recover on his claim. This view was adopted by the Supreme Court of Kansas in *Allen v. Brown, supra,* in which the court reasoned:

> As is often the case in the purchase of a new automobile, the purchaser on discovering mechanical conditions which do not seem to be normal in the operation of the motor vehicle, will return the automobile to the dealer from whom the purchase was made. The particular defect is usually unknown to the purchaser and it is upon the dealer that he relies for discovery of the defect causing the unusual mechanical functioning of the vehicle.

> * * *

> Under an express warranty as alleged in the petition, it would place a tremendous burden upon the purchaser of a new motor vehicle to find the precise part or parts of the

vehicle which were defective and direct the dealer to replace them or remedy the defect. If the operation of such
vehicle is mechanically defective and the automobile is
returned to the dealer for the purpose of correcting these
defects, it is incumbent upon the dealer to find such defective part or parts and replace them pursuant to the terms of
the warranty . . . .

181 Kan. at 307, 310 P. 2d at 927–928. *Accord, Rice v. Chrysler
Motors Corporation,* 198 N.W. 2d 247 (N.D. 1972).

The testimony of plaintiff and his witnesses concerning the
persistent oil leak is sufficient to permit the inference that
some defect in the truck was the cause, even though the precise
cause has eluded discovery by Ford mechanics. As to plaintiff's
complaint of loss of power on going up inclines, however, his
own mechanic testified that the apparent cause of such loss of
power was the van installed on the rear of the truck which
increased wind resistance and placed a greater strain on the
engine. Unlike the evidence concerning the oil leak, none of
plaintiff's evidence would support an inference that this was
the result of a defect covered by the warranty.

Also, there is sufficient evidence presented in the record
from which the jury could infer that Green Ford, Inc. either
refused to perform further repairs on plaintiff's truck, or that it
failed to make proper repair of defective parts on the truck
within a reasonable time, thereby causing plaintiff to seek repairs from another Ford dealer. In either event, both defendants' liability for breach would attach, and the plaintiff's refusal to return the vehicle to the selling dealer for further
repairs would not preclude him from recovery. *See, Cannon v.
Pulliam Motor Company, supra.* The facts of this case distinguish it from those presented in *Lilley v. Motor Co.,* 262 N.C. 468,
137 S.E. 2d 847 (1964), upon which defendants rely. In *Lilley,* our
Supreme Court held that, in the absence of evidence that repairs or replacements made by the selling dealer were unsatis-
factory, plaintiff's refusal to permit the selling dealer to comply
further with the warranty was fatal to his action. In the present case, such evidence is present.

Because the directed verdicts in favor of the selling dealer and the manufacturer were erroneously granted on plaintiff's breach of warranty claim, the case must be remanded for a new trial. For the guidance of the trial court, we discuss the measure of damages to which plaintiff would be entitled in the event that a breach of warranty by Green Ford and Ford Motor Company is found. The written warranty expressly limits the remedy available to the purchaser in the event of breach to repair or replacement of parts. Such a contractual limitation of remedy is permitted by G.S. 25-2-719 which provides as follows:

(1) Subject to the provisions of subsections (2) and (3) of this section . . . .

(a) the agreement may provide for remedies in addition to or in substitution for those provided in this article and may limit or alter the measure of damages recoverable under this article, as by limiting the buyer's remedies ... to repair and replacement of non-conforming goods or parts; and

(b) resort to a remedy as provided is optional unless the remedy is expressly agreed to be exclusive, in which case it is the sole remedy.

(2) Where circumstances cause an exclusive or limited remedy to fail of its essential purpose, remedy may be had as provided in this chapter.

(3) Consequential damages may be limited or excluded unless the limitation or exclusion is unconscionable. Limitation of consequential damages for injury to the person in the case of consumer goods is prima facie unconscionable but limitation of damages where the loss is commercial is not.

Although the statute declares such limitations valid, subsection (2) specifies that the contractual limitation will not apply "[w]here circumstances cause an exclusive or limited remedy to fail of its essential purpose." As the Official Comment to G.S. 25-2-719 makes clear, "it is of the very essence of a sales con-

tract that at least minimum adequate remedies be available."
Where, as in the present case, there is a defect which is not or
cannot be repaired within a reasonable period as required by
the warranty, courts in other jurisdictions have concluded that
the limited, exclusive remedy "fails of its essential purpose"
within the meaning of § 2-719(2) of the Uniform Commercial
Code and have permitted the buyer to recover damages as
otherwise provided by the Code. *See, Givan v. Mack Truck, Inc.,
supra;* 67 Am. Jur. 2d Sales § 534, pp. 718-719 and cases cited
therein.

[3] The general measure of damages for breach of warranty
allowed by the Uniform Commercial Code under G.S. 25-2-714
is "the difference at the time and place of acceptance between
the value of the goods accepted and the value they would have
had if they had been as warranted, *unless special circumstances
show proximate damages of a different amount.*" (emphasis
added). The burden of proving the difference in value, of course,
rests upon the purchaser. To the extent that plaintiff in the
present case "accepted" the truck by continued use in spite of
its "nonconformity", *see* G.S. 25-2-606, the date of acceptance
preceded the time when numerous repairs were made in full
compliance with the warranty. At the end of the warranty
period, the only nonconformity of which plaintiff complains and
of which there is evidence of defective parts or workmanship is
the oil leakage. Under the special facts of this case, we hold,
then, that an appropriate measure of damages would be the
difference in the fair market value of the truck in its condition
at the time and place of acceptance, increased by the value of
repairs and replacements made in compliance with the warranty, and its fair market value had it been as warranted. *See, Transportation, Inc. v. Strick Corp,* 283 N.C. 423, 196 S.E. 2d 711 (1973).
This, in effect, would permit plaintiff to recover damages com-
pensating him for the loss in value due to the persistent oil
problem, while preventing him from receiving windfall damages for defects which were subsequently successfully repaired.

As to the recovery of incidental and consequential damages
for breach of warranty, recovery of these is generally permitted
by G.S. 25-2-714. G.S. 25-2-719, however, expressly permits

contractual limitation of such damages unless the limitation or exclusion is unconscionable. The warranty in the present case contains such a limitation: "Under this warranty, repair or replacement of parts is the only remedy, and loss of use of the vehicle, loss of time, inconvenience, commercial loss or consequential damages are not covered." Although we have held that the limitation of remedy to repair and replacement of parts here fails of its essential purpose, we do not deem the failure of that one remedy to invalidate the contractual limitation on the recovery of consequential damages. We hold, therefore, that the contractual limitation on damages of this kind would be effective to limit plaintiff's recovery in the event breach of warranty is found to the difference in fair market value as stated above. See *Cox Motor Car Company v. Castle*, 402 S.W. 2d 429 (Ky. 1966).

DIRECTED VERDICT ON DEFENDANT FORD MOTOR CREDIT COMPANY'S COUNTERCLAIM

In its counterclaim filed as an amended answer, Ford Motor Credit Company sought judgment against plaintiff in the amount of $7,486.08, representing the unpaid balance allegedly due on the Retail Installment Contract executed by plaintiff. At trial Louis Hubbard, branch manager of defendant's Greensboro office, testified that the credit company had purchased the installment contract from Green Ford on 6 April 1976 for $6,500.00, the amount financed under the terms of the contract. Mr. Hubbard stated that between May and October 1976, plaintiff made six monthly payments of $178.24, or a total of $1069.44. The last payment made was on 13 October 1976. In accordance with the terms of the contract on default, Ford Motor Credit Company accelerated the debt, leaving the amount of $7,486.08 due and payable under the contract. Taking into account the rebate of the unearned portion of the interest charge, defendant's witness testified that the "payoff" to which Ford Motor Credit Company was entitled was $7,190.80. After granting Ford Motor Credit Company's motion for a directed verdict, the trial court entered judgment in the company's favor in the amount of $7,190.80.

Stutts v. Green Ford, Inc.

[4] The question raised by this portion of the appeal is whether a verdict was properly directed for the party with the burden of proof. Our Supreme Court has held that a trial judge may not direct a verdict in favor of the party having the burden of proof when his right to recover depends upon the credibility of his witnesses. *Cutts v. Casey*, 278 N.C. 390, 180 S.E. 2d 297 (1971). The court has more recently recognized that there are rare instances in which credibility may be established as a matter of law, as where the non-movant admits the truth of the facts upon which movant's claim rests, where the controlling evidence is documentary and the non-movant does not deny the authenticity of or correctness of the document, or where there are only latent doubts as to the credibility of oral testimony. *Bank v. Burnette*, 297 N.C. 524, 256 S.E. 2d 388 (1979).

[5] The present case does not fall within one of those rare exceptions. Although Ford Motor Credit Company's principal evidence was documentary, that evidence was directly contradicted by plaintiff's testimony that he paid seven monthly installments between May and November 1976, rather than six. The credibility of the witnesses, and the conflicts in the evidence were for the jury to assess and resolve, and it was error for the court to direct a verdict on defendant's counterclaim.

CONCLUSION

For the reasons stated, the judgment is vacated, and the cause is remanded for further proceedings not inconsistent with this opinion.

Vacated and remanded for a New Trial.

Judges ARNOLD and WEBB concur.

QUAIL HOLLOW EAST CONDOMINIUM ASSOCIATION, Plaintiff, v.
DONALD J. SCHOLZ COMPANY and HAROLD COOLER, Defendants,
and HAROLD COOLER, Third Party Plaintiff v. INDOOR COMFORT OF
RALEIGH, INC., a corporation, and HOLLAND CONSTRUCTION COM-
PANY, INC., a corporation, Third Party Defendants and HAROLD
COOLER, Third Party Plaintiff, v. REA BROTHERS, INC., Additional
Third Party Defendants

No. 7926SC558

(Filed 15 July 1980)

1. Architects § 3; Contracts § 15; Negligence § 2– condominium owners – action
against architect – negligent design and supervision

    An association of condominium owners could properly maintain an ac-
tion against an architect for the negligent design and preparation of plans
and specifications and the negligent supervision of construction of the condominium complex although no contractual privity existed between the
architect and the association of condominium owners.

2. Architects § 3; Limitation of Actions § 4.2; Rules of Civil Procedure § 15– action
against architect – statute of limitations – amendment of complaint – relation
back to time of original complaint

    Where defects in an underground water pipe system serving a condomin-
ium complex were discovered for the first time on or about 9 October 1974,
an action instituted on 13 June 1977 against defendant architect for negligent supervision of the installation of the system was brought within the
three-year statute of limitations of G.S. 1-52(5) and within the six year outer
limit of G.S. 1-50(5). Furthermore, an amendment of plaintiffs' complaint
filed on 1 February 1979 alleging defendant's negligent design of the water
pipe system related back to the date of the original complaint pursuant to
G.S. 1A-1, Rule 15(c) and was therefore not barred by the statute of limitations, since the original complaint gave defendant notice of the transactions
or occurrences to be proved pursuant to the amendment.

3. Architects § 3– condominium owners – action against architect – genuine issue
of material fact

    In an action brought by an association of condominium owners against
defendant architect for negligent design and supervision of installation of
an underground water pipe system for the condominium complex, the evidence on motion for summary judgment presented questions of fact as to the
duties arising between the parties where plaintiff's materials tended to
show that defendant drew the plans for the piping system; defendant had
the authority to interrupt the construction process so that design and construction errors could be remedied; defendant knew or should have known
that the piping system would deteriorate if proper methods of sealing the
pipes were not followed; defendant knew at the time of construction that
certain prescribed methods of construction were not being followed; and
defendant did not exercise his authority to prevent or correct the problems

that appeared on the construction site; and where defendant denied such assertions by plaintiffs and asserted that he was never obligated by contract or otherwise to oversee the construction in a supervisory capacity and that the plans and specifications drawn and approved by him were in all respects proper.

APPEAL by plaintiff from *McConnell, Judge.* Judgment entered 12 February 1979 in Superior Court, MECKLENBURG County. Heard in the Court of Appeals 16 January 1980.

Plaintiff, Quail Hollow East Condominium Association (Condominium Association), commenced this action, pursuant to G.S. 47A-26, seeking damages for economic injury allegedly resulting from the substandard condition of the underground water pipe system serving the condominium complex. In its complaint, plaintiff Condominium Association alleged that defendant Harold Cooler, an architect, entered into a contract in 1971 with defendant Donald J. Scholz Company (Scholz), a general contracting firm, "to prepare plans and specifications" for the construction of Quail Hollow East Condominiums in Charlotte, North Carolina, and "to supervise and administer the construction of the condominiums." Plaintiff further alleged that Cooler filed his plans with the Register of Deeds of Mecklenburg County, thus representing that construction would be in accordance with those plans. Plaintiff alleged that certain underground hot and cold water pipes had deteriorated since their installation, causing leaks and necessitating extensive repairs. In an amendment to its complaint, plaintiff alleged that the "deterioration and the resulting damage was caused by failure to comply with the building code, failure to comply with the plans and specifications, failure to properly install, and failure to properly test said piping system." According to plaintiff, defendant Cooler "was negligent in that he failed to properly supervise and inspect the construction of the premises, thus allowing substandard water piping to be installed throughout the complex." Plaintiff alleged that Cooler knew that the purchasers of the condominiums were relying on his expertise and his representations as to the plans and specifications, and that he knew plaintiff would ultimately be responsible for maintenance and upkeep of the water system and other common areas. Plaintiff prayed for recovery of $150,000, the cost of replacement of the underground piping system. Plaintiff subsequently amended its complaint to reflect a demand of $230,000.

Plaintiff alleged a separate cause of action for fraud and deceit and false representation in the procurement of purchase agreements entered into by its members. This count, however, was subsequently abandoned and is not relevant to this appeal.

Defendant Cooler answered, averring that plaintiff's complaint fails to state a claim upon which relief can be granted, and that he never had any contract with, or any obligation to, plaintiff or any members of the Condominium Association. Defendant Cooler denied that he represented having anything to do with the construction or that the construction would be in accordance with the plans. Defendant specifically denied having "any obligation to anyone to supervise or inspect the construction as it progressed."

As a third defense to both counts in plaintiff's complaint, defendant Cooler averred that plaintiff's action is barred by the statute of limitations as set forth in G. S. 1-52, which provides that actions must be commenced within three years of the date of accrual. As a fourth defense to both counts, defendant pled the provisions of G. S. 1-50, averring that plaintiff failed to commence the action within the six years allowed by that statute.

Defendant Cooler also filed a third party complaint against Indoor Comfort of Raleigh, Inc., and Holland Construction Co., Inc., seeking indemnity if held liable, alleging that "[i]f there were any defects or deficiencies in connection with the pipes . . . and if the underground water system was not constructed in accordance with plans and specifications or did not meet the standards of the construction industry in North Carolina, or if there was a failure to properly supervise the job, such defects or deficiencies were due to failure of Indoor Comfort of Raleigh, Inc. and Holland Construction Co., Inc., one or both of them, to properly perform the duties and obligations which they had undertaken." Defendant Cooler's third party claim is not a subject of this appeal.

After extensive discovery, and on 19 September 1978, defendant Cooler filed a motion for summary judgment, supported by the pleadings; admissions; interrogatories; affidavits of Cooler, C. Craven Hughes, who was Vice-President of Scholz, and T.W. Porter, an engineer employed by Cooler; the depositions of Cooler and others; and certain exhibits. On 12 February 1979, judgment was entered allowing defendant Cooler's motion for summary judgment, dismissing the action. Plaintiff appeals.

Jones, Hewson and Woolard, by Hunter M. Jones and Harry C. Hewson, for defendant and third party plaintiff appellee Harold Cooler.

Weinstein, Sturges, Odom, Bigger, Jonas and Campbell, by Allan W. Singer and L. Holmes Eleazer, Jr., for plaintiff appellant.

MORRIS, Chief Judge.

Plaintiff preserves only one assignment of error on appeal: The trial court improperly granted summary judgment in favor of defendant Cooler. In order for defendant to prevail on his motion, the "pleadings, depositions, answers to interrogatories, and admissions on file, together with the affidavits, if any [must] show that there is no genuine issue as to any material fact and that any party is entitled to a judgment as a matter of law." G. S. 1A-1, Rule 56(c); *Moore v. Fieldcrest Mills, Inc.*, 296 N.C. 467, 251 S.E. 2d 419 (1979). Plaintiff contends that there are genuine issues of material fact concerning the negligence of defendant Cooler in the performance of his professional obligations as an architect employed by Quail Hollow East Condominiums.

I. *Architect Liability*

[1] The primary question raised by this appeal is whether a homeowner's association may sue an architect for the negligent design and preparation of plans and specifications and the negligent supervision of construction of a condominium complex where there exists no contractual privity between the

architect and the homeowner's association. Recently becoming
an area of enormous concern within the legal community, the
scope of liability of an architect for the negligent performance
of his professional duties has undergone considerable expansion. This broadening of scope has been seen principally in the
relaxation of the traditional requisite of contractual privity. As
a general proposition of the law of torts, it is settled that, under
certain circumstances, one who undertakes to render services
to another which he should recognize as necessary for the protection of a third person, or his property, is subject to liability to
the third person, for injuries resulting from his failure to exercise reasonable care in such undertaking. Restatement
(Second) of Torts § 324A (1965); W. Prosser, Handbook of the Law
of Torts § 93 (4th ed. 1971). This principle was applied in the
recent decision of *Davidson and Jones, Inc. v. County of New
Hanover*, 41 N.C. App. 661, 255 S.E. 2d 580 (1979), *cert. den.* 298
N.C. 295, 259 S.E. 2d 911 (1979), wherein Judge Erwin wrote for
this Court the following:

The law imposes upon every person who enters upon an
active course of conduct the positive duty to exercise ordinary care to protect others from harm and calls a violation of
that duty negligence. *Council v. Dickerson's, Inc.*, 233 N.C.
472, 64 S.E. 2d 551 (1951); *Stroud v. Transportation Co.*, 215
N.C. 726, 3 S.E. 2d 297 (1939). The duty to protect others
from harm arises whenever one person is by circumstances
placed in such a position towards another that anyone of
ordinary sense who thinks will at once recognize that if he
does not use ordinary care and skill in his own conduct with
regard to those circumstances, he will cause danger of injury to the person or property of the other. *Insurance Co. v.
Sprinkler Co.*, 266 N.C. 134, 146 S.E. 2d 53 (1966); *Honeycutt
v. Bryan*, 240 N.C. 238, 81 S.E. 2d 653 (1954). The duty to
exercise due care may arise out of contractual relations.
However, a complete binding contract between the parties
is not a prerequisite to a duty to use due care in one's
actions in connection with an economic relationship, nor is
it a prerequisite to suit by a contractor against an
architect. *See Detweiler Bros., Inc. v. John Graham & Co.*,
412 F. Supp. 416 (E.D. Wash. 1976); *see also* 57 Am. Jur. 2d,
Negligence, § 49, p. 398.

An architect, in the performance of his contract with his employer, is required to exercise the ability, skill, and care customarily used by architects upon such projects. 5 Am. Jur. 2d, Architects, § 8, pp. 669-70. Where breach of such contract results in foreseeable injury, economic or otherwise, to persons so situated by their economic relations, and community of interests as to impose a duty of due care, we know of no reason why an architect cannot be held liable for such injury. Liability arises from the negligent breach of a common law duty of care flowing from the parties' working relationship.

41 N.C. App. at 666-67, 255 S.E. 2d at 584. In a more recent case, *Industries, Inc. v. Construction Co.*, 42 N.C. App. 259, 257 S.E. 2d 50, *cert. denied*, 298 N.C. 296, 259 S.E. 301 (1979), we stated that "the position and authority of a supervising architect are such that he ought to labor under a duty to the prime contractor [third party] to supervise the project with due care under the circumstances, even though his sole contractual relationship is with the owner." 42 N.C. App. at 266, 257 S.E. 2d at 55. We concluded there as follows:

The additional defendant (architect) here entered upon performance of an undertaking and, by doing so, entered into a relation with the contractor and others giving rise to a duty to those who must reasonably rely upon his professional performance. The arrangement presented here of an architect having general supervisory responsibility over the contractor and other subcontractors on a construction project of this nature is a normal one in this commercial age. Each of the various participants must, to some degree, rely upon the professional performance of the other and each therefore has the responsibility of performing his task with due care. Clearly, the incidental fact of the existence of the contract between the architect and the property owner should not negative the responsibility of the architect when he enters upon a course of affirmative conduct which may be expected to affect the interest of third parties.

42 N.C. App. at 271-72, 257 S.E. 2d at 59.

In *Browning v. Levien & Co.*, 44 N.C.App. 701, 262 S.E. 2d 355 (1980), we applied *Davidson and Jones, Inc.* and *Industries, Inc.* in again considering the scope of architect liability. In *Browning*, plaintiffs were members of a limited partnership formed to build an apartment complex, having obtained a construction loan from the First National City Bank of New York. First National employed defendant and his architectural firm to inspect the construction at the time of each progress payment request and to certify the progress according to the applicable plans and specifications. Upon default by the building contractor under the loan agreement, the limited partners brought suit against defendants, alleging that defendants had been negligent in certifying the work done by the contractor. As a cross assignment of error on appeal, defendants argued that the action was improper because there was no contractual privity between plaintiffs and defendants. This Court rejected that contention and held that "when the defendants undertook to perform services for the bank, it could be reasonably foreseen that the owners of the property, the plaintiffs in this case, might rely on the certification of defendants." 44 N.C.App. at 705, 262 S.E. 2d at 358. In so holding, we recognized the general rule evolving from recent decisions that "an architect who contracts to perform services is liable for damages proximately caused by his negligence to anyone who can be reasonably foreseen as relying on that architect's performing services in a reasonable manner." 44 N.C.App. at 704-5, 262 S.E. 2d at 358. This rule is applicable to actions arising both from negligent supervision and from the negligent preparation of plans and specifications. *Industries, Inc. v. Construction Co., supra.*

We must now determine whether these particular plaintiffs — an association of condominium purchasers — may maintain this action for damages resulting from negligent design and supervision. We find language from *United Leasing Corp. v. Miller*, 45 N.C.App. 400, 263 S.E. 2d 313, 318 (1980), instructive:

Whether ... a party has placed himself in such a relation with another so that the law will impose upon him an obligation, sounding in tort and not in contract, to act in such a way that the other will not be injured calls for the balancing of various factors: (1) the extent to which the transaction was intended to affect the other person; (2) the foreseeability of harm to him; (3) the degree of certainty that he suffered injury; (4) the closeness of the connection between the defendant's conduct and the injury; (5) the moral blame attached to such conduct; and (6) the policy of preventing future harm. (Citations omitted.)

Proper application of these factors requires that we consider the materials presented by both plaintiff and defendant on motion for summary judgment. From our review of those materials, it is evident that plaintiff's members fall within the range of potential plaintiffs contemplated by our earlier decisions abolishing the privity requirement. It is obvious that any architect's involvement in residential construction is intended to affect the ultimate consumer-purchaser in that the buyer anticipates and expects sound construction and solid workmanship. In addition, it is certainly foreseeable that any defect in design or negligence in supervision may bring harm to the homeowner, who is met daily with any deficiencies that may develop. Further, in this case, it is certain that the homeowners have suffered injury, as evidenced by the exhibits showing the water damage caused to the various condominium units and the extensive repairs that have already taken place within the condominium complex. We find that the allegations are sufficient to bring defendant within the purview of holdings in *Davidson and Jones, Inc., Industries, Inc.,* and *Browning.* The allegations are supported, at least nominally, by evidence presented on hearing of the motion for summary judgment. Although *Davidson and Jones, Inc.,* and *Industries, Inc.,* involved plaintiffs who were directly involved with the architect during the construction phases of the structures in those cases, in *Browning* plaintiffs were the owners of the property on which the construction took place. Under *Browning,* although the plaintiff's members did not purchase the units until after the allegedly defective pipe system had been installed, it seems entirely appropriate that third party purchasers would rely on the architect's certifications during construction as evidence that proper construction materials and methods were utilized. We, therefore, hold that, under the decisions previously discussed, plaintiff has standing to sue for damages resulting from the alleged negligence of an architect in the design and supervision of the construction of Quail Hollow East Condominiums.

Defendant argues, however, that plaintiff is barred from suit because this action involves economic loss rather than damage to property, relying on *Drilling Co. v. Nello L. Teer Co.*, 38 N.C.App. 472, 248 S.E. 2d 444 (1978). We find such a distinction neither dispositive nor persuasive. In *Industries, Inc. v. Construction Co., supra*, we distinguished *Drilling Co.* on this precise point, stating that "we do not believe the action is one for mere 'loss of profits'. Assuming, *arguendo*, that there is validity to that subtle distinction, the cause of action here is for an economic loss as a result of alleged *property damages*." 42 N.C. App. at 271, 257 S.E. 2d at 58. We find this decision applicable to the facts before us, and accordingly dismiss defendant's contention.

II. *Statute of Limitations*

[2]   We now consider whether plaintiff's claim is barred by the statute of limitations applicable to an action in tort against an architect for negligence arising out of a construction project. Plaintiff cites several statutes which it argues are controlling in this instance, which we discuss below.

The statute limiting tort actions in this State is G. S. 1-52(5), which provides that actions involving "any other injury to the person or rights of another, not arising on contract and not hereafter enumerated" must be brought within three years from the time the right of action accrues. G. S. 1-15(b), as it read at all times pertinent to this appeal, provided:

> Except where otherwise provided by statute, a cause of action, other than one for wrongful death, having as an essential element bodily injury to the person or a defect in or damage to property which originated under circumstances making the injury, defect or damage not readily apparent to the claimant at the time of its origin, is deemed to have accrued at the time the injury was discovered by the claimant, or ought reasonably to have been discovered by him, whichever event first occurs; provided that in such cases the period shall not exceed 10 years from the last act

of the defendant giving rise to the claim for relief.

G. S. 1-50(5), allowing for a six-year period of limitation for actions to recover for damages to realty applicable to architects and building contractors, provides:

> No action to recover damages for any injury to property, real or personal, or for an injury to the person, or for bodily injury or wrongful death, arising out of the defective and unsafe condition of an improvement to real property, nor any action for contribution or indemnity for damages sustained on account of such injury, shall be brought against any person performing or furnishing the design, planning, supervision of construction or construction of such improvement to real property, more than six (6) years after the performance or furnishing of such services and construction. This limitation shall not apply to any person in actual possession and control as owner, tenant or otherwise, of the improvement at the time the defective and unsafe condition of such improvement constitutes the proximate cause of the injury for which it is proposed to bring an action.

The effect of these statutes is that date of the accrual of a cause of action is deemed to be the date of discovery of the defective or unsafe condition of a structure, and that the action must be brought within three years thereafter. Finally, G.S. 1-50(5) sets an outside limit on the right to sue, requiring that the action be brought within six years after construction is completed, except that it is not applicable "to any person in actual possession and control as owner, tenant or otherwise, of the improvement at the time the defective and unsafe condition of such improvement constitutes the proximate cause of the injury for which it is proposed to bring an action." *See generally Smith v. American Radiator & Standard Sanitary Corp.*, 38 N.C.App. 457, 248 S.E. 2d 462 (1978), *cert. denied*, 296 N.C. 586, 254 S.E. 2d 33 (1979). The defects were discovered for the first time on or about 9 October 1974. This action was instituted on 13 June 1977. It is evident that plaintiff brought its action, at least with respect to its claim for negligent supervision, within the limits prescribed in these sections, and defendant properly does not contend otherwise.

Defendant does, however, dispute the timeliness of this action with respect to plaintiff's claim based on defendant's allegedly negligent design of the plans and specifications used in the construction project. Plaintiff's claim here is based on an amendment to its complaint filed on 1 February 1979, alleging that defendant "failed to design adequate piping systems as to both plans and specifications." The date of the commencement of this claim is well beyond the three years allowed by G.S. 1-52(5), and the six years allowed by G.S. 1-50(5). Plaintiff contends, however, that the claim is timely in that it relates back to the date of the original complaint under G.S. 1A-1, Rule 15(c) of the North Carolina Rules of Civil Procedure. Defendant argues, on the other hand, that this amendment introduces "a new cause of action essentially in conflict with the cause of action previously alleged and that the previous pleadings gave no notice of the transactions and occurrences to be proved pursuant to the proposed amendment," contrary to the requirements of G.S. 1A-1, Rule 15(c).

Without deciding whether plaintiff's amendment to its complaint constitutes a new cause of action, it is our opinion that the amendment was properly allowed and that it relates back to the original complaint under Rule 15(c). In *Humphries v. Going,* 59 F.R.D. 583 (1973), the Court recognized that in North Carolina even a new cause of action can relate back to the original complaint so as to defeat the effect of a statute of limitations. The test is whether defendant ought to have known from the original complaint the facts which plaintiff attempts to add by its amendment. "A claim asserted in an amended pleading is deemed to have been interposed at the time the claim in the original pleading was interposed, *unless the original pleading does not give notice of the transactions, occurrences, or series of transactions or occurrences to be proved pursuant to the amended pleading.*" (Emphasis added.) G. S. 1A-1, Rule 15(c). *See also* Comment, Section (c) to Rule 15. We hold that in this case defendant was afforded notice of the "transactions, occurrences, or series of transactions or occurrences" contemplated by plaintiff's lawsuit.

III. *Evidence Presented on Motion for Summary Judgment.*

[3]   Finally, defendant argues that summary judgment was properly entered because plaintiff's evidence is insufficient to present a genuine issue as to any material fact concerning negligent supervision and negligent design. In the materials presented on motion for summary judgment, we find some evidence which tends to show that defendant Cooler drew the plans for the piping system; that he had the authority, if not the responsibility, to interrupt the construction process so that design and construction errors could be remedied; that defendant knew or should have known that the piping system would deteriorate if proper methods of sealing the pipes were not followed; that defendant knew at the time of construction that certain prescribed methods of construction were not being followed; and that defendant did not exercise his authority to prevent or correct the problems that appeared on the construction site. These assertions are denied by defendant, who asserts he was never obligated by contract or otherwise to oversee the construction in a supervisory capacity, and that the plans and specifications drawn and approved by him were in all respects proper. Thus, the evidence presents questions of fact as to the duties arising between the parties to this lawsuit. This question is one for the jury to resolve in its sound discretion, and in light of the standard of reasonableness previously set forth in this opinion and the decisions cited herein.

Reversed and remanded.

Judges MARTIN (Harry C.) and HILL concur.

JOHN E. MARSHALL, MARNA J. MARSHALL, DEVON G. BELL, RHONDA
T. ROGERS, EDWARD L. HOWELL, AMON G. STEWART, BETTY J. STE-
WART AND G.C. BROWN v. ERNEST W. MILLER, AND WIFE, JANE D. MIL-
LER, INDIVIDUALLY AND D/B/A SPANISH TRAILS, ALIAS SPANISH TRAILS
MOBILE HOME PARK, AND IRA GROSSMAN

No. 7918DC1113

(Filed 15 July 1980)

1. **Landlord and Tenant § 6.1– leased spaces in trailer park – facilities and services furnished under lease – credibility of witnesses in issue – directed verdict improper**

    In an action to recover damages for breach of agreements under which defendants leased spaces in a trailer park to plaintiffs', the trial court erred in directing verdict for plaintiffs since issues of credibility were raised where the evidence tended to show that some of the plaintiffs had previously had written leases; other plaintiffs had never had written leases but had moved into and remained at the park only under oral agreements that they pay monthly rental; none of the plaintiffs relied upon a written lease agreement; to establish the nature and extent of defendants' agreements to furnish facilities and services in exchange for the payment of monthly rental, plaintiffs presented evidence of newspaper advertisements, rules and regulations promulgated by defendants, and oral representations made by park managers and employees; and to establish defendants' breach of agreements, plaintiffs presented their own testimony and that of other witnesses.

2. **Trusts § 19– mobile home parts retained by defendants – insufficiency of evidence of constructive fraud**

    In an action to recover for mobile home wheels, tires, and axles which defendants allegedly wrongfully sold or converted to their use, the trial court erred in imposing a constructive trust and in directing verdict that defendants had breached the trust, since evidence presented by defendants, if believed, would tend to show that the contested tires, wheels, and axles were never included in the original sales of mobile homes to plaintiffs; evidence presented by plaintiffs, if believed, would tend to establish either that the defendants had failed to deliver the contested items as agreed at the time of the original sales of the mobile homes or that, although delivered at that time, they were later retained by defendants and stored in another area of the trailer park; and therefore no constructive trust arose on this evidence.

3. **Unfair Competition § 1– unfair or deceptive trade practice – rental of mobile home spaces – trade or commerce**

    Rental of spaces in a mobile home park is trade or commerce within the meaning of G.S. 75-1.1.

Marshall v. Miller

4. **Unfair Competition § 1– single course of conduct – breach of contract – unfair and deceptive trade practice – damages for both improper**

Where the same course of conduct gives rise to a traditionally recognized cause of action, as, for example, an action for breach of contract, and as well gives rise to a cause of action for violation of G.S. 75-1.1, damages may be recovered either for the breach of contract or for violation of G.S. 75-1.1, but not for both.

5. **Unfair Competition § 1– furnishing services in trailer park – no bad faith – no unfair or deceptive trade practice – treble damages inappropriate**

Absent a finding of some bad faith, the jury's answer as to whether defendant, without the intent or ability to perform, led plaintiffs to believe that he would provide certain facilites in a trailer park would not support a violation of G.S. 75-1.1 and an award of treble damages under G.S. 75-16.

6. **Unfair Competition § 1– treble damages sought by private party – good faith relevant**

Although good faith may be irrelevant where injunctive relief is sought by the Attorney General under G.S. 75-14, it should be relevant where a private party seeks treble damages under G.S. 75-16.

APPEAL by defendants from *Alexander, (Elreta M.), Judge.* Judgment entered 5 October 1978 in District Court, GUILFORD County. Heard in the Court of Appeals 15 May 1980.

Plaintiffs, residents in Spanish Trails, a mobile home park owned and operated by the defendant Ernest W. Miller, brought this action on 7 October 1977 seeking to recover damages for (1) breach of agreements under which defendants leased to the several plaintiff's spaces in the park for use as sites for their respective mobile homes, (2) breach of agreements under which defendants sold mobile homes to the several plaintiffs, and (3) violations of G.S. 75-1.1(a). Defendants filed answer in which they denied violating any agreement with plaintiffs, denied that any plaintiff held under a long-term lease in the park, admitted that defendants sold trailers to plaintiffs but denied any breach of the sales contracts, and denied violations of G.S. 75-1.1(a). Defendants also denied that the defendant Jane D. Miller had any involvement whatsoever in the park as partner, agent, or owner.

At trial before a jury plaintiffs presented evidence in the form of advertisements of the park facilities made by defendants, printed rules and regulations furnished by defendants to persons renting spaces in the park, and testimony as to oral representations made by defendants concerning the facilities, services, and amenities which a person becoming a resident in the park could expect to enjoy, and they presented evidence of defendants' continued failure to furnish the facilities, services, and amenities as represented. Plaintiffs also presented evidence tending to show that included in the sale of each mobile home made by defendants to the several plaintiffs were wheels, tires, and axles; that these had been affixed to the mobile homes when they were brought into the park but had been detached and removed by defendants when the homes were set up on the respective sites in the park occupied by the several plaintiffs; that when plaintiffs inquired about the wheels, tires, and axles they were first told that these were being stored for them in a storage area in the park but were later told that they had been sold; and that defendants had refused, after demand made upon them, to deliver to plaintiffs either the wheels, tires, and axles or the proceeds from their sale.

Defendants presented evidence to show that at the time of the commencement of this action none of the plaintiffs held under a long-term lease but each occupied space in the park only under a month-to-month tenancy, that the facilities and services furnished to residents in the park were substantially as they had been represented except in instances where, through no fault of defendants, this could not be done, and that operation of the park had resulted in a substantial loss to its owner. Concerning the wheels, tires, and axles, defendants' testimony tended to show that these items had not been included in the original sale of the mobile homes.

At close of the evidence the court permitted plaintiffs to amend their complaint to allege, as an alternative to the claim for breach of contract of sale of the mobile homes, that defendants had "willfully failed to honor the trust created by the delivery of the plaintiffs' tires, wheels and axles to the defendants as alleged."

The court submitted issues which were answered by the jury as follows:

Marshall v. Miller

1. Was Mrs. Jane Miller a partner in Spanish Trails all of the times complained of as alleged?

ANSWER: YES.

2. How much, if any, are the following plaintiffs entitled to recover of the defendant for breach of the constructive trust to return the tires, wheels and axles?

(a) Mrs. Betty Stewart.

ANSWER: $1,350.00

(b) Mr. G.C. Brown

ANSWER: $900.00

(c) Mr. E.L. Howell

ANSWER: $900.00

(d) Mr. Devon G. Bell

ANSWER: $900.00

3. How much, if any, are the following plaintiffs entitled to recover of the defendant for breach of lease from October 7, 1974 to October 7, 1977?

(a) Mr. and Mrs. John E. Marshall

ANSWER: $630.00

(b) Mr. and Mrs. A.G. Stewart

ANSWER: $630.00

(c) Mrs. Rhonda T. Rogers

. . . . . .

ANSWER: $630.00

(e) Mr. Edward L. Howell

ANSWER: $577.50;

4. Did the defendant, after October 7, 1974, without the intent and/or the ability to perform lead the plaintiffs or any of them to believe that he would provide the following equipped facilities for their use, reasonable wear and tear accepted (sic)?

(a) Two playgrounds

ANSWER: YES.

(b) One basketball court

ANSWER: YES.

(c) One swimming pool

ANSWER: YES.

(d) Household water

ANSWER: NO.

(e) Adequate garbage facilities and pickup

ANSWER: YES.

(f) Complete yard care, that is, mowing and trimming

ANSWER: YES.

(g) Paved streets

ANSWER: YES.

(h) Lighted streets

ANSWER: YES.

(i) Common facilities

ANSWER: YES.

5. If so, has the defendant within the period specified, that is, after October 7, 1974, failed to reasonably provide any and all of the following:

(a) Two playgrounds

ANSWER: YES.

(b) One basketball court

ANSWER: YES.

. . . . . .

ANSWER: YES.

(d) Household water

ANSWER:

(e) Adequate garbage facilities and pickup

ANSWER: YES.

(f) Complete yard care, that is mowing and trimming

ANSWER: YES.

(g) Paved streets

ANSWER: YES.

(h) Lighted streets

ANSWER: YES.

(i) Common facilities

ANSWER: YES.

6. If so, did any or all of the following plaintiffs reasonably expect the defendant to comply with the foregoing after October 7, 1974?

(a) Mr. and Mrs. John E. Marshall

ANSWER: YES.

(b) Mr. Devon G. Bell

ANSWER: YES.

(c) Ms. Rhonda T. Rogers

ANSWER: YES.

(d) Mr. Edward L. Howell

ANSWER: YES.

(e) Mr. and Mrs. Amon G. Stewart

ANSWER: YES.

(f) Mr. G.C. Brown

ANSWER: YES.

7. If so, what, if any, damages have plaintiffs sustained by reason thereof, such plaintiffs being the ones to which you answered "yes" in the preceding Issue No. 6?

(a) Mr. and Mrs. John E. Marshall

ANSWER: $540.00

Marshall v. Miller

(b) Mr. Devon G. Bell

ANSWER: 540.00

(c) Ms. Rhonda T. Rogers

ANSWER: $540.00

(d) Mr. Edward L. Howell

ANSWER: 495.00

. . . .   .   .

ANSWER: $540.00

(f) Mr. G.C. Brown

ANSWER: $540.00

The court entered judgment in which, based on the findings of the jury with respect to Issues 4, 5, 6, and 7, the court concluded that

> the acts of the defendants complained of by the plaintiffs constitute unfair or deceptive acts or practices in or affecting commerce within the meaning of North Carolina General Statues § 75-1.1, and therefore, pursuant to North Carolina General Statues § 75-16, the damages assessed by the jury in answer to Issue No. 7 above should be and are hereby trebled.

Accordingly, the court entered judgment that

1. The plaintiffs, Mr. and Mrs. John E. Marshall, have and recover of the defendants the sum of $2,250.00;

2. The plaintiffs, Mr. and Mrs. Amon Glenn Stewart, have and recover of the defendants the sum of $3,600.00;

3. The plaintiff, Ms. Rhonda T. Rogers, have and recover of the defendants, the sum of $2,250.00;

4. The plaintiff, Mr. G.C. Brown, have and recover of the defendants the sum of $3,150.00;

5. The plaintiff, Mr. Devon G. Bell, have and recover of the defendants the sum of $3,150.00;

6. The plaintiff, Mr. Edward L. Howell, have and recover of the defendants the sum of $2,962.50;

The court also taxed the costs of the action, including a fee of $5787.50 for plaintiffs' attorney, against the defendants.

From this judgment, defendants appealed.

Edwards, Greeson, Weeks & Turner, by Joseph E. Turner, attorneys for plaintiff appellees.

Kathryn K. Hatfield, attorney for defendant appellants.

PARKER, Judge.

[1] In regard to plaintiffs' first claim for relief, being the claim to recover damages for breach of agreements under which defendants leased spaces in the park to several plaintiffs, the court announced at the close of the evidence that it would "grant the motion of the plaintiffs for a directed verdict in regard to the breach of lease as to each of the plaintiffs from the period of October 7, 1974, to October 7, 1977, and submit to the jury the issue of how much damages, if any, is each of the plaintiffs entitled to recover therefor." Consistent with the ruling, the court instructed the jury that "the court has concluded that there was a substantial breach of the lease agreement between the parties." The court then submitted to the jury in regard to plaintiffs' first claim for relief only Issue No. 3 as to what amount of damages, if any, each plaintiff was entitled to recover for breach of lease. In directing a verdict in plaintiffs' favor on the issue of breach of lease, the court committed error.

In prosecuting their first claim for relief, plaintiffs had the burden of proving first, the nature and extent of the contractual agreements made between the parties concerning facilities and services to be furnished by defendants in exchange for payment of monthly rental by plaintiffs and, second, defendants' breach of those agreements. By directing verdict in plaintiffs' favor on those issues, the court directed verdict in favor of the parties having the burden of proof. Under some circumstances, this may be proper. *See Bank v. Burnette*, 297 N.C. 524, 256 S.E. 2d 388 (1979). We do not find it so in the present instance. Evidence in this case shows that, although some of the plaintiffs previously had written leases, other plaintiffs had never had written leases, but had moved into and remained at the park only under oral agreements that they pay monthly rental. None of the plaintiffs relied upon a written lease agreement. To establish the nature and extent of defendants' agreements to furnish facilities and services in exchange for the payment of monthly rental, plaintiffs presented evidence of newspaper advertisements, rules and regulations promulgated by defendants, and oral representations made by park managers and employees. To establish defendants' breach of the agreements, plaintiffs presented their own testimony and that of other witnesses. Although much of plaintiffs' evidence was uncontradicted, issues of credibility remained for resolution by the jury, and it was error for the court to direct verdict in plaintiffs' favor.

[2] For their second claim for relief, each of the plaintiffs, Stewart, Brown, Howell, and Bell, alleged in their original complaint that after the defendants had sold to each of them a mobile home, including the undercarriage consisting of axles, wheels, and tires, defendants removed these items and either sold or otherwise intentionally converted them to defendants' use. Plaintiffs prayed to recover damages in the amount of the fair market value of the items allegedly wrongfully taken by the defendants. After close of the evidence, the court permitted the plaintiffs to amend their complaint to allege as an alternative to their second claim for relief that defendants had "wilfully failed to honor the trust created by the delivery of the plaintiffs' tires, wheels and axles to the defendants as alleged." The court then allowed the plaintiffs' motion for a directed verdict "as to the breach of the constructive trust to return the wheels, tires and axles." Consistent with these rulings, the court submitted

to the jury in regard to plaintiffs' second claim for relief only Issue No. 3 as to what amount, if any, the named plaintiffs were entitled to recover of the defendants "for breach of the constructive trust to return the tires, wheels and axles." In imposing a constructive trust and in directing verdict that defendants had breached the trust, the court committed error.

No constructive trust arose on the evidence in this case. Evidence presented by defendants, if believed, would tend to show that the contested tires, wheels, and axles were never included in the original sales of the mobile homes to the plaintiffs. Evidence presented by plaintiffs, if believed, would tend to establish either that the defendants had failed to deliver the contested items as agreed at the time of the original sales of the mobile homes or that, although delivered at that time, they were later retained by defendants and stored in another area of the park. If the latter, the relationship between the named plaintiffs and the defendants with respect to such items became that of bailors and bailees, in which event defendants' liability for loss or damage to the property would be governed by a determination of the question of for whose benefit the property was being stored. *See Clott v. Greyhound Lines*, 278 N.C. 378, 180 S.E. 2d 102 (1971). Plaintiffs had the burden of proving either their original claim that defendants had breached their contracts of sale by failing to deliver the contested items as agreed, or that defendants had breached their duty as bailees of the contested property. It was error for the court to impose a constructive trust and to direct verdict that defendants had breached the trust thus imposed.

We now turn to plaintiffs' claim based upon defendants' alleged violations of G.S. 75-1.1(a). At the time defendants committed the acts which plaintiffs allege as the basis of their claim, the statute read as follows:

Unfair methods of competition and unfair or deceptive acts or practices in the conduct of any trade or commerce are hereby declared unlawful.[1]

[3] Interpreting this statute, this Court has held that the rental of residential housing is "trade or commerce" under G.S. 75-1.1. *Love v. Pressley*, 34 N.C. App. 503, 239 S.E. 2d 574 (1977). We now hold that rental of spaces in a mobile home park is also "trade or commerce" within the meaning of the statute. The question remains whether defendants' conduct constituted "unfair or deceptive acts or practices" in the conduct of that trade or commerce. To resolve this question, the trial court, complying with the directive of our Supreme Court in *Hardy v. Toler*, 288 N.C, 303, 218 S.E. 2d 342 (1975), ruled that it was for the jury to determine the facts, and based on the jury's findings, the court would then determine as a matter of law whether defendants engaged in unfair or deceptive acts or practices in the conduct of trade or commerce. For this purpose the court submitted Issues 4, 5, 6, and 7 to the jury, and on the basis of the jury's answers to those issues, the court ruled as a matter of law that defendants had violated G.S. 75-1.1 We find error both in the issues submitted and in the court's instructions with regard thereto.

[4] While charging the jury with respect to Issue No. 7, which concerned the amount of damages which the jury could find

---

[1]Effective 27 June 1977, which was prior to institution of the present action but subsequent to the commission by defendants of the acts complained of, G.S. 75-1.1(a) and (b) were rewritten by Ch. 747 of the 1977 Session laws to read as follows:

G.S. 75-1.1

(a) Unfair methods of competition in or affecting commerce, and unfair or deceptive acts or practices in or affecting commerce, are declared unlawful.

(b) For purposes of this section, "commerce" includes all business activities, however denominated, but does not include professional services rendered by a member of a learned profession.

plaintiffs sustained because of defendants' alleged violations of
G.S. 75–1.1(a), the court instructed the jury:

> Now the fact that you will answer — would have
> answered something for the breach of lease, don't worry
> about that. *You may use some of the same elements in
> answering this.*

> This becomes a question of law. If you decide — you get
> to this, you are not required to get to this issue, the burden
> is on the plaintiffs to satisfy you from the evidence and
> greater weight thereof, you should get to this issue, *you
> should answer this in some sum you find the plaintiffs sus-
> tained or any of them by reason of the defendants' failure to
> provide the facilities listed in the preceding items.* (Em-
> phasis added).

In giving this instruction, the court committed error. The effect
of this instruction was to permit the jury to assess damages
against the defendants twice for the same default. The error
was compounded when the court, acting under G.S. 75-16, gave
judgment for treble the amount of the damages fixed by the
jury's answer to issue No. 7 in addition to the amounts already
fixed by the jury's answer to Issue No. 3. The net result is that
some of the plaintiffs were given judgment for quadruple damages. We do not believe that the legislature intended any such
result when it enacted G.S. 75-1.1(a). Where the same course of
conduct gives rise to a traditionally recognized cause of action,
as, for example, an action for breach of contract, and as well
gives rise to a cause of action for violation of G.S. 75-1.1, damages may be recovered either for the breach of contract, or for
violation of G.S. 75-1.1, but not for both.

[5] We also find error in the form of Issue No. 4 as submitted to
the jury. It was possible for the jury to answer that issue in the
affirmative, thus furnishing a portion of the basis on which the
court concluded there had been a violation of G.S. 75-1.1, if the
jury found that defendants, even though acting in good faith,
became financially unable to fulfill all of their contractual
obligations. We hold that, absent a finding of some bad faith, the
jury's answer to Issue No. 4 would not support a violation of

Marshall v. Miller

G.S. 75-1.1 and an award of treble damages under G.S. 75-16. In so holding, we note the distinction between the private method of enforcement and the public methods of enforcement provided for in the legislative scheme of Chapter 75.

The present action based on a violation of G.S. 75-1.1 was brought pursuant to G.S. 75-16, which grants a private right of action to any person injured by any act in violation of Chapter 75 of the General Statutes. Chapter 75 also contains provisions for enforcement of G.S. 75-1.1 in suits brought by the Attorney General, provisions which substantially follow the federal scheme for enforcement of § 5 of the Federal Trade Commission Act. G.S. 75-14 (actions brought by Attorney General to obtain mandatory orders); G.S. 75-15.2 (imposition of civil penalties in suits brought by the Attorney General where the "acts or practices which constituted the violation were, when committed, specifically prohibited by a court order or knowingly violative of a statute."). Unlike our own statutory scheme, however, the FTC Act confers no private right of action upon an injured party, *Federal Trade Commission v. Klesner*, 280 U.S. 19, 50 S. Ct. 1, 74 L. Ed. 138 (1929), and the sole means of enforcement is through the Federal Trade Commission which is empowered to issue a complaint whenever it has reason to believe that a violation of the Act has occurred and that a proceeding "would be to the interest of the public." 15 U.S.C. § 45(b). The issuance of a cease and desist order by the FTC pursuant to such a complaint is warranted upon proof that an act or practice has a capacity or tendency to deceive, that it offends public policy, or that it is substantially injurious to consumers, *see, e.g., Spiegel, Inc. v. F.T.C.*, 540 F. 2d 287 (7th Cir. 1976); *Koch v. Federal Trade Commission*, 206 F. 2d 311 (6th Cir. 1953); *D.D.D. Corporation v. Federal Trade Commission*, 125 F. 2d 679 (7th Cir. 1942), and the presence of good faith is immaterial to the question of whether an order should issue. *Koch v. Federal Trade Commission, supra.*

[6] Our Supreme Court has held that our courts should look for guidance to federal decisions interpreting the FTC Act. *Johnson v. Insurance Co.*, 300 N.C. 247, 266 S.E. 2d 610 (1980); *Edmisten, Attorney General v. Penney Co.*, 292 N.C. 311, 233 S.E. 2d 895 (1977). However, to the extent that good

or bad faith has been held irrelevant to a determination of a violation of the FTC Act, the applicability of that principle in suits based on alleged violations of our own G.S. 75-1.1 should be determined with reference to our dual statutory scheme of enforcement. Thus, although good faith may be irrelevant where *injunctive* relief is sought by the Attorney General under G.S. 75-14, it should be relevant where a private party seeks *treble damages* under G.S. 75-16. *See, Trust Co. v. Smith*, 44 N.C. App. 685, 262 S.E. 2d 646 (1980); *United Roasters, Inc. v. Colgate-Palmolive Co.*, 485 F. Supp. 1049 (E.D.N.C. 1980). In the former type of case, a defendant against whom a mandatory order is issued is thereafter on notice that civil penalty may be imposed should his conduct continue, and a defendant who knowingly violates G.S. 75-1.1 and must pay a civil penalty pursuant to G.S. 75-15.2 needs no such notice. In the latter type of case, however, treble damages should not be assessed against a defendant who acts in good faith where he is not otherwise on notice that his conduct violates G.S. 75-1.1. This interpretation of the legislative intent is supported by the language employed by the legislature in enacting G.S. 25A-44(4),which made the "knowing and willful violation" of any provision of G.S. Ch. 25A, the Retail Installment Sales Act, an unfair trade practice under G.S. 75-1.1.

For the errors above noted, defendants are entitled to a

New Trial.

Judges VAUGHN and ERWIN concur.

JESSE THOMAS LEE V. WOODROW WILSON REGAN

No. 7914SC1087

(Filed 15 July 1980)

1. **Damages § 3– aggravation of preexisting disease**
   Where plaintiff presented competent medical evidence that his preexisting syringomyelia was aggravated by a collision resulting from the negligence of defendant, defendant is liable for the damages due to enhancement or aggravation of the condition.

Lee v. Regan

2. Damages § 3.1– hospitalization costs – determination of preexisting disease –
   competency

   Where plaintiff's action for damages arising from an automobile accident was based on a cervical sprain and aggravation of his existing syringomyelia, hospitalization costs following the accident to determine whether
   plaintiff indeed had syringomyelia were competent evidence of plaintiff's
   damages resulting from the accident.

3. Damages § § 12, 13– items of damages – causal connection to accident – sufficiency of complaint

   There was a sufficient causal connection between plaintiff's injuries
   suffered in an automobile accident and evidence of why plaintiff and his wife
   stopped teaching, of bladder problems, of salary since the accident, of days
   missed from his teaching job and of pain and suffering and mental anguish
   since the accident so that such evidence was properly admitted where plaintiff presented expert medical testimony that the accident could have aggravated his preexisting degenerative disease, syringomyelia, and such evidence was directly related to the worsening syringomyelia for which defendant was liable to the extent his negligence aggravated the preexisting
   condition. Furthermore, such items of damages were adequately pled by
   plaintiff where he alleged that he "suffered extensive injuries, great pain of
   the body and mind, was prevented from transacting his business and incurred expenses for medical attention, hospitalization and damages to his person in an amount not yet determined," and a subsequent amendment alleged
   damages of $75,000.

4. Evidence §§ 49.1, 50.2; Damages § 16.1– hypothetical question – competency of
   response

   Plaintiff's hypothetical question to a medical expert as to whether a
   cervical sprain received by plaintiff in the accident in question could have
   aggravated plaintiff's preexisting disease of syringomyelia was not improper where it included only facts in evidence or which the jury could have
   inferred from the evidence, and the expert's response that the cervical
   sprain "can or could" aggravate the syringomyelia and "hasten the development of fresh worsening of neurological signs" was not so speculative as to
   be inadmissible to show causation where the witness further testified that
   he was speaking of what was medically possible and what will happen and
   that "it would be less likely" that the accident would not have aggravated
   the syringomyelia.

APPEAL by defendant from *Farmer, Judge.* Judgment entered 4 June 1979 in Superior Court, DURHAM County. Heard in
the Court of Appeals 13 May 1980.

This action arises out of an accident occurring about 9:40
p.m. on 21 April 1976 at the intersection of Duke and Frasier
Streets in Durham, North Carolina. Plaintiff's complaint

alleged that defendant negligently caused the accident and injuries by driving at an excessive speed, failing to stop for a stop sign at the intersection and driving while under the influence of alcohol. Plaintiff alleged he had "suffered extensive injuries, great pain of the body and mind, was prevented from transacting his business and incurred expenses for medical attention, hospitalization and damage to his personal property in an amount not yet determined." He prayed for $30,000.00 in damages. Defendant filed an answer denying any negligence on his part and alleging as a defense to the action the contributory negligence of plaintiff in failing to decrease speed at the intersection and in driving with improper lighting. Plaintiff's complaint was subsequently amended with the permission of the trial court to request the sum of $75,000.00 in damages. A jury trial was held where the following evidence was presented.

Defendant was called as an adverse witness. He testified that he stopped at the intersection in question and, seeing no other cars, proceeded to enter the intersection where he was struck by plaintiff's car which was travelling between sixty and seventy miles per hour without lights. Defendant admitted he was charged with driving under the influence and failing to stop for a stop sign. He denied entering pleas of guilty but admitted paying a fine. The Chief Clerk of the Durham County District Court testified that according to court records charges arising out of this accident were brought against defendant who had pled guilty to reckless driving and a stop sign violation and was fined $100.00 and costs.

Plaintiff testified to the following. On the night of the collision, he was approaching the intersection at a speed of about thirty miles per hour with his car lights on. When he noticed defendant's car, he slowed down and, when he realized defendant was not going to stop for the stop sign, he swerved to avoid the impact. After the collision, his knees were pinned to the dashboard, his abdomen was in the steering wheel and he had pain in his neck, back and head for which he was hospitalized for twelve or thirteen days following the collision at a cost of $651.00. Prior to the collision, he was hospitalized in 1965 for an infection to his left index finger and in 1970 for a limp and headaches. A 1973 automobile collision from which he received a whiplash injury did not result in hospitalization. Before the 1976 collision, he could walk without a cane, mow the lawn, climb steps, cook, use shop tools and raise his right hand. After the 1976 collision, he could do none of these things. He was unable to button his shirt or tie his shoes and neckties. His wife had to quit her job to take care of him. He has continuous pain in his neck and back. He has also suffered from urinary tract problems. He has a monthly drug bill of $21.00. In August 1976, defendant was again hospitalized at a cost of $1,511.16. He had further expenses of $740.00 to the Durham Clinic, $35.00 for ambulance service and $57.00 for the Durham Urology Clinic, all of which he indicated were related to the 1976 collision. Plaintiff continued teaching school until 1978 when his doctor told him to stop.

On cross-examination, plaintiff's testimony was to the following effect. During the hospitalization following the accident, he was treated by Dr. Robert E. Price, Jr., a neurosurgeon at the Durham Clinic. Dr. Price diagnosed a cervical sprain injury as a result of the 1976 accident. In 1964, plaintiff began having trouble with his knees locking. In 1965, he had prostate trouble. In 1970, he noticed the muscles in his left hand were weakening and that when he was hospitalized in 1970 for headaches and a limp, he was diagnosed as having syringomyelia, a chronic progressive disease of the spinal cord.

An eyewitness to the accident testified that he was following plaintiff's car which had its taillights on and that defendant failed to stop. The investigating officer testified that when he arrived on the scene, he observed plaintiff fall as he attempted to get out of his car. The officer testified that he smelled alcohol on the breath of defendant who registered a blood alcohol level of .20 when given a breathalyzer test following the accident. According to the officer, the front of defendant's truck struck the left side of plaintiff's car.

A teacher who worked with plaintiff testified that in 1975 plaintiff walked slowly with a limp and occasionally had trouble holding things. After the 1976 accident, according to this witness, plaintiff walked with a cane, moved slower and had great difficulty holding things. Testimony was introduced on the progressive number of workdays plaintiff missed following the accident and that his 1978 monthly teacher's salary was over $1,100.00.

Dr. Ng Khye Weng testified about his treatment of plaintiff which began on 19 May 1978. Plaintiff had been referred to Dr. Weng by Dr. Price for reevaluation of the neurogenic bladder and advanced syringomyelia diagnosis made at the time of the August 1976 hospitalization of plaintiff. In response to a hypothetical question, Dr. Weng stated that the cervical sprain plaintiff suffered in the 1976 collision "can or could" aggravate the syringomyelia and "hasten the development of fresh worsening of neurological signs" and that plaintiff's condition will not improve with time. On cross-examination, Dr. Weng testified.

I have used the word could or might in response to Mr. Darsie's questions and this in connection with the automobile accident of April 21 and the plaintiff's existing condition of syringomyelia and as to whether in expressing my opinion and using could or might as to whether I mean it is possible that the trauma of the accident could have aggravated Mr. Lee's existing condition of syringomyelia, and as to when I responded to counsel's questions I meant to say that it is possible that that could have aggravated Mr. Lee's existing active condition of syringomyelia, my answer is yes sir. I cannot be sure. As to whether I cannot state an opinion that it did, my answer is no sir. I cannot state absolutely, because I did not see him then. And so, just basing it on the stories that happened in the past and knowing that Mr. Lee has a cervical syringomyelia, any trauma like a neck sprain or a whiplash could aggravate the condition, but I cannot say it definitely did it, because I wasn't around.

He further testified that when he was using the word "could," he was speaking in the sense that it was medically possible. In his opinion, "it would be less likely" that the accident trauma would not aggravate his condition. Dr. Weng testified that the August 1976 hospitalization had nothing to do with the cervical sprain but was solely to reevaluate the syringomyelia diagnosis.

Lee v. Regan

Other witnesses, including defendant's wife, offered testimony which tended to corroborate the previously described testimony about the accident and its effect on plaintiff.

Defendant then presented evidence of four witnesses, two of whom set the foundation for the introduction into evidence of certain medical records and one of whom lived near the intersection in question and could testify about the scene immediately after the accident. The fourth witness for defendant was Dr. Robert E. Price. He testified that on the night of the collision, he treated plaintiff in the emergency room and that he had plaintiff admitted to the hospital for a possible cervical fracture which was ultimately diagnosed as a sprain. In his opinion, plaintiff's complaints are related to the syringomyelia and have nothing to do with the cervical sprain. According to his testimony,

I do have an opinion satisfactory to myself as to whether [plaintiff's] complaints could in any way be related to the cervical sprain which I treated on April 21, 1976, and my opinion is that all of the symptoms that he has described are symptoms of the progressive disease of syringomyelia and it is my opinion that whatever happened with regard to his neurological disorder related to the accident would have been immediate and that these complaints are related to his syringomyelia and have nothing whatsoever to do with the cervical sprain.

The urinary tract problems are, according to Dr. Price, a result of the syringomyelia.

At the close of the evidence, plaintiff was allowed to amend his complaint to allege that as a further result of said collision, he had "suffered permanent aggravation of his pre-existing condition and permanent injury." The jury found that plaintiff was injured and damaged by the negligence of defendant and that plaintiff did not contribute to his injuries by his own negligence. The jury awarded plaintiff $70,123.00 in damages. Defendant filed motions for judgment notwithstanding the verdict and a new trial which were denied. Defendant appeals.

Charles Darsie; Archbell and Cotter, by James B. Archbell, for plaintiff appellee.

Haywood, Denny and Miller, by James H. Johnson III, for defendant appellant.

VAUGHN, Judge.

[1] Defendant has brought forward eight arguments on appeal. All eight address one issue, the evidence and proof of damages, particularly the evidence and proof of damages relating to the preexisting syringomyelia. Our State recognizes the "special sensitivity" or "thin skull" rule. According to this rule, a negligent defendant is subject to liability for harm to the plaintiff although a physical condition of plaintiff which is neither known nor should be known to defendant makes the injury greater than that which defendant as a reasonable man should have foreseen as a probable result of his conduct. Restatement of Torts 2d § 461 (1965). As stated by our Supreme Court.

> [t]he general rule is that if the defendant's act would not have resulted in any injury to an ordinary person, he is not liable for harmful consequences to one of peculiar susceptibility, except insofar as he was on notice of the existence of such susceptibility, but if his misconduct amounts to a breach of duty to a person of ordinary susceptibility, he is liable for all damages suffered by plaintiff notwithstanding the fact these damages are unusually extensive because of peculiar susceptibility.

Lockwood v. McCaskill, 262 N.C. 663, 670, 138 S.E. 2d 541, 546 (1964). This case is but an application of this rule to a case where a preexisting condition has been aggravated. Plaintiff has presented competent medical evidence that his preexisting syringomyelia was aggravated by the collision which resulted from the negligence of defendant. Defendant is liable for the damages due to enhancement or aggravation of the condition.

    An injured person is entitled to recover all damages proximately caused by the defendant's negligence. Even so, when his injuries are aggravated or activated by a pre-existing physical or mental condition, defendant is liable only to the extent that his wrongful act proximately and naturally aggravated or activated plaintiff's condition. "The defendant is not liable for damages ... attributable solely to the original condition."

Potts v. Howser, 274 N.C. 49, 54, 161 S.E. 2d 737, 742 (1968). We now deal with the separate arguments of defendant addressed to this general principle of liability for the resulting damages.

[2] Defendant questions evidence of certain medical bills and expenses which plaintiff incurred. Over his objection, the trial court admitted testimony about a $1,511.06 bill for hospitalization in August 1976 and clinic treatment costs related to this hospitalization of $740.00 to his doctors and $57.00 to urologists. Defendant contends no competent medical testimony or evidence was presented by plaintiff to show that those medical bills were for treatment of injuries suffered as a result of defendant's negligence. Such evidence relating the damages to the injury caused by the defendant is required. *Ward v. Wentz*, 20 N.C. App. 229, 201 S.E. 2d 194 (1973); *Graves v. Harrington*, 6 N.C. App. 717, 171 S.E. 2d 218 (1969). Defendant points to the testimony of Dr. Weng where in discussing the August 1976 hospitalization he said, "the reason for the hospitalization in August of 1976 ... had nothing to do with the cervical sprain he received in the accident and this was to establish whether he did or did not have syringomyelia and that was the sole purpose of that hospitalization." This does not indicate as defendant contends that these medical costs are not damages for which defendant was liable. Plaintiff's case was based on damages which arose from the accident in two forms — a cervical sprain and aggravation of his syringomyelia. Thus, hospitalization costs in August 1976 following the accident to determine whether plaintiff indeed had syringomyelia were competent evidence of plaintiff's damages resulting from the accident.

[3] Defendant contends the trial court committed error in permitting plaintiff's evidence of why plaintiff and his wife stopped teaching, of bladder problems, of salary since the 1976 accident, of days missed from his teaching job and of pain and suffering

and mental anguish since the 1976 accident. He contends there is no causal connection between this testimony and the injuries suffered in the 1976 collision and that these items are in effect items of special damages not specifically pled by plaintiff as required by our Rules of Civil Procedure. G.S. 1A-1, Rule 9(g). The objected to evidence is directly related to the worsening syringomyelia for which defendant is liable to the extent his negligent conduct aggravated the preexisting condition. *Potts v. Howser, supra; Howell v. Nichols*, 22 N.C. App. 741, 207 S.E. 2d 768, *cert. den.*, 286 N.C. 211, 209 S.E. 2d 316 (1974). The expert testimony on causation of Dr. Weng and Dr. Price, is in conflict. The testimony presented a jury question and, if the jury chose to take Dr. Weng's opinion on the relationship of the worsened state of plaintiff's preexisting degenerative disease to the 1976 accident over that of Dr. Price, this evidence is causally related to the 1976 accident. According to Dr. Weng,

> If a patient has syringomyelia in the area where the cord is swollen up in its sheath, it will increase pressure and it will cause further extension of the canal. It will be like increasing a jet of water on the river bank and it will wash away more of the soil of the river bank and so the whiplash injury can or could aggravate the problem. It may hasten the development of fresh-worsening of neurological signs.

He went on to say that the accident could have aggravated the syringomyelia. His testimony to this effect is not too speculative as defendant contends. The doctor also testified that the collision could or might have caused a permanent cervical sprain. The evidence objected to is lay testimony supported by competent expert testimony tending to prove damages resulting from the accident. We find no merit to defendant's contention that these damages were not adequately pled by plaintiff. Plaintiff alleged that he "suffered extensive injuries, great pain of the body and mind, was prevented from transacting his business and incurred expenses for medical attention, hospitalization and damages to his person in an amount not yet determined." A subsequent amendment alleged damages to be $75,000.00. This is sufficient specific pleading under our Rules of Civil Procedure of these damages for which proof was offered. *See also Sparks v. Holland*, 209 N.C. 705, 184 S.E. 552 (1936).

[4] Defendant contends the hypothetical question to Dr. Weng contained facts not supported by competent evidence and that the opinion of Dr. Weng was based on speculation about medical possiblility as opposed to reasonable certainty or probability. The hypothetical question was acceptable in that it included only facts in evidence or which the jury might logically infer from the evidence. *Thompson v. Lockhert*, 34 N.C. App. 1, 237 S.E. 2d 259, *cert. den.*, 293 N.C. 593, 239 S.E. 2d 264 (1977). The response of Dr. Weng was not so speculative as to be inadmissible as competent evidence of causation. The case at hand is factually distinguishable from *Garland v. Shull*, 41 N.C. App. 143, 254 S.E. 2d 221 (1979) which is relied upon by defendant. The testimony of the medical expert in *Garland* in response to a hypothetical question was, "The headaches *may* persist for years at least. An indefinite period of time." *Id.* at 147, 254 S.E. 2d at 223 (emphasis added). The Court held the admission of this doctor's opinion with regard to possible pain and suffering which plaintiff might suffer in the future to be error. There was no amplification or explanation of the expert opinion in *Garland*. Dr. Weng, in the case at hand, stated that he was speaking of what was medically possible and what *will* happen. On cross-examination, he stated that "it would be less likely" that the accident would not have aggravated the syringomyelia. The evidence in the case at hand goes far beyond that offered in *Garland*. As stated by our Supreme Court in *Lockwood*,

> [t]he opinion is based on the reasonable probabilities known to the expert from scientific learning and experience. A result in a particular case may stem from a number of causes. The expert may express the opinion that a particular cause "could" or "might" have produced the result — indicating that the result is capable of proceeding from the particular cause as a scientific fact, *i.e.*, reasonable probability in the particular scientific field. If it is not reasonably probable, as a scientific fact, that a particular effect is capable of production by a given cause, and the witness so indicates, the evidence is not sufficient to establish *prima facie* the causal relation, and if the testimony is offered by the party having the burden of showing the causal relation, the testimony, upon objection, should not be admitted and, if admitted, should be stricken. The trial judge is not, of

course, required to make subtle and refined distinctions and he has discretion in passing on the admissibility of expert testimony, and if in the exercise of his discretion it reasonably appears to him that the expert witness, in giving testimony supporting a particular causal relation, is addressing himself to reasonable probabilities according to scientific knowledge and experience, and the testimony *per se* does not show that the causal relation is merely speculative and mere possibility, the admission of the testimony will not be held erroneous.

Id. at 262 N.C. at 668-69, 138 S.E. 2d at 545-46. The testimony of Dr. Weng satisfies the prerequisites for expert opinion set forth in *Lockwood.*

Defendant's remaining arguments are without merit. Amendment of the complaint at the close of the evidence to conform to the proof was properly allowed by the trial court. G.S. 1A-1, Rule 15(b). The jury instructions were proper in all respects, particularly the instructions on damages for aggravation of a preexisting injury wherein the instruction complied with the law in *Lockwood* and *Potts v. Howser.* The trial court properly denied defendant's motion for a new trial.

No error.

Judges PARKER and HEDRICK concur.

———————

STATE OF NORTH CAROLINA v. ROBERT JONES

No. 8012SC155

(Filed 15 July 1980)

1. **Criminal Law § 92.3– failure to join charges – no error**

   The trial court did not err in denying defendant's motion to dismiss for failure to join related offenses where the indictments in the present case were returned against defendant after two mistrials had been entered, and there could have been no joinder of offenses because, when the first offenses were tried, there was no other offense to join with the first.

State v. Jones

---

2. **Criminal Law § 92.3– motion to dismiss for failure to join offenses – offense as indictment**

    As used in G.S. 15A-926(c)(2), which requires the granting of a defend-ant's motion to dismiss a charge of a joinable offense when he has been tried for one offense and has made a timely motion to dismiss, the word "offense" may be construed to mean "indictment."

3. **Criminal Law § 34.5– defendant's guilt of other offenses – admissibility to show identity**

    In a prosecution for sale and delivery of heroin, the trial court did not err in admitting into evidence testimony concerning charges of misconduct by defendant several days after the crime with which he was charged, since such evidence was admissible to prove the identity of defendant.

4. **Conspiracy § 6– conspiracy to sell and deliver heroin – sufficiency of evidence**

    In a prosecution for conspiracy to sell and deliver heroin, evidence was sufficient to be submitted to the jury where it tended to show that two undercover narcotics agents met defendant at his address and went with him in a car to another house; there defendant met with a person and briefly conversed with him; and that person handed defendant a small package of heroin which defendant then sold to one of the agents.

5. **Criminal Law § 86.4– cross-examination of defendant – other offenses – impeachment**

    Defendant who was charged with narcotics offenses could properly be asked if he filed income tax returns for a given year, since a defendant may be cross-examined for impeachment purposes as to other criminal or degrad-ing conduct; moreover, defendant had already answered the question once in the absence of an objection by his counsel, thereby curing any possible error in its admission.

6. **Criminal Law § 113.1– court's recapitulation of evidence – no error**

    Defendant was not prejudiced by the trial court's recapitulation of the evidence that after defendant met with another person and had a brief conversation with him, the other person handed defendant a small tinfoil package and defendant in turn handed the package to an undercover narco-tics agent, since defendant's counsel did not call to the court's attention any error; the evidence did show that defendant was handed a tinfoil package which he then handed to the agent; and the court cautioned the jury to take the evidence as they recalled it and not as he summarized it for them.

7. **Criminal Law § 122.2– failure of jury to reach verdict – instructions not prejudi-cial**

    When the jury informed the court that it was divided ten to two, the court's response that the jury could continue to deliberate that night, could return to deliberate the next day, and had two more days in which delibera-tions could take place did not coerce the jury into reaching a decision, particularly in light of the court's instruction the following morning that the jury should reach a unanimous verdict if possible without surrendering their conscientious convictions; furthermore, the court's instruction that a disagreement meant "that if this case is not brought to a verdict as I previously instructed you that another judge and another jury in another week will try this case again" was not erroneous since an isolated mention of the necessity to retry the case does not warrant a new trial unless the charge as a whole is coercive.

8. Criminal Law § 122.1– jury's request to have testimony read again – refusal not abuse of discretion

The trial judge did not abuse his discretion in refusing to allow the jurors to have certain testimony read back to them after deliberations had begun, since the judge explained that the witness whose testimony was requested by the jury was one of a number of witnesses, and the court did not want to give special emphasis to any particular witness.

APPEAL by defendant from *Preston, Judge.* Judgment entered 25 October 1979 in Superior Court, CUMBERLAND County. Heard in the Court of Appeals 10 June 1980.

Defendant appeals from a judgment of imprisonment entered after verdicts of guilty were returned by the jury on charges of possession with intent to sell and deliver heroin, sale and delivery of heroin, and conspiracy to sell and deliver heroin. These offenses occurred on 21 September 1978; defendant was indicted on the charges 26 March 1979.

Defendant had earlier been indicted for possession with intent to sell and deliver heroin and the sale and delivery of heroin, offenses which allegedly occurred on 29 August and 1 September 1978. Trials on these charges, held 30 January and 6 March 1979, resulted in mistrials. On 10 April 1979 these charges against defendant were dismissed by the state because the state had no new evidence to warrant another trial.

Defendant moved to have the remaining charges, on which he was ultimately convicted, dismissed pursuant to N.C.G.S. 15A-926(c) for failure of the state to join them with the previous offenses. After defendant presented evidence on the pretrial motion, the court denied the motion.

The state presented testimony by Mary Patterson, an undercover agent for the SBI, and Ottis Alexander Rousseau, a federal narcotics agent, that on 21 September 1978 they met the defendant at 708 Campbell Terrace, Fayetteville, North Carolina. After talking with him, they drove to a house where defendant had a brief conversation with another person. After receiving a "small tinfoil package" from that person, defendant handed it to Rousseau in exchange for $350 in marked bills. The SBI lab subsequently determined that the package contained heroin.

Defendant's motion for dismissal at the close of the state's evidence was denied.

Defendant presented evidence to show that he did not live at 708 Campbell Terrace in Fayetteville. He travels up and down the East coast as a disc jockey. He had never seen either Rousseau or Mary Patterson before his trial. He neither possessed, sold, nor conspired to sell heroin, on 21 September 1978 or at any other time.

Defendant's motion for dismissal at the close of all the evidence was denied. Motions for dismissal after the verdicts and after judgment were also denied.

Attorney General Edmisten, by Assistant Attorney General Thomas H. Davis, Jr., for the State.

Pope, Reid, Lewis & Deese, by Renny W. Deese, for defendant appellant.

MARTIN (Harry C.), Judge.

Defendant brings forward ten assignments of error. After a careful review of them, however, we conclude that defendant's trial was free of prejudicial error.

[1] Defendant first argues that the court erred in denying his motion to dismiss for failure to join related offenses. He relies upon N.C.G.S. 15A-926(c)(2), which requires the granting of a defendant's motion to dismiss a charge of a joinable offense when he has been tried for one offense and made a timely motion to dismiss, with three exceptions. It is unnecessary that we discuss these statutory exceptions in an attempt to find one

applicable to this case. Based on this Court's reasoning in *State
v. Cox*, 37 N.C. App. 356, 246 S.E. 2d 152, *disc. rev. denied, appeal
dismissed*, 295 N.C. 649, 248 S.E. 2d 253 (1978), *cert. denied*, 440
U.S. 930 (1979), we do not believe that this statute mandates the
dismissal of the charges on which defendant was tried and
convicted. As the Court stated: "At the outset, we note that
defendant had not been charged with the offense of accessory
after the fact to armed robbery. There could be no joinder of
offenses in the absence of a second offense to join with the
first." *Id.* at 361, 246 S.E.2d at 154. Here, defendant was indicted
for the present offenses on 26 March 1979; these indictments
were returned against defendant *after* the two mistrials of 30
January and 6 March. There could have been no joinder of
offenses because when the first offenses were tried, there was
no other offense to join with the first. In parallel circumstances,
our Supreme Court found that N.C.G.S. 15A-926 simply did not
apply. In *State v. Furr*, 292 N.C. 711, 235 S.E. 2d 193, *cert. denied*,
434 U.S. 924 (1977), defendant was tried for murder on 12 January 1976. At that time no indictments had yet been returned
against him for solicitation. On 9 February 1976 bills of indictment for solicitation were returned. The Court held that the
latter bills could not have been joined with the murder charge.

[2] We note additionally that contrary to defendant's contention that "offense" should not be construed as meaning "only
indictments," the Courts in *Furr* and *Cox* construed the word to
mean "indictment." Defendant's first assignment of error is
overruled.

[3] Next, defendant contends the court erred by allowing into
evidence uncharged acts of misconduct by defendant. At trial
the district attorney questioned a witness for the state about
defendant's actions on 25 September 1978, four days after the
date on which the charged offenses occurred. Over objections,
the court allowed evidence of a telephone call to defendant and
a subsequent meeting with defendant to arrange another
purchase of heroin. The court then sustained defendant's continuing objections and, on its own initiative, instructed the jury
that the "sole purpose of the line of questioning concerning any
event that may have occurred on the 25th of September, 1978, is

State v. Jones

for the purpose of identifying the defendant, if in fact, you find that it does." Again the court stated that the evidence "has to do solely with respect to identification if in fact, you find that it does."

Defendant concedes that there is case authority for the principle that evidence of prior or subsequent purchases of drugs is relevant and admissible to show modus operandi, guilty knowledge, or defendant's state of mind. His argument is that in this case the evidence was not offered or admitted for any of these authorized purposes. It is clear, however, that evidence of other misconduct is admissible to prove the relevant fact of identity. 1 Stansbury's N.C. Evidence § 92 (Brandis rev. 1973). This assignment of error is overruled.

[4] Defendant assigns error to the court's denial of his motions to dismiss, questioning the sufficiency of the evidence to take the case to the jury solely as it relates to the conspiracy charge. Defendant accurately capsulizes the task the state undertakes in attempting to prove a criminal conspiracy: it must show an agreement between two or more persons to do an unlawful act or to do a lawful act in an unlawful way. *State v. Bindyke*, 288 N.C. 608, 220 S.E. 2d 521 (1975). The familiar test to be applied upon a motion to dismiss is whether there is substantial evidence of all material elements of the offense, considering all the evidence admitted in the light most favorable to the state and with the state entitled to every reasonable inference therefrom. *Stave v. Furr, supra; State v. Barbour*, 43 N.C. App. 143, 258 S.E. 2d 475 (1979). Applying this test to the present case, we find the trial court did not err in allowing the conspiracy charge to go to the jury. The state's evidence showed that Mary Patterson and Rousseau met defendant on 21 September 1978 at his address and went with him in a car to another house. There defendant met with a person and briefly conversed with him. That person handed defendant a small package of heroin, which defendant then sold to Rousseau. This evidence was sufficient to survive the motion to dismiss. It does not, as defendant contends, leave in the realm of conjecture the crucial question whether an unlawful agreement existed. This assignment of error cannot be upheld.

[5] On cross-examination of defendant by the district attorney, he was asked whether he filed income tax returns for 1978. Without objection, defendant answered no. Defendant's counsel then objected to a repetition of the question. Defendant excepted to the court's overruling his objection and assigns it as error. In addition to the fact that defendant had already answered the question in the absence of an objection by his counsel, thereby curing any possible error in its admission, *State v. Van Landingham*, 283 N.C. 589, 197 S.E. 2d 539 (1973), it was within the discretion of the court to permit the question. On cross-examination of defendant in a criminal case, it is permissible for impeachment purposes to ask disparaging questions concerning collateral matters relating to his criminal and degrading conduct, and such questions are permissible within the discretion of the court. *State v. Black*, 283 N.C. 344, 196 S.E. 2d 225 (1973). Clearly, no abuse of discretion is evident here. There is no merit in this assignment of error.

Three of defendant's assignments of error criticize the court's instructions to the jury.

[6] Defendant argues the court erred in recapitulating the state's evidence to the jury. He takes exception to the court's statement that after defendant met with another person and had a brief conversation with him, "[t]he other person handed the defendant a small tinfoil package and the defendant in turn handed the small tinfoil package to Agent Rousseau." His contention is that the record is totally void of any such evidence, and he attempts to rely on the principle that although ordinarily the court should be informed of an inaccuracy in the recapitulation of the evidence in time for correction, a statement of a material fact not in evidence will constitute reversible error, whether or not defendant's counsel called it to the court's attention. *State v. Barbour*, 295 N.C. 66, 243 S.E. 2d 380 (1978). In *Barbour*, the court's instruction indicated that when defendant entered a room he had a pistol in his hand. The only witness to the shooting, however, had nowhere testified that she saw a gun in defendant's hand when he entered the room. The instruction was found to be highly misleading and prejudicial. In the case sub judice, one witness testified that after defendant talked with another man, that man went into a house across the

street and came out in less than five minutes. The witness continued:

> He then came back across the street and handed Robert Jones (defendant) something in his hand. I did not see what it was. The other man and Robert Jones were talking briefly and the other man seemed a little angry. Then Robert Jones came to the car and handed Agent Rousseau a package of aluminum paper, tinfoil, or whatever you call it.

Another witness similarly testified that the man whom defendant met unlocked the door to a residence across the street and went inside for three to five minutes. Then he came out, and the witness "observed him to have a foil package in his hands which he put in his front pocket." He then walked across the street and conferred with defendant. "I saw their hands meet . . . I did not see what was in their hands . . . . Then Robert Jones walked to where I was in my vehicle . . . handed me a tinfoil package which I opened and observed to contain white powder."

We do not think the court committed prejudicial error in its summary of this evidence. Defendant's counsel did not call to the court's attention any error, and the rule in *Barbour* is not applicable because the evidence does show that defendant was handed a tinfoil package, which he then handed to Rousseau. Further, in his charge to the jury the trial judge cautioned as follows:

> The law provides, members of the jury, that I give you a brief resume of the evidence. I caution you at the outset that you will take the evidence as you recall it and not as I recall it nor these attorneys. Though, I told you earlier that they could comment upon the evidence and the law requires me to give you a brief resume but you are to consider all of the evidence and not just what I mention some of it tends to show.

Considering the charge as a whole, we do not find prejudice. This assignment of error is overruled.

[7] Defendant's next two assignments of error focus on the

court's instructions relevant to the jury's deliberations. After retiring and taking a vote, the jury returned and informed the court that it was divided ten to two. The court responded:

> Okay. Well, would you think further deliberations tonight would be of benefit or do you wish to come back tomorrow and continue your deliberations. We have got Thursday and we have got Friday.

After the foreman gave his opinion that it would do no good to deliberate any longer, that night or the next day, the court released the jurors until the next morning.

Defendant contends that because of the court's comments the jury was distinctly impressed with the prospect of an un- reasonably lengthy deliberation unless it reached a unanimous verdict and, therefore, the jury's deliberations were "coercively affected." Defendant argues that N.C.G.S. 15A-1235(c) was violated. We cannot agree. Not only is a two-day period not an unreasonable length of time under the statute, but the court's instruction to the jurors when they assembled the next morn- ing was free of coercion:

> I don't want to intimate coercion at all but I do tell you that it is your sworn duty to try to reach a verdict, unanimous verdict. To try to reconcile your differences but you must do so if at all without surrendering your own conscientious convictions. You have heard the evidence and you have heard the charge of the court, you have heard the argu- ments of counsel and I fully realize, after fourteen years of this, that there are instances in which twelve good people cannot agree as to what the facts are in seeking to reach a unanimous verdict but it is your duty to do whatever you can to reason the matter together as reasonable men and women and to reconcile your differences if such is possible without surrendering your conscientious convictions, and so, I will send you back in and let you continue to deliberate.

We also find, contrary to defendant's contention, that the court did not err in instructing the jury that a disagreement means "that if this case is not brought to a verdict as I previously instructed you that another judge and another jury in another week will try this case again." Isolated mention of the necessity to retry the case does not warrant a new trial unless the charge as a whole is coercive. *State v. Alston*, 294 N.C. 577, 243 S.E. 2d 354 (1978). Further, this instruction is not on a par with that held to be reversible error in *State v. Lamb*, 44 N.C. App. 251, 261 S.E. 2d 130 (1979). In *Lamb* the trial court had made the following statements:

> "Both the State and the defendants have a tremendous amount of time and money invested in this case.
>
> "If you don't reach a verdict, it means that it will have to be tried again by another jury in this county and that involves a duplication of all the expense and all of the time."

Id. at 252, 261 S.E. 2d at 130. In the instruction given by the court in the present case, there is no emphasis on the time, money, and expense involved; in fact, no mention is made of any of these factors. This assignment of error is overruled.

[8] The eighth question raised by defendant is whether the court erred in refusing to allow the jurors to have certain testimony read back to them after deliberations had begun, especially after a photograph had been allowed into the jury room upon request. N.C.G.S. 15A-1233(a) clearly provides that it is within the judge's discretion to direct that requested parts of the testimony be read to the jury. The judge explained to the jury his reason for not allowing Rousseau's statement to be read back: "[H]e is one of a number of witnesses and the court would not want to give special emphasis to any particular witness." There was no abuse of discretion by the trial court.

We find no merit in defendant's ninth assignment of error. We agree with the state's argument that unlike Mary Patterson, a convicted felon who had become an undercover agent through a beneficial agreement with the state, federal agent Rousseau had no considerable interest in the outcome of the case. The court, therefore, did not commit prejudicial error in instructing on the possible interest Mary Patterson had and in failing to instruct on any interest Rousseau might have.

Finally, defendant contends the court erred in failing to instruct on the limited purpose of the corroborating evidence offered by agent Rousseau, after so instructing regarding testimony of Mary Patterson. During the trial the court did instruct the jury that testimony given by William Wolak, special agent with the SBI, was for the purpose of corroborating Mary Patterson's testimony and Rousseau's testimony. Furthermore, it was not error for the court to fail to give a limiting instruction in the charge when defendant did not specifically request such an instruction. *State v. Sauls*, 291 N.C. 253, 230 S.E. 2d 390 (1976), *cert. denied*, 431 U.S. 916 (1977).

In the defendant's trial, we find

No error.

Judges HEDRICK and MARTIN (Robert M.) concur.

LONA P. LONG, WIDOW, LONA P. LONG, GUARDIAN AD LITEM OF TODD LONG, Minor Child; GEORGE E. LONG, DECEASED, EMPLOYEE, PLAINTIFFS V. ASPHALT PAVING COMPANY OF GREENSBORO, EMPLOYER, AND STANDARD FIRE INSURANCE COMPANY, CARRIER, DEFENDANTS

No. 7910IC1050

(Filed 15 July 1980)

1. **Master and Servant § 56– workers' compensation – airplane crash in Florida – accident arising out of and in course of employment**

    There was sufficient competent evidence to support the Industrial Commission's findings and conclusion that decedent was on a business trip to Florida in connection with his duties as an employee of defendant asphalt paving company at the time he was killed in an airplane crash and that decedent suffered the fatal injury by accident arising out of and in the course of his employment.

2. **Evidence § 33.2– conduct of decedent not hearsay**

    Testimony that the witness observed deceased and another walking around the woods of a subdivision during their trip to Florida was not hearsay and was properly admitted into evidence to show the business nature of decedent's trip, since decedent did not intend his conduct as a positive assertion of anything.

3. **Evidence § 33.2– testimony not offered to show truth of matter asserted – no hearsay**

 A witness's testimony that he heard a third person tell decedent, when they passed an asphalt processing plant in Florida, that "this is where you can get the asphalt," and another witness's testimony that the third person introduced him to decedent in Florida and told him that decedent "is in the paving business" did not constitute inadmissible hearsay since the testimony of neither witness was offered to show the truth of the matter asserted but was offered to show that business was transacted by decedent during his trip to Florida.

4. **Evidence § 33.2– intent of decedent to go on business trip – admissibility as exception to hearsay rule**

 Testimony by decedent's wife that, on the night before decedent left for Florida, decedent told her that he and another person "had to go to Florida on business" was admissible under the exception to the hearsay rule permitting the admission of the statements of a person, deceased at the time of the trial, as to his present intention to do something in the immediate future. The testimony was also admissible under the exception to the hearsay rule founded upon (1) necessity and (2) a reasonable probability of truthfulness.

APPEAL by defendants from the opinion and award of the North Carolina Industrial Commission filed 20 August 1979. Heard in the Court of Appeals 23 April 1980.

George E. Long was President of defendant Asphalt Paving Company of Greensboro. On 19 June 1977 Long and Floyd H. (Sam) Martin, President of C.O. Martin & Sons, Inc., flew in a small plane owned by the Martin corporation to Apopka, Florida. On 22 June 1977, when the party was departing to return to North Carolina, their airplane clipped a tree and crashed just after takeoff, killing the two men. The decedents' next of kin filed claims against their respective employers, including the defendant, for workers' compensation benefits. The claims were consolidated for hearing. After the hearing, Deputy Commissioner William L. Haigh denied plaintiffs' claim, concluding that

 1. The activities of deceased, George Long, with respect to the subdivision property did not further, directly or indirectly, to an appreciable degree the business of Asphalt Paving Company of Greensboro.

 2. Deceased, George Long, did not at the time com-

plained of sustain an injury by accident arising out of and in the course of his employment with defendant employer and, therefore, plaintiffs are not entitled to the benefits of the Workmen's [sic] Compensation Act. G.S. 97-2 (6).

Upon appeal, the Full Commission reversed the determination of the Deputy Commissioner and made an award to the plaintiff, concluding:

> 1. The decedent on 22 June 1977 suffered an injury by accident arising out of and in the course of his employment, such injury resulting in his immediate death.

* * *

From the opinion and award of the Full Commission, defendants appeal.

Douglas, Ravenel, Hardy, Crihfield & Bullock, by John W. Hardy, for the plaintiff appellees.

Smith, Moore, Smith, Schell & Hunter, by J. Donald Cowan, Jr. and William L. Young, for the defendant appellants.

WELLS, Judge.

[1] The principal issue which defendants raise on appeal is whether there was sufficient *competent* evidence to support the Full Commission's findings of fact and conclusion that the decedent was on a business trip to Florida in connection with his duties as an employee of defendant Asphalt Paving Company at the time of the accident and that the decedent suffered a fatal injury by accident arising out of and in the course of his employment. Pursuant to G.S. 97-2 (6), a compensable injury under the North Carolina Workers' Compensation Act must be one "arising out of and in the course of the employment." An accident is said to arise out of and in the course of the employment when it occurs while the employee is engaged in some activity or duty which he is authorized to undertake and which is calculated to further, directly or indirectly, the employer's business. *Martin v. Bonclarken Assembly*, 296 N.C. 540, 251 S.E. 2d 403 (1979).

Whether an injury results from an accident arising out of and in the course of the employment is a mixed question of law and fact. *Bryan v. Church*, 267 N.C. 111, 147 S.E. 2d 633 (1966); *Insurance Co. v. Curry*, 28 N.C. App. 286, 221 S.E. 2d 75 (1976), *disc. rev. denied*, 289 N.C. 615, 223 S.E. 2d 396 (1976). The Commission's findings of fact are conclusive if supported by any competent evidence. *Perry v. Bakeries Co.*, 262 N.C. 272, 136 S.E. 2d 643 (1964).

We hold that there was sufficient competent evidence to support the operative findings and conclusion of the Full Commission. The following testimony was received without objection: Defendant Asphalt Paving Company was engaged in the business of paving subdivision streets, driveways, and parking lots. George Long's duties as defendant's president included estimating the cost of paving contracts and supervising the work. The defendant company had worked together with the construction company C.O. Martin & Sons, Inc. in the past. The Martin company usually subcontracted paving jobs. Sam Martin owned nine acres of property in Florida on which he had previously constructed several houses. The visit to Florida had been planned for months. Both Martin and Long took their clothes in which they worked on the trip and Martin took a briefcase containing papers concerning the subdivision in Florida. Long did not take any dress clothes. Martin, Long and their sons travelled to Florida on a small plane owned by the Martin company. Long was wearing coveralls when he departed. Immediately upon their arrival in Florida, Long, Martin and their sons were driven first, to the "job site", and then to a motel. The next day, while the boys were visiting Disney World, Long, dressed in his work coveralls, and Martin rented a car and visited the job site. They were on the property four or five hours. Long was employed by the defendant company at the time of his death.

We deal now with testimony which defendant argues should have been excluded by the Deputy Commissioner as inadmissible hearsay. Our courts have defined "hearsay" as an out-of-court statement which is offered to prove the truth of the matter asserted therein. *Potts v. Howser*, 274 N.C. 49, 161 S.E. 2d 737

(1968).[1] Under the rule against hearsay, when a proper objection has been raised, a statement which is hearsay is inadmissible in evidence unless it falls within a recognized exception to the rule. *See e.g., State v. Jackson,* 287 N.C. 470, 215 S.E. 2d 123 (1975). The justifications which are commonly stated for the rule are that the declarant of the out-of-court statement was not under oath and could not be confronted or cross-examined. *See generally,* 1 Stansbury's N.C. Evidence § 139, pp. 461-465 (Brandis rev. 1973). We have determined that much of the testimony, the admissibility of which is disputed by defendants in this case, falls into the following three categories, each of which we shall discuss below: (1) conduct of the deceased, not intended as assertions, which does not fall under the hearsay rule; (2) statements of the deceased, not offered to prove the truth of the matters asserted therein, which do not come within the prohibition of the hearsay rule; and (3) statements of the deceased to his spouse made shortly before his departure to Florida concerning the business nature of his trip, which were hearsay, but admissible under two exceptions to the hearsay rule laid down in *State v. Vestal,* 278 N.C. 561, 180 S.E. 2d 755 (1971).

[2] An example of the first category of alleged hearsay admitted over defendants' objection was that of Terrell Weeks, a resident of Apopka, Florida, who testified that he observed Martin and Long walking around the woods of the Walker Subdivision during their trip. While it is generally agreed that conduct may sometimes be considered hearsay, the trend is not to consider it as such and to allow its admission into evidence when the conduct is not intended by the actor as an assertion about the fact proved. 1 Stansbury's N.C. Evidence § 142, pp. 472-475 (Brandis rev. 1973); Wigmore on Evidence §§ 267; 459; 1362, n. 1 (Chadbourn rev. 1974); McCormick on Evidence § 250, pp. 596-601 (2d ed. 1972); Powers, *The North Carolina Hearsay Rule and the Uniform Rules of Evidence,* 34 N.C. L. REV. 171, 180 (1956). *See, e.g.,* Federal Evidence Rule 801 (a)(2) (a "statement" which may be the basis of a hearsay declaration includes

---

[1]   Similarly, Rule 801 (c) of the Federal Rules of Evidence defines hearsay as, "a statement, other than one made by the declarant while testifying at the trial or hearing, offered in evidence to prove the truth of the matter asserted."

"nonverbal conduct of a person, if it is intended by him as an assertion"). Clearly, Long and Martin, in walking around the subdivision, did not intend their conduct as a positive assertion of anything, much less as an assertion that they were discussing business. We therefore hold that Weeks' testimony was not hearsay and was properly admitted into evidence.

[3]   The second category of reputedly inadmissible hearsay also concerns testimony which is not, in fact, hearsay. Clarence Tuttle testified that he overheard Sam Martin and George Long conversing in their car en route to their Florida motel. Tuttle stated, "We passed an asphalt processing place and Sam said, 'George, that is where you can get the asphalt.' "[2] Terrell Weeks testified that he was introduced to Long by Martin as follows: "This is Mr. Long, Mr. Weeks ... Mr. Long is in the paving business."

It is well recognized that an out-of-court statement which is offered for any purpose other than to prove the truth of the matter asserted in the statement is not hearsay. *State v. Caddell*, 287 N.C. 266, 215 S.E. 2d 348 (1975); 1 Stansbury's N.C. Evidence, *supra*, § 141, pp. 467-472; Wigmore on Evidence §§ 1361, 1766 (Chadbourn rev. 1974); McCormick on Evidence § 246, pp. 584-586 (2d ed. 1972). The reason such statements are admissible is not that they fall under an exception to the rule, but that they simply are not hearsay — they do not come within the above legal definition of the term. Viewed in this light, Tuttle's testimony was not hearsay because Martin's statement as to the place Long could obtain his asphalt was not offered to show where Long could find asphalt, but that business was transacted on the trip. Similarly, Weeks' testimony that "Mr. Long is in the paving business" was not offered to show the business in which Long was engaged. The statement was offered to show that business was transacted during the

---

[2]   Plaintiffs argue that even if this statement was hearsay it may still have been admissible as part of the *res gestae*. While continuing to recognize the vitality of many of the individual exceptions to the rule against hearsay comprising what has previously been labeled the "*res gestae*" exception, we recently expressed disapproval over the confusion which the use of this phrase has generated. *State v. Hammonds*, 45 N.C. App. 495, 263 S.E. 2d 326 (1980).

Florida trip. As such, this testimony was not hearsay. For the same reason, Martin's other inquiries as to the places where asphalt could be obtained were likewise admissible as nonhearsay.

[4] The third category of evidence into which we have divided the disputed testimony relates to statements which are hearsay, but nonetheless admissible under exceptions to the rule. An example of such a statement occurred when Long's widow testified that the night before Long and Martin left for Florida, Long said that he and Martin "had to go to Florida on business." Long's statement, that he had to go to Florida on business, was offered to prove that he did in fact go to Florida on business. Clearly, the statement was hearsay. However, the testimony was admissible if it qualified under an exception to the rule.

We hold that Long's statement was admissible under the exception to the rule permitting the admission of the statements of a person, deceased at the time of trial, as to his present intention to do something in the immediate future. *State v. Vestal*, 278 N.C. 561, 180 S.E. 2d 755 (1971). The *Vestal* Court emphasized that although such statements are not admissible as part of the *res gestae*[3] doctrine where they are not connected with the immediate departure of the declarant, they are nonetheless admissible in their own right to show the decedent's intent. *See also, State v. Cawthorne*, 290 N.C. 639, 227 S.E. 2d 528 (1976). While the decedent's *intent* to transact business is not directly in issue, it is logically relevant in that it is more probable than not that the decedent actually did what he said he was going to do:

> We see no plausible basis for holding such a statement admissible if shouted back to the wife as the car leaves the driveway, but inadmissible if told to her at the dinner table or while packing the traveler's suitcase. The sound basis for its admission is not the *res gestae* doctrine, but the

---

[3] *See*, n. 2, *supra*.

exception to the hearsay rule permitting the admission of declarations of the decedent to show his intention, when the intention is relevant *per se* and the declaration is not so unreasonably remote in time as to suggest the possibility of a change of mind.

State v. Vestal, supra, 278 N.C. at 587, 180 S.E. 2d at 772.[4]

Defendant argues that the cases of *Gassaway v. Gassaway & Owen, Inc.*, 220 N.C. 694, 18 S.E. 2d 120 (1942), and *Little v. Brake Co.*, 255 N.C. 451, 121 S.E. 2d 889 (1961), are controlling. In these cases our Supreme Court held that the statements of a deceased person as to the purpose and destination of the trip were not admissible under the Workers' Compensation Act because they were not part of the *res gestae*. In *Vestal*, however, the Court limited the holding of these two cases on this issue to their facts. *State v. Vestal, supra*, 278 N.C. at 586, 180 S.E. 2d at 771. As to *Gassaway*, the *Vestal* Court said that the statement offered to show that the defendant's purpose in taking the trip was compensable under the Act "threw no light whatever on that matter." As to the *Little* case, the *Vestal* Court noted that the statement offered to show that the decedent traveled to a specific location did not disclose where the customer which he was to visit resided. It is clear from Justice Lake's opinion in *Vestal* that *Gassaway* and *Little* no longer state the law as to the admissibility of a decedent's declarations to his spouse of his intent to go on a business trip, independent of what was formerly labeled the *res gestae* exception to the rule against hearsay.

The hearsay statement involved in the present case is also admissible under the two-fold basis for exceptions to the rule enunciated by the Supreme Court in *Vestal*. This exception is founded upon: (1) necessity; and (2) a reasonable probability of truthfulness. *State v. Vestal, supra*, 278 N.C. at 582, 180 S.E. 2d at 769. *Accord, State v. Cobb*, 295 N.C. 1, 243 S.E. 2d 759 (1978);

---

[4]   The *Vestal* case relies on the venerable cases of *Mutual Life Insurance Co. v. Hillmon*, 145 U.S. 285, 36 L.Ed. 706, 12 S.Ct. 909 (1892), and *People v. Alcalde*, 24 Cal. 2d 177, 148 P. 2d 627 (1944).

State v. Parks, 41 N.C. App. 514, 255 S.E. 2d 216 (1979), *disc. rev. denied*, 298 N.C. 303, 259 S.E. 2d 916 (1979). As in *Vestal*, the decedent's death in the case *sub judice* satisfies the requirement of necessity. Furthermore, as in *Vestal*, the requirement that the statement possess a reasonable probability of truthfulness is satisfied by the high degree of reliability attached to an individual's statement to his or her spouse as to the destination and purpose of travel away from the home.

It is the normal, natural, customary routine for a man leaving his home, or office, upon an out-of-town trip to inform some member of his family, or an employee or business associate, of where he is going, with whom and when he will return. Of course, the particular declarant on the particular occasion may falsely state these matters to his wife or to his business associate. The credibility of his statement on the particular occasion is always open to question, but that is a question for the jury. The fact that in the overwhelming preponderence of such instances the statement is true, because it has no purpose or significance except to promote the orderly conduct of the declarant's domestic or business affairs, supplies that reasonable probability of truth in the particular instance which justifies the Court in permitting the jury to hear the statement and determine its truth or falsity.

State v. Vestal, supra, 278 N.C. at 588-589, 180 S.E. 2d at 773.

We conclude that there was ample and sufficient competent evidence to support the Full Commission's operative findings of fact, that the findings of fact support and justify the Commission's conclusion of law, and that the order and award of the Full Commission must be

Affirmed.

Chief Judge MORRIS and Judge PARKER concur.

JAMES H. SESSOMS v. WILLIAM V. ROBERSON

No. 797SC1116

(Filed 15 July 1980)

Automobiles §§ 62.2, 83.4– striking of pedestrian – negligence and contributory negligence

In an action to recover for injuries received by plaintiff highway construction worker when he was struck by defendant's automobile while crossing the highway at a point beyond an intersection, plaintiff's evidence was sufficient to be submitted to the jury on issues of defendant's negligence in (1) failing to drive on the right side of the road in violation of G.S. 20-146(a); (2) failing to decrease his speed to avoid colliding with a person on the highway in violation of G.S. 20-141(m); (3) operating his automobile at an unreasonable speed under the conditions then and there existing in violation of G.S. 20-141; (4) failing to reduce his speed as he entered an intersection in violation of G.S. 20-141; (5) failing to warn plaintiff by sounding his horn in violation of G.S. 20-174(e); and (6) failing to keep a proper lookout and to keep his automobile under proper control. Furthermore, plaintiff's evidence failed to show his contributory negligence as a matter of law but presented issues as to whether plaintiff was contributorily negligent in failing to yield the right-of-way and in stepping into the path of defendant's automobile.

APPEAL by plaintiff from *Barefoot, Judge.* Judgment entered 11 July 1979 in Superior Court, NASH County. Heard in the Court of Appeals on 15 May 1980.

By a verified complaint filed 22 November, 1978, plaintiff instituted this action to recover damages for personal injuries he suffered as the result of a collision in which the car being driven by defendant struck the plaintiff as plaintiff was crossing the highway. Plaintiff alleged that the accident was proximately caused by the negligence of the defendant in that defendant failed to drive on the right side of the highway, failed to heed highway signs warning that construction work was in progress in that area, drove at an unreasonable speed under the conditions then and there existing, failed to reduce his speed as he approached and entered an intersection, failed to warn the plaintiff by sounding the car's horn, failed to keep a proper lookout and to properly control his car, and drove in a careless and reckless manner.

Defendant filed answer generally denying that he was negligent and averring that plaintiff was contributorily negligent as a matter of law in that plaintiff failed to yield the right-of-way and stepped suddenly and without warning from the shoulder of the road into the path of defendant's car.

At trial the plaintiff offered evidence tending to show the following:

Plaintiff is employed by the North Carolina Highway Commission and, on 23 November 1977, was part of a three-man crew assigned to a road project at the intersection of Rural Paved Road (RPR) 1004 and RPR 1414 in Nash County. Their task was to lay additional joints of pipe on each side of the intersection, and they had begun their job the day before by digging out the ditch to expose the pipe already there. Plaintiff's first responsibility upon arriving at the job site on November 23, as was the case the day before, was to position warning signs to the south and north of the intersection. The signs were typical road construction hazard signs, that is, they were diamond-shaped, bright orange in color, and bore the legend "Road Construction Ahead."

Testimony of various witnesses, as well as photographs and diagrams, established that RPR 1004 is a two-lane, paved secondary road that runs north and south. RPR 1414 is also a two-lane, paved road which comes into RPR 1004 from the east to form a "T" intersection. Thus, if one is travelling north on RPR 1004, RPR 1414 turns off to the right. Also, if one is travelling north on RPR 1004, approximately 300 to 400 feet south of the intersection, RPR 1004 curves slightly to the right.

Plaintiff testified that when he arrived on the job site the morning of November 23, he picked up a warning sign from the pile of dirt at the intersection, threw it over his shoulders, and headed south on Road 1004. By his calculations, he placed the sign 96 or 97 yards south of the intersection on the shoulder of Road 1004 so that it would be visible to northbound traffic. Plaintiff then returned to the intersection and picked up the second sign. He threw it across his shoulders and started walking north on the shoulder about 14 or 15 feet and then turned to cross Road 1004 so that he could place the sign on the opposite shoulder for the benefit of southbound traffic. Before starting to cross the road, plaintiff said he stopped on the edge and looked to his left, that is, he looked back down Road 1004 to the south. He saw a car approaching in the northbound lane approximately at the point where he had placed the first sign, but "had plenty of chance to get across the road" and walked across. Plaintiff testified that he crossed the center line of Road 1004 — that is, he walked out of the northbound lane of travel and into the southbound lane — walked two to three feet into the southbound lane, and then turned right. About that time, the car driven by defendant struck him.

Plaintiff was wearing a blue uniform and a white hard hat at the time of the accident. The sign he was carrying was between him and the defendant's car. He said that "[f]rom the time I saw the vehicle and before I started across the road until the time I was struck, I did not hear a horn blow." He suffered injuries to his back, hip and face, was hospitalized for 18 days, and had to have a steel plate inserted into his hip.

State Highway Patrolman L.E. Raynor investigated the accident. He testified that it was "drizzling rain" when he arrived on the scene; that the plaintiff had already been taken to the hospital; but that the defendant was still there. The car driven by defendant, a 1976 Ford Thunderbird, was located approximatley 100 feet north of the intersection. It was headed north, but was situated in the southbound lane of travel across the center line. Trooper Raynor observed slight damage to the "left front of the vehicle where the paint was scratched . . . ." He recalled that the warning sign placed south of the intersection for northbound traffic was clearly visible and could be seen "before you got into that curve" on Road 1004.

Trooper Raynor talked to the defendant who told him that the collision had occurred "just left of the center line" in the southbound lane of travel on Road 1004. Defendant told the officer that the plaintiff walked in front of him and that he hit the plaintiff when he swerved his car to the left to try to avoid hitting the plaintiff. Defendant estimated his speed to be about 40 miles per hour just prior to the accident.

Plaintiff also offered the testimony of Barry Driver, a member of the crew assigned to this particular road project and plaintiff's superior on the job. Driver testified that he was standing on Road 1414 talking to the other crew member, that he "glimpsed" the car as it passed the intersection, and turned to face Road 1004 just as the car passed. He described what he saw as follows:

> When I first turned around, James [plaintiff] was in the right-hand lane, northbound lane of Road 1004, probably a couple of steps from the center line. . . . He was walking kind of diagonally when I first saw him across there and he kept walking and from the time I looked at him, he kept walking before the car hit him. Yes, I saw the car when it actually struck Mr. Sessoms. Mr. Sessoms was across the center line when the car struck him. The car was approximately straddle of the center line of the road when it hit James.
>
> .   .   .
>
> From the time I glimpsed the car to where it hit James, the car was in the center of the road. . . .

In Driver's opinion the car was travelling at approximately 40 miles per hour when he first saw it and about 15 miles per hour when it struck the plaintiff. He said he did not hear a horn blow. Driver also testified that the warning sign which plaintiff had placed south of the intersection for northbound traffic was situated 110 yards from the intersection, that the distance from where he was standing on Road 1414 to where plaintiff was struck on Road 1004 was approximatley 50 yards, and that he was standing about 30 feet from the center of Road 1004. He said the road was wet.

Plaintiff called defendant as an adverse witness, and he testified in substance that he didn't remember seeing any kind of sign along the highway; that he first saw the plaintiff when he came out of the curve on Road 1004; and that he slowed down to 40 or 45 miles per hour as he came around the curve because it was raining. When defendant was asked whether he had stated in his deposition that plaintiff was in the center of the highway when he passed the intersection, defendant replied, "Possible. I could have said that....I don't know for sure. He was around the center lane somewhere."

Defendant testified further that he "tooted" his horn when he first saw the plaintiff standing on the shoulder, that plaintiff stepped out onto the highway and he "tooted" his horn again and proceeded, and that he blew the horn about the same time he applied his brakes. He said he tried to turn his car to the right when he saw the plaintiff in the middle of the road, but that the car "went into a slide...it just skidded straight." He testified that there were no cars ahead of him, nor were there any obstructions either on the paved portion of the highway or on the shoulder.

At the close of the plaintiff's evidence, the court allowed the defendant's motion for a directed verdict. From a judgment entered thereon, plaintiff appealed.

Biggs, Meadows, Batts, Etheridge & Winberry, by William D. Etheridge and Auley M. Crouch III, for the plaintiff appellant.

Battle, Winslow, Scott & Wiley, by Robert L. Spencer, for the defendant appellee.

ERWIN, Judge.

The sole issue presented by this appeal is whether the entry of a directed verdict for defendant was appropriate. We say, no.

The legal standard for gauging the evidence on a motion for a directed verdict is well established and hardly needs repeating: "[A]ll evidence which supports plaintiff's claim must be taken as true and viewed in the light most favorable to him, giving him the benefit of every reasonable inference which may legitimately be drawn therefrom, and with contradictions, conflicts and inconsistencies being resolved in his favor." *Maness v. Fowler-Jones Construction Co.*, 10 N.C. App. 592, 595, 179 S.E. 2d 816, 818, *cert. denied*, 278 N.C. 522, 180 S.E. 2d 610 (1971). The issue in the case at bar is thus refined to a determination, first, whether the plaintiff has offered sufficient evidence which, considered in accordance with the above test, tends to show that his injuries were proximately caused by the negligence of the defendant, and, nevertheless, whether the evidence establishes as a matter of law that the plaintiff failed to exercise the requisite degree of ordinary care for his own safety. *See Ryder v. Benfield*, 43 N.C. App. 278, 258 S.E. 2d 849 (1979). In our opinion, the evidence is such as to permit different inferences reasonably to be drawn as to each issue and, thus, both questions should have been submitted to the jury.

It cannot be denied that certain duties existing by virtue of statute as well as the common law were imposed upon both plaintiff and defendant under the factual situation present in this case. For example, pertinent provisions of G.S. § 20-174 require pedestrians who cross a roadway "at any point other than within a marked crosswalk or within an unmarked crosswalk at an intersection" to yield the right-of-way to all vehicles upon the roadway. Notwithstanding this duty imposed upon the pedestrian, the statute mandates that "every driver of a vehicle shall exercise due care to avoid colliding with any pedestrian upon any roadway, and shall give warning by sounding the horn when necessary... ." G.S. § 20-141 also imposes a general standard of due care with respect to speed and requires that a motorist not operate his vehicle "at a speed greater than is reasonable and prudent under the conditions then existing." Obviously, this duty exists notwithstanding that the motorist's actual speed is less than the posted speed limit. *See Kolman v. Silbert*, 219 N.C. 134, 12 S.E. 2d 915 (1941). Moreover, this provision of our highway law requires the motorist to decrease his speed when special hazards exist by reason of weather and highway conditions, to the end that others using the highway may not be injured. *Williams v. Tucker*, 259 N.C. 214, 130 S.C. 2d 306 (1963).

The evidence in this case also clearly implicates the following provisions of G.S. § 20–146:

> (a) Upon all [highways] of sufficient width a vehicle shall be driven upon the right half of the highway . . .
>
> . . . .

(d) Whenever any street has been divided into two or more clearly marked lanes for traffic, the following rules in addition ... shall apply.

(1) A vehicle shall be driven as nearly as practicable entirely within a single lane and shall not be moved from such lane until the driver has first ascertained that such movement can be made with safety.

The purpose of the above–quoted statute is to proctect occupants of other vehicles and pedestrians. *Powell v. Clark*, 255 N.C. 707, 122 S.E. 2d 706 (1961). Our Courts have consistently held that the violation of this section constitutes negligence *per se*, and when it is the proximate cause of injury or damage, such violation is actionable negligence. *See, e.g., Reeves v. Hill* 272 N.C. 352, 158 S.E. 2d 529 (1968). Whether the violation is the proximate cause of an injury is for the jury to determine. *Stephens v. Southern Oil Company of North Carolina, Inc.*, 259 N.C. 456, 131 S.E. 2d 39 (1963). "When a plaintiff suing to recover damages for injuries sustained in a collision offers evidence tending to show that the collision occurred when the defendant was driving to his left of the center of the highway, such evidence makes out a *prima facie* case of actionable negligence." *Anderson v. Webb.* 267 N.C. 745, 749, 148 S.E. 2d 846, 849 (1966). Of course, the defendant may rebut the inferences arising from such evidence by showing that he was driving on the wrong side of the road for reasons other than his own negligence, but, in such a case, such showing by the defendant serves merely to raise an issue of credibility for the jury to resolve. *See Smith v. Kilburn* 13 N.C. App. 449, 186 S.E. 2d 214, *cert. denied*, 281 N.C. 155, 187 S.E. 2d 586 (1972).

In the case before us, all the evidence shows that defendant's car struck the plaintiff to the left of the center line. Indeed, defendant concedes that as a fact. However, he sought to explain that he crossed the center line in an attempt to avoid hitting the plaintiff. In our opinion, this evidence alone, on the authority of *Anderson v. Webb* and *Smith v. Kilburn, supra* is sufficient to require the submission of this case to the jury.

Additionally, we find the evidence, when considered in the

light most favorable to the plaintiff, sufficient to raise *inter alia* the following inferences:

1. That the defendant operated his car at a speed that was greater than was reasonable and prudent under the conditions then and there existing, with respect to weather conditions and possible road construction hazards, in violation of G.S. § 20-141.

2. That the defendant failed to decrease his speed as he approached, entered and transversed an intersection, in violation of G.S. § 20-141.

3. That the defendant failed to decrease his speed as necessary to avoid colliding with a person on or entering the highway, in violation of G.S. § 20-141(m).

4. That the defendant failed to sound his horn to warn the plaintiff of his approach, in violation of G.S. § 20-174(e).

5. That the defendant failed to exercise due care to avoid hitting the plaintiff in that he failed to keep a proper lookout, or to keep his car under proper control.

From these inferences the jury could find that the defendant was negligent and that his negligence was a proximate cause of plaintiff's injuries.

Defendant contends, however, that the evidence establishes as a matter of law that the plaintiff was contributorily negligent so as to bar plaintiff's right to recover. We agree that the evidence is sufficient to raise an inference, among others, that the plaintiff failed to yield the right-of-way and that, without due regard for his own safety, he stepped into the path of the defendant's car. But, as we have shown above, the evidence in this case is such as to raise a number of reasonable inferences. Rational persons could logically draw different conclusions as to whether plaintiff's injuries proximately resulted from the negligence of the defendant or from the plaintiff's contributory

negligence. "[O]nly when 'all the evidence so clearly establishes [plaintiff's] failure to yield the right of way as one of
the proximate causes of his injuries *that no other reasonable conclusion is possible,*'" *Ragland v. Moore,* 229 N.C.
360, 369, 261 S.E. 2d 666, 671 (1980) [emphasis added] [quot-
ing from *Blake v. Mallard,* 262 N.C. 62, 136 S.E. 2d 214
(1964), will a directed verdict against the plaintiff be
appropriate. In this case the evidence is for the jury as to
plaintiff's contributory negligence, if any, as well as defendant's negligence, if any. We cannot imagine a more clear-
cut case for the twelve.

The judgement directing a verdict for the defendant is
reversed.

Reversed.

Judges PARKER and VAUGHN concur.

ERVIN BAER PERSONAL REPRESENTATIVE OF THE ESTATE OF MICHAEL J.
PAROBY, JR., DECEASED v. WILLIAM R. DAVIS, PERSONAL REPRESENTATIVE OF
THE ESTATE OF SHARON JEAN SAXON, DECEASED, AND JEROME KARL PERSON,
PERSONAL REPRESENTATIVE OF THE ESTATE OF GARY LYNN SCHRECKENDGUST, DE-
CEASED.

No. 8012SC40

(Filed 15 July 1980)

Death § 4– wrongful death – action barred by statute of limitations

Plaintiff's claim for wrongful death was barred by the six month limitation of G.S. 28A-19-3 (b)(2), since plaintiff's claim arose on 23 October 1976, the
date of intestate's death, but plaintiff did not present his claim until some 15
months later.

APPEAL by plaintiff from *Braswell, Judge.* Order entered 15
August 1979 in Superior Court, CUMBERLAND County. Heard in
the Court of Appeals 3 June 1980.

Plaintiff's and defendants' intestates drowned on 23 October 1976 when the car in which they were riding overturned and

sank in a pond. Plaintiff brings this wrongful death action and defendants bring wrongful death actions as counterclaims. By the pre-trial order the parties stipulated that the only written notice of these claims they gave to each other was by service of the pleadings in this action in January 1978. Defendants in their answers and plaintiff in his replies allege as pleas in bar the six month statute of limitations established by G.S. 28A-19-3(b)(2). Prior to trial the court ruled on these pleas in bar and dismissed plaintiff's action and the counterclaims with prejudice. Plaintiff appeals.

Pollock, Fullenwider & Cunningham, by Bruce T. Cunningham, Jr., for plaintiff appellant.

Bryan, Jones & Johnson, by Robert C.'Bryan, for defendant appellee Person.

ARNOLD, Judge.

Plaintiff argues on appeal that it is the statute of limitations established by G.S. 28A-19-3 (a) which is pertinent to this case, and not that of G.S. 28A-19-3 (b)(2). G.S. 28A-19-3 (a) applies to claims arising prior to a decedent's death while G.S. 28A-19-3 (b)(2) applies to claims arising at or after his death.

However, plaintiff's argument is of no avail since the issue of the applicability of G.S. 28A-19-3 (a) was not raised before the trial court. *See Wallace Men's Wear, Inc. v. Harris,* 28 N.C. App. 153, 220 S.E. 2d 390 (1975), *cert. denied* 289 N.C. 298, 222 S.E. 2d 703 (1976). It is clear from the trial court's order and the pleadings of the parties that it is G.S. 28A-19-3 (b)(2) which the parties alleged as a plea in bar and upon which the trial court ruled. The sole question for our review is whether the trial court ruled correctly that G.S. 28A-19-3 (b)(2), as it existed prior to amendment in 1979, bars plaintiff's action.

G.S. 28A-19-3(b)(2) provides that with an exception not pertinent here all claims against a decedent's estate arising at or after the death of the decedent must be presented within six months after the claim arises. A cause of action for wrongful death accrues at the date of death, G.S. 1-53 (4), in this case 23

October 1976, and the claim was not presented until some 15 months later.

Plaintiff argues that since no administrators were appointed for the estates of defendants' intestates until January of 1978, he was only required to file his claim within six months of the appointment of the administrators, but we find this argument to be without merit. As defendants point out, plaintiff could have applied for letters of administration in the estates of defendants' intestates, see G.S. 28A-4-1 (b)(5) and (6), or sought to have the public administrator appointed, see G.S. 28A-12-4 (3), before the six-month statute of limitations established by G.S. 28A-19-3 (b)(2) had run. In fact, it was at plaintiff's instigation that administrators were finally appointed for the estates. The trial court correctly ruled that plaintiff's claim was barred by the statute of limitations.

Affirmed.

Judges MARTIN (Robert M.) and HILL concur.

CASES REPORTED WITHOUT PUBLISHED OPINION

Filed 1 July 1980

BARROW v. BARROW No. 808DC101	Lenoir (78CVD1253)	Appeal Dismissed
BILLINGS v. BULLARD No. 8020SC104	Moore (78CVS461)	Affirmed
GRACE & CO. v. HARDEE No. 8016DC82	Robeson (78CVD1177)	Affirmed
HENDERSON v. HENDERSON No. 7928DC633	Buncombe (78CVD1151)	Affirmed
JACKSON v. JACKSON No. 7927DC427	Gaston (77CVS1049)	Affirmed
JOHNSON v. BOARD OF EDUCATION No. 8019SC96	Cabarrus (78CVS1664)	Appeal Dismissed
KNOX v. BOARD OF ADJUSTMENT No. 8018SC181	Guilford (79VS3368)	Affirmed
LONG v. WILSON No. 8022SC163	Davidson (78SP257)	Affirmed
MORGAN v. WOOD No. 8018SC159	Guilford (79CVS5123)	Affirmed
POLLARD v. INSURANCE CO. No. 8010IC164	Ind. Comm. (G-9526)	Affirmed
STATE v. BEYAH No. 8014SC232	Durham (79CRS21223)	New Trail
STATE v. BILLINGS No. 8021SC89	Forsyth (79CR27007)	No Error
STATE v. BOLT No. 8026SC55	Mecklenburg (78CRS151224) (79CRS8449)	Dismissed
STATE v. BOYD No. 8017SC215	Washington (79CRS526)	No Error

STATE v. CAMACK No. 7918SC1018	Guilford (78CRS50938)	No Error
STATE v. COFFEY No. 7925SC938	Caldwell (79CRS2761) (79CRS1342)	No Error
STATE v. COX No. 7926SC1048	Mecklenburg (79CR010310)	No Error
STATE v. CRAVEN No. 8019SC201	Randolph (79CRS6297)	No Error
STATE v. DELLINGER No. 8027SC224	Lincoln (79CRS5936)	No Error
STATE v. ELLIS No. 804SC211	Onslow (79CRS15806) (79CRS15807)	No Error
STATE v. GEDDINGS No. 8026SC90	Mecklenburg (79CRS026050) (79CRS026057) (79CRS026065)	No Error
STATE v. JAMES No. 798SC1189	Wayne (78CR20068)	No Error
STATE v. LOGUE No. 8018SC170	Guilford (79CRS17057) (79CRS17061) (79CRS17065)	No Error
STATE v. McDOWELL No. 8027SC190	Gaston (79CRS14749) (79CRS14750) (79CRS14751)	No Error
STATE v. MODLIN No. 792SC1154	Martin (79CRS1439)	No Error
STATE v. RUCKER No. 8017SC119	Rockingham (78CRS9130)	No Error
STATE v. WAINWRIGHT No. 802SC122	Beaufort (79CRS7103)	No Error
STATE v. WALKER No. 8017SC215	Rockingham (79CR9991)	No Error

STATE v. WILLIAMS No. 8021SC103	Forsyth (79CRS16759) (79CRS16760)	No Error
STATE v. WILSON No. 7918SC1128	Guilford (78CRS47235)	No Error
WAYSIDE FURNITURE v. LEE No. 8017DC16	Rockingham (78CVD126)	Affirmed
WILSON v. WILSON No. 7930SC857	Macon (76SP16)	Reversed and Remanded

Fisher v. Ladd

VIRGINIA C. FISHER, Successor Trustee Under the Will of OLIVER D.
FISHER; ANNIE CLEE HIGH FISHER, Widow; ROBERT L. FISHER and
wife, VIRGINIA H. FISHER; RANDOLPH D. FISHER and wife, VIRGIN-
IA C. FISHER, individually; MARGARET F. JONES, Widow; HAZEL F.
GRIFFIN and husband, GEORGE R. GRIFFIN; BUCK FISHER and wife,
DORIS L. FISHER; CAROLYN F. JOYNER and husband, G. HERMAN
JOYNER; PEGGY F. SNIPES and husband, SIDNEY B. SNIPES; BILLY
THORPE FISHER and wife, EVELYN T. FISHER; KATHERINE T.
FISHER, Widow; CHRISTOPHER B. FISHER, Unmarried; and KIMBER-
LY B. FISHER, an unmarried minor; LILLY ANN FISHER, an unmarried
minor; AMY L. FISHER, an unmarried minor, and JENNY K. FISHER, an
unmarried minor, all of said minors acting herein as plaintiffs through
ROY A. COOPER, JR., their Guardian ad Litem, appointed pursuant to
Court Order; and LOTTIE F. CURTIS, Widow; ROBERT E. CURTIS, Un-
married; JIMMY CURTIS, Unmarried; DAVID CURTIS, Unmarried;
RUTH F. LADD and husband, ARTHUR N. LADD; DAVID L. LADD and
wife; DIXIE F. LADD; TODD E. LADD, Unmarried; PAMELA SUE LADD,
Unmarried; JOANNE F. YOUNG and husband, GARY ALLEN YOUNG,
CHARLOTTE J. STRUM and husband, JACK H. STRUM; JACKIE GRAY
STRUM, Unmarried; LOTTIE GENEVA STRUM, Unmarried; BOBBIE J.
WOLLETT and husband, THEODORE R. WOLLETT, JR.; THEODORE R.
WOLLETT, III, Unmarried; MARGARET J. HARRIS and husband,
ROBERT LOWELL HARRIS; OLIVER DANIEL GRIFFIN and wife, VIR-
GINIA O. GRIFFIN; WAYNE GRIFFIN and wife, RITA M. GRIFFIN;
WILLIAM CLIFTON GRIFFIN and wife, MARIE B. GRIFFIN; ROBERT
DEWEY GRIFFIN and wife, LINDA M. GRIFFIN, GWENDOLYN J. DEW
and husband, ROBERT E. DEW; TOMMY GEORGE JOYNER and wife,
SUE B. JOYNER; JERRY RANDLOPH JOYNER and wife, BETTY E.
JOYNER; HERMAN STEVEN JOYNER and wife, TAM F. JOYNER;
KATHY J. BENNETT and husband, JAMES LEWIS BENNETT; SANDRA
S. WATSON and husband, JACK STEVENS WATSON; and JENNIFER S.
SOWELL and husband, JAMES M. SOWELL, JR. v. JENNIFER YVONNE
LADD; TWANA SUE WRIGHT; GARY SCOTT YOUNG; MARY ESTHER
WOLLETT; JIM ALBERT HARRIS; MONICA LEE HARRIS; CINDY
GRIFFIN; MARVIN DEAN GRIFFIN; KELLY RENEE GRIFFIN;
CHRISTOPHER GRIFFIN; DONALD RAY DANIEL; TAMMY KAYE
GRIFFIN; TIMOTHY CRAIG FISHER; TRACY LYNN DEW; MELISSA
CAROL DEW; CINDY CAROL JOYNER; TOMMY GEORGE JOYNER, JR.;
SHANNON RENEE JOYNER; JASON SCOTT JOYNER; ASHLEY
STEVEN JOYNER; JOSHUA SIDNEY WATSON; MATTHEW JAMES
WATSON; HOPE FISHER; all unmarried minors, ANY UNBORN DE-
SCENDANT OF OLIVER D. FISHER, INCLUDING BUT NOT LIMITED
TO ANY CHILD HEREAFTER BORN TO OR ADOPTED BY Robert L.
Fisher, Lottie F. Curtis, Robert E. Curtis, Jimmy Curtis, David Curtis,
Randloph D. Fisher, Ruth F. Ladd, David L. Ladd, Todd E. Ladd, Pamela
Sue Ladd, Jennifer Yvonne Ladd, Joanne F. Young, Twana Sue Wright,
Gary Scott Young, Margaret F. Jones, Charlotte J. Strum, Jackie Gray
Strum, Lottie Geneva Strum, Bobbie J. Wollett, Theodore R. Wollett,
III, Mary Esther Wollett, Margaret J. Harris, Jim Albert Harris, Moni-

CA LEE HARRIS, HAZEL F. GRIFFIN, OLIVER DANIEL GRIFFIN, CINDY GRIFFIN, MARVIN DEAN GRIFFIN, WAYNE GRIFFIN, KELLEY RENEÉ GRIFFIN, CHRISTOPHER GRIFFIN, WILLIAM CLIFTON GRIFFIN, TAMMY KAYE GRIFFIN, ROBERT DEWEY GRIFFIN, BUCK FISHER, TIMOTHY CRAIG FISHER, CAROLYN F. JOYNER, GWENDOLYN J. DEW, TRACY LYNN DEW, MELISSA CAROL DEW, TOMMY GEORGE JOYNER, CINDY CAROL JOYNER, TOMMY GEORGE JOYNER, JR., JERRY RANDOLPH JOYNER, SHANNON RENEÉ JOYNER, HERMAN STEVEN JOYNER, JASON SCOTT JOYNER, ASHLEY STEVEN JOYNER, KATHY J. BENNETT, PEGGY F. SNIPES, SANDRA S. WATSON, JOSHUA SIDNEY WATSON, MATTHEW JAMES WATSON, JENNIFER S. SOWELL, BILLY THORPE FISHER, HOPE FISHER, CHRISTOPHER B. FISHER, AMY L. FISHER, KIMBERLY B. FISHER, JENNY K. FISHER AND LILLY ANN FISHER; ANY UNKNOWN DESCENDANT OF OLIVER D. FISHER, INCLUDING BUT NOT LIMITED TO ANY UNKNOWN DESCENDANTS OF ROBERT L. FISHER, LOTTIE F. CURTIS, ROBERT E. CURTIS, JIMMY CURTIS, DAVID CURTIS, RANDOLPH D. FISHER, RUTH F. LADD, DAVID L. LADD, TODD E. LADD, PAMELA SUE LADD, JENNIFER YVONNE LADD, JOANNE F. YOUNG, TWANA SUE WRIGHT, GARY SCOTT YOUNG, MARGARET F. JONES, CHARLOTTE J. STRUM, JACKIE GRAY STRUM, LOTTIE GENEVA STRUM, BOBBIE J. WOLLETT, THEODORE R. WOLLETT, III, MARY ESTHER WOLLETT, MARGARET J. HARRIS, JIM ALBERT HARRIS, MONICA LEE HARRIS, HAZEL F. GRIFFIN, OLIVER DANIEL GRIFFIN, CINDY GRIFFIN, MARVIN DEAN GRIFFIN, WAYNE GRIFFIN, KELLY RENEÉ GRIFFIN, CHRISTOPHER GRIFFIN, WILLIAM CLIFTON GRIFFIN, TAMMY KAYE GRIFFIN, ROBERT DEWEY GRIFFIN, BUCK FISHER, TIMOTHY CRAIG FISHER, CAROLYN F. JOYNER, GWENDOLYN J. DEW, TRACY LYNN DEW, MELISSA CAROL DEW, TOMMY GEORGE JOYNER, CINDY CAROL JOYNER, TOMMY GEORGE JOYNER, JR., JERRY RANDOLPH JOYNER, SHANNON RENEÉ JOYNER, HERMAN STEVEN JOYNER, JASON SCOTT JOYNER, ASHLEY STEVEN JOYNER, KATHY J. BENNETT, PEGGY F. SNIPES, SANDRA S. WATSON, JOSHUA SIDNEY WATSON, MATTHEW JAMES WATSON, JENNIFER S. SOWELL, BILLY THORP FISHER, HOPE FISHER, CHRISTOPHER B. FISHER, AMY L. FISHER, KIMBERLY B. FISHER, JENNY K. FISHER AND LILLY ANN FISHER

No. 797SC1104

(Filed 15 July 1980)

Trusts § 10.1– consent of all beneficiaries to termination of trust – termination proper

In N.C. if all the beneficiaries of a trust consent and none of them is under incapacity, they can compel the termination of the trust, even though the period fixed by its terms has not expired; therefore, the trial court did not err in terminating a trust and ordering sale of the trust property and division of the trust assets where testator set up a trust with his wife and children as beneficiaries; the will contained no language that testator intended that a child had to survive the life tenant, testator's wife, in order to acquire an interest in the property; pursuant to the will the wife and children took vested interests in the income and corpus of the trust estate, these interests being determined upon the death of the testator; and all beneficiaries agreed to the termination of the trust.

APPEAL by defendants from *Peel, Judge.* Judgment entered 10 October 1979 in Superior Court, NASH County. Heard in the Court of Appeals 14 April 1980.

In this declaratory judgment action, plaintiffs seek the termination of a testamentary trust established by Oliver D. Fisher, who died on 27 November 1958. The portion of that will establishing the trust, relevant to this appeal, provides as follows:

THIRD: It is my wish to adequately provide for my wife and minor children to the best of my ability and it is my opinion that this can best be done by giving the remainder of my estate to a competent Trustee to manage for her. I therefore give, bequeath and devise all the rest and residue of my property of every kind and description and wheresoever the same may be situate to my brother, John T. Fisher, of the County of Nash, State of North Carolina, not for his own use but as Trustee with the powers and for the purposes and upon the trusts herein set forth.

FOURTH: My Trustee is empowered to receive, hold, manage and control the said property until the trust herein created shall be terminated, as hereinafter provided: to invest any and all moneys constituting a part of said trust estate as he shall see fit; to sell at public or private sale, for cash or on time and without order of court, any part of the personal property as my Trustee shall consider for the best interest of my estate and to reinvest the proceeds as he sees fit; to operate my farm in such manner as he considers for the best interest of my estate and to do any and all things incident or necessary to carry out the provisions of this trust. In the event my Trustee is unable to serve or should die I then direct that his successor be appointed by the clerk of the Superior Court of Nash County.

FIFTH: My Trustee shall deliver to my wife, during her life and widowhood, in convenient installments, the net income from my said trust estate in order that she may use the same for the maintenance and support of herself and such of my minor children as she thinks need help.

SIXTH: If at any time the income is insufficient for my wife and minor children to have the necessities of life my Trustee is then empowered to use so much of the principal as may be necessary to insure their comfort and welfare, considering always the size of my estate and the probable time that the trust is to run. If my wife or any of my children shall meet with any unforseen calamity or if they are in need because of prolonged sickness or other misfortune, then my Trustee is authorized to make such provision as he deems expedient and as to this he shall be the sole judge.

SEVENTH: The trust herein created shall continue during the life and widowhood of my said wife. Upon her death or remarriage the trust herein created shall terminate and my said estate shall be divided equally among my children, the issue of any deceased child to take the share its parent would have taken if living. I have heretofore advanced to my son, Robert L. Fisher, certain money, as evidenced by notes which are now in my possession. It is my desire that these notes be cancelled and that the same shall not be charged against the share of my son, Robert L. Fisher.

On 8 December 1978 a Family Settlement Agreement was executed by all the living adult children and spouses of the children of testator and the successor trustee which provided that the widow and surviving children would seek termination of the trust and a division of the trust assets. The agreement was also executed by all of the living adult descendants and spouses of descendants of testator. On 13 April 1979, plaintiffs filed the present action pursuant to that agreement. Guardians ad litem were appointed for the minor descendants and the unknown and unborn lineal descendants of testator, all filing answers denying the propriety of plaintiffs' petition. On hearing, the trial court made findings of fact, which are not the subject of this appeal, and concluded as a matter of law that the above quoted portion of testator's will "created an active trust, and the laws of North Carolina permit an active trust to be terminated if all of the beneficiaries of the trust have a vested interest and agree to termination." The court entered further conclusions of law:

2. The Will of Oliver D. Fisher . . . created a vested life estate in Anne Clee High Fisher, subject to being divested by her remarriage.

3. The Trust under the Will of Oliver D. Fisher vested a remainder interest in the children of Oliver D. Fisher, as of the death of Oliver D. Fisher.

4. The descendants of Oliver D. Fisher, other than his widow and children, took no interest under the Will of Oliver D. Fisher.

The trial court then ordered that the trust be terminated and the assets distributed in accordance with the Family Settlement Agreement. Defendants appeal, assigning error to the court's conclusions of law supporting the order of termination.

Davenport and Fisher, by John E. Davenport, for plaintiff appellees.

Ralph G. Willey III, Robert D. Kornegay, Jr. and John S. Williford, Jr., for Guardian Ad Litem defendant appellants.

MORRIS, Chief Judge.

This appeal involves the principles of law relating to the termination of testamentary trusts prior to their natural expiration. Defendants assert as grounds for reversal of the trial court's ruling that the testamentary trust was improperly terminated in that there was given no consent by all parties having an interest in the trust, and that several parties did not have a vested interest in the trust which would enable them to give effective consent to early termination. In North Carolina, if all the beneficiaries of a trust consent and none of them is under incapacity, they can compel the termination of the trust, even though the period fixed by its terms has not expired. *Solon Lodge v. Ionic Lodge,* 247 N.C. 310, 101 S.E. 2d 8 (1957); *Wachovia Bank and Trust Co. v. Laws,* 217 N.C. 171, 7 S.E. 2d 470 (1940); *Wachovia Bank and Trust Co. v. Sevier,* 41 N.C. App. 762, 255 S.E. 2d 636, *cert. denied,* 298 N.C. 304, 259 S.E. 2d 305 (1979). *See generally* 76 Am. Jur. 2d, *Trusts* §§ 75, 76, 80 (1975).

We note at the outset that neither the validity of the Family Settlement Agreement nor the percentage amounts given to each party therein is before us for consideration. Defendants have not excepted to the findings of fact by the trial judge, and those findings are deemed conclusive on appeal. *See Moss v. City of Winston-Salem*, 254 N.C. 480, 119 S.E. 2d 445 (1961). We are not, however, necessarily bound by the findings of fact which go to the nature of the interests held by the various beneficiaries. The nature of a trust beneficiary's interest is a question of law to be determined in light of the distributive provisions of the instrument itself.

The will of testator is utterly devoid of any language which would indicate that the testator intended that a child had to survive the life tenant in order to acquire an interest in the property. The testator's direction with respect to representation merely referred to the time the estate could be enjoyed in possession. It is clear that, under the will of Oliver D. Fisher, the wife and children took vested interests in the income and corpus of the trust estate, these interests being determined upon the death of the testator. *Roberts v. Northwestern Bank*, 271 N.C. 292, 156 S.E. 2d 229 (1967); *Pinnell v. Dowtin*, 224 N.C. 493, 31 S.E. 2d 467 (1944); *Witty v. Witty*, 184 N.C. 375, 114 S.E. 482 (1922). All these beneficiaries consented to the termination of the trust.

No other interests passed by the will, although testator provided for representation by the children of any of testator's children who predecease the life tenant. The children of the deceased son of testator, Georgie B. Fisher, share in the trust proceeds by this provision, and all have agreed to the termination of the trust.

Where the beneficiaries under a will validly contract with other interested persons in regard to their respective interests in the estate, such agreement constitutes an effective compromise of their claims. *Reynolds v. Reynolds*, 208 N.C. 254, 180 S.E. 70 (1935). These agreements have long been favored by our courts. *See Spencer v. McCleneghan*, 202 N.C. 662, 163 S.E. 753 (1932).

We conclude and so hold that the judgment terminating the trust and ordering the sale of the trust property and subsequent division of the trust assets in accordance with the settlement agreement was fair and proper with respect to all the parties.

Affirmed.

Judges PARKER and WELLS concur.

RAM TEXTILES, INC., A CORPORATION v. HILLVIEW MILLS, INC.; A.I.R. INDUSTRIES, INC.; HENRY A. SINGE: AND RICHARD G. LEVINE TEXLAND INDUSTRIES, INC. v. HILLVIEW MILLS, INC.; A.I.R. INDUSTRIES, INC.; HENRY A. SINGE; AND RICHARD G. LEVINE

No. 8026SC34

(Filed 15 July 1980)

1. Corporations § 1.1– one corporation not alter ego of another

Defendant corporation was not the alter ego of a now insolvent corporation so as to make defendant liable for the purchase price of yarn sold to the insolvent corporation, although plaintiff creditors showed a certain degree of relationship among the stockholders and officers of the two corporations, where the evidence showed that defendant was one of about 200 customers of the insolvent corporation, that the insolvent corporation's manufacture of goods for defendant accounted for only 15% of its employees' time and that the president and sole shareholder of the insolvent corporation made all the policy decisions of that company, and where there was no evidence of fraudulent representations or wrongs by defendant or its employees to plaintiff creditors.

2. Fraudulent Conveyances § 3.4– insufficient evidence of fraudulent conveyance

Defendant corporation is not liable to plaintiffs for the purchase price of yarn sold to an insolvent corporation on the ground that defendant participated in a fraudulent conveyance of assets of the insolvent corporation where plaintiffs presented no evidence of any conveyance of the assets owned by the bankrupt corporation to defendant; the assets plaintiffs allege were fraudulently conveyed were purchased by defendant from a creditor of the bankrupt corporation which sold them pursuant to a security agreement; and there was no evidence that the sale of such assets constituted a collusive or fraudulent conveyance made with the intent to defraud other creditors.

APPEAL by defendant from *Ervin, Judge.* Judgments entered 20 August 1979 in Superior Court, MECKLENBURG County. Heard in the Court of Appeals 3 June 1980.

Ram Textiles sold $92,299.65 worth of yarn to Hillview Mills. Texland Industries sold $58,334.17 worth of yarn to Hillview Mills. Both Ram Textiles and Texland Industries brought actions against Hillview Mills, A.I.R. Industries, Henry A. Singe and Richard G. Levine when they were unable to collect payment from Hillview Mills. Plaintiffs alleged A.I.R. Industries should be held liable for the Hillview Mills debt of approximately $150,000.00 on the grounds that it was an alter ego of Hillview Mills and had participated in a fraudulent conveyance of the assets of Hillview Mills. The cases were consolidated for trial where the following evidence was presented by plaintiffs.

Richard Levine was president of Hillview Mills and vice-president and secretary of A.I.R. Industries. Henry Singe was a former treasurer of A.I.R. Industries and vice-president and later plant manager for Hillview Mills. James Hanrahan is president of A.I.R. Industries. Hillview Mills had operated a hosiery mill in Midland, North Carolina since 1972. All financial policy decisions for Hillview Mills were made by Levine who apparently owns all the stock of that company. Hanrahan and Levine had known each other for about twenty years in 1975 when they formed A.I.R. Industries with each owning half of the stock. Later, Singe was given five percent of the stock leaving Levine with forty-five percent and Hanrahan with fifty percent.

A.I.R. Industries had patents on certain surgical hosiery items which it supplied under a sales agreement to Zimmer, U.S.A. In October 1975, in order to provide these surgical hosiery items, A.I.R. Industries entered into a manufacturing contract with Hillview Mills which would manufacture the products for sale to A.I.R. Industries which would then sell the goods to Zimmer. Levine signed the manufacturing agreement on behalf of Hillview Mills, and Hanrahan signed on behalf of A.I.R. Industries. Some of the terms of the contract were as follows. A.I.R. Industries had no obligation to purchase any minimum quantity from Hillview Mills and could purchase from other manufacturers. Hillview Mills was required to meet A.I.R. Industries' requirements for the goods. A.I.R. Industries could assign its contract rights but Hillview could not. A.I.R. Industries could terminate the contract upon ten days' notice but no such termination provision was provided for Hillview Mills. The price paid to Hillview Mills was to be fifty percent of the net price received by A.I.R. Industries from its largest customer which thus assured a one hundred percent profit to A.I.R. Industries on the sale of surgical goods since it had only one customer. Payment to Hillview Mills was to come only after A.I.R. Industries had received payment on its resale of the goods.

The only activity of A.I.R. Industries was the selling of the surgical goods manufactured, packaged and shipped by Hillview Mills. Hillview Mills on the other hand manufactured hosiery products for approximately 200 other customers which accounted for approximately eighty-five percent of Hillview Mills' employee time.

Hillview Mills had 250 employees while A.I.R. Industries had four. At the time of the October 1975 agreement, Hanrahan became an employee of Hillview Mills though he did not distinguish between his Hillview Mills employee duties and his presidential duties at A.I.R. Industries. The other three A.I.R. Industries employees were Levine, Singe and a bookkeeper who was also employed by Hillview Mills. The business records of A.I.R. Industries were kept in the New York City corporate headquarters of Hillview Mills.

In April 1976, Hillview Mills entered into a lease of machines used in the manufacture of the surgical hosiery. Hanrahan, the president of A.I.R. Industries, was personal guarantor of the $72,000.00 yearly lease. The lease was put in A.I.R. Industries' name three months later but the equipment remained in the Hillview Mills plant. Another machine and raw materials titled in A.I.R. Industries were also in the Hillview Mills plant. While most of the products manufactured for A.I.R. Industries were manufactured on this equipment loaned to Hillview Mills, other products were manufactured on machinery owned by Hillview Mills.

In February 1977, A.I.R. Industries agreed to an assignment of the Hillview Mills manufacturing agreement to Hillview Manufacturing, a then nonexistent corporation, which was incorporated in April 1977 with Levine the president and owner. The manufacturing agreement of Hillview Mills with A.I.R. Industries was assigned to Hillview Manufacturing in June 1977. The surgical goods were still made for A.I.R. Industries at the Hillview Mills plant in Midland until March 1978.

In mid-1977, Hillview Mills became slow in paying Ram Textiles' invoices. A.I.R. Industries made some payments to Ram Textiles for yarns used in the manufacture of the surgical goods. The Hillview Mills corporate charter was suspended on 30 September 1977.

In October 1977, the payments by A.I.R. Industries for the manufacture of surgical goods were made to Hillview Manufacturing. The goods paid for were manufactured in the Hillview Mills plant in Midland. Over a four month period from October 1977 through January 1978, Levine as president of Hillview Manufacturing and vice-president and secretary of A.I.R. Industries had over $240,000.00 paid to Hillview Manufacturing for the manufacture of surgical goods.

In October 1977, checks given to creditors by Hillview Mills began to bounce. A representative of the two plaintiff creditors in this suit questioned Henry Singe about the financial situation. Singe reassured them about their credit on the basis of the highly profitable surgical line.

In March 1978, at a New York City meeting of Levine, Hanrahan and Singe, Levine announced that Hillview Mills was insolvent. To avoid any interruption in the production of surgical goods, they decided that the equipment used in the surgical goods manufacture should be moved. Congress Factors, a company which lent money to both Hillview Mills and A.I.R. Industries on the security of invoices and which had a lien on the equipment of both companies used in the manufacture of surgical goods, approved and authorized the move of the equipment.

In March 1978, Hillview Mills employees moved the equipment used in the manufacture of surgical goods from the Midland plant to a Concord plant which opened under the name of A.I.R. Industries. The Midland plant was left in a shambles. In April or May 1978, A.I.R. Industries purchased the Hillview Mills equipment in the Concord plant from Congress Factors. Approximately forty of the Hillview Mills employees went to work in the Concord plant. The remainder were let go and Hillview Mills ceased operation. The money owed to the creditors bringing suit in this case was mostly if not entirely for materials purchased in operations other than the surgical goods manufacturing.

At the close of plaintiffs' evidence, A.I.R. Industries moved for directed verdict which was granted. Plaintiffs appeal.

Casey and Bishop, by Jeffrey L. Bishop, for plaintiff appellants.

Moore and Van Allen, by Jeffrey J. Davis, for defendant appellee.

VAUGHN, Judge.

Plaintiffs' claims against A.I.R. Industries were based on the grounds that it was the alter ego of Hillview Mills and that it had engaged in fraudulent conveyances of the assets of Hillview Mills. We hold that the evidence considered in a light most favorable to plaintiffs does not entitle them to have the jury pass on the alter ego and fraudulent conveyance claims against A.I.R. Industries.

[1] Plaintiffs contend we should extend the liability for the obligations of Hillview Mills beyond the confines of its own separate existence and hold another separate corporate entity, A.I.R. Industries, liable for the debts of Hillview Mills. Plaintiffs' evidence in a light most favorable to them must show that Hillview Mills and A.I.R. Industries were mere instrumentalities or alter egos of defendant Levine and a shield for the purpose of defrauding creditors in violation of the public policy of this State. If this were proven, Levine, Hillview Mills

and A.I.R. Industries should be treated as one. *Henderson v. Finance Co.*, 273 N.C. 253, 160 S.E. 2d 39 (1968). Plaintiffs' evidence in a light most favorable to them does not show that A.I.R. Industries dominated the policies and business practices of Hillview Mills to the extent that Hillview Mills had no existence of its own.

The evidence shows that A.I.R. Industries' products accounted for approximately fifteen percent of the employee time of Hillview Mills' 250 employees. A.I.R. Industries was one of about 200 customers of Hillview Mills. Levine, the president and apparently the sole shareholder, and not A.I.R. Industries made all the policy decisions for the company. He possibly had the company as his alter ego and so used it as a mere instrumentality of his ends. There is, however, no evidence that A.I.R. Industries had such control.

Plaintiffs have shown a certain degree of relationship among the officers and stockholders of Hillview Mills and A.I.R. Industries. The president and sole shareholder of Hillview Mills, Levine, was a forty-five percent shareholder in A.I.R. Industries. This common ownership, however, is not enough to place liability for Hillview Mills' debts on A.I.R. Industries. Some additional circumstances of fraud are needed. *Huski-Bilt, Inc. v. Trust Co.*, 271 N.C. 662, 157 S.E. 2d 352 (1967). No such additional circumstances arise on the evidence of this case. There is no evidence of fraudulent representations or wrongs by A.I.R. Industries or its employees to plaintiffs. A.I.R. Industries at one point apparently paid for some of the raw material purchased from Ram Textiles and used in the production of the surgical goods manufactured for A.I.R. Industries. This does not indicate a fraud. The trial court properly directed a verdict on the claim.

[2] We turn now to plaintiffs' claim of fraudulent conveyance. A conveyance made with the actual intent to defraud creditors of the grantor which is participated in by the grantee is void. *Aman v. Walker*, 165 N.C. 224, 81 S.E. 162 (1914). Plaintiffs presented no evidence of any conveyance of assets owned by Hillview Mills to A.I.R. Industries. The assets plaintiffs allege were fraudulently conveyed were purchased in April or May 1978 by

A.I.R. Industries from Congress Factors which sold them pursuant to a security agreement it had with Hillview Mills. There is no evidence that Congress Factors' authorization of the transfer of the property in which it had a security interest in March 1977 and its subsequent sale of that property was a collusive or fraudulent conveyance made with the intent to defraud creditors. If it were, Congress Factors, which was not a party in this action, would be the defrauding party.

There is no question that plaintiffs lost money in dealing with Hillview Mills but A.I.R. Industries, on the evidence presented, is not liable to them for that loss.

Finally, we note that plaintiffs brought forward on appeal several assigned errors to the trial court's rulings on certain offers of evidence. We find the trial court's rulings proper.

Affirmed.

Judges PARKER and HEDRICK concur.

IN THE MATTER OF THE FORECLOSURE OF THE DEED OF TRUST OF A. C. BURGESS, JR., SINGLE TO L.B. HOLLOWELL, JR., TRUSTEE FOR GASTONIA MUTUAL SAVINGS AND LOAN ASSOCIATION RECORDED IN THE GASTON COUNTY PUBLIC REGISTRY IN DEED OF TRUST BOOK 1467 AT PAGE 287

No. 7927SC1201

(Filed 15 July 1980)

Mortgages and Deeds of Trust § 25– foreclosure by exercise of power of sale in deed of trust – amount owed in dispute

G.S. 45-21.16(d)(i) permits the clerk to find a "valid debt of which the party seeking to foreclose is a holder" if there is competent evidence that the party seeking to foreclose is the holder of some valid debt, irrespective of the exact amount owed, and G.S. 45-21.16(d)(iii) permits the clerk to find a "right to foreclose under the instrument" if there is competent evidence that the terms of the deed of trust permit the exercise of the power of sale under the circumstances of the particular case.

APPEAL by respondents Horace M. Dubose III, Trustee, and Robert J. Bernhardt, Trustee, from *Thornburg, Judge.* Order entered 27 November 1979 in Superior Court, GASTON County. Heard in the Court of Appeals 18 March 1980.

This is an appeal by respondents, purchasers of certain property at a sheriff's execution sale, from an order of the superior court entered after hearings held pursuant to G.S. 45-21.16 authorizing foreclosure of a deed of trust on that property.

On 30 May 1978, A.C. Burgess, Jr., owner of five lots in the Longwood Subdivision in Gaston County, North Carolina, executed a deed of trust conveying said lots to L.B. Hollowell, Jr., as trustee for Gastonia Mutual Savings and Loan Association. The deed of trust was given to secure a note in the amount of $56,000.00 and to secure future obligations and future advances in accordance with the terms of a construction loan agreement executed by the parties. The note was payable in monthly installments of principal and interest in the amount of $450.59, with payments to begin 1 May 1979.

Prior to 1 May 1979, certain judgment creditors of A.C. Burgess Jr., through their trustees, Horace M. DuBose, III and Robert J. Bernhardt, sought execution upon the five lots subject to the deed of trust. Those trustees were permitted to bid the value of the judgments at a sheriff's sale, and as the successful bidders they received a sheriff's deed for the property on 13 February 1979. The validity of that deed was subsequently challenged in an independent action brought by holders of mechanics' liens junior to the judgment liens, Case No. 79CVS1113, and the deed was set aside by order of superior court dated 12 October 1979. DuBose and Bernhardt timely appealed from that order.

On 12 October 1979, L.B. Hollowell, Jr., Trustee for Gastonia Mutual Savings and Loan Association, served notice of hearing on Horace M. DuBose, III, and Robert J. Bernhardt, as trustees, personally, and on A.C. Burgess, Jr., by publication, that Hollowell, as trustee under the deed of trust dated 30 May 1978 would appear before the clerk of superior court in Gaston County on 7 November 1979 to petition for authority to commence foreclosure proceedings pursuant to the power of sale contained in that deed of trust. Respondents DuBose and Bernhardt responded with a motion that the proceeding be stayed pending a disposition by this Court of the title dispute in Case No. 79CVS1113.

Following the hearing on 7 November 1979 at which Gastonia Mutual Savings and Loan Assocation, Horace M. DuBose, III and Robert J. Bernhardt appeared, the clerk of superior court entered an order finding that L.B. Hollowell, Jr., Trustee, was authorized to commence foreclosure proceedings in accordance with the terms of the deed of trust.

On appeal by respondents for hearing de novo before the judge of superior court in Gaston County, the parties stipulated to the following facts: Gastonia is the owner and holder of the note and deed of trust in controversy. Pursuant to the terms of the note and the deed of trust, Gastonia had advanced $36,884.00 as a construction loan between 28 June 1978 and 15 September 1978. In addition, Gastonia made advancements of $3,290.00 which were charged to that loan, with interest calculated and charged from the date of advancement. Payments had been made to Gastonia as follows:

Date	Amount	Purpose
7/20/78	$ 4.54	Interest
8/4/78	83.92	Interest
5/22/79	450.59	Principal and Interest
5/22/79	207.00	Insurance
6/12/79	450.59	Principal and Interest
Total	$1,196.64	

No installments of principal and interest were paid after 12 June 1979. The parties stipulated that Gastonia contended that the balance due on the note and deed of trust as of 8 November 1979 was $43,495.02 plus interest to date and that respondents contended that the balance on that date was not in excess of $37,794.76 plus interest to date.

At the hearing before Judge Thornburg on 27 November 1979, petitioner offered evidence that the balance due on the note as of that date was $43,238.09, taking into account a reimbursement to Gastonia for insurance payments which had not been included in the earlier computations. Respondents attempted to introduce evidence concerning the dispute over the balance due on the note and the deed of trust and over title; however, the trial court excluded the evidence on the grounds of relevancy. On 27 November 1979, Judge Thornburg entered an order finding that a deed of trust had been executed by A.C. Burgess, Jr. securing payment of a note, that default in the payment of principal, interest and insurance had occurred, that the deed of trust empowered the trustee named therein to sell the property in the event of default, that notice had been served upon all those entitled to such, and that the blance due and owing on the note and deed of trust as of 28 November 1979 was $43,238.09. Based on these findings, the court ordered that L.B. Hollowell, Jr., Trustee, be authorized to proceed with foreclosure in accordance with the terms of the deed of trust. From that order respondents appealed.

James C. Windham, Jr. for petitioner appellee.

Horace M. DuBose III and Robert J. Bernhardt for respondent appellants.

PARKER, Judge.

At issue in the present case is the scope of the procedures under G.S. 45-21.16 for hearing prior to the exercise of a power of sale under a deed of trust. G.S. 45-21.16(d), after providing for a hearing before the clerk of court in the county where the land is located, provides:

> If the clerk finds the existence of (i) valid debt of which the party seeking to foreclose is the holder, (ii) default, (iii) right to foreclose under the instrument, and (iv) notice to those entitled to such under subsection (b), then the clerk shall further find that the mortgagee or trustee can proceed under the instrument, and the mortgagee or trustee can give notice of and conduct a sale pursuant to the provisions of this Article.

On appeal from a determination by the clerk that the trustee is authorized to proceed, the judge of the district or superior court having jurisdiction is limited to determining the same four issues resolved by the clerk. *In re Watts*, 38 N.C. App. 90, 247 S.E. 2d 427 (1978). Respondents concede that the hearing is so limited, but contend that evidence that the amount due on the note was in dispute and that the mortgagee had been invited, but refused, to intervene in the litigation over the title to the subject property was relevant to a determination under G.S. 45-21.16(d)(iii) of a "right to foreclose under the instrument." Because the court failed to make findings of fact relating to the title litigation or the balance dispute, respondents argue that the requirements of G.S. 45-21.16(d) have not been met and that they have been denied due process of law. We disagree.

Historically, foreclosure under a power of sale has been a private contractual remedy. *Brown v. Jennings*, 188 N.C. 155, 124 S.E. 150 (1924); *Eubanks v. Becton*, 158 N.C. 230, 73 S.E. 1009 (1912). The intent of the 1975 General Assembly in enacting the notice and hearing provisions of G.S. 45-21.16 was not to alter the essentially contractual nature of the remedy, but rather to satisfy the minimum due process requirements of notice to interested parties and hearing prior to foreclosure and sale which the district court in *Turner v. Blackburn*, 389 F. Supp. 1250 (W.D.N.C. 1975), held that our then existing statutory procedure lacked. *In re Foreclosure of Sutton Investments*, 46 N.C. App. 654, 266 S.E. 2d 686 (1980). In light of this background, we construe G.S. 45-21.16 (d)(i) to permit the clerk to find a "valid debt of which the party seeking to foreclose is the holder" if there is competent evidence that the party seeking to foreclose is the holder of some valid debt, irrespective of the exact amount owed. Similarly, we construe G.S. 45-21.16(d)(iii) to permit the clerk to find a "right to foreclose under the instrument" if there is competent evidence that the terms of the deed of trust permit the exercise of the power of sale under the circumstances of the particular case. Thus, the fact that respondents in the present case dispute the balance owed on the note and deed of trust is irrelevant to the required findings under G.S. 45-21.16(d).

The parties' stipulations that Gastonia is the owner and holder of a duly executed note and deed of trust and that there was some amount outstanding on that debt amply supports the court's finding under G.S. 45-21.16(d)(i). It is true that the trial judge in the present case went beyond the required finding of a valid debt to conclude that the balance due and owing as of 28 November 1979 was $43,238.09. Because we hold that the determination of the amount owed on a debt is beyond the scope of the hearing under G.S. 45-21.16, that finding is mere surplusage and should be stricken. Similarly, in light of the express language in the deed of trust authorizing the trustee, upon application of the morgagee, to sell the encumbered property in the event of default, the court's finding of a "right to foreclose under the instrument" is also fully supported.

Contrary to respondents' contentions, a limited reading of G.S. 45-21.16(d) such as we adopt here neither deprives them of due process of law nor leaves them without remedy to their prejudice. Having received the notice and hearing intended by the statute, respondents are now able to utilize the procedure of G.S. 45-21.34 to enjoin the mortgage sale "upon [any] legal or equitable ground which the court may deem sufficient". If and when respondents choose to apply for injunctive relief, the dispute over the balance due on the note and deed of trust and the manner in which the balance was computed will certainly be relevant to the issue of respondents' right to relief. As to the title dispute, we note that the 12 October 1979 order of superior court declaring the sheriff's deed to DuBose and Bernhardt null and void was reversed by this Court in *Questor Corp. v. DuBose*, 46 N.C. App. 612, 265 S.E. 2d 501 (1980) and the cause was remanded with direction to dismiss the action challenging the validity of that deed.

Respondents have also challenged the setting of bond to cover appeal in the amount of $43,238.09 as excessive. Assuming arguendo that the bond was excessive, respondents have failed to show prejudice. The bond was in fact posted, and the appeal has been heard. As yet no motion has been made or other proceeding instituted to recover on the bond. Only when this is done should the rights and obligations of the several parties to the bond be determined.

The order appealed from authorizing the trustee to proceed with foreclosure under the terms of the power of sale contained in the deed of trust is modified by striking therefrom Finding of Fact No. 5 that "the balance due and owing on said note and deed of trust as of November 28, 1979 is Forty-three thousand two hundred thirty-eight and 09/100 ($43,238.09) Dollars," and as so modified, the order is affirmed.

Modified in part,

Affirmed in part.

Judges MARTIN (Harry C.) and HILL concur.

WILLIAM S. WOJSKO and MARCIA WOJSKO v. STATE OF NORTH CARO-
LINA; RUFUS EDMISTEN, ATTORNEY GENERAL; PERRY POWELL, DIREC-
TOR, NORTH CAROLINA JUSTICE ACADEMY

No. 804SC129

(Filed 15 July 1980)

1. State § 4.4– alleged breach of employment contract by State – application of sovereign immunity

Plaintiff's alleged claim for breach of a contract of employment with the State accrued on the date he was discharged, 1 August 1975. Therefore, the decision of *Smith* v. *State*, 289 NC 303, which abrogated the doctrine of sovereign immunity and is to be applied prospectively after 2 March 1976, did not apply to plaintiff's action, and it was barred by the doctrine of sovereign immunity.

2. State § 5.1– claim against State for intentional torts – application of sovereign immunity

Plaintiff's claim against the State and its agents for damages for the intentional torts of false representation and fraudulent inducement were barred by the doctrine of sovereign immunity since suits against the State, its agencies and its officers for alleged tortious acts can be maintained only to the extent authorized by the Tort Claims Act, and intentional torts are not compensable under the Tort Claims Act.

APPEAL by plaintiff, William S. Wojsko, from *Llewellyn*, *Judge.* Judgment entered 16 November 1979 in Superior Court, SAMPSON County. Heard in the Court of Appeals on 9 June 1980.

   In a complaint filed 1 March 1978 plaintiff purported to allege three causes of action against the State of North Carolina, Attorney General Edmisten, and director of the North Carolina Justice Academy Perry Powell, based on a contract of employment entered into between plaintiff and defendants on 20 January 1975. First, plaintiff claimed that, when he was hired as Director of Program Development and Evaluation for the Justice Academy, he was promised a certain status and "supervisory authority" which never materialized; that instead he was "relegated" to a status which was inferior to that promised; that he "had no real professional function . . . as promised"; and that such constituted a breach of his employment contract. Second, plaintiff alleged that by false representations the defendants had fraudulently induced him and his wife to leave their home and his job in Florida and to accept employment at the Justice Academy. Third, plaintiff alleged that he was wrongfully discharged from his employment on 1 August 1975. He claimed that his termination was motivated by defendants' "desire to punish" him because he had relayed to the "proper authorities" information concerning alleged illegal conduct at the Justice Academy "by certain high ranking individuals."

   Defendants moved to dismiss the complaint for its failure to state a claim for which relief could be granted, G.S. § 1A-1, Rule 12(b)(6), and for the reason that the doctrine of sovereign immunity barred the action. On 21 June 1978 the motion was allowed as to the plaintiff Marcia Wojsko and denied as to the plaintiff William Wojsko. Thereafter, defendants filed an answer admitting the contract, but denying that it had been breached in any particular.

   On 2 April 1979 defendants moved for summary judgment and supported their motion with, *inter alia*, the affidavit of William L. Brewer, Jr., who was business officer of the Justice Academy at the times pertinent to this lawsuit. In his affidavit, Brewer outlined the "organizational hierarchy" of the Academy to show that his position as business officer and plaintiff's position as director of program development and evaluation, as well as the chairmanship positions of two other departments, "were at the same level, and the persons occupying them were equal in responsibilities and authority," although they were subordinate to the director who had general supervision over the facility. Brewer also explained certain conduct and practices at the Academy which plaintiff had challenged as improper or illegal and related in detail the incident giving rise to plaintiff's termination of employment. Brewer avowed that on 29 July 1975 he was acting as director of the Academy in the absence and at the direction of the defendant Powell as evidenced by a memo to that effect prepared by Powell and posted by Powell's secretary; that plaintiff and his staff were preparing the Academy newsletter for mailing that day; that the mailing was supposed to be taken to the post office by 3:00 p.m.; and that a few minutes before 3:00, plaintiff came by his [Brewer's] office carrying the newsletters. Brewer described the ensuing incident as follows:

> I reminded him of the time deadline for mailing and directed him to take the newsletters to the Post Office. Mr. Wojsko then became abusive and insulting to me. He threw the newsletters down on the floor in front of my office. I told him to remove them and mail them. He cursed me and said that if I wanted the letters mailed, I could do it myself .... Following his outburst, he left the Academy for the remainder of the day.

Brewer reported the incident to Powell, whose deposition testimony was also relied on by defendants to support their summary judgment motion. Powell testified in substance that plaintiff had been offered the position of director of program development and evaluation at an annual salary of $15,468; that plaintiff had been hired for and was occupying that position when his employment with the Academy terminated; and that plaintiff had been asked to resign as a result of the incident regarding the newsletters which Powell had determined was an act of insubordination.

Powell testified further that the plaintiff's charges of misconduct related primarily to the practice of placing certain items of personal property belonging to the Academy in the homes of certain Academy employees. He said the essential reasons for so doing were (1) to guard against stealing which initially had been a serious problem at the facility, and (2) to provide accommodations for out-of-town visitors to the facility. In each instance challenged by plaintiff, Powell testified, the practice had been approved by the Attorney General's office.

In opposition to the defendants' motion for summary judgment, plaintiff submitted his affidavit and the affidavit of his wife, Marcia. Plaintiff detailed the allegations of his complaint, asserting that the position he had been promised was the "number 2 man" to the director and that he was supposed to be superior in authority to all personnel except the director. Instead, he said he found out after he came to the Academy that his position was inferior to the other directorial slots and that he was not second in command. He averred that the defendant Powell had a "personal grudge" against him and that he had maliciously been labeled a "trouble maker." With respect to the incident giving rise to his termination, plaintiff avowed that Brewer, not plaintiff, had become "abusive and insulting" when plaintiff brought the newsletters to Brewer's office. Brewer demanded that plaintiff put the newsletters down, and he did "just that." Then Brewer told plaintiff to remove the newsletters. Plaintiff stated, "I could see I could do no more with him because he was at this point red in the face, cursing and I simply left and went about my business." Plaintiff contended that his actions did not constitute insubordination for the reason that Brewer had no authority to give plaintiff "direct orders." Plaintiff and his wife also alleged that she had been promised a job as "Food Supervisor" at the Academy, that the promise was falsely made and had fraudulently induced them to leave Florida and come to North Carolina.

Plaintiff's deposition testimony was substantially the same, although he conceded that all he had been promised when the job offer was actually made was "just the job, the title and the money," and that he expected to be fired as a result of the incident with Brewer. Plaintiff reiterated his charges that "crimes" were being committed at the Academy, but stated, "I am not saying that the discovery of crimes at the Academy by me were [sic] the only reason for my termination."

On 19 November 1979, after considering "the briefs of counsel ... and the Complaint, the Answer, the Depositions ... , and the Affidavits . . . ," the trial court entered summary judgment for the defendants. Plaintiff appealed.

Bruce H. Robinson, Jr., for the plaintiff appellant.

Attorney General Edmisten, by Senior Deputy Attorney General Andrew A. Vanore, Jr., and Assistant Attorney General Kaye R. Webb, for the defendant appellees.

HEDRICK, Judge.

Plaintiff contends that the court erred in granting the defendants' motion for summary judgment for that the materials considered by the trial judge demonstrate that genuine issues of material fact exist with respect to each cause of action asserted. Assuming *arguendo* that the record before us does disclose issues of material fact with respect to the three claims asserted, summary judgment for defendants, nevertheless, was appropriate since the evidence in support of and in opposition to the motion affirmatively establishes that plaintiff's alleged claims are barred by the doctrine of sovereign immunity.

[1] Plaintiff's first cause of action alleges a claim for damages for the defendants' supposed breach of the terms of plaintiff's contract of employment with the State of North Carolina. Plaintiff denominates and consistently refers to this first cause of action as a claim for breach of contract. In similar fashion, plaintiff's third cause of action asserts a claim for damages for defendants' alleged breach of plaintiff's contract in wrongfully causing plaintiff to terminate his employment.

As recently settled by our Supreme Court, plaintiff's alleged claim for breach of contract accrued on the date he was discharged, which was 1 August 1975. *See MacDonald v. University of North Carolina*, 299 N.C. 457, 263 S.E. 2d 578 (1980). On 1 August 1975, the doctrine of sovereign immunity was alive and well in this State and operated to preclude suits against the State, its agencies and its officers for alleged breaches of contracts entered into with the State. Such a suit simply would not lie. Some four years ago, however, the doctrine was abrogated

in its entirety by our Supreme Court which held as follows in
Smith v. State, 289 N.C. 303, 320, 222 S.E.2d 412, 423-24 (1976):

> [W]henever the State of North Carolina, through its autho-
> rized officers and agencies, enters into a valid contract, the
> State implicitly consents to be sued for damages on the
> contract in the event it breaches the contract. Thus, in this
> case, and *in causes of action on contract arising after the
> filing date of this opinion, 2 March 1976*, the doctrine of
> sovereign immunity will not be a defense to the State.

[Emphasis added.] The abrogation of the doctrine was clearly
declared to be prospective only, and the subsequent decision in
MacDonald v. University of North Carolina, supra, resolved any
lingering doubts to the contrary. As the *MacDonald* Court
observed, 299 N.C. at 463, 263 S.E.2d at 582: "[W]e reaffirm the
conclusion of *Smith* in favor of a wholly prospective application
of the abrogation of the doctrine of sovereign immunity." Thus,
in the present case plaintiff's first and third claims arising out
of the alleged breach of his employment contract with the State
are barred by the doctrine of sovereign immunity.

[2] By his second cause of action, plaintiff asserts a claim for
damages for alleged false representations made by defendants
to fraudulently induce plaintiff to leave his home and his job in
Florida. This second claim clearly sounds in tort. Suits against
the State, its agencies and its officers for alleged tortious acts
can be maintained only to the extent authorized by the Tort
Claims Act, G.S. § 143-291 *et seq.*, and that Act authorizes recovery only for negligent torts. Intentional torts committed by
agents and officers of the State are not compensable under the
Tort Claims Act. *See, e.g., Givens v. Sellars*, 273 N.C. 44, 159
S.E.2d 530 (1968); *Braswell v. North Carolina A & T State University*, 5 N.C. App. 1, 168 S.E.2d 24 (1969).

Plaintiff in the present case seeks to recover damages for
the intentional torts of false representation and fraudulent
inducement. It has been observed by our Supreme Court that
"[i]n no forum is the [State] liable for fraudulent misrepresentations." *Davis v. North Carolina State Highway Commission*, 271
N.C. 405, 408, 156 S.E. 2d 685, 688 (1967). In *Davis* plaintiffs

alleged that the Highway Commission by false representations fraudulently and unnecessarily induced them to vacate their home two years before it was required for highway purposes. Noting that neither intentional misrepresentation nor fraud is negligence, the Court held that the plaintiffs' allegations were insufficient to state a cause of action against the Highway Commission. We find the decision in *Davis* plainly apposite to and dispositive of the question posed by the present plaintiff's second claim for relief. Consequently, that claim, too, is barred by the sovereign immunity of the State, its agencies and its officers.

We hold that the trial court correctly granted the defendants' motion for summary judgment and the judgment entered thereon is

Affirmed.

Judges MARTIN (Robert M.) and MARTIN (Harry C.) concur.

F.H. HOOD T/A HOOD CONSTRUCTION COMPANY v. SAMUEL A. FAULKNER ET UX DOLLY RUTH FAULKNER

No. 794DC1115

(Filed 15 July 1980)

1. **Contracts § 27.1– construction of house – recovery for additional labor and materials – sufficiency of evidence of contract**

In plaintiff's action to recover for additional labor and additional material which he allegedly supplied during the course of constructing a home for defendants, the trial court properly denied defendant's motion for a directed verdict where plaintiff established the existence of a contract whereby defendants were to pay him for extra work or additional materials required to be undertaken or supplied in building defendants' house; plaintiff offered plenary evidence of the nature and extent of additional work and services rendered; defendants accepted the services but refused to pay for all the additional work performed; plaintiff was therefore entitled to nominal damages at least, and the mere paucity of evidence as to the value of plaintiff's services would not entitle defendants to a directed verdict.

2. **Quasi Contracts and Restitution § 2.2– recovery for house construction – no agreement as to compensation – quantum meruit – failure to show reasonableness of charges**

   Where the parties' written agreement failed to address the question of how much plaintiff would be paid for extra work he performed or additional services he rendered in the construction of defendants' house, and the parties did not otherwise agree as to the amount of compensation plaintiff would receive, plaintiff's action to recover for the extra work was based on quantum meruit, and the proper measure of his recovery was the reasonable value of the services rendered to and accepted by defendants; therefore, defendants are entitled to a new trial where the judge at no point instructed the jury that it must determine from all the evidence the reasonable worth of the additional services rendered by plaintiff and that it could award plaintiff only an amount that represented a reasonable value, and plaintiff did not offer sufficient evidence of the reasonable value of the services for which he sought to hold defendants accountable.

APPEAL by defendant from *Erwin (E. Alex), Judge.* Judgment entered 24 August 1979 in District Court, ONSLOW County. Heard in the Court of Appeals on 15 May 1980.

This is a civil action wherein plaintiff seeks to recover $2,437.54 from defendants for "additional labor" and "additional material" which plaintiff allegedly supplied during the course of constructing a home for defendants. Plaintiff alleged in a verified complaint that he had entered into a written contract with the defendant Samuel Faulkner on 3 March 1976 "to partially construct a home for the Defendants"; that the contract provided that labor and materials supplied by plaintiff which were not specified in the agreement would be at extra cost to defendants; and that plaintiff had performed additional work and furnished additional materials the "charges and costs" of which amounted to a total due plaintiff of $2,437.54.

Answering, defendants denied the essential allegations of the complaint, alleged that they had fully paid plaintiff for all work performed by him pursuant to their contract, and asserted a counterclaim for damages of $7,000. In the counterclaim, defendants alleged that the plaintiff had breached the contract by failing to fully perform so that defendants found it necessary "to employ others to furnish and complete the work, etc., agreed to be performed and furnished by the plaintiff."

At the subsequent trial before a jury, the plaintiff's evidence in summary tended to show the following:

Plaintiff is a subcontractor and has been in the business "since the late fifties." He has worked on several buildings for the defendants on prior occasions. With respect to the contract involved in this case, the written agreement called for plaintiff to do the framing and inside and outside trim on the defendants' new house; to pour the concrete garage floor and the front and rear porches; and to install at specified places "premanufactured ornamental decoration." The contract price for the enumerated services was $13,000. According to plaintiff, defendant was to pay for the work "on the basis of [$700] a week, and he was to pay for extras as they were done." At the time of trial, defendant had paid plaintiff $9,400 of the contract total.

Plaintiff testified in considerable detail concerning the work he did and the materials he furnished in addition to the work which the contract called for him to perform. He said that all the extra work was requested and authorized by defendant, and that defendant promised to pay for the extras each time they discussed the matter.

On or about 8 June 1976 plaintiff presented defendant with a bill listing the extra work he had performed and showing a total of $2,428.67, "plus ten percent, . . . for office and bookkeeping." Defendant told plaintiff he would not pay "that much." Plaintiff then "pulled off the job site," leaving the inside trim work still to be done. He told defendant he was "quitting" until he collected for the extras. Defendant has paid him nothing on the bill, although he had paid plaintiff $1,814 "for the extras that I did do prior to the time that I presented him with this bill."

Two of plaintiff's employees on the job for defendant corroborated plaintiff's testimony concerning the extra work that was performed.

Defendant testified that he is a building contractor and has been in the business 15 to 20 years. He admitted that he had agreed to pay plaintiff extra for work he performed in addition

to that called for in the contract and said that he had paid
plaintiff for several extra things. However, with respect to the
extra work listed on the bill at issue in this lawsuit, he denied
approving everything listed, testified that some of the extra
work for which plaintiff was attempting to charge him was in
reality work necessary to correct plaintiff's mistakes, and
stated that he and plaintiff had never discussed or agreed on
the price of the extras claimed on the bill. In defendant's opinion, plaintiff had "overcharged" and had submitted a "dishonest bill." After plaintiff quit the job, defendant had to hire
another man to finish the work called for in the written contract.

At the conclusion of the evidence, the judge submitted the
following issues to the jury which were answered by it as indicated:

1. Was there an agreement that the plaintiff, F.H. Hood,
would receive compensation for the materials and services
furnished to the defendant, Samuel A. Faulkner?

ANSWER: YES.

2. Did the defendant, Samuel A. Faulkner breach the
agreement or contract with the plaintiff, F.H. Hood?

ANSWER: YES.

3. [W]hat amount of damages, if any, has the plaintiff,
F.H. Hood, sustained?

ANSWER: $2,437.54.

4. Did the plaintiff, F.H. Hood, fail to substantially
perform his obligations arising out of the agreement or
contract?

ANSWER: No.

From judgment entered on the verdict, defendant
appealed.

Gaylor & Edwards, by Jimmy F. Gaylor, for the plaintiff appellee.

Turner & Harrison, by Fred W. Harrison, for the defendant appellant.

HEDRICK, Judge.

[1] Initially, defendant contends that the court erred in refusing to grant his motion for a directed verdict. He argues that there was no "proper evidence" from which the jury could determine damages since there was no evidence as to the value of the services rendered by plaintiff other than his bill. We disagree that the mere paucity of evidence as to the value of plaintiff's services in connection with the extra work performed entitles the defendant to a directed verdict. Plaintiff established the existence of a contract whereby defendant was to pay him for extra work or additional materials required to be undertaken or supplied in building defendant's house. Plaintiff offered plenary evidence of the nature and extent of additional work and services rendered. Defendant accepted the services, but has refused to pay for all the additional work performed. "The law implies a promise to pay for services rendered by one party to another where the recipient knowingly and voluntarily accepts the services and there is no showing that the services were gratuitously given." *Harrell v. W. B. Lloyd Construction Co.*, 41 N.C. App. 593, 595, 255 S.E.2d 280, 281 (1979). *See also Johnson v. Sanders*, 260 N.C. 291, 132 S.E.2d 582 (1963). In such a case, plaintiff is entitled at least to nominal damages. *Bryan Builders Supply v. Midyette*, 274 N.C. 264, 162 S.E.2d 507 (1968); *Gales v. Smith*, 249 N.C. 263, 106 S.E.2d 164 (1958). Thus, the trial court properly denied defendant's motion for a directed verdict. *See Harrell v. W.B. Lloyd Construction Co., supra; Pilot Freight Carriers, Inc. v. David G. Allen Co., Inc.*, 22 N.C. App. 442, 206 S.E.2d 750 (1974), *cert. denied*, 423 U.S. 1055 (1976).

[2] However, error in the charge requires that we reverse the judgment of the District Court and remand the matter for a new trial. It is uncontradicted that the written agreement between these parties failed to address the question of how much the plaintiff would be paid for extra work he performed or

additional services he rendered in the construction of defendant's house. Neither does the evidence support even an inference that the parties ever agreed otherwise as to the amount of
compensation plaintiff would receive. Plaintiff's action, then,
clearly sounds in *quantum meruit* and is based on the promise
to pay which the law implies. The proper measure of plaintiff's
recovery in such a case is the reasonable value of the services
rendered to and accepted by the defendant. "[W]hen there is no
agreement as to the amount of compensation to be paid for
services, the person performing them is entitled to recover
what they are reasonably worth, based on the time and labor
expended, skill, knowledge and experience involved, and other
attendant circumstances, . . ." *Turner v. Marsh Furniture Co.*,
217 N.C. 695, 697, 9 S.E.2d 379, 380 (1940). *See also Austin v.
Raines*, 45 N.C. App. 709, 264 S.E.2d 121 (1980). *See generally,* 5
A. Corbin, *Contracts* § 1112 (1964); 66 Am. Jur. 2d, *Restitution
and Implied Contracts* §§ 24, 28 (1973).

With respect to the issue of damages in the case before us,
the judge charged as follows:

> A party injured by a breach of contract is entitled to be
> placed insofar as this can be done by money in the same
> position he would have occupied if the contract had been
> performed. The party injured by the breach is entitled to
> recover for gains prevented as well as losses sustained
> because of the breach. Now the plaintiff contends of course
> that he has been damaged in the amount of $2,437.54, *that's
> the value of his services* and materials that he has indicated
> that were expended on behalf of the defendant for services
> requested and materials provided.

> . . .

> So I finally instruct you on this issue that if you find by
> the greater weight of the evidence that F.H. Hood has
> sustained some amount of damages under the rule that I
> have explained to you, and if you find by the greater weight
> of the evidence that the damages were reasonably foresee-
> able at the time the contract was made, then you would
> answer the issue by writing that amount in the blank space
> provided. [Our emphasis.]

Hood v. Faulkner

The portion of the charge quoted above constitutes the court's entire instruction regarding the measure of damages recoverable in this case. It obviously is erroneous since at no point did the judge instruct the jury that it must determine from all the evidence adduced the reasonable worth of the additional services rendered by plaintiff and that it could award plaintiff only an amount that represented a reasonable value. Indeed, the charge amounts almost to a peremptory instruction that the jury award plaintiff the total sum shown on his bill. While the plaintiff's bill is some evidence of the value of his services, it is by no means conclusive and, standing alone, is insufficient to support an award for the amount shown. *Harrell v. W.B. Lloyd Construction Co., supra; Pilot Freight Carriers, Inc. v. David G. Allen Co., Inc., supra.* Nor is the plaintiff's opinion that the amount of his bill is reasonable sufficient to sustain an award for such sum. *Austin v. Raines, supra.* The reasonable value of services rendered is an objective measure and "is determined largely by the nature of the work and the customary rate of pay for such work in the community and at the time the work was performed." 66 Am. Jur. 2d, *supra* § 28 at 973. *Accord, Cline v. Cline,* 258 N.C. 295, 128 S.E.2d 401 (1962); *Harrell v. W.B. Lloyd Construction Co., supra.*

In our opinion the plaintiff in this case did not offer sufficient evidence of the reassonable value of the services for which he sought to hold defendant accountable. His testimony that the rates shown on the bill were customary for him, and that he based the total amount on the hourly rate he paid his employees plus ten percent, establishes no more than a formula by which he arrived at a total and a reiteration of his opinion that his bill was reasonable. There is no independent evidence or objective indicia by which to gauge whether the plaintiff's rates were customary and reasonable in the business, in the community, and at the time. For this reason as well as for error in the charge, defendant is entitled to a

New trial.

Judges PARKER and VAUGHN concur.

VERNON M. HOLT v. VERDIE R. HOLT and WILLIAM S. HOLT

No. 8020SC151

(Filed 15 July 1980)

1. Executors and Administrators § 33– family settlement agreement – construction – statute of frauds

A jury question was presented as to whether a family settlement agreement provided that one defendant was to receive a larger share of testatrix's real estate which would be accomplished by probating testatrix's will but not a codicil thereto and executing deeds to complete the transaction or whether the agreement was that plaintiff and defendants would share equally in the real estate and this would be accomplished by probating the will but not the codicil. If the agreement required the execution of deeds, it is a partially executed agreement to convey real estate and is barred by the statute of frauds.

2. Executors and Administrators § 33.1– family settlement agreement – absence of exigency not contemplated by testatrix

A family settlement agreement was not invalid because an exigency or emergency not contemplated by the testatrix did not exist.

3. Executors and Administrators § 33– family settlement agreement – agreement not to probate codicil

A family settlement agreement was supported by consideration and was not void as against public policy because it included an agreement not to probate a codicil to testatrix's will.

APPEAL by a plaintiff from *Wood, Judge.* Judgment entered 1 November 1979 in Superior Court, STANLY County. Heard in the Court of Appeals 11 June 1980.

This action was commenced by the filing of a complaint in which the plaintiff alleged he had entered into a family settlement agreement with the defendants which the defendants had refused to carry out. The defendants answered pleading, among other things, the statute of frauds and illegal consideration. Both sides moved for summary judgment. The pleadings and affidavits filed for and against the motions for summary judgment established that the parties to this action are the only children of Annie H. Holt, deceased. On 29 October 1964, Annie H. Holt executed a will which left her estate equally to her three sons. On 11 September 1969, Annie H. Holt executed a codicil to her will which excluded the plaintiff from any participation in her estate. Annie H. Holt died on 25 March 1977. Shortly after the death of Mrs. Holt, her three sons met in the office of S. Craig Hopkins, an attorney in Albemarle, North Carolina. Mr. Hopkins read the will and the codicil to the three sons of Mrs. Holt. An argument ensued between the three sons and other members of the family who were present. Mr. Hopkins explained to them that they could divide the estate equally if that were the wishes of the three sons. The three sons agreed to do this. Verdie R. Holt and William S. Holt each said in affidavits the following:

"[We] were informed by Attorney S. Craig Hopkins that we would allow Vernon M. Holt to share in the estate in this matter by probating only the Will, destroying the Codicil, and executing Deeds along with Vernon that divided the estate into three shares; that it was agreed that this would be done and that it was further agreed that . . . William S. Holt, would receive the largest share because of a prior conveyance of some land to [Verdie R. Holt] by our father, James Marshall Holt."

Vernon M. Holt stated in an affidavit the following:

"[A]fter a discussion among and between myself and my two brothers, the Defendants, I and my two brothers, the Defendants, agreed . . . I and my two brothers, the Defendants, would share equally in my Mother's Estate and that the will, Exhibit A, would constitute the Last Will and Testament of Annie H. Holt.

* * *

That after reaching said Agreement, we were informed by S. Craig Hopkins that this Agreement could be carried out simply by probating only the will . . . ."

The codicil was torn and the pieces given to Mr. Hopkins who kept them. The will was probated on 28 March 1977. A division deed was drawn for Annie H. Holt's property, but the plaintiff did not feel he was being treated fairly in the division and refused to sign it. When the plaintiff refused to sign, the defendants reconstituted the codicil and offered it for probate. The codicil was probated on 4 August 1977. Verdie R. Holt was appointed executor of the estate.

The court granted summary judgment for the defendants.

Lefler and Bahner, by John M. Bahner, Jr., and James E. Griffin, for plaintiff appellant.

Brown, Brown and Brown, by Richard Lane Brown III and Steven F. Blalock, for defendant appellees.

WEBB, Judge.

[1] It is clear from the evidence produced by both sides that there was a family settlement agreement in the case sub judice. There is a conflict as to what constituted the agreement. The defendants contend in their affidavits that the agreement was that William S. Holt would receive the largest share and deeds would be drawn accordingly after the will, but not the codicil, was probated. The plaintiff contends that the agreement was that the parties would share equally in the estate and this would be accomplished by probating the will but not the codicil. The part of the family settlement agreement that involved a conveyance or division of the real estate would be governed by the statute of frauds. A partially executed contract to convey real estate is subject to the statute of frauds. *Pickelsimer v. Pickelsimer,* 257 N.C. 696, 127 S.E. 2d 557 (1962); *Duckett v. Harrison,* 235 N.C. 145, 69 S.E. 2d 176 (1952); *Ebert v. Disher,* 216 N.C. 36, 3 S.E. 2d 301 (1939). A fully executed contract is not subject to the statute of frauds. *Dobias v. White,* 240 N.C. 680, 83 S.E. 2d 785 (1954). We hold that it is an issue for the jury as to whether the defendants' version of the agreement is correct, that is, whether William S. Holt was to receive a larger share of the real estate which would be accomplished by probating the will but not the codicil and executing deeds to complete the transaction, or whether the plaintiff's version is correct, that is, the agreement was that the three brothers would share equally in the real estate and this would be accomplished by probating the will but not the codicil. If the defendants' version is correct, the family settlement agreement, so far as the real estate is

concerned, is a partially executed agreement to convey real estate and is barred by the statute of frauds. If the plaintiff's version is correct, it is a fully executed agreement and is not subject to the statute of frauds. As to the personal property, all the evidence is that the parties agreed to share equally. The plaintiff was entitled to have his motion for summary judgment allowed as to the personal property in the estate.

The appellant contends that the family settlement agreement is nothing more than a renunciation of a devise and is not covered by the statute of frauds. He cites *Reese v. Carson*, 3 N.C. App. 99, 164 S.E. 2d 99 (1968) for this proposition. *Reese* involved the renunciation of a bequest of personal property. If the action of the defendants in the case sub judice was a renunciation of a devise, its effect was to convey real estate to the plaintiff, and we hold the statute of frauds must be taken into account.

[2] The defendants contend the family settlement agreement in the case sub judice is not valid because an exigency or emergency not contemplated by the testatrix does not exist. Defendants cite *O'Neil v. O'Neil*, 271 N.C. 106, 155 S.E. 2d 495 (1967) for this proposition. It is true that *O'Neil* contains language that a "will or testamentary trust may be modified by a family settlement agreement only where there exists some exigency or emergency not contemplated by the testator." The case sub judice is factually distinguishable from *O'Neil*. In that case, the beneficiaries of a trust attempted to change the terms of the trust to postpone the vesting of the minors' interest. In the case sub judice, all the parties who made the family settlement agreement had reached their majorities. The language of *O'Neil* is inconsistent with many cases. *See Wagner v. Honbaier*, 248 N.C. 363, 103 S.E. 2d 474 (1958). We hold it does not govern in the case sub judice.

[3] The defendants also contend the family settlement agreement is based on illegal and unlawful consideration, if on any consideration at all, and is not binding. The defendants argue that an agreement not to probate a codicil is illegal and against public policy and should not be enforced. We believe *In re Will of Pendergrass*, 251 N.C. 737, 112 S.E. 2d 562 (1960) governs this point. That case involved an agreement not to probate a will.

The Court pointed out it is against public policy and a misdemeanor under G.S. 14-77 to conceal or destroy a will fraudulently. It held that the agreement should be enforced in that case, saying the rights of creditors were not impaired and the agreement was openly and fairly made between adults. As for consideration, the Court said, "[t]he mutual promises for the sake of family harmony and good will, the settlement of controversies and the purpose to avoid further litigation outweigh mere pecuniary considerations." We hold that under *Pendergrass*, the family settlement agreement in the case sub judice was supported by sufficient consideration and is not against public policy.

The defendants next argue that the policy underlying family settlement agreements, that is the promotion of family harmony, would not be promoted by the enforcement of this agreement. The defendants point out that the agreement has not brought harmony to the Holt family. We do not believe this is sufficient reason to set aside the agreement. The policy of promoting family harmony remains, if it has not succeeded for the Holt family, and perhaps it may do so yet.

The appellees' last contention is that there was no agreement but simply a "ruse" by the plaintiff to get the defendants to give him a part of their inheritance. Whatever the motive of the plaintiff, all the evidence shows the parties came to an agreement and the parties are bound by it so far as it is not barred by the statute of frauds.

For the reasons stated in this opinion, we reverse and remand to the superior court for a judgment in plaintiff's favor as to an equal division of personal property in the estate and for trial on the issue of a family settlement agreement as to the real property.

Reversed and remanded.

Judges PARKER and CLARK concur.

State v. Dunbar

STATE OF NORTH CAROLINA v. MERRITTE L. DUNBAR

No. 8025SC125

(Filed 15 July 1980)

1. **Constitutional Law § 50– delay between indictment and trial – forgery indictments – no relation to earlier indictments for false pretense**

    There was no merit to defendant's contention that he was not tried within the period provided in G.S. 15A-701(a1)(1) in that he had been indicted more than 120 days prior to the trial, since defendant was indicted for forgery on 20 August 1979 and tried on 4 September 1979, and the 20 August 1979 bills of indictment for forgery did not relate back to 30 April 1979 indictments for false pretense, though both sets of indictments arose out of the same transactions.

2. **Forgery § 2.2– fictitious name signed to check – showing not required – no authority to sign check shown**

    In a prosecution for forgery it was not necessary for the State to prove that the name "B. Hansely" signed by defendant to three checks was that of a fictitious person or a real person, since the evidence showed that the instrument was executed without authority, as neither "B. Hansely" nor the name of defendant appeared on the signature card of the S & M Paint Company account, upon which the checks in question were written; moreover, proof that no person bearing the name signed to a check has any right to draw on the party to whom it is directed is prima facie evidence that the name is fictitious.

3. **Forgery § 2– false instrument – signature on check not on signature card – instructions proper**

    The trial court in a forgery prosecution properly charged the jury on the element that the instrument be false where the court instructed the jury that executing a check on a bank account by signing a name not authorized by the signature card would be a false making of a check.

APPEAL by defendant from *Kirby, Judge.* Judgment entered 5 September 1979 in Superior Court, CATAWBA County. Heard in the Court of Appeals 9 June 1980.

In 13 bills of indictment proper in form, defendant was charged with 12 counts of forgery and 1 count of forgery and uttering. Defendant was tried and convicted on 3 counts of forgery. From judgment imposing sentence, defendant appeals.

Attorney General Edmisten, by Special Deputy Attorney General Isaac T. Avery III, for the State.

J. Bryan Elliott for defendant appellant.

MARTIN (Robert M.), Judge.

[1] Defendant by his first assignment of error contends that he was not tried within the period provided in G.S. 15A-701(al)(1) in that he had been indicted more than 120 days prior to the trial.

The procedural events upon which defendant grounds his argument are as follows: Defendant was originally indicted on 22 August 1977 for obtaining property by false pretense. These charges were dismissed with leave by the State on 29 June 1978 because the defendant failed to appear for arraignment and could not be found. On 12 April 1979 an order for arrest was served upon defendant for five true bills of indictment returned by the grand jury for the crime of false pretenses which order was issued on 24 August 1977. After the order for arrest was executed, warrants for arrest on the false pretenses charges were served on 17 April 1979. These warrants were subsequently dismissed on 8 May 1979 because five true bills of indictment for the offenses of false pretenses had been returned on 30 April 1979. Defendant was served with the indictments for false pretenses on 7 May 1979.

Thereafter, defendant was indicted on 20 August 1979 on 12 counts of forgery and 1 count of forgery and uttering arising from the same transactions on which the false pretenses indictments were based. These bills were served on defendant on 27 August 1979. Defendant was tried on three of the forgery charges on 4 September 1979.

G.S. 15A-701(al)(1) provides that

Notwithstanding the provisions of G.S. 15A-701(a) the trial of a defendant charged with a criminal offense who is arrested, served with criminal process, waives an indictment or is indicted, on or after October 1, 1978, and before October 1, 1980, shall begin within the time limits specified below:

(1) Within 120 days from the date the defendant is arrested, served with criminal process, waives an indictment, or is indicted, whichever occurs last; . . .

It is clear that the trial of defendant on 4 September 1979 for the offenses of forgery was within 120 days from the date from the indictments for those offenses on 20 August 1979 and service of the indictments on 27 August 1979. The crux of defendant's argument is that the 20 August 1979 bills of indictment for forgery upon which defendant was tried would relate back to the 30 April 1979 indictments for false pretense since both sets of indictments arose out of the same transactions. Defendant cites no authority for the proposition that the time limit relates back and we do not accept such a proposition. We note further that the provision of G.S. 15A-703 that a dismissal with prejudice shall bar further prosecution of the defendant for the same offense or an offense based on the same act or transaction has no application to the present case since at the time of the trial on 4 September 1979 there had been no dismissal of the charges of false pretenses or the remaining charges of forgery.

The defendant by his second assignment of error contends the court erred in failing to grant defendant's motion to dismiss pursuant to G.S. 15A-1227. A motion pursuant to G.S. 15A-1227 tests the sufficiency of the evidence to sustain a conviction and in that respect is identical to a motion for judgment as in the case of nonsuit under G.S. 15-173. *State v. Smith*, 40 N.C. App. 72, 252 S.E. 2d 535 (1979). In determining the sufficiency of the State's evidence, the court must consider the evidence "in the light most favorable to the State, all contradictions and discrepancies therein must be resolved in its favor and it must be given the benefit of every reasonable inference to be drawn from the evidence." *State v. Yellorday*, 297 N.C. 574, 578, 256 S.E. 2d 205, 209 (1979) (quoting from *State v. Cutler*, 271 N.C. 379, 382, 156 S.E. 2d 679, 681 (1967)). If there is substantial evidence that the offense charged in the bill of indictment, or a lesser offense included therein has been committed, and that the defendant committed it, the case is properly for the jury. *State v. Burke*, 36 N.C. App. 577, 244 S.E. 2d 477 (1978).

In the present case, defendant was tried on three indictments charging him with forgery of checks each in the amount of $136.44. Three elements are necessary to constitute a forgery: (1) a false making or alteration of some instrument in writing; (2) a fraudulent intent; and (3) the instrument must be apparently capable of effecting a fraud. *State v. Phillips*, 256 N.C. 445, 124 S.E. 2d 146 (1962), *State v. Dixon*, 185 N.C. 727, 117 S.E. 170 (1923). As to the first requirement of the offense, defendant contends that the State failed to prove that the instrument was false, that is executed without authority.

> If the name signed to a negotiable instrument ... is fictitious, of necessity, the name must have been affixed by one without authority. ... However, if the purported maker is a real person and actually exists, the State is required to show not only that the signature in question is not genuine, but was made by defendant without authority.

State v. Phillips, 256 N.C. 445, 448, 124 S.E. 2d 146, 148 (1962). Defendant argues that because the State failed to offer any evidence as to the identity or existence of the purported maker of the checks, B. Hansely, there was no proof that the signing of the check was false and unauthorized. We do not agree. The critical element is not the identity of the maker, real or fictitious, but whether the maker had authority to execute the instrument.

The State's evidence in the present case showed that an account had been opened at the First National Bank of Catawba County for S & M Paint Company on 13 September 1976. The signature of Sherman Dunbar appears on the signature card for that account. On 24 September 1976 three checks were written on the S & M Paint Company account. All of the checks bore the name of B. Hansely as maker and all were made out to and endorsed by Sherman Dunbar. The testimony of the FBI handwriting expert was omitted from the record on appeal by stipulation of the State and the defendant. The defendant further stipulated in the record on appeal that he had signed the checks "as the maker thereof by placing the name 'B. Hansely' upon said checks as the maker thereof."

State v. Dunbar

[2] The State's evidence that neither B. Hansley nor the defendant appear on the signature card of the S & M Paint Company account is sufficient evidence from which the jury could find that neither B. Hansely nor the defendant had any authority from the owner of the checks to sign them. *See State v. Greenlee,* 272 N.C. 651, 159 S.E. 2d 22 (1968). Under these circumstances, it is not necessary for the State to prove that the name B. Hansely signed by defendant is that of a fictitious person or a real person. In either case, the evidence shows the instrument was executed without authority. Moreover, we note that proof that no person bearing the name signed to a check has any right to draw on the party to whom it is directed is *prima facie* evidence that the name is fictitious. 37 C.J.S. Forgery § 95.

[3] Defendant by his fourth assignment of error contends the court erred in its definition of forgery by failing to require the State to show whether defendant made a false instrument by affixing an actual person's name without authority. As outlined above, the essential element is that the instrument be false, i.e. made without authority.

"The fact that the drawer of a check lacks authority is one characteristic which renders an instrument false, and an instruction including the requirement that there be a false making encompasses the requirement that the instrument be drawn by one who lacks authority". *State v. McAllister,* 287 N.C. 178, 188, 214 S.E. 2d 75, 83 (1975). The trial court charged the jury as follows:

> First, the State must prove that the defendant falsely made a check.

> Executing a check on a bank account with a specific account number, with a specific authorized signature, by the signing of another name to the check not authorized by the signature card would be a false making of a check.

We hold the court has properly charged on the element that the instrument be false, that is made without the authority of the owner, where evidence tends to show defendant signed a name to a check which was not authorized by the signature card.

Defendant by his third assignment of error contends the trial court's summary of the evidence contained a statement of material fact not in evidence which prejudiced the defendant. In its summary of the evidence, the court stated:

> In this case, members of the jury, there has been evidence offered which tends to show but what it does show is for you to decide, . . . that these checks were then sent to the bank but not paid by the bank because of the lack of authorized signature on the checks; . . . Now that very briefly is just what some of the evidence tends to show but members of the jury is for you to say what if anything the evidence does in fact show, you are the triers of the facts.

The State's evidence showed that only the signature of Sherman Dunbar was on the signature card; that none of the checks were honored by the bank and that records show there were insufficient funds on deposit to pay the three checks. In light of our holding that the absence of defendant's or B. Hansely's name on the signature card is sufficient circumstantial evidence from which the jury could conclude that defendant lacked authorization to draw the check, we do not think the court's charge contained a misstatement of material fact to the prejudice of the defendant. Defendant received a fair trial free of prejudicial error.

No error.

Judges HEDRICK and MARTIN (Harry C.) concur.

GOODMAN TOYOTA, INC. v. CITY OF RALEIGH

No. 7910SC921

(Filed 15 July 1980)

Injunctions § 5– sign control ordinance – erroneous preliminary injunction

   The trial court erred in entering a temporary restraining order enjoining defendant city from enforcing its sign control ordinance by prohibiting plaintiff's use of a blimp and searchlight where plaintiff alleged only that the enforcement of the ordinance against it will "irreparably injure the property rights of this plaintiff" and "will cost it thousands of dollars in loss of property and profits," and the record contains no facts to show the extent to which plaintiff's business or goodwill may be damaged by enforcement of the ordinance against plaintiff or that plaintiff will suffer irreparable harm by such enforcement.

APPEAL by defendant from *Bailey, Judge.* Judgment and order entered 14 May 1979 in Superior Court, WAKE County. Heard in the Court of Appeals 26 March 1980.

Plaintiff brought this action to restrain the City of Raleigh from enforcing a recently enacted sign control ordinance, Ordinance No. (1979) 982 TC 96, as it "relates or might relate to the operation by the plaintiff of a helium filled blimp and a searchlight." The ordinance was meant to regulate all types of signs within the city, and specifically prohibited windblown devices, flashing signs, and temporary portable signs. In its complaint, plaintiff alleged that the blimp and searchlight "have come to form a distinctive logo or trade symbol in the minds of the public and portray to the public the idea of a special sale and special prices at Goodman Toyota, Inc., when the sales promotions are carried out . . . ." Plaintiff alleged that enforcement of the ordinance against it, and requiring it to remove and abandon the blimp and searchlight will "irreparably injure the property rights of this plaintiff" and "will cost it thousands of dollars in loss of property and profits."

A temporary restraining order was granted enjoining defendant from enforcement of its ordinance, and a hearing was scheduled for the purpose of determining whether the restraining order should be continued until the final determination of plaintiff's action. On hearing, plaintiff presented its verified complaint, memoranda of legal authority and an exhibit. Defendant offered oral evidence which tended to show plaintiff's blimp and searchlight are subject to the ordinance and that if plaintiff is allowed "to maintain its windblown device and searchlight," enforcement of the sign ordinance will be significantly impaired. Defendant also submitted exhibits explaining the background of the sign control ordinance, and a memorandum of law relating to the ordinance and its application. On 14 May 1979, the trial court issued a preliminary injunction after making certain findings, including the following to which defendant excepts:

5. That at the hearing, a showing was made which raised serious questions, under (a) the Raleigh ordinances, (b) state and federal law, and (c) the federal and state constitutions as to the legality of the ordinance as applied to plaintiff's operations.

EXCEPTION NO. 1

6. That enforcement of the act, pending final hearing, would inflict irreparable damage upon the plaintiff.

EXCEPTION NO. 2

7. That the Court further finds as a fact that the plaintiff does not have any other adequate remedy at law at the present stage of this matter.

EXCEPTION NO. 3

IT IS THEREFORE ORDERED AND DECREED that the defendant be, and it is hereby restrained and enjoined until a final hearing of the cause on its merits from interfering with the operation of the plaintiff's blimp and searchlight.

EXCEPTION NO. 4

Defendant filed motions pursuant to North Carolina Rules of Civil Procedure 52 and 59 requesting the court to amend its findings, or, alternatively, to grant a new hearing on the matter, which were denied. Defendant appeals, assigning error to the trial court's granting the preliminary injunction prohibiting enforcement of defendant's sign control ordinance.

Blanchard, Tucker, Twiggs & Denson, by Charles F. Blanchard and Charles H. Mercer, Jr., for plaintiff appellee.

City Attorney Thomas A. McCormick, Jr., by Associate City Attorney Ira J. Botvinick, for defendant appellant.

MORRIS, Chief Judge.

Defendant argues that the preliminary injunction is improper in that enforcement of the ordinance will not irreparably injure plaintiff; that plaintiff, in its application for a preliminary injunction, failed to set out with particularity facts showing irreparable injury; and that any injunction restraining the enforcement of the ordinance is contrary to prior decisions involving injunctions and sign regulations. We agree with defendant that plaintiff has failed to set forth with particularity facts to support its claim of irreparable injury, and accordingly reverse the trial court's granting a preliminary injunction prohibiting the enforcement of defendant's sign control ordinance.

In *United Telephone Co. of the Carolinas, Inc. v. Universal Plastics*, 287 N.C. 232, 235, 214 S.E. 2d 49, 51 (1975), we find the following language pertinent to the case before us:

A prohibitory preliminary injunction is granted only when irreparable injury is real and immediate. Its purpose is to preserve the status quo of the subject matter involved until a trial can be had on the merits. 4 Strong, N.C. Index 2d, Injunctions § 1, p. 388 (1968); *In re Reassignment of Albright*, 278 N.C. 664, 180 S.E. 2d 798 (1971); *Hall v. Morganton*, 268 N.C. 599, 151 S.E. 2d 201 (1966); *Starbuck v. Havelock*, 252 N.C. 176, 113 S.E. 2d 278 (1960). The issuing court, after weighing the equities and the advantages and disadvantages to the parties, determines in its sound discretion whether an interlocutory injunction should be granted or refused. The court cannot go further and determine the final rights of the parties which must be reserved for the trial of the action. 2 McIntosh, North Carolina Practice and Procedure 2d, § 2219 (1956); *In re Reassignment of Albright, supra; Grantham v. Nunn*, 188 N.C. 239, 124 S.E. 309 (1924). "In passing on the validity of an interlocutory injunction the appellate court is not bound by the findings of fact made by the issuing court, but may review the evidence and make

its own findings . . . ." *In re Reassignment of Albright, supra.*
*Accord, Conference v. Creech and Teasley v. Creech and
Miles,* 256 N.C. 128, 123 S.E. 2d 619 (1962); *Lance v. Cogdill,*
238 N.C. 500, 78 S.E. 2d 319 (1953).

An applicant for a preliminary injunction has the burden of
showing a reasonable probability of substantial and irreparable injury to the applicant from the continuance of the activity
of which it complains to the final determination of the action.
Board of Provincial Elders v. Jones, 273 N.C. 174, 159 S.E. 2d 545
(1968). The applicant must do more than merely allege that
irreparable injury will occur. "The applicant is required to set
out with particularity facts supporting such statements so the
court can decide for itself if irreparable injury will occur." *United Telephone Co. of the Carolinas, Inc. v. Universal Plastics,
Inc., supra,* 287 N.C. at 236, 214 S.E. 2d at 52.

The record in the present case fails to disclose any facts
from which we can determine that plaintiff will suffer irreparable harm if defendant's sign control ordinance is enforced
against it. We find only the allegation that plaintiff will suffer
injury in that "removal and abandonment [of the blimp and
searchlight] will cost it many thousands of dollars in loss of
property and profits," and that it will either have to remove the
objects or "subject itself to daily arrest and fines . . . ." There is
nothing which would permit us to know the extent to which
plaintiff's business or goodwill may be damaged by the imposition of defendant's ordinance. The lack of particularity in plaintiff's application is in stark contrast to other decisions where
our courts have upheld the granting of a preliminary injunction
dealing with alleged business losses. *See, e.g., Schloss v. Jami-
son,* 258 N.C. 271, 128 S.E. 2d 590 (1962). *Cf. United Telephone Co.
of the Carolinas, Inc. v. Universal Plastics, Inc., supra* (issuance
of preliminary injunction on facts alleged held error).

It is not necessary for us to determine whether plaintiff has
the right to the continued use of its blimp and searchlight in the
face of defendant's ordinance prohibiting such activity. This
and all other issues raised by the pleadings will be determined
at the final hearing of this action.

We are aware of *State v. School*, 299 N.C. 351, 261 S.E. 2d 908 (1980), where the Court, in a unanimous opinion, said that unless a substantial right of appellant is endangered, appeal from the granting of a preliminary restraining order cannot be maintained. While we do not think appellant here has shown deprivation of a substantial right, we have, nevertheless, entertained the appeal. Future appeals of this nature will be examined in the light of *State v. School, supra*.

For the reasons stated, the order of the trial court granting the preliminary injunction is reversed and the case is remanded for trial on its merits.

Reversed and remanded.

Judges PARKER and WELLS concur.

STATE OF NORTH CAROLINA v. RANDY ANSON CULPEPPER and TREVOR DALE GURGANUS

No. 801SC132

(Filed 15 July 1980)

Criminal Law § 50.1– opinion testimony – witness's knowledge of facts not shown – no proper hypothetical question

   In a prosecution of defendants for conspiring to burn a building and personal property therein with intent to prejudice the insurer, the trial court properly excluded a witness's testimony as to his opinion that the char pattern on the floor of the second story of the building did not indicate the use of an accelerant and that there was only one origin to the fire for the reason that defendants failed to demonstrate the witness's personal knowledge of essential facts, and defendants did not ask the witness's opinion in response to a hypothetical question which included the essential facts to be assumed.

APPEAL by defendants from *Brown, Judge*. Judgments entered 12 June 1979 in Superior Court, PASQUOTANK County. Heard in the Court of Appeals on 9 June 1980.

Defendants were indicted on two counts of conspiring with each other to burn a building in which a nightclub and tavern establishment was located, and for conspiring to burn the personal property located therein with the intent to prejudice the insurer of said property. Defendants were also indicted on two counts each of the substantive offenses of burning a building and burning personal property.

Defendants were found guilty as charged on all counts.

From judgments imposing prison sentences of not less than nor more than 15 years on the count which charged burning of a building, 5 years on the count which charged burning of personal property, and 2 years on the counts which charged conspiracy to burn a building and conspiracy to burn personal property, each defendant appealed.

Attorney General Edmisten, by Special Deputy Attorney General John R.B. Matthis and Assistant Attorney General Acie L. Ward, for the State.

Twiford, Trimpi, Thompson & Derrick, by C. Everett Thompson, for defendant appellants.

HEDRICK, Judge.

Although the record in these cases contains 573 pages in two volumes, and 44 assignments of error based on 147 exceptions, defendants have brought forward and argued in their brief only six assignments of error, all of which relate to the exclusion of testimony.

First, defendants argue that the trial judge erred in not allowing their expert witness, Harley June, to give his opinion that "the charred floor on the second floor of the building" was not caused by the use of an "accelerant" and that there was but one point of origin to the fire. The State offered the testimony of three expert witnesses tending to show that the char pattern on the floor in question indicated the use of an accelerant and that there were three points of origin to the fire.

Expert testimony upon "practically any facet of human knowledge and experience" is admissible to aid the jury's understanding of the evidence provided (1) the witness is qualified as an expert in the field in question, *and* (2) the witness is qualified as an expert in the particular case based on personal knowledge gained from first-hand study of the aspects of the case for which his or her expert opinion is sought, or based on facts assumed in a properly framed hypothetical question. 1 Stansbury's N.C. Evidence, *Opinion* § 134 at 438 (Brandis rev. 1973). *See Teague v. Duke Power Co.*, 258 N.C. 759, 129 S.E. 2d 507 (1963). Applying this principle to the case before us, the witness was qualified as an expert in his field and indeed was tendered and apparently accepted as an expert in the "causes of fires." However, in our opinion, Judge Brown properly excluded this witness's testimony as to his opinion that the char pattern on the floor of the second story did not indicate the use of an accelerant and that there was only one origin to the fire for the reason that defendants failed to demonstrate the witness's personal knowledge of essential facts nor did defendants ask the witness's opinion in response to a hypothetical question which included the essential facts to be assumed. The witness did not examine the premises until 13 January 1979, some 97 days after the fire on 6 October 1978. While other witnesses testified as to the condition of the premises before the fire and, in particular, as to the fact that paint thinner had been stored on the second floor, the defendants failed to show that their expert possessed any personal knowledge concerning the location of the paint thinner, nor did they seek to elicit his opinion by asking him a hypothetical question which included this essential fact. *See State v. Smith*, 34 N.C. App. 671, 239 S.E. 2d 610 (1977). Additionally, defendants failed to lay a proper foundation for this witness's opinion either by offering evidence that the condition of the building as he observed it, and upon which he based his opinion, was substantially the same as it was immediately after the fire, nor was this essential fact contained in a properly framed hypothetical question. *See State v. Smith, supra; State v. Reavis*, 19 N.C. App. 497, 199 S.E. 2d 139 (1973); *State Highway Commission v. Matthis*, 2 N.C. App. 233, 163 S.E. 2d 35 (1968). Unless the witness demonstrates that he personally knows of or is hypothetically made familiar with those facts necessary for him to form an opinion, then his opinion lacks probative value and is properly excluded.

Even assuming *arguendo*, however, that the challenged testimony was erroneously excluded, we perceive no prejudicial error thereby since defendants' second expert witness, Dr. Donald M. Oglesbe, whose credentials were impressive, testified in response to a properly framed hypothetical question which included all the essential facts that, in his opinion, the fire had only one point of origin and that no accelerant was poured on the second-story floor causing the char patterns described by Harley June and the State's experts. For these reasons, this assignment of error is not sustained.

Defendants next contend the trial court erred in not allowing the owner/lessor of the building in question to testify on cross-examination if he knew whether the building had a fire in it prior to the date of this fire. The record discloses that the witness was allowed to testify that he *knew* whether the building had had a fire in it, but it does not disclose that the witness was ever asked whether it in fact had had a fire. Thus, we cannot determine if the exclusion of the testimony was prejudicial. Nevertheless, the question called for clearly irrelevant testimony. This assignment of error is not sustained.

By assignment of error number 37, based on nine exceptions duly noted, defendants argue the court erred in "not allowing the defendant, Trevor Gurganus, to testify that the defendants had purchased beer through another nightclub operated by defendants and used these beer purchases in the Boardwalk nightclub," which was the establishment that burned. Again, assuming the relevancy of the excluded testimony, its exclusion was not prejudicial since almost identical evidence had been previously elicited from this same witness. This assignment of error is meritless.

Defendants' next assignment of error challenges a ruling of the trial court by which defendants contend testimony that there were no fires in the building after the date of the fire in question was erroneously excluded. To the contrary, the record reveals that this evidence, which defendants strenuously contend should have been admitted, was in fact admitted. That is, the witness did testify that there were no fires in the building to his knowledge after 6 October 1978. This assignment of error borders on the frivolous.

By assignment of error number 40, defendants assert the trial court erred in not allowing their expert, Harley June, to testify "as to the structural supports of the men's restroom and the significance of the char pattern on the supports." The two exceptions upon which this assignment of error is based indicate that the following testimony was stricken:

Q. State whether or not this support member was on top of or below the perpendicular support members that crossed it.

A. Well, it would be on top, the, the ceiling was fastened to a support member that would go like this (indicating) across and that (indicating). And, covered —

MR. TEAGUE: Motion to Strike what the ceiling was attached to.

SUSTAINED.

. . .

Q. Mr. June, you have just testified as to what in your opinion the significance of the burning pattern of the supports in the upper part of the men's room false ceiling was. Can you explain that answer please.

A. The upper cross members or support members showed heavy charring all the way around, side, bottom and top. The heavy charring was on the side and on the top. The lower supports directly underneath was [sic] heavy charred on the sides and on the top but was [sic] very well isolated or insulated by the paneling of the ceiling.

MR. TEAGUE: OBJECTION. MOTION TO STRIKE.

SUSTAINED. MOTION ALLOWED.

However, the record reveals that this witness testified in great detail concerning the structural supports and the char patterns on the supports, and with respect to the significance of the char pattern, the witness testified as follows, without objection, immediately upon the court's striking the last-quoted answer above:

> The significance of the char pattern is the heavy charring on the top and on the sides indicates extreme high heat from the top down and as the bottom is also charred, but not as heavily, there had to be fire from below, causing that charring.

Obviously, this is the answer which defendants sought to elicit by their questions, and they have no room to complain that the court struck the previous unresponsive answer. This assignment of error is patently without merit.

Finally, defendants contend the court erred in not setting aside the verdict. In their brief, they state that the basis for this assignment of error is "cited in the above assignments of error," that is, the defendants' motion to set aside the verdict was apparently bottomed on the alleged errors in evidentiary rulings which we have treated in this opinion. At any rate, that is the defendants' position on this appeal. Since we have found no error in the rulings challenged on appeal, *a fortiori* we find no error in the trial court's denial of the motion.

We hold the defendants had a fair trial free from prejudicial error.

No error.

Judges MARTIN (Robert M.) and MARTIN (Harry C.) concur.

NOVA UNIVERSITY v. THE UNIVERSITY OF NORTH CAROLINA; THE BOARD OF GOVERNORS, UNIVERSITY OF NORTH CAROLINA; WILLIAM FRIDAY, PRESIDENT, UNIVERSITY OF NORTH CAROLINA; WILLIAM JOHNSON, CHAIRMAN, BOARD OF GOVERNORS, UNIVERSITY OF NORTH CAROLINA; MRS. HOWARD HOLDERNESS; DR.

Nova University v. University of North Carolina

E.B. TURNER; IRWIN BELK; F.P. BODENHEIMER; HUGH CANNON; PHILIP G. CARSON; LAURENCE A. COBB; T. WORTH COLTRANE; WAYNE A CORPENING; MRS. KATHLEEN R. CROSBY; DR. HUGH DANIEL, JR.; WILLIAM A. DEES, JR.; CHARLES Z. FLACK, JR.; JACOB H. FROELICH, JR.; DANIEL C. GUNTER, JR.; GEORGE WATTS HILL; LUTHER H. HODGES, JR.; JAMES E. HOLMES; ROBERT L. JONES; JOHN R. JORDAN, JR.; MRS. JOHN L. McCAIN; REGINALD McCOY; WILLIAM D. MILLS; MRS. HUGH MORTON; J. AARON PREVOST; LOUIS T. RANDOLPH; HARLEY F. SHUFORD, JR.; MACEO A. SLOAN; DAVID J. WHICHARD, II; MRS. GEORGE D. WILSON, MEMBERS OF THE BOARD OF GOVERNORS, UNIVERSITY OF NORTH CAROLINA

No. 8010SC176

(Filed 15 July 1980)

Colleges and Universities § 2– Florida institution – teaching program in N.C. – degrees granted in Florida – no right of U.N.C. Board of Governors to regulate

The Board of Governors of the University of North Carolina does not have the authority under G.S. 116-15 to license or regulate Nova University, a Florida institution, in its teaching program in this State which leads to degrees granted in Florida.

APPEAL by plaintiff and defendants from *Hobgood (Hamilton H.), Judge.* Orders entered 15 and 19 October 1979 in Superior Court, WAKE County. Heard in the Court of Appeals 12 June 1980.

This is an appeal by plaintiff from an order denying its motion for summary judgment and by defendant from an order allowing discovery by the plaintiff. This court allowed certiorari to determine both questions.

Nova University is chartered in the State of Florida. It offers "external degree" programs in which instruction is given off-campus. Candidates for such degrees are not required to fulfill a university residence requirement. It has offered four "external degree" programs in North Carolina which would lead to graduate degrees given in the State of Florida. Three of the degrees would be in the field of education and one would be in criminal justice. Students meet in "clusters" of 25 to 30 persons at sites relatively near their homes and the faculty is brought in for weekend sessions. The students listen to lectures, take notes, have class discussions, and take final examinations. The students are also required to complete research projects. The first external program offered by Nova in this state was taught in the fall of 1973.

In 1976, Nova applied to the Board of Governors of the University of North Carolina for a license to conduct its programs in this state. A team of examiners was appointed by the Board of Governors who recommended on 31 October 1977 that the application be denied. On 7 December 1978, the Board of Governors' Committee on Educational Planning, Policies and Programs recommended to the Board of Governors that the application be denied, and on 8 December 1978, the Board of Governors denied Nova's application for a license. Plaintiff filed what it denominated a petition and complaint in the Superior Court of Wake County asking for a hearing *de novo* and a declaratory judgment that "[p]laintiff may teach in North Carolina and confer its degrees in Florida without interference" from the Board of Governors of the University of North Carolina. Plaintiff moved for summary judgment, and it was denied. The court then entered an order which allowed the plaintiff to conduct discovery.

The plaintiff petitioned this Court for certiorari as to the order denying its motion for summary judgment and the defendants petitioned for a writ of certiorari as to the order allowing discovery. We allowed both petitions.

Powe, Porter, Alphin and Whichard, by E.K. Powe, Willis P. Whichard and Charles R. Holton; Glassie, Pewett, Dudley, Beebe and Shanks, by Hershel Shanks and Michael A. Gordon, for plaintiff appellant and appellee.

Attorney General Edmisten, by Assistant Attorney General Elizabeth C. Bunting and Assistant Attorney General Marvin Schiller, for defendant appellants.

WEBB, Judge.

The Board of Governors of the University of North Carolina is empowered to license nonpublic educational institutions by G.S. 116-15 which provides in part:

(a) No nonpublic educational institution created or established in this State after December 31, 1960, by any person, firm, organization, or corporation shall have power or authority to confer degrees upon any person except as provided in this section. For the purposes of this section, the term "created or established in this State" or "established in this State" shall mean, in the case of an institution whose principal office is located outside of North Carolina, the act of issuance by the Secretary of State of North Carolina of a certificate of authority to do business in North Carolina. The Board of Governors shall call to the attention of the Attorney General, for such action as he may deem appropriate any institution failing to comply with the requirements of this section.

(b) The Board of Governors, under such standards as it shall establish, may issue its license to confer degrees in such form as it may prescribe to a nonpublic educational institution established in this State after December 31, 1960, by any person, firm, organization, or corporation; but no nonpublic educational institution established in the State subsequent to that date shall be empowered to confer degrees unless it has income sufficient to maintain an adequate faculty and equipment sufficient to provide adequate means of instruction in the arts and sciences, or in any other recognized field or fields of learning or knowledge.

The question posed by this appeal is whether under G.S. 116-15 the Board of Governors of the University of North Carolina has the power to license Nova University, a Florida institution, to conduct classes in this state which lead to degrees granted in Florida.

The Board of Governors concedes it would have no power to regulate the teaching of courses in this state if the granting of degrees were not involved. It also concedes it has no power to control the licensing of institutions in Florida for the granting of degrees. The Board contends that G.S. 116-15(b) which empowers the Board to issue licenses to confer degrees by out-of-state institutions includes the power to issue licenses for

in-state instruction which leads to out-of-state degrees. The
Board argues that this power is inherent in the language of G.S.
116-15(b). The Board contends that it is specifically given the
power to license the "conferral of degrees" and unless it also
has the authority to license degree programs, Nova will successfully "end run" the grasp of the statute. The Board argues
further that the purpose of Chapter 116 of the General Statutes
is the planning and development in this state under the guidance of the Board of a "coordinated system of higher education" and this can only be accomplished if the Board has the
authority to regulate "degree programs" as well as the "conferral of degrees."

    The difficulty we have with the Board's position is that the
statute does not specifically grant the power it seeks. What they
ask is the power to regulate and license Nova's right to teach
which is a restriction on freedom of speech. As Nova points out,
other constitutional questions would also arise if we interpreted the statute as contended by the Board. We do not believe
we should find a power in the statute by implication which could
lead to such constitutional problems. If the General Assembly
wants to give the Board the power to so restrict teaching in this
state, it may do so specifically and the constitutional questions
may then be raised. The statute is not clear in giving the Board
the power it seeks. We do not believe we should find this power
by implication. We hold that under G.S. 116-15(b) the Board of
Governors does not have the power to license or regulate Nova
University in its teaching program in this state so long as Nova
does not confer degrees in this state.

    We do not reach the questions raised by the defendants'
appeal.

    We reverse and remand to the superior court for a judgment
consistent with this opinion.

    Reversed and remanded.

    Judges PARKER and CLARK concur.

ARCHIE ROSE v. HERRING TRACTOR & TRUCK CO. AND INTERNATION-
AL HARVESTER COMPANY

No. 798SC1034

(Filed 15 July 1980)

Automobiles § 68.1– accident caused by defective brakes – plaintiff negligent as matter of law

In an action to recover damages resulting from an accident involving a truck manufactured by one defendant and sold to plaintiff by the other defendant, the trial court properly directed verdict for defendants where the evidence tended to show that plaintiff was negligent as a matter of law because plaintiff's employee continued to drive the truck on a public highway with knowledge that the brakes were not in proper working order and were unsafe. G.S. 20-124.

APPEAL by plaintiff from *Barefoot (Napoleon B.), Judge.* Judgment entered 8 June 1979 in Superior Court, WAYNE County. Heard in the Court of Appeals 22 April 1980.

This is a civil action against defendants, Herring Tractor and Truck Company (herein "Herring Tractor") and International Harvester Company, wherein, the plaintiff, owner of a trucking company involved in hauling products, seeks to recover damages resulting from an accident that occurred on 1 September 1976 involving one of his trucks which was manufactured by defendant International Harvester Company and sold to plaintiff by Herring Tractor on 24 February 1976. The plaintiff's evidence tends to show that within two weeks of the purchase of the vehicle, plaintiff became aware that there was a loss of air when the brakes were applied and complaints were made to defendant Herring Tractor about the malfunctioning of the brakes as indicated by the brake light and the loss of air. The tractor was involved in a first unrelated accident which caused the tractor to be in the repair shop from 20 May 1976 to 26 July 1976. In August 1976, the truck was taken to Herring Tractor for brake repairs. On Sunday, 29 August 1976, Timmy Phelps, an employee and driver of Rose Poultry Company, took the tractor for a test drive. As stated by Phelps:

"I took it down Highway 117 South and my wife was with me. When I put on the brakes, I would lose air and it had a bumping to it. I felt like there was a hard knot and it kept on and it felt like you were running over rocks or something like that. As to what effect it had on my ability to control the truck, you just could not stop it like it should stop. It was unsafe.

When I got back, I told Mr. Rose that the brakes were losing air and that they had a knock in it and that it was unsafe to drive. It would bump when you put on the brakes and it felt like it was bumping and it was losing air. When I applied the brake, it would have a hissing sound and the air pressure was dropping and the truck would not stop."

Dennis Rose took the tractor back to Herring Tractor on Monday, 30 August 1976, for brake repairs. The repair order of 30 August 1976 indicated, "Check DOST 121 brakes for not holding properly, check all air valves for not braking together, found okay." The tractor was picked up by Dennis Rose on 30 August 1976. He was assured by Ronald Grant and Donald Page of Herring Tractor that the truck was "okay" when he picked it up; however, when Dennis Rose picked up the truck on the evening of 30 August 1976, and drove the truck back to Goldsboro, he noticed that "the brakes were the same way." Nonetheless, on the next day, 31 August 1976, Dennis Rose told Timmy Phelps to take the truck to Patterson, New Jersey. Timmy Phelps testified that:

"... I picked it up on Tuesday and I drove it on Tuesday. I had the same problems on Tuesday that I had with it when I road-tested it on Sunday. My boss told me to go to Patterson, New Jersey and I went. I knew in my mind that I still had the same problem with it and in my opinion the vehicle was unsafe."

While returning from New Jersey, the defendant had an accident in LaPlanta, Maryland, which accident allegedly resulted from brake failure.

At trial, the defendant moved for a directed verdict at the end of the plaintiff's evidence and this motion was granted by the trial court.

Barnes, Braswell & Haithcock by Michael A. Ellis and W. Timothy Haithcock for plaintiff appellant.

Taylor, Warren, Kerr & Walker by Robert D. Walker, Jr. and John H. Kerr III for defendant appellee, Herring Tractor and Truck Company.

Smith, Anderson, Blount, Dorsett, Mitchell & Jernigan by C. Ernest Simons, Jr. for defendant appellee, International Harvester Company.

CLARK, Judge.

The plaintiff does not bring forth any argument or assignment of error or make any argument in his brief on the issues of breach of warranty or on the question of liability of International Harvester. The plaintiff therefore waives any assignment of error on these questions. N.C. App. R. 28; *Crockett v. First Federal Savings and Loan Association,* 289 N.C. 620, 224 S.E. 2d 580 (1976); *State v. Wilson,* 289 N.C. 531, 223 S.E. 2d 311 (1976).

The only question properly raised for review by this Court is whether the trial court erred in directing a verdict for the defendants. The defendants contend that the plaintiff was guilty of negligence as a matter of law because plaintiff's employee continued to drive the tractor on a public highway with knowledge that the brakes were not in proper working order and were unsafe. On the other hand, plaintiff contends that he was not contributorily negligent because he was acting in reasonable reliance upon the statements or representations of the employees of Herring Tractor that the tractor brakes were in proper working order. We do not agree with plaintiff's contentions.

"The right to rely upon the assumption that another will exercise due care is not absolute ... and must yield to the realities of the situation to the extent that if the plaintiff observes a violation of duty which imperils him, he must be vigilant in attempting to avoid injury to himself." *Harris v. Bingham,* 246 N.C. 77, 79, 97 S.E. 2d 453, 455 (1957). "[W]here a person *sui juris* knows of a dangerous condition and voluntarily goes into the place of danger, he is guilty of contributory negligence, which will bar his recovery." *Dunnevant v. R.R.*, 167 N.C. 232, 234, 83 S.E. 347, 348 (1914); *Cook v. Winston-Salem*, 241 N.C. 422, 85 S.E. 2d 696 (1955), (quoting the above language, held nonsuit properly allowed at close of plaintiff's evidence). There is no dispute about the relevant facts as quoted in the statement of facts above: plaintiff's partner and employee both knew of the defective condition of the brakes and nonetheless caused the tractor to be operated on a public highway. "Here, according to plaintiff's [evidence], the alleged known defective condition was obvious, not latent; and such defective condition was of such nature that the hazards reasonably foreseeable from the continued use and operation of the [tractor] were patent." *Nationwide Mutual Insurance Co. v. Don Allen Chevrolet Co.*, 253 N.C. 243, 251, 116 S.E. 2d 780, 786 (1960). The willingness of plaintiff's employee-driver and partner-owner to operate the tractor on a public highway with defective or malfunctioning brakes and knowledge thereof is negligence as a matter of law. G.S. 20-124; *Wilcox v. Glover Motors, Inc.*, 269 N.C. 473, 153 S.E. 2d 76 (1967) (duty on both owner and driver who have knowledge); *Tysinger v. Coble Dairy Products*, 225 N.C. 717, 36 S.E. 2d 246 (1945). The entry of directed verdict for the defendant was proper.

Affirmed.

Judges VAUGHN and MARTIN (Harry C.) concur.

LEOPOLD HERMAN HAANEBRINK AND JACQUELINE E. CORNEY HAANEBRINK v. LOUIS B. MEYER, TRUSTEE, AND THE LELY CORPORATION OF DELAWARE

No. 807SC19

(Filed 15 July 1980)

Usury § 4– forfeiture of interest for usury – statute of limitations

The two-year statute of limitations on the forfeiture of all interest for usury, G.S. 1-53(3), begins to run at the time an agreement or charge for usurious interest is first made. Therefore, plaintiff's action for the forfeiture of all interest on a promissory note was barred by the statute of limitations where the note was signed on 7 June 1976 and the action was instituted on 21 August 1979.

APPEAL by defendant from *Reid, Judge.* Judgment entered 23 October 1979 in Superior Court, WILSON County. Heard in the Court of Appeals 22 May 1980.

This is an action for declaratory judgment in which plaintiffs request the court to determine the rights of the parties with respect to a promissory note executed by plaintiffs to the corporate defendant and deed of trust securing the note. Plaintiffs seek to have the interest in the promissory note declared usurious and to have the deed of trust cancelled by the trustee upon payment by the plaintiffs to the corporate defendant of the principal without interest. From summary judgment in favor of plaintiffs, defendant Lely Corporation of Delaware appealed.

Narron, Holdford, Babb, Harrison & Rhodes, by William H. Holdford, for plaintiff appellees.

Parker, Miles & Hinson, by C. David Williams, Jr., for defendant appellant.

MARTIN (Robert M.), Judge.

The issue presented by this appeal is when the two year statute of limitations on the forfeiture of all interest for usury begins to run.

G.S. 24-2 on the penalty for usury provides in pertinent part:

> The taking, receiving, reserving or charging a greater rate of interest than permitted by this chapter or other applicable law, either before or after the interest may accrue, when knowingly done, shall be a forfeiture of the entire interest which the note or other evidence of debt carries with it, or which has been agreed to be paid thereon. And in case a greater rate of interest has been paid, the

person ... by whom it has been paid, may recover back twice the amount of interest paid in an action in the nature of action for debt.

G.S. 1-53 contains the applicable statute of limitations:

Within two years —

* * *

(2) An action to recover the penalty for usury.

(3) The forfeiture of all interest for usury.

It is well settled that the statute of limitations on the recovery of twice the amount of interest paid begins to run upon payment of the usurious interest. The right of action to recover the penalty for usury paid accrues upon each payment of usurious interest giving rise to a separate cause of action to recover the penalty therefor, which action is barred by the statute of limitations at the expiration of two years from such payment. *Henderson v. Finance Co.*, 273 N.C. 253, 160 S.E. 2d 39 (1968); *Ghormley v. Hyatt*, 208 N.C. 478, 181 S.E. 242 (1935); *Trust Co. v. Redwine*, 204 N.C. 125, 167 S.E. 687 (1933).

The question, however, of when the statute of limitations begins to run on the forfeiture of all interest has not been directly addressed by this Court. G.S. 1-53(3) pertaining to the forfeiture of interest was enacted in 1931. Prior to 1931, the statute of limitations mentioned only an action to recover the penalty for usury, the recovery of twice the amount of interest paid, and was held inapplicable to a defense demanding the forfeiture of interest in *Pugh v. Scarboro*, 200 N.C. 59, 156 S.E. 149 (1930). As a result of that decision the two year statute was amended to add "the forfeiture of all interest for usury."

It is indicated that the time runs from forfeiture, and this would seem to take place when an agreement or charge for usurious interest is first made. If this is the proper construction, the statute will bar the forfeiture in many cases before the principal debt matures, unless the debtor brings an action for forfeiture within the two years.

1 T. Wilson & J. Wilson, McIntosh N.C. Practice and Procedure § 502 (2nd ed. 1956). We are persuaded that this is indeed the proper construction.

There shall be no forfeiture of interest for usury after the expiration of two years from the date of forfeiture under the provisions of G.S. 24-2. *Trust Co. v. Redwine*, 204 N.C. 125, 167 S.E. 687 (1933). The forfeiture under G.S. 24-2 is the "taking, receiving, reserving or charging" of a usurious rate of interest. In *Smith v. Building and Loan Assn.*, 119 N.C. 249, 255 26 S.E. 41, 42 (1896), the Court stated that "[t]he statute makes the charging or contracting for usury a forfeiture of all interest ..." and in *Mortgage Co. v. Zion Church*, 219 N.C. 395, 397, 14 S.E. 2d 37, 38 (1941) the Court stated that "[a]s exaction for the release, the defendants were required to promise to pay a part of the old as well as additional usury. This was a clear imposition upon the borrower. All interest is forfeited when usury is knowingly exacted." Similarly in *Kessing v. Mortgage Corp.*, 278 N.C. 523, 180 S.E. 2d 823 (1971), the Court confirmed that the "charging" which constitutes a forfeiture is the contract, promise or agreement to a usurious rate of interest as opposed to the actual payment of that interest. In *Kessing*,

> [a] greater rate of interest than allowed by law was charged by means of the partnership agreement required, but no profit has yet inured to the defendant under this agreement. The only interest actually paid by Kessing Company was the 8% provided for in the note. This in itself was a legal rate. No usurious interest has been paid, and Kessing Company is not entitled to recover double the amount of the interest. (Citations omitted). The statutory penalty for *charging* usury is the forfeiture of *all* interest on the loan. The charging of usurious interest as provided for by the partnership agreement in this case is sufficient to cause a forfeiture of all the interest charged.

Id. at 532, 180 S.E. 2d at 828-29. Therefore, the two year statute of limitations begins to run from the time an agreement or charge for usurious interest is first made.

The case of *Grant v. Morris*, 81 N.C. 150 (1879) relied on by plaintiffs is not to the contrary. In *Grant*, the court did not consider "the mere entry of a usurious claim upon the account as either 'a taking, receiving, reserving or charging.' within the meaning of the amending act. These words imply something more to be done, to the loss or detriment of the debtor, than the mere presentation of an illegal claim which is neither recognized nor paid." *Id.* at 154. In *Grant,* however, there was no usurious stipulation found in the contract itself, plaintiff did not otherwise agree to a usurious rate of interest and none was paid. After advances were made to the plaintiff by defendant, the defendant in an account rendered to plaintiff included a charge of usurious interest to which the plaintiff objected. Because there was no promise to pay a usurious interest rate by the debtor in exchange for the advance of money by the lender, there was no detriment to the debtor. A usurious rate of interest is charged when the debtor agrees or promises to pay it. Hence, the signing of a note calling for usurious interest is a charging within the meaning of the statute which would cause the period of limitation to begin.

In the present case, the plaintiff signed a promissory note for $13,185.83 bearing interest at the commercial prime lending rate of interest, plus four percent per annum on 7 June 1976. According to the deposition of the corporate defendant's vice president, the prime commercial lending rate plus 4% was approximately 12% at that time. The maximum legal interest rate under G.S. 24-1.1(3) was 9%. Defendant's third assignment of error that it lacked the necessary "corrupt intent" to charge a greater rate of interest than allowed by law is without merit. *Kessing v. Mortgage Co.,* 278 N.C. 523, 180 S.E. 2d 823 (1971); *Equilease Corp. v. Hotel Corp.,* 42 N.C. App. 436, 256 S.E. 2d 836, *cert. denied* 298 N.C. 568, 261 S.E. 2d 121 (1979).

We find that the charging of usurious interest dates from the agreement on 7 June 1976. Plaintiffs brought this action for the forfeiture of all interest on 21 August 1979. Consequently, plaintiffs' action is barred by the two year statute of limitations.

Summary judgment in favor of plaintiffs is

Tinkham v. Hall

Reversed.

Judges ARNOLD and HILL concur.

━━━━━━━━━━━

D.J. TINKHAM, D/B/A TINKHAM CONSTRUCTION COMPANY v. RODAN-
THE P. HALL, INDIVIDUALLY; GREAT AMERICAN INSURANCE COM-
PANY, A CORPORATION; ROY R. BARNES, JR., IN HIS CORPORATE CAPACITY;
DAN PITTMAN, D/B/A DAN PITTMAN INSURANCE AGENCY; AND
ELMO PEELE, INDIVIDUALLY

No. 806DC127

(Filed 15 July 1980)

1. **Appeal and Error § 28.1– findings of fact – no exceptions in record – findings binding on appeal**

   When findings of fact are not challenged by exceptions in the record, they are presumed to be supported by competent evidence and are binding on appeal.

2. **Process §§ 7, 12– process – corporate defendant – deceased individual – leaving with individual defendant's sister – insufficiency of service**

   Evidence was sufficient to support the trial court's findings that defendants were not properly served with process where the evidence tended to show that: (1) service of process upon the corporate defendant was attempted by delivering copies of the summons and complaint to an individual who at that time was neither the agent of the corporate defendant nor authorized to receive service of process in its behalf; (2) service upon one of the individual defendants was attempted by delivering copies of the summons and complaint to his sister who neither resided with him nor was present in his home when the papers were delivered to her; and (3) one of the individual defendants upon whom service was attempted had been deceased since 1965; his estate had been settled for many years; and service was attempted by delivery of summons and complaint to an individual who was not the personal representative of the estate of the deceased.

3. **Principal and Agent § 11– person sued in representative capacity – no claim stated against individual**

   Because the complaint in this action stated a claim against an individual defendant solely in his representative capacity, it could not state a claim for which relief could be granted against him personally as well.

APPEAL by plaintiff from *Long, Judge.* Orders entered 13 November and 15 November 1979 in District Court, HERTFORD County. Heard in the Court of Appeals 9 June 1980.

Plaintiff commenced this civil action against the multiple defendants on 31 October 1978, alleging indebtedness on a delinquent open account, breach of contract, and fraud arising out of construction repairs and services rendered by plaintiff to defendant Rodanthe Hall. Partial default judgment was eventually entered against defendant Hall; she is not, however, a party to this appeal. On 5 December 1978 defendants Great American Insurance Company, Roy R. Barnes, Jr., and Dan Pittman, d/b/a Dan Pittman Insurance Agency, moved to dismiss the action for lack of personal jurisdiction, insufficiency of process, and insufficiency of service of process. Defendant Elmo Peele moved to dismiss for failure to state a claim against him for which relief can be granted. On the basis of affidavits, other evidence, and arguments of counsel, Judge Long granted these motions and entered an order of dismissal as to these defendants on 13 November 1979. Plaintiff then filed a motion requesting a reasonable period of time in which to refile his action against these defendants. On 15 November 1979 the judge denied plaintiff's motion. Plaintiff appeals.

Rosbon D.B. Whedbee for plaintiff appellant.

Leroy, Wells, Shaw, Hornthal, Riley & Shearin, by L.P. Hornthal, Jr., for defendant appellees.

MARTIN (Harry C.), Judge.

[1] In its order of dismissal dated 13 November 1979, the court made findings of fact upon which it based its conclusion of law that attempted service of process upon the defendants Great American Insurance Company, Roy Barnes, and Dan Pittman was insufficient and defective, that the court did not have personal jurisdiction over those defendants, and that plaintiff's complaint failed to state a claim for which relief could be granted against the defendant Elmo Peele. Plaintiff made no exceptions to any of these findings of fact. When findings of fact are not challenged by exceptions in the record, they are pre-

sumed to be supported by competent evidence and are binding on appeal. *Phillips v. Alston*, 257 N.C. 255, 125 S.E. 2d 580 (1962); *Jackson v. Collins*, 9 N.C. App. 548, 176 S.E. 2d 878 (1970).

[2] Plaintiff did appeal this order of dismissal and, without an exception to the findings of fact or to the evidence, presents for appellate review only the question whether the facts found support the order. *Hinson v. Jefferson*, 287 N.C. 422, 215 S.E. 2d 102 (1975). In this case, unquestionably the facts found support the order of dismissal.

The court found that as to defendant Great American Insurance Company, the record shows that service of process upon it was attempted by delivering copies of the summons and complaint to Roy Barnes, "who at that time was neither the agent of the defendant Great American nor authorized to receive service of process in its behalf." Clearly, this attempted service failed to comply with N.C.G.S. 1A-1, Rule 4(j)(6). *Simms v. Stores, Inc.*, 285 N.C. 145, 203 S.E. 2d 769 (1974). The defendant corporation was not effectively served with process.

The court found that service upon Roy Barnes was attempted by delivering copies of the summons and complaint to his sister, "who neither resides at the dwelling house of the defendant Barnes nor was present therein when such papers were delivered to her." N.C.G.S. 1A-1, Rule 4(j)(1)(a), which prescribes one of the methods of service of process required to exercise personal jurisdiction over a natural person, was not followed in this case. The court, therefore, correctly concluded that the service was defective and insufficient to obtain personal jurisdiction over Barnes. *See Guthrie v. Ray*, 293 N.C. 67, 235 S.E. 2d 146 (1977); *Williams v. Hartis*, 18 N.C. App. 89, 195 S.E. 2d 806 (1973).

As to the defendant Dan Pittman, the court found as a fact that he had been deceased since 1965 and his estate had been settled "many years prior to 1976." Furthermore, service upon Mr. Pittman had been attempted by delivery of the summons and complaint to Elmo Peele, "who is not contended to be the personal representative of the estate of the defendant Pittman." Under N.C.G.S. 28A-18-1 and 28A-18-3, only the personal representative of Mr. Pittman could have had this action brought against him.

[3] The court also made the finding that plaintiff's counsel "conceded in open court that no personal claim was being made against the defendant Elmo Peele, but that the Complaint stated a claim against him solely in his representative capacity as agent of the Dan Pittman Insurance Agency." Based on this finding, the court concluded that the complaint failed to state a claim against Peele for which relief could be granted. This conclusion of law was not erroneous. Because the complaint stated a claim against Peele solely in his representative capacity, it could not state a claim for which relief could be granted against him personally as well. *Satterfield v. McLellan Stores,* 215 N.C. 582, 2 S.E. 2d 709 (1939).

We hold the order of dismissal is supported by the facts found by the trial court. Furthermore, we find no merit in plaintiff's contentions that defendants waived their defenses of insufficiency of service of process and jurisdiction by dilatory action. Defendants filed their motion to dismiss on 5 December 1978 in response to plaintiff's complaint, filed 31 October 1978. The motion specifically stated the grounds for dismissal as lack of personal jurisdiction, insufficiency of process, and insufficiency of service of process. Moreover, plaintiff's argument that Barnes had "actual notice" of the pending action cannot be sustained. *Distributors v. McAndrews,* 270 N.C. 91, 153 S.E. 2d 770 (1967); *Stone v. Hicks,* 45 N.C. App. 66, 262 S.E. 2d 318 (1980).

Plaintiff's other assignment of error is that the court committed a prejudicial abuse of discretion in denying plaintiff's timely motion under N.C.G.S. 1A-1, Rule 41(b), for a reasonable extension of time in which to refile this action and to obtain new service upon defendants. Plaintiff recognizes that this motion was addressed to the sound discretion of the court and will not be disturbed absent a showing of abuse of that discretion. The more precise test is whether there has been a clear abuse of discretion, *Welch v. Kearns,* 261 N.C. 171, 134 S.E. 2d 155 (1964), but in this case no abuse has been shown.

The orders of the trial court are

Affirmed.

Judges HEDRICK and MARTIN (Robert M.) concur.

QUENTIN GREGORY, JR. v. PERDUE, INCORPORATED

No. 796SC998

(Filed 15 July 1980)

Contracts § 3– no meeting of minds as to essential terms

    Plaintiff's evidence on motion for summary judgment was insufficient to show a binding contract with defendant where plaintiff's materials alleged at most an agreement by him to grow an unspecified quantity of chickens for defendant in the future under certain quality conditions in return for which defendant agreed to guarantee plaintiff a stated minimum profit and to aid him in remodeling his chicken houses, since it is clear that plaintiff and defendant never reached a mutual understanding as to how many chickens plaintiff would grow, time of delivery, or compensation.

APPEAL by plaintiff from *Small, Judge.* Judgment entered 6 August 1979 in Superior Court, HALIFAX County. Heard in the Court of Appeals 17 April 1980.

This action was brought to recover damages for breach of contract. In his verified complaint, plaintiff alleged that in December 1976, he began dismantling and remodeling six of his chicken houses at the instruction of defendant and in reliance on defendant's promise that plaintiff would receive a contract to grow chickens for defendant in the houses. In reliance on defendant's promises, plaintiff made physical changes in the houses and applied for a $50,000 loan to remodel them. In June 1977, defendant promised plaintiff a contract for the six houses in return for which plaintiff promised that all six houses would be operational by 1 January 1978. As a condition precedent to the contract, defendant insisted that plaintiff hire a man capable of supervising the six houses, which plaintiff did at considerable expense. Defendant guaranteed plaintiff $10,000 per house per year net income on the contract. Defendant instructed plaintiff to borrow $85,000 in additional funds, and defendant agreed to escrow profits to repay this loan. In October 1977, defendant cancelled all contractual relationships with plaintiff, causing plaintiff to sustain damages in the sum of $125,000.

Defendant filed an unverified answer in which it denied the essential allegations of the complaint and asserted as a further defense that the only agreement between defendant and plaintiff was for plaintiff to grow chickens for defendant in one house on a flock to flock basis. Defendant alleged that plaintiff's poor management and growing practices caused it to withdraw from this arrangement.

The cause came on for hearing before Judge Small on defendant's motion for summary judgment. In support of its motion, defendant offered the affidavit of its employee, Gerald Jackson, and the deposition of plaintiff. Following the hearing, the trial judge entered summary judgment for defendant, from which plaintiff appeals.

Allsbrook, Benton, Knott, Cranford & Whitaker, by William O. White, Jr., for plaintiff appellant.

Pritchett, Cooke & Burch, by Stephen R. Burch and Jonas M. Yates, for defendant appellee.

WELLS, Judge.

On motion for summary judgment, the question before the court is whether the pleadings, depositions, answers to interrogatories, and admissions on file, together with the affidavits, if any, show that there is no genuine issue as to any material fact and that a party is entitled to judgment as a matter of law. G.S. 1A-1, Rule 56(c); *Page v. Sloan,* 281 N.C. 697, 190 S.E. 2d 189 (1972). The burden upon the moving party is to establish that there is no genuine issue as to any material fact remaining to be determined. *Savings & Loan Assoc. v. Trust Co.,* 282 N.C. 44, 191 S.E. 2d 683 (1972). This burden may be carried by a movant by proving that an essential element of the opposing party's claim is nonexistent or by showing through discovery that the opposing party cannot produce enough evidence to support an essential element of his claim. *Moore v. Fieldcrest Mills, Inc.,* 296 N.C.

467, 251 S.E. 2d 419 (1979); *Zimmerman v. Hogg & Allen*, 286 N.C. 24, 209 S.E. 2d 795 (1974). The purpose of summary judgment is to eliminate formal trials where only questions of law are involved by permitting penetration of an unfounded claim or defense in advance of trial and allowing summary disposition for either party when a fatal weakness in the claim or defense is exposed. *Moore v. Fieldcrest Mills, Inc., supra; Caldwell v. Deese*, 288 N.C. 375, 218 S.E. 2d 379 (1975).

We now determine the propriety of summary judgment for defendant in this case by applying these principles to the record before us. The forecast of plaintiff's evidence must be gleaned from his verified complaint and his deposition, as he submitted no other papers in opposition to defendant's motion. Considered in the light most favorable to him, plaintiff, in both his verified complaint and deposition, at most alleges an agreement by him to grow an unspecified quantity of chickens for defendant in the future under certain quality conditions in return for which defendant agreed to guarantee plaintiff a stated minimum profit and to aid him in remodeling his chicken houses. Consequently, the acceptance of a proposition to make a contract, the terms of which are to be subsequently fixed, does not constitute a binding obligation. *Construction Co. v. Housing Authority*, 1 N.C. App. 181, 160 S.E. 2d 542 (1968). An offer to enter into a contract in the future must, to be binding, specify all of the essential and material terms and leave nothing to be agreed upon as a result of future negotiations. *Smith v. House of Kenton Corp.*, 23 N.C. App. 439, 209 S.E. 2d 397 (1974), *cert. denied*, 286 N.C. 337, 211 S.E. 2d 213 (1974). To constitute a valid contract, the parties must assent to the same thing in the same sense, and their minds must meet as to all the terms. If any portion of the proposed terms is not settled, or no mode agreed on by which they may be settled, there is no agreement. *Boyce v. McMahan*, 285 N.C. 730, 208 S.E. 2d 692 (1974).

From plaintiff's deposition, it is manifestly clear that plaintiff and defendant never reached a mutual understanding as to how many chickens plaintiff would grow, the time or times they would be delivered by defendant to plaintiff for growing or delivered by plaintiff to defendant after growing, or the compensation to be paid by defendant to plaintiff. There simply was no meeting of the minds. Under these circumstances, summary judgment was properly entered and the judgment of the trial court must be

Affirmed.

Chief Judge MORRIS and Judge PARKER concur.

STATE OF NORTH CAROLINA v. GARY DAN MAXWELL

No. 8018SC233

(Filed 15 July 1980)

1. **Criminal Law § 86.4– prior crimes of defendant – admissibility for impeachment**

    The trial court properly allowed defendant to be questioned about unrelated crimes for the purpose of impeachment.

2. **Rape and Allied Offenses § 19– taking indecent liberties with child – constitutionality of statute**

    G.S. 14-202.1 making it a crime to take indecent liberties with a female under the age of 16, the offender being over 16 years old and more than five years older than the female child, is not unconstitutionally vague.

3. **Rape and Allied Offenses § 19– taking indecent liberties with child – willfulness – failure to instruct – harmless error**

    In a prosecution of defendant for taking indecent liberties with a female under the age of 16, defendant being over 16 years old and more than five years older than the female child, the jury, by finding that defendant committed the crime, necessarily found that he acted willfully and accordingly the court's failure to charge on willfulness was harmless beyond a reasonable doubt.

APPEAL by defendant from *Seay, Judge.* Judgment entered 1 November 1979 in Superior Court, GUILFORD County. Heard in the Court of Appeals 13 June 1980.

Defendant was indicted for taking indecent liberties with a female under the age of 16, he being over 16 years old and more than five years older than the female child (G.S. 14-202.1(a)(1)). He was convicted and sentenced to 5-7 years. Defendant appeals.

Attorney General Edmisten, by Assistant Attorney General James E. Magner, Jr., for the State.

Jack Floyd and Stephen W. Earp for defendant appellant.

ARNOLD, Judge.

[1] Defendant contends that the trial court erred in allowing the State to question him about unrelated crimes. Defendant argues that this court should follow what is now probably the majority rule in this country, embodied in Rule 608(b) of the Federal Rules of Evidence. This rule gives the court discretion to permit cross-examination concerning instances of unrelated conduct, but only if such instances of conduct are probative of the witness's truthfulness or untruthfulness. While there may be merit in defendant's argument, we do not feel that this court has the prerogative to adopt or follow such a rule.

The questions defendant challenges relate to two separate occurrences. First defendant was asked, "[I]f in the summer of 1973 you weren't in a motel room in Greenville, South Carolina, with a fourteen year old girl?" Defendant denied that he had been. Then he was asked "[w]hether or not on [6 September 1979 at 1413 Grove Street in Greensboro] you struck Alton Ray McQueen about the head and face and removed $550.00 in good and lawful money from him?" Defendant denied this also.

The latter question is clearly correct as impeachment, relating as it does to a specific act of misconduct on defendant's part. See 4 Strong's N.C. Index 3d, Criminal Law §§ 86.1 and 86.5. In light of our Supreme Court's decision in *State v. Purcell*, 296 N.C. 728, 252 S.E. 2d 772 (1979), we have some doubt as to whether the former question was sufficiently specific. (In *Purcell*, the court held improper the questioning of the defendant as to whether he had "ever killed anybody.") Even if this question was improper, however, we do not find it to have been a prejudicial error. In view of the evidence of defendant's guilt we do not believe that this one question about an unrelated event could have influenced the jury's verdict, and we find no prejudicial error.

[2] Defendant attacks the statute under which he was charged as unconstitutionally vague, and therefore void. We have previously found that G.S. 14-202.1 is not void for vagueness, *State v. Vehaun*, 34 N.C. App. 700, 239 S.E. 2d 705 (1977), *cert. denied* 294 N.C. 445, 241 S.E. 2d 846 (1978), and that decision is the correct one. Defendant argues that our opinion in *Vehaun* did not address the standard set out in *Grayned v. City of Rockford*, 408 U.S. 104, 92 S.Ct. 2294, 33 L.Ed. 2d 222 (1972), and *Smith v. Goguen*, 415 U.S. 566, 94 S.Ct. 1242, 39 L.Ed. 2d 605 (1974), that to avoid being unconstitutionally vague a statute must provide standards to guide those who enforce the law. We do not find, however, that G.S. 14-202.1(a)(1) is unconstitutional on this basis, and we note that this statute is much more specific than the ordinance which was held unconstitutional in *Goguen*. Defendant's argument as to unconstitutionality is without merit.

We find no merit in defendant's fourth argument, which is addressed to the trial court's restriction of his questioning of potential jurors. Regulation of the inquiry on voir dire rests in the court's discretion, and in order to show reversible error in the exercise of that discretion defendant must show both prejudice and a clear abuse of discretion. *State v. Young*, 287 N.C. 377, 214 S.E. 2d 763 (1975), *death penalty vacated*, 428 U.S. 903, 49 L.Ed. 2d 1208, 96 S. Ct. 3207 (1976). Neither of these appears in this case.

[3] Finally, defendant argues that the trial court erred in failing to charge the jury that they must find as an essential element of the crime that defendant *willfully* took indecent liberties with the child. Defendant is correct that G.S. 14-202.1(a)(1) requires that the taking of indecent liberties be willful, and the court should have charged on willfulness as an element. (North Carolina Pattern Jury Instruction — Criminal 226.85, upon which the court appears to have relied, inadvertently omits this element.) However, in this case all the evidence shows that if defendant took indecent liberties with the child he did so willfully, that is, purposely and without justification or excuse. *See State v. Arnold*, 264 N.C. 348, 141 S.E. 2d 473 (1965). In fact, we cannot imagine a situation in which the taking of indecent liberties for the purpose of arousing or gratifying sexual desire could be other than willful, and we fail to

see what the element of willfulness adds to this statutory crime. This is a very different situation from that of abandonment and nonsupport addressed in *State v. Yelverton*, 196 N.C. 64, 144 S.E. 534 (1928), upon which defendant relies. We hold that in this case the jury by finding that defendant committed the crime necessarily found that he acted willfully, and accordingly the omission in the charge was harmless beyond a reasonable doubt.

No error.

Judges ERWIN and HILL concur.

PORSH BUILDERS, INC. v. CITY OF WINSTON-SALEM, A NORTH CAROLINA MUNICIPAL CORPORATION, WAYNE A. CORPENING, MAYOR; JON B. DeVRIES; EUGENE F. GROCE; ERNESTINE WILSON; VIRGINIA H. NEWELL; JOHN J. CAVANAGH; ROBERT S. NORTHINGTON, JR.; VIVIAN K. BURKE; LARRY D. LITTLE, MEMBERS OF THE BOARD OF ALDERMAN FOR THE CITY OF WINSTON-SALEM, AND THE REDEVELOPMENT COMMISSION OF WINSTON-SALEM, A POLITICAL SUBDIVISION OF THE CITY OF WINSTON-SALEM

No. 7921SC320

(Filed 15 July 1980)

Municipal Corporations § 4.5– sale of property by redevelopment commission – necessity for accepting high bid

   Where the high bidder for property being sold by a municipal redevelopment commission to private developers has submitted a proposal for use of the property that complies with the zoning law and has been approved as being in conformity with the redevelopment plan, the municipal board of aldermen does not have the discretion to accept a lower bid for the property. G.S. 160A-514.

   Judge MARTIN (Harry C.) dissents.

APPEAL by plaintiff from *Walker (Ralph A.), Judge*. Judgment entered 20 November 1978 in Superior Court, FORSYTH County. Heard in the Court of Appeals 27 November 1979.

   This is an action by the plaintiff for an order requiring the Mayor and Board of Aldermen of the City of Winston-Salem to accept a bid made by plaintiff on a certain parcel of real estate in the City of Winston-Salem. The Winston-Salem Redevelopment Commission had acquired certain property in the City of Winston-Salem. On 22 September 1975, the Commission adopted the Crystal Towers Community Development Plan (CTCDP) for that property. Pursuant to that plan, the Commission offered for sale a parcel of real estate designated Parcel 1, Crystal Towers Community Development Area. The plaintiff submitted a bid of $6,550.00 for the property. One other bid was submitted by John Ozmun for $4,750.00. Both bidders submitted proposals for the development of the property. Plaintiff proposed to build six apartment units, and Ozmun proposed to move a single family dwelling onto the property. The City of Winston-Salem Planning Staff determined that both proposals met the requirements of the zoning district and the residential nature of the CTCDP. The planning staff determined that Mr. Ozmun's proposed proposal "more nearly" complied with the redevelopment plan for the area as it would increase home ownership. The planning staff recommended that the Board of Aldermen accept the Ozmun bid on the condition that he transfer an option he held on a certain lot to the City. The Board of Aldermen accepted the Ozmun bid and rejected the plaintiff's bid. The court granted the defendant's motion for summary judgment. Plaintiff appealed.

Frye, Booth and Porter, by Leslie G. Frye, for plaintiff appellant.

Womble, Carlyle, Sandridge and Rice, by Roddey M. Ligon, Jr., for defendant appellees.

WEBB, Judge.

The sale to private developers of property owned by the Winston-Salem Redevelopment Commission is governed by G.S. 160A-514 (c) and (d) which provide in part:

> (c) A commission may sell, exchange, or otherwise transfer real property or any interest therein in a redevelopment project area to any redeveloper for residential, recreational, commercial, industrial or other uses or for public use in accordance with the redevelopment plan, sub-

ject to such covenants, conditions and restrictions as may be deemed to be in the public interest or to carry out the purposes of this Article; provided that such sale, exchange or other transfer, and any agreement relating thereto, may be made only after, or subject to, the approval of the redevelopment plan by the governing body of the municipality and after public notice and award as specified in subsection (d) below.

(d) Except as hereinafter specified, no sale of any property by the commission or agreement relating thereto shall be effected except after advertisement, bids and award as hereinafter set out. The commission shall, by public notice, by publication once a week for two consecutive weeks in a newspaper having general circulation in the municipality, invite proposals and shall make available all pertinent information to any persons interested in undertaking a purchase of property or the redevelopment of an area or any part thereof. The commission may require such bid bonds as it deems appropriate. After receipt of all bids, the sale shall be made to the highest responsible bidder. All bids may be rejected. All sales shall be subject to the approval of the governing body of the municipality.

The question posed by this appeal is whether the Board of Aldermen may, in their discretion, accept a lower bid if the high bidder has submitted a proposal for the use of the lot that complies with the zoning law and has been approved as being in conformity with the redevelopment plan. We hold that they may not do so. This case turns on the construction of the sentence from the statute "[a]fter receipt of all bids, the sale shall be made to the highest responsible bidder." We hold that the plain words of the statute require in the case sub judice that if a bid is to be accepted it must be the bid of Porsh, which was the high bid. The appellees contend that the word "responsible" gives the Aldermen discretion to accept a lower bid if the Aldermen determine the lower bidder will make a more effective contribution to the redevelopment plan. We believe "responsible" means that the bidder must have the resources and ability to do what he has agreed to do in his proposal.

The defendants contend the statute gives the Board of Aldermen the discretion to decide which plan is more consistent with the CTCDP, that the Board can take into account the overall financial effect upon the City in determining which bid to accept, and the Board took into account several germane factors in exercising its discretion in rejecting the plaintiff's bid. We believe that to accept these arguments of the defendants, we would have to overrule the plain words of the statute.

The Board of Aldermen had the option of rejecting both bids, but if it is to accept a bid, it must be the bid of plaintiff which was the "highest responsible" bid.

We reverse the superior court and remand for a judgment consistent with this opinion.

Reversed and remanded.

Judge VAUGHN concurs.

Judge MARTIN (Harry C.) dissents.

———————

CARLTON L. HASKINS, JR., BY GUARDIAN AD LITEM, CARLTON L. HASKINS, SR. v. CAROLINA POWER AND LIGHT COMPANY

No. 7911SC397

(Filed 15 July 1980)

Negligence § 35.1– cable across private driveway – minor driving without lights after dark – contributory negligence as matter of law

In an action to recover for injuries sustained by plaintiff, a 15 year old, when he drove his motorbike into a steel cable which was stretched across defendant's roadway, the trial court properly granted defendant's motion for summary judgment since plaintiff was contributorily negligent as a matter of law in driving his motorbike on defendant's private roadway after dark without a light.

APPEAL by plaintiff from *Smith (Donald L.), Judge.* Judgment entered 31 January 1979 in Superior Court, HARNETT County. Heard in the Court of Appeals 4 December 1979.

The minor plaintiff, by his guardian ad litem, instituted this action for personal injuries as the result of an accident which occurred on a roadway owned by the defendant. The minor plaintiff drove his motorbike into a steel cable which was stretched across the roadway. Defendant made a motion for summary judgment, contending that plaintiff was contributorily negligent as a matter of law. The papers filed in support and in opposition to the motion for summary judgment established the following facts. On 22 April 1977 between 9:00 and 9:30 p.m., plaintiff, 15-year-old boy, drove his motorbike onto the defendant's private roadway. The roadway was unpaved and led to the defendant's substation near Erwin. The motorbike did not have a headlight. Plaintiff was very familiar with the roadway, having operated his motorbike on it "hundreds of times" over a period of several years. Plaintiff had not been on the roadway for approximately two weeks. Approximately three days prior to 22 April 1977, defendant had installed a steel cable across the roadway. The operator of the substation testified by affidavit that the cable was put up each night to prevent vandalism and was in place approximately three feet above the roadway when he left the premises at approximately 5:00 p.m. on 22 April 1977. He also stated in his affidavit that "[a]ttached to the cable was a metal red and white sign with the word 'Danger' on it, a red flag such as used to mark the end of power poles when they are transported by trailer, and a piece of orange surveyor's ribbon or tape." Plaintiff drove his motorbike into this cable and was injured. Plaintiff stated that when he looked at the cable after the accident, he saw only a small "danger" sign on the cable.

The court granted defendant's motion for summary judgment. Plaintiff appealed.

Pope, Tilghman and Tart, by Patrick H. Pope, for plaintiff appellant.

Fred D. Poisson, and Johnson and Johnson, by W.A. Johnson, for defendant appellee.

WEBB, Judge.

If the documents filed in support and in opposition to the motion for summary judgment forecast evidence, which if offered at trial would entitle the defendant to a directed verdict, the motion for summary judgment was properly allowed. *Moore v. Fieldcrest Mills, Inc.*, 296 N.C. 467, 251 S.E. 2d 419 (1979). If the only reasonable conclusion the jury could make is that the plaintiff, by driving his motorbike on the defendant's roadway after dark without a light, did something a reasonable 15-year-old boy would not have done under the circumstances and he should reasonably have seen that he might collide with a cable or something else on the roadway, the plaintiff was contributorily negligent as a matter of law. *See* 9 Strong's N.C. Index 3d, Negligence §§ 1, 8, and 13 (1977) for definitions of negligence, contributory negligence, and proximate cause. We hold that this is the only reasonable conclusion the jury could make. We believe that at age 15, a person should know that it is dangerous to ride a motorbike at night without lights and that a cable or other object is likely to be on a private roadway which can cause a collision and injury. Summary judgment for defendant was proper.

The plaintiff argues that it could be inferred that he was operating the motorbike at a safe rate of speed; that he was operating it in a prudent manner; that he had it under proper control and used a proper lookout. In answer to these arguments, it was not speed which was the cause of the collision; it was not in a prudent manner to drive without lights; and he could not keep a proper lookout if he did not have a light on the motorbike. Plaintiff also argues that it may be inferred that he could not have seen the cable if it had been daylight or if he had a spotlight on the motorbike. We do not believe we should speculate on either of these hypotheticals. In the case *sub judice*, the plaintiff was not able to see the cable in the dark. *See Starr v. Clapp*, 40 N.C. App. 142, 252 S.E. 2d 220 (1979).

Affirmed.

Judges VAUGHN and MARTIN (Harry C.) concur.

STATE OF NORTH CAROLINA v. WALTER CARNELL MULLEN

No. 801SC93

(Filed 15 July 1980)

Robbery § 5.2– nun-chuckas as dangerous weapon per se – erroneous instruction

The trial court in a prosecution for attempted armed robbery erred in instructing the jury that nun-chuckas allegedly used by defendant would be a dangerous weapon where the State presented evidence that nun-chuckas are two sticks joined by a chain; the victim testified that the sticks were 12 inches long and the chain perhaps 12 inches long; a policeman testified that nun-chuckas are eight to ten inch sticks connected by a six inch chain; no evidence was presented as to the weight or circumference of the sticks or chain; and the sticks and chain were not introduced into evidence.

APPEAL by defendant from *Barefoot, Judge.* Judgment entered 7 November 1979 in Superior Court, PASQUOTANK County. Heard in the Court of Appeals 3 June 1980.

Defendant was indicted for attempted armed robbery. The State presented evidence that at about 12:45 a.m. on 14 September 1979, Sheila Simpson went to pick up her brother Shelton Spence at the Sonic Drive-In where he worked as night manager. The business was closed and she stopped at the front door with her lights on and engine running. She saw defendant crouched outside the building, near the front door where Spence usually came out. This time Spence came out the back door of the business, carrying the day's receipts in an attache case as he usually did, and ran toward the car. Defendant ran behind Spence and began hitting him about the head and arm with "two sticks with a chain, nun-chuckas," using "tremendous force." Spence threw the attache case into the car and Simpson tried to sit on it. Defendant leaned into the car and tried to get the attache case from her. Simpson had known defendant in school, and she tried to talk him out of what he was doing. Defendant then "back[ed] up and ran" and jumped over a fence behind the place of business.

Defendant presented alibi and reputation evidence and denied that he had tried to rob the Sonic Drive-In. The jury returned a verdict of guilty of attempted armed robbery with a dangerous weapon, and defendant was sentenced to 12-15 years. He appeals.

Attorney General Edmisten, by Assistant Attorney General Daniel F. McLawhorn, for the State.

White, Hall, Mullen, Brumsey & Small, by G. Elvin Small III, for defendant appellant.

ARNOLD, Judge.

One of the essential elements of attempted armed robbery under G.S. 14-87(a) is the use of a "dangerous weapon . . . whereby the life of a person is endangered or threatened." In the present case the trial court charged the jury that "nun-chuckas, such as has been described in the evidence that has been used in this case would be a dangerous weapon," and defendant assigns error on the ground that the nun-chuckas were not a dangerous weapon *per se.*

We are compelled to find that defendant is correct. The State presented evidence that nun-chuckas are two sticks joined by a chain. Spence, the victim, testified that the sticks were 12 inches long and the chain perhaps 12 inches long. Ralph Williamson, an Elizabeth City policeman, testified that nun-chuckas are "eight to ten inch sticks connected by a six inch chain." No evidence was presented as to the weight or circumference of the sticks or chains, and they were not introduced into evidence. Our courts have held that assault with a deadly weapon is a lesser included offense in armed robbery, *State v. Richardson,* 279 N.C. 621, 185 S.E. 2d 102 (1971), so a "deadly" weapon is synonymous with a "dangerous" one, and cases addressing the question of whether a particular weapon was deadly *per se* are pertinent to the question now before us.

We find a close analogy to the present situation in the case of *State v. Buchanan,* 28 N.C. App. 163, 220 S.E. 2d 207 (1975), *cert. denied* 289 N.C. 452, 223 S.E. 2d 161 (1976). There the defendant was charged with assault with a deadly weapon, a policeman's nightstick, with intent to kill inflicting serious injury. No verbal description of the nightstick was given in the record, nor was the nightstick included as an exhibit on appeal. We awarded the defendant a new trial for the court's error in removing from the jury the question of whether the nightstick was a deadly weapon. Here, as in *Buchanan,* neither the meager description of the weapon nor the manner of its use is sufficient to permit the court to say as a matter of law that these nun-chuckas were a dangerous weapon within the meaning of the statute. For error in the charge to the jury, defendant is entitled to a new trial.

It follows from our ruling on this question that the trial court also erred in failing to charge the jury on the lesser included offense of attempted common law robbery, since if the jury were to find that the nun-chuckas were not a dangerous weapon, upon the evidence here they could find defendant guilty of attempted common law robbery. *See State v. Bailey,* 278 N.C. 80, 178 S.E. 2d 809 (1971), *cert. denied* 409 U.S. 948, 34 L.Ed. 2d 218, 93 S.Ct. 293 (1972). However, there is no evidence to support an instruction on assault with a deadly weapon or simple assault. All the State's evidence tended to show an attempted robbery rather than an assault. *See State v. Hicks,* 241 N.C. 156, 84 S.E. 2d 545 (1954) (The court should charge on a lesser included offense only when there is evidence of that offense. The contention that the jury might accept the State's evidence in part and reject it in part is not sufficient.).

Defendant's argument that he was entitled to a judgment as of nonsuit is without merit.

New trial.

Judges MARTIN (Robert M.) and HILL concur.

STATE OF NORTH CAROLINA v. ZEBEDEE MILBY AND STATE OF NORTH CAROLINA v. CHARLES LINWOOD BOYD

No. 809SC208

(Filed 15 July 1980)

1. **Criminal Law § 86.4– evidence of prior crimes – admissibility for impeachment**

The trial court did not err in admitting evidence of other unrelated crimes, since such evidence was admissible for impeachment purposes.

2. **Criminal Law § 42.4– armed robbery – guns taken from defendants five weeks later – no connection with crime – admission erroneous**

   In a prosecution for armed robbery, the admission of handguns taken from defendants five weeks after the crime with which they were charged was prejudicial error, since there was no evidence that either gun matched the description given by a witness concerning one gun used in the robbery, and there was no other evidence to connect the guns to the robbery for which defendants were on trial.

APPEAL by defendants from *Tillery, Judge.* Judgments entered 11 October 1979 in Superior Court, VANCE County. Heard in the Court of Appeals 11 June 1980.

Defendants were indicted for armed robbery for the theft of money from an A & P Store on 21 April 1979. They were found guilty and each was sentenced to 20-25 years. Defendants appeal.

Attorney General Edmisten, by Associate Attorney General Lucien Capone III, for the State.

Perry, Kittrell, Blackburn & Blackburn, by George T. Blackburn II, for defendant appellant Boyd.

Linwood T. Peoples for defendant appellant Milby.

ARNOLD, Judge.

[1] The robbery with which defendants are charged occurred on 21 April 1979. Defendants contend that the court erred by admitting evidence of other unrelated crimes, but in this they are mistaken. The testimony as to crimes on 20 August 1978 and 27 January 1979 was elicited on cross-examination of defendant Boyd and was proper as impeachment. See 4 Strong's N.C. Index 3d, Criminal Law §§ 86.1 and 86.5. The challenged testimony relating to 27 May 1979 was not evidence of a crime, and while the testimony objected to may have been irrelevant, we do not find that it was prejudicial.

[2] On 27 May 1979 officers stopped the vehicle which defendant Boyd was driving and in which defendant Milby was a passenger and arrested the defendants on a fugitive warrant. A

search of defendant Boyd revealed a handgun, and a second handgun was found in the passenger seat where defendant Milby had been sitting. These guns were admitted into evidence and defendants assign error, arguing that no connection was established between the guns and the robbery five weeks earlier.

We agree with defendants that admission of these handguns was prejudicial error. There was no evidence that either gun matched the description given by the witness Juanita Fuller that one gun used in the robbery was "a long, narrow gun" with "sort of a brass look." This case is different from those in which a witness testifies that the object admitted into evidence is at least similar to that involved in the crime. *See, e.g., State v. King,* 287 N.C. 645, 215 S.E. 2d 540 (1975), *death penalty vacated,* 428 U.S. 903, 49 L.Ed. 2d 1209, 96 S.Ct. 3208 (1976); *State v. Patterson,* 284 N.C. 190, 200 S.E. 2d 16 (1973). See generally 1 Stansbury's N.C. Evid. § 118 (Brandis rev. 1973). There was no other evidence to connect these guns to the robbery for which defendants were on trial. "The general rule is that weapons may be admitted in evidence 'where there is evidence tending to show that they were used in the commisson of a crime.'" *Id.* at 194, 200 S.E. 2d 19 quoting *State v. Wilson,* 280 N.C. 674, 678, 187 S.E. 2d 22, 24 (1972). The question of whether the court's error in admitting the guns into evidence was prejudicial is a close one, since there was substantial evidence that defendants were the prepetrators of the robbery. The State's evidence was not so overwhelming, however, that we can say this error was harmless beyond a reasonable doubt. Accordingly, defendants must be granted a new trial.

We find no merit in defendants' further assignments of error.

New trial.

Judges ERWIN and HILL concur.

State v. McLean

STATE OF NORTH CAROLINA v. NATHAL McLEAN

No. 7912SC747

(Filed 15 July 1980)

1. **Searches and Seizures § 23– affidavit for search warrant – statement that defendant "sexually assaulted" daughter – probable cause**

    An officer's affidavit, including a statement that defendant had "sexually assaulted" his daughter, stated sufficient facts from which a magistrate could properly find probable cause that a crime had been committed by defendant and that evidence of the crime might be found on his premises.

2. **Searches and Seizures § 4– nontestimonial identification evidence – use of search warrant**

    In addition to a nontestimonial identification order pursuant to Art. 14 of G.S. Ch. 15A, a search warrant is a proper method to obtain nontestimonial identification evidence from a defendant.

3. **Searches and Seizures § 4– blood and hair samples from defendant – probable cause for search warrant**

    An officer's affidavit was sufficient to support the magistrate's finding of probable cause for the issuance of a search warrant to permit public hair and a blood sample to be taken from defendant where the affidavit stated that defendant had sexually assaulted his daughter, listed several items of evidence which had been collected, including pubic hair and possible semen from the bed linen, and alleged that samples of defendant's pubic hair and blood were needed for comparison with the pubic hair and semen found in the linen.

APPEAL by defendant from *Gavin, Judge.* Judgment entered 11 April 1979 in Superior Court, CUMBERLAND County. Heard in the Court of Appeals 15 January 1980.

The defendant appeals from active prison sentences imposed after he was convicted of second degree rape, incest, and attempted incest.

Attorney General Edmisten, by Special Deputy Attorney General John R.B. Matthis and Assistant Attorney General Acie L. Ward, for the State.

Gregory A. Weeks for defendant appellant.

WEBB, Judge.

[1] The defendant in one assignment of error argues the in-
validity of two separate search warrants. He contends that
certain evidence seized under these warrants should have been
excluded from evidence. The first search warrant was issued on
16 January 1979 and was based in part on the following portion
of an affidavit which the defendant contends was not sufficient:

> "The applicant swears to the following facts to estab-
> lish probable cause for the issuance of a search warrant: On
> January 16, 1979 Angela Michelle McLean was sexually
> assaulted by her father on two occasions: at about 12:30 AM
> and again at about 2:30 AM in his bedroom of the above
> described residence. At the time of the assaults the victim
> was wearing a blue housecoat and red pajamas. During the
> assaults Nathel [sic] McLean (the father) withdrew from
> the body of Angela Michele [sic] McLean and ejaculated
> upon the bed linens. A second daughter brought into the
> same bedroom and an attempt to sexually assualt her was
> committed. [Angela Mechelle [sic] McLean stated to this
> officer that she was threatened by her father with a .25
> caliber pistol, that he had been drinking.]"

Defendant contends the statement in the affidavit that the
defendant had sexually assaulted Angela Michelle McLean is a
conclusion and does not state facts from which the magistrate
could determine a crime had been committed. We hold the words
"sexually assaulted" are specific enough that a more detailed
account was not necessary in order for the magistrate to determine what had happened. *Aguilar v. Texas,* 378 U.S. 108, 84 S.Ct.
1509, 12 L.Ed. 2d 723 (1964) involved a search warrant. In that
case, unlike the case sub judice, the applicant for a search
warrant relied on an unidentified informant. We believe the
rule of *Aguilar,* as applied to the case sub judice, is that in order
to issue a search warrant the magistrate must be able to find
probable cause from facts or circumstances shown in the affidavit submitted to him that a crime has been committed and
evidence of the crime may be on the premises to be searched. In
Aguilar, the Court held that since the affiant was relying on an
unidentified informant, the affidavit must contain facts from
which the magistrate could find probable cause (1) that the
informant is reliable and (2) that the informant spoke with

personal knowledge of the things he related. This has been called the two prong test of *Aguilar*. In the case sub judice the affiant was not relying on an unidentified informant. It is obvious from reading the affidavit that the affiant was relying on Angela Michelle McLean, the daughter of the defendant. The affidavit stated with specificity what had happened. We hold that from this affidavit the magistrate could find probable cause that a sexual assault had been committed by defendant and that evidence of the assault might be found on his premises. The first search warrant was properly issued.

[2] The second search warrant was issued to take blood samples and pubic hairs from the defendant. The investigating officers elected not to use Art. 14 of Chapter 15A of the General Statutes to obtain this nontestimonial identification from the defendant. G.S. 15A-272 provides:

> A request for a nontestimonial identification order may be made prior to the arrest of a suspect or after arrest and prior to trial. Nothing in this Article shall preclude such additional investigative procedures as are otherwise permitted by law.

We hold that a search warrant is one method in addition to Art. 14 of Chapter 15A to obtain nontestimonial identification evidence from defendants.

[3] The affidavit supporting the second search warrant stated that a sexual assault on Angela Michelle McLean had been committed by defendant and listed several items of evidence which had been collected including pubic hair and possible semen from the bed linen. The applicant, through the affidavit, asked to be allowed to take pubic hair and a blood sample from the defendant to compare with the pubic hair and semen on the linen for identification purposes. We hold that this was sufficient for the magistrate to find probable cause that a crime had been committed and evidence of the crime might be gained by taking pubic hair and a blood sample from the defendant. The second search warrant was properly issued.

No error.

Judges PARKER and ARNOLD concur.

———————————

SEASHORE PROPERTIES, INC. v. EAST FEDERAL SAVINGS AND LOAN
ASSOCIATION OF KINSTON, AND JOHN L. GRAY, JR., TRUSTEE

No. 803SC10

(Filed 15 July 1980)

Mortgages and Deeds of Trust § 26– notice of foreclosure – record owner defined

The term "record owner" in G.S. 45-21.16, which provides for the giving of notice of foreclosure proceedings, refers either to the original mortgagor of the property or to a present owner who has purchased property subject to a mortgage; therefore, plaintiff was not a record owner and was not entitled to notice when a recorded management agreement promised to convey to plaintiff a 50% interest in the real property after two promissory notes were repaid but not later than five years.

APPEAL by plaintiff from *Rousseau, Judge.* Order entered 10 October 1979 in Superior Court, CARTERET County. Heard in the Court of Appeals 22 May 1980.

This is an appeal from a partial summary judgment for defendants in an action to have a foreclosure set aside.

On 1 April 1976 East Federal Savings and Loan Association of Kinston sold a certain tract of land in Carteret County, North Carolina, referred to as Captain's Bridge Motel to O.C.G. Enterprises, Inc. The deed of trust and deed were recorded on 1 April 1976 in the Carteret County Register of Deeds Office. After O.C.G. Enterprises, Inc., purchased the property from East Federal Savings and Loan Association, but on the same day, 1 April 1976, O.C.G. Enterprises, Inc. executed a document entitled "Management Agreement" with plaintiff, Seashore Properties, Inc., regarding the management of Captain's Bridge Motel. This document was recorded on 23 April 1976 in the Carteret County Register of Deeds Office.

The management agreement provides in Article 11 and Article 15 that, in addition to other considerations, the plaintiff was to receive a 50% interest in the real and personal property comprising Captain's Bridge Motel as compensation for its management services. This interest was to be conveyed to plaintiff as soon as certain notes were paid, or after five years, whichever came first. The agreement was to be construed so as to create in plaintiff, Seashore Properties, Inc., a property interest in the above mentioned real and personal property.

Thereafter on 31 March 1977, foreclosure proceedings were instituted. Plaintiff did not receive notice of hearing or notice of the foreclosure sale. Defendants' motion for summary judgment was granted on the question of whether plaintiff was entitled to receive notice of the foreclosure. Plaintiff appealed.

Michael E. Mauney and Timothy E. Oates for plaintiff appellant.

Ward and Smith, by Michael P. Flanagan, for defendant appellees.

MARTIN (Robert M.), Judge.

The sole question presented for review is whether the trial court erred in granting partial summary judgment in favor of defendants on the ground that as a matter of law plaintiff was not entitled to receive notice of the foreclosure made reference to in plaintiff's first claim for relief.

At the time of the foreclosure proceedings instituted on 31 March 1977, the relevant portion of G.S. 45-21.16(b) then in effect read as follows:

(b) Notice of hearing shall be sent to:

* * *

(3) To the record owner or owners (including owners in tenancy by the entirety) of the real estate at the time of the giving of the notice.

We note that the above section of the statute was amended in 1977. Session Laws 1977, c. 359, s. 18, provides: "This act shall become effective on October 1, 1977, and shall apply only to those foreclosure actions commenced on or after that date." Session Laws 1977, c. 359, s. 17 provides that this act shall not apply to pending litigation.

Plaintiff contends that by virtue of the recorded management agreement, which promises to convey to plaintiff a 50% interest in the real property to be conveyed after two promissory notes are repaid but not later than five years and which creates in plaintiff a property interest in the real property, it was a record owner within the meaning of the statute and as such was entitled to notice. We do not agree.

G.S. 45-21.16 does not contain a definition of "record owner or owners." In interpreting G.S. 45-21.16, this Court has stated:

The intent of the legislature controls the interpretation of a statute. In ascertaining this intent the courts should consider the language of the statute and what it sought to accomplish. (Citations omitted) G.S. 45-21.16 was enacted in response to *Turner v. Blackburn*, 389 F. Supp. 1250 (W.D.N.C. 1975) In *Turner*, the court held that the statutory procedures governing foreclosure under a power of sale did not comport with due process because the procedures did not provide adequate notice or a hearing prior to foreclosure and the mortgagor had not waived notice and hearing.

In re Watts, 38 N.C. App. 90, 93, 247 S.E. 2d 427, 429 (1978). Thus, the Legislature was responding to the specific due process requirement laid down in *Turner* that personal notice of foreclosure be given to the *mortgagor*. 389 F. Supp. at 1257-59.

In light of the legislative history, we hold that the term "record owner" in G.S. 45-21.16 was intended to refer to either the original mortgagor of the property or a present owner who has purchased property subject to a mortgage. This interpretation is supported by G.S. 45-21.16A which contains the following language:

Contents of Notice of Sale. — The notice of sale shall — (1) Describe the instrument pursuant to which the sale is held, by identifying the *original* mortgagors and recording date, and if different from the *original mortgagors* shall list the *record owner* of the property, as reflected on the records of the register of deeds not more than 10 days prior to posting the notice, who may be identified as *present owners*, and may reflect the owner not reflected on the records if known. (Emphasis added)

Because plaintiff was neither the original mortgagor nor the present owner of the property, it was not entitled to notice of the foreclosure under G.S. 45-21.16 then in effect and summary judgment was properly granted on this issue.

Affirmed.

Judges ARNOLD and HILL concur.

_____

NOMIE JEAN DOSS STEWART v. RICHARD LEE STEWART

No. 8018DC120

(Filed 15 July 1980)

Appeal and Error § 9– Rule 60 motion to set aside portion of prior order – moot question

The question presented by plaintiff's Rule 60 motion to set aside the portion of a January 1979 order vacating child custody and support provisions of a prior order was moot where plaintiff filed a second action in March 1979 and the status of the children was settled in a child custody and support order entered in May 1979 before plaintiff filed her Rule 60 motion.

APPEAL by plaintiff from *Campbell, Judge.* Judgment entered 29 August 1979 in District Court, GUILFORD County. Heard in the Court of Appeals 5 June 1980.

In April 1977 the trial court entered an order awarding to the plaintiff alimony pendente lite, child support, and custody of the parties' two minor children. In October 1978 defendant moved to vacate this order on the ground that since their separation and the entry of the order the parties had had intercourse, and thus plaintiff had condoned any misconduct on his part which had been a basis for the 1977 order. Responding to defendant's motion, plaintiff alleged that the acts of intercourse between the parties had been without her consent; that defendant had threatened her and forced himself upon her. In January 1979 the trial court entered its order on defendant's motion, ruling that, the parties having resumed the marital relationship, the 1977 order was void. No appeal was taken from the January 1979 order.

In August 1979 plaintiff moved under Rule 60 for partial relief from the January order, contending that intercourse between the parties should not invalidate the custody and support portions of the 1977 order. Ruling on the motion, the court found that plaintiff had filed a second action in this matter in March 1979, and that in that action she had been awarded custody of one of the children, child support, and alimony pendente lite. The court held that by bringing the March action plaintiff had waived her right to a favorable ruling on her Rule 60 motion, and denied the motion. Plaintiff appeals.

Samuel M. Moore and Douglas P. Dettor for plaintiff appellant.

Tate & Bretzmann, by C. Richard Tate, Jr., for defendant appellee.

ARNOLD, Judge.

Plaintiff contends that the trial court erred in denying her Rule 60 motion, because she is entitled to relief from the court's order of January 1979. She argues that the court could not by its January 1979 order vacate the custody and support portions of the 1977 order and thus leave the status of the children *in fieri*. As defendant points out, however, since the entry of the January 1979 order the status of the children has been settled by the court's order in plaintiff's action filed in March 1979, and as a result the question plaintiff raises by her motion is now moot.

The situation here is much like that in *Utilities Comm. v. Southern Bell Telephone Co.*, 289 N.C. 286, 221 S.E. 2d 322 (1976). There, the telephone company sought a rate increase, and received only about one-quarter of what it requested. While the company's appeal was pending, it filed a new application and received the entire rate increase. Our Supreme Court took judicial notice of the later proceeding and dismissed the appeal from the original rate increase as moot.

In the present case, plaintiff seeks relief from the January 1979 order on the ground that the status of the children may not be left *in fieri*, but that the trial court in ruling on her motion properly took judicial notice of the action filed by plaintiff in March 1979. The order entered in that action in May 1979 settled the status of the children, and at the time plaintiff filed her Rule 60 motion in August 1979 the question of whether the trial court acted improperly by the entry of its January 1979 order was moot. Accordingly, the order denying plaintiff's motion for relief was proper.

Affirmed.

Judges MARTIN (Robert M.) and HILL concur.

LUCILLE GLORIA WESLEY v. GREYHOUND LINES, INC.

No. 7910SC733

(Filed 5 August 1980)

1. **Carriers § 19.2– sexual assault on bus passenger – action against carrier – type of area surrounding station**

   In an action against a bus company to recover damages allegedly resulting from defendant's negligent failure to protect plaintiff passenger from sexual assault in the women's restroom of defendant's bus station, testimony that defendant's station was located in a high crime area, that bums, prostitutes, and their pimps frequented the bus station, that fights from area night clubs frequently spilled into the streets, that drug arrests were common in the neighborhood, and that some of these very same characters were loiterers-in-residence at defendant's bus station was competent to show defendant's knowledge of the need for insuring adequate protection of passengers going to, going from, and waiting in the bus station.

Wesley v. Greyhound Lines, Inc.

---

2. Carriers § 19.2– sexual assault on bus passenger – action against carrier – instruction on absence of denial that plaintiff sustained injury – harmless error

In an action against a bus company to recover damages allegedly resulting from defendant's negligent failure to protect plaintiff passenger from sexual assault in the women's restroom of defendant's bus station, the trial court erred in instructing the jury that defendant did not deny that the plaintiff was a victim of a criminal assault at its Raleigh terminal "or that she sustained injury or damage" where defendant did not stipulate or admit that plaintiff sustained injury or damage from the assault. However, defendant was not prejudiced by such error where (1) the jury could not have been misled by the misstatement; (2) the trial court thereafter instructed that it was for the jury to determine whether plaintiff sustained injury or damage; and (3) the trial court summarized the contentions of both parties as to the issue of injury and damage.

3. Trial § 32.2– instruction to ignore previous charge on negligence issue

There is no merit in defendant's contention that the trial court erred in instructing the jury to ignore its original instructions on the first issue of negligence because the jury could have disregarded the previously given instructions on the nature of the lawsuit, proximate cause, and the burden of proof.

4. Appeal and Error § 50.2; Negligence § 40– instructions on proximate cause – use of "probable cause"

The trial court's *lapsus linguae* in using the term "probable cause" instead of "proximate cause" in one instance in the charge was not prejudicial error.

5. Evidence § 48; Damages § 3.4– permanency of psychological effects of sexual assault – testimony by clinical psychologist

A clinical psychologist was not prohibited by the statute precluding the practice of medicine without a license, G.S. 90-18, from testifying as to the permanency of psychological effects on plaintiff resulting from a sexual assault. Furthermore, the psychologist's testimony was not too speculative for admission, although she used the word "guess" in stating her opinion, where her opinion was not a mere guess but was a statement of probability.

6. Damages § 3.4; Evidence §48– expert testimony by psychologist – sufficient contact with plaintiff to provide basis for opinion

A clinical psychologist's contact with plaintiff was not so minimal as to provide an insufficient basis for her opinion testimony as to the permanency of psychological effects on plaintiff from a sexual assault where the psychologist first saw plaintiff on 7 July 1976 approximately one month after the assault; subsequent meetings were held on 15 July 1976, 4 October 1976, 1 January 1979 and 2 February 1979; at the time of these meetings, plaintiff was suffering from severe mental damage and, in keeping with psychological practices in such cases, was being seen only upon request; and the trial court did not find that the psychologist's examinations of plaintiff were solely for trial purposes and not for treatment.

7. **Carriers § 19.2; Damages § 3.4– psychological and physical effects from sexual assault – compensable injury**

   In an action against a bus company to recover damages allegedly resulting from defendant's negligent failure to protect plaintiff passenger from
sexual assault in the women's restroom of defendant's bus station, plaintiff
suffered a compensable injury where her evidence tended to show that, since
the sexual assault on her, she has had difficulty sleeping, has had nightmares, has awakened at night afraid that some other person was in the room
threating to harm her, and has been unable to participate in or enjoy the
sexual pleasures which she had previously experienced, since plaintiff has
suffered a physical impact resulting in mental distress or emotional disturbance.

8. **Damages §§ 3.5, 17.5– lost wages and reduced earning capacity – unemployed plaintiff**

   In an action to recover for damages allegedly resulting from defendant
bus company's negligent failure to protect plaintiff passenger from sexual
assault in the women's restroom of defendant's station, the trial court did
not err in instructing the jury on loss of wages and reduced capacity to earn
because plaintiff was unemployed before the incident.

9. **Carriers § 19.2– sexual assault on bus passenger – liability of carrier – standard of care**

   The trial court's instruction that a common carrier must exercise the
highest degree of care in foreseeing the imminence of a criminal assault on
its passengers will not be held erroneous where such instruction is in accord
with the rule stated in one line of prior N.C. cases, although another line of
cases states that a carrier is only required to exercise ordinary or due care in
foreseeing the imminence of a criminal assault on its passengers, since it is
for the Supreme Court to determine which rule of law will govern when there
is a conflict of rules.

10. **Carriers § 19.2; Evidence § 42– sexual assault on bus passenger – action against carrier – characterizations of persons observed around bus station – shorthand statements of fact – relevancy to show notice**

    A witness's testimony that over a period of time he observed bums, winos
and panhandlers hanging around a bus station and disturbing people was
competent as a shorthand statement of fact and was relevant to show notice
and knowledge by the bus company of the imminence of a sexual assault on a
passenger in its station.

11. **Carriers § 19.2; Evidence § 48– expert in security – adequacy of carrier's security measures**

    In an action to recover for damages allegedly resulting from defendant
bus company's negligent failure to protect plaintiff passenger from sexual
assault in the women's restroom of defendant's station, opinion testimony
by an expert witness in the field of law enforcement and security as to the
adequacy of defendant's security measures on the date of the sexual assault
did not invade the province of the jury and was properly admitted.

Wesley v. Greyhound Lines, Inc.

12. Carriers § 19.2– sexual assault on bus passenger – action against carrier –
evidence of need and availability of security guards and devices

In an action to recover damages allegedly resulting from defendant bus
company's negligent failure to protect plaintiff passenger from sexual
assault in the women's restroom of defendant's station, testimony that an
officer had talked to defendant's agents about the need for and the availability of security guards was competent to prove notice to and knowledge of the
need for adequate security measures by defendant, and testimony concerning the availability of security devices was relevant to the issue of negligence.

13. Witnesses § 5.2– cross-examination of plaintiff – subsequent evidence of good
character

Plaintiff could properly present evidence of her good character after her
credibility had been impeached by defendant's cross-examination of her.

14. Carriers § 19.2– sexual assault on bus passenger – negligence by bus company –
sufficiency of evidence

Plaintiff's evidence was sufficient for the jury on the issue of defendant
bus company's negligence in failing to protect plaintiff passenger from sexual assault in defendant's station where it tended to show that plaintiff
arrived at defendant's station by bus at 3:00 a.m.; while waiting in the
women's restroom for her cousin to pick her up, she was forcibly compelled at
knife point and against her will to submit to the sexual advances of a loiterer
in the station; the assailant had bothered female passengers on other occasions as they waited in the bus terminal and had pulled a gun on defendant's
employee when he sought to intervene on one occasion; the employee had
run the assailant out of the station about fifty times prior to the assault on
plaintiff; the assailant had also been asked to leave the station on other
occasions by defendant's district manager and by its terminal manager; the
entrance to the women's restroom was not observable by any of defendant's
employees although technological means were available to permit such
observations; pimps, prostitutes, transvestites, bums, winos and loiterers
were allowed to linger in the bus station where they frequently pestered
defendant's passengers and were out of view of defendant's employees;
fights, narcotics arrests and criminal activities abounded in the neighborhood, and persons committing the crimes were free to enter and to leave the
bus station at their discretion; a police officer had talked with defendant's
agents about the need for and availability of security guards, but defendant
had not instituted such measures; defendant's national security director
had not issued any directive pertaining to securing the bus station, and
defendant's local agents had in many instances failed to report incidents
such as assaults in the bus station; since the assault plaintiff has difficulty
sleeping, has nightmares, is unable to interact with people, takes valium to
calm her nerves, and is unable to enjoy a normal sex life or affectionate
embraces from male suitors; and plaintiff will suffer permanent psychological effects from the assault. However, such evidence was insufficient for
submission to the jury of issues of willful and wanton negligence and punitive damages.

APPEAL by plaintiff and defendant from *Godwin, Judge.* Judgment entered 16 March 1979 in Superior Court, WAKE County. Heard in the Court of Appeals 21 March 1980.

On 6 June 1976, plaintiff, a resident of Bishopville, South Carolina, purchased a bus ticket from defendant, Greyhound Lines, Inc. (hereinafter Greyhound), to travel from Bishopville to Raleigh. The bus on which she was traveling pulled into defendant's Raleigh bus station at approximately 3:00 a.m. on 7 June 1976. While sitting in the lounge of the ladies' restroom in the Raleigh terminal awaiting her ride, plaintiff was sexually assaulted by one Darnell Banks, a loiterer in the bus station. Plaintiff sued defendant Greyhound for negligence in not protecting her from the assault.

At trial, plaintiff asked the trial court to submit an issue as to punitive damages. The trial court refused. The jury returned a verdict of $150,000 in plaintiff's favor.

Plaintiff and defendant appealed. Other facts pertinent to this appeal are set out in the opinion.

Thorp, Anderson & Slifkin, by William L. Thorp and Anne R. Slifkin, for plaintiff.

Johnson, Patterson, Dilthey & Clay, by I. Edward Johnson, Robert W. Kaylor, and Alene M. Mercer, for defendant.

ERWIN, Judge.

DEFENDANT'S APPEAL

[1] Defendant's initial assignment of error is that the trial court erred in permitting testimony concerning the neighborhood surrounding its bus station and the type of individuals who frequented the area. We find no error.

The sole basis for defendant's objection is that the objected to testimony was highly prejudicial. It is the rule of law in our State that all relevant evidence is admissible unless excluded by some specific rule, 1 Stansbury's N.C. Evidence (Brandis rev.

1973), § 77, and relevant evidence will not be excluded simply because it may tend to prejudice the opponent for the cause of the party who offers it. 1 Stansbury's N.C. Evidence (Brandis rev. 1973), § 80. Here, plaintiff offered the objected to testimony to show that defendant had knowledge or should have had knowledge which would have forewarned it of the imminency of attack or assault on one of its passengers — the plaintiff. In 1 Stansbury's N.C. Evidence (Brandis rev. 1973), § 83, p. 259, it is stated: "Knowledge may be proved by the conduct and statements of the party himself, by statements made to him by other persons, by evidence of reputation which it may be inferred had come to his attention, and by various circumstances from which an inference of knowledge might reasonably be drawn." (Footnotes omitted.)

Evidence that defendant's bus station was located in a high crime area, that bums, prostitutes, and their pimps frequented the bus station, that fights from area night clubs frequently spilled into the streets, that drug arrests were common in the neighborhood, and that some of these very same characters were loiterers-in-residence at defendant's bus station was clearly admissible and relevant to show defendant's knowledge of the need for insuring adequate protection of passengers going to, going from, and waiting in the bus station. This is especially the case where a carrier is concerned, for the law imposes upon a carrier a special duty to protect passengers from assault, abuse, or injury at the hands of fellow passengers or third persons, and the carrier is responsible to a passenger for a wrong inflicted by an intruder, as in the instant case, at least, where the carrier or its servants knew or ought to have known that it was threatened. See *Pride v. R.R.*, 176 N.C. 594, 97 S.E. 418 (1918). We are reluctant to state the rule in its entirety, since we are called on to examine and clarify it at a later point herein. For now, we believe the portion as cited will suffice. Furthermore, we overrule defendant's contention that the trial court erred in instructing the jury on the foregoing evidence.

[2] As its next assignment of error, defendant contends that the trial court erred in stating in its charge to the jury that "it does not deny that the plaintiff was a victim of a criminal

assault at its Raleigh terminal, or that she sustained injury and damage."

In a pretrial order signed by respective counsel and approved by Judge Godwin, defendant stipulated that "[p]laintiff was sexually assaulted in the lounge of the women's restroom of the Greyhound Bus Station by Darnell Banks. Darnell Banks was found guilty of this attack."

Nowhere in the pretrial order or at trial did defendant stipulate that plaintiff sustained injury or damage. Ordinarily, a charge on the law relative to facts not shown in the evidence is prejudicial. 1 Strong's N.C. Index 3d, Appeal and Error, § 50.1, p. 320. However, no prejudicial error warranting a new trial occurs where it is clear from the charge, as here, that: (1) the jury could not have been misled by the misstatement; (2) the trial court at a later point in the charge instructed the jury that it was for them to determine whether plaintiff had sustained injury and damage; and (3) the trial court summarized both parties' contentions arising from the evidence as to the issues of injury and damage. *See* 1 Strong's N.C. Index 3d, Appeal and Error, § 50.2, p. 321.

[3] Defendant contends that the trial court erred in instructing the jury to ignore its original instructions on the first issue submitted, because the jury could reasonably thereafter have disregarded the previously given instructions on the nature of the lawsuit, proximate cause, greater weight of the evidence, *et al.*

While the trial court's instruction might have been more artfully drawn, we do not believe that the jury was misled. Immediately after the contested instruction, the jury's foreman asked: "Your Honor, this morning there was a question on the word imminent, and I anticipate that the same question will come up again when we go back. Does that refer to time span or likelihood?" This incident would indicate that the jury was very well aware of its continuing duty to consider the court's earlier instructions as they related to burden of proof, proximate cause, *et al.*, and correctly disregarded the court's instructions as to the other matters. We find no prejudicial error.

[4] Similarly, we reject defendant's contention that the trial court's use of the term *probable cause* instead of *proximate cause* in one instance was prejudicial error. The trial court had correctly set out and defined the term proximate cause previously. In reiterating its previous instructions to the jury, the trial court committed a mere *lapsus linguae* in saying probable cause when he meant to say proximate cause. The instruction was altogether correct in all other respects, and we find no prejudicial error, for the trial court's error was mere inadvertence.

[5] As a further assignment of error, defendant contends that the trial court erred in permitting testimony by a clinical psychologist as to the permanency of plaintiff's injuries and the indicatory symptoms. We disagree.

A psychologist in the rendering of professional psychological services may apply psychological principles and procedures for the purposes of understanding, *predicting*, or influencing the behavior of individuals. G.S. 90-270.2(e). A diagnosis by a psychologist that an external occurrence such as a sexual assault may have permanent psychological effects is clearly within his or her realm of competence. We are aware that G.S. 90-18 generally precludes the practice of medicine by an individual not licensed in accordance with the provisions of Article 1 and that a person is regarded as practicing medicine within the meaning of Article 1 if he "shall diagnose or attempt to diagnose . . . or attempt to treat . . . any human ailment, physical or mental." G.S. 90-18. While not specifically exempted by G.S. 90-18, a psychologist who limits himself to the practice of psychology and the rendering of professional psychological services as defined in G.S. 90-270.2(d) and (e) is exempt from G.S. 90-18 to that extent, and we so hold. *Cf. Maloney v. Hospital Systems*, 45 N.C. App. 172, 262 S.E. 2d 680 (1980) (nurse who was an expert in field of intravenous therapy competent to testify, even though she was not licensed to diagnose illness or injury or prescribe treatment).

Defendant's exception to Dr. Cogwell's expert testimony on the permanency of plaintiff's injuries on the ground that it is speculative is meritless. Defendant relies on our decision in

Garland v. Shull, 41 N.C. App. 143, 254 S.E. 2d 221 (1979). In *Garland*, a physician was allowed to testify over defendant's objection that plaintiff's "headaches may persist for years at least. An indefinite period of time." We granted defendant a new trial on the grounds that:

" '[A] physcian testifying as an expert to the consequences of a personal injury should be confined to certain consequences or probable consequences, and should not be permitted to testify as to possible consequences.' *Fisher v. Rogers*, 251 N.C. 610, 614, 112 S.E. 2d 76, 79 (1960). *See generally*, Annot., 75 A.L.R. 3d 9 (1977). Testimony tending to indicate that an event may occur is an indication that the occurrence of the event is certain or probable."

Id. at 147, 254 S.E. 2d at 223.

In the instant case, when asked about the permanency of plaintiff's injuries, Dr. Cogwell stated:

"My opinion is that some of the problems are probably not permanent and that others are. The ones that I would guess to be permanent include a generally increased fearfulness, particularly around strangers and particularly around men. A generally decreased level of people in general, but particularly in people that she does not know well. I would expect her to continue to have occasional nightmares, although I would expect those to continue to decrease as time goes on and I would expect there to be a continuing fearfulness in physical situations that are similar to the one in which she was attacked."

While Dr. Cogwell did use the word, "guess," in her answer, we do not perceive the same speculativeness or conjecture in her answer as evidenced in *Garland*. It is clear that Dr. Cogwell's opinion was not a mere guess, but rather a statement of probability. We find no error in the admission of her testimony. Moreover, Dr. Cogwell's testimony as to the permanency of some of plaintiff's injuries was sufficient basis for introduction of the mortuary tables, and the trial court's jury charge as to these matters was not error. *See Gillikin v. Burbage*, 263 N.C.

317, 139 S.E. 2d 753 (1965), and *McCoy v. Dowdy*, 16 N.C. App. 242, 192 S.E. 2d 81 (1972).

[6] An ancillary argument presented by defendant is that Dr. Cogwell's contact with plaintiff was so minimal as to provide an insufficient basis for admitting her testimony. Defendant calls to our attention our decision in *Ward v. Wentz*, 20 N.C. App. 229, 201 S.E. 2d 194 (1973).

In *Ward v. Wentz, supra,* we upheld the trial court's exclusion of testimony by a physician that plaintiff's injuries were of a permanent nature where the physician's prognosis was based upon an examination made of plaintiff the day before the trial; the physician had last treated plaintiff for her injuries nearly four years before her trial; and her visit to the physician on the day before trial was not for the purpose of treatment, but rather to obtain evidence for use at trial. In upholding the exclusion of the physician's testimony, we held that under the circumstances of the case, plaintiff suffered no prejudicial error. While the facts in the instant case are somewhat similar to those in *Ward v. Wentz, supra,* we find no prejudicial error in the court's admission of the testimony in this case.

Dr. Cogwell testified:

"It is important that persons involved in crisis intervention counseling see the victim of an assault as often as the victim wants to be seen, which may not be as often as counselor can see them. It is also important for the counselor not to intrude on the victim during periods where the victim does not wish to be seen. In rape and sexual assault situations there usually is a period following the assault when a person attempts to block it all out and does not want counseling for a while."

The record indicates that Dr. Cogwell first saw plaintiff on 7 July 1976, approximately one month after the sexual assault. Subsequent meetings were held on 15 July 1976, on 4 October 1976, around 1 January 1979, and on 2 February 1979. At the times these meetings were held, plaintiff was suffering from severe mental damage, and in keeping with psychological practices in such cases, was being seen only upon request. Unlike the situation in *Ward v. Wentz, supra,* the trial court did not find that Dr. Cogwell's examinations were sought solely for trial purposes, not for treatment. We find no prejudicial error in its admission.

[7] Defendant's next assignment of error is that plaintiff did not suffer a compensable injury. We disagree.

Plaintiff presented evidence that since the sexual assault, she has had difficulty sleeping, has had nightmares, and has awakened at night afraid that some other person was in the room threatening to harm her. Since the assault, she has been unable to participate in or enjoy the sexual pleasures that she had previously experienced. When viewed properly, plaintiff's evidence indicates that she has suffered mental trauma or emotional disturbance.

In *Williamson v. Bennett,* 251 N.C. 498, 503, 112 S.E. 2d 48, 52 (1960), our Supreme Court stated:

"It is almost the universal opinion that recovery may be had for mental or emotional disturbance in ordinary negligence cases where, coincident in time and place with the occurrence producing the mental stress, some actual physical impact or genuine physical injury also resulted directly from defendant's negligence."

Although the court denied recovery in *Williamson,* it did so because the plaintiff's injury was thought not to have been the proximate result of defendant's acts, not because of a disavowal of the universal rule. That that was the case is evidenced by reiteration of the rule in *King v. Higgins,* 272 N.C. 267, 158 S.E. 2d 67 (1967). It is significant that under the rule, a plaintiff may recover if there is "some actual physical impact or genuine physical injury." This alternative mode of proof justifying recovery is important because of the difficulty of defining "physical injury." *See Kimberly v. Howland,* 143 N.C. 398, 55 S.E. 778 (1906). Under whichever test used, we have no difficulty in finding that plaintiff has suffered a compensable injury. As a proximate result of the sexual assault by Darnell Banks, allegedly facilitated by defendant's negligent act, plaintiff has suffered a physical impact resulting in mental distress or emotional disturbance.

When viewed under the test of physical injury, plaintiff has shown such a wrecking of her nervous system as to come within the rule so eloquently stated and explained in *Kimberly v. Howland*, 143 N.C. 398, 403-04, 55 S.E. 778, 780 (1906):

> "The nerves are as much a part of the physical system as the limbs, and in some persons are very delicately adjusted, and when 'out of tune' cause excruciating agony. We think the general principles of the law of torts support a right of action for physical injuries resulting from negligence, whether wilful or otherwise, none the less strongly because the physical injury consists of a wrecked nervous system instead of lacerated limbs."

[8] Defendant's assignment of error, that the trial court erred in instructing the jury on loss of wages and reduced capacity to earn because plaintiff was unemployed before the incident, is without merit and is overruled. *See Johnson v. Lewis*, 251 N.C. 797, 112 S.E. 2d 512 (1960), and *Purgason v. Dillon*, 9 N.C. App. 529, 176 S.E. 2d 889 (1970).

[9] We next consider defendant's assignment of error that the trial court's charge to the jury regarding the degree of care owed by a common carrier was erroneous, in that, it held defendant to a higher standard of care than is required by North Carolina law.

The trial court instructed the jury in pertinent part:

> "I instruct you that if you find that the plaintiff has satisfied you by the greater weight of the evidence that on and prior to June 6, 1976, Greyhound Lines, Incorporated, its officers, agents, or servants knew or *the exercise of the highest degree of care* for the safety of its passengers *should have known*, that a criminal assault on plaintiff or some other of its passengers in its ladies' restroom at its Raleigh terminal was imminent and that it had or in the exercise of

the highest degree of care for the safety of its passenbers [sic], should have had such knowledge long enough in advance of June 6, 1976, to have prevented the assault on plaintiff with the manpower and physical resources at hand;

And further that Greyhound Lines, Incorporated, failed and neglected to exercise the highest degree of care for the safety of plaintiff in [his] Raleigh terminal on June 6, 1976 as far as was consistent with the practical operation of its business and that such failure and neglect proximately resulted in the June 6, 1976 criminal assault on plaintiff, you will answer the first issue yes in favor of the plaintiff.

As we understand it, defendant's objection is based on the fact that the trial court instructed the jury that a common carrier must exercise the *highest degree* of *care* in *foreseeing* the imminence of a criminal assault on its passengers. Defendant argues that a carrier is only required to exercise *ordinary care* or *due care* in foreseeing the imminence of a criminal assault on its passengers.

Which standard is applicable is a matter not free from doubt.

In *Daniel v. R.R.*, 117 N.C. 592, 602, 23 S.E. 327 (1895), our Supreme Court stated the law in pertinent part, thusly: "Common carriers are insurers, subject to a few reasonable exceptions. They are held to exercise the greatest practicable care, the highest degree of prudence, and the utmost human skill and foresight which have been demonstrated by experience to be practicable." Relying on the Court's decision in *Daniel v. R.R.*, *supra*, the trial court, in *Hollingsworth v. Skelding*, 142 N.C. 246, 55 S.E. 212 (1906), charged the jury in the Supreme Court's language. Nevertheless, the Supreme Court found error. Expressly overruling its decision in *Daniel v. R.R.*, the Supreme Court opined:

"We doubt if any better definition of the duty of a carrier owes the passenger can be found than that of *Lord Mansfield in Christie v. Griggs*, 2 Camp., 29: 'As far as human care and foresight could go, he must provide for their safe conveyance.' In commenting upon this case Mr. Barrow says: 'It must not be supposed, however, that the law requires the carrier to exercise every device that the ingenuity of man can conceive. Such interpretation would act as an effectual bar to the business of transporting people for hire.' "

Hollingsworth v. Skelding, 142 N.C. 246, 248-49, 55 S.E. 212, 213 (1906). Based on the Court's decision in *Hollingsworth*, a new trial was ordered in *Perry v. Sykes*, 215 N.C. 39, 200 S.E. 923 (1939), when the trial court instructed the jury as in *Daniel v. R.R., supra;* yet when presented with the same charge in *Horton v. Coach Co.*, 216 N.C. 567, 5 S.E. 2d 828 (1939), the Supreme Court found no error. Thus, two rules of law were recognized. A third rule was established in a line of cases beginning with *Britton v. R.R.*, 88 N.C. 536, where our Supreme Court established a converse proposition that:

"According to the uniform tendency of these adjudications which we admit as authorities, the carrier owes to the passenger the duty of protecting him from the violence and assaults of his fellow-passengers or intruders, and will be held responsible for his own or his servant's neglect in this particular, when, by the exercise of proper care, the acts of violence might have been foreseen and prevented; and while not required to furnish a police force sufficient to overcome all force, when unexpectedly and suddenly offered, it is his duty to provide ready help sufficient to protect the passenger against assaults from every quarter which might reasonably be expected to occur under the circumstances of the case and the condition of the parties." (Citations ommitted.)

Id. at 544. *See also Leake v. Coach Co.*, 270 N.C. 669, 155 S.E. 2d 161 (1967); *Harris v. Greyhound Corporation*, 243 N.C. 346, 90 S.E. 2d 710 (1956); *Smith v. Cab Co.*, 227 N.C. 572, 42 S.E. 2d 657 (1947); *Pride v. R.R.*, 176 N.C. 594, 97 S.E. 418 (1918); *Mills v. R.R.*, 172 N.C. 266, 90 S.E. 221 (1916); *Pruett v. R.R.*, 164 N.C. 3, 80 S.E. 65 (1913); *Stanley v. R.R.*, 160 N.C. 323, 76 S.E. 221 (1912) (Brown, J. dissenting opinion); *Seawell v. R.R.*, 132 N.C. 856, 44

S.E. 610 (1903). In fact, many of these cases also espouse, in part, the standard set forth in *Hollingsworth v. Skelding, supra,* requiring a carrier to provide for the safe conveyance of its passengers as far as human care and foresight can go, consistent with practical operation of the business, *e.g., Leake v. Coach Co., supra,* and *Smith v. Cab Co., supra;* while other cases simultaneously embrace the standard approved in *Daniel v. R.R., supra,* that a carrier must exercise the utmost human skill and foresight in providing for the safe conveyance of its passengers. *See, e.g., Mills v. R.R., supra.* That a conflict exists between the various rules of law as stated by the Supreme Court was recognized in Torts — Negligence — Common Carriers — Degree of Care owed Passengers, 17 N.C.L. Rev. 453, 457-58 (1939), where it is stated:

"In *Pruett v. Southern Ry.*[28] the court seems to apply both the 'high degree of care' rule and the 'reasonable care' rule. It uses this language, 'A common carrier ... is required only to exercise *proper care* to guard them [its passengers] against injuries which *may reasonably be anticipated.*' On page five of the official report the court quotes with approval as follows, ' "The rule that it is *the duty of a carrier to use the highest degree of care* to protect the passenger from wrong or injury by a fellow-passenger applies only when the carrier has knowledge of the existence of the danger, or of facts and circumstances from which the danger may be *responsibly anticipated.*" ' This language indicates that a carrier must use the highest degree of care to guard against known dangers and those of which he reasonably should know but is only required to use reasonable care to foresee danger. In a later case, *Mills v. Atlantic Coast Line Ry.,*[29] the court holds that the following language, which seems to be squarely *contra* to that set out above, correctly describes the duty owed by a common carrier to its passengers, 'Railroad companies ... are held to a high degree of care in looking after the safety of passengers on their trains ... and the company is responsible for

[28]164 N.C. 3, 4, 80 S.E. 65, 66 (1913).

[29]172 N.C. 266, 267, 90 S.E. 221 (1916).

actionable wrongs committed upon them by other passengers or third persons *which could have been provided against or prevented by the utmost vigilance and foresight* ... these companies are not insurers of the safety of passengers and are not liable for injuries which in the exercise of *such care* [this must refer to the italicized language set out above] their ... employees ... could not *reasonably have prevented.*' "

In conclusion, the author states:

"In view of the fact that jury verdicts may go one way or the other depending on the language used to describe the degree of care owed by common carriers to their passengers and the fact that the North Carolina court has used so many different phrases to designate this degree of care it seems that we would secure more uniform verdicts, and have fewer appeals, if the supreme court would definitely and finally put its stamp of approval on one consistent group of words which could be confidently used by trial courts in cases involving this question."

Where there is a conflict of rules of law and no factual distinctions can be made, as here, it is for the Supreme Court to determine which rule will govern. 1 Strong's N.C. Index 3d, Appeal and Error, § 2, pp. 180-81. Since the trial court's instruction here was in accord with at least the two rules of law imposing a high degree of care in foreseeing the imminence of an assault on a carrier's passenger, we affirm it and find no prejudicial error. We note, however, that in instructing the jury, the trial court stated that defendant Greyhound must have been able to foresee the likelihood of an assault on plaintiff or some other passenger in the ladies' restroom before liability could be imposed. This portion of the instruction was erroneous, since all that any of the standards enumerated require is the foreseeability of the imminence of an assault anywhere within the terminal. This error was favorable to the defendant, and it cannot now complain.

Defendant assigns as error the trial court's permitting the plaintiff to testify concerning future plans, feelings about sex, and relations with other individuals. In view of our previous holding that plaintiff sustained a compensable injury, this assignment of error is overruled. *See also* Loss of Enjoyment of Life — Should It be a Compensable Element of Personal Injury Damages?, 11 Wake Forest L. Rev. 459 (1975).

Similarly, we find defendant's assignment of error relating to the testimony of witness Cherry to be meritless.

Mr. Franklin Cherry, a newspaper salesman at defendant's bus station, testified that he was present on the night of 6 June 1976 and had seen Darnell Banks after the time they had gone to school together. Defendant's Exception No. 21 is based on relevancy. We glean from the question asked that plaintiff was seeking to prove that Darnell Banks habitually frequented the bus station, inclusive of the night of 6 June 1976. His answer and the question were relevant and admissible.

[10] Defendant's Exception No. 22 is based on the following:

"Q. Can you tell us between the period of time from three a.m. to five or six a.m. during the years 1975 to June '76, can you tell us what people you saw there?

MR. JOHNSON: OBJECTION.

A. Yes.

COURT: He may say what people he saw, if he knows.

Q. Go ahead, sir.

DEFENDANT APPELLANT'S EXCEPTION NO. 22

A. I saw different types of people hanging around, messing around, just panhandling and doing different types of things; just observed people, you know, upset and disturbing people passing through the terminal."

We find no error in the admission of this testimony, since it relates to the issue of notice and knowledge of the imminency of an assault discussed previously herein. Exception Nos. 23 and 24 are of the same import, and we find no prejudicial error in the court's rulings. Mr. Cherry's use of the terms, bums, winos, panhandlers, and disturbing people, was a shorthand statement of facts. *See State v. Hunter*, 299 N.C. 29, 261 S.E. 2d 189 (1980). Consequently, defendant's Exception No. 25 assigning as error the trial court's failure to exclude the testimony and denial of his motion to strike the testimony is overruled.

[11] Defendant assigns as error the trial court's allowing Dr. Bopp, an expert witness in the field of law enforcement and security, to testify. The basis of this assignment of error is that Dr. Bopp's testimony invaded the province of the jury in giving his opinion as to the adequacy of defendant's security measures.

> "It has been said that expert testimony to be admissible must relate to some trade or pursuit requiring special skill or knowledge, but the wide range of subject matter to which expert opinion has been directed in North Carolina disproves the existence of any such limitation and demonstrates that the only question is whether the particular matter under investigation is one on which the witness can be helpful to the jury because of his superior knowledge." (Footnotes omitted.)

1 Stansbury's N.C. Evidence (Brandis rev. 1973), § 134, p. 433. It is further stated: "It seems abundantly clear that, despite occasional technical roadblocks erected by the 'rule' against invading the jury's province and by notions about the jury's sublime capacity to draw its own inferences, there can be expert testimony upon practically any facet of human knowledge and experience." *Id.* at 438. We overrule this assignment of error.

[12] Defendant assigns as error the trial court's permitting the witness Womble to testify in regard to the availability of security guards. This assignment is likewise without merit. The testimony was competent to prove notice to and knowledge of the need for adequate security measures by defendant. Here, the witness is merely reporting his actions, and his testimony was competent for that purpose.

Defendant's assignment of error relating to the testimony of the witness Olsen regarding the availability of security devices is overruled, since the testimony was relevant to the issue of negligence, *i.e.*, the standard of care imposed by law upon a carrier in the protection of its passengers and the breach thereof.

[13] Next, defendant assigns as error the trial court's permitting evidence concerning plaintiff's character.

A civil action for assault and battery is not a proceeding where character is in issue. *Smithwick v. Ward*, 52 N.C. (7 Jones) 64. The general rule in civil suits is that unless the character of a party be put directly in issue by the nature of the proceeding, evidence of his character is not admissible. *McRae v. Lilly*, 23 N.C. (1 Ired.) 118. An exception to the general rule precluding the introduction of character evidence in a civil action exists after the credibility of the party seeking to offer it has been impeached, *see* 1 Stansbury's N.C. Evidence (Brandis rev. 1973), § 50, and cross-examination is one form of impeachment. *Id.* At trial, defendant cross-examined plaintiff. Once this was done, plaintiff was free to prove her good character, although there was no direct attack upon it. *Id.* at 145. This assignment of error is overruled.

[14] The final assignment of error which we need to consider on defendant's appeal is whether the trial court erred in denying defendant's motion for a directed verdict.

> " 'On a motion by a defendant for a directed verdict in a jury case, the court must consider all the evidence in the light most favorable to the plaintiff and may grant the motion only if, *as a matter of law*, the evidence is insufficient to justify a verdict for the plaintiff.' " (Citations omitted.)

Kelly v. Harvester Co., 278 N.C. 153, 158, 179 S.E. 2d 396, 398 (1971). When plaintiff's evidence is viewed in this light, it was clearly sufficient to withstand the motion for a directed verdict.

Plaintiff's evidence tended to show: On 6 June 1976, plaintiff left Bishopville, South Carolina by Greyhound bus arriving at the Raleigh terminal in the early morning hours of 7 June 1976. Upon arrival, she telephoned her cousin for a ride and waited for the ride in the ladies' lounge. While sitting in the lounge (restroom) reading, plaintiff was accosted by one Darnell Banks, a known loiterer at the bus station, who pulled a knife on her and forcibly compelled her, at knife point and against her will, to submit to his sexual advances, including the act of fellatio. Only after he had ejaculated did Banks flee.

Since the assault, plaintiff has difficulty sleeping; she has nightmares; she is unable to interact with people; she takes valium to calm her nerves; and she is unable to enjoy a normal sex life or affectionate embraces from male suitors because of the frightening sexual assault. Her injury has been psychological in nature, resulting in irreparable damage, for which she is entitled to compensation. Defendant's former employee, Wayne Braswell, testified that Banks, on prior occasions, had bothered female passengers as they waited in the bus terminal and had pulled a gun on him when he sought to intervene on one occasion. Braswell had run Banks out of the station approximately 50 times, and on several occasions prior to the incident on 6 June 1976, Mr. Fred Mock, defendant's district manager of the Raleigh Division, and Mr. Shirley Gresham, defendant's Raleigh terminal manager, had asked Banks to leave. Indicative of Banks' activities is the testimony related by Wayne Braswell in the record:

"A. Right. The reason that I would ask him to leave, more so than anything, in one instance I had walked up to the baggage area where you set the baggage right beside the ticket counter. A girl got up and walked towards me at the same time and he started towards the front door and told me that he told her if she didn't leave with him he was going to cut her. So from then on, I more or less watched him. I heard several of the other employees say that, you know, they had heard —

Mr. Kaylor: Objection to what anyone else has said.

Mr. Thorp: Goes to notice, Your Honor.

Court: Overruled.

DEFENDANT APPELLANT'S EXCEPTION NO. 151

A. The other employees had told me from time to time that on different shifts when we would come in and discuss what had happened, that he would leave during the night and sometime with a girl and the girl would come back crying. They would ask her why she was crying and they would say he told me if I didn't leave with him he was going to shoot me or cut me, he had a gun. They said why didn't you sign a warrant. They always lived out of town, didn't have time for court and would rather forget it, just leave."

Defendant's terminal was structured so that the entrance to the ladies' restroom where the lounge was located was not observable by any of Greyhound's employees, even though technological means were available to do so. Pimps, prostitutes, transvestites, bums, winos, and loiterers, like Banks, were allowed to linger in the bus station where they frequently pestered defendant's passengers and were out of view of defendant's employees. Fights, narcotics arrests, as well as other criminal activities abounded in the neighborhood, and persons committing these crimes were free to enter, to linger, and to leave the bus terminal at their discretion.

A police officer, Officer Womble, called to the premises to remove these persons, had talked with defendant's agents about the provision and need for security guards, but defendant had not instituted such measures. Defendant's national security director had not issued any directives pertaining to securing the bus terminal, and defendant's local agents had in many instances failed to report incidents such as assaults in the bus station.

This evidence was more than sufficient to show defendant's negligent breach of its duty to protect its passengers from assaults by intruders, regardless to which standard of care in foreseeing harm defendant is held, *i.e.*, "the utmost human skill and foresight," *see Daniel v. R.R.*, 117 N.C. 592, 23 S.E. 327 (1895); "as far as human care and foresight could go," *Hollingsworth v. Skelding*, 142 N.C. 246, 55 S.E. 212 (1906); or "with the proper [reasonable] care." *See Pride v. R.R.*, 176 N.C. 594, 97 S.E. 418 (1918).

Defendant's other assignments of error have been reviewed and are without merit.

Plaintiff's Appeal

Plaintiff contends the trial court erred in failing to submit to the jury the issues of (1) whether the plaintiff was injured by the willful and wanton conduct of the defendant and (2) whether plaintiff was entitled to punitive damages. We disagree.

Plaintiff's evidence as set forth in the foregoing portion of our opinion was insufficient for the submission to the jury of the issues of willful and wanton negligence and punitive damages.

Conclusion

The judgment entered below is

Affirmed.

Judges Martin (Robert M.) and Clark concur.

WESTERN AUTO SUPPLY COMPANY v. JAMES OLIVER VICK, Trading and Doing Business as a Western Auto Associate Store

No. 807SC58

(Filed 5 August 1980)

1. Usury § 1– findings unsupported by evidence
    In an action in which defendant store owner contended that transactions involving the assignment of chattel paper to plaintiff Western Auto fell within the purview of the usury laws, there was no evidence in the record to support the trial court's findings that (1) "Without regard to whether payment for merchandise purchased by [defendant] from [plaintiff] . . . was made in cash or with chattel paper, the amounts for which [defendant] was given cash or chattel paper — equivalent credit upon his account(s) were no longer deemed by [plaintiff] or [defendant] to be owed by [defendant] to [plaintiff] for the merchandise purchases by [defendant] reflected in his account(s)," and (2) plaintiff and defendant "intended and viewed the transactions between them as the purchase and sale of merchandise and the

purchase and sale of chattel paper," since to the extent that defendant paid for his purchases from plaintiff with chattel paper, defendant continued to be obligated or indebted to plaintiff for the payments reflected in the chattel paper until defendant remitted cash to plaintiff equivalent to those installments.

2. **Usury § 1– purchase of Western Auto Store – payment of individual debtors' debts – usurious transactions**

Transactions pursuant to an agreement whereby defendant purchased the assets of a Western Auto Store which had previously been operated by plaintiff were usurious and could not be considered the sale of chattel paper at a discount where the evidence tended to show that defendant was responsible for collecting and forwarding amounts due from individual installment debtors to plaintiff; defendant was required to pay to plaintiff all installments when due, whether or not the installments were paid by the individual debtors; defendant was required to repurchase all chattel paper from plaintiff on accounts more than ninety days in arrears even though he had been making the payments as they became due to plaintiff; plaintiff obtained a security interest in the chattel paper collateralizing defendant's debt; for the period specified in each installment contract, plaintiff refrained from collecting from defendant sums due under the contract; as defendant paid off the deferred installment payments under the chattel paper, he was credited only with that portion of the installments attributed to principal, plus 30 or 35% of the finance charge; and plaintiff kept for itself 65 or 70% of the finance charge.

3. **Usury § 1.3– amount of interest – amount financed determined on transaction-by-transaction basis**

Where defendant contended that the transactions between the parties were usurious, there was no merit to plaintiff's contention that, since the total balance which defendant owed was considered to be in excess of $300,000, the parties were free to agree on any rate of interest under G.S. 24-1.1(5), as that statute was in effect at that time, since the only reasonable interpretation of that statute is that the principal amount financed must be determined on a transaction-by-transaction basis, at least where the transactions are not contemporaneous, and not on the basis of the aggregate amount owing between the parties.

4. **Usury § 1– corrupt intent – sufficiency of evidence**

Defendant showed the requisite corrupt intent on the part of plaintiff for the transactions in question to be held usurious, since the corrupt intent required to constitute usury is simply the intentional charging of more for money lent than the law allows, and plaintiff intended to exact the interest which it did by keeping 65 or 70% of the unearned finance charge on each of the contracts "assigned."

5. **Usury § 1– usurious transactions – no time-price sales**

Transactions between the parties which defendant claimed were usurious did not fall within the "time-price" exception to the usury statutes

Auto Supply v. Vick

since the transactions complained of did not involve the bona fide sale of chattel paper; defendant's obligation to plaintiff was not finally determined when contracts were assigned to plaintiff, but only when installments were paid under the contracts; the contracts themselves were merely regarded by the parties as security for the advancement of credit by plaintiff to defendant; and the transactions possessed none of the attributes commonly associated with time-price sales.

APPEAL by defendant and plaintiff from *Browning, Judge.* Order entered 10 July 1979 and judgment entered 29 June 1979 in Superior Court, NASH County. Heard in the Court of Appeals 4 June 1980.

Based upon the extensive stipulations of the parties and the evidence adduced at the trial below, the factual background of this case is as follows. Plaintiff Western Auto is engaged in the business of selling various merchandise at wholesale to the owners of Western Auto Associate Stores in North Carolina. In 1971, Western Auto and Vick reached an agreement for Vick to purchase the assets of a Western Auto Store in Rocky Mount, North Carolina, which had previously been operated by Western Auto for its own account. In connection with this agreement the parties executed three documents: (1) a "Western Auto Associate Store Contract", governing the terms of the franchise; (2) a "Purchase Agreement", regulating the assignment of conditional sales contracts by Vick to Western Auto and the respective liabilities of the parties with respect to such transactions; and (3) a security agreement granting Western Auto a security interest in much of Vick's presently owned and after acquired property, including conditional sales contracts entered into between Vick and his customers.

In connection with his acquisition of the store assets, Vick also purchased and became legally responsible for the collection of chattel paper generated from the operation of the company-owned store, then having a total outstanding unpaid balance of about $175,000. The parties had the understanding that the chattel paper would be treated as though generated by Vick in the operation of his store and assigned to Western Auto under the purchase agreement.

After Vick purchased the store from Western Auto, it became a Western Auto Associate Store, meaning that it was owned and operated by Vick independent of any control of Western Auto. At the time that Vick commenced operation of his store, he was furnished with a supply of retail installment sales agreement forms to be used by Vick in connection with the documentation of any sale of merchandise to his retail customers that involved a time payment arrangement. Vick was also given a supply of transmittal forms to be used by him in submitting his retail installment sales agreements (chattel paper) to Western Auto for credit on his account.

The Western Auto system of accounts involved several account categories under which charges made to Vick might be entered: (1) a "regular" account; (2) a "trade acceptance" account; (3) a "dating terms" account; and (4) a "floor plan" account. On 29 December 1972 a memorandum was issued by Western Auto to Vick which specified that as to charges made to Vick's regular account, payment would be due not later than the tenth day of the month for charges reflected in the statement of account issued by Western Auto around the first of the month and the payment would be due not later than the twenty-fifth day of the month on the statements of account issued by Western Auto at mid-month.

Vick satisfied the charges made to his regular account, and in some instances the charges made to his trade acceptance, floor plan and dating terms accounts, by either sending to Western Auto cash payments or by submitting to Western Auto chattel paper generated from his store operations. The chattel paper was attached to a letter of transmittal, which listed all of the agreements attached to it and specified certain information about the amounts due upon and finance charges applicable to each of such agreements. Letters of transmittal were so structured that Vick would compute the amount of credit that he was requesting under each such letter. This computation involved the deduction from the total amount due on each contract of either sixty-five percent or seventy percent (depending upon the terms of the particular agreement) of the finance charges specified in each agreement as the portion of such finance charges Western Auto was to retain for itself when the sums due under the chattel paper were collected. One copy of the transmittal letters was returned to Vick with a notation on it by Western Auto as to the amount of credit that was being made to his accounts pursuant to the letter. The amount of the credit given by Western Auto as to each letter of transmittal was noted on the copy returned to Vick and corresponded to a credit shown on the next statement of account issued by Western Auto to Vick.

Statements of account were periodically furnished by Western Auto to Vick. In the early part of the relationship between the parties, these statements of account were issued as often as weekly, but after January 1977, they were issued semi-monthly. The statements of account detailed all the charges to each of Vick's accounts, *i.e.*, regular, trade acceptance, dating terms and floor plan, and showed the credit given on each of these accounts. As to all chattel paper assigned by Vick, Western Auto submitted to Vick each month an "installment billing" for the aggregate of all payments due during that month on the chattel paper, the aggregate amount due also being detailed on his statement of account under the heading "installment." If Vick failed to collect the total amount due under the chattel paper from Vick's customers, Vick was required to remit to Western Auto the difference. It was Vick's responsibility to see that all payments due under the chattel paper were collected, to send out any delinquency notices that were required, and to repossess any merchandise if monthly payments were not forthcoming as required under the agreement. Auditors of Western Auto periodically examined the ledger cards maintained by Vick as to each amount and if any customer was found to be in arrears more than ninety days, Vick was required to pay to Western Auto the entire balance due on the particular account, notwithstanding the fact that the monthly payments on such accounts made by Vick to Western Auto were on a current basis. Upon Vick's making such payoff, the chattel paper was returned to him. The billings for these payoffs were called special installment billings and were detailed on the statements of account submitted by Western Auto to Vick.

No transaction in which chattel paper was submitted to Western Auto involved an amount equal to or greater than

$50,000. In July 1975 Vick executed a deed of trust to Robert L. Spencer, trustee for Western Auto, to secure Vick's indebtedness to Western Auto of $72,056.00. During the time Vick was a Western Auto dealer, he was free to transfer his chattel paper to entities other than Western Auto. In connection with the transfer of chattel paper by Vick to Western Auto, Vick never received any money from Western Auto.

Western Auto filed this action against Vick, claiming he was in default of his obligations under the purchase agreement. Vick answered, denying that the agreement was in default. Vick further defended and counterclaimed, alleging that the practices of Western Auto with respect to the assignment of chattel paper were corruptly intended by Western Auto to collect interest from Vick at an unlawful and usurious rate. By consent of the parties, Vick's counterclaim for usury was ordered severed from the remainder of the action and tried without a jury. At the trial of this counterclaim the trial court denied Western Auto's motion for an involuntary dismissal under G.S. 1A-1, Rule 41(b), but nevertheless granted judgment for it on the counterclaim itself. The judgment was certified for immediate appellate review under Rule 54(b). From the judgment granted in favor of the plaintiff Western Auto, defendant Vick appeals. Plaintiff cross-appeals from the court's denial of its Rule 41(b) motion.

Smith, Anderson, Blount, Dorsett, Mitchell & Jernigan, by Michael E. Weddington and Carl N. Patterson, Jr., for the plaintiff appellee.

Biggs, Meadows, Batts, Etheridge & Winberry, by Samuel W. Johnson, for the defendant appellant.

WELLS, Judge.

[1] Defendant first assigns as error two findings of fact made by the trial court on grounds that they were not supported by any evidence. The court's findings of fact are conclusive on appeal if supported by any competent evidence, even though there may be evidence in the record to support contrary findings. *Henderson County v. Osteen*, 297 N.C. 113, 254 S.E. 2d 160

(1979). However, if there is no evidence in the record to support findings to which proper exceptions have been entered, they must be set aside. *See, Insurance Co. v. Lambeth,* 250 N.C. 1, 108 S.E. 2d 36 (1959). The two challenged findings read as follows:

> 10. Without regard to whether payment for merchandise purchased by Vick from Western Auto and reflected on a "statement of account" rendered by Western Auto to Vick was made in cash or with chattel paper, the amounts for which Vick was given cash or chattel paper — equivalent credit upon his account(s) were no longer deemed by Western Auto or Vick to be owed by Vick to Western Auto for the merchandise purchases by Vick reflected in his account(s).

> * * *

> 16. From the written agreements entered into between Western Auto and Vick and their course of dealing thereunder, which was not inconsistent therewith, it is clear that Western Auto and Vick intended and viewed the transactions between them as the purchase and sale of merchandise and the purchase and sale of chattel paper.

We find that there is no evidence in the record to support these findings. The purchase agreement entered into between the parties contained provisions requiring Vick to repurchase chattel paper upon the occurrence of certain events, to collect all the installments as they came due from the customers, and to remit all such installment payments to Western Auto whether or not they had been paid by the customers. The agreement also contains the following key provision: "The Company shall have all of the rights of the Dealer, and the Dealer shall remain liable to the Company for any deficiency on such Chattel Paper, including the Company's reasonable expenses and attorney fees." As to collection and remittance arrangements and practices, Vick testified:

> When I sent chattel paper to Western Auto, they kept the original and sent me back a copy. Collections were made on the payments due on the paper by people coming to the store and making payments or mailing the payments in or

in some cases we'd have to go to see them to pick up the payments. Western Auto was not involved in any way with the collection of payments from my customers. Western Auto did not send out any notices of delinquencies and it did not have any representatives call on my customers and attempt to collect payments. I maintained collection records by keeping a ledger card posted up to date for each customer and I kept a separate ledger card on each contract that was sent in to Western Auto. When I collected payments from customers I noted the collections on the ledger card and put the money into a special bank account and sent it to Western Auto. If a customer didn't pay me one month I had to make the payment for him to Western Auto. Western Auto sent me a statement each month showing all the customers and how much they owed, and that is the way we paid that. The auditors of Western Auto came around and checked my ledger cards every now and then. If they found a customer was behind over 90 days, I would have to pay the account off in full. All the auditor did was check the ledger card and call for a pay-off on certain ones if they were behind, and they checked the credit information if it was a new account.

As to the treatment of the chattel paper sent to Western Auto by Vick, Western Auto's auditor testified as follows:

Q. Now, Mr. Gallimore, I believe in response to questions put to you by Mr. Weddington that you have said that merchandise charged to Mr. Vick's Regular account can be paid by cash or by the chattel papers.

A. Yes, sir.

Q. And that when you got the chattel paper in that you credited his account with, his Regular account wiped it out, you said, that much of the charge.

A. Yes, sir.

Q. I believe that is what you said.

A. Right.

Q. And I believe you said that he didn't owe you that amount. Is that what you meant to say?

A. I said what?

Q. That as soon as he got that credited he didn't owe it anymore.

A. That is correct. This eliminated that charge, that portion of the charge on his Regular account.

Q. Now what you mean is he didn't owe it under that account.

A. That is correct.

Q. But he was still obligated to pay it, wasn't he, until that chattel paper was paid out?

A. He owed the amount of the paper, yes.

Q. So that was, as you said, just a paper transaction. You credited that, and debited him somewhere else.

A. That is correct.

The factual pattern that thus emerged from the record is that to the extent Vick paid for his purchases of merchandise from Western Auto with chattel paper, Vick continued to be obligated or indebted to Western Auto for the payments reflected in the chattel paper until *Vick* remitted cash to Western Auto equivalent to those installments. We believe the following chart of events and transactions expresses in shorthand fashion the undisputed evidence before the trial court.

Substance of the Transactions

I. Extension of Credit and Payment of Principal

A. Vick makes wholesale purchases from Western Auto on open credit accounts which may be collected as due on ten days notice.

B. Vick pays for the items due on account with cash or by assigning Western Auto what is in effect the installments due under the chattel paper.

C. Vick remains responsible for collecting and forwarding amounts due from individual installment debtors to Western Auto. Vick must pay to Western Auto all installments when due, whether or not the installments were paid by the individual debtors, and Vick must repurchase all chattel paper from Western Auto on accounts more than ninety days in arrears even though he has been making the payments as they became due to Western Auto.

D. Western Auto obtains a security interest in the chattel paper collateralizing Vick's debt.

II. Forbearance

A. For the period specified in each installment contract, Western Auto refrains from collecting from Vick sums due under the contract.

III. Interest

A. As Vick pays off the deferred installment payments under the chattel paper, he is credited only with that portion of the installments attributed to principal, plus thirty or thirty-five percent of the finance charge. Western Auto keeps for itself sixty-five or seventy percent of the finance charge.

We find no evidence in the record in support of the trial court's Findings of Fact Nos. 10 and 16, and defendant's exception to these findings must accordingly be sustained. *Accord, Morse v. Curtis*, 276 N.C. 371, 172 S.E. 2d 495 (1970).

[2] Vick maintains that the transactions between the parties with respect to the chattel paper fall within the purview of the usury laws. The elements of usury are: (1) a loan or forbearance of money; (2) an understanding that the money loaned shall be returned, or the credit extended shall be repaid after the forbearance; (3) payment or an agreement to pay a greater rate of interest than that allowed by law; and (4) a corrupt intent to take more than the legal rate for the use of the money. *See, Henderson v. Finance Co.*, 273 N.C. 253, 160 S.E. 2d 39 (1968). The trial court concluded that: the transactions complained of did not involve a loan or forbearance; if any amount was owed by Vick to Western Auto it was in excess of $300,000 and not subject to interest limitations under G.S. 24-1.1A(e); no interest payments were made by Vick; Vick was not required to make any interest payments out of his own funds; Western Auto did not intend to reserve for itself any interest in the transactions; and the time-price doctrine prevented the transactions from falling under the usury statutes. We hold that the complained-of transactions fall clearly within the purview of the usury laws.

Western Auto extended Vick credit for Vick's purchases of merchandise and had the authority to collect all amounts due on Vick's regular account on ten days notice. The term "forbearance" has been defined as

> a contractual obligation of a lender or creditor to refrain during a given period of time from requiring a borrower or debtor to pay a loan or debt that is due and payable. In case of a forbearance, it is not necessary that it be preceded by an actual loan, provided a debt has already been created; the usury will consist in the agreement for excessive interest in order to secure an extension of time.

45 Am. Jur. 2d, Interest and Usury § 117, p. 102 (1969). Western Auto accepted the chattel paper as security for its extension of credit and collected from Vick sixty-five or seventy percent of the unearned finance charge as the charge for its forbearance. Western Auto's retention of a portion of the unearned finance charge on each contract is analogous to a service charge taken by Western Auto for its forbearance from collecting on a portion

of a debt owed to it by Vick. We have previously held such a forbearance subject to the usury laws. *Supply, Inc. v. Allen,* 30 N.C. App. 272, 227 S.E. 2d 120 (1976).

The assignment of the chattel paper to Western Auto under the conditions in this case is clearly distinguishable from the pure sale of paper at a discount. Since Vick was required to pay all installments under each contract to Western Auto when they came due and to repurchase all chattel paper which became more than ninety days overdue, Vick, in effect, guaranteed payment of all the contracts.

As to the character and effect of such a transaction the authorities present some four different views. Some courts have held such a transaction to be clearly usurious, and that the usurious indorsee takes no rights against any of the parties to the instrument. Others have held that while the transaction between the indorser and indorsee is usurious, the defense of usury is personal to the indorser and is not available to the prior parties. A third view, while holding the transfer not usurious, limits the right of recovery against the vendor-indorser to the amount received by him with lawful interest, and gives the purchaser recourse against prior parties to the full amount of the obligation. In still other jurisdictions such a transaction is regarded as a valid sale of a chattel with a warranty of its soundness, and the purchaser is allowed to enforce the obligation to its full extent against his own indorser and all prior indorsers.

91 C.J.S., Usury § 19 (a)(3), p. 595 (1955). At least as between indorser and indorsee, such transactions have been subject to the usury laws in North Carolina for over a hundred years. *See, Bynum v. Rogers,* 49 N.C. 399 (1857); Annot., *Usury as Predicated Upon Transaction In Form of a Sale or Exchange of Commercial Paper or Other Choses In Action,* 165 A.L.R. 626 (1946).

We agree with Vick that *Associated Stores, Inc. v. Industrial Loan & Invest. Co.,* 202 F. Supp. 251 (E.D.N.C. 1962), *aff'd per curiam,* 326 F. 2d 756 (4th Cir. 1964), *cert. denied,* 379 U.S. 830, 13 L.Ed. 2d 39, 85 S. Ct. 60 (1964), is in point. In the *Associated* case, Associated was in the business of selling home appliances and occasionally needed to borrow money. The money was furnished by Industrial through its purchase from Associated of conditional sales contracts which Industrial bought at an eleven percent discount. However, Associated guaranteed payment of the contracts by indorsement. Judge Craven held that the fact that neither of the parties regarded the transactions as loans was not determinative under the usury laws of North Carolina:

> "It has been repeatedly held, in this State, that while one may buy a note from another, at any price that may be agreed upon, the bargain being free from fraud or unlawful imposition, if the purchaser requires the indorsement of the seller as a guaranty of payment, the transaction, as between the immediate parties thereto, is in effect a loan, and will be so considered, within the meaning and purport of our laws against usury." *Bynum v. Rogers*, 49 N.C. 399; *Ballinger v. Edwards*, 39 N.C. 449; *McElwee v. Collins*, 20 N.C. 350; *Sedbury v. Duffy*, 158 N.C. 362. [sic]

> "A profit, greater than the lawful rate of interest, intentionally exacted as a bonus for the loan of money, imposed upon the necessities of the borrower in a transaction where the treaty is for a loan and the money is to be returned at all events, is a violation of the usury laws, it matters not what form or disguise it may assume." *Doster v. English*, 152 N.C. 339, 67 S.E. 754; *Monk v. Goldstein*, 172 N.C. 516, 90 S.E. 519.

> It is a half-truth to call the transactions between Associated and Industrial "sales at a discount" ....

* * *

> A rose is a rose is a rose, and smells the same by any other name. The parties contemplated and contracted that in all events Industrial was to get back all of its monies advanced plus approximately 11 per cent. This invokes the application of the Usury law of North Carolina — if other essential elements are present. The shorthand way of expressing this conclusion is to call it a loan transaction, which conclusion of law I adopt and confirm.

202 F. Supp. at 253. Associated received cash in return for the contracts, which gave the transactions examined in that case the appearance of being loans, rather than forbearances. In the present action, for each contract assigned, Vick received Western Auto's agreement to forbear from collecting a certain sum until the installments came due. The North Carolina usury statutes cover forbearances from the collection of debts as well as loans. *See,* G.S. 24-1.1 *et seq; Ausband v. Trust Co.,* 17 N.C. App. 325, 194 S.E. 2d 160, *cert. denied,* 283 N.C. 257, 195 S.E. 2d 689 (1973). We detect the same scent of roses in this case that Judge Craven found in *Associated.* To summarize, the undisputed evidence of Vick's continuing obligation with respect to the payment of the installments due under the chattel paper as well as Vick's guarantee of those payments and the fact that Vick had the sole responsibility for collecting the installments due under these installment contracts, clearly differentiate these transactions from the *bona fide* sale and purchase of chattel paper.

While the law may be contrary in other jurisdictions, it is clear that in North Carolina such transactions fall within the protection of the usury statutes. *Compare, Lake Hiwassee Development Co., Inc. v. Pioneer Bank,* 535 S.W. 2d 323 (Tenn. 1976); *A.B. Lewis Co. v. National Investment Corp. of Houston,* 421 S.W. 2d 723 (Tex. Civ. App. 1967). The vitality of the usury statutes would not be maintained by allowing creditors to charge unlawful interest rates merely by disguising the form of their transactions. We must be concerned with substance and not form, *Bank v. Merrimon,* 260 N.C. 335, 132 S.E. 2d 692 (1963), and we consider the "assignment" of the chattel paper and retention of a portion of the unearned finance charge as they were viewed by Western Auto — as security and payment for Western Auto's forbearance from collecting on Vick's debt.

[3] The third element of usury is the charging of interest at an unlawful rate. Western Auto argues that since the total balance which Vick owed was considered to be in excess of $300,000, the parties were free to agree on any rate of interest under G.S. 24-1.1A(e), as that statute was in effect at that time. We hold that the only reasonable interpretation of this statute is that the principal amount financed must be determined on a transac-

tion-by-transaction basis, at least where the transactions are not contemporaneous, and not on the basis of the aggregate amount owing between the parties. Since the parties have stipulated that the precise amount of interest paid by Vick which was subject to the usury statutes is to be determined at a later time, we do not reach the issue as to which section of Chapter 24 is applicable to each of the transactions presented in this case.

[4] We also hold that Vick has shown the requisite corrupt intent on the part of Western Auto for the suspect transactions to be held usurious. "The corrupt intent required to constitute usury is simply the intentional charging of more for money lent than the law allows." *Kessing v. Mortgage Corp.*, 278 N.C. 523, 530, 180 S.E. 2d 823, 827 (1971). The evidence contained in the record leads to the unmistakable conclusion that Western Auto intended to exact the interest which it did by keeping sixty-five or seventy percent of the unearned finance charge on each of the contracts "assigned." Nothing more need be proven under our Supreme Court's analysis in *Kessing* than Western Auto's deliberate exaction of the charges made.

[5] Finally, Western Auto argues that the transactions complained of fall within the "time-price" exception to the usury statutes. As Judge (now Justice) Brock stated in *Supply, Inc. v. Allen*, 30 N.C. App. 272, 279-280, 227 S.E. 2d 120, 125 (1976), in holding the time-price doctrine inapplicable to the otherwise usurious forbearance presented in that case:

> Usury only pertains to a loan or forbearance of money, not a *bona fide* sale. In recent years the definition of bona fide sale has been expanded to include credit sales in which the difference between the cash price and the credit or time price is greater than the allowable rate of interest.
>
> > "A vendor may fix on his property one price for cash and another for credit, and the mere fact that the credit price exceeds the cash price by a greater percentage than is permitted by the usury laws is a matter of concern to the parties and not to the courts, barring evidence of bad faith. (Citations omitted.)

.   .   .   .

"If there is a real and bona fide purchase, not made
as the occasion or pretext for a loan, the transaction
will not be usurious even though the sale be for an
exorbitant price, and a note is taken, at legal rates, for
the unpaid purchase money. The reason is that the
statute against usury is striking at, and forbidding, the
extraction or reception of more than a specified legal
rate for the hire of money, and not for anything else;
and a purchaser is not, like the needy borrower, a victim of a rapacious lender, since he can refrain from the
purchase if he does not choose to pay the price asked by
the seller." *Bank v. Merrimon*, 260 N.C. 335, 132 S.E. 2d
692 (1963). Thus it appears that the sale of merchandise
is not usurious when the sale is made for one price if
cash is paid and for a higher price if payment is deferred or made in future installments, so long as the
transaction is not a subterfuge to conceal a usurious
loan.

See also, Bank v. Hanner, 268 N.C. 668, 151 S.E. 2d 579 (1966);
Bank v. Merrimon, supra.

We hold that from the substance of the transactions presented in this case the time-price doctrine is inapplicable. As we
stated previously, the transactions complained of here did not
involve the *bona fide* sale of chattel paper. Vick's obligation to
Western Auto was not finally determined when the contracts
were assigned to Western Auto, but only when installments
were paid under these contracts. The contracts themselves
were merely regarded by the parties as security for the
advancement of credit by Western Auto to Vick.

Furthermore, the suspect transactions possessed none of
the attributes commonly associated with time-price sales. Fun-
damentally, the time-price doctrine requires that the cash price
and time-price be fixed and quoted to the buyer at the time of
the sale in order to afford the buyer a genuine choice. *Supply,
Inc. v. Allen, supra.* In the present action, Vick was never
quoted a *fixed* time-price since, even after the assignment, Vick

remained liable to Western Auto for each installment debtor's default on the underlying contract. Vick alone assumed the risk of the individual debtor's default.

In *Ripple v. Mortgage Corp.*, 193 N.C. 422, 424, 137 S.E. 156, 157-158 (1927), our Supreme Court enunciated the general standard by which the courts of our State must examine allegedly usurious transactions:

> Our courts do not hesitate to look beneath the forms of transactions alleged to be usurious in order to determine whether or not such transactions are in truth and in reality usurious ... . Where a transaction is in reality a loan of money, whatever may be its form, and the lender charges for the use of his money a sum in excess of interest at the legal rate, by whatever name the charge may be called, the transaction will be held to be usurious. The law considers the substance and not the mere form or outward appearance of the transaction in order to determine what it in reality is. If this were not so, the usury laws of the State would easily be evaded by lenders of money who would exact from borrowers with impunity compensation for money loaned in excess of interest at the legal rate.

From the testimony, instruments, and stipulated practices of the parties, we find that the only reasonable conclusions which may be drawn in the case *sub judice* are that the complained-of transactions involve the payment of interest in return for a forbearance in the collection of money owed on account, and that these transactions invoke the protection of our State's usury statutes. Our opinion makes it unnecessary to reach plaintiff's cross-assignment of error. We reverse the judgment of the Superior Court on defendant's appeal, affirm the court's judgment with respect to plaintiff's appeal, and remand the case with instructions that the court make findings and enter judgment consistent with this opinion.

Reversed in part and affirmed in part.

Judges WEBB and MARTIN (Harry C.) concur.

DEBRA WATSON, Administratrix of CHARLES EUGENE WATSON, JR., Deceased (Docket TA-5894), ROGER DALE WYATT (Docket TA-5757), ELZENA WALKER, Administratrix of ARCHIE LEE WILLIAMS, Deceased (Docket TA-5766), RICKEY SHUMATE, (Docket TA-5775), CARL MOODY, (Docket TA-5797), BRENDA RICE, Administratrix of DAVID RICE, Deceased (Docket TA-5930), SAMMY RAY PORTER (Docket TA-5774), JAMES DAVID CARPENTER (Docket TA-5779), MARION D. WESLEY, Administratrix of RONALD DENNY (Docket TA-5876), QUENTIN MAURICE LUCAS (Docket TA-5855), DAVID HORNE (Docket TA-5820), FREDDIE B. LEWIS (Docket TA-5771), FRANK J. HAMMONDS (Docket TA-5773), HENRY CARSON REECE (Docket TA-5772) and WILLIAM M. JORDAN (Docket TA-5780) v. NORTH CAROLINA DEPARTMENT OF CORRECTION

No. 7910IC188

(Filed 5 August 1980)

1. **Convicts and Prisoners § 3; State § 8.3– injuries to prison inmates in fire – use of polyurethane mattresses – no negligence by Deputy Director of Prisons**

   In a tort claim action to recover for deaths and injuries to prison inmates in a fire which occurred when inmates, in furtherance of an escape attempt, set fire to several mattresses piled on and around a table in a prison dormitory, the Deputy Director of Prisons was not negligent in placing inmates in a prison dormitory with polyurethane mattresses when he knew that the mattresses were combustible when continuously exposed to a combustion source since it was not foreseeable that the inmates would pile mattresses on and around a table and then provide the combustion which would cause them to burn rapidly.

2. **Convicts and Prisoners § 3; State § 8.3– injuries to prison inmates in fire – no negligence by lieutenant and sergeant**

   In a tort claim action to recover for deaths and injuries to prison inmates in a fire which occurred when inmates set fire to several mattresses piled on and around a table in a prison dormitory, plaintiffs' evidence was insufficient to show negligence on the part of the lieutenant or the sergeant at the prison unit where it tended to show that the inmates planned an escape by starting a fire and rushing the guards when they came in to put it out; debris was placed under a picnic table and ignited; the sergeant called the lieutenant to come to the dormitory because of a disturbance and gave him the dormitory keys; the lieutenant and sergeant saw smoke in the dormitory but did not see any flame; mattresses on the table were not near the smoke; the lieutenant told the inmates to put out the fire and was told that if he wanted the fire out to come in and put it out; both the lieutenant and the sergeant feared the fire had been started as part of an escape plan; the lieutenant, sergeant and three guards in the dormitory did not have guns; the lieutenant told the inmates that if they would not put out the fire he would go and get help; the lieutenant directed the sergeant to man the tower; the sergeant opened the safe in his station to obtain guns and other riot equipment but did

---

---

not obtain the keys from the lieutenant for the emergency doors; after the officers left the dormitory, inmates began throwing mattresses on and around the table, and one of their number ignited the mattresses; the lieutenant telephoned his supervisor, and his call was interrupted by a guard's call for help advising that the place was on fire; the lieutenant and sergeant ran back to the dormitory, and the lieutenant gave the keys to the sergeant, telling him to get the inmates out and that he would go man the tower; the lieutenant went to the tower and called the sheriff's department for assistance; the fire raged out of control within a very few minutes; the key to the emergency door would not work because glass had fallen into the lock; the sergeant then opened the dormitory door and yelled for the inmates to come out; and previous fires at the unit, including those involving polyurethane mattresses such as those used on the date in question, had been put out by inmates or prison personnel with water or by separating the burning material from the flame.

APPEAL by plaintiffs and defendant from a decision and order of the North Carolina Industrial Commission filed 24 October 1978. Heard in the Court of Appeals 22 October 1979.

These are actions brought under the provisions of G.S. 143-291 *et seq.*, the Tort Claims Act. The actions were consolidated for hearing before the Industrial Commission. Separate opinions were issued, and separate appeals were taken to the full Commission. The actions have been consolidated for appellate review. All of the actions arose from a fire at the McDowell County Prison Unit of the Department of Correction near Marion, North Carolina. The fire occurred on the evening of 30 June 1976, when inmates, in furtherance of an escape attempt, set fire to several mattresses piled on a table in B Dormitory at the Prison. The hearing examiner found negligence on the part of the prison officials, allowed recovery for some of the plaintiffs and denied recovery to others on the basis of contributory negligence. The full Commission reversed the finding of negligence on the part of the Deputy Director, but concurred in the finding of negligence on the part of the Lieutenant and Sergeant, and concluded that all plaintiffs were guilty of contributory negligence, thus denying recovery to all plaintiffs. One commissioner dissented.

The findings of fact of the hearing examiner were adopted in toto by the full Commission, and those which are pertinent to these appeals are discussed in the opinion. The findings are identical in all cases except that in those cases in which the hearing examiner denied recovery, findings with respect to contributory negligence were added.

For clarity, the record on appeal is divided into Group A and Group B. Group A is composed of the plaintiffs who were allowed recovery by the hearing examiner and Group B is composed of plaintiffs who were denied recovery. We have found that characterization of the two groups helpful.

All plaintiffs appealed from the decision and order of the Commission, and the appellee has set out exceptions and cross assignments of error.

Attorney General Edmisten, by Sandra M. King, Assistant Attorney General, and Russell and Greene, by J. William Russell, for North Carolina Department of Correction, appellee.

Robert H. West, for Rickey Shumate, Carl Moody, Sammy Ray Porter, James David Carpenter, Freddie E. Lewis, Frank J. Hammonds, Henry Carson Reece, and William M. Jordan, appellants.

Wilson and Palmer, by Bruce L. Cannon, for Debra Watson, Administratrix of Charles Eugene Watson, appellant.

Goldsmith and Goldsmith, by C. Frank Goldsmith, Jr., for Elzena Walker, Administratrix of the Estate of Archie Lee Williams, appellant.

S. Thomas Walton, for Roger Dale Wyatt and Brenda Rice, Administratrix of David Rice, appellants.

R. Lewis Ray for David Horne, appellant.

Alvis A. Lee, for Quentin Maurice Lucas and Marion D. Wesley, Administratrix of Ronald Denny, appellants.

MORRIS, Chief Judge.

[1] Plaintiff appellants first assign error to the Commission's striking Deputy Commissioner Denson's conclusion of law No. 3, which concluded that Deputy Director of Prisons, W.L. Kautzky was negligent "in that he improperly maintained polyurethane mattresses in the Unit which he knew were highly inflammable and presented a hazard to anyone exposed to a burning mattress, when he could reasonably foresee that fires would be intentionally set by inmates to those mattresses", contending that the greater weight of the evidence reveals negligence as a matter of law. Plaintiffs did not except to any finding of fact except those findings of contributory negligence with respect to each plaintiff in Group B.

This tragic occurrence took place on 30 June 1976, and the claims were filed at various times in 1976 and 1977. At all times pertinent to these claims, under the provisions of G.S. 143-291, the Industrial Commission, which was constituted a court to hear and pass upon tort claims against departments, institutions, and agencies of the State, was given the responsibility of determining whether the claim before it "arose as a result of a negligent act of any officer, employee, involuntary servant or agent of the State while acting within the scope of his office, employment, service, agency or authority, under circumstances where the State of North Carolina, if a private person, would be liable to the claimant in accordance with the laws of North Carolina." Effective 1 July 1979, the section was amended to require the Commission to determine whether the claim "arose as a result of the negligence of any officer, employee, involuntary servant or agent of the State ..." We are not concerned with the amended statute, which obviously enlarges the rights of persons seeking to recover for injuries resulting from State employees' negligence.

The right of prisoners to seek recovery under the Tort Claims Act is established in *Ivey v. North Carolina Prison Dept.*, 252 N.C. 615, 114 S.E. 2d 812 (1960).

In *Mackey v. Highway Comm.*, 4 N.C. App. 630, 167 S.E. 2d 524 (1969), plaintiff sought to recover for injuries sustained when she stepped in a hole on the shoulder of the State highway. She alleged that her injury was caused solely and proximately by the negligent conduct of a named employee in removing large posts which had been placed along the shoulder of the highway, leaving unfilled holes, into one of which she stepped and was injured. In holding that the creation of a hole was a negligent act, and not a negligent omission, we said:

> Under the State Tort Claims Act recovery is permitted for injuries resulting from a *negligent act*, but not those resulting from a *negligent omission* on the part of State employees. G.S. 143-291; *Flynn v. Highway Commission*, 244 N.C. 617, 94 S.E. 2d 571. In *Flynn* the claim denied was based upon the alleged negligent failure of named employees of the State to repair a hole or break in the surface of a State road *caused by public travel over it.* "In order to authorize the payment of compensation, the Industrial Commission's findings must include (1) a negligent act, (2) on the part of a State employee, (3) while acting in the scope of his employment, etc. The first requirement is that the claimant show a *negligent act.* Is a failure to repair a hole in the highway caused by ordinary public travel a negligent act? The requirement of the statute is not met by showing negligence, for negligence may consist of an act or an omission. Failure to act is not an act." *Flynn v. Highway Commission, supra.*

4 N.C. App. at 633, 167 S.E. 2d at 526. The statement in *Flynn* accurately reflected the law at the time these plaintiffs received their injuries. *See also Midgett v. Highway Commission*, 265 N.C. 373, 144 S.E. 2d 121 (1965) (failure to keep highway drains free of sand and debris); *Etheridge v. Graham*, 14 N.C. App. 551, 188 S.E. 2d 551 (1972) (allegations that damages resulted from the failure of the Commissioner to perform certain duties).

Since the Tort Claims Act is in derogation of sovereign immunity from liability for torts, it must be strictly construed with strict adherence to its terms, *Floyd v. Highway Commission*, 241 N.C. 461, 85 S.E. 2d 703 (1955). Thus the allegations that the injuries resulted from the failure of Deputy Director Kautzky to replace the petroleum based product mattresses with cotton mattresses do not bring these claims within the purview of the Tort Claims Act.

Although the allegations in the affidavits were couched in language indicating negligent acts of omission, Commissioner Denson, in her conclusion of law No. 3, used language indicating negligent acts of commission when she concluded that "Mr. Kautzky was negligent in that he improperly maintained polyurethane mattresses in the Unit which he knew were highly inflammable and presented a hazard to anyone exposed to a burning mattress, when he could reasonably foresee that fires would be intentionally set by inmates to those mattresses."

In *Lawson v. Highway Commission*, 248 N.C. 276, 103 S.E. 2d 366 (1958), the allegations were that the employee of the State "was negligent in not ascertaining that the prisoners under his supervision could work in safety, he having knowledge that electric wires were down in the vicinity in which they were working; that his negligence in not calling the power companies and requesting them to switch the electricity from the wires which were down was the proximate cause of the death of Cleo Lawson, without contributory negligence on the part of plaintiff. . . ." To defendant's argument that the negligence, if any, consisted of omission, not acts, the Court, speaking through Bobbitt, J. (later C.J.), said:

While the findings of fact established Barefoot's negligent failure to ascertain whether the prisoners under his supervision could work in safety in the area to which he assigned them, his omissions in this respect constituted the circumstances under which he acted, not the cause of Lawson's death. The basis of plaintiff's claim is Barefoot's act, in the light of such circumstances, in putting the prisoners, including Lawson, to work in an area of hidden danger when he should have reasonably foreseen that they might and probably would unwittingly come in contact with a live wire. In our view, the findings support the Commission's composite conclusion of fact and law, set forth in its Conclusions of Law, that the negligence of Barefoot was the proximate cause of Lawson's death.

Greene v. Board of Education, 237 N.C. 336, 75 S.E. 2d 129, and *Lyon & Sons v. Board of Education*, 238 N.C. 24, 76 S.E. 2d 553, involved proceedings under G.S. 143-291 et seq., where injury was inflicted by the negligent operation of a school bus. In each, plaintiff recovered. The driver's failure to exercise due care to observe the child in front of the bus (*Greene* case) or the [sic] automobile behind the bus (*Lyon* case) did not proximately cause the injury or damage. The fact that the driver operated the bus under such circumstances was the negligent act that proximately caused the injury or damage.

248 N.C. at p. 281, 103 S.E. 2d at p. 370.

In *Spicer v. Williamson*, 191 N.C. 487, 490, 132 S.E. 291, 293 (1926), Justice Connor said: "The prisoner by his arrest is deprived of his liberty for the protection of the public; it is but just that the public be required to care for the prisoner, who cannot by reason of the deprivation of his liberty, care for himself." The duty of the State to its prisoners was stated thusly by Justice Clark, in his concurring opinion in *State v. Mincher*, 172 N.C. 895, 902, 90 S.E. 429, 432 (1916), "The State owed him protection from violence, especially from its own agents, sufficient food and clothing, and good treatment."

If Deputy Director Kautzky, acting for the State, negligently violated the duty of the State to furnish its prisoners protection from violence, or if Mr. Kautzky placed prisoners "in a place of known danger where injury would probably result", *Gordon v. Highway Commission*, 250 N.C. 645, 647, 109 S.E. 2d 376, 378 (1959), then the State should respond in damages to one whose injuries proximately result from that negligent violation. Deputy Commissioner Denson concluded that the Deputy Director was negligent in allowing polyurethane mattresses, "which he knew are highly inflammable", to be used in Dormitory B, and that this negligence was a proximate cause of the injuries to the plaintiffs. We do not agree and are of the opinion that the full Commission properly struck this conclusion.

The evidence is clear and uncontradicted that Mr. Kautzky knew the polyurethane mattresses were combustible. Indeed, he had recommended that the Department request the General Assembly to appropriate sufficient funds to replace that type of mattress with flame retardant cotton mattresses. It is uncontradicted that he knew that there had been other fires in various units when these mattresses were burned. He testified that he did not know they were very flammable, but he had conducted tests which proved that "when the mattress was continuously exposed to a combustion source" it would be completely consumed in flames in about three minutes. "However, if you remove the source of combustion, it would immediately go out" and would not burn. To charge Mr. Kautzky with the duty of foreseeing that the use of polyurethane mattresses would result in a conflagration such as happened here is requiring more of him than the law does or should require.

We must apply the rules of common law negligence. By these rules, the duty owed is ordinary care under the circumstances. Whether a person so acts is to be determined upon the facts as they appeared at the time and not by a judgment from the actual consequences which were not then to be apprehended by an ordinarily prudent person. *Williams v. Boulerice*, 268 N.C. 62, 149 S.E. 2d 590 (1966). In order for negligence to be actionable, it must be tested by the *reasonable* foreseeability of an event which might have resulted in injury and exists where there is a failure to guard against a *reasonably* to be expected danger. The law does not require prescience — merely reasonable foreseeability.

Tested by these well-established principles, we are convinced that the placing of inmates in Dormitory B with polyurethane mattresses on the bunks was not an act from which Mr. Kautzky could have and should have foreseen that the inmates would pile mattresses on and around a table and then provide the combustion which would cause them to burn rapidly. We are of the opinion that the injuries to plaintiffs were so unforeseeable that reasonable minds could not differ thereon, and the Commission properly struck the Deputy Commissioner's conclusion of law No. 3.

[2] By cross assignments of error Nos. 9 and 10, defendant urges that the Commission erred in adopting as its own the Deputy Commissioner's conclusions of law Nos. 4 and 5 by which the Deputy Commissioner concluded, on facts found, that Lt. Wilson and Sgt. Macopson were negligent in the respects set out in the order as follows:

4. Lt. Wilson was negligent in his improper response to the situation with which he was presented when he was called to the dormitory. Such negligence occurred in the following specifics:

(a) The Lieutenant took with him the keys, effectively closing the prisoners inside the cellblock with a fire, when he could reasonably foresee that the fire could develop and become life-threatening.

(b) The Lieutenant ordered the Sergeant to come with him when, as chief custodial officer at the Unit, the Sergeant's responsibility was to remain in the corridor and see to the safety of the inmates.

(c) The Lieutenant's action in making telephone calls to superior officers was an improper response to the situation with which he had been presented. The proper response was obviously to call the Sheriff's Department and ask for help.

At the time the Lieutenant left the dormitory, he was not confronted with a sudden emergency and cannot avail himself of that doctrine to require a lesser degree of care.

Such negligence as herein specified of Lt. Wilson was a proximate cause of the injury sustained by the plaintiff and was not intervened nor insulated by subsequent negligence of any person.

5. Sgt. Macopson was negligent in the following respects:

(a) He improperly exercised his primary duty to supervise the inmates for their safekeeping and safety in that he failed to request the keys from the Lieutenant and he left the corridor rather than remain and supervise the custody situation.

(b) The Sergeant's actions at the Sergeant's Station were inappropriate. Rather than secure the emergency door keys and the fire extinguisher, he secured the keys to the gun locker in order to get weapons and riot equipment.

At the time the Sergeant left the dormitory, he was not confronted with a sudden emergency and cannot avail himself of that doctrine to require a lesser degree of care.

Such negligence as herein specified by Sgt. Macopson was a proximate cause of the injury sustained by the plaintiff and was not intervened nor insulated by subsequent negligence of any person.

From the findings of fact, the following sequence of events appears: there were five employees at the Unit the night of the fire: Lt. Wilson, Sgt. Macopson, and three guards, Mr. Brooks, Mr. Buckner, and Mr. Cox. The Unit had one dormitory building which housed A and B dormitories and B Dormitory at that time housed 33 inmates. During the afternoon of 30 June 1976, Sgt. Macopson and Mr. Buckner went into B Dormitory to confiscate radios because some inmates had been playing them without using earphones. One inmate smashed his radio rather than turning it over to the authorities. Afer the evening meal, the inmates discussed the course they should follow to protest. The leader asked all inmates to refuse to undress and go to bed at 10:00 p.m. After that meeting, a group of inmates met, hidden from the view of the guards, planned an escape. The plan was to start a fire and rush the guards when they came in to put it out. About 7:30, this plan was initiated. Some debris was placed under a picnic table at a position farthest from the bars. It was ignited. Guards Brooks and Buckner saw the smoke, and Mr. Brooks called Sgt. Macopson. He told the Sergeant that the inmates were piling mattresses on the table and that there was going to be trouble. Sgt. Macopson responded to the call and saw three mattresses on the table. He turned toward the inmates and looked at them, whereupon two of the inmates removed their mattresses. The Sergeant called Lt. Wilson, who was working in the Superintendent's office, and told him he thought there would be trouble because the inmates had started a little fire. The Sergeant went to the locked gate and let the Lieutenant in the fenced-in area of the compound and handed the Lieutenant his keys, including the key to the two dormi-

tories. After pulling the plug on the television sets so the noise
would not interfere, Lt. Wilson motioned for the inmates to
come to the bars. At his second request, most of the inmates
came to the front. The Lieutenant and Sergeant sensed a tense-
ness among the inmates. The inmates who came to the front
listened to the Lieutenant. Those who did not come could not be
seen. The leader of the inmates related their grievances and the
Lieutenant told him the actions by the inmates were not the
proper and appropriate way to settle their problems. The
Lieutenant and the Sergeant saw the smoke but did not see any
flame, although Mr. Buckner, who was standing where he could
look around the inmates, did see a flame. Any mattresses on the
table were at the front of the table and not near the flame or the
smoke. Lt. Wilson told the inmates to put out the fire. The
response was that if he wanted the fire out to come in and put it
out. This was, of course, in keeping with the escape plan.
Although there was a fire extinguisher in the corridor, no inmate asked for it. Both the Lieutenant and Sergeant understood or feared that the fire which had been started was a part
of an escape plan. The Lieutenant told the inmates that if they
would not put out the fire, he would go and get help. He directed
the Sergeant to come man the towers and the Sergeant ordered
Mr. Buckner to come help. Lt. Wilson had the keys and they
went to the Sergeant's station. After they left an inmate, Joe
Bright, said "let's burn this m---- f---- down!"[1.] The Sergeant
opened the safe in his station containing guns and other riot
equipment. He did not get the keys to the emergency doors at
that time. The Lieutenant attempted to contact his immediate
supervisor by phone. He was not successful, and he then telephoned the next superior officer. Their conversation was interrupted by Mr. Brook's call for help advising that the place was
going up. It was then that they ran back to the dorm. Lieutenant handed the keys to the Sergeant telling him to get the
inmates out and that he would go man the tower. The Lieutenant went to the tower near the visitor's gate and from there

---

1. The findings of fact do not indicate at what time this statement was
made, but the evidence is clear that it was after the officers left without falling
victims to the escape plan, a turn of events which angered the inmates, and they
began wildly throwing mattresses on and around the table, after which one of
their number ignited the mattresses.

called the Sheriff's Department and asked for them to send the necessary assistance. The fire raged out of control within a very few minutes. The key to the emergency room door would not work because glass had fallen into the lock and obstructed its opening. When the Sergeant ran in to open the doors he had the key to Dormitory A in his hand, opened that first, ran back out to get a breath of air, returned and opened the door to B Dormitory and yelled for the inmates to come out. The rules and regulations required that the persons manning the towers be armed. The Guidebook (regulations) of the defendant contained the following instructions with respect to emergencies:

> *Alarms* — The officer in charge of the prison shall be notified as soon as an emergency develops. This notification shall be given by the most direct method available, but caution should be exercised to prevent disturbing inmates in other areas. The officer in charge shall take immediate steps to activate the appropriate established plan without waiting to contact higher ranking officials; however, if Prison Department Headquarters can be notified immediately about a major emergency, this shall be done before local law enforcement agencies are notified.

> As soon as possible, the immediate superior of the officer in charge of the prison shall be notified. This officer shall determine whether the situation warrants the immediate notification of higher ranking officials in the chain of command. In all cases where the officer in charge of the prison is unable to make contact with his immediate superior soon after an emergency develops, the next officer in the chain of command shall be notified.

Previous fires at the Unit, even those involving polyurethane mattresses, had been put out by the inmates or prison personnel with water or by separating the burning material from the flame.

We fail to see negligent action on the part of Lt. Wilson and Sgt. Macopson, or either of them. It is quite clear that they were aware of the purpose of the fire. A pertinent part of the Guidebook is found in the Deputy's findings of fact: "In handling emergencies arising in the State Prison System, competing interests shall be considered in the following priority order: (1) the general public safety; (2) the safety and welfare of hostages; (3) prevention of loss of life or injury to other personnel; (4) inmate welfare; (5) protection of property." It is obvious to us, from the findings of fact alone without reference to other supportive evidence in the Record not included in the findings, that had the two men gone into that dormitory, the inmates would have overpowered them and taken them hostage, injured, or killed them and that the same treatment would have then been accorded Guards Brooks and Buckner as the inmates made their way out of the prison and back into society again to prey upon the general public, committing other crimes of violence as they went. There is absolutely no conflict in the evidence that neither Lt. Wilson nor Sgt. Macopson could see anything but a little smoke. There was nothing to warn them of the holocaust which was to occur in a very few minutes. Neither they nor Brooks and Buckner and Cox had guns. The findings of fact relate that "in a very short time" the fire was completely out of control with flames shooting to the ceiling. The evidence is not in conflict on that point. It took only a very few minutes. To charge these men with negligence for refusing to risk their lives and the lives of other personnel in a futile attempt to prevent an escape is, we think, totally unrealistic. We, therefore, reverse the action of the Commission in adopting as its own the Deputy Commissioner's conclusions Nos. 4 and 5.

Because we fail to find actionable negligence on the part of the prison officials, we do not discuss the question of the contributory negligence of the inmates, plaintiffs' only other assignment of error. Nor do we discuss the defendant's remaining cross assignments of error.

Upon the plaintiffs' appeal, the striking of the Deputy Commissioner's conclusion No. 3, resulting in the decision of the Industrial Commission that Deputy Director was not negligent, is affirmed.

Upon the defendant's cross appeal, the adoption by the Industrial Commission of Deputy Commissioner's conclusions

State v. Greenwood

of law Nos. 4 and 5, resulting in the decision of the Commissioner that Lt. Wilson and Sgt. Macopson were negligent, is reversed.

Judges PARKER and MARTIN (Robert M.) concur.

STATE OF NORTH CAROLINA v. MICHAEL BARXLEY GREENWOOD

No. 7918SC1032

(Filed 5 August 1980)

1. Searches and Seizures § 12– defendant sitting in automobile – investigatory
   stop or seizure

   In a prosecution for possession of marijuana, felonious breaking and
   entering a motor vehicle, and larceny of a pocketbook, there was no merit to
   defendant's contention that his initial detention by a police officer as he sat
   in his car in a church parking lot constituted a "forcible stop" or "seizure" of
   his person which violated his reasonable expectation of privacy, since the
   evidence tended to show that the officer received a call between 7:00 and 8:00
   p.m. requesting him to investigate a "suspicious person" on the church
   premises; as he arrived he was directed by churchgoers toward defendant
   who was alone in an automobile parked in the corner of the lot; and the
   totality of the circumstances afforded the officer the basis of authority to
   approach defendant's automobile and direct defendant to roll down his
   window for the limited purpose of investigating a report that a suspicious
   person was on the premises.

2. Searches and Seizures § 11– marijuana odor in automobile – warrantless
   search of vehicle – probable cause

   An officer's warrantless search of defendant's automobile was based on
   probable cause and was therefore proper where the officer, trained in the
   identification of marijuana by its odor, detected the distinct odor of marijuana emanating from defendant's automobile, and it was reasonable for the
   officer to assume that the odor originated from defendant's vehicle and that
   the vehicle contained marijuana.

3. Arrest and Bail § 3.4– possession of controlled substance – warrantless arrest –
   probable cause

   Where an officer conducted a proper warrantless search of defendant's
   vehicle and found cigarette butts and a "roach clip" which apparently contained marijuana, the officer had probable cause to believe that defendant
   had committed the offense of possession of a controlled substance, and his
   warrantless arrest was therefore lawful.

4. **Searches and Seizures § 37– pocketbook on rear seat of car – warrantless search incident to arrest for marijuana possession**

Search of a pocketbook found on the rear seat of defendant's automobile subsequent to defendant's warrantless arrest for possession of marijuana was improper, since the pocketbook was obviously a repository for personal items, and a warrantless search thereof was in violation of the Fourth Amendment prohibition against unreasonable searches and seizures.

APPEAL by defendant from denial of Motion to Suppress entered by *Crissman, Judge,* on 14 December 1978. Judgment entered by *Davis, Judge,* on 8 June 1979 in Superior Court, GUILFORD County. Heard in the Court of Appeals 24 March 1980.

Defendant was charged under G.S. 90-95(a)(3) with the misdemeanor possession of marijuana and under G.S. 14-56 and G.S. 14-72 with felonious breaking and entering a motor vehicle and with larceny and receiving of a pocketbook. Defendant moved for the suppression of the marijuana and pocketbook.

At the suppression hearing, the State presented evidence which tended to show the following: On 27 November 1977, at approximately 8:00 p.m., Officer M. L. Simpson of the High Point Police Department was called to the Church of God at 209 West Ward Street in High Point to investigate a report that a suspicious person was on the premises. Upon his arrival at the church, Officer Simpson was directed by some people standing nearby toward a particular vehicle parked in the corner of the church parking lot, which Officer Simpson observed as a 1966 blue Ford Mustang. Defendant was sitting in the driver's seat of the vehicle.

Officer Simpson approached the vehicle and directed defendant to roll the window down, and defendant complied. Officer Simpson then asked defendant to present his driver's license. At this time, the officer detected the odor of marijuana in and around the vehicle. Officer Simpson asked defendant to get out of the vehicle and, after defendant did so, the officer advised defendant of his *Miranda* rights. Officer Simpson then told defendant that he was going to search the vehicle for marijuana. The officer collected several fragments of cigarette butts which were later determined to contain marijuana. Officer Simpson also discovered a "roach clip" with some marijuana residue on it. Defendant was then placed under arrest for possession of marijuana. Officer Simpson advised defendant that, according to departmental rules and regulations, his duty was to store and inventory defendant's vehicle. Officer Simpson proceeded to inventory the vehicle. On the rear seat of defendant's vehicle the officer found a light brown pocketbook under some jackets. The pocketbook was searched and the contents inventoried, which revealed that the pocketbook did not belong to defendant. Defendant was then charged with breaking and entering a motor vehicle and with larceny and receiving. Defendant's vehicle was subsequently removed by a wrecker and stored.

At the conclusion of the suppression hearing, the court denied defendant's motion, concluding that under G.S. 20-29 the officer had the right, under the circumstances, to request that defendant present his driver's license; that, pursuant to his duty, the officer had the right to search defendant's vehicle for marijuana without a search warrant; and that the officer "had the right to impound the car to keep it from getting away." Defendant thereafter pleaded no contest to the charges of misdemeanor possession of marijuana and misdemeanor breaking and entering. Pursuant to this plea arrangement, defendant was given a suspended prison sentence of not less than eighteen nor more than twenty-four months, placed on unsupervised probation for a period of two years, and ordered to pay fines and costs in each case. Execution of the sentence was stayed pending this appeal by defendant of the denial of his motion to suppress.

Attorney General Edmisten, by Associate Attorney William R. Shenton, for the State.

Assistant Public Defender Robert L. McClellan for the defendant appellant.

MORRIS, Chief Judge.

Defendant's various assignments of error are presented in his brief under the general contention that the trial court erred by failing to grant defendant's pretrial motion to suppress. We consider defendant's appeal by examining his arguments with respect to the various aspects of the police officer's conduct on this occasion, from the initial contact with defendant through the subsequent arrests.

Defendant argues that his initial detention by Officer Simpson in the church parking lot constituted a "forcible stop" or "seizure" of his person, and that under the circumstances the officer had no authority to intrude upon his "reasonable expectation of privacy" as he sat in his automobile with the windows rolled up.

With respect to defendant's claim of an expectation of privacy, our United States Supreme Court recently stated that an individual operating an automobile does not lose all reasonable expectation of privacy simply because the automobile and its use are subject to government regulation. *Delaware v. Prouse*, 440 U.S. 648, 59 L.Ed. 2d 660, 99 S.Ct. 1391 (1979). Indeed, just as people do not waive their Fourth Amendment protections against unreasonable searches and seizures when they step from their homes onto public sidewalks, *Terry v. Ohio*, 392 U.S. 1, 20 L.Ed. 2d 889, 88 S.Ct. 1868 (1968), neither do they lose those protections when they step from the sidewalks into their automobiles. *Adams v. Williams*, 407 U.S. 143, 32 L.Ed. 2d 612, 92 S.Ct. 1921 (1972). *See also Katz v. United States*, 389 U.S. 347, 19 L.Ed. 2d 576, 88 S.Ct. 507 (1967). Even assuming in the case before us that defendant enjoyed a reasonable expectation of privacy while in his automobile parked in the church parking lot, we are of the opinion that the police officer acted properly when he approached defendant in his vehicle for the purposes of a limited investigation.

In *Delaware v. Prouse, supra*, the Court stated that "the permissibility of a particular law enforcement practice is judged by balancing its intrusion on the individual's Fourth Amendment interests against its promotion of legitimate governmental interests. Implemented in this manner, the reasonableness standard usually requires, at a minimum, that the facts upon which an intrusion is based be capable of measurement against 'an objective standard', whether this be probable cause or a less stringent test." 440 U.S. at 654, 59 L.Ed. 2d at

667-68, 99 S.Ct. at 1396. Both the United States Supreme Court and our own North Carolina Supreme Court have recognized the limited right of police officers, in appropriate circumstances, to approach an individual for purposes of investigating "possible criminal behavior", even though there is no probable cause to make an arrest. *Terry v. Ohio, supra; State v. Streeter*, 283 N.C. 203, 195 S.E. 2d 502 (1973). The "stop and frisk" rule, as applied in North Carolina is explained in *State v. Streeter, supra,* as follows:

> [I]f the totality of circumstances affords an officer reasonable grounds to believe that criminal activity may be afoot, he may temporarily detain the suspect. If, after the detention, his personal observations confirm his apprehension that criminal activity may be afoot and indicate that the person may be armed, he may then frisk him as a matter of self-protection. [Citations omitted.]

283 N.C. at 210, 195 S.E. 2d at 507. (In this case, we are only concerned with the "stop" element of this rule, that is, the "forcible stop" or "seizure" of defendant's person while he sat in his automobile.) This rule has been extended to persons travelling in automobiles, *Adams v. Williams, supra,* where there is "at least articulable and reasonable" suspicion that a motorist or his vehicle is somehow subject to seizure for violation of law. *Delaware v. Prouse, supra.* This right to conduct an investigatory stop or seizure of an individual has been approved in many decisions since *State v. Streeter, supra,* on different facts. *E.g., State v. Buie,* 297 N.C. 159, 254 S.E. 2d 26, *cert. denied,* 444 U.S. 971, 62 L.Ed. 2d 386, 100 S.Ct. 464 (1979); *State v. Thompson,* 296 N.C. 703, 252 S.E. 2d 776, *cert. denied,* 444 U.S. 907, 62 L.Ed. 2d 143, 100 S.Ct. 220 (1979); *State v. McZorn,* 288 N.C. 417, 219 S.E. 2d 201 (1975), *death sentence· vacated,* 428 U.S. 904, 49 L.Ed. 2d 1210, 96 S.Ct. 3210 (1976); *State v. Sadler,* 40 N.C. App. 22, 251 S.E. 2d 902, *cert. denied and appeal dismissed,* 297 N.C. 303, 254 S.E. 2d 924 (1979); *State v. Stanfield,* 19 N.C. App. 622, 199 S.E. 2d 741 (1973), *appeal dismissed,* 284 N.C. 622, 201 S.E. 2d 692 (1974). *See also Gaines v. Craven,* 448 F. 2d 1236 (9th Cir. 1971) and *United States v. Unverzagt,* 424 F. 2d 396 (8th Cir. 1970) (where it was held that police officers acted properly by conducting an investigatory

stop of a "suspicious individual" under circumstances in which the officers had a reasonable belief that further investigation was necessary to test information which had been given to them.) This standard was refined in the recent decision of *State v. Thompson, supra*, where the Court applied both *Terry v. Ohio, supra*, and *Adams v. Williams, supra*. The Court stated:

> The standard set forth in *Terry* for testing the conduct of law enforcement officers in effecting a warrantless "seizure" of an individual is that "the police officer must be able to point to specific and articulable facts, which taken together with rational inferences from those facts, reasonably warrant [the] intrusion." *Id.* at 21, 88 S.Ct. at 1880, 20 L.Ed. 2d at 906. In *Adams v. Williams*, 407 U.S. 143, 146, 92 S. Ct. 1921, 1923, 32 L.Ed. 2d 612, 617 (1972), the Court reaffirmed the principle of *Terry* that "[a] brief stop of a suspicious individual, in order to determine his identity or to maintain the status quo momentarily while obtaining more information, may be most reasonable in light of the facts known to the officer at the time." The standard set forth in *Terry* and reaffirmed in *Adams* clearly falls short of the traditional notion of probable cause, which is required for an arrest. We believe the standard set forth requires only that the officer have a "reasonable" or "founded" suspicion as justification for a limited investigative seizure. *United States v. Constantine*, 567 F. 2d 266 (4th Cir. 1977); *United States v. Solomon*, 528 F. 2d 88 (9th Cir. 1975).

296 N.C. at 706, 252 S.E. 2d at 779.

[1] Under the facts before us, it is our view that the "totality of the circumstances" afforded Officer Simpson the basis of authority to approach defendant's automobile parked in the parking lot of a church and direct defendant to roll down his window for the limited purpose of investigating a report that a "suspicious person" was on the premises. The evidence on voir dire shows that the officer received a call between 7:00 p.m. and 8:00 p.m. on 27 November 1977 requesting him to investigate a "suspicious person" on the church premises. As he arrived, he was directed by churchgoers toward defendant, who was alone in an automobile parked in the corner of the lot.

State v. Greenwood

We find these facts controlled by the recent decision of *State v. Thompson, supra.* There, police officers approached and detained defendants, who occupied a van parked in a public parking area in the early morning. Evidence showed that the officers were aware that criminal activity in the area involving a van had been recently reported. The Court, in upholding convictions based on evidence seized from the van, concluded that the facts and inferences drawn therefrom justified a reasonable suspicion that the occupants of the van might be engaged in or connected with criminal activity. The Court, therefore, found that the officers acted properly in approaching the van and seeking identification from its occupants.

Such conduct is similarly appropriate in the instant case. It appears that, based on the totality of circumstances as they were perceived through the eyes of Officer Simpson; the officer was justified in his belief that further investigation of defendant was necessary to test out the report previously given him. *See Gaines v. Craven, supra; United States v. Unverzagt, supra.*

In so holding, we reject as inapplicable defendant's argument that any authority given to police officers to detain motorists under G.S. 20-29 has been overruled by our United States Supreme Court in *Delaware v. Prouse, supra,* wherein the Court stated:

> [W]e hold that except in those situations in which there is at least articulable and reasonable suspicion that a motorist is unlicensed or that an automobile is not registered, or that either the vehicle or an occupant is otherwise subject to seizure for violation of law, stopping an automobile and detaining the driver in order to check his driver's license and registration of the automobile are unreasonable under the Fourth Amendment.

440 U.S. at 663, 59 L.Ed. 2d at 673, 99 S.Ct. at 1401. Rather, under the decisions of *Terry v. Ohio, supra, Adams v. Williams, supra, State v. Thompson, supra,* and *State v. Streeter, supra,* we find from these facts a sufficient basis upon which Officer Simpson's investigatory stop of defendant's person was appropriate, independently of the officer's authority pursuant to G.S. 20-29 to

detain motorists for the purposes of inspection on the public streets. This result is, furthermore, entirely consistent with the standard of "articulable and reasonable suspicion" announced in *Delaware v. Prouse, supra.*

[2] We next consider whether the search of defendant's automobile was proper. The State argues that the search was proper in that the officer, upon detecting the odor of marijuana in and around defendant's car at the time defendant rolled down his window, had probable cause to believe that a controlled substance was contained within defendant's automobile. Defendant argues, on the other hand, that the alleged odor of marijuana, standing alone, did not provide probable cause to search defendant's vehicle for the presence of a controlled substance, absent a search warrant.

Whether the odor of an illegal substance alone provides a sufficient basis to justify the warrantless search for such substances has been an issue of considerable debate. There appears to be a split of authority among the jurisdictions which have decided this question. *Compare, e.g., Johnson v. United States,* 333 U.S. 10, 92 L.Ed. 436, 68 S.Ct. 367 (1948); *State v. Schoendaller,* 578 P. 2d 730 (S.Ct. Mont. 1978); and *People v. Hilber,* 403 Mich. 312, 269 N.W. 2d 159 (1978) *with United States v. Martinez-Miramontes,* 494 F. 2d 808 (9th Cir.), *cert. denied,* 419 U.S. 897, 42 L.Ed. 2d 141, 95 S.Ct. 176 (1974), and *United States v. Barron,* 472 F. 2d 1215 (9th Cir.) *cert. denied,* 413 U.S. 920, 37 L.Ed. 2d 1041, 93 S.Ct. 3063 (1973). In *United States v. Mullin,* 329 F. 2d 295 (4th Cir. 1964), defendants were convicted of possessing nontaxpaid whiskey. On appeal, the Court of Appeals for the Fourth Circuit reversed, holding that there was not probable cause to justify warrantless search:

> Odors associated with contraband that lead a reasonable man to believe that a crime has been committed have been recognized as a valid basis on which to seek a search warrant. [Citations omitted.] The Supreme Court has recently reaffirmed the principle, however, that such observations, while furnishing probable cause for the issuance of a warrant, will not suffice to justify a search and seizure without a warrant. [Citation omitted.]

329 F. 2d at 297. The *Mullin* Court relied heavily on *Johnson v. Unites States, supra,* where the Supreme Court explained the rationale behind its distinction between evidence sufficient for a search warrant as opposed to probable cause to justify a warrantless search:

> The point of the Fourth Amendment which often is not grasped by zealous officers, is not that it denies law enforcement the support of the usual inferences which reasonable men draw from evidence. Its protection consists in requiring that those inferences be drawn by a neutral and detached magistrate instead of being judged by the officer engaged in the often competitive enterprise of ferreting out crime. Any assumption that evidence sufficient to support a magistrate's disinterested determination to issue a search warrant will justify the officers in making a search without a warrant would reduce the Amendment to a nullity and leave the people's homes secure only in the discretion of police officers.

333 U.S. at 13-14, 92 L.Ed. at 440, 68 S.Ct. at 369.

This zealous regard for review by a disinterested judicial official has been carried over into the modern era where state police officers and federal officials are engaged in the same "competitive enterprise", only with different types of contraband. In *People v. Hilber, supra,* cited by defendant, defendant was stopped for speeding by a Michigan State trooper, and was requested to present his driver's license and registration. A subsequent search of defendant's vehicle revealed a substantial quantity of marijuana. At a suppression hearing, the Circuit Court found that the trooper's detection of the odor of marijuana justified the search of the automobile. The Court of Appeals disagreed with this finding and reversed defendant's conviction. On appeal to the Supreme Court, the State argued that the odor of burned marijuana provided reasonable cause to believe that defendant had smoked the marijuana that caused the odor and that there was unsmoked marijuana in the automobile. The Court distinguished between marijuana that was unburned, burning, and burned, and the possible inferences to be drawn therefrom and compared the habit of smoking marijuana to that of smoking cigarettes. After criticizing the "indefinite and indeterminate" terminology used by the trooper to describe his suspicions about defendant, the Court concluded that even if it was reasonable to believe that a marijuana smoker would have in his possession or in his automobile a supply of unsmoked marijuana, it was unreasonable in this case to conclude that defendant was the smoker, and, therefore, that the trooper was not justified in searching defendant's vehicle. Similarly, in *State v. Schoendaller, supra,* police officers approached defendant in his automobile while defendant was stopped in the street blocking traffic. While standing beside the open driver's window of defendant's automobile, one officer detected the odor of marijuana and incense. Based on this detection, the officers searched defendant's vehicle and found contraband substances, including marijuana. The Montana Supreme Court ruled the search invalid, concluding as follows:

> The police conducted their warrantless search on the basis of ". . . a strong odor of marijuana in the car along with that of some incense or something . . ." and lacking an exigent circumstances, such perception falls closer to the realm of bare suspicion than probable cause. We do not deny police officers the right to rely on these [sic] sense of smell to confirm their observations. However, to hold that an odor alone, absent evidence of visible contents, is deemed equivalent to plain view might very easily mislead officers into fruitless invasions of privacy where there is no contraband.

578 P. 2d at 734. *Accord: State v. Olson,* 589 P. 2d 663 (S.Ct. Mont. 1979). In both *Hilber* and *Schoendaller* there were strong dissents which supported the view that the odor of marijuana is in itself enough to provide probable cause to search.

Recent decisions from jurisdictions other than North Carolina have held generally that the detection of odor of marijuana emanating from a automobile constitutes probable cause to search the vehicle for the presence of marijuana. *E.g., State v. Zamora,* 114 Ariz. 75, 559 P. 2d 195 (1977); *United States v. Solomon,* 528 F. 2d 88 (9th Cir. 1975); *United States v. Barron, supra; United States v. Garcia-Rodriguez,* 558 F. 2d 956 (9th Cir. 1977),

State v. Greenwood

cert. denied, 434 U.S. 1050, 54 L.Ed. 2d 802, 98 S.Ct. 900 (1978); *United States v. Stricklin,* 534 F. 2d 1386 (10th Cir.), *cert. denied,* 429 U.S. 831, 50 L.Ed. 2d 95, 97 S.Ct. 92 (1976); *United States v. Fontecha,* 576 F. 2d 601 (5th Cir. 1978); *Rose v. City of Enterprise,* 52 Ala. App. 437, 293 So. 2d 862 (1974); *State v. Harrison,* 111 Ariz. 508, 533 P. 2d 1143 (1975); *State v. Ballesteros,* 23 Ariz. App. 211, 531 P. 2d 1149 (1975), *cert. denied,* 423 U.S. 870, 46 L.Ed. 2d 100, 96 S.Ct. 135 (1975); *People v. Gale,* 108 Cal. Rptr. 852, 511 P. 2d 1204 (1973); *Mattson v. State,* 328 So. 2d 246 (Fla. App. 196); *People v. Gremp,* 20 Ill. App. 3d 78, 312 N.E. 2d 716 (1974); *State v. Gilson,* 116 N.H. 230, 356 A. 2d 689 (1976); *State v. Binns,* 194 N.W. 2d 756 (N.D. 1972); *State v. Childers,* 13 Or. App. 622, 511 Pa. 2d 447 (1973). In most, if not all, of these decisions, probable cause to search was grounded on the expertise and sound judgment of the investigating officer in assessing the probability that the odor detected is that of a contraband substance and that it is reasonable to assume that a search of a vehicle will reveal the substance. We find these decisions persuasive and believe that they represent a suitable resolution to the issue presented here.

Applying the rationale underlying these decisions, we conclude that the search by Officer Simpson of defendant's automobile was, although without a warrant, based on probable cause and, therefore, proper. The law is settled in North Carolina that a law enforcement officer may conduct a warrantless search of an automobile if the officer has a reasonable belief that the automobile contains contraband materials. *State v. Jefferies* and *State v. Person,* 41 N.C. App. 95, 254 S.E. 2d 550, *cert. denied,* 297 N.C. 614, 257 S.E. 2d 438 (1979); *State v. Bunn,* 36 N.C. App. 114, 243 S.E. 2d 189, *cert. denied,* 295 N.C. 261, 245 S.E. 2d 778 (1978); *State v. Walker,* 25 N.C. App. 157, 212 S.E. 2d 528, *cert. denied,* 287 N.C. 264, 214 S.E. 2d 436, *cert. denied,* 423 U.S. 894, 46 L.Ed. 2d 126, 96 S. Ct. 193 (1975), and cases there cited. Such probable cause to search is established where, from the surrounding circumstances, there exists at least a "probability" that contraband substances are contained within the vehicle. *Cf., State v. McLeod,* 36 N.C. App. 469, 244 S.E. 2d 716, *cert. denied,* 295 N.C. 555, 248 S.E. 2d 733 (1978). Here, the officer, trained in the identification of marijuana by its odor, detected the distinct odor of marijuana emanating from defendant's automobile. In our view, it was reasonable for the officer to assume that the odor originated from defendant's vehicle and that the vehicle contained marijuana. Further, the subtle distinctions created by other courts concerning the possible inferences to be drawn from unburned, burning, and burned marijuana are not, we believe, based on the best logic and, in addition, are not dispositive in any particular case. *See People v. Hilber, supra* (Williams, Justice, dissenting). In addition, we find sufficient exigencies in this case to justify the officer's failure to procure a search warrant before searching defendant's vehicle, in that, had Officer Simpson left defendant to get a warrant, it is highly unlikely that defendant would have been in the parking lot when he returned. In concluding that the search of defendant's automobile was based upon probable cause and conducted under exigent circumstances, we reiterate the words of Justice Huskins in *State v. Riddick*, 291 N.C. 399, 406, 230 S.E. 2d 506, 511 (1976), that "probable cause means a reasonable ground to believe that the proposed search will reveal the presence, upon the premises to be searched, of the objects sought and that those objects will aid in the apprehension or conviction of the offender." We believe those criteria have been met in this case.

[3] Defendant next argues that his arrest on the charge of possession of a controlled substance was unlawful. We disagree. Pursuant to his proper search of defendant's vehicle, the officer found cigarette butts and a "roach clip" which apparently contained marijuana. The officer then had probable cause to believe that defendant had committed the offense of possession of a controlled substance. G.S. 90-95(a)(3). Defendant's arrest was, therefore, proper under G.S. 15A-401(b)(2), in that the circumstances led the officer to believe that defendant had "committed a misdemeanor" and would "not be apprehended unless immediately arrested." Defendant's contention that under G.S. 90-95(d)(4) he was guilty at most of a misdemeanor and subject only to a fine of not more than $100, and that his arrest was an unlawful deprivation of liberty is, therefore, without merit.

[4] Defendant's remaining contentions relate to the suppression of a pocketbook found on the rear seat of defendant's automobile. We are of the opinion that, even if the further search

after defendant's arrest for possession of marijuana was proper, evidence concerning the pocketbook obtained by a search of its contents should have been suppressed.

Controlling in this instance is our recent decision of *State v. Cole*, 46 N.C. App. 592, 265 S.E. 2d 507 (1980). In *Cole*, the Court held that the warrantless search of a jacket found on the rear seat of defendant's automobile was in violation of the Fourth Amendment prohibition against unreasonable searches and seizures under the rules established initially in *United States v. Chadwick*, 433 U.S. 1, 53 L.Ed. 2d 538, 97 S.Ct. 2476 (1977), and followed in the recent case of *Arkansas v. Sanders, supra*. The Court characterized defendant's jacket as a "repository for personal items when one wishes to transport them", citing *United States v. Meier*, 602 F. 2d 253, 255 (10th Cir. 1979) and *Arkansas v. Sanders, supra*. We adhere to these principles in the present case involving a pocketbook, which is obviously a repository for personal items, and hold that a warrantless search of the pocketbook was improper. This result obtains regardless of whether the pocketbook was seized from defendant's automobile. *See Arkansas v. Sanders, supra*.

The trial court's order denying defendant's motion to suppress with respect to the controlled substance, is affirmed.

The trial court's order denying defendant's motion to suppress, with respect to the contents of the pocketbook, is reversed.

Affirmed in part; reversed in part.

Judges PARKER and WELLS concur.

IONA S. MOORE, Employee v. J. P. STEVENS & COMPANY, INC. Employer
LIBERTY MUTUAL INSURANCE COMPANY, Carrier

No. 7910IC777

(Filed 5 August 1980)

1. **Master and Servant § 68– worker's compensation – occupational disease – proof of causation**

    One element of a claimant's right to compensation for an occupational disease under G.S. 97-53(13) and G.S. 97-52 is proof of causation.

2. **Master and Servant § 68– worker's compensation – occupational disease – necessary findings**

    Where the Industrial Commission awards compensation for disablement due to an occupational disease emcompassed by G.S. 97-53(13), the opinion and award must contain explicit findings as to the characteristics, symptoms and manifestations of the disease from which the plaintiff suffers, as well as a conclusion of law as to whether the disease falls within the statutory provision; however, such findings should not be necessary upon the Commission's finding that the disease, whatever its manifestations and whatever its symptoms, was not due to causes or conditions characteristic of the particular employment in which the employee was engaged.

3. **Master and Servant § 68– worker's compensation – finding that exposure to cotton dust not cause of disease – denial of claim**

    A finding by the Industrial Commission that plaintiff textile worker's chronic obstructive pulmonary disease was not due to her exposure to cotton dust and lint in her employment with defendant employer provided a sufficient basis for the Commission's denial of compensation to plaintiff for an occupational disease.

4. **Master and Servant § 68– worker's compensation – finding that exposure to cotton dust not cause of disease – sufficiency of evidence**

    A finding by the Industrial Commission that plaintiff's chronic pulmonary disease "is not due to her exposure to cotton dust and lint in her employment with defendant employer" was supported by the evidence where plaintiff's expert witness testified that, although plaintiff had been employed in an area of cotton manufacturing in which the incidence of employment-related chronic lung disease is highest, plaintiff did not exhibit the usual history of onset and progression symptoms classical for this problem, and where plaintiff's expert, in explaining his opinion testimony that plaintiff's respiratory disease "could or might have been caused by her occupational exposure," stated that his opinion referred to "possibility" rather than "probability."

5. **Master and Servant § 68– workers' compensation – pulmonary problems – findings as to effect of weather**

    The evidence supported a finding by the Industrial Commission that plaintiff's pulmonary problems were worse in the fall and winter months and that cold weather adversely affected those problems.

APPEAL by plaintiff from Opinion and Award of the North Carolina Industrial Commission filed 5 March 1979. Heard in the Court of Appeals 4 March 1980.

This is a claim for benefits under the Workers' Compensation Act for alleged occupational disease resulting from exposure to cotton dust. The jurisdictional facts were stipulated. The case was heard before Deputy Commissioner Denson on 4 January 1978 in Roanoke Rapids and on 24 May 1978 in Chapel Hill.

At the hearings the parties further stipulated that plaintiff last worked for defendant employer on 14 May 1976 and that for the periods 1925 to 1934 and 1941 to 1945 plaintiff employee had worked in the spinning room at defendant's Roanoke Rapids plant, and for the period 1945 to 1976 in the weave room.

Evidence was presented at the hearing to show the following: Dr. John W. Boone, a specialist in family practice who treated plaintiff for a number of years after December 1965, testified that during that period plaintiff suffered from a variety of medical problems including headaches, nervous tension, gastritis, arthritis, dizziness, upper respiratory tract infection and bronchitis. In 1968 plaintiff suffered from chest discomfort, which Dr. Boone diagnosed as myocardial ischemia and treated with nitroglycerin. Between 1965 and 1977 plaintiff had two episodes of coughing blood, which Dr. Boone attributed to her bronchitis because it cleared with antibiotics. He stated that based on his diagnoses of her condition at the time of the hearing, plaintiff was disabled from work primarily because of her heart difficulties and chest pain.

On cross-examination by plaintiff's attorney, Dr. Boone testified that chest pain, such as that from which plaintiff suffered, is "one symptom of dust disease or lung disease." However, in a letter dated 19 December 1977 to defendant's insurance carrier he stated that he was not aware of her symptoms on exposure to cotton dust and was not familiar with the section of the mill in which she worked.

Plaintiff testified that she began working for defendant employer at the age of 13 in the spinning room. During her years in the spinning room, there was always lint dust in the air of the work area. In 1946 plaintiff began working in the weave room which was also filled with lint dust. She had no serious illness prior to starting work in the weave room except bronchitis. The temperature and humidity in the weave room in which she worked varied considerably. In 1950 plaintiff began smoking. When she suffered lung problems, she stayed out from work. Plaintiff stopped working on 14 May 1976 because of weakness and shortness of breath. Dr. Boone, her personal physician, recommended that defendant employer remove her from an area where there was lint and dust. Plaintiff attempted to return to work in November 1976 after her leave of absence, but was told by defendant's plant personnel manager that she could not continue to work because he understood that she had lung problems. After May 1977 plaintiff sought other employment, and by the time of the hearing she had worked on and off part-time as a laundry attendant at minimum wage. She continues to suffer from shortness of breath and weakness and attacks of bronchitis. Although the bronchitis attacks do not occur monthly, they occur regularly, especially when she is exposed to dampness, air conditioning or fans. In 1976 plaintiff was given a brown lung breathing test and was referred by the Brown Lung Association to Dr. William Z. Wood, a pulmonary disease specialist, who is also a member of the medical faculty at the University of North Carolina at Chapel Hill and a member of the Industrial Commission's Textile Occupational Disease Panel.

Dr. Wood testified in Chapel Hill at a later stage of the hearings. During his examination of plaintiff on 18 November 1976 he conducted several lung function tests which revealed a reduction in the forced vital capacity of the lung and a reduction in the volume of forced exhalation, as well as a mild reduction in the oxygen level of the arterial blood gases. Dr. Wood concluded that, although there was a problem with the ability of the patient properly to perform the tests, the studies showed lung dysfunction due to chronic bronchitis and emphysema of nonspecific etiology. He did testify that in his report filed with the Industrial Commission following his examination of plaintiff that she had been employed in the phase of textile manufacturing where cotton dust hypersensitivity, *i.e.* chronic lung disease and byssinosis, is high in incidence. However, in that same report Dr. Wood indicated that plaintiff did not show the classic symptomatic history of onset and progression of the textile occupational disease. Plaintiff did not indicate that her episodes of bronchitis were brought on after exposure to cotton dust, but rather that they occurred in cooler and damper weather and that she could not tolerate air conditioners, which indicated an irritated reaction. Dr. Wood stated that her occupational exposure could or might have caused, *i.e.* was possibly a cause of her respiratory problems, but that he did not know the initiating cause.

Deputy Commissioner Denson made findings concerning plaintiff's work history, her medical history and treatment and tests, and her present employment. She further found that "[p]laintiff's chronic obstructive pulmonary disease is not due to her exposure to cotton dust and lint in her employment with defendant employer." She concluded as a matter of law that plaintiff had not contracted an occupational disease arising out of and in the course of her employment, and accordingly denied compensation. On appeal to the full Industrial Commission from the Opinion and Award of the Deputy Commissioner, the Commission affirmed the denial of compensation and adopted that Opinion and Award as its own. From this Opinion and Award plaintiff appeals.

Davis, Hassell & Hudson by Charles R. Hassell, Jr. and Robin E. Hudson for plaintiff appellant.

Maupin, Taylor & Ellis by Richard M. Lewis, for defendant appellees.

PARKER, Judge.

Plaintiff bases her claim for disability benefits under the North Carolina Workers' Compensation Act upon the provisions of G.S. 97-53(13) and G.S. 97-52. G.S. 97-53 lists the diseases and conditions deemed to be "occupational diseases." Subsection (13) includes the following as an "occupational disease":

Any disease, other than hearing loss covered in another
subdivision of this section, which is proven to be due to
causes and conditions which are characteristic of and
peculiar to a particular trade, occupation or employment,
but excluding all ordinary diseases of life to which the
general public is equally exposed outside of the employment.

Under G.S. 97-52, "disablement" of an employee resulting from
an "occupational disease" described in G.S. 97-53 is to be
"treated as the happening of an injury by accident within the
meaning of the North Carolina Workers' Compensation Act,"
thus triggering the award of benefits.

[1] In *Booker v. Medical Center*, 297 N.C. 458, 256 S.E. 2d 189
(1979) our Supreme Court discussed at length the elements
necessary to prove the existence of the compensable "occupational disease" defined by G.S. 97-53(13). The first two elements,
that a disease be "characteristic" of a trade or occupation and
that it not be an ordinary disease of life "to which the general
public is equally exposed outside of the employment" are expressly required by the language of the statute. The third element was stated by the court in *Booker v. Medical Center*,
supra, as follows:

The final requirement in establishing a compensable claim
under subsection (13) is proof of causation. It is this limitation which protects our Workmen's Compensation Act from
being converted into a general health and insurance benefit act. *Bryan v. Church*, 267 N.C. 111, 115, 147 S.E. 2d 633,
635 (1966). In *Duncan v. Charlotee*, 234 N.C. 86, 91, 66 S.E. 2d
22, 25 (1951) we held that the addition of G.S. 97-53 to the Act
"in nowise relaxed the fundamental principle which requires proof of causal relation between injury and employment. And nonetheless [sic], since the adoption of the
amendment, may an award for an occupational disease be
sanctioned unless it be shown that the disease was incident
to or the result of the particular employment in which the
workmen was engaged."

297 N.C. at 475, 256 S.E. 2d at 200.

The rule of causation in the field of workers' compensation where the right to recover is based on injury by accident has been that the employment need not be the sole causative force to render an injury compensable. If the employee, "by reason of constitutional infirmities is predisposed to sustain injuries while engaged in labor, nevertheless the leniency and humanity of the law permit him to recover compensation if the physical aspects of the employment contribute in some reasonable degree to bring about or intensify the condition which renders him susceptible to such accident and consequent injury." *Vause v. Equipment Co.*, 233 N.C. 88, 92, 63 S.E. 2d 173, 176 (1951). A similar rule of causation has been implied in cases where compensation for occupational disease is sought; however, if a disease is produced by some extrinsic or independent agency, it may not be imputed to the occupation or the employment. *Duncan v. Charlotte*, 234 N.C. 86, 66 S.E. 2d 22 (1951).

Plaintiff contends on this appeal that the Commission failed to make proper findings of fact regarding compensability under G.S. 97-53(13) on the grounds that no findings were made with respect to the cause of plaintiff's chronic bronchitis and pulmonary emphysema or to the issue of whether her years of occupational exposure exposed plaintiff to a greater risk of contracting pulmonary disease than the general public.

It is well established that the Industrial Commission must make specific findings of fact as to each material fact upon which the rights of the parties in a case involving a claim for compensation depend. *Wood v. Stevens & Co.*, 297 N.C. 636, 256 S.E. 2d 692 (1979); *Thomason v. Cab Co.*, 235 N.C. 602, 70 S.E. 2d 706 (1952). If the findings of fact of the Commission are insufficient to enable the court to determine the rights of the parties upon the matters in controversy, the cause must be remanded to the Commission for proper findings of fact. *Young v. Whitehall, Co.*, 229 N.C. 360, 49 S.E. 2d 797 (1948); *Gaines v. Swain & Son, Inc.*, 33 N.C. App. 575, 235 S.E. 2d 856 (1977).

[2, 3] In the present case, were it not for the Commission's Finding of Fact No. 12, we would agree with plaintiff's contention that there were insufficient findings to support the Commission's denial of compensation, principally because a number

of the other "findings" are mere recitals of the opinions of the medical experts which, in themselves, could not properly form the basis for conclusions of law as to compensability. *See, Gaines v. Swain & Son, Inc., supra.* Finding of Fact No. 12 recites:

> Plaintiff's chronic obstructive pulmonary disease is not due to her exposure to cotton dust and lint in her employment with defendant employer.

Although cast in the form of a negative finding, it does provide a sufficient basis for the conclusion of law that plaintiff's disablement is noncompensable because, as indicated in *Booker v. Medical Center, supra,* a claimant's right to compensation for an occupational disease under G.S. 97-53(13) and G.S. 97-52 depends upon proper proof of causation, and the burden of proving each and every element of compensability is upon the plaintiff. *Richards v. Nationwide Homes,* 263 N.C. 295, 139 S.E. 2d 645 (1965), *Aylor v. Barnes,* 242 N.C. 223, 87 S.E. 2d 269 (1955). It is true that, where the Commission awards compensation for disablement due to an occupational disease encompassed by G.S. 97-53(13), the opinion and award must contain explicit findings as to the characteristics, symptoms and manifestations of the disease from which the plaintiff suffers, as well as a conclusion of law as to whether the disease falls within the statutory provision. *Wood v. Stevens, supra.* However, such findings should not be necessary upon the Commission's finding that the disease, whatever its manifestations and whatever its symptoms, was not due to causes or conditions characteristic of the particular employment in which the employee was engaged. The denial of compensation may be predicated upon the failure of the claimant to prove any one of the elements of compensability.

[4] Having determined that Finding of Fact No. 12 is sufficient to support the Commission's denial of plaintiff's claim, we consider whether that finding is supported by competent evidence in the record. If so, it is conclusive and binding upon this Court. *Cole v. Guilford County,* 259 N.C. 724, 131 S.E. 2d 308 (1963); *Vause v. Equipment Co., supra.* Dr. William Z. Wood, Jr., the pulmonary disease specialist and member of the Industrial

Commission's Textile Occupational Disease Panel, testified at length concerning plaintiff's medical condition. Although he stated that plaintiff had been employed in an area of cotton manufacturing in which the incidence of employment-related chronic lung disease is highest, he also testified that plaintiff did not exhibit the usual symptomatic history of symptoms onset and progression classical for this problem:

> By that I mean that the usual and classical onset is one of increasing symptoms in the onset of symptoms on the first day returning to work after a period away from the mill. The symptoms usually described is [sic] a sensation of tightness and difficulty breathing which may be associated with cough. This seems to improve with continued exposure so by the second, third, fourth day the symptoms are much less or may be completely absent. That's generally referred to as Grade one-half. And then, as the continued progression of the symptoms occur the symptoms may be present on more than one day after returning to work. That is, I think, usually given the Grade one to the point it is present throughout the work week, with evidence of lung dysfunctions, Grade two and then, failure to improve even after being away from work is referred to as Grade three, with symptoms of tightness, shortness of breath, often times accompanied by cough and sputum production. I am saying that Mrs. Moore did not give that progression of symptoms, that is correct. Her major complaint has been that of cough and shortness of breath. There has been some sputum production that has fluctuated in intervals throughout some forty years-thirty or forty years of her history. The major symptom being shortness of breath. She also indicated frequent episodes of what she called bronchitis, that is the story she gave to me. Yes, sir. She also told me that these episodes came on in cooler and damper periods of time and that she could not tolerate air conditioners or cool or damp weather. That indicated to me that she has airways that are sensitive to temperature and climatic change. This is frequently seen in people who have a variety of lung diseases.

* * *

She did not indicate that these episodes were brought on after exposure to cotton dust. In fact, an air conditioner or the cooler, damper weather that brought on these symptoms could be classified as an irritant.

Further, in explaining his response to a hypothetical question posed by plaintiff's counsel in which he stated that, in his opinion, plaintiff's respiratory disease "could or might have been caused by her occupational exposure," Dr. Wood stated that that opinion referred to "possibility" rather than "probability." In light of Dr. Wood's testimony, the Commission was justified in finding that plaintiff's chronic pulmonary disease "is not due to her exposure to cotton dust and lint in her employment with defendant employer."

[5] Plaintiff has also excepted and made the basis of an assignment of error on the grounds of the insufficiency of the evidence to support it a portion of finding of fact no. 5 which recites: "Beginning in March of 1966 [plaintiff] complained to [her family practitioner] of upper respiratory problems and these problems or problems [sic] which he diagnosed as bronchial problems continued more or less constantly to the present time. This happened more often during the fall and winter months and Dr. Boone connected it with a viral infection or some other irritant or allergic reaction to cold weather." Although this "finding" is certainly not a clear statement of fact, there is some evidence to support it. Dr. Boone testified:

> I mentioned several times that she had bronchitis. I think it seemed to be more severe at certain times of the year, say in the Fall. Looking back, she had one spell first in December, the hemoptysis occurred in December. She had a spell here in October, another in October. She had a year-round problem but — here is one in June. So she had it at other times. One in November. I think it is more common in everyone, people with normal lungs as well as people with lung disease, in the fall and winter months, to have bronchitis flareups. It is sort of to be expected. I think the weather has something to do with it. It would not be suggestive of an allergy. No, more like an infection, the type of thing she had.

Thus, the record supports the finding that plaintiff's respiratory problems seemed to worsen in colder weather. Although there are inaccuracies in the Commission's reference to the infection as being "viral" and in the reference to an "allergic" reaction to cold weather, these inaccuracies do not detract from the main thrust of Finding of Fact No. 5, *i.e.* that plaintiff's pulmonary problems were worse in the fall and winter months and that the cold weather adversely affected those problems.

Finally, plaintiff challenges the Commission's inaccurate statement of the stipulation of the parties regarding plaintiff's work history. The parties stipulated that she had worked from 1925-1935 in the spinning room of defendant's mill, but the findings of fact reflect only that she worked from 1941-1976. Although such an omission is clearly erroneous, it does not require a rehearing of this case. Plaintiff's claim was denied on the ground of her failure to prove causation. The testimony of the expert witnesses, Dr. Boone and Dr. Wood, upon which the Commission based its finding that plaintiff's chronic obstructive pulmonary disease is not due to occupational exposure, discloses that their opinions were based upon their knowledge of plaintiff's full employment history, including the ten-year period inadvertently omitted from the Commission's finding.

Thus, the Commission's crucial finding is supported by sufficient evidence to justify the denial of compensation in the present case. The Opinion and Award of the Full Commission is

Affirmed.

Judges MARTIN (Harry C.) and HILL concur.

U.S. INDUSTRIES, INC. v. LOTON E. THARPE, Administrator of the Estate of CRYSTAL FAYE THARPE and ARCHIE DALE BARKER v. KENNETH ROGER PULASKI

No. 8023SC145

(Filed 5 August 1980)

1. **Automobiles § 74– entering highway in front of oncoming truck – contributory negligence as matter of law**

	In defendant's third party action to recover against a truck driver for wrongful death, evidence was sufficient to show that defendant's negligence so clearly contributed as at least one of the proximate causes of the collision that she would be barred as a matter of law from any recovery based on the alleged negligence of the third party defendant, where such evidence tended to show that defendant drove an automobile directly into the path of the third party defendant's oncoming tractor-trailer which clearly had the right of way at a time when the truck was only 100 yards away and when the driver of the rig, third party defendant, could not have avoided hitting the car even though he took evasive action.

2. **Automobiles § 109– owner as passenger – negligence of driver imputed to owner**

	In defendant car owner's third party action to recover for personal injuries sustained in an automobile accident, negligence of the driver was imputed to defendant owner so as to bar his claim, since defendant's presence in the car, coupled with his command to the driver to stop, demonstrated his attempts to retain and to exercise his right to control the actual operation of the car, and application of the owner-occupant doctrine was therefore proper.

3. **Appeal and Error § 49– evidence excluded – similar evidence previously and subsequently admitted**

	Defendant was not prejudiced by the exclusion of evidence on two occasions since similar evidence was admitted both before and after the exclusion in question.

4. **Rules of Civil Procedure § 48; Trial § 42– majority verdict – time for entering agreement**

	An agreement made pursuant to G.S. 1A-1, Rule 48, that a verdict of a stated majority of the jurors will be accepted as the verdict need not be made before the jury begins its deliberations but may be made at any time, and defendant who agreed to accept a verdict of less than twelve could not complain when the verdict ultimately rendered was eleven to one, and the court accepted it as the verdict.

APPEAL by defendant Archie Dale Barker from *Burroughs, Judge.* Judgment entered 13 September 1979 in Superior Court, WILKES County. Heard in the Court of Appeals on 10 June 1980.

Plaintiff U.S. Industries, Inc., instituted this action against the defendants Loton E. Tharpe, Administrator of the estate of Crystal Faye Tharpe, and Fred F. Barker, Guardian of Archie Dale Barker, seeking to recover $28,784.64 for damages which allegedly resulted to its truck when the truck collided with an automobile owned and operated by the defendants on 27 November 1977. The defendants filed answers denying negligence and asserting a counterclaim against the plaintiff and a third-party claim against plaintiff's driver, Kenneth Roger Pulaski, for wrongful death and personal injuries.

At the close of all the evidence the trial judge directed a verdict for the plaintiff and third-party defendant Pulaski as to defendants' claims for wrongful death and personal injuries.

With respect to plaintiff's claim the following issues were submitted to and answered by the jury as indicated:

1. Was the plaintiff, U.S. Industries, Inc., damaged by the negligence of the Defendants, Crystal Faye Tharpe and Archie Dale Barker?

ANSWER: YES.

2. Did the plaintiff, U.S. Industires, Inc., by its own negligence contribute to its damage?

ANSWER: NO.

3. What amount, if any, is the Plaintiff U.S. Industries, Inc., entitled to receive for damages to personal property?

ANSWER: $24,401.95.

4. What amount, if any, is the Plaintiff, U.S. Industries, Inc., entitled to recover for loss of use of its International Tractor and Brown trailer?

ANSWER: $3201.00.

From a judgment directing a verdict as to his claim against the plaintiff and third-party defendant, and from the judgment entered on the verdict as to plaintiff's claim, defendant Fred F. Barker, Guardian of Archie Dale Barker, appealed.

Tuggle, Duggins, Meschan, Thornton & Elrod, by Joseph E. Elrod, III and Joseph F. Brotherton, for plaintiff appellee and third-party defendant appellee.

Finger, Park and Parker, by M. Neil Finger and Raymond A. Parker, II, for defendant appellant Archie Dale Barker.

HEDRICK, Judge.

Defendant assigns error to the judgment directing a verdict for the plaintiff and the third-party defendant with respect to defendant's counterclaim and cross claim. The evidence offered at trial tends to show the following:

The collision giving rise to this cause occurred about 9:00 p.m. on 27 November 1977 at the intersection of U.S. Highway 21 Bypass and Poplar Springs Road between a tractor-trailer owned by plaintiff and driven by plaintiff's agent, Pulaski, third-party defendant, and a Mustang Cobra automobile owned by the defendant, Barker, and driven by the defendant, Tharpe. U.S. Highway 21 in the vicinity of its intersection with Poplar Springs Road contains four lanes divided by a median 45 feet wide with two lanes for traffic moving south and two lanes for traffic moving north. Poplar Springs Road at that point has two lanes and runs east and west.

Pulaski testified that he was driving plaintiff's rig south over U.S. Highway 21. He was thoroughly familiar with the intersection of Highway 21 and Poplar Springs Road. As he approached the intersection Pulaski saw two cars on Poplar Springs Road approaching Highway 21 from his left and moving in a westerly direction. The first vehicle on Poplar Springs Road passed through the intersection and was not really a concern to Pulaski, although he took his foot off the accelerator and steered slightly left to be sure that the car had plenty of room to get across. He may have placed his foot on the brake pedal, but he did not apply the brakes. Pulaski turned the rig he was driving back to the right as the second car (defendant's automobile) crossed the median. At that point Pulaski was driving approximately 55 m.p.h. in a 55 m.p.h. zone. Pulaski testified that he did not think the defendant's automobile would attempt to pass in front of him and he therefore did not attempt to reduce his speed. Defendant's vehicle appeared to stop momentarily, and then moved forward directly in front of him. Pulaski testified he steered his truck to the right in an effort to avoid a collision and applied his brakes just before striking the right front of defendant's vehicle with the left front of the truck.

Further evidence showed that earlier that evening, defendant Barker and a friend, Hudspeth, met the defendant Crystal Tharpe in Elkin. Tharpe wanted to drive Barker's new car. Barker allowed her to drive and she, Barker, and Hudspeth went to visit a friend. On the way back the defendant Tharpe was driving the defendant Barker's automobile in a westerly direction along Poplar Springs Road approaching the intersection with U.S. Highway 21. Barker was riding in the right front seat of his automobile with Tharpe driving. Hudspeth was riding in the rear seat. Hudspeth testified as follows:

. . .

She came up to the stop sign. Then I looked. I didn't see anything coming, I looked in both directions. I always do that. From that point that we were sitting there, you could see north to the top of the hill. That would be approximately 350 yards to the top of the hill. Then, Crystal Tharpe decided to cross the northbound lane, went into a median. As — come out of the median, I seen the truck coming under the flashing light. I hollered "Stop."

Q. Who hollered "Stop?"

A. All of us — me and Archie hollered, "Stop."

. . .

A. Okay, I —

Q. Just a minute —

. . .

Q. Who hollered, "Stop?"

A. Me and Archie.

. . .

A. Okay.

. . .

Q. All right, now, upon your and Archie hollering, "Stop," what did Crystal Faye Tharpe do?

A. She stopped, or to the best of my knowledge, she did stop just a second and the truck — the time she stopped — she accelerated again. And she went straight across — truck was coming straight at us — he was turning to right, it looked like to me, to miss us — I don't know. Anyway, he was turning to the right as the truck slammed into us.

Q. All right, sir, how far up the highway was the truck at the time that you first saw the truck?

A. Coming under the flashing lights about 200 yards.

Q. About 200 yards? Where was the truck at the time that Crystal Faye Tharpe stopped her motor vehicle, or the motor vehicle?

A. About a hundred yards.

Q. All right. You may state what you did after Crystal Faye Tharpe stopped the motor vehicle.

A. I turned around and turned my head back.

Q. All right, sir, what did you see?

A. I seen the truck coming straight at us and I looked at the truck 'til it hit us.

Q. All right. Now, do you have an opinion satisfactory to yourself as to the speed that the tractor-trailer was going at the time that you observed it coming along the 100 yards until it collided with the motor vehicle in which you were riding?

.   .   .

Q. Do you have an opinion?

A. Yeah, I have an opinion, looking at the truck —

.   .   .

Q. What is that opinion?

A. My opinion, I'd say sixty miles an hour.

.   .   .

I observed the truck coming into the car in which I was riding. As the truck crashed into the car, the last thing that I remember, I thought I felt glass hit me in the face. After everything come to a stop, I don't know where I was at, but I got up and grabbed hold of something to stand up. The next thing I remember, I was in the hospital. This was the next day.

I think Crystal Faye Tharpe came to a stop — I think the time she stopped, she accelerated just about as fast as she stopped. She came to that stop about halfway out into the right lane of the southbound travel, inside lane. It was the inside lane.

I am familiar with the diagram over there a little bit.

.   .   .

Q. All right, how about stepping over here and looking at the diagram and see if you can —

A. You want me to point out where we stopped —

. . .

Q. ... Can you point out here on this diagram where you stated that Crystal Faye Tharpe stopped her motor vehicle?

[A]. The front of the car was about halfway out into the inside lane. In other words, the car — half of it was in the turn lane and the other half of it was in the inside lane here.

Defendant argues that the court erred in directing a verdict for the plaintiff and the third-party defendant Pulaski on his claims against them because the record contains evidence sufficient to raise an inference that Pulaski was negligent, and that his negligence was a proximate cause of the collision; that the evidence, when considered in the light most favorable to the defendant, does not show contributory negligence as a matter of law on the part of the defendant Tharpe; and that, even if the evidence does not establish contributory negligence as a matter of law as to the defendant Tharpe, such negligence is not imputed as a matter of law to the defendant Barker. Our decision with respect to the last two contentions of the defendant makes it unnecessary for us to discuss the first. However, since contributory negligence presupposes negligence upon the part of the one against whom a claim is asserted, *Dennis v. Voncannon*, 272 N.C. 446, 158 S.E. 2d 489 (1968), we want to point out that our discussion of the defendant Tharpe's "contributory negligence" is not to be understood as a holding upon our part that the evidence in this record raises an inference that the third-party defendant, Pulaski, was negligent in the operation of the plaintiff's truck and that such negligence was a proximate cause of the collision.

We turn then to the issue whether the evidence proves contributory negligence as a matter of law on the part of the defendant Tharpe. The rule is simply stated:

When the evidence establishes contributory negligence "so clearly that no other conclusion may be reasonably drawn therefrom," *Holland v. Malpass*, 255 N.C. 395, 398, 121 S.E. 2d 576, 578 (1961); *see also Ragland v. Moore*, 299 N.C. 360, 261 S.E.

2d 666 (1980), then a directed verdict for the defendant [Pulaski in this case] is not only appropriate, it is mandated. *Rouse v. Snead*, 271 N.C. 565, 157 S.E. 2d 124 (1967). The negligence of the plaintiff [defendant Tharpe in this case] need not be the sole proximate cause of the injury; if such negligence contributes as *one* of the proximate causes of the injury, then it suffices to bar any recovery. *Holland v. Malpass, supra; Cook v. City of Winston-Salem*, 241 N.C. 422, 85 S.E. 2d 696 (1955).

Our Courts have held time and again that "where a person *sui juris* knows of a dangerous condition and voluntarily goes into the place of danger, he is guilty of contributory negligence, which will bar his recovery." *Dunnevant v. Southern Railway Co.*, 167 N.C. 232, 234, 83 S.E. 347, 348 (1914); *see also Cook v. City of Winston-Salem, supra; Gordon v. Sprott*, 231 N.C. 472, 57 S.E. 2d 785 (1950). This principle is plainly applicable to the factual situation presented by the case before us.

It is elementary that one who is entering or seeking to enter or cross a dominant highway from a servient street must yield the right of way to traffic traveling upon the dominant road. G.S. § 20-158. The driver who is required to stop should not proceed, with oncoming vehicles in view, until in the exercise of due care he has determined that he can proceed safely. *Satterwhite v. Bocelato*, 130 F. Supp. 825 (E.D.N.C. 1955); *Badders v. Lassiter*, 240 N.C. 413, 82 S.E. 2d 357 (1954); *see* G.S. § 20-158. Furthermore, "[n]othing else appearing, the driver of a vehicle having the right of way at an intersection is entitled to assume and to act, until the last moment, on the assumption that the driver of another vehicle, approaching the intersection, will recognize his right of way and will stop or reduce his speed sufficiently to permit him to pass through the intersection in safety." *Dawson v. Jennette*, 278 N.C. 438, 445, 180 S.E. 2d 121, 126 (1971). The motorist who is required to stop and ascertain whether he can proceed safely is deemed to have seen what he would have been able to see had he looked. "[H]is liability to one injured in a collision with his vehicle is determined as it would have been had he looked, observed the prevailing conditions and continued to drive as he did." *Raper v. Byrum*, 265 N.C. 269, 274, 144 S.E. 2d 38, 41 (1965).

[1] When we apply these principles of law to the facts of this case, we find only one conclusion reasonable: Defendant Tharpe's own negligence so clearly contributed as at least one of the proximate causes of the collision that she would be barred as a matter of law from any recovery based on the alleged negligence of the third-party defendant, Pulaski. It follows that any recovery from the plaintiff on the theory of *respondeat superior* would also be barred. While it is undisputed that Tharpe did stop upon first arriving at the intersection of Poplar Springs Road and Highway 21 in obedience to the stop sign there erected, G.S. § 20-158, it is also undisputed that she thereafter failed to stop sufficiently and to yield the right of way at the intersection of the median strip and the southbound lanes of Highway 21 as required by G.S. § 20-155(a). The evidence of record in this case establishes beyond question that the defendant Tharpe drove the automobile directly into the path of the oncoming tractor-trailer which clearly had the right of way at a time when the truck was only 100 yards away and when the driver of the rig, Pulaski, could not have avoided hitting the car even though he took evasive action.

We find the case of *Raper v. Byrum, supra,* factually indistinguishable from the one we decide today. In *Raper* the evidence established that plaintiff's intestate, even though he came to a stop in obedience to the stop sign, thereafter drove at a slow rate of speed into the intersection "when the automobile of the defendants was so near to it that a collision was a virtual certainty." 265 N.C. at 275, 144 S.E. 2d at 42. *See also Snider v. Dickens,* 293 N.C. 356, 237 S.E. 2d 832 (1977). We agree with the *Raper* Court that, in *Raper* as in the case at hand, "[i]t might well be concluded that this was the sole proximate cause of the collision." *Id.* In any event, even if the negligence of Tharpe in driving into the intersection under the circumstances established by all the evidence was not the sole proximate cause of the collision, it was one of the proximate causes and therefore would be sufficient to bar any recovery by Tharpe.

[2] The issue thus becomes whether the defendant Barker's claim is also barred by the doctrine of imputed negligence. That is, must the negligence of the defendant-driver Tharpe be im-

puted to the owner-occupant Barker so as to bar his right to recover as a matter of law? We answer this issue in the affirmative.

The owner-occupant doctrine, so-called, holds that when the owner of the automobile is also an occupant while the car is being operated by another with the owner's permission or at his request, negligence on the part of the driver is imputable to the owner. *Harper v. Harper*, 225 N.C. 260, 34 S.E. 2d 185 (1945). Such is the case because the owner maintains the legal right to control the operation of the vehicle. *Randall v. Rogers*, 262 N.C. 544, 138 S.E. 2d 248 (1964); *Siders v. Gibbs*, 39 N.C. App. 183, 249 S.E. 2d 858 (1978). That the owner does not exercise control or is physically incapable of exercising control is of no consequence. *See, e.g., Tew v. Runnels*, 249 N.C. 1, 105 S.E. 2d 108 (1958); *Baird v. Baird*, 223 N.C. 730, 28 S.E. 2d 225 (1943); *Etheridge v. Norfolk Southern Railway Co.*, 7 N.C. App. 140, 171 S.E. 2d 459, *cert. denied*, 276 N.C. 327 (1970). Indeed, the right of the owner to control the operation of the car can be inferred from the presence of the owner in the car. *Tew v. Runnels, supra.* To avoid the operation of the doctrine, the owner of the vehicle must prove that he relinquished, "for the time being, the incidents of ownership and the right to control the manner and methods of its use." *Shoe v. Hood*, 251 N.C. 719, 724, 112 S.E. 2d 543, 548 (1960).

In the instant case the undisputed and unchallenged facts illustrate a classic case of the owner-occupant doctrine. Furthermore, even if we assume that Barker, as defendant insists, yelled for Tharpe to stop, such action is not sufficient to avoid the operation of the doctrine. There is no evidence that the defendant Barker by any conduct released the *right* to control his car. Manifestly, his presence, coupled with his command to the driver to stop, demonstrates his attempts to retain and to exercise his right to control the actual operation of the car. We hold the negligence of the driver Tharpe under the circumstances of this case is imputed to the owner Barker as a matter of law. Thus, the trial judge correctly directed a verdict for the plaintiff and the third-party defendant as to defendant Barker's claims.

[3] We consider now the defendant's assignments of error with respect to the trial of the plaintiff's claim. Defendant first assigns as error and argues the court erred in not allowing the witness Hudspeth to testify that he [defendant Barker] yelled, "Stop," when it became obvious that Tharpe was not going to stop for the truck. While the court sustained objections on two occasions to questions inquiring of Hudspeth what the defendant Barker said to Tharpe as she proceeded across the median, it appears from the record that Hudspeth testified numerous times on both direct and cross-examination before and after the challenged rulings that Barker yelled "Stop" to Tharpe. Clearly, any "[e]rror in excluding evidence will almost always be cured by allowing its admission later in the trial, . . . " 1 Stansbury's N.C. Evidence, *Witnesses* § 28 at 74 (Brandis rev. 1973). *See, e.g., Continental Insurance Co. v. Foard*, 9 N.C. App. 630, 177 S.E. 2d 431 (1970). With respect to this assignment of error, the defendant's position is untenable. If the judge erred in twice excluding the evidence, the error obviously was not prejudicial error entitling defendant to a new trial.

Defendant next argues the court erred in its instructions to the jury on the doctrine of imputed negligence by instructing the jury "that the negligence of Crystal Faye Tharpe would be imputed to the defendant Archie Dale Barker." Our disposition above of the issue regarding imputed negligence obviously resolves the question raised by this assignment of error. We find no error in the charge.

[4] Finally, the defendant contends the court erred in accepting "less than a majority verdict," even though the record proves that he agreed during the time the jury was deliberating to "take a verdict of nine or more." The verdict ultimately rendered was eleven to one, and based on the prior agreement of all counsel, the court accepted it as the verdict, pursuant to G.S. § 1A-1, Rule 48, which provides:

> Except in actions in which a jury is required by statute, the parties may stipulate that the jury shall consist of any number less than 12 *or that a verdict* or a finding *of a stated majority of the jurors shall be taken as the verdict* or finding of the jury. [Emphasis added.]

Industries, Inc. v. Tharpe

Defendant argues that the agreement must be made before the jury begins its deliberations, although he admits he has no authority to support his interpretation of the statutory language. We cannot agree. The statute does not by its terms restrict the time at which the parties may stipulate to accept a stated majority verdict. In our opinion a fair interpretation of the language allows such an agreement to be made at any time. Defendant voluntarily agreed to accept a verdict of less than twelve, although he certainly could have held out for nothing less than a verdict of the twelve. He will not now be heard to complain.

The result is: The Judgment directing a verdict for the plaintiff and the third-party defendant Pulaski on the defendant appellant's claims is affirmed. With respect to the judgment for the plaintiff entered on the jury verdict, we find in the trial thereof no error.

Affirmed in part; no error in part.

Judges MARTIN (Robert M.), and MARTIN (Harry C.) concur.

CASES REPORTED WITHOUT PUBLISHED OPINION

(Filed 15 July 1980)

BARNES v. INSURANCE CO. No. 794SC927	Duplin (78CVS258)	New Trial
COLEMAN v. COLEMAN No. 7913SC813	Columbus (77CVS676)	Affirmed
ELLER v. ELLER No. 7915DC1126	Alamance (77CVD479)	Affirmed
FULLER v. FULLER No. 8015DC178	Orange (79CVD195)	Affirmed
HARRIS v. STACY RACING, INC. and HYDE v. STACY RACING, INC. No. 7919SC1046	Cabarrus (78CVS0641) (78CVS0824)	 Reversed Affirmed
IN RE SUDDRETH No. 8025SC23	Caldwell (79SP140)	Affirmed
PARRISH v. PARRISH No. 8015DC140	Orange (78CVD044)	Vacated and Remanded
STATE v. ALLEN No. 7911SC1031	Johnston (79CRS2230) (79CRS2231)	No Error
STATE v. BEAN No. 808SC5	Wayne (79CR6771) (79CR6772) (79CR6773) (79CR6774) (79CR6775) (79CR6776)	No Error
STATE v. GRAVES No. 8017SC152	Rockingham (79CR1741A) (79CR1741B)	No Error
STATE v. HOOD No. 8026SC157	Mecklenburg (79CRS17462)	No Error
STATE v. LOCKLEAR No. 7918SC909	Guilford (79CRS12559) (78CRS12560) (78CRS12561)	No Error

STATE v. McNEIL	Warren	No Error
No. 809SC17	(79CRS1117)	
STATE v. MARTIN	Guilford	No Error
No. 8018SC183	(78CRS66714)	
STATE v. RICH	Randolph	No Error
No. 8019SC124	(79CRS3885)	

ANALYTICAL INDEX

WORD AND PHRASE INDEX

TOPICS COVERED IN THIS INDEX

Titles and section numbers in this Index correspond with titles and section numbers in the N.C. Index 3d.

ABORTION

§ 4. Elective Abortions

In administering State funds appropriated by the General Assembly for the State Abortion Fund through the county department of social services, a county acts pursuant to administrative rules governing the Fund which were enacted pursuant to statutory authority. *Stam v. State*, 209.

A human fetus is not a "person" within the meaning of Art. I, §§ 1 and 19 of the N.C. Constitution, and the protections of those sections thus do not apply to the fetus so as to prohibit State funding for elective abortions. *Ibid.*

ADMINISTRATIVE LAW

§ 8. Scope of Judicial Review

Trial court did not err in ruling that it did not have jurisdiction over the subject matter of this action by a discharged fire department employee on the ground that executive actions in personnel matters are not appealable on a writ of certiorari to the courts. *Foust v. City of Greensboro*, 159.

APPEAL AND ERROR

§ 6.2. Finality as Bearing on Appealability; Premature Appeals

Partial summary judgment holding that third party defendant must indemnify defendant for any judgment on plaintiff's claim is interlocutory and not appealable. *Cook v. Tobacco Co.*, 187.

§ 9. Moot Questions

The question presented by plaintiff's Rule 60 motion to set aside the portion of a January 1979 order vacating child custody and support provisions of a prior order was moot where plaintiff filed a second action in March 1979 and the status of the children was settled in a child custody and support order entered in May 1979 before plaintiff filed her Rule 60 motion. *Stewart v. Stewart*, 678.

§ 21. Appellate Review by Certiorari When No Right of Appeal is Provided

Trial court did not err in ruling that it did not have jurisdiction over the subject matter of this action by a discharged fire department employee on the ground that executive actions in personnel matters are not appealable on a writ of certiorari to the courts. *Foust v. City of Greensboro*, 159.

§ 45.1. Effect of Failure to Discuss Exceptions and Assignments of Error in Brief

Defendants' appeal is dismissed where they failed to set forth in their brief assignments of error and the exception pertinent to their argument. *Lloyd v. Carnation Co.*, 203.

ARCHITECTS

§ 3. Liability for Defective Conditions

An association of condominium owners could properly maintain an action against an architect for the negligent design and preparation of plans and the negligent supervision of construction of the condominium complex although no contractual privity existed between the architect and the association. *Condominium Assoc. v. Scholz Co.*, 518.

ARCHITECTS – Continued

An action against an architect for negligent supervision of the installation of an underground water pipe system brought within three years after the defects in the system were discovered was brought within the statute of limitations. *Ibid.*

ARREST AND BAIL

§ 3.4. Legality of Arrest for Possession of Narcotics

An officer's warrantless arrest of defendant was lawful where the officer conducted a proper warrantless search of defendant's vehicle and found cigarette butts and a roach clip which apparently contained marijuana. *S.v. Greenwood*, 731.

§ 5.2. Right of Officer to Enter Dwelling

An officer had probable cause to arrest defendant at the home of a friend without a warrant. *S. v. Graham*, 303.

ASSAULT AND BATTERY

§ 3.1. Sufficiency of Evidence in Civil Assault Actions

In an action to recover damages for assault and battery and to recover alimony, evidence was sufficient for the jury where it tended to show that defendant deliberately struck plaintiff on the head with a baseball bat after threatening to kill her. *Clarke v. Clarke*, 249.

Defendant is entitled to a new trial in a civil assault action because of the trial court's improper instructions which led the jury to believe that negligence was an issue. *Ibid.*

Summary judgment was appropriate in an action to recover for sexual assault where the evidence tended to show that plaintiff did not remember having had sexual intercourse and there was no evidence that plaintiff feared or knew that harmful or offensive contact might occur. *McCraney v. Flanagan*, 498.·

ATTORNEYS AT LAW

§ 7.5. Fees as Part of Costs

In a proceeding to determine the right of a spouse to dissent, trial court erred in taxing attorneys' fees against the estate of testator. *In re Kirkman*, 479.

Where the trial court made no finding or conclusion with respect to whether a caveat proceeding was without substantial merit, the court on appeal could not determine whether the trial court properly exercised its discretion in awarding fees to caveators' counsel. *In re Ridge*, 183.

AUTOMOBILES

§ 46. Opinion Testimony as to Speed

In an action to recover for the wrongful death of a pedestrian, trial court

AUTOMOBILES – Continued

erred in excluding testimony by an eyewitness concerning the speed of defendant's vehicle. *Oliver v. Powell*, 59.

§ 62.2. Negligence in Striking Pedestrians While Crossing Other Than at Intersections

In an action to recover for the wrongful death of a pedestrian who was struck by defendant's vehicle, evidence was sufficient to be submitted to the jury and did not show that the pedestrian was contributorily negligent as a matter of law. *Oliver v. Powell*, 59.

Plaintiff highway construction worker's evidence was sufficient to be submitted to the jury on the issue of defendant's negligence in striking plaintiff while he was crossing the highway at a point beyond an intersection. *Sessoms v. Roberson*, 573.

§ 68.1. Defective Vehicles, Brakes and Tires

In an action to recover damages resulting from an automobile accident, plaintiff was negligent as a matter of law because plaintiff's employee continued driving a truck on a public highway with knowledge that the brakes were not in proper working order and were unsafe. *Rose v. Truck Co.*, 643.

§ 74. Contributory Negligence in Entering Highway

Evidence showed that defendant was contributorily negligent as a matter of law in driving into the path of third party defendant's oncoming tractor-trailer which had the right of way. *Industries, Inc. v. Tharpe*, 754.

§ 109. Imputation of Driver's Negligence to Nondriving Owner

In defendant car owner's third party action to recover for personal injuries sustained in an automobile accident, negligence of the driver was imputed to defendant owner so as to bar his claim since the owner was present in the car and commanded the driver to stop. *Industries, Inc. v. Tharpe*, 754.

BANKS AND BANKING

§ 4. Joint Accounts

Summary judgment for plaintiff was proper in an action to recover, as joint legatee, funds withdrawn by defendant, another legatee, from a bank account which named testatrix and defendant as joint depositors. *Herbin v. Farrish*, 193.

BILLS AND NOTES

§ 8. Makers and Persons Primarily Liable

Trial court erred in determining that there was a presumption of gift from plaintiff husband to defendant wife where both executed a promissory note and plaintiff paid the note, and that plaintiff failed to rebut that presumption. *Grimes v. Grimes*, 353.

BROKERS AND FACTORS

§ 8. Licensing and Regulation

A shareholder is not an owner of realty of the corporation in which the

BROKERS AND FACTORS – Continued

shares are held so as to bring the shareholder within the "owner" exemption provisions of the real estate brokers and salesmen licensing statutes. *Cox v. Real Estate Licensing Board*, 135.

BURGLARY AND UNLAWFUL BREAKINGS

§ 5.1. Sufficient Evidence of Identity of Defendant as Perpetrator

Evidence was sufficient for the jury in a burglary case where it tended to show that defendant was apprehended by police at the crime scene, immediately after the crime, dressed the same as the intruder seen by the occupant. *S. v. Callihan*, 360.

§ 6.2. Instructions on Felonious Intent

Trial court in a burglary case did not err in instructing the jury that "the fact of entry alone in the nighttime accompanied by flight when discovered is some evidence of guilt and in the absence of any other proof or evidence of other intent ... may warrant a reasonable inference of guilty intent." *S. v. Callihan*, 360.

CARRIERS

§ 2.7. Granting of Operating Authority

The Utilities Commission properly granted an application for authority to operate as a contract carrier under contract with Reynolds Metal Company to transport metal containers to all intrastate points. *Utilities Comm. v. Delivery Services*, 418.

§ 5.1. Motor Carrier Rates

The dedicated service provision in the tariff schedule for motor vehicle common carriers of petroleum products is discriminatory and preferential in violation of G.S. 62-140. *Utilities Comm. v. Oil Co.*, 1.

§ 19.2. Liability for Assaults on Passengers

In an action against a bus company to recover damages allegedly resulting from defendant's negligent failure to protect plaintiff passenger from sexual assault in the women's restroom of defendant's bus station, testimony as to the type of area surrounding the bus station was competent to show defendant's knowledge of the need for insuring adequate protection of passengers at the station. *Wesley v. Greyhound Lines, Inc.*, 680.

Plaintiff suffered a compensable injury where her evidence tended to show permanent psychological effects from a sexual assault upon her in the restroom of defendant's bus station. *Ibid.*

Opinion testimony by an expert witness in the field of law enforcement and security as to the adequacy of defendant's security measures at its bus station on the date of a sexual assault on plaintiff did not invade the province of the jury and was properly admitted. *Ibid.*

Trial court's instruction that a common carrier must exercise the highest degree of care in foreseeing the imminence of a criminal assault on its passengers will not be held erroneous where such instruction is in accord with the rule stated in one line of N.C. cases. *Ibid.*

CARRIERS – Continued

Plaintiff's evidence was sufficient for the jury on the issue of defendant bus company's negligence in failing to protect plaintiff from sexual assault in defendant's bus station. *Ibid.*

COLLEGES AND UNIVERSITIES

§ 2. Control of Private Institutions

The Board of Governors of the University of N.C. does not have authority to license or regulate Nova University in its teaching program in this State which leads to degrees granted in Florida. *Nova University v. University of N.C.*, 638.

CONSPIRACY

§ 6. Sufficiency of Evidence of Criminal Conspiracy

In a prosecution for conspiracy to sell controlled substances, evidence was sufficient to establish a conspiracy where it tended to show a close association between defendant and his female coconspirator. *S. v. Cooley*, 376.

Evidence was sufficient for the jury in a prosecution for conspiracy to sell and deliver heroin. *S. v. Jones*, 554.

§ 17. Personal and Civil Rights Generally

A human fetus is not a "person" within the meaning of Art. I, §§ 1 and 19 of the N.C. Constitution, and the protections of those sections thus do not apply to the fetus so as to prohibit State funding for elective abortions. *Stam v. State*, 209.

CONSTITUTIONAL LAW

§ 24.7. Jurisdiction Over Foreign Corporations and Nonresident Individuals

Trial court did not acquire personal jurisdiction over a foreign corporation's cause of action arising out of a contract made in N.C. where defendant denied the making of any contract. *Allen Co. v. Quip-Matic, Inc.*, 40.

A foreign corporation had insufficient minimum contacts with N.C. to justify personal jurisdiction over it. *Ibid.*

Trial court obtained personal jurisdiction over the nonresident defendant in an action for alimony based on abandonment and for child custody and support where defendant was served with process by registered mail. *Brown v. Brown*, 323.

§ 28. Due Process in Criminal Proceedings

Defendant was not denied due process of law when he was compelled to exhibit himself to the jury for the purpose of allowing a police officer to identify certain physical characteristics on his person. *S. v. McNeil*, 30.

§ 34. Double Jeopardy

Testimony by an SBI agent, though hearsay, constituted sufficient basis for the trial court to find that up to three jurors could have been tampered with, and defendant's constitutional rights were not violated where the court declared a mistrial and ordered retrial of defendant. *S. v. Cooley*, 376.

CONSTITUTIONAL LAW – Continued

§ 40. Right to Counsel
Defendant was not prejudiced by the fact that he may not have been informed of his right to be represented by counsel before he entered a guilty plea. *S. v. Grimes*, 476.

§ 48. Effective Assistance of Counsel
Defendant failed to show that he was denied effective assistance of counsel because his attorney also represented his codefendant who was charged with the same offenses. *S. v. Johnson*, 297.

§ 53. Speedy Trial, Delay Caused by Defendant
Defendant was not denied his right to a speedy trial where he was charged on 28 June 1978 and tried in September 1979. *S. v. Mackins*, 168.

CONTRACTS

§ 3. Definiteness and Certainty of Agreement
Plaintiff's evidence was insufficient to show a binding contract to grow chickens for defendant. *Gregory v. Perdue, Inc.*, 655.

§ 4.1. Sufficient Consideration
Plaintiff was not entitled to recover tuition paid to defendant school in advance on the ground of failure of consideration because plaintiff's former wife would not let the child attend the school after the school year had begun. *Brenner v. School House, Ltd.*, 19.

§ 15. Suit by Third Person for Negligent Breach of Contract
An association of condominium owners could properly maintain an action against an architect for the negligent design and preparation of plans and the negligent supervision of construction of the condominium complex although no contractual privity existed between the architect and the association. *Condominium Assoc. v. Scholz Co.*, 518.

§ 20.1. Impossibility of Performance
A contract which required plaintiff to pay tuition in advance with no refund in order for defendant to hold a place in defendant's school for plaintiff's child was not subject to rescission because of frustration when plaintiff's former wife would not permit the child to attend defendant's school. *Brenner v. School House, Ltd.*, 19.

§ 27.1. Sufficiency of Evidence of Existence of Contract
In plaintiff's action to recover for additional labor and material which he allegedly supplied during the course of constructing a home for defendants, trial court properly denied defendant's motion for a directed verdict. *Hood v. Faulkner*, 611.

§ 27.2. Sufficiency of Evidence of Breach of Contract
Trial court properly denied defendant's motion for directed verdict in an action for breach of contract where there was sufficient evidence to show that a dam and pipe system as constructed did not conform to the terms of the agreement. *Silver v. Board of Transportation*, 261.

CONTRACTS – Continued

§ 27.3. Damages for Breach of Contract

Failure of the trial court to award nominal damages for breach of contract did not constitute prejudicial error. *Marsico v. Adams*, 196.

CONVICTS AND PRISONERS

§ 3. Negligent Injury to Prisoners

In a tort claim action to recover for injuries to prison inmates in a fire which occurred when inmates set fire to several mattresses piled around a table in a prison dormitory, the Deputy Director of Prisons was not negligent in placing inmates in a prison dormitory with polyurethane mattresses, and plaintiff's evidence was insufficient to show negligence on the part of the lieutenant and sergeant at the prison unit where the fire occurred. *Watson v. Dept. of Correction*, 718.

CORPORATIONS

§ 1.1. Disregarding Corporate Entity

Defendant corporation was not the alter ego of a now insolvent corporation so as to make defendant liable for the purchase price of yarn sold to the insolvent corporation. *Textiles v. Hillview Mills*, 593.

COSTS

§ 1.2. Recovery of Costs in Particular Actions

Trial court should have taxed the costs to plaintiff where defendants were entitled to recover nominal damages for breach of contract. *Marsico v. Adams*, 196.

COUNTIES

§ 5.5. County Subdivision Ordinance

The names "Springdale Gardens" and "Springdale Woods" closely approximate the name "Springdale Estates," an existing subdivision, so that the use of such names for subdivisions violates the Wake County Subdivision Regulations. *Springdale Estates Assoc. v. Wake County*, 462.

§ 6.2. Expenditure of Funds

In administering State funds appropriated by the General Assembly for the State Abortion Fund through the county department of social services, a county acts pursuant to administrative rules governing the Fund which were enacted pursuant to statutory authority. *Stam v. State*, 209.

CRIMINAL LAW

§ 5. Mental Capacity in General; Insanity

There was no merit to defendant's contention that he was entitled to a directed verdict because he offered plenary evidence of insanity which was uncontradicted. *S. v. Flowers*, 457.

CRIMINAL LAW – Continued

§ 5.1. Instructions on Insanity
Where the trial court defined insanity as not knowing the nature and quality of one's act or not knowing that it was wrong, the court was not required to instruct that defendant must have the will and ability to control his conduct. *S. v. Hodgen*, 329.

§ 17. Jurisdiction of Federal and State Courts
The courts of this State had jurisdiction over the crimes of breaking and entering a post office and larceny of property therefrom. *S. v. Graham*, 303.

§ 18.1. Sufficiency of Record to Show Jurisdiction in Superior Court
Appeal from conviction of a misdemeanor in superior court is dismissed for failure of the record to show jurisdiction in superior court. *S. v. Felmet*, 201.

§ 23. Plea of Guilty
Even if an electric coffee maker was illegally seized from defendant's apartment pursuant to an invalid warrant, defendant's plea of guilty of felonious larceny of certain business machines and the coffee maker by breaking and entering was supported by evidence relating to the business machines which were seized from the basement of the apartment house in which defendant lived pursuant to a search conducted with the landlord's written permission. *S. v. Williams*, 205.

§ 26. Plea of Former Jeopardy
Defendant was not twice placed in jeopardy when he was tried and convicted of kidnapping for the purpose of facilitating flight following his participation in an armed robbery and of armed robbery. *S. v. Martin*, 223.

§ 26.6. Former Jeopardy; Same Acts or Transaction Violating Different Statutes
In a prosecution of defendant for armed robbery and larceny, judgment of the trial court imposing sentence for misdemeanor larceny of the victim's automobile must be arrested since the evidence necessary to convict defendant of both offenses was substantially the same, and inherent in the jury's verdict finding defendant guilty of armed robbery was a finding that defendant took and carried away property consisting of the victim's cash and automobile. *S. v. Martin*, 223.

§ 34.5. Admissibility of Other Offenses to Show Identity
In a prosecution for sale and delivery of heroin, trial court properly admitted evidence of defendant's guilt of other offenses to prove the identity of defendant. *S. v. Jones*, 554.

§ 35. Evidence Offense Was Committed by Another
In a prosecution for kidnapping and crime against nature, an autopsy report and pathologist's testimony regarding the murder of the victim's ten year old sister shortly before defendant's trial were not admissible to bolster the credibility of defendant's testimony that a third party forced him at gunpoint to commit the crimes charged and threatened to harm defendant, the victim and their families if they told of the third party's involvement in the crimes. *S. v. Winston*, 363.

CRIMINAL LAW – Continued

§ 42.4. Admissibility of Weapons; Connection With Crime

In a prosecution for armed robbery, the admission of handguns taken from defendants five weeks after the crime with which they were charged was prejudicial error. *State v. Milby*, 669.

§ 50.1. Admissibility of Expert Opinion Testimony

Trial court properly excluded a witness's testimony concerning a fire where the witness's personal knowledge of the essential facts was not shown and the witness's opinion was not asked for in response to a hypothetical question. *S. v. Culpepper*, 633.

§ 63. Evidence as to Sanity of Defendant

Statement by defendant to a police officer who investigated the crime was inadmissible to show insanity. *S. v. Flowers*, 457.

Statements made by defendant to a psychiatrist concerning his use of drugs were inherently reliable and the trial court did not err in allowing them into evidence. *Ibid.*

§ 66.1. Evidence of Identity by Sight; Opportunity for Observation

An assault victim who had ample opportunity for observation at the time of the crime could properly make an in-court identification of defendant. *S. v. Mackins*, 168.

§ 66.12. Confrontation in Courtroom

Defendant was not denied due process of law when he was compelled to exhibit himself to the jury for the purpose of allowing a police officer to identify certain physical characteristics on his person. *S. v. McNeil*, 30.

§ 75.2. Confessions; Effect of Statements by Officer

Trial court properly admitted defendant's confession where the record shows that defendant stated he wanted to talk to a lawyer but changed his mind and then signed a written waiver of counsel, and the court found upon conflicting evidence that the officer did not induce defendant's confession by saying he would put in a good word for defendant in court. *S. v. Graham*, 303.

§ 82.2. Physician-Patient Privilege

The physician-patient privilege does not preclude a psychiatrist, who examines a criminal defendant to determine his capacity to proceed, from testifying at trial on the insanity issue. *S. v. Hodgen*, 329.

§ 86.4. Impeachment of Defendant; Prior Misconduct or Crimes

Defendant who was charged with narcotics offenses could properly be asked if he filed income tax returns for a given year for impeachment purposes. *S. v. Jones*, 554.

The trial court did not err in admitting evidence of other unrelated crimes, since such evidence was admissible for impeachment purposes. *S. v. Milby* and *S. v. Boyd*, 669.

The trial court properly allowed defendant to be questioned about unrelated crimes for the purpose of impeachment. *S. v. Maxwell*, 658.

CRIMINAL LAW – Continued

§ 91.6. **Continuance to Obtain Evidence**

Trial court did not err in denying defendant's motion for continuance to interview witnesses where defendant already had available the identical information he sought to obtain from the witnesses. *S. v. Winston,* 363.

§ 92.3. **Consolidation of Charges Against Same Defendant**

Trial court did not err in denying defendant's motion to dismiss for failure to join related offenses. *S. v. Jones,* 554.

§ 101. **Misconduct Affecting Jury**

Testimony by an SBI agent, though hearsay, constituted sufficient basis for the trial court to find that up to three jurors could have been tampered with, and defendant's constitutional rights were not violated where the court declared a mistrial and ordered retrial of defendant. *S. v. Cooley,* 376.

§ 101.2. **Exposure of Jurors to Evidence Not Formally Introduced**

Trial court in a homicide case properly found that no evidence came to the attention of the jurors which would violate defendant's right of confrontation where defendant contended that one of the jurors stated in the jury room that he realized during the trial that he knew about defendant and that she was not fit to walk the streets and should receive the maximum sentence. *S. v. Gilbert,* 316.

§ 102. **Number of Jury Arguments**

Trial court did not violate G.S. 84-14 in permitting a defendant who introduced evidence to present only one jury argument. *S. v. McCaskill,* 289.

§ 102.6. **Particular Comments in Argument to Jury**

There was sufficient evidence of use of drugs by defendant at the time of the crime charged so that the district attorney could argue it to the jury, and the court should have mentioned it in the charge. *S. v. Flowers,* 457.

§ 111.1. **Form and Sufficiency of Instructions in General**

The prohibition against reading the pleadings to the jury is inapplicable to the judge's charge. *S. v. McNeil,* 30.

Trial judge did not improperly refer to the bills of indictment returned against defendant while informing prospective jurors about the case where the judge summarized the indictments and explained to the jury circumstances under which defendant was being tried. *Ibid.*

§ 114.2. **No Expression of Opinion in Statement of Evidence**

Trial court did not express an opinion by stating that defendant had "confessed." *S. v. Graham,* 303.

§ 117.2. **Charge on Interested Witnesses**

Trial court did not err in charging the jury that it should scrutinize defendant's testimony in light of his interest in the outcome of the case, though the court did not give similar instructions to scrutinize testimony of other witnesses. *S. v. Johnson,* 297.

CRIMINAL LAW – Continued

§ 122.1. **Jury's Request For Additional Instructions**

Trial judge did not abuse his discretion in refusing to allow the jurors to have certain testimony read back. *S. v. Jones*, 554.

§ 122.2. **Additional Instructions Upon Failure to Reach Verdict**

When the jury informed the court that it was divided, the court's response that the jury could continue to deliberate that night, could return to deliberate the next day, and had two more days in which deliberations could take place did not coerce the jury into reaching a decision. *S. v. Jones*, 554.

§ 130. **New Trial for Misconduct Affecting Jury**

Though there was some evidence of jury tampering, an order of mistrial under G.S. 15A-1062 would have been improper since there was no evidence of any connection between defendant or his attorney and the alleged jury tampering. *S. v. Cooley*, 376.

By the enactment of G.S. 15A-1062 and G.S. 15A-1063 the General Assembly did not intend to limit the authority of trial judges to order a mistrial where events not instigated by defendant or his lawyer have nevertheless colored the proceedings in such a way as to prevent an impartial trial. *Ibid.*

§ 134.4. **Youthful Offenders**

Trial court's order did not show that defendant's age at the time of his resentencing was a primary reason for failure of the court to resentence defendant as a committed youthful offender. *S. v. Safrit*, 189.

§ 138.11. **Different Punishment On Retrial**

The harsher punishment statute was not violated where defendant was given the same indeterminate term of imprisonment at his resentencing as that imposed at his original sentencing. *S. v. Safrit*, 189.

§ 142.4. **Improper Conditions of Probation**

The imposition of a fine is not restitution or reparation within the meaning of G.S. 148-33.2 (c). *S. v. Alexander*, 502.

§ 143.10. **Violation of Probation Condition as to Payments**

Evidence supported the court's revocation of defendant's probation for violation of conditions that she make monthly payments on costs, fines and restitution and that she remain gainfully employed. *S. v. Freeman*, 171.

DAMAGES

§ 3. **Compensatory Damages for Personal Injuries**

Where plaintiff presented competent medical evidence that his preexisting syringomyelia was aggravated by a collision resulting from the negligence of defendant, defendant is liable for the damages due to enhancement or aggravation of the condition. *Lee v. Regan*, 544.

§ 3.4. **Pain, Suffering and Mental Anguish**

A clinical psychologist was not prohibited by statute from testifying as to the permanency of psychological effects on plaintiff resulting from a sexual assault, and such testimony was not too speculative for admission although she

DAMAGES – Continued

used the word "guess" in stating her opinion. *Wesley v. Greyhound Lines, Inc.*, 680.

A clinical psychologist's contact with plaintiff was not so minimal as to provide an insufficient basis for her opinion as to the permanency of psychological effects on plaintiff from a sexual assault. *Ibid.*

Plaintiff suffered a compensable injury where her evidence tended to show permanent psychological effects from a sexual assault upon her in the restroom of defendant's bus station. *Ibid.*

§ 3.5. Loss of Earnings

Trial court did not err in instructing the jury on loss of wages and reduced earning capacity because plaintiff was unemployed before the incident. *Wesley v. Greyhound Lines, Inc.*, 680.

§ 16.1. Evidence of Causation of Injuries

An expert's testimony that a cervical sprain "can or could" aggravate plaintiff's preexisting condition and "hasten the development of fresh worsening of neurological signs" was not so speculative as to be inadmissible to show causation. *Lee v. Regan.* 554.

DEATH

§ 4. Time Within Which Action Must Be Instituted

Plaintiff's claim for wrongful death was barred by the six month limitation of G.S. 28A-19-3(b)(2). *Baer v. Davis*, 581.

§ 4.3. Time for Instituting Action in Cases Involving Qualification of Administrators

Trial court did not err in denying motion of plaintiff, the duly qualified Virginia administratrix of her daughter's estate, to amend her pleadings in a wrongful death action to allege her subsequent appointment as ancillary administratrix in N.C. and to have her amendment relate back to the original institution of the action so that her claim would not be barred by the statute of limitations. *Burcl v. Hospital*, 127.

DIVORCE AND ALIMONY

§ 2. Process

Trial court obtained personal jurisdiction over the nonresident defendant in an action for alimony based on abandonment and for child custody and support where defendant was served with process by registered mail. *Brown v. Brown*, 323.

§ 14.2. Testimony by Spouse Concerning Adultery

Trial court in a divorce case erred in permitting defendant to be cross-examined as to whether she had undressed in front of or with various men since such cross-examination clearly implied that defendant had committed adultery. *Horner v. Horner*, 334.

DIVORCE AND ALIMONY – Continued

§ 16.6.   Sufficiency of Evidence in Alimony Action

The evidence in an action for divorce from bed and board and alimony did not require the court to submit to the jury the issue of whether defendant was a spendthrift. *Odom v. Odom*, 486.

§ 17.1.   Alimony Without Divorce; Pleadings and Proof

In an action to recover damages for assault and battery and to recover alimony, evidence was sufficient for the jury where it tended to show that defendant deliberately struck plaintiff on the head with a baseball bat after threatening to kill her. *Clarke v. Clarke*, 249.

Trial court did not err in refusing to submit to the jury issues as to plaintiff's status as a dependent spouse and defendant's status as the supporting spouse. *Ibid.*

That portion of the trial court's order granting a divorce from bed and board must be vacated since plaintiff's complaint alleged a claim for alimony without divorce. *Ibid.*

§ 18.12.   Findings as to Right to Alimony Pendente Lite

Trial court's conclusions in an alimony pendente lite action that defendant constructively abandoned plaintiff and subjected her to such indignities as to render her condition intolerable and her life burdensome were supported by the court's findings. *Cornelison v. Cornelison*, 91.

§ 18.13.   Amount of Alimony Pendente Lite

Evidence was sufficient to support the court's order requiring defendant husband to pay plaintiff wife $335 per month as alimony pendente lite and $1250 for counsel fees. *Cornelison v. Cornelison*, 91.

§ 18.18.   Effect of Alimony Pendente Lite Decree

Defendant's contention that a pendente lite order remained in effect and could be enforced by contempt proceedings in district court until the validity of the final judgment should be finally determined on appeal was without merit. *Clarke v. Clarke*, 249.

§ 21.5.   Contempt for Violation of Alimony Order

Where defendant appealed from final judgment entered on 9 November 1977 providing for divorce from bed and board, alimony and child support, two orders dated 22 December 1977 punishing defendant for contempt were void. *Clarke v. Clarke*, 249.

§ 24.1.   Amount of Child Support

Trial court did not abuse its discretion in ordering child support because the court first announced the support would be $200 per month and then changed it to $250 per month. *Horner v. Horner*, 334.

§ 27.   Attorney's Fees

The court erred in awarding counsel fees to the wife in a child support action where the court made no findings as to the wife's ability to pay or the reasonableness of the fees. *Horner v. Horner*, 334.

Trial court erred in ordering defendant to pay a portion of plaintiff's attor-

EVIDENCE – Continued

§ 33.2. Hearsay Testimony
Testimony by defendant's wife that on the night before defendant left for Florida he told her that he and another person had to go to Florida on business was admissible as an exception to the hearsay rule. *Long v. Paving Co.*, 564.

§ 48. Competency and Qualification of Experts
A clinical psychologist was not prohibited by statute from testifying as to the permanency of psychological effects on plaintiff resulting from a sexual assault, and such testimony was not too speculative for admission although she used the word "guess" in stating her opinion. *Wesley v. Greyhound Lines, Inc.*, 680.

A clinical psychologist's contact with plaintiff was not so minimal as to provide an insufficient basis for her opinion as to the permanency of psychological effects on plaintiff from a sexual assault. *Ibid.*

Opinion testimony by an expert witness in the field of law enforcement and security as to the adequacy of defendant's security measures at its bus station on the date of a sexual assault on plaintiff did not invade the province of the jury and was properly admitted. *Ibid.*

§ 50.2. Medical Testimony as to Cause of Death
An expert's testimony that a cervical sprain "can or could" aggravate plaintiff's preexisting condition and "hasten the development of fresh worsening of neurological signs" was not so speculative as to be inadmissible to show causation. *Lee v. Regan*, 544.

EXECUTORS AND ADMINISTRATORS

§ 3. Appointment of Ancillary Administrators
Trial court did not err in denying motion of plaintiff, the duly qualified Virginia administratrix of her daughter's estate, to amend her pleadings in a wrongful death action to allege her subsequent appointment as ancillary administratrix in N.C. and to have her amendment relate back to the original institution of the action so that her claim would not be barred by the statute of limitations. *Burcl v. Hospital*, 127.

§ 33. Family Settlement Agreements
A jury question was presented as to the construction of a family settlement agreement. *Holt v. Holt*, 618.

A family settlement agreement was not void as against public policy because it included an agreement not to probate a codicil to testatrix's will. *Ibid.*

§ 33.1. Necessity for Bona Fide Controversy as to Validity of Will
A family settlement agreement was not invalid because an exigency or emergency not contemplated by the testatrix did not exist. *Holt v. Holt*, 618.

FORGERY

§ 2. Instructions
Trial court in a forgery prosecution properly charged the jury on the element that the instrument be false. *S. v. Dunbar*, 623.

FORGERY – Continued

§ 2.2.   Sufficiency of Evidence

In a prosecution for forgery it was not necessary for the State to prove that the name signed by defendant to three checks was that of a fictitious person or a real person. *S. v. Dunbar*, 623.

FRAUD

§ 5.   Reliance on Misrepresentation

In an action to recover for fraud in the sale of a house and lot, trial court erred in directing verdict for defendants since there was a jury question as to whether plaintiff's reliance on defendant's representations was reasonable. *Vickery v. Construction Co.*, 98.

§ 12.   Sufficiency of Evidence

Evidence was sufficient for the jury in an action to recover for fraud in the sale of a house and lot where the realtor made misrepresentations as to the inclusion of a driveway with the land conveyed. *Vickery v. Construction Co.*, 98.

FRAUDS, STATUTE OF

§ 5.1.   Original Promise; Main Purpose Rule

In an action to recover upon defendant's alleged oral guarantee to pay the debt of a corporation in which defendant was alleged to possess a substantial interest, there was a genuine issue of material fact as to whether defendant had such a personal, immediate and pecuniary interest in the transaction so as to bring his promise within the operation of the main purpose rule and thus exempt it from the statute of frauds. *Furniture Industries v. Griggs*, 104.

FRAUDULENT CONVEYANCES

§ 3.4.   Sufficiency of Evidence

Defendant corporation is not liable to plaintiffs for the purchase price of yarn sold to an insolvent corporation on the ground that defendant participated in a fraudulent conveyance of assets of the insolvent corporation. *Textiles v. Hillview Mills*, 593.

HOMICIDE

§ 3.   Deadly Weapon

Trial court in a second degree murder case properly refused to instruct the jury that a tire tool found in deceased's possession was a deadly weapon as a matter of law. *S. v. McGee*, 280.

§ 12.   Indictment

There was no merit to defendant's contention that the bill of indictment for murder in the second degree should be quashed because it did not contain the word "aforethought" modifying malice. *S. v. McGee*, 280.

§ 19.   Evidence Competent on Question of Self-Defense

Evidence as to the nature and customs of the area in which a homicide

HOMICIDE – Continued

occurred was not admissible to show defendant's state of mind in relation to his plea of self-defense. *S. v. Harris*, 121.

§ 19.1. Evidence of Character or Reputation

Defendant's objections to the State's rebuttal evidence of deceased's reputation for peace and quiet based only on the witnesses' knowledge of deceased "on the job" ordinarily would have been well taken, but defendant abandoned her objections by failing to pursue them and move to strike the answers. *S. v. Gilbert*, 316.

§ 21.7. Sufficiency of Evidence of Second Degree Murder

Evidence was sufficient for the jury in a second degree murder case where it tended to show that defendant shot deceased. *S. v. McGee*, 280; that defendant stabbed deceased. *S. v. Harris*, 121.

§ 24.1. Instructions on Presumptions Arising from Use of Deadly Weapon

Trial court, in instructing on the presumptions of malice and unlawfulness, did not fail to place the burden of proof on the State in instructing that "if nothing else appears the defendant would be guilty of second degree murder." *S. v. Harris*, 121.

Trial court's instructions on presumptions arising from use of a deadly weapon were proper. *S. v. Johnson*, 297.

§ 28.2. Instructions on Self-Defense; Existence of Necessity to Take Life

In a homicide case in which defendant testified that decedent's husband was holding her by the hair while decedent attempted to hit her with a rock, trial court did not err in instructing the jury that, in determining the reasonableness of defendant's apprehension of death or great bodily harm, it should consider the size, age, and strength of decedent rather than of both decedent and her husband. *S. v. Gilbert*, 316.

HUSBAND AND WIFE

§ 1.1. Liability for Debts

Trial court erred in determining that there was a presumption of gift from plaintiff husband to defendant wife where both executed a promissory note and plaintiff paid the note, and that plaintiff failed to rebut that presumption. *Grimes v. Grimes*, 353.

§ 10. Requisites and Validity of Separation Agreement

The wife's acknowledgment of a separation agreement was fatally defective under former G.S. 52-6 where there was no private examination of the wife and where the acknowledgment was certified by a Judge Advocate in the Marine Corps who did not qualify as a certifying officer. *DeJaager v. DeJaager*, 452.

INDICTMENT AND WARRANT

§ 17.2. Variance as to Time

There was no fatal variance between an indictment charging defendant with felonious possession of a stolen trailer in Duplin County on 21 January 1979 and evidence showing defendant possessed the trailer in Columbus County on 18 February 1979. *S. v. Currie,* 446.

INJUNCTIONS

§ 5. To Restrain Enforcement of Ordinance

The trial court erred in entering a temporary restraining order enjoining defendant city from enforcing its sign control ordinance by prohibiting plaintiff's use of a blimp and search light. *Goodman Toyota v. City of Raleigh,* 628.

INSURANCE

§ 136. Actions on Fire Policies

Trial court properly submitted an issue as to whether plaintiff intentionally misrepresented the extent of her fire loss for the purpose of defrauding defendant insurer. *Hanks v. Insurance Co.,* 393.

Error, if any, in the admission of testimony concerning a prior fire loss to property owned by plaintiff in Virginia was harmless. *Ibid.*

JURY

§ 1.3. Waiver of Right to Jury Trial

A party may waive his right to a jury trial by failing to appear at trial. *Frissell v. Frissell,* 149.

KIDNAPPING

§ 1. Elements of Offense

Defendant was not twice placed in jeopardy when he was tried and convicted of kidnapping for the purpose of facilitating flight following his participation in an armed robbery and of armed robbery. *S. v. Martin,* 223.

§ 1.3. Instructions

Trial court in an armed robbery and kidnapping case sufficiently instructed the jury that the armed robbery offense must have been completed prior to the beginning of the kidnapping offense. *S. v. Martin,* 223.

There was no merit to defendant's contention that the trial court erred in failing to submit the issue of a kidnapping victim's age to the jury, since the victim's age is not an essential element of the crime of kidnapping itself. *Ibid.*

The trial court in an armed robbery and kidnapping case sufficiently instructed the jury that the armed robbery offense must have been completed prior to the beginning of the kidnapping offense. *Ibid.*

LABORERS' AND MATERIALMEN'S LIENS

§ 7. Sufficiency of Notice or Claim

Plaintiff cannot establish a lien for labor and materials as a prime contrac-

LABORERS' AND MATERIALMEN'S LIENS – Continued

tor when its own notice of claim of lien and judicial findings to which plaintiff consented established it is a subcontractor. However, plaintiff is entitled to try its claim for a money judgment against defendant owner. *Contractors, Inc. v. Forbes*, 371.

LANDLORD AND TENANT

§ 6.1. Construction of Lease; Premises Demised

Trial court erred in directing a verdict for plaintiffs in an action to recover damages for breach of agreements under which defendants leased space in a trailer park to plaintiffs since issues of credibility were raised. *Marshall v. Miller*, 530.

§ 18. Forfeiture for Nonpayment of Rent

Defendant's use of the words "Legal Notice" on a padlocking notice posted on the doors of tenants who were late paying their rent did not violate G.S. 75-54. *Spinks v. Taylor*, 68.

There was no merit to plaintiff's contention that the termination provision of their lease, which allowed for padlocking of the premises upon failure to pay rent and after notice by the landlord, was unconscionable and therefore unenforceable as violative of public policy. *Ibid.*

§ 19. Rent and Actions Therefor

A landlord can lawfully exercise peaceful, nonviolent self-help in N.C. to regain possession of leased premises where the tenant fails to pay rent. *Spinks v. Taylor*, 68.

LARCENY

§ 1.1. Elements of Crime; Taking

In a prosecution of defendant for armed robbery and larceny, judgment of the trial court imposing sentence for misdemeanor larceny of the victim's automobile must be arrested since the evidence necessary to convict defendant of both offenses was substantially the same; and inherent in the jury's verdict finding defendant guilty of armed robbery was a finding that defendant took and carried away property consisting of the victim's cash and automobile. *S. v. Martin*, 223.

§ 7.3. Sufficiency of Evidence; Ownership of Property Stolen

There was no fatal variance where a larceny indictment alleged that stolen property was the property of a post office and the evidence showed the property belonged to the postmaster. *S. v. Graham*, 303.

LIBEL AND SLANDER

§ 5.2. Imputations Affecting Profession

Alleged false statements made by a defendant calling a plaintiff dishonest or charging that plaintiff was untruthful and an unreliable employee are not actionable per se. *Stutts v. Power Co.*, 76.

LIBEL AND SLANDER – Continued

§ 6. Publication

In an action for slander, trial court properly determined that any publication of an alleged defamatory statement by the individual defendant which would bring defendant power company, an employer of the individual defendant, within the statute of limitations was not attributable to defendant power company. *Stutts v. Power Co.,* 76.

§ 14. Pleadings

In an action for slander, plaintiff's failure to state the defamatory words verbatim in the complaint did not render it fatally defective. *Stutts v. Power Co.,* 76.

LIMITATION OF ACTIONS

§ 4.2. Accrual of Cause of Action in Negligence Actions

An action against an architect for negligent supervision of the installation of an underground water pipe system brought within three years after the defects were discovered was brought within the statute of limitations. *Condominium Assoc. v. Scholz Co.,* 518.

§ 4.3. Accrual of Cause of Action for Breach of Contract

Plaintiff's action to recover for breach of contract to construct a dam and pipe system on plaintiff's property was not barred by the three year statute of limitations. *Silver v. Board of Transportation,* 261.

§ 8.1. Ignorance of Cause of Action as Exception to Operation of Limitation Laws

Plaintiff's action to reform a deed on the ground of mistake six years after it was executed was not barred by the statute of limitations. *Hice v. Hi-Mil, Inc.,* 427.

LIS PENDENS

§ 1. Generally

Plaintiff's filing of notice of lis pendens did not constitute an act of malicious prosecution or an injurious falsehood or slander of title. *Whyburn v. Norwood,* 310.

Plaintiff's filing of notice of lis pendens which included defendant's entire subdivision did not constitute abuse of process where plaintiff brought an action to remove a cloud on his title to lands constituting a portion of a subdivision which was being developed by defendants. *Ibid.*

MALICIOUS PROSECUTION

§ 6. Termination of Prosecution

Plaintiff's filing of notice of lis pendens did not constitute an act of malicious prosecution. *Whyburn v. Norwood,* 310.

MASTER AND SERVANT

§ 10. Duration and Termination of Employment Contract

A contract which did not specify the duration of plaintiff's employment was terminable at will. *Mumford v. Hutton & Bourbonnais Co.,* 440.

MASTER AND SERVANT – Continued

§ 17. Strikes and Picketing

Trial court erred in entering a permanent injunction prohibiting defendant union from mass picketing and other activities at plaintiff's plant where the permanent injunction was entered almost two years after the settlement of the strike which gave rise to the action for the injunction. *General Electric Co. v. Union*, 153.

§17.1. Picketing; Federal Pre-emption of State Court Jurisdiction

The courts of this State had jurisdiction of an action to enjoin defendant union from mass picketing at plaintiff's plant and to prohibit the union from interfering with ingress and egress at the plant or assaulting or intimidating workers. *General Electric Co. v. Union*, 153.

§ 26.1. Employer's Liability for Injury to Domestic Servants

Summary judgment was properly entered for defendants in an action to recover for injuries suffered by plaintiff when a stairstep in defendants' dwelling collapsed and caused plaintiff to fall while she was doing domestic work for defendants. *Whitaker v. Blackburn*, 144.

§ 56. Workers' Compensation; Causal Relation Between Employment and Injury

Evidence was sufficient to support determination by the Industrial Commission that decedent was on a business trip to Florida in connection with his duties as an employee of defendant asphalt paving company at the time he was killed in an airplane crash and that he suffered the fatal injury by accident arising out of and in the course of his employment. *Long v. Paving Co.*, 564.

§ 65.1. Workers' Compensation; Hernia

Evidence was sufficient to support the Industrial Commission's finding that repair of plaintiff's third hernia was not a loss of or permanent injury to an important organ or part of his body in view of his prior operations. *Porterfield v. RPC Corp.*, 140.

§ 68. Workers' Compensation; Occupational Diseases

The Industrial Commission's finding that plaintiff's chronic pulmonary disease was not due to her exposure to cotton dust and lint in her employment was supported by evidence and provided a sufficient basis for the denial of compensation to plaintiff for an occupational disease. *Moore v. Stevens & Co.*, 744.

Plaintiff was entitled to compensation for total disability where the Industrial Commission found that plaintiff was totally disabled to work and that 55% of her disability was due to her occupational disease and 45% of her disability was due to physical infirmities not related to her work. *Morrison v. Burlington Industries*, 50.

§ 69. Workers' Compensation; Amount of Recovery

A lump sum award under G.S. 97-44 need not be commuted to the present value of the future installments which would otherwise be due but can be the uncommuted total of those installments. *Harris v. Paving Co.*, 348.

Evidence supported the Industrial Commission's finding that this is an

MASTER AND SERVANT – Continued

"unusual case" which permits an award directing a lump sum payment of death benefits under G.S. 97-44 to the widow of a deceased employee. *Ibid.*

§ 74. Workers' Compensation; Recovery for Disfigurement

The dependents of a deceased employee who suffered a serious bodily disfigurement due to an accident covered by the Workers' Compensation Act but who died due to an unrelated cause are entitled to a post mortem award for serious bodily disfigurement based on the best possible medical estimate as to the probable residual disability that would have remained had the employee lived. *Wilhite v. Veener Co.*, 434.

§ 87.1. Workers' Compensation; Cases Not Within Operation of Statute

The death of plaintiff's intestate who drowned in defendant employer's swimming pool after he had completed his day's work and while he was attending a birthday party for another employee was not compensable under the Workers' Compensation Act. *Brown v. Motor Inns*, 115.

§ 108. Right to Unemployment Compensation Generally

Claimant voluntarily left work as a county social worker for good cause attributable to her employer and was thus entitled to unemployment compensation where she resigned because she was instructed to initiate custody proceedings for certain children after she had secured an agreement from the mothers to place their children in temporary custody of others upon her assurance to the mothers that the children would be returned to them on request. *In re Clark*, 163.

Claimant's evidence was sufficient to raise a factual issue as to whether she left her job because of racial discrimination practiced against her by her employer. *In re Bolden*, 468.

§ 111.1. Conclusiveness and Review of Findings by Employment Security Commission

The superior court erred in reversing a decision of the Employment Security Commission on the ground that the Commission did not properly apply the law to the facts found by the Commission "and other facts in evidence." *In re Bolden*, 468.

MORTGAGES AND DEEDS OF TRUST

§ 25. Foreclosure by Exercise of Power of Sale in the Instrument

G.S. 45-21.16(d)(i) permits the clerk to find a "valid debt of which the party seeking to foreclose is a holder" if there is competent evidence that the party seeking to foreclose is the holder of some valid debt, irrespective of the exact amount owed. *In re Foreclosure of Burgess*, 599.

§ 26. Notice and Advertisement of Sale

Plaintiff was not a record owner and was not entitled to notice of foreclosure proceedings where a recorded management agreement promised to convey to plaintiff a 50% interest in the real property after two promissory notes were repaid but not later than five years. *Properties, Inc. v. Savings and Loan Assoc.*, 675.

MORTGAGES AND DEEDS OF TRUST – Continued

§ 37. Election Between Suit to Set Aside Foreclosure and Action for Damages for Wrongful Foreclosure

By plaintiffs' failure to assign error to the trial court's order that a foreclosure sale be set aside they elected to treat the sale as a nullity, and the trial court correctly found that plaintiffs proved no damages as a result of the institution of foreclosure proceedings. *Parker v. Sheldon*, 493.

MUNICIPAL CORPORATIONS

§ 4.5. Power Over Housing and Urban Development

A municipal board of aldermen does not have the discretion to accept a lower bid for property being sold by a municipal redevelopment commission where the high bidder has submitted a proposal for use of the property that complies with the zoning law and the redevelopment plan. *Builders, Inc. v. City of Winston-Salem*, 661.

§ 30.9. Spot Zoning

The rezoning of an 11.42 acre tract from a residential classification to a light industrial classification constituted spot zoning. *Lathan v. Bd. of Commissioners*, 357.

§ 30.11. Zoning; Restrictions as to Specific Businesses or Structures

In an action to enjoin the operation of a ready mix concrete batching plant on the ground that such use was not permitted under the city zoning ordinance, trial court properly placed the burden on defendant of proving that the city had made a determination six years before the action was brought that the operation was permissible and did not violate the zoning ordinance, but the court erred in instructing on the purpose for which the action was brought and erred in excluding certain evidence. *City of Winston-Salem v. Concrete Co.*, 405.

NARCOTICS

§ 4. Sufficiency of Evidence

In a prosecution for conspiracy to sell controlled substances, evidence was sufficient to establish a conspiracy where it tended to show a close association between defendant and his female coconspirator. *S. v. Cooley*, 376.

§ 4.5. Instructions

Trial court was not required to instruct that defendant's possession of a controlled substance must be unlawful in order to convict him of that offense. *S. v. McNeil*, 30.

NEGLIGENCE

§ 2. Negligence Arising From Performance of a Contract

An association of condominium owners could properly maintain an action against an architect for the negligent design and preparation of plans and the negligent supervision of construction of the condominium complex although no contractual privity existed between the architect and the association. *Condominium Assoc. v. Scholz Co.*, 518.

NEGLIGENCE – Continued

§ 5. Dangerous Agencies and Instrumentalities

A chemical which can cause serious injury upon contact with the skin is a dangerous instrumentality or substance, and the manufacturer thereof will be subject to liability under a negligence theory for damages which proximately result from failure to provide adequate warnings as to the product's dangerous propensities or for failure to provide adequate directions for the foreseeable user. *Davis v. Siloo Inc.*, 237.

§ 5.2. Dangerous Agencies; Degree of Care Required

Plaintiff stated no claim for relief against defendant distributor for negligence in the death of plaintiff's intestate allegedly caused by a product distributed by defendant. *Davis v. Siloo Inc.*, 237.

§ 30.3. Nonsuit; Foreseeability

Directed verdict was proper in an action to recover for personal injuries received by plaintiff when defendant's forklift operator started forward and a metal sheet on which plaintiff was standing was jerked forward, causing plaintiff to fall, since there was insufficient evidence of foreseeability. *Poythress v. Burlington Industries*, 199.

§ 35.1. Particular Cases Where Evidence Discloses Contributory Negligence as a Matter of Law

Trial court properly granted defendant's motion for summary judgment in a personal injury action since plaintiff was contributorily negligent as a matter of law in driving his motorbike on defendant's private roadway after dark without lights. *Haskins v. Power and Light Co.*, 664.

§ 40. Instruction on Proximate Cause

The trial court's *lapsus linguae* in using the term "probable cause" instead of "proximate cause" in one instance in the charge was not prejudicial error. *Wesley v. Greyhound Lines, Inc.*, 680.

PARTITION

§ 3.1. Jurisdiction of Proceeding for Judicial Partition

The courts of this State do not have jurisdiction to order partition of real property located in Florida. *Parslow v. Parslow*, 84.

PARTNERSHIP

§ 7. Actions by Partners Against Third Person

An individual partner may sue to recover damages for his personal injuries which proximately result from the breach of warranty on goods purchased by the partnership with partnership funds. *Barnes v. Chain Co.*, 488.

PRINCIPAL AND AGENT

§ 4. Proof of Agency Generally

In an action to recover for fraud, negligence, breach of contract, and deceptive trade practices, trial court erred in directing verdict in favor of defendants where there was a jury question as to whether the realty company employee

PRINCIPAL AND AGENT – Continued

who sold the property to plaintiff was an agent of the land owner or the realty company. *Vickery v. Construction Co.*, 98.

§ 5.2. Authority in Particular Matters

Evidence was sufficient to take the case to the jury on plaintiffs' cause of action for breach of contract against defendant landowner where plaintiffs' evidence tended to show that defendant realtor had represented to plaintiffs that the land in question included a driveway, and the realtor was acting as the owner's agent. *Vickery v. Construction Co.*, 98.

§ 11. Liabilities of Agent to Third Persons

Because the complaint stated a claim against an individual defendant solely in his representative capacity, it could not state a claim for which relief could be granted against him personally as well. *Tinkham v. Hall*, 651.

PROCESS

§ 1.2. Defects in Copy Delivered to Served Party

Where an action was validly commenced by filing a complaint but attempted service of summons was defective in that a copy of the summons delivered to defendant incorrectly indicated the action was pending in Pitt rather than Bertie County, plaintiff's action was continued in existence as to defendant by an alias summons until valid service of summons was obtained upon defendant. *Ellis v. Kimbrough*, 179.

§ 7. Personal Service on Resident Individuals

An individual was not properly served with process where copies of the summons and complaint were delivered to his sister who neither resided with him nor was present in his home when they were delivered to her. *Tinkham v. Hall*, 651.

§ 9. Personal Service on Nonresident Individuals in Another State

Trial court obtained personal jurisdiction over the nonresident defendant in an action for alimony based on abandonment and child custody and support where defendant was served with process by registered mail. *Brown v. Brown*, 323.

§ 10.2. Service by Publication; Sufficiency as to Diligence to Ascertain Defendant's Whereabouts

There was no merit to defendant's contention that service of process by publication was improper because plaintiff failed to exercise due diligence to discover defendant's address, whereabouts, dwelling house or usual place of abode. *Emanuel v. Fellows*, 340.

§ 12. Service on Domestic Corporations

A corporate defendant was not properly served with process where copies of the summons and complaint were delivered to an individual who was neither an agent of the corporate defendant nor authorized to receive service of process on its behalf. *Tinkham v. Hall*, 651.

§ 19. Actions for Abuse of Process

Plaintiff's filing of notice of lis pendens which included defendant's entire

REFERENCE – Continued

§ 7. Report of Referee

The referee in a compulsory reference is required to file a transcript of the evidence with his report, and the referee's notes summarizing the testimony of the witnesses in the hearing before him are not a proper substitution for the transcript. However, the requirement of the transcript may be waived by the parties. *Synco, Inc. v. Headen,* 109.

REFORMATION OF INSTRUMENTS

§ 1.1. Mutual Mistake

Plaintiff's action to reform a deed on the ground of mistake six years after it was executed was not barred by the statute of limitations. *Hice v. Hi-Mil.,* 427.

§ 7. Sufficiency of Evidence

Evidence was sufficient to show a mutual mistake in a deed from plaintiff to defendant's predecessors in title where plaintiff's homeplace was improperly included in the deed. *Hice v. Hi-Mil, Inc.,* 427.

§ 9. Rights of Third Persons

In plaintiff's action to reform a deed, defendant was not an innocent bona fide purchaser for value. *Hice v. Hi-Mil, Inc.,* 427.

ROBBERY

§ 1.2. Relation to Other Crimes

Defendant was not twice placed in jeopardy when he was tried and convicted of kidnapping for the purpose of facilitating flight following his participation in an armed robbery and of armed robbery. *S. v. Martin,* 223.

In a prosecution of defendant for armed robbery and larceny, judgment of the trial court imposing sentence for misdemeanor larceny of the victim's automobile must be arrested since the evidence necessary to convict defendant of both offenses was substantially the same, and inherent in the jury's verdict finding defendant guilty of armed robbery was a finding that defendant took and carried away property consisting of the victim's cash and automobile. *Ibid.*

§ 3.2. Competency of Evidence; Physical Objects

In a prosecution for armed robbery, even if an exhibit of the State was not in fact the same shotgun used by defendant, in view of defendant's own testimony that it was "like" the one he possessed, any error in its admission was harmless. *S. v. Martin,* 223.

§ 4.3. Armed Robbery Cases Where Evidence Held Sufficient

Evidence was sufficient for the jury in a prosecution for armed robbery. *S. v. Martin,* 223.

§ 5. Instructions

The trial court in an armed robbery and kidnapping case sufficiently instructed the jury that the armed robbery offense must have been completed prior to the beginning of the kidnapping offense. *S. v. Martin,* 223.

ROBBERY – Continued

§ 5.2. Instructions Relating to Armed Robbery

Trial court in a prosecution for attempted armed robbery erred in instructing the jury that nun-chuckas allegedly used by defendant would be a dangerous weapon. *S. v. Mullen*, 667.

§ 5.4. Instructions on Lesser Offenses

Trial court in an armed robbery case was not required to instruct on lesser included offenses where the victim testified that the taking was by two men, one of whom had a gun which he pointed at them. *S. v. Allen*, 482.

The fact that defendant left his pistol in his belt or pants instead of pointing it directly at the victim did not require the court in an armed robbery case to instruct on lesser included offenses. *Ibid.*

RULES OF CIVIL PROCEDURE

§ 4. Process

Where an action was validly commenced by filing a complaint but attempted service of summons was defective in that a copy of the summons delivered to defendant incorrectly indicated the action was pending in Pitt rather than Bertie County, plaintiff's action was continued in existence as to defendant by an alias summons until valid service of summons was obtained upon defendant. *Ellis v. Kimbrough*, 179.

§ 5. Service and Filing of Pleadings and Other Papers

Defendant made a general appearance in an alimony and child custody and support action by filing an answer and counterclaim, and a contempt show cause order was properly served on defendant by hand delivery to his attorney. *Brown v. Brown*, 323.

§ 15. Amended Pleadings

An action against an architect for negligent supervision of the installation of an underground water pipe system brought within three years after the defects in the system were discovered was brought within the statute of limitations; and an amendment of the complaint alleging negligent design of the system related back to the date of the original complaint so that it was not barred by the statute of limitations. *Condominium Assoc. v. Scholz Co.*, 518.

§ 33. Interrogatories

Trial court did not err in ruling that plaintiff need not answer interrogatories which were not filed in apt time. *Clarke v. Clarke*, 249.

§ 38. Jury Trial of Right

A party may waive his right to a jury trial by failing to appear at trial. *Frissell v. Frissell*, 149.

§ 41. Dismissal of Actions

There was no merit to plaintiff's contention that the trial court treated defendant's motion to dismiss under G.S. 1A-1, Rule 12(b)(6) as a hearing on a motion for summary judgment where the judge asked plaintiff if he desired to present additional evidence or amend his complaint, and the judge was doing

SEARCHES AND SEIZURES – Continued

§ 11   Search and Seizure of Vehicles on Probable Cause

An officer's warrantless search of defendant's automobile was based on probable cause and was therefore proper where the officer, trained in the identification of marijuana by its odor, detected the distinct odor of marijuana emanating from defendant's automobile. *S. v. Greenwood*, 731.

§ 12.   "Stop and Frisk" Procedures

There was no merit to defendant's contention that his initial detention by a police officer as he sat in his car in a church parking lot constituted a forcible stop or seizure of his person which violated his reasonable expectation of privacy. *S. v. Greenwood*, 731.

§ 23.   Application for Warrant; Sufficiency of Showing Probable Cause

An officer's affidavit, including a statement that defendant had "sexually assaulted" his daughter, stated sufficient facts from which a magistrate could properly find probable cause that a crime had been committed by defendant and that evidence of the crime might be found on his premises. *S. v. McLean*, 672.

§ 37.   Scope of Search Incident to Arrest; Vehicles

Search of a pocketbook found on the rear seat of defendant's automobile subsequent to defendant's warrantless arrest for possession of marijuana was improper. S. v. Greenwood, 731.

SEDUCTION

§ 3.   Sufficiency of Evidence

Summary judgment was appropriate in an action to recover for seduction where the evidence tended to show that plaintiff willingly went to a field, willingly drank alcoholic beverages, and remembered nothing until she found herself back in town and subsequently discovered she had had intercourse. *McCraney v. Flanagan*, 498.

STATE

§ 4.4.   Actions Against the State

The doctrine of sovereign immunity barred plaintiff's action for breach of a contract of employment with the State which occurred on 1 August 1975. *Wojsko v. State*, 605.

§ 5.1.   Tort Claims Act; Intentional Injuries

Plaintiff's claim against the State for damages for the intentional torts of false representation and fraudulent inducement were barred by the doctrine of sovereign immunity since suits against the State based on intentional torts are not compensable under the Tort Claims Act. *Wojsko v. State*, 605.

§ 8.3.   Negligence of State Employee; Action by Prisoners

In a tort claim action to recover for injuries to prison inmates in a fire which occurred when inmates set fire to several mattresses piled around a table in a prison dormitory, the Deputy Director of Prisons was not negligent in placing inmates in a prison dormitory with polyurethane mattresses, and plaintiff's

TRUSTS – Continued

§ 19. Action to Establish Constructive Trust; Sufficiency of Evidence

In an action to recover for mobile home wheels, tires, and axles which defendants allegedly wrongfully sold or converted to their use, trial court erred in imposing a constructive trust and in directing verdict that defendants had breached the trust. *Marshall v. Miller*, 530.

UNFAIR COMPETITION

§ 1. Unfair Trade Practices in General

Rental of spaces in a mobile home park is trade or commerce within the meaning of G.S. 75-1.1. *Marshall v. Miller*, 530.

Where the same course of conduct gives rise to a traditionally recognized cause of action and as well gives rise to a cause of action for violation of G.S. 75-1.1, damages may be recovered upon only one cause of action. *Ibid.*

Absent a finding of some bad faith, the jury's answer as to whether defendant, without the intent or ability to perform, led plaintiffs to believe that he would provide certain facilities in a trailer park would not support a violation of G.S. 75-1.1 and an award of treble damages. *Ibid.*

Although good faith may be irrelevant where injunctive relief is sought by the Attorney General under G.S. 75-14, it should be relevant where a private party seeks treble damages under G.S. 75-15. *Ibid.*

UNIFORM COMMERCIAL CODE

§ 10. Warranties in General

Defendant did not through its advertising create either an express or implied warranty that a carburetor and metal cleaner was safe for human use. *Davis v. Siloo, Inc.*, 237.

§ 11. Express Warranties

A manufacturer or other warrantor may be liable for breach of warranty when it repeatedly fails within a reasonable time to correct a defect as promised. *Stutts v. Green Ford, Inc.*, 503.

§ 12. Implied Warranties

G.S. 25-2-318 does not contemplate extending implied warranties to employees of purchasers. *Davis v. Siloo Inc.*, 237.

§ 25. Buyer's Remedy for Breach of Warranty

Directed verdicts in favor of the seller and manufacturer of a truck were erroneously granted on plaintiff's breach of warranty claim where there was evidence from which the jury could infer that either defendant refused to perform repairs on plaintiff's truck or that it failed to make proper repair of defective parts within a reasonable time. *Stutts v. Green Ford, Inc.*, 503.

§ 26. Breach of Warranty; Measure of Damages

Where a defect in a truck was not or could not be repaired within a reasonable period as required by a warranty limiting the remedy available to the purchaser in the event of a breach to repair or replacement of parts, the limited, exclusive remedy fails of its essential purpose, and the purchaser is entitled to recover damages as otherwise provided by the Uniform Commercial Code. *Stutts v. Green Ford, Inc.*, 503.

UNIFORM COMMERCIAL CODE – Continued

§ 32. Commercial Paper; Liability of Parties

Trial court erred in determining that there was a presumption of gift from plaintiff husband to defendant wife where both executed a promissory note and plaintiff paid the note, and that plaintiff failed to rebut that presumption. *Grimes v. Grimes*, 353.

§ 45. Default and Enforcement of Security Interest

In an action to recover damages allegedly resulting from breach of warranty where one defendant counterclaimed for an amount which represented the unpaid balance on the retail installment contract executed by plaintiff, trial court erred in directing verdict for defendant where there was a dispute as to the number of payments which had been made. *Stutts v. Green Ford, Inc.*, 503.

USURY

§ 1. What Constitutes Usury

Transactions pursuant to an agreement whereby defendant purchased the assets of a Western Auto Store which had previously been operated by plaintiff were usurious and could not be considered the sale of chattel paper at a discount. *Auto Supply Co. v. Vick*, 701.

Transactions between the parties which defendant claimed were usurious did not fall in the time-price exception to the usury statutes. *Ibid.*

§ 1.3. Excess of Legal Maximum

There was no merit to plaintiff's contention that since the total balance which defendant owed was considered to be in excess of $300,000 the parties were free to agree on any rate of interest under G.S. 24-1.1(5) since the principal amount financed should be determined on a transaction-by-transaction basis. *Auto Supply Co. v. Vick*, 701.

§ 4. Limitations on Right of Action to Assert Usury

Plaintiff's action for the forfeiture of all interest on a promissory note was barred by the statute of limitations. *Haanebrink v. Meyer*, 646.

WILLS

§ 16. Caveat; Parties

Trial court properly dismissed a caveat by an orphanage on the ground that caveator had no standing pursuant to G.S. 31-32 to file a caveat. *In re Calhoun*, 472.

§ 61. Dissent of Spouse

In a proceeding to determine the right of a spouse to dissent, trial court erred in taxing attorneys' fees against the estate of testator. *In re Kirkman*, 479.

WITNESSES

§ 5.2. Evidence of Character and Reputation

Plaintiff could present evidence of her good character after her credibility had been impeached by defendant's cross-examination of her. *Wesley v. Greyhound Lines, Inc.*, 680.

WORD AND PHRASE INDEX

ABORTION

No constitutional bar to State funding of abortions, *Stam v. S.*, 209.

ADULTERY

Spouse's testimony implying adultery inadmissible in divorce case, *Horner v. Horner*, 334.

ALIAS SUMMONS

Continuance of action, *Ellis v. Kimbrough*, 179.

ALIMONY

Alimony pendente lite —
    constructive abandonment and indignities, *Cornelison v. Cornelison*, 91.
    order superseded by final judgment, *Clarke v. Clarke*, 249.
Husband as spendthrift, insufficiency of evidence, *Odom v. Odom*, 486.
Minimum contacts test, abandonment of wife in N.C., *Brown v. Brown*, 323.
Permanent alimony, waiver of jury trial by failure to appear, *Frissell v. Frissell*, 149.
Violation of order being appealed, punishment improper, *Clarke v. Clarke*, 249.
Without divorce prayed for, granting of divorce from bed and board improper, *Clarke v. Clarke*, 249.

AMENDMENT OF PLEADINGS

Qualification as ancillary administrator, no amendment permitted, *Burcl v. Hospital*, 127.

ANCILLARY ADMINISTRATOR

Qualification by nonresident, no amendment of pleadings, *Burcl v. Hospital*, 127.

APPEAL

Partial summary judgment not appealable, *Cook v. Tobacco Co.*, 187.

APPEARANCE

General appearance by answer and counterclaim, *Brown v. Brown*, 323.

ARCHITECTS

Negligent design of condominiums, *Condominium Assoc. v. Scholz Co.*, 518.

ARMED ROBBERY

Gun stuck in belt or pants, *S. v. Allen*, 482.
Instruction on lesser offenses not required, *S. v. Allen*, 482.
Money given to defendant by victim, *S. v. Martin*, 223.

ARREST

Probable cause for warrantless arrest of defendant at friend's home, *S. v. Graham*, 303.
Warrantless arrest for possession of marijuana, *S. v. Greenwood*, 731.

ASSAULT

Jury instructions in civil action improper, *Clarke v. Clarke*, 249.

ATTORNEYS' FEES

Improper taxing in proceeding to determine spouse's right to dissent, *In re Kirkman*, 479.
Insufficient findings in caveat proceeding, *In re Ridge*, 183; in child support action, *Horner v. Horner*, 334.

AUTOMOBILES

Accident caused by defective brakes, *Rose v. Truck Co.*, 643.

Entering highway in front of oncoming truck, *Industries, Inc. v. Tharpe*, 754.

Minor driving without lights after dark, *Haskins v. Power and Light Co.*, 664.

Negligence of driver imputed to owner passenger, *Industries, Inc. v. Tharpe*, 754.

Opinion testimony as to speed, *Oliver v. Powell*, 59.

Striking of pedestrian, *Oliver v. Powell*, 59.

Warrantless search for marijuana, *S. v. Greenwood*, 731.

BANKS

No right of survivorship in joint account, *Herbin v. Farrish*, 193.

BILL OF INDICTMENT

Court's summary to prospective jurors, *S. v. McNeil*, 30.

Reading during jury charge, *S. v. McNeil*, 30.

BLOOD SAMPLES

Use of search warrant to obtain, *S. v. McLean*, 672.

BRAKES

Plaintiff's knowledge of defect, *Rose v. Truck Co.*, 643.

BREACH OF WARRANTY

Suit by individual partner proper, *Barnes v. Chain Co.*, 488.

BURGLARY

Defendant apprehended at crime scene, *S. v. Callihan*, 360.

Instruction on evidence of intent, *S. v. Callihan*, 360.

BUS PASSENGER

Sexual assault on in restroom of bus station, *Wesley v. Greyhound Lines, Inc.*, 680.

CARBURETOR CLEANER

Liability of manufacturer for injuries caused by, *Davis v. Siloo Inc.*, 237.

CAVEAT PROCEEDING

Insufficient findings to support award of fees, *In re Ridge*, 183.

No standing of orphanage to file, *In re Calhoun*, 472.

CHAR PATTERN

Opinion testimony inadmissible in arson case, *S. v. Culpepper*, 633.

CHARACTER EVIDENCE

Reputation of deceased, knowledge of deceased only on the job, *S. v. Gilbert*, 316.

CHECK

Fictitious name signed to, *S. v. Dunbar*, 623.

CHICKENS

No valid contract concerning growth of, *Gregory v. Perdue, Inc.*, 655.

CLINICAL PSYCHOLOGIST

Testimony as to psychological effects of sexual assault, *Wesley v. Greyhound Lines, Inc.*, 680.

CODICIL

Validity of agreement not to probate, *Holt v. Holt*, 618.

COMMITTED YOUTHFUL OFFENDER

Resentencing proceeding, *S. v. Safrit*, 189.

COMPULSORY REFERENCE

Necessity for transcript of evidence, *Synco, Inc. v. Headen*, 109.

CONCRETE MIXING FACILITY

Permitted use under zoning ordinance, *City of Winston-Salem v. Concrete Co.*, 405.

CONDOMINIUMS

Action against architect for negligent design, *Condominium Assoc. v. Scholz Co.*, 518.

CONFESSIONS

Court's reference to statement as "confession," no expression of opinion, *S. v. Graham*, 303.

Request for counsel, subsequent written waiver, *S. v. Graham*, 303.

CONFRONTATION, RIGHT TO

Statements by juror in jury room not violation of, *S. v. Gilbert*, 316.

CONSPIRACY

Sale and delivery of heroin, *S. v. Jones*, 554.

To burn building and personal property, *S. v. Culpepper*, 633.

To sell contraband, *S. v. Cooley*, 376.

CONTEMPT

Punishment for violations of orders being appealed improper, *Clarke v. Clarke*, 249.

CONTINUANCE

Denial of motion based on time to interview witnesses, *S. v. Winston*, 363.

CONTRABAND

Sufficiency of evidence of conspiracy to sell, *S. v. Cooley*, 376.

CONTRACT CARRIER

Transportation of metal containers, *Utilities Commission v. Delivery Services*, 418.

CONTRACTS

Accrual of cause of action for breach, *Silver v. Board of Transportation*, 261.

Breach of, failure to award nominal damages not prejudicial error, *Marsico v. Adams*, 196.

Failure of child to attend private school, no impossibility of performance, *Brenner v. School House, Ltd.*, 19.

No meeting of minds as to essential terms, *Gregory v. Perdue, Inc.*, 655.

CORPORATIONS

One corporation not alter ego of another, *Textiles v. Hillview Mills*, 593.

COSTS

Unnecessary material in record on appeal, *Clarke v. Clarke*, 249.

COUNSEL, RIGHT TO

Failure to inform non-indigent defendant of right to counsel, *S. v. Grimes*, 476.

COUNTY SUBDIVISION ORDINANCE

Name approximating name of existing subdivision, *Springdale Estates Assoc. v. Wake County*, 462.

COURT DOCUMENT

Padlocking notice not simulation of, *Spinks v. Taylor* and *Richardson v. Taylor*, 68.

CUSTOMS

Area customs incompetent in homicide case, *S. v. Harris*, 121.

DAM

Breach of contract to construct, *Silver v. Board of Transportation*, 261.

DAMAGES

Breach of contract, failure to award nominal damages not prejudicial error, *Marsico v. Adams*, 196.

DANGEROUS INSTRUMENTALITY

Carburetor cleaner, *Davis v. Siloo Inc.*, 237.

DEADLY WEAPON

Nun-chuckas were not as matter of law, *S. v. Mullen*, 667.
Presumptions arising from use, *S. v. Johnson*, 297.
Tire tool was not as matter of law, *State v. McGee*, 280.

DEED

Reformation for mutual mistake, *Hice v. Hi-Mil, Inc.*, 427.

DEED OF TRUST

Foreclosure by exercise of power of sale, *In re Foreclosure of Burgess*, 599.

DEFENSE OF HABITATION

Instruction not required in second degree murder case, *S. v. McGee*, 280.

DIRECTED VERDICT

Impropriety when credibility of witnesses in issue, *Marshall v. Miller*, 530.

DISMISSAL OF ACTION

Dismissal with prejudice, no abuse of discretion, *Mumford v. Hutton & Bourbonnais Co.*, 440.
Failure to comply with invalid order of reimbursement, *Thornburg v. Lancaster*, 131.

DIVORCE

Decree regular on face of record, no collateral attack, *Maxwell v. Woods*, 495.
Divorce from bed and board where alimony without divorce prayed for, *Clarke v. Clarke*, 249.
Spouse's testimony implying adultery, *Horner v. Horner*, 334.

DOUBLE JEOPARDY

Conviction for armed robbery and kidnapping was not, conviction for armed robbery and larceny was, *S. v. Martin*, 223.

DRIVEWAY

Minor driving into cable across, *Haskins v. Power and Light Co.*, 664.
Misrepresentation by realtor, *Vickery v. Construction Co.*, 98.

DUE PROCESS

Defendant compelled to exhibit self to jury, *S. v. McNeil*, 30.

EASEMENTS

Permit executed by life tenant invalid upon tenant's death, *Williams v. Telegraph Co.*, 176.

EFFECTIVE ASSISTANCE OF COUNSEL

Codefendants represented by same counsel, *S. v. Johnson*, 297.

EMBEZZLEMENT

Court's reference to defendant as employee, no invasion of province of jury, *S. v. McCaskill*, 289.

EMPLOYMENT CONTRACT

Duration not specified, *Mumford v. Hutton & Bourbonnais Co.*, 440.

EQUITABLE LIEN

Contributions to improvements on wife's properties, *Parslow v. Parslow*, 84.

ESTOPPEL

Estoppel of school board to deny career teacher status, *Meachan v. Board of Education*, 271.

EXPRESSION OF OPINION

Court's reference to statement as "confession," *S. v. Graham*, 303.

FAMILY SETTLEMENT AGREEMENT

Absence of emergency not contemplated by testatrix, *Holt v. Holt*, 618.

Agreement not to probate codicil, *Holt v. Holt*, 618.

FETUS

Human fetus is not person within meaning of N.C. Constitution, *Stam v. S.*, 209.

FINE

No restitution or reparation, *S. v. Alexander*, 502.

FIRE DEPARTMENT

No judicial review of departmental hearing on personnel matters, *Foust v. City of Greensboro*, 159.

FIRE INSURANCE

Evidence of prior fire loss by insured, harmless error, *Hanks v. Insurance Co.*, 393.

Fraudulent misrepresentation of extent of loss, *Hanks v. Insurance Co.*, 393.

FORECLOSURE

By exercise of power of sale in deed of trust, *In re Foreclosure of Burgess*, 599.

No damages shown resulting from institution of proceedings, *Parker v. Sheldon*, 493.

Record owner defined, *Properties, Inc. v. Savings and Loan Assoc.*, 675.

FOREIGN CORPORATION

Contract not made in N.C., no personal jurisdiction, *Allen Co. v. Quip-Matic, Inc.*, 40.

Insufficient minimum contacts, *Allen Co. v. Quip-Matic, Inc.*, 40.

FORGERY

False instrument, instructions proper, *S. v. Dunbar*, 623.

Necessity for showing name was fictitious, *S. v. Dunbar*, 623.

FORKLIFT

Foreseeability of injury from operation, *Poythress v. Burlington Industries*, 199.

FRAUD

Misrepresentation by realtor, *Vickery v. Construction Co.*, 98.

FRAUDULENT CONVEYANCES

Insufficient evidence of fraudulent conveyance of corporate assets, *Textiles v. Hillview Mills*, 593.

INJUNCTIONS

Erroneous preliminary injunction against sign control ordinance, *Goodman Toyota v. City of Raleigh*, 628.

INSANITY

Defendant's statements to police inadmissible to show, *S. v. Flowers*, 457.

Instruction on commitment procedure, *S. v. Flowers*, 457.

Instruction on the will and ability to control conduct not required, *S. v. Hodgen*, 329.

Issue for jury determination, *S. v. Flowers*, 457.

INSURANCE

Settlement as partial or complete, question of fact, *Thornburg v. Lancaster*, 131.

INTENT

Intent of decedent to go on business trip, *Long v. Paving Co.*, 564.

INTERESTED WITNESSES

Charge on scrutiny of testimony not given, *S. v. Johnson*, 297.

INTERROGATORIES

Failure to serve in apt time, *Clarke v. Clarke*, 249.

JOINDER

Failure to join charges not error, *S. v. Jones*, 554.

JOINT BANK ACCOUNT

No right of survivorship, *Herbin v. Farrish*, 193.

JUDGE ADVOCATE

Improper certifying officer for separation agreement, *DeJaager v. DeJaager*, 452.

JURY

Refusal of request to have testimony read again, *S. v. Jones*, 554.

Summary of indictment to prospective jurors, *S. v. McNeil*, 30.

JURY ARGUMENT

Permitting only one argument by defendant, no violation of statute, *S. v. McCaskill*, 289.

JURY INSTRUCTIONS

Further instructions upon failure to reach verdict, *S. v. Jones*, 554.

Reading indictment, *S. v. McNeil*, 30.

JURY TAMPERING

Mistrial proper though events not instigated by defendant, *S. v. Cooley*, 376.

JURY TRIAL

Waiver by failure to appear in alimony action, *Frissell v. Frissell*, 149.

KIDNAPPING

Age of victim, submission of issue not required, *S. v. Martin*, 223.

LABORERS' AND MATERIALMEN'S LIENS

No right to lien as prime contractor, *Contractors, Inc., v. Forbes*, 371.

LANDLORD AND TENANT

Exercise of self-help for failure to pay rent, *Spinks v. Taylor and Richardson v. Taylor*, 68.

LARCENY

Ownership of stolen property, no fatal variance, *S. v. Graham*, 303.

LIS PENDENS

Inclusion of entire subdivision, no abuse of process, *Whyburn v. Norwood*, 310.

MAIN PURPOSE RULE

Oral guaranty to pay corporation's debt, *Furniture Industries v. Griggs*, 104.

MAJORITY VERDICT

Time for entering agreement, *Industries, Inc. v. Tharpe*, 754.

MALICIOUS PROSECUTION

Filing of notice of lis pendens was not, *Whyburn v. Norwood*, 310.

MANSLAUGHTER

Fine, improper condition for parole or work release, *S. v. Alexander*, 502.

MARIJUANA

Warrantless search of vehicle for, *S. v. Greenwood*, 731.

MINIMUM CONTACTS TEST

Abandonment of wife in N.C., *Brown v. Brown*, 323.

Insufficient contacts by foreign corporation, *Allen Co. v. Quip-Matic, Inc.*, 40.

MISDEMEANOR

Trial in superior court, failure of record to show jurisdiction, *S. v. Felmet*, 201.

MOBILE HOME PARK

Rental as trade or commerce, *Marshall v. Miller*, 530.

MOOT QUESTION

Order vacating child custody and support provisions of prior order, *Stewart v. Stewart*, 678.

MOTORBIKE

Minor driving without lights after dark, *Haskins v. Power and Light Co.*, 664.

NARCOTICS

Failure to instruct on unlawfulness of possession and sale, *S. v. McNeil*, 30.

NON-TESTIMONIAL IDENTIFICATION EVIDENCE

Use of search warrant to obtain, *S. v. McLean*, 672.

NOVA UNIVERSITY

No right of UNC Board of Governors to regulate, *Nova University v. University of North Carolina*, 638.

NUN-CHUCKAS

No dangerous weapon per se, *S. v. Mullen*, 667.

OPINION TESTIMONY

No proper hypothetical question, *S. v. Culpepper*, 633.

Witness's knowledge of facts not shown, *S. v. Culpepper*, 633.

ORAL GUARANTY

Main purpose rule, *Furniture Industries v. Griggs*, 104.

ORPHANAGE

No standing to file caveat, *In re Calhoun*, 472.

RETAIL SALES CONTRACT

Number of payments made in dispute, *Stutts v. Green Ford, Inc.*, 503.

ROBBERY

Guns not connected with the crime improperly admitted, *S. v. Milby* and *S. v. Boyd*, 669.

Nun-chukas not dangerous weapon per se, *S. v. Mullen*, 667.

SCHOOL TEACHER

Disability retirement benefits, resignation by implication, *Meachan v. Board of Education*, 271.

SCHOOL TUITION

Failure of child to attend private school, tuition not refundable, *Brenner v. School House, Ltd.*, 19.

SEARCHES AND SEIZURES

Guilty plea not vitiated by illegal search, *S. v. Williams*, 205.

Use of search warrant to obtain blood and hair samples, *S. v. McLean*, 672.

Warrantless search based on marijuana odor, *S. v. Greenwood*, 731.

Warrantless search of house, *State v. Mackins*, 168.

Warrantless search of pocketbook in car improper, *S. v. Greenwood*, 731.

SECOND DEGREE MURDER

Instructions on presumptions of malice and unlawfulness, *S. v. Harris*, 121.

SEDUCTION

Willing plaintiff, *McCraney v. Flanagan*, 498.

SELF-DEFENSE

Sufficiency of instructions on reasonable apprehension of death or great bodily harm, *S. v. Gilbert*, 316.

SEPARATION AGREEMENT

No private examination of wife, improper certifying officer, *DeJaager v. DeJaager*, 452.

SETTLEMENT

Issue of fact as to whether partial or complete, *Thornburg v. Lancaster*, 131.

SEXUAL ASSAULT

Passenger in bus station restroom, *Wesley v. Greyhound Lines, Inc.*, 680.

SIGN CONTROL ORDINANCE

Erroneous preliminary injunction, *Goodman Toyota v. City of Raleigh*, 628.

SLANDER

Publication of employee's statements not attributable to employer, *Stutts v. Power Co.*, 76.

Slanderous words not alleged verbatim in complaint, *Stutts v. Power Co.*, 76.

SLANDER OF TITLE

Filing of lis pendens was not, *Whyburn v. Norwood*, 310.

SOCIAL WORKER

Unemployment compensation after resignation, *In re Clark*, 163.

SOVEREIGN IMMUNITY

Alleged breach of contract of employment with State, *Wojsko v. S.*, 605.

TRUCKING

Rates for petroleum products, dedicated service provision, *Utilities Comm. v. Oil Co.*, 1.

TRUST

Consent of beneficiaries to termination, *Fisher v. Ladd*, 587.

TUITION

Failure of child to attend private school, tuition not refundable, *Brenner v. School House, Ltd.*, 19.

UNC BOARD OF GOVERNORS

No authority to regulate Nova University, *Nova University v. University of North Carolina*, 638.

UNEMPLOYMENT COMPENSATION

Alleged racial discrimination by employer, *In re Bolden*, 468.

Failure to apply law to "other facts in evidence," *In re Bolden*, 468.

Resignation of social worker, cause attributable to employer, *In re Clark* 163.

UNFAIR OR DECEPTIVE TRADE PRACTICE

Furnishing services in trailer park, *Marshall v. Miller*, 530.

UNION

Permanent injunction against picketing after strike ended, *General Electric Co. v. Union*, 153.

UNJUST ENRICHMENT

Improper jury instructions, *Wright v. Wright*, 367.

Lien for contributions to improvements on wife's properties, *Parslow v. Parslow*, 84.

USURY

No time-price sales, *Auto Supply v. Vick*, 701.

Purchase of Western Auto Store, *Auto Supply v. Vick*, 701.

UTILITY EASEMENT

Permit executed by life tenant invalid upon tenant's death, *Williams v. Telegraph Co.*, 176.

VERDICT

Agreement to accept stated majority verdict, *Industries, Inc. v. Tharpe*, 754.

VOLUNTARY DISMISSAL

New action not based on same claim, *Stutts v. Power Co.*, 76.

WARRANTIES

Duty of warrantor to correct defect, *Stutts v. Green Ford, Inc.*, 503.

Oil leak in truck, *Stutts v. Green Ford, Inc.*, 503.

Warranty of carburetor cleaner not created through advertising, *Davis v. Siloo Inc.*, 237.

WILLS

No standing of orphanage to file caveat, *In re Calhoun*, 472.

Proceeding to determine spouse's right to dissent, *In re Kirkman*, 479.

WORK RELEASE

Fine improper condition for, *S. v. Alexander*, 502.

WORKERS' COMPENSATION

Airplane crash in Florida, *Long v. Paving Co.*, 564.